Race and Crime

RACE AND CRIME

Geographies of Injustice

Elizabeth Brown and George Barganier

UNIVERSITY OF CALIFORNIA PRESS

University of California Press, one of the most distinguished university presses in the United States, enriches lives around the world
by advancing scholarship in the humanities, social sciences, and
natural sciences. Its activities are supported by the UC Press Foundation and by philanthropic contributions from individuals and
institutions. For more information, visit www.ucpress.edu.

University of California Press
Oakland, California

Library of Congress Cataloging-in-Publication Data

Names: Brown, Elizabeth, 1976– author. | Barganier, George,
    1976– author.
Title: Race and crime : geographies of injustice / Elizabeth Brown
    and George Barganier.
Description: Oakland, California : University of California Press,
    [2018] | Includes bibliographical references and index. |
Identifiers: LCCN 2018009971 (print) | LCCN 2018016608 (ebook) |
    ISBN 9780520967403 (E-book) | ISBN 9780520294189 (pbk. : alk.
    paper)
Subjects: LCSH: Racism in criminology—United States. | Criminal
    justice, Administration of—United States. | Imprisonment—
    United States. | Human geography—United States.
Classification: LCC HV6197.U6 (ebook) | LCC HV6197.U6 B76 2018
    (print) | DDC 363.3/400973—dc23
LC record available at https://lccn.loc.gov/2018009971

Manufactured in the United States of America

26 25 24 23 22 21 20 19 18
10 9 8 7 6 5 4 3 2 1

Contents

Illustrations

Preface

This book emerged from our collective experiences of teaching a course at San Francisco State University called Race, Crime, and Justice. Taught to over two hundred students each year, this course examines how race impacts the workings of the criminal justice system. While seemingly a simple task, from our perspectives as interdisciplinary scholars of the crime, law, and justice systems, this was anything but. Instead, we came to view this course as a preliminary introduction, not just to how race is experienced in the criminal justice system but to why this topic is important for understanding the very workings of the criminal justice system today.

Any student of criminal justice knows just how important race is to the system—the staggering statistics showing that the United States leads the world in incarceration, and that this incarceration is concentrated among black and Latinx* communities. Yet, in comparison to the wealth of textbooks on criminal justice systems in general, only a few books examine just how this came to be and why this reality in the criminal justice system is so important to the history and idea of race. Even fewer direct this at an undergraduate audience and not at scholars of race in the field. Textbooks that do examine race and crime tend to consider race nothing more than a series of outcomes in the system, produced primarily through the lack of controls on discretion or the perceived pathologies of incarcerated communities.

Our training as scholars of race, first and foremost, and not as criminologists means that we see this picture of race, crime, and justice as severely limited. Race is something that emerged just over five hundred years ago with the birth of colonialism but has often been approached in books on race and crime as an ahistorical concept. Connections between historical lineages of race and the emergence of racialized mass incarceration today have been few and far between in introductory books. Further, issues of race in the criminal justice system have often been treated as merely one issue in the system and not as constitutive of the system itself. We longed for a text that understood that how we view crime today is inseparable from the history of race in the United States and colonial conquest more broadly. We sought a text that was not limited to a tour of criminal justice institutions and their racial outcomes but rather provided a strong foundation for understanding what race is, where it comes from, how it changed over time, and why it has come to so easily dominate the criminal justice system today.

---

* We use the term *Latinx* in order to provide a gender-neutral term for referring to communities commonly referred to as *Latina/o;* we also refer to people as *Latino, Latina,* or *Latinx* instead of *Hispanic* as the latter term originated in the tactics of colonization we discuss in this book. Graphs that refer to Latinx communities often use this term even when the original data source uses the term *Hispanic.*

These limitations in texts meant that we were tasked with teaching a subject with very few introductory primers for students. We each cobbled together a series of readings and lectures that represented a more holistic approach to the understanding of race and the criminal justice system, but students still did not have access to any readings that translated our overarching approach into a single text. This book emerged from that gap.

In chapter 1, we introduce readers to the macrostructural perspective of race in the criminal justice system by introducing the idea of racialized mass incarceration and the key terms and theoretical construct of the book. Drawing on scholars of colonialism and race, we develop the key term of coloniality to guide readers as to the practices that reproduce racial hierarchies today. In chapter 2, we embark on an in-depth exploration of how race emerged from colonialism, and how this created a structure of human/nonhuman imbued throughout emerging European and U.S. state forms. We discuss in this chapter where race came from, how race was conceived, and how these trends shaped what we know about racial history in the United States today.

Chapter 3 examines explicitly the role of race in the field of criminal justice historically. Beginning with the scientific invention of race, this chapter traces the emergence of regimes of scientific racism from the early 1800s to eugenics in the 1930s. These histories of race, while antiquated, are nevertheless instructional as to how certain behaviors, bodies, and places are infused with racial meanings today.

Chapter 4 builds on this history by examining how racial science influenced the development of social science and the birth of what today are known as "social problems." Social problems were integral to redefining the state and to transitioning the state from the explicit racial apartheid of the slavery era to the less

explicit, though nonetheless trenchant, racial structures of today. As a result of this redefinition of state power, critical criminal justice institutions emerged, such as the juvenile court and the uniformed urban police. As we trace at the end of this chapter, these institutions identified poor, nonwhite communities as the primary source of social problems, an identification that continues today.

Chapter 5 turns to the geography of race that emerged in the post-WWII period with the advent of the suburb and the decline and disinvestment of urban spaces. This chapter sets the stage for understanding how geography continues to play a critical and necessary role in the continuation of mass incarceration and how our ideas about space and place are critical forces within practices of racialization.

In chapter 6, we move to the emergence of the logics of crime control buildup in the 1960s by tracing the role of political elites in responding to political protests and crises. In the 1960s and the 1970s, we get our first glimpse of the logics of the "law and order" discourse and a fundamentally new way of thinking about the role of the state relative to social issues. Here we detail the emergence of the war on drugs, the redefinition of federal law enforcement, and the reallocation of state resources toward prison building, policing, and incarceration.

We then turn in chapters 7–10 to examining how these historicized power relations affected the various institutions of criminal justice. The first agency we examine is law enforcement in chapter 7. Urban policing is arguably one of the most important agencies for how criminal justice institutions act to produce race and often one that is overlooked. This chapter details the role of various geographical policing schemes critical to understanding policing in the twenty-first century. From "broken windows" and community policing to SWAT team drug raids, the police act as a critical agency for furthering colonial power relations into the seemingly color-blind postracial era.

Chapter 8 looks at the role of courts in continuing the colonial order through practices of public defense, inadequate counsel, and what has come to be known as tactics of spatial governmentality. By using space and one's presence in it as an arbiter of criminality, tactics of spatial governmentality created "no-go" and hyperpoliced zones that in many ways mimic the spatial restrictions of well-known racist political projects of the past.

Chapter 9 examines the role of race in imprisonment and considers how the contemporary prison system mimics the institutional and racial structures of chattel slavery. Practices of dehumanization first mastered in the slavery era are reborn within the dehumanizing practices of imprisonment that extend beyond even the walls of the prison. Chapter 10 examines the ultimate act of dehumanization by examining race and the death penalty. Unsurprisingly, given the history of race in the United States, the death penalty was critical to continuing what commentators call "legal lynching" even as lynching became explicitly criminalized. Here, the connection between colonialism and violent, sovereign elimination of the racial "other" is most clearly on display, but execution also provides a telling look into how the larger structural trends examined in each previous chapter are amplified in the use of the death penalty.

Finally, we conclude by looking at how the city is changing today, and the role that larger forces play today in remaking race. As we discuss in the conclusion, mass incarceration has somewhat plateaued nationally, and we may be moving toward a decarcerated era. Yet, as the practices of decarceration and the remaking of the city today both show, race, class, and gender remain salient, entrenched, and consequential in criminal justice practices. Thus, we contend

that even as the power of coloniality and race-making shifts and restructures, it is likely to continue influencing the criminal justice system for generations to come.

This book is the product of so many conversations and intellectual debts that are not named or cited in this text. We especially thank all of those whose insights, arguments, and pointed commentaries helped us to grapple with the world around us—from our very first instructors in undergraduate to our mentors, inspiration, and cheerleaders today—and eventually resulted in this book. We hope to provide this opportunity to our readers. We especially want to thank the many reviewers who read drafts of this book and provided exceedingly helpful comments, even those that were critical of its first iterations. We are especially indebted in this regard to Randall G. Shelden, Sandra Browning, Natalie Byfield, Gary Smith, Joseph Margulies, Brian Jordan Jefferson, Fawn Ngo, and Tim Robicheaux. Without reviewers advising us to consider the work of particular scholars, concepts, and historical events, we would not have deepened our own understandings of the twists and turns that led to race and crime today, and as such, this book. Many thanks as well to Maura Roessner and the entire editorial team at UC Press, whose encouragement and enthusiasm for the project guided us throughout. We could not have completed this book, however, without the expert guidance and advice of Sarah Calabi, whose patience, gentle questioning, and organizational suggestions made this a stronger and clearer book than we could have done on our own. All the omissions and errors are ours alone. Many thanks as well to Tony Sparks, Askari Barganier, and Amirah Qureshi, who endured our late nights of writing, weekends without us, and constant inattention.

Race, Crime, and Justice: Definitions and Context

LEARNING OUTCOMES

▶ Explain what mass incarceration is and how it impacts race in the United States today.

▶ Summarize the connection between racialized mass incarceration and strides toward racial justice in the United States.

▶ Define terms key to understanding race, crime, and justice in the United States.

▶ Demonstrate how race and crime are socially constructed.

KEY TERMS

▶ mass incarceration
▶ coloniality
▶ sovereign force
▶ state power
▶ knowledge production
▶ premature death
▶ social construction
▶ white supremacy

White nationalist protesters in the United States marched through the streets with torches, wantonly inflicting violence and even death when a member charged the group. As they marched, they chanted, "Blood and Soil," a Nazi slogan. One protester plowed into a group of counterprotesters, hurting at least twenty people and killing one. Racial taunts, shoving, and fighting led the governor to declare a state of emergency and the National Guard to descend upon the city. The president of the country refused to condemn the violence and instead noted that "bad dudes" on "both sides" were to blame for the violence. He further sided with the protesters, declaring monuments to white supremacy "beautiful" and part of the "history and culture" of the United States. No, this is not sometime in the 1800s or even the 1960s but August 2017, when white nationalists amassed to protest the removal of a statue that commemorated the slaveholding southern United States in Charlottesville, North Carolina.

You might ask why we would open a book titled *Race and Crime* with a discussion of white nationalist violence and its resurgence in the United States. Seventy years ago, though, this question might not have been asked. One of the first "wars on crime" in the 1940s sought not to fight drugs or gangs, as we often declare today, but to define crime as white racial violence and the criminal justice system as the responsible state institution for protecting the nation against these acts (Murakawa 2014). For reformers in the 1940s, the events in Charlottesville would have had everything to do with race and crime.

The events in Charlottesville themselves, though, might have seemed odd to reformers in the post-WWII era. At the end of the 1940s, the United States was embarking on an era where the traditional structures of race-based exclusion—such as explicit racial segregation in housing and schools—would be eroded and ultimately overturned. Over the next two decades, Supreme Court decisions would mandate protections for those most disenfranchised, especially in the criminal court, by providing state-funded attorneys for poor people and requiring Fourth Amendment protections against the actions of local (not just federal) police. And in 1964, the nation would pass the Civil Rights Act, which explicitly prohibited racial discrimination. This time would be remembered as a period when the civil rights movement made extraordinary inroads in exposing and changing the systems of white supremacy that marked the pre–civil rights era. For the reformers in the 1940s seeking to define the criminal justice system as the foremost institution in the fight against racial hatred and violence, the events in 2017 in Charlottesville would not have seemed likely.

With the passage of the Civil Rights Act, affirmative action remedies in the 1970s and 1980s, and the election of Barack Obama as president in 2008, many today were even poised to declare the ascendance of the "postracial" moment in the United States. The *New York Times* headline the day after the election proclaimed "Obama Elected President as Racial Barrier Falls." *Time* magazine asserted that his election signaled that "the economy is trumping race" and that "worried white voters [were] turning toward Obama."

Yet, only a little over eight years separate the events in Charlottesville from the election of Obama. Arguably, Obama's election was generations in coming—starting with the first moments of the civil rights movement (and likely earlier). Could something with that amount of historical significance really change in just eight short years? Could the events of today really be such a backlash to Obama's election that the prior half century of racial justice work would be obliterated? Could we really have gone so quickly from a postracial future to the resurgence of a violent, white supremacist past? Or is something else going on?

We argue that something else is going on, and this something else is found within the criminal justice system. By examining the institutions of criminal justice, we reveal how and why the criminal justice system emerged as the paramount institution of racial governance in the United States. We also explore why this happened at a time when reformers might not have expected it, and when many were primed to declare the past few decades as the ascendance of a postracial future.

POSTRACISM AND MASS INCARCERATION

Let's consider a critical transformation in the criminal justice system that happened at the same time as the postracial future was being built. For an entire century prior to the civil rights movement, the rate of incarceration was nearly constant (Cahalan 1986). And while black and brown communities were certainly recipients of undue criminal justice attention, policing, and violent force, whites routinely made up the majority of people in prison (Cahalan 1986; Johnson, Dobrzanska, and Palla 2005). With this historical background, we might have expected the criminal justice system to be the exemplar institution of the postracial era, emerging out of the civil rights moment in the 1960s as a model of racial equality, justice, and fairness. Something else happened, though.

Mass Incarceration

That something else is what is often called **mass incarceration.** Mass incarceration is defined by David Garland (2001, 1) as "a rate of imprisonment . . . that is markedly above the historical and comparative norm" for a given society. With mass incarceration, imprisonment "ceases to be the incarceration of individual offenders and becomes the systematic imprisonment of whole groups of the population."

Today, 25 percent of the world's total prisoners are held in the United States, though it has just 5 percent of the global population (Sentencing Project 2015). Its rate of incarceration is far above any comparable nation, with almost 700 people incarcerated per 100,000 residents (see figure 1.1). The next highest rate among OECD countries is Chile's 256 per 100,000. (The Organization for Economic Cooperation and Development, begun by the United States, Canada, and European countries in the 1960s, includes thirty-five nations.) Among all the countries in the world, the United States remains the leader, with Rwanda coming in second with 492 people incarcerated per 100,000 (Sentencing Project 2015). Indeed, the United States incarcerates more people than the top thirty-five European countries combined! And the United States' incarceration rate does not include the 360,000 people incarcerated in immigrant detention facilities in 2016 (Detention Watch Network 2018).

This level of incarceration is unprecedented compared not only to other countries but also in the history of incarceration in the United States. Figure 1.2 shows the *rate* of incarceration, or how many people are incarcerated relative to the total population, in this case, per 100,000 people. Just like the total number of people incarcerated, the rate of incarceration also substantially increased and demonstrated that even with population increases, incarceration in the 1980s was both historically unprecedented and drastic. Between 1900 (when reliable national record keeping began) and the 1970s, the rate of incarceration including jails was also relatively constant, averaging around 100

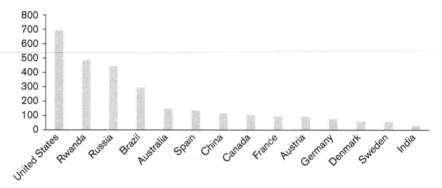

Figure 1.1 International rates of imprisonment, per 100,000 residents. Source: Data from Sentencing Project, *Trends in U.S. Corrections*, 2015.

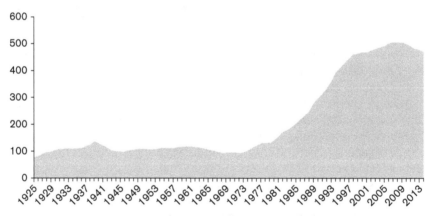

Figure 1.2 State and federal imprisonment rate (excluding jails) in the United States per 100,000, 1925–2014. Sources: E. Ann Carson and Daniela Golinelli, *Prisoners in 2012: Trends in Admissions and Releases, 1991–2012*, Bureau of Justice Statistics Bulletin (Washington, DC: U.S. Department of Justice, December 2013 [revised September 2014]); Danielle Kaeble, Lauren Glaze, Anastasios Tsoutis, and Todd Minton, *Correction Populations in the United States, 2014*, Bureau of Justice Statistics Bulletin (Washington, DC: U.S. Department of Justice, December 2015 [revised January 2016]), www.bjs.gov/content/pub/pdf/cpus14.pdf; Margaret Warner Cahalan and Lee Anne Parsons, *Historical Corrections Statistics in the United States, 1850–1984*, NCJ-102529 (Washington, DC: U.S. Department of Justice, Bureau of Justice Statistics, December 1986), www.bjs.gov/content/pub/pdf/hcsus5084.pdf.

per 100,000. Yet, after the 1970s, this rose to a global high of 755 per 100,000 in 2008 (the peak) and about 693 per 100,000 today.

The current U.S. rates of incarceration are certainly unprecedented, unparalleled, and anomalous. Yet measures of incarceration do not reveal the entire story. As incarceration rates rose, so did probation and parole. Today, over

6 million people are under some sort of criminal justice supervision—a number that shows just how widespread and entrenched the mass incarceration complex is in U.S. society.

Race and Mass Incarceration

The term *mass incarceration* suggests a widespread application, yet mass incarceration is not widely applied, and it does not apply to an amorphous, nonracialized conception of society. In a country that is over 77 percent white, more than 60 percent of people in jail and prison are persons of color. In 2013, whites made up just 34.3 percent of the prison population, while black people made up 37.4 percent and Latinxs 22.3 percent (Sentencing Project 2015). The chance of incarceration for a black person is six times that of a white person, and Latinxs are 2.3 times more likely to be incarcerated than whites (Sentencing Project 2015).

At the height of mass incarceration, among every 100,000 residents, almost 2,300 black people were incarcerated and almost 1,100 Latinxs, compared to just over 320 whites. In 2016, 274 whites per 100,000 were incarcerated, compared to almost six times more blacks at 1,608, and over three times as many Latinxs at 856 per 100,000 (see figure 1.3). Among every 100,000 male U.S. residents, 2,724 black men are incarcerated, 1,091 Latino men, and just 465 white men. For white women, just 53 in every 100,000 are incarcerated, compared to 64 in 100,000 Latinas, and 109 in 100,000 black women. Today, one in three black people and one in seven Latinxs are under some sort of criminal justice supervision, but only one in twenty-three whites! Indeed, in some cities, such as Baltimore, Milwaukee, and Washington DC, the rate of criminal justice supervision for black men is one in two (Mauer 2006). And this increase in incarceration, probation, and parole for black people and Latinxs happened at a time when the postracial moment was seemingly building in other areas of the country.

Incarceration and the (Racialized) Life Experience

There is no doubt that the management of crime today plays a significant, if not defining, role in creating the racial experience (Cole 2000). The most commonly cited incarceration statistics provide just a glimpse of one aspect of the carceral complex that is directed at black and brown communities (Mauer 2006). It fails to include the effects of living in a hyperpoliced community or among unregulated criminal markets or under a general pattern of suspicion, distrust, and extraordinary attention—not just violence—directed at one's community (Chesney-Lind and Mauer 2003; Travis and Waul 2003).

Bird's-eye views of incarceration statistics fail to convey how incarceration has become a normal part of the life course for some groups (Petit and Western 2004). For example, while white men have a one-in-seventeen chance of being incarcerated in their lifetimes, Latino men have a one-in-six chance and black

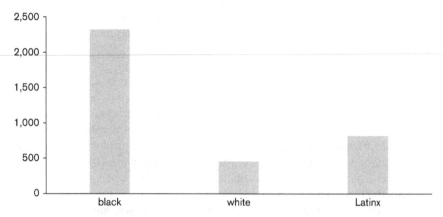

Figure 1.3 Rates of incarceration (including prison and jails) by race and ethnicity, per 100,000. Source: E. Ann Carson, 2018. *Prisoners in 2016*, US Department of Justice, Bureau of Justice Statistics, table 6. www.bjs.gov/content/pub/pdf/p16.pdf.

men have a one–in-three chance (Mauer 2006). For black men ages 30–34, the age group with the most concentrated incarceration, 6,412 men per 100,000 are incarcerated. For Latinos in that age bracket, the rate is 2,457; for whites, it's just 1,111 (Carson 2015).

Postracial? The Case of Crime

When viewed from the vantage point of racial gains, the emergence of racialized mass incarceration seems anomalous. Many might not suspect that racial disparity would pervade a government institution as thoroughly as it has done in the criminal justice system. To the extent that race did emerge as a defining feature, we might expect that this could be easily corrected by appeal to the law or through court cases, congressional lobbying, or some other remediation. Yet, there has been no comprehensive reform package, congressional action, or presidential mandate to end racialized mass incarceration. Even in the era of plateauing incarceration rates, racial disproportionalities in the incarceration experience remain trenchant.

How can this be, particularly when so many see such strides being made in racial justice? The answer to this question is the subject of this book. Robert Allen (2005) has argued that two strategies developed simultaneously to maintain white racial power in the wake of the civil rights movement: (1) a mechanism of inclusion that permitted the development of a black and nonwhite intermediary class consisting of professionals and bureaucrats and (2) the expansion of the punitive state to target and continue the subjugation and oppression of a nonwhite disenfranchised populace.

While the number of black elected officials has increased from a few hundred in the early 1960s to around 10,000 today, black politicians hold only 2 percent of the total number of elected offices in the United States (Brown-Dean et al. 2015). The disparity is especially stark next to numbers of people incarcerated and suppressed by the criminal justice system cited earlier in this chapter (Allen 2005). The election of Obama and the gains of the civil rights movement were certainly significant, but they were set amid a larger expansion of political disenfranchisement due to the effects of criminalization. Thus, political gains by the black middle class have been relatively insignificant compared to the much larger, often hidden processes by which black and brown communities became embedded within the criminal justice system.

This book tells the story of how the criminal justice system became the newest institution managing racial governance in the United States. The criminal justice system is part of a broader legacy of state institutions—from slavery to Jim Crow—through which race has been created, reproduced, and managed. This book tells how this happened and explains why we should not be entirely shocked by the events in Charlottesville in 2017. Instead, we argue, Charlottesville represents an extreme example of what has been one of the most continuous trends in the history of the United States—white racial domination. Though Charlottesville is considered extreme and unrepresentative of the U.S. populace, it is connected to the ways that white racial structures are sublimated through the institutions of everyday life. Even while many—including whites—work toward a postracial future, the policies, practices, and assumptions underwriting state institutions reflect this racialized worldview.

This happened even though the policies and structures of state institutions, including the justice system, are formally race neutral. This race neutrality, however, is not divorced from the broader social context, and thus the race-defined ways we think about crime are baked into the ways policies are implemented, even in the seemingly postracial era. To demonstrate, let's consider how the criminalization of race happens through the emergence today of seemingly race-neutral, "objective," and "rational" approaches to policing.

POSTRACIAL POLICING: COMPSTAT AND THE CRIMINALIZATION OF RACE

Criminology and criminal justice practice today take a seemingly much more objective and scientific approach to the study of crime than in generations past. Police, for instance, have embraced forms of policing based on statistical models and evidence-based practices. This, we might hope, more evenly distributes policing across the population, reflecting an even distribution of criminal activity across racial lines (Hagan and Foster 2004; Beckett and Sasson 2007).

Yet, even one of the most celebrated and seemingly objective, rational approaches to policing was embedded in a racialized imagination of the world.

One widely known example of this new form of policing is COMPSTAT, which was developed in New York (McDonald and Greenberg. 2002; Smith and Bratton 2001). COMPSTAT stands for "compare statistics" and is a police management practice of using statistical information to identify "hot spots" of crime and then targeting enforcement accordingly. Prior to COMPSTAT, policing was riddled with examples of racially discriminatory policing, and police regularly used force to subjugate and oppress communities of color, some of which we describe in subsequent chapters. COMPSTAT was intended to allow police to focus on areas where they were most needed. As a result, police embarked on a new model of policing based on crime rates and their distribution over urban areas.

With COMPSTAT, authorities could identify hot-spot neighborhoods where crime concentrated (Braga and Bond 2008). This move made policing more "rational" and less tied to stereotypes and subjective assumptions considered a product of earlier models of policing. This also moved policing into what many considered a color-blind or postracial era, where police are deployed strategically in response to crime rates and not because of the racial threat of a particular community.

COMPSTAT, for many, is an achievement of the values of democracy, equality, and justice in policing. Yet, the data used to produce crime maps in COMPSTAT is not reflective of objective rates of crime. The data in COMPSTAT is based primarily on *reports* of crime to the police, not on actual crime taking place. Thus, the data is in actuality a measure of *police activity,* not of crime.

Consider how the data is compiled. COMPSTAT does examine all reports of crime, but most crime is reported to the police in one of two ways. The first way is when people call the police to report a crime. This leaves out the many crimes that go undetected or unreported. Measures of crime victimization show the actual crime rate is almost three times higher than measures of police activity indicate (Beckett and Sasson 2007). COMPSTAT data primarily focuses on crime that happens in public places—those hot spots of criminal activity. Much crime, however, happens behind closed doors, in private spaces. These types of crimes are least likely to be reported. For instance, if a person is assaulted in public by an unknown assailant, the person is likely to call the police. However, if the person is assaulted by a loved one in their home, there is a good chance that the person will not call the police. Data plotted on crime maps thus overrepresents crimes people are more likely to report to the police—that is, crimes committed by strangers—but these are the crimes we are least likely to be victimized by (e.g., Bachman and Saltzman 1994).

The second source of reports of crime is from police patrolling and making arrests as a result of their surveillance. Police patrols, however, are not evenly distributed across a jurisdiction. Consider this question: where in an urban area are police most likely to be found, outside of police stations? Most people would suggest a neighborhood that likely is poor and less white; few would respond with a predominantly white, wealthy neighborhood. It would be quite strange to find regular police patrols in these neighborhoods. But police don't encounter crime on patrol in neighborhoods they aren't surveilling, so crime in wealthier, whiter neighborhoods often goes undetected. Consequently, *where* police patrol largely determines who gets targeted, surveilled, and arrested—and thus, which places end up in police data. COMPSTAT thus has a circular effect: increased police activity in a neighborhood results in higher rates of crime which then justifies further policing in those same places.

New York's COMPSTAT is often seen as a rational and objective source of evidence for police activity, yet this evidence also reinforces a racially disparate experience of criminal justice agencies. A notable recent example was the use of "stop and frisk." Stop and frisk was developed as part of the COMPSTAT crackdown on crime and was used extensively by the New York Police Department to stop and search almost anyone. The intention was to combat weapons and drug crimes, but relying on COMPSTAT data, the police focused their efforts on "high-crime neighborhoods"—where the population was more likely to be black or brown and lower income (Ward 2014).

With COMPSTAT and other criminological technologies, the "objective" or "rational" coding of space thus hides deeply contextual, relational, and embedded forms of knowledge. What is "objective" is actually the result of highly mediated processes—such as determining what constitutes crime, what types of crime are the most deserving of attention, and how to respond to crime. These processes all have important consequences for who gets policed, how they get policed, and why they get policed. Without a doubt, COMPSTAT is considerably more sophisticated and often based on much larger and different types of data than earlier policing efforts. Yet, the result is the same—the deployment of police in the very same communities and against the very same individuals that have historically borne the brunt of policing.

The story of COMPSTAT is a microcosm of the story we tell in this book about race and crime. It's a story that considers how good intentions, racial redress, and an entire national history predicated on equality and liberty result in centuries of racial subjugation. Thus, even though criminal justice agencies embraced newly emerging scientific techniques of crime investigation, the problem of racialized mass incarceration continued. Indeed, we argue that what we see when we look at criminal justice is not the workings of a fundamentally just but somewhat flawed criminal justice system in need of reform. Rather, it is the effect of the systematic equation of race and crime and the criminalization of race in the United States, a history that began several centuries ago.

The cause is not racist police, nor other racist criminal justice officials, but rather the ways in which the narratives of white racial domination have been sublimated into structures and institutions. Narratives of white racial domination were explicitly demonstrated in Charlottesville, but they can also be found in the institutions that make up our everyday lives, from the school to the economy to the criminal justice system. This began when race was invented in the era of colonialism and continues to shape how we address crime and justice today.

CRIMINALIZING RACE: COLONIALISM, RACE, AND CRIME

Colonialism may seem an odd place to start a textbook on the intersections between race and crime, especially as the supposed date of "discovery" of the Americas in 1492 was almost five centuries ago. Many likely see colonialism as far removed from contemporary politics of race and crime. Yet the origins of colonialism are critical for understanding the emergence, ascendance, and continuation of race in society today.

Coloniality

Racial inequalities today are the result of practices that began in the colonial era and make up what we call **coloniality.** This term, coined by Aníbal Quijano (2000), refers to the processes by which colonial-era mechanisms of power were subsumed and integrated into the social order. Coloniality has been described as the "darker side of modernity," where "human lives became expendable to the benefit of increasing wealth, and such expendability was justified by the naturalisation of the racial ranking of human beings" (Mignolo 2007, 41). Coloniality consists of two dominant practices: (1) violent geographical appropriation of resources, places, and people and (2) racial and patriarchal knowledge production.

Sovereign Force

Colonialism was ultimately a geographical project—centered on the conquest, acquisition, and shaping of space, place, and people. Closely linked to the idea of colonial conquest is the notion of sovereign force. *Sovereignty* refers to the power of a ruler over land and territory. In a monarchy, the king is sovereign and holds sway over the land, while in a democracy, the people's rule is sovereign. **Sovereign force** refers to the process by which rulers use instruments of violence—conquest, war, and even the criminal justice system—to rule over others. In colonial conquest, sovereign force meant the violent appropriation of people and places for the health, wealth, and continued domination of the sovereign. In this book, we will examine how sovereign force—or what we will call more simply **state power**—is used to protect the health, wealth, and continued appropriation of people and places for the continuity of white racial domination.

Knowledge Production

Colonialism is also about what we say and think about colonized places, or what we call, in shorthand, practices of knowledge production. **Knowledge production** refers to the methods by which truth claims are asserted and the processes by which those claims are bolstered and disseminated. Knowledge production is going on around us all the time, such as when someone makes a truth claim about another person and then disseminates that to others. This is often called "gossip." But it is a practice of knowledge production, with a method of dissemination. It also, importantly, has a broader impact, shaping the relational structures between friends, which can even alter the future social, political, and economic contexts of those involved. For instance, consider how a rumor can lead to someone losing social standing. In this book, we are concerned with the practices of knowledge production about race and crime and how these practices shape the social, cultural, political, and economic contexts of colonial conquest, both historically and today.

Knowledge production was integral to colonial conquest. Colonialism initiated the Age of Enlightenment, as contact with new places and people resulted in an explosion of interest in the mapping, classification, and ordering of places, people, animals, and plants (Mitchell 2002). Colonialist appropriation and practice continued not because the use of sovereign force continued to expand but because the techniques of classification and ordering produced evidence for the colonial order.

It was much easier, for instance, to appropriate the bodies of black people when Africa was classified, even by very smart people like the philosopher Georg Hegel, as a place "properly understood" as the "Unhistorical, Undeveloped Spirit, still involved in the conditions of mere nature" (1857, 103). Thinking of an entire continent and its people as "mere nature" meant that they could be transplanted, weeded, cultivated, and even abandoned and killed, just as one would treat a flower bed. This knowledge production about Africa allowed whites to reconcile claims of equality with racial subjugation, even as this subjugation was intended to "liberate," "civilize," and otherwise enact seemingly benevolent outcomes.

Coloniality and Criminal Justice

COMPSTAT gives us a glimpse into how the techniques of sovereign force are deployed domestically through law enforcement. Criminal justice systems are domestic institutions of sovereign force and use the same tactics and techniques as colonial powers, such as police patrols, courts, and administrative procedures. Law, as Robert Cover (1986) notes, "takes place in a field of pain and death," and there is little doubt that lives are affected, disrupted, and even ended as a consequence of the practice of law.

COMPSTAT also gives us a glimpse into tactics of knowledge production about crime. Khalil Gibran Muhammad (2010) traces how crime knowledge emerged during the era of scientific racism in the 1800s, a topic discussed in detail in chapter 3. Today, criminology continues to obsess about why "some" are so different from the rest of "us," and why the "criminal," like the colonized "savage," is considered a threat to society. Colonialist senses of places and people are eerily similar to the ways space, place, people, and especially crime are thought about in the era of crime mapping. Urban neighborhoods, where the vast majority of arrests take place, are often thought to be "unsafe," "unruly," and even "uncivilized" neighborhoods in need of revitalization and redevelopment. The criminal persona is often imagined as a savage human being, with little respect for or adherence to society's values. COMPSTAT institutionalizes this knowledge in the crime map, which distinguishes places where "they," "the savage," and "crime" dominate from those where "we," "the civilized," and "safety" must be protected. And then police are deployed in ways that make this knowledge reality.

Today, coloniality is alive and well, hidden in plain sight in the criminal justice system. For instance, sexual assault of black and brown women today is underpoliced, underprosecuted, and given much less media attention and outrage (Ritchie 2006). During colonialism and slavery, black and brown women were considered "unrapeable" by white men, meaning that any assault on them was not often legally defined as rape. As recent events have shown, like the choking to death by New York police of Eric Garner for selling single cigarettes or the "rough ride" in a Baltimore police van that killed Freddie Gray, black and brown people, especially men, are subject to greater use of force by agents of the state such as the police. During colonial conquest and slavery, black and brown people were also killed with impunity and subject to repeated violent assaults. Crime knowledge and the geographical practices of controlling crime thus are not as unlike colonialism as they might seem at first glance.

Indeed, no other institution plays such a defining role in mediating, often literally, the line between life and death as the justice system does today. The subjection, as Ruth Wilson Gilmore (2002, 2006) calls it, of black Americans to **"premature death"** is not a figure of speech but names a reality in which the criminal justice system organizes the early death of many nonwhites, especially black Americans. The criminal justice system and its attendant logics surrounding crime articulate and organize the racial experience. They create a knowledge about race that is as deep and insidious as earlier historical logics that we might today disregard. They continue a deep divide, created through the conquest of some, through the deployment of criminal justice resources.

To explain the contemporary coloniality of criminal justice, we trace two sometimes distinct but often intersecting social, political and economic developments in the United States: (1) race as a category shaping and dominating U.S. society and (2) crime and criminal justice as key institutions in the U.S. political landscape. While some might argue that these two only collude in the contemporary moment, both embed a racial logic into institutions that reproduces and transforms again and again. We argue that today both race and crime/criminal justice are based in a colonial model of power, where the subjugation, expropriation, and elimination of some are considered natural and right. The significance of these two together today is not accidental, but instead reflective of a broader embedding within a racialized state logic that began in the colonial era. This collusion also certainly happens within other institutions, and in another era, an institution other than criminal justice may ascend as a new racial management institution. Yet, this will not mean that race will lose its significance in U.S. society, but rather that its institutional, popular, and political manifestations will shift.

Before we embark on this explanation, however, we turn to a brief definition of the two terms that are at the heart of the topic: race and crime. Both of these terms have histories that will be revisited in subsequent chapters, but below we provide a brief sketch not only of how these terms are used in this book, but why the struggle and contestation over these terms is critical to understanding their intersection.

WHAT IS RACE?

When instructing about race, we commonly teach that race is a social construction, but what this means is more elusive and complex than this simple expression connotes. We often also repeat another common refrain to remedy a historically deeply held misconception about race: race is not biology. Yet these two maxims—race is a social construction and not biology—are often hard to reconcile with the manifestation of race today. How can race be a social construction when it is based (in part) on a clearly visible and mostly immutable bodily characteristic? How can race not be biology when it is passed down to people through the very biological practice of birth? How can race be a social construction when it has such clear roots in the body? Indeed, the ability of race to seem natural, biological, and even predestined reveals just how deep this social construction runs (Smedley and Smedley 2005).

Paying attention to the social construction of knowledge means paying attention to the world in which we live. Take for example the amount of time one is expected to spend at work. In the United States, it is common to refer to the "forty-hour week," but this standard is by no means global. How does this happen? Cultural custom defines expectations about work, which are subsequently translated in legislative mandates about work. Legislation defines the meaning of *full time* and whether any benefits accrue to this status. Vacation, sick leave, parental leave, and all sorts of other accommodations vary by jurisdiction. Some countries, such as the United States, do not have paid parental leave, while other countries mandate that parents receive sometimes as much as two years of leave after the birth of a child. Political agitation by workers and capitalist owners has meant struggle over the meaning of the workweek and the quality of working conditions, leading to yet more labor legislation. What constitutes the workweek is thus subject to change across space and time, political contestation, and social, cultural and economic norms. In short, **social construction** is meaning making by society.

The social construction of race thus means that it is—and can be—built through institutional structures, ideological struggle, and individual proclivities and habits. Race emerges from these meaning-making processes, and this textbook provides an understanding of how the meaning-making processes that constitute race came to infuse and permeate issues and institutions of crime and justice.

Race Is Not . . .

Race is constituted by historical, economic, social, and geographical processes, and seems to be quite literally everywhere and nowhere at once. It is one of the most defining constructs in American society, yet discussions of race often lack any real specificity. Some see it as a by-product of capitalism or a historical holdover from an earlier era. Others see it as reflective of cultural difference or ethnic heritage, reducible to cultural norms and practices. Since race is not biology and thus not "real," it is often easy to suggest that its origins come from something else—the economy, culture, or some other place. Other arguments claim that race is the by-product of explicit prejudice or racial hatred and the result of extreme or fringe elements in society. For these reasons, before we define what race *is,* we begin with what we think race *is not.*

Race Is Not Biology

One common misperception is that race is the result of biological difference. This is often based on a historical idea of race that classified the entire world into three "races"—white, Asiatic, and black. As we discuss in chapter 3, biological ideas of race have long been discounted. One frequently cited statistic is the probability that we can be more genetically like someone of another "race" than someone within our own racial group. Much of what we "see" as "clear" racial difference is the result of gradual changes from one place to the next, and not the result of "different races" (McChesney 2015).

Further, there is no scientific basis to the idea that certain racial "characteristics" are reflective of innate capacities, behaviors, or predilections. Traits that are seemingly simple—like the color of eyes or hair—are in fact incredibly complex. Height, for instance, is influenced by over 180 genetic loci (McChesney 2015). Though it is popular to argue that there is a racial "bell curve" for intelligence, this argument is based on a single measure—the IQ test. The IQ test, however, has been shown to be culturally biased, and when environmental context and influences are taken into account, racial differences in results disappear. Scientists looking for a genetic basis for intelligences have had little luck, confirming that "the direct evidence indicates that the differences between the races [in disease, IQ, or other similar traits] is entirely due to environmental factors" (Nisbett et al. 2012, 146). Even medical scientists today are warning against the use of race in understanding genetic research as it "can lead to serious medical errors" and that "once race is presumed, the ways in which multiple genetic inheritances interact with the environment within that individual seem to disappear" (Braun et al. 2007, 1426).

Thinking of race as biology often leads people to define racism as someone who holds a set of stereotypes or prejudices about a group of people, often based in the idea of biology (or another reason below). Racism in this context is simply acting on those prejudices to disadvantage an individual or a group of people. Often-cited examples of racism using this definition are people or groups who murder or explicitly discriminate against someone because of their "race." Calls to racially profile Arab Americans, for instance, are examples of explicit racism or racism as prejudice. Murdering people because of skin color is another example. These are important types of racialized behaviors, but they do not encapsulate the entirety of race nor explain where race comes from or why it survives. They tell us one experience of race—the experience of prejudice or racial hatred—but they do not tell us about race as a social practice, a system of knowledge making, or a host of other things about race.

This definition of race sees race as ancillary to society and not part of seemingly race-neutral practices. When race is equated with biology, and racism as prejudice or hate, individual people are racist, and these racists are discrete, nameable, and seen as outside the "normal" functioning of society. Take the example of schooling. Education is not seen as integral to race-making, yet historically, it was used as a marker of humanity, defined as educated, white, male, and property owning. Education has been denied to many historically—nonwhites, women, the poor, and others nonconforming to this conception of citizenship (Leonardo 2009; Spring 1994). Education taught fundamental skills like reading and math, but it also was a vehicle for the normalization and dissemination of white sensibilities that shaped our conceptions of race, gender, class and sexuality. Students were taught how to comport themselves in dress, bodily mannerisms, and speech. Educational practice quite explicitly created a white racial culture by including topics like moral education and the most appropriate way for young women to keep a home.

Education is not the only institution responsible for racialization and merely provides an example of how pervasive race-making is to institutional function.

Race is not just rooted in people and groups that espouse hate or prejudice but is inseparable from institutional practice. While institutions are certainly made up of the people and groups that populate them, institutions are also critical to structuring and organizing people and groups across space and time. Institutions are also sites invested with critical significance in understanding and making the social world. Institutions are social anchors—and as such are critically important to the production and reproduction of social life. If race were solely the result of white supremacist or any other groups, it would not affect the lives of so many people. Racial hate would have little social significance and ultimately little social purchase. Yet, race continues, not because of individual racists but because of its institutional embedding. And, importantly, it is this institutional entrenchment that provides social support for racial hatred.

Race Is Not Culture

Often, the move away from the biological definition of race leads commentators to argue that even though race is not biological, it still has intractable roots that act a lot like biological determinism. For example, it used to be believed that the biological processes that resulted in someone's skin being a particular color were also responsible for making people "lazy" or "rational." For those who say that race is culture, these traits stem not from biology but from culture. Examples of this type of logic that you may be familiar with include that people of a certain "race" have more babies because of their ethnic/cultural heritage; that people of a certain "race" are more likely to be cheap, thrifty, or economically untrustworthy because of their cultural upbringing; that growing up in certain types of conditions, like poverty, creates and reinforces certain cultures of responding to conflict through actions like violence and criminality; or that wealth accumulation in certain races is the result of a culture of hard work, struggle, and sacrifice.

Race-as-biology proponents might have argued that whites had a biological predisposition toward industriousness and rationality. Race-as-culture proponents argue that those same whites produce a culture of industriousness and rationality through the influence of certain traits found more often in white racial groups. The influence of wealth accumulation, colonial state practice, history, and geography on the creation of opportunity is obfuscated and erased by race-as-culture arguments. This framework is problematic not only for the obvious reason that it merely reproduces biological determinism, but also because it fails to understand race itself as the result of meaning-making processes that vary across space and time.

Anthropologists have taught us that culture and cultural difference exist, but as a determinant for the emergence and continuity of race, they are a poor explanation. Culture emerges from social interaction, not from any innate processes, and it can change throughout history, is different in different places, and has both large (e.g., "American" culture) and small (e.g., the culture of the lunchroom) manifestations (Geertz 1973). While this book cannot provide an in-depth look at what culture is, relying on culture to explain race often reproduces many of the same logics of the biological definition of race. Instead of being rooted in the body, as the biological definition of race portends, race is instead rooted in the imprint that social embedding leaves on the body—the ethnic or racial heritage that marks people as from a "different culture" and thus "different" in their entirety. This argument is developed in more detail in chapter 4, where we discuss the transition in criminology and social policy from biological conceptions of race to cultural ones.

Race Is Not Class

Race is not reducible to class or a by-product of capitalism. Economic-determinist arguments often claim that what is regarded as "race" is in reality class structure. Yet, race exists outside, above, and beyond class structure. Race is also not just an economic reality but also a social, cultural, political, historical, and geographical concept. Economics also does not determine the expression of race in these realms. Instead, race is a reality that extends across all classes and categories in the United States—it is intersectional and informed by gender, class, and sexuality, to name a few of the most important dimensions. Race is thus, like many other social categories, a complex and complicated social structure.

This social structure is revealed through several social outcomes that show the pervasiveness of race and not class over our lives. Race, more than class, determines whether one is exposed to environmental hazards and trauma, where one lives, and what schools one attends. Race, not class, has been shown to determine who gets pulled over by police, who gets arrested, who juries are more likely to convict, and who is more likely to get the death penalty. Race, more than class, even determines one's life expectancy. This is not to suggest that class does not matter. Rather, race and class are inseparably tangled, and considerations of race necessarily include how political economy and wealth accumulation influence the distribution of resources, such as criminal justice institutions. Or as noted earlier, class—and the accumulation of wealth by some and the expendability of others—is the result of the "naturalisation of the racial ranking of human beings" (Mignolo 2007, 41).

Often, race is used as an ideological tool to explain and justify class cleavages. According to this tradition, race serves two central functions. First, during the era of chattel slavery it served to reconcile a glaring contradiction: the emerging democracy was supposedly based on the idea that all men are created equal, yet some were permanently excluded. Those who were excluded from democratic participation had their civil and natural rights repeatedly, violently, and systematically infringed through the institution of slavery. Some claim that it was this contradiction—and the need to continue this economic exploitation for the good of the nation—that led to race (Marable 2000). Race in this context is merely a justification for economic exploitation (Fields 1990). Yet, this explanation misses the role that race plays in creating societal cleavages that justify and legitimate the emergence of a class-based system. Without the hierarchy of "civilization" and "savage," or what we call between the "human" and the "nonhuman," class politics and wealth accumulation may not have been possible.

Second, those who argue that race just obfuscates economic forces argue that the real function of racial classification is to break solidarity within the working class (e.g., Roediger 1999). Race is considered an ideological tool of the dominant class, utilized to mystify economic exploitation and obscure structures of capitalist domination. Proponents of this view cite the use of black Americans as strikebreakers in the North, prohibitions against black membership in many unions, and higher rates of virulent racism amongst the white working class than among the white upper class. Calling attention to race undermines class solidarity by causing white workers to identify with the white capitalist elite rather than with their natural allies, working-class nonwhites. Race then is ultimately just a tool to continue capitalist oppression and stymie worker revolt.

This definition, however, fails to explain how race itself is an organizing principle of political economy (Quijano 2000). Many suggest that exploitation of people, such as the institution of slavery, happened because people were motivated by profit. Yet the historical record suggests otherwise. As we show in chapter 2, people did not necessarily desire to exploit others for profit. Rather, enslavement had an underlying logic based not in the appropriation of land or resources but in the idea that the people being exploited were not deserving of the same protections as the conquerors. Instead, enslaving people, even in ancient times, was seen as ordained by God and as something that could only befall particular people. As we show in detail in chapter 2, the accumulation of profit based on the exploitation of others began with a racial logic (Grosfoguel 2003).

Race Is Not Reducible to Color Racism

Perhaps the greatest obstacle to critical engagement with conceptions of race is that race is usually understood as color racism, meaning that it is seen merely as discrimination based on the color of someone's skin. "Color," though, is not the primary logic animating race, but rather the shorthand signifier of race on a daily basis. Color racism is but one form of racism. Hierarchical racial relations are based on far wider and more extensive understandings than color. Take the stereotypes discussed above about what it means to be white. Whiteness is not about color per se but about being cast as morally upright, industrious, and responsible. These are not necessarily attributes of those who have white skin—there are plenty of immoral, lazy, and irresponsible white people—but those with white skin are the recipients of the assumption that they possess these traits. Color racism is then the result of a larger process of race making, whereby all sorts of attributes, behaviors, predilections, and practices have racialized meaning.

Race Is . . .

Race is then, a system of classification that organizes the world's population into a hierarchy of human/nonhuman (Delaney 2001; Grosfoguel 2007; Hepburn and Anderson 1995; Quijano 2000). Humans are those who have evolved, are civilized, and ultimately are "white," while the nonhuman is the savage, the predator, and ultimately "black."

The structure of race, therefore, is a hierarchy of superiority/inferiority in relation to the line of humanity. Race is the logic that infuses humanity not by signifying a biological species classification of *Homo sapiens* but by signifying a set of ideals of consciousness, behavior, and logic supposedly absent in other species. Some people identified as "humans" are nevertheless repeatedly, consistently, and violently sorted into this nonhuman category. And that is the basis of race.

We trace this classification to a set of ideas and material practices that are born within but transcend the era of colonial conquest. While some people argue that we have emerged from colonialism and are in a postcolonial era, the power structures initiated by colonization, conquest, and subjugation are still salient today (Maldonado-Torres 2007). Today, colonial power structures are hidden behind ideologies that do not use the language of colonialism and thus are often harder to recognize.

The theoretical construct of coloniality provides a way to highlight race as the consequence of several practices: knowledge production, material practice, and geographical expression (Ndlovu-Gatsheni 2013, Mignolo 2002, Quijano 2000). Race is the product of what we know, how we act, and what we build. Tracing race today from colonial logics provides us with a way to understand race simultaneously as both a material practice (what we build and how we act) and ideological practice (what we know and how we justify and rationalize it). Further, it provides a lens to see race as something that is rooted in place. What race is has a lot to do with *where* one is. Consider the issue of race in the 1800s. If a black person was in Chicago, he or she was a free person. If, however, that same person had been just to the south, in the same nation, then it was likely that he or she would not be free but instead enslaved. That does not mean that racial differences were not also practiced in Chicago; it means that they looked different. But both together contributed to the specific ideas about race and racial difference that make up the national history of the United States. Race thus looks and acts differently across space and time *and* has lasting historical and geographical importance.

Race is also *productive,* meaning that it creates certain ways of knowing the world. It does this across a range of geographical spaces, from the body and people to families and homes and groups and communities. Race makes and marks people. Consider how we know ourselves as racialized beings—when did you come to know that you had a race? That's the power of race: it creates. It also creates groups and belonging within particular groupings—such as black and white, but also Chinese, Latinx, and so on. Finally, it also creates the spaces that we know and that shape how we live, grow, and reproduce.

Race, though, is not alone in this process. Race is lived through other vectors of social difference such as gender, sexuality, class, and age. Race is thus intersectional—and projects of race are never related to race alone. Race also *needs* these other vectors to operate. It does not work without constructions of heterosexual middle-class womanhood, for instance, which is a common identity invoked for the justification and rationalization of intense racial violence. As we will show throughout this book, racial logics occur within constructs of gender, sexuality, and class.

Race is thus constituted by a multiplicity of logics and is multifaceted in its expression. Throughout this book, you will find that the human/nonhuman divide leads to all sorts of practices that produce gender or sexuality or class differences. Race is not epiphenomenal, but the result of deliberate, intentional, and rationalized actions that take place in a world that is simultaneously gendered, sexualized, classed, and aged. The particular manifestation that race takes is a matter of historical particularity, which is why race is so central to our investigation of the criminal justice system.

The social structure of race has stayed remarkably consistent throughout time, even as the dividing line between human and nonhuman has shifted institutional anchors, transcended geographical space, and reconstituted identities and life experiences. As we detail in later chapters, the criminal justice system played a critical role in organizing racial experience throughout history, but it is only today that it has achieved such a significant and defining role in this process.

Given this definition of race, we routinely refer in this book to how state, political, and cultural practices contribute to white supremacy. While *white supremacy* is often used to refer to the ideology of fringe racists, we contend they are not the source of the majority of practices and beliefs that sustain racial hierarchies, and we use the term in a different manner. As Zeus Leonardo (2004) notes, white supremacy differs from white privilege in that "the conditions of white supremacy make white privilege possible. In order for white racial hegemony to saturate everyday life, it has to be secured by a process of domination" (137). **White supremacy** thus for us refers also to the larger structural practices by which whiteness as a system of lived advantage and privilege is reproduced and sustained. Thus, the practices that sustain white supremacy as an organizing logic are not limited to those committed by those we—and broader society—call white supremacists. By terming the structural logics that position some as human and others as nonhuman *white supremacy,* we are intending to call attention to the myriad ways that even the sometimes most insignificant practices contribute to the continuation of racial hierarchies in the United States.

We turn now from the definition of race and toward how the discourse of crime and the practice of the criminal justice system came to be so easily defined with organizing and articulating race in the postracial era.

WHAT IS CRIME?

Crime, like race, is a social construction. *Crime* is defined as a behavior or practice that is forbidden by law and subject to punishment, in our society, by the government. A process of social construction is integral to this definition. Crime is an act that must be forbidden, which suggests an active process. In the United States, in order for an act to be forbidden as a crime, this means that it must be defined in a legislative statute—that is, a law—as a felony or misdemeanor. The series of laws that define particular behaviors as crimes is defined as the criminal or penal code. These codes vary across space and time because crime is socially constructed.

Take the case of marijuana. If, in 2018, you were in California, Washington, Oregon, or Colorado, of age, and found with a joint, you were most likely engaging in a perfectly legal activity. Step over the border to Idaho or Utah or find yourself on federal land, and you would suddenly be committing a crime, one that might be severely punished by years in prison. State differences in the definition of crime highlight the role of society in defining crime. What we call crime is the result of social negotiation and, unsurprisingly, often reflects how we construct social inequalities.

Crime is also something that demands a response, particularly from the state. It must be "forbidden" and "punished." Crime must not only be something society wants to address, but also something it wants to address with the state's monopoly on (legitimate) violence. Crime does not apply to all problematic behaviors, and as we discuss below, significant harms are excluded from this definition.

Crime is thus socially constructed on at least two fronts—both in terms of what gets defined as crime in the penal code (and the related issues of what is enforced, punished more harshly, or ignored altogether) and what society comes to deem as the most important types of behavior deserving of exercise of state violence. This means that the particular types of behaviors called crimes and the various responses to them through the criminal justice system have long been key sites for political contestation and negotiation.

Socially Constructing Crime: The Case of Alcohol Prohibition

One example of how the definition of crime is politically contested and negotiated is the prohibition of alcohol in the United States in the 1920s. Alcohol was not elevated to an illegal activity demanding the violence of the state until white, middle-class Progressive reformers associated its consumption with a whole variety of social ills. Alcohol, according to early-twentieth-century Progressive reformers, brought about the downfall of the family, led to the moral degradation of young women, resulted in the proliferation of crime, and contributed to social inefficiency. Its prohibition through a constitutional amendment was one of the crowning achievements of Progressivism.

Federal police were deployed to stop the trade in alcohol across the U.S.-Canadian border. Prison populations and imprisonment rates swelled (though nowhere close to today). Rampant disobedience of Prohibition prevailed, and soon, alcohol prohibition proved unenforceable (Levine 1985). Prohibition's repeal just a few years later was a redefinition of crime, this time though of what crime is not.

The political, social, and violent resistance to alcohol prohibition is also a larger story of how power, race, and capitalist crises came together. Unlike opium prohibition in the early twentieth century (see chapter 6), which specifically targeted the opium ingestion habits of the Chinese, alcohol prohibition affected white working-class communities. In *Profits, Power and Prohibition*, John Rumbarger (1989) reveals how the anti-liquor movement was supported by capitalist interests seeking to create a disciplined, sober, and reliable labor force in order to secure steady and predictable profits. Immigrants and other factory workers were seen as in need of control by the criminal justice system in order to secure capitalist interests. Rumbarger writes that the U.S. capitalist class "first perceived customary drinking as an obstacle to the orderly transformation of society, and to achieve that transformation, it sought first to remove drink from the interstices of the workday and to inculcate a social habit of abstemiousness entailing the acceptance of the unending need to produce for profit" (187). The anti-liquor movement largely failed because the interests of the white working class aligned with white rural interests and created a formidable force against capitalist interests. Indeed, Rumbarger notes that an organized and sober working class was much more dangerous to the interests of the capitalist class than a working class that was allowed to imbibe in their spare time. Race and class politics together helped construct the definition of crime, and race and class politics also helped undo this construction.

Socially Constructing Crime: The Case of Race

Like Prohibition, mass incarceration stemmed from the social construction of crime, but in this case, it began with race. But this is not a story about how black and brown communities came to be more criminal and thus overrepresented within crime statistics. It is rather about the history of race in the United States and "a race problem that was criminalized" and became inflected throughout the institutions of criminal justice (Murakawa 2014, 3). Or, as one scholar puts it, today "talking about crime *is* talking about race" (Barlow 1998, 149).

How did race and crime become synonymous? This was not always the case, but racialized mass incarceration is inextricably linked to the fight for racial justice. In the 1940s and 1950s, crime was not seen as a problem restricted to black youth; instead, crime was seen as a problem of cities, white and black. When discussing the civil rights movement, most representations during this era "were primarily characterized by the themes of white mob violence and the police as ineffectual in preventing the violence" (Barlow 1998, 158). As we mentioned earlier, this meant that the problem of race and crime was seen as a problem of white racial violence and the inability of state policies and practices to protect black and brown communities.

Crime reports shifted, though, in 1965. By 1965, black political violence was equated with crime in cities, and the tone of crime reports changed, describing crime as a "malignant enemy," "epidemic," and ultimately as the province of "Negro slums." One particular example is what is popularly known as the Watts Riots, which were sparked by an encounter between white police officers and a young black man in South Central Los Angeles (see chapters 6 and 7). Stories blamed a "slum mentality," the lack of Negro leadership, and civil rights leaders inciting violence. Discussion of police brutality and racial injustice were absent.

This shift in discourse placed the blame for violence and crime squarely within the province of black, and not white, power. Other news stories furthered the ideological connection between black communities and crime, and in 1970, the first use of the term "young black male" in relation to crime appeared in *Time* magazine (Barlow 1998). In a just a few decades, the entire tenor of news reporting changed from viewing violence committed by whites as an unfortunate consequence of ideological transformation to viewing black political violence and, indeed, the issue of crime in its entirety as a problem of black communities, especially young black men. This is a construction that continues today—when we see young black men, we often don't think "race" but "crime."

Today, these ideas of crime are commonplace, and a whole corpus of scholarship and field of study has grown up around how media depictions of crime are racialized (e.g., Callanan 2005; Oliver and Fonash 2002; Chiricos and Eschholz 2002). Scholars note that crimes of black Americans, especially against white Americans, are reported on more frequently, punished more severely, and considered more heinous by Americans (Chiricos and Eschholz 2002; Dixon, Azocar, and Casas 2003). The linkage between blackness and crime is so strong that in one study of news reports, participants reported seeing black mug shots even when no mug shot was shown in the report (Peffley, Shields, Williams 1996). Study after study reveals how robust this linkage is: black Americans are regarded as worthier of suspicion and seen as the primary contributors to urban disorder. They are even more likely to be shot in split-second decision tests (Correll et al. 2007; Eberhardt et al. 2004; Fagan and Davies 2000; Quillian and Pager 2001; Sadler et al. 2012; Sampson and Raudenbush 2004). This reality is the direct result of the representation of crime and its transformation.

The term *crime* is thus unstable, and its meaning often exceeds the behaviors and actions that warrant the term. This instability, however, leads to several questions we answer in this book: Why is crime able to have such rhetorical flexibility? How could the term shift in such dramatic fashion in a just a few decades? And how does this shift help to organize the behaviors of crime control institutions—police, courts, prison, execution—in ways that produce race as an identifiable and salient category?

Our answer to these questions is that crime has been socially constructed as race, or what is called the criminalization of race. Consider the definition of crime a bit more closely. Does how we define crime reflect the greatest harms we face or the greatest cost from harms? In other words, are we protecting ourselves from the things that are most likely to harm us, either physically or economically?

Jeffrey Reiman in *The Rich Get Richer and the Poor Get Prison* (2007) says no, and that popular culture's conception of crime is a "carnival mirror" reflecting a distorted image of the harms that affect us. According to Reiman, today's criminal justice system is a distorted reflection "created more by the shape of the mirror than by the reality reflected," and this distortion is the reason why when we look at the prison system, we see primarily black and brown faces (2007, 62).

Reiman argues that this distorted mirror is based on an image he calls the "Typical Criminal," or the socially constructed criminal in the United States. This image is reflected in media accounts of crime, citizens' conception of who is involved in crime, and the material practices of criminal justice that target, police, monitor, imprison, and kill black and brown people more. Yet our conceptions of the harms we supposedly face from this mythological character are far out of proportion to the real harms we face every day.

Reiman opens his book with the statistic that by the time the reader has finished the first chapter, two murders will have taken place, but during that same time, more than six Americans will die from unsafe or unhealthy work conditions that are often entirely preventable (2007, 82). Many more will die from preventable medical malpractice, environmentally caused health conditions, including pollution and food additives, the harms of poverty, and a host of other social ills. In tables 1.1 and 1.2, we reproduce two of Reiman's tables

Table 1.1   **How Americans are murdered, 2014**

Total murders where weapon is known	Firearms	Knife or other cutting instrument	Other weapons: blunt objects, arson, strangulation, poison, etc.	Personal weapons: hands, fists, etc.
11,961	8,124	1,567	1,610	660

SOURCE: Reiman and Leighton 2017, 92.

Table 1.2   **How Americans are *really* murdered, 2014**

Total murders where weapon is known	Occupational hazard or disease	Firearms	Knife or other cutting instrument	Other weapons: blunt objects, arson, strangulation, poison, etc	Personal weapons: hands, fists, etc.
166,237	54,276	8,124	13,567	89,610	660

SOURCE: Reiman and Leighton 2017, 93.

contrasting official statistics on murder and how people are really murdered by including the range of ways people are killed by medical malpractice, workplace safety violations, and other preventable harms. Together, these two tables demonstrate how much harm in the United States is not captured by our definitions of crime or the criminal justice system. Despite these preventable harms, rarely are they dealt with in the criminal justice system.

This definition of crime has huge racial consequences (Murray 2003). Black and brown workers are the ones most likely to face workplace harms, as they are more likely to work in dangerous professions and in workplace environments lacking safety protections. It further benefits white accumulation of wealth, as the lack of safety protections for workers is often the direct result of attempts to increase profits. Since whites are the majority of those who own businesses, especially multinational corporations in the United States, they stand to disproportionately benefit from the lack of enforcement.

Enforcement of workplace harms is further bastardized compared to the criminal justice system. If a safety violation is found on a worksite, it is not even dealt with by the criminal justice system and is instead under the jurisdiction of the Occupational Health and Safety Administration (OSHA). If workplaces fail to abide by safety regulations, often the only punishment, if any, is a fine.

Unlike the criminal justice system, which has substantial resources at its disposal, OSHA is woefully underfunded and understaffed. Charles Jeffress (2002), the head of OSHA in the 1990s, noted that under the OSHA act, willful negligence that results in death is only a misdemeanor. Even further, Jeffress notes that whether someone is injured or killed has little bearing on the penalty, because a safety violation with no injury is often assessed the same penalty as a safety violation with an injury. Further, OSHA does not directly prosecute if someone is killed, and in 2003, of the over 200,000 deaths investigated by OSHA since its founding, only 151 cases were referred for prosecution, and only 8 resulted in incarceration (Frontline 2003). All of the sentences were a year or less (only one was a year, and the rest were under six months), a far cry from the sentences meted out for other crimes in the criminal justice system.

Some might point to the recent prosecution of factory owner Stewart Parnell who knowingly distributed salmonella-tainted peanut butter, which caused the deaths of 9 people and 714 to fall ill. Facing seventy-two counts, Parnell was eventually sentenced to twenty-eight years in prison, heralded as the largest penalty ever faced for a food-borne illness (McCoy 2015). It was also the *first* time that a food executive has been convicted for a food-borne illness (Basu 2015). Many might see this as a step toward greater equality in the definition of crime and as a moment when the definition expands to include the most important harms that face us. Yet, even this sentence is far out of proportion to what many in the criminal justice system face for equivalent crimes.

Killing nine would almost invariably make someone eligible for the death penalty, especially combined with the hundreds who fell ill as a result of his actions. Many people are in jail for much longer for far lesser crimes. Clarence Aaron, for instance, received three life sentences for introducing his cousins to some of his friends at college who then, without Aaron's involvement or knowledge, allegedly transported drugs across state lines (no drugs were ever weighed or entered into evidence) (Linzer 2012). Duc Ta, a youth of 16, was driving a car when his friend shot a gun out the window (Elliott 2005). No one was injured, Duc did not do the shooting, and he was only a teen, yet he received thirty-five years in prison for this single crime alone. There are countless cases of nonviolent offenders receiving sentences for behaviors that did not result in death that were two or three times longer than that of the anomalous peanut executive (Beckett and Sasson 2003).

Crime and the response by the criminal justice system are thus highly mediated and, at their core, are socially constructed processes. Though many use the term *social construction* to point to how ideas and things are imbued with social meaning, often this is seen as tainted by politics, economics, or other social forces. This would mean that perhaps crime and the criminal justice system could exist outside social construction, and our real job as scholars of crime is to find its true meaning. However, as we show in the case of murder in box 1.1, crime is always socially constructed, even if done in a way that is seen as equitable and just.

While rehabilitators and punishers might respond to crime differently, both work to socially construct crime. And both start with the idea that people involved in crime are ultimately in need of intervention *themselves*. We differ from this perspective in seeing the process of constructing crime as a meaning-making process in itself—and what is defined as crime, criminals, rehabilitation, and even punishment as the outcome of that process. Crime and its criminal justice complex then are critical institutions for mediating the line between "us" and "them," between the "human" and the "nonhuman." Defining crime and the work of the criminal justice system is central to the institutional process by which the human and nonhuman are constituted domestically. As we show in the coming chapters, it is not surprising that the tactics of colonization that introduced the concept of race to the modern world are again on display in the practices of the criminal justice system.

CONCLUSION

Many popular pundits argue that race has gone away and thus that the enormous racial differences in the criminal justice system are not an example of the continuation of racial oppression. Many argue that today both political society and legal doctrine protect sufficiently against racial oppression. The passage of the Civil Rights Act in 1964 is one example that many point to as evidence of the end of racism in the United States. Further, the election of President Barack Obama signaled to many that the postracial era has not only arrived, but that equality has been reached. Finally, many suggest that the Fourteenth Amendment's equal protection clause is enough legal protection to guard against discrimination in the criminal justice system.

President Obama's election and the existence of formal legal protections against racist behavior represent not a postracial era where race does not matter, but rather the normalization and obfuscation of race as a particular set of social and cultural proclivities. As we detail in coming chapters, significations of race change over space and time, but race as colonial structure of human/nonhuman continues, even today. And it is no accident that many of those killed by the police today come from similar socioeconomic classes and have similar skin pigmentation to those who were exploited in the past.

Examining the intersections between race and crime thus illuminates how race acts as a cleavage between the "human" and the "nonhuman" and how criminalization and racialization are mutually constituted today. In contemporary American society, the structure of race remains the same but is even more dangerous because it is hidden. We aim to bring this hidden history to the forefront by turning to the origins of race within U.S. political society. We embark on this journey by turning in the next chapter to the historical emergence of race.

BOX 1.1   **Defining Crime: The Case of Murder**

When confronted with the definitional instability of the term *crime,* many people turn to the prohibition on murder as an example of stability in the definition of crime. Often the argument is that murder has been prohibited across time and space and among a myriad of diverse political communities and practices. We are not suggesting that there is not some ideological stability to definitions across time—indeed, crime would not be understandable as the unique and interesting political complex that it is if there was not some internal coherence. Rather, we suggest that this coherence is always partial and contingent. By this we mean that in every society, both ones with extensive laws against murder and ones without, there are some forms of violence and death that do not get equated with murder. And these actions and behaviors are not stable across space and time.

Today, one of the more controversial examples of the self-defense doctrine is what are called "stand-your-ground" laws. The infamous case of Trayvon Martin, who was killed by a self-styled neighborhood watch member, demonstrates this pernicious logic. Martin was on his way back from a local convenience store when the neighborhood watch member reported him to police as a suspicious person. Before police arrived, the killer alleged that he followed Martin, but then Martin turned and confronted him. Martin was shot by the killer in the altercation and died at the scene. The killer was not arrested by police that night and was instead let go under the provisions of Florida's controversial stand-your-ground law. He was eventually charged but used that same law as his defense and was ultimately acquitted by a jury. He never alleged that he did not shoot and kill Martin, only that he did so in the name of self-defense.

One of the most important examples in the Western context (and others as well) of violence that is not considered murder is self-defense, where the defense against imminent danger is a legitimate excuse for killing another. In this popular conception of self-defense, imminent danger is considered objectively and materially present. Stand-your-ground laws are a permutation of this type of logic. The Florida law, passed in 2005, authorizes citizens to "meet force with force, including deadly force" in situations where they are in fear of "great bodily harm." As Ta-Nehisi Coates (2013) puts it, this means "effectively, I can bait you into a fight and if I start losing I can legally kill you, provided I 'believe' myself to be subject to 'great bodily harm'." Coates further cites the instructions given to the jury in the Martin killing case that the danger "need not have been actual" and that "based upon appearances . . . one must have actually believed that the danger was real." An analysis of stand-your-ground provisions found that white-on-black homicides were eleven times more likely to be ruled self-defense than black-on-white homicides were. Moreover, states with stand-your-ground laws also had considerably more white-on-black homicides ruled self-defense than states without such laws.

Jody Armour (1997) called this type of defense the "reasonable racism" defense, where the racial construction of threat is enough to establish that it is reasonable to believe that some members of a race are likely to kill you in any confrontation. Before the controversial Martin case, and even before the ascendance of stand-your-ground laws, reasonable-racism defenses played a role in acquitting whites for the killing and some would call murder of nonwhite individuals. One of the most famous examples of the reasonable-racism discourse is the 1984 case of Bernhard Goetz, who shot four young men on the New York subway when they tried to mug him. Goetz admitted to the shooting, indicating that "my intention was to murder them, to hurt them, to make them suffer as much as possible" (Drogin 1987). Despite admitting to murder and telling police, "If I had more bullets, I would have shot them all again and again," Goetz was acquitted of all charges except carrying a concealed weapon. Dubbed the "subway vigilante" by the media, Goetz was considered a hero to those who represented New York as under siege from crime and violence.

The Goetz and Martin cases both illustrate how behaviors that might seem to be always labeled crimes—like murder—are in reality also subject to social and political construction. Both Martin's killer and Goetz joined a long line of whites for whom killing black, brown, and other nonwhite people is considered "rational" and meets the legal definition of reasonableness. While law is often considered to be objective, rational, and predictable, cases like these demonstrate just how contingent this claim is on a particular racialized construction of who can kill with impunity.

Sources: Jody David Armour, *Negrophobia and Reasonable Racism: The Hidden Costs of Being Black in America* (New York: NYU Press, 1997); Ta-Nehisi Coates, "Trayvon Martin and the Irony of American Justice," *Atlantic*, July 15, 2013, www.theatlantic.com/national/archive/2013/07/trayvon-martin-and-the-irony-of-american-justice/277782/; Bob Drogin, "Recording Played at Trial in Subway Shootings of Four," *Los Angeles Times*, April 30,1987, http://articles.latimes.com/1987-04-30/news/mn-2897_1_subway-gunman; LaKerri R. Mack and Kristie Roberts-Lewis, "The Dangerous Intersection between Race, Class and Stand Your Ground," *Journal of Public Management & Social Policy* 23, no. 1 (2016): 4.

REFERENCES

Allen, Robert. 2005. "Reassessing the Internal (Neo)Colonialism Theory." *Black Scholar* 35, no. 1 (Spring): 2–11.
Anderson, Kay. 1995. " 'The Beast Within': Race, Humanity, and Animality." *Environment and Planning D: Society and Space* 13, no. 6.
Armour, Jody David. 1997. *Negrophobia and Reasonable Racism: The Hidden Costs of Being Black in America.* New York: NYU Press,
Bachman, Ronet, and Linda E. Saltzman. 1994. *Violence against Women.* Vol. 81. Washington, DC: U.S. Department of Justice, Office of Justice Programs, Bureau of Justice Statistics.
Barlow, Melissa Hickman. 1998. "Race and the Problem of Crime in *Time* and *Newsweek* Cover Stories, 1946 to 1995." *Social Justice* 25, no. 2 (Summer): 149–83.
Basu, Moni. 2015. *For First Time, Company Owner Faces Life Sentence for Food Poisoning Outbreak.* CNN Online, September 21, 2015. www.cnn.com/2015/09/20/us/peanut-butter-salmonella-trial/
Beckett, Katherine. 2000. *Making Crime Pay: Law and Order in Contemporary American Politics.* New York: Oxford University Press.
Beckett, Katherine, and Theodore Sasson. 2003. *The Politics of Injustice: Crime and Punishment in America.* Thousand Oaks, CA: Sage.

Bjornstrom, E. E., R. L. Kaufman, R. D. Peterson, and M. D. Slater. 2010. "Race and Ethnic Representations of Lawbreakers and Victims in Crime News: A National Study of Television Coverage." *Social Problems* 57, no. 2, 269–93.

Bonilla-Silva, Eduardo. 2006. *Racism without Racists: Color-blind Racism and the Persistence of Racial Inequality in the United States.* Lanham, MD: Rowman & Littlefield.

Braga, Anthony A., and Brenda J. Bond. 2008. "Policing Crime and Disorder Hot Spots: A Randomized Controlled Trial." *Criminology* 46, no. 3: 577–607.

Braun, Lundy, Anne Fausto-Sterling, Duana Fullwiley, Evelynn M. Hammonds, Alondra Nelson, William Quivers, Susan M. Reverby, and Alexandra E. Shields. 2007. "Racial Categories in Medical Practice: How Useful Are They?" *PLoS Medicine* 4, no. 9: e271.

Brown, Elizabeth. 2014. "Expanding Carceral Geographies: Challenging Mass Incarceration and Creating a 'Community Orientation' towards Juvenile Delinquency." *Geographica Helvetica* 69, no. 5: 377.

Cahalan, Margaret Werner. 1986. *Historical Corrections Statistics in the United States, 1850–1984.* Washington, DC: U.S. Department of Justice, Office of Justice Programs, Bureau of Justice Statistics.

Callanan, Valerie J. 2005. *Feeding the Fear of Crime: Crime-Related Media and Support for Three Strikes.* New York: LFB Scholarly Publishing.

Carson, E. Ann. 2015. *Prisoners in 2014.* Washington, DC: U.S. Department of Justice, Office of Justice Programs, Bureau of Justice Statistics.

Carson, E. Ann, and Daniela Golinelli. "Prisoners in 2012: Trends in Admissions and Releases, 1991–2012." 2013. *Bureau of Justice Statistics Bulletin* (December, rev. September 2014). Washington, DC: U.S. Department of Justice Programs, Bureau of Justice Statistics.

Chesney-Lind, Meda, and Marc Mauer, eds. 2003. *Invisible Punishment: The Collateral Consequences of Mass Imprisonment.* New York: New Press.

Chiricos, Ted, and Sarah Eschholz. 2002. "The Racial and Ethnic Typification of Crime and the Criminal Typification of Race and Ethnicity in Local Television News." *Journal of Research in Crime and Delinquency* 39, no. 4: 400–420.

Coates, Ta-Nehisi. 2013. "Trayvon Martin and the Irony of American Justice." *Atlantic,* July 15, 2013. www .theatlantic.com/national/archive/2013/07/trayvon-martin-and-the-irony-of-american-justice/277782/.

Cole, David. 2000. *No Equal Justice: Race and Class in the American Criminal Justice System.* New York: New Press.

Cover, Robert M. 1986. "Violence and the Word." *Yale Law Journal* 95, no. 8: 1601–29.

Correll, J., B. Park, C. M. Judd, B. Wittenbrink, M. S. Sadler, and T. Keesee. 2007. "Across the Thin Blue Line: Police Officers and Racial Bias in the Decision to Shoot." *Journal of Personality and Social Psychology* 92, no. 6: 1006.

Brown-Dean, Khalilah, Zoltan Hajnal, Christina Rivers, and Ismail White. 2015. *50 Years of the Voting Rights Act: The State of Race in Politics.* Washington DC: Joint Center for Political and Economic Studies. http://jointcenter.org/sites/default/files/VRA%20report%2C%203.5.15%20%281130%20 am%29%28updated%29.pdf.

Delaney, David. 2001. "Making Nature/Marking Humans: Law as a Site of (Cultural) Production." *Annals of the Association of American Geographers* 91, no. 3: 487–503.

Detention Watch Network. 2018. *Immigration Detention 101.* Washington, DC. www.detentionwatchnetwork .org/issues/detention-101.

Dixon, Travis L., Cristina L. Azocar, and Michael Casas. 2003. "The Portrayal of Race and Crime on Television Network News." *Journal of Broadcasting & Electronic Media* 47, no. 4: 498–523.

Drogin, Bob. 1987. "Recording Played at Trial in Subway Shootings of Four : 'Intention Was to Murder,' Goetz Says on Tape." *Los Angeles Times,* April 30, 1987. http://articles.latimes.com/1987–04–30/news/mn-2897_1_ subway-gunman.

Eberhardt, J. L., P. A. Goff, V. J. Purdie, and P. G. Davies. 2004. "Seeing Black: Race, Crime, and Visual Processing." *Journal of Personality and Social Psychology* 87, no. 6: 876.

Elliott, Stephen. 2005. *Juvies: Michael Duc Ta.* Huffington Post, July 3, 2005. www.huffingtonpost.com/stephen-elliott/juvies-michael-duc-ta_b_3598.html.

Fagan, Jeffrey, and Garth Davies. 2000. "Street Stops and Broken Windows: Terry, Race and Disorder in New York City." *Fordham Urban Law Journal* 28, no. 2: 457–504.

Farlie, Robert W. 2005. *Are We Really a Nation Online?: Ethnic and Racial Disparities in Access to Technology and Their Consequences.* Report for the Leadership Conference on Civil Rights Education Fund. September 20, 2005. www.freepress.net/sites/default/files/fp-legacy/lccrdigitaldivide.pdf.

Fields, Barbara Jeanne. 1990. "Slavery, Race and Ideology in the United States of America." *New Left Review* 181, no. 1: 95–118.

Fraser, Mark W. 1997. *Risk and Resilience in Childhood: An Ecological Perspective.* Washington, DC: NASW Press.

Frontline. 2003. "Criminal Prosecution of Workplace Fatalities." In *A Dangerous Business.* WGBH, PBS. Airdate January 9, 2003. www.pbs.org/wgbh/pages/frontline/shows/workplace/osha/.

Garland, David. 2001. *The Culture of Control.* Oxford: Oxford University Press.

Geertz, Clifford. 1973. *The Interpretation of Cultures: Selected Essays.* New York: Basic Books.

Gilmore, Ruth Wilson. 2002. "Fatal Couplings of Power and Difference: Notes on Racism and Geography." *Professional Geographer* 54, no. 1: 15–24.

———. 2006. *Golden Gulag: Prisons, Surplus, Crisis, and Opposition in Globalizing California.* American Crossroads 21. Berkeley: University of California Press.

GoGwilt, Christopher Lloyd. 1995. *The Invention of the West: Joseph Conrad and the Double-Mapping of Europe and Empire.* Stanford, CA: Stanford University Press.

Grosfoguel. Ramon. 2003. *Colonial Subjects: Puerto Ricans in a Global Perspective.* Berkeley: University of California Press.

———. 2007. "The Epistemic Decolonial Turn." *Cultural Studies* 21, no. 2: 211–23.

Hagan, John, and Holly Foster. 2006. "Profiles of Punishment and Privilege: Secret and Disputed Deviance during the Racialized Transition to American Adulthood." *Crime, Law, and Social Change* 46, no. 1–2: 65–85.

Hegel, Georg Wilhelm Friedrich. 1857. *Lectures on the Philosophy of History, 1770–1831.* London: Henry G. Bohn. https://hdl.handle.net/2027/uc1.$b288580.

Hepburn, Katherine, and Kay Anderson. 1995. "'The Beast Within': Race, Humanity, and Animality." *Environment and Planning D: Society and Space* 13, no. 6.

Jeffress, Charles. 2002. "Interview with Charles Jeffress," September 30, 2002. In *A Dangerous Business.* Frontline. WGBH, PBS. www.pbs.org/wgbh/pages/frontline/shows/workplace/osha/jeffress.html.

Jencks, Christopher, and Meredith Phillips, eds. 2011. *The Black-White Test Score Gap.* Washington, DC: Brookings Institution Press.

Johnson, Robert, Ania Dobrzanska, and Seri Palla. 2005. "The American Prison in Historical Perspective: Race, Gender, and Adjustment." In *Prisons: Today and Tomorrow,* edited by Jocelyn M. Pollock, 26–51. 2nd ed. Burlington, MA: Jones & Bartlett Learning.

Johnston, Ron, Michael Poulsen, and James Forrest. 2007. "Ethnic and Racial Segregation in U.S. Metropolitan Areas, 1980–2000: The Dimensions of Segregation Revisited." *Urban Affairs Review* 42, no. 40: 479–504.

Kaeble, Danielle, Lauren Glaze, Anastasios Tsoutis, and Todd Minton. 2015. "Correction Populations in the United States, 2014." *Bureau of Justice Statistics Bulletin* (December, rev. January 2016). Washington, DC: U.S. Department of Justice Programs, Bureau of Justice Statistics. www.bjs.gov/content/pub/pdf/cpus14.pdf.

Krysan, Maria. 2002. "Community Undesirability in Black and White: Examining Racial Residential Preferences through Community Perceptions." *Social Problems* 49, no. 4: 521–43.

Krysan, Maria, and Michael Bader. 2007. "Perceiving the Metropolis: Seeing the City through a Prism of Race." *Social Forces* 86, no. 2: 699–733.

Leonardo, Zeus. 2009. *Race, Whiteness, and Education.* New York: Routledge.

Levine, Harry Gene. 1985. "Birth of American Alcohol Control: Prohibition, the Power Elite, and the Problem of Lawlessness." *Contemporary Drug Problems* 12 (Spring): 63–115.

Linzer, Dafna. 2012. "Clarence Aaron Was Denied Commutation, but Bush Team Wasn't Told All the Facts." *Washington Post,* May 13, 2012. www.washingtonpost.com/investigations/clarence-aaron-was-denied-commutation-but-bush-team-wasnt-told-all-the-facts/2012/05/13/gIQAEZLRNU_story.html.

Maldonado-Torres, Nelson. 2007. "On the Coloniality of Being." *Cultural Studies* 21, no. 2: 240–70.

Massey, Douglas S., and Nancy A. Denton. 1993. *American Apartheid: Segregation and the Making of the Underclass.* Cambridge, MA: Harvard University Press.

Marable, Manning. 2000. *How Capitalism Underdeveloped Black America: Problems in Race, Political Economy, and Society.* South End Press Classics 4. Updated ed. Cambridge, MA: South End Press.

Mauer, Marc. 2006. *Race to Incarcerate.* New York: New Press.

Mauer, Marc, and Ryan S. King. 2007. *Uneven Justice: State Rates of Incarceration by Race and Ethnicity.* Washington, DC: Sentencing Project.

McChesney, Kay Young. 2015. "Teaching Diversity: The Science You Need to Know to Explain Why Race Is Not Biological." *SAGE Open* 5, no. 4: 1–13.

McCoy, Kevin. 2015. *Peanut Exec in Salmonella Case Gets 28 Years.* USAToday online, September 21, 2015. www.usatoday.com/story/money/business/2015/09/21/peanut-executive-salmonella-sentencing/72549166/.

McDonald, Phyllis P., and Sheldon Greenberg. 2002. *Managing Police Operations: Implementing the New York Crime Control Model CompStat.* Belmont, CA: Wadsworth.

Mignolo, Walter D. 2002. "The Geopolitics of Knowledge and the Colonial Difference." *South Atlantic Quarterly* 101, no. 1 (Winter): 57–96.

———. 2007. "Coloniality: The Darker Side of Modernity." *Cultural Studies* 21, no. 2–3: 39–49.

Mitchell, Timothy. 2002. *Rule of Experts: Egypt, Techno-politics, Modernity.* Berkeley: University of California Press.

Muhammad, Khalil Gibran. 2010. *The Condemnation of Blackness.* Cambridge, MA: Harvard University Press.

Murakawa, Naomi. 2014. *The First Civil Right: How Liberals Built Prison America.* New York: Oxford University Press.

Murray, Linda Rae. 2003. "Sick and Tired of Being Sick and Tired: Scientific Evidence, Methods, and Research Implications for Racial and Ethnic Disparities in Occupational Health." *American Journal of Public Health* 93, no. 2: 221–26.

Ndlovu-Gatsheni, Sabelo J. 2013. "Why Decoloniality in the 21st Century?" *Thinker* 48 (February): 10–16

Nisbett, Richard E., Joshua Aronson, Clancy Blair, William Dickens, James Flynn, Diane F. Halpern, and Eric Turkheimer. 2012. "Intelligence: New Findings and Theoretical Developments." *American Psychologist* 67, no. 2: 130.

Oliver, Mary Beth, and Dana Fonash. 2002. "Race and Crime in the News: Whites' Identification and Misidentification of Violent and Nonviolent Criminal Suspects." *Media Psychology* 4, no. 2: 137–56.

OSHA (Occupational Safety and Health Administration). 2000. "Conditions at Tyler Pipe: OSHA Inspection Report." In *A Dangerous Business*. Frontline. WGBH, PBS. www.pbs.org/wgbh/pages/frontline/shows /workplace/mcwane/osha.html.

Orfield, G., D. Losen, J. Wald, and C. B. Swanson. 2004. *Losing Our Future: How Minority Youth Are Being Left Behind by the Graduation Rate Crisis*. Cambridge, MA: The Civil Rights Project at Harvard University. Contributors: Urban Institute, Advocates for Children of New York, and The Civil Society Institute. https://files.eric.ed.gov/fulltext/ED489177.pdf.

Peffley, Mark, Todd Shields, and Bruce Williams. 1996. "The Intersection of Race and Crime in Television News Stories: An Experimental Study." *Political Communication* 13, no. 3: 309–27.

Pettit, Becky, and Bruce Western. 2004. "Mass Imprisonment and the Life Course: Race and Class Inequality in US Incarceration." *American Sociological Review* 69, no. 2: 151–69.

Quijano, Aníbal. 2000. "Coloniality of Power, Eurocentrism and Latin America." *Nepantla: Views from the South* 1, no. 3: 533–80.

Quillian, Lincoln, and Devah Pager. 2001. "Black Neighbors, Higher Crime? The Role of Racial Stereotypes in Evaluations of Neighborhood Crime." *American Journal of Sociology* 107, no. 3 (November): 717–67.

Reiman, Jeffrey. 2007. *The Rich Get Richer and the Poor Get Prison: Class, Ideology and Criminal Justice*. New York: Pearson/Allyn.

Reiman, Jeffrey, and Paul Leighton. 2017. 11th ed. *The Rich Get Richer and the Poor Get Prison: A Reader*. New York: Routledge.

Rex, John. 2013. *Race, Colonialism and the City*. Abingdon, UK: Routledge.

Ritchie, Andrea J. 2006. "Law Enforcement Violence Against Women of Color." In *Color of Violence: The INCITE! Anthology*, edited by INCITE! Women of Color Against Violence. 138–56. Durham, NC: Duke University Press.

Roberts, Dorothy E. 1992. "Crime, Race, and Reproduction." *Tulane Law Review* 67: 1945.

Roediger, David R. 1999. *The Wages of Whiteness: Race and the Making of the American Working Class*. London: Verso.

Rumbarger, John. 1989. *Profits, Power, and Prohibition: Alcohol Reform and the Industrializing of America, 1800–1930*. SUNY Series in New Social Studies on Alcohol and Drugs. Albany: State University of New York Press.

Sadler, M. S., J. Correll, B. Park, and C. M. Judd. 2012. "The World Is Not Black and White: Racial Bias in the Decision to Shoot in a Multiethnic Context." *Journal of Social Issues* 68, no. 2, 286–313.

Said, Edward W. 1993. *Culture and Imperialism*. New York: Vintage.

Sampson, Robert J., and Stephen W. Raudenbush. 2004. "Seeing Disorder: Neighborhood Stigma and the Social Construction of 'Broken Windows.'" *Social Psychology Quarterly* 67, no. 4: 319–42.

Schept, Judah. 2013. "'A Lockdown Facility . . . with the Feel of a Small, Private College': Liberal Politics, Jail Expansion, and the Carceral Habitus." *Theoretical Criminology* 17, no. 1 (February): 71–88.

Sentencing Project. 2015. *Trends in U.S. Corrections*. Fact sheet. Washington, DC: Sentencing Project.

Simon, Jonathan. 2007. *Governing through Crime: How the War on Crime Transformed American Democracy and Created a Culture of Fear*. New York: Oxford University Press.

Smedley, Audrey, and Brian D. Smedley. 2005. "Race as Biology Is Fiction, Racism as a Social Problem Is Real: Anthropological and Historical Perspectives on the Social Construction of Race." *American Psychologist* 60, no. 1: 16–26.

Smith, C., A. J. Lizotte, T. P. Thornberry, and M. D. Krohn. 1995. "Resilient Youth: Identifying Factors That Prevent High-Risk Youth from Engaging in Delinquency and Drug Use." *Current Perspectives on Aging and the Life Course* 4: 217–47.

Smith, Dennis C., and William J. Bratton. 2001. "Performance Management in New York City: CompStat and the Revolution in Police Management." In *Quicker, Better, Cheaper: Managing Performance in American Government*, edited by Dall Forsyth, 453–82. New York: Rockefeller Institute Press.

Spring, Joel. 1994. *Deculturalization and the Struggle for Equality: A Brief History of the Education of Dominated Cultures in the United States*. New York: McGraw-Hill.

Stoler, Ann Laura. 2002. *Carnal Knowledge and Imperial Power: Race and the Intimate in Colonial Rule*. Berkeley: University of California Press.

Travis, Jeremy, and Michelle Waul, eds. 2003. *Prisoners Once Removed: The Impact of Incarceration and Reentry on Children, Families, and Communities*. Washington, DC: Urban Institute.

Truman, Jennifer L. 2010. "Criminal Victimization, 2009." *Bureau of Justice Statistics Bulletin*, NCJ 231327. October 2010. Washington, DC: U.S. Department of Justice, Office of Justice Programs. www.bjs.gov /content/pub/pdf/cv09.pdf.

Ward, Stephanie Francis. 2014. "Has 'Stop and Frisk' Been Stopped?" *ABA Journal*, March 1, 2014. www .abajournal.com/magazine/article/has_stop_and_frisk_been_stopped.

Zeus, Leonardo. 2004. "The Color of Supremacy: Beyond the Discourse of 'White Privilege.'" *Educational Philosophy and Theory* 36, no. 2: 137–52.

Race, Colonialism, and the Emergence of Racial Democracy

LEARNING OUTCOMES

▶ Explain what colonialism is and how it structured a global economy based on race.

▶ Analyze the impact of colonialism on the newly emerging democratic state form.

▶ Illustrate how enslavement, westward expansion, and U.S. imperialism abroad were based on racial logics.

▶ Summarize how colonial endeavors that led to the accumulation of wealth in Western Europe and the United States continue to facilitate national development today.

▶ Describe the construct of coloniality and explain its impact on the development of the United States, particularly white racial identity.

KEY TERMS

▶ colonialism

▶ papal bull

▶ Valladolid debate

▶ global economy

▶ capitalism

▶ feudalism

▶ indentured servitude

▶ slave codes

▶ manifest destiny

▶ Indian Removal Act

▶ Trail of Tears

▶ white man's burden

▶ imperialism

▶ zones of being and nonbeing

According to the schoolchildren's saying, "In 1492, Columbus sailed the ocean blue"—and shortly thereafter the Americas were "discovered." Though this recounting is now regarded as a tale that omits significant historical realities (such as the many peoples already living in the newly "discovered" lands), 1492 was critical for the birth of something else: a technological innovation in power premised on the idea we today call "race."

This innovation began with projects initiated by Columbus and his contemporaries including discovery, conquest, and expansion—or what is commonly called **colonialism,** defined as the occupation and domination of a foreign territory and people. Colonialism may seem an odd place to look to understand the issues of race and crime today, especially as 1492 is almost five centuries before the era of "mass incarceration."

Yet, colonialism is critical to understanding contemporary state forms and power relations among differently situated groups. At its simplest, colonialism was a geographical project that consisted of conquering other people, settling in foreign lands, and extracting natural resources, including people and labor, from colonies. Colonialism, however, was also a project of knowledge production, spurred in part from some of the very first encounters between colonizers and other people. These ideas shaped how early colonizers thought about people and places, and as we show throughout this book, had an enormously important effect on how we think about race, and thus, on how we think about crime today.

Colonialism's connection to mass incarceration begins with two very different but twinned projects that made up the colonial era. First, colonialism is ultimately a violent process, where the power of nation-states is brutally displayed. Through private citizens, militias, and military fleets, places are "discovered," forcefully conquered, and named as colonies of the invading force. This type of force is called *sovereign force,* or *sovereignty.*

Sovereign force is often associated with military power, but there is a domestic corollary: the criminal justice system. Through the institutions of policing, courts, the prisons, and the death penalty, some state agents are allowed to use violent force against others, even take lives. Colonialism is often associated with initial acts of war and conquest, but the mechanisms of domestic sovereignty have also been critical tools in securing everyday life and relations between colonizers and the colonized (Stoler 2002).

Second, colonialism came about when Europeans were undergoing a revolution in the tactics of knowledge production, something facilitated by colonial encounter. Consider the discipline of geography. Mapmaking emerged before anyone thought of geography as an area of study, but it was through European colonial conquest that mapmaking took on importance to more than just exploration. Maps became a way of knowing the world, and early colonial maps mapped everything from differences in flora and fauna to temperatures and disease. This period also saw the emergence of a European approach to the study of the world that privileged classification and ordering as the preeminent tools of knowledge production (Mitchell 2002). These tactics and techniques produced the empirical "evidence" for the colonial order.

Race emerged as the consequence of both of these practices: colonial conquest and knowledge produced about the colonial world. But colonialism did not produce just the logic of race. It also produced a state form that integrated racial thinking into the very foundations of the state. Colonial conquest—by Europeans, the United States, and settler colonialists—was premised on a racial understanding of the colonizer's superiority. As the state continued to develop and the mechanisms of colonial conquest became normalized in the day-to-day practice of nation-states, the racial logic of colonial conquest was integrated within state practices.

COLONIALISM, RELIGIOUS AUTHORITY, AND THE CONQUEST OF OTHERS

Colonialism is critical to the creation of the U.S. state, but colonialism first emerged not from the actions of the state, but from religious authorities. During the period of colonial contact, political authority and knowledge were held by the church. Monasteries established by Christians during the Roman Empire were critical to cultural history, including art, history, and language. The power of the Roman Catholic Church continued to rise as it accumulated wealth and control, until the seventeenth century, when the nation-state became the center of political authority.

Religious Authority and Enslavement

Beginning in 1452, Pope Nicholas V issued a series of **papal bulls.** A papal bull is an order or decree of the church, similar to a law or regulation defining a new state policy (see an example in figure 2.1). One of the papal bulls issued by Nicholas gave Portugal's king, Afonso V, "full and free permission to invade, search out, capture, and subjugate the Saracens and pagans and any other unbelievers and enemies of Christ wherever they may be, as well as their kingdoms, duchies, counties, principalities, and other property . . . and to reduce their persons into perpetual servitude." This bull legitimated the practices of conquest of the Portuguese monarchy that were taking place across Europe and northern Africa at the time. This particular papal bull granted the monarchy the power not only to "invade, search out, capture, and subjugate" others but also to reduce them into "perpetual servitude," or what we call slavery. Notably, this power was extended not because of race but because of the religious leanings of the "Saracens" and "pagans." Colonial conquest thus first began as a practice to establish religious, not racial, dominance. Religious domination, however, was also

Figure 2.1 Papal bull of Pope Urban VIII, 1637. Urban was a great patron of Catholic foreign missions. Source: George Powell of Nanteos Bequest to the University of Wales, Aberystwyth, in 1882.

premised on what would become the logic of racial difference—that some people were less than "human," or Christian in this case, and could thus be subject to different treatment than those within the religious community. Religious logic thus served as the foundation for later conceptions of race.

Papal bulls were critical to the division of power in colonialism. Africa was declared the property of the Portuguese, and in 1493 another bull gave portions of lands of the Americas to Spain. Religion was again critical to colonial conquest and the bull ordering lands of the Americas to Spain declared that "the Catholic faith and the Christian religion be exalted and be everywhere increased and spread, that the health of souls be cared for and that barbarous nations be overthrown and brought to the faith itself." Colonialism was an opportunity for resource accumulation, but it importantly also needed to fulfill a higher purpose in order to succeed. This higher purpose was religious expansion and Catholic indoctrination. Caring for the health of souls and bringing barbarous nations to the faith thus meant, in practice, colonialism and enslavement, often carried out through the settlement of "mission" territories.

Unsurprisingly, colonizers took the Pope's instruction to "invade, search out, capture, and subjugate" indigenous people to heart. The theft of land and resources by one group from another requires the implementation of a system of violence that assures its vitality and longevity. Colonialism is the political system implemented by European powers in Africa, Asia, and what is now known as the Americas that would ensure their control of these territories.

Those whose nonhumanity was established by the papal bulls were violently subjugated and enslaved, such as in "missions" throughout the United States. Missions were religious establishments set up in colonized lands that facilitated colonial authority. Specifically, the goal was to convert "heathens" to Christianity, but this conversion often consisted of little more than enslavement, forced labor, and control by the church and colonial authorities over indigenous populations. For instance, the missions of California are now well-known as particularly brutal places where Indigenous peoples were subject to forced labor, brutal punishment, and forced religious conversion.

Religious colonial exploration is the origin of race as a fundamental structure of colonial power. The enslavement and dehumanization of the colonized depended on religious authority declaring these groups "heathens." This relegated them to a class of people whose souls could not be "saved," and thus they could be perpetually forced to labor on behalf of those who could. The religious sanction of this idea meant that colonizers could enslave others without contradicting their religious beliefs.

The Valladolid Debate

Racism is a colonial construct. As we discussed above, the question of indigenous and African humanity was used as the justification for the colonial expansion of Europe. Church authorities, though, regularly debated the question of enslaving indigenous peoples, with many prominent church authorities arguing against their enslavement. These debates raged throughout the 1400s and 1500s.

In 1537, the papal bull *Sublimis Deus* countered earlier papal bulls and established the rationality of indigenous peoples. It declared

> that the Indians are truly men and that they are not only capable of understanding the Catholic Faith but, according to our information, they desire exceedingly to receive it. Desiring to provide ample remedy for these evils, We define and declare . . . that, notwithstanding whatever may have been or may be said to the contrary, the said Indians and all other people who may later be discovered by Christians, are by no means to be deprived of their liberty or the possession of their property, even though they be outside the faith of Jesus Christ; and that they may and should, freely and legitimately, enjoy their liberty and the possession of their property; nor should they be in any way enslaved.

This declaration, along with further agitation by religious authorities, led to the passage of what were called the "new laws" in Spain. They outlawed the enslavement of indigenous people and ended the *encomienda* system, in which colonizing settlers were granted a specific number of conquered people as their slaves. (Little actually changed in the day-to-day life of colonies, however, because enslavement as a form of conversion and tribute was still sanctioned practice.)

Convinced by the arguments of religious authorities, the king of Spain ordered military conquest to cease in 1450 until the issue of the souls of natives, enslavement, and conquest were decided. He assembled a group of intellectuals and theologians to debate the matter and issue a ruling on whether indigenous peoples belonged in the category of human. This was called the **Valladolid debate** and is considered the first debate on colonialism and human rights in European history. It was the culmination of years of work by theologians and religious authorities opposing forced conversation by conquered populations. These debates were represented by Bartolomé de las Casas, a religious authority who had worked for years to end encomienda and opposed forced conversion, and Juan Ginés de Sepúlveda, a philosopher and humanist.

Sepúlveda's arguments demonstrate one of the first articulations of race, rather than religion, as a system of human and nonhuman. His argument began with the religious question of the soul of indigenous peoples but quickly turned to what we would identify today as questions of race. He argued:

> The Spanish have a perfect right to rule these barbarians of the New World and the adjacent islands, who in prudence, skill, virtues, and humanity are as inferior to the Spanish as children to adults, or women to men, for there exists between the two as great a difference as between savage and cruel races and the most merciful, between the most intemperate and the moderate and temperate and, I might even say, between apes and men. . . . War against these barbarians can be justified not only on the basis of their paganism but even more so because of their abominable recklessness, their unusual sacrifice of human victims, the extreme harm that they inflicted on innocent persons, their horrible banquets of human flesh, and the impious cult of their idols.

Sepúlveda's arguments reveal one of the first articulations of racial logic: the "war" of conquest was justified "not only on the basis" of religious difference but also on perceived attributes, such as "abominable recklessness." These "barbarians" were to Sepúlveda "as inferior to the Spanish" as the "savage and cruel races" and "apes" were. Their inferiority is based not just in religion but in their "prudence, skill, virtues, and humanity."

Sepúlveda's primary opponent, Las Casas, did not contradict this racial construction; he argued instead that although the indigenous were savages, it was the duty of the Spanish empire to civilize them. Here, the debate reveals how religious authority was making way for the ascendance of race as the dominant logic, something influenced also by the emergence of the Enlightenment period, discussed in the next chapter. Las Casas believed that through civilizing endeavors, indigenous people would adopt Christianity and could be integrated into colonial society. He replied to Sepúlveda that "from the fact that the

Indians are barbarians it does not necessarily follow that they are incapable of government and have to be ruled by others, except to be taught about the Catholic faith and to be admitted to the holy sacraments."

The winner of the Valladolid debate is unclear. Little changed in the Spanish Crown's approach to the indigenous peoples of the Americas. But this debate had lasting consequences and shaped the relations between Spanish colonizers and the indigenous populations of the Americas and set the foundation for race for the next 450 years. Las Casas and Sepúlveda fundamentally agreed that indigenous people were (or could be, in the case of Las Casas) barbarians, but they had different ideas about what should be done in response to that. One believed in enslavement, and the other in assimilation. Both, however, presupposed the elimination and obliteration of *indigenous* ways of being.

By casting indigenous practices and people out of the realm of humanity, at least in current form, the Valladolid debate set the stage for a system of racism justified by many in fundamentally benevolent terms. Enslavement happened not just because people were inferior biologically, culturally, or historically but also because white European Christians were seeking to "save," "civilize," and "convert" people to their ways of being.

Here we find the two main discourses of racism that would shape the way we have thought about race for the past 450 years: (1) the idea of nonwhites as nonhumans who can be exploited and even eliminated, and (2) the idea that those subhumans may be redeemable, able to be civilized and assimilated. Although the term *race* did not emerge until later, racism, as a structure of power that organizes groups of human beings into a hierarchy of human and nonhuman, was established within the religious context of colonialism. To this day, this structure still serves as the foundation for racial classification.

Colonialism, however, did not just depend on the construct of race for its continuation. This construct was used to justify the most important aspect of colonialism: pillaging resources and wealth from colonies and the colonized. Colonialism created a global economic system where some benefitted from the labor and wealth of others. In the United States, this system depended on the ultimate extraction of wealth: enslaving human labor.

COLONIALISM, SLAVERY, AND THE GLOBAL ECONOMY

Spanish and Portuguese success in Africa and South America kicked off a global competition for control of the new lands and resources. In a quest for the riches provided by colonial conquest, the Netherlands, England, and France would establish their own colonies, using the same concepts of European superiority over indigenous people that the papal bulls and Sepúlveda relied on. The conception of Africans and peoples of the Americas as nonhumans justified Dutch, English, and French colonialism and helped create a global structure of domination.

Colonialism and Access to New Resources

Colonialism enabled colonizers to amass great economic wealth. Silver and gold mined in colonies ended up in the coffers of colonial powers. Colonizers also amassed wealth through agricultural products that could be sold throughout Europe, such as tea from India, coffee from Brazil, and sugarcane from the West Indies. Colonialism was accomplished not just through the sovereign force of states but also through the actions of private companies seeking profit through global trade. Estimates of the wealth accumulated vary widely, but most estimates agree that colonialism provided the basis for the accumulation of wealth that facilitated European and U.S. industrialism.

Colonialism facilitated wealth accumulation not just through colonial endeavors but through domestic ones as well. For instance, coal mined in Uganda by British entrepreneurs was transferred back to the United Kingdom to provide energy for industrial enterprises. The buying and selling of the coal enabled banks to accumulate wealth.

The buying and selling of goods across the world led powers to invest in transportation routes, such as trains and waterways. This marked the emergence of the global economy—and it began not in the 1970s, but in 1492. The **global economy** is the interconnected practices of buying and selling goods across national borders. National and regional economies were dependent upon resources extracted from other places, such as coal mined by enslaved people in the United States to fuel the industrial centers of the Northeast and Britain. And the global market in sugarcane production led traders to travel across the Atlantic Ocean to buy and sell it. The creation of the global economy allowed for massive accumulation of wealth for nation-states, private individuals, and corporations.

Capitalism, Feudalism, and Labor

The accumulation of wealth in the hands of a few countries and private individuals is known as capitalism. **Capitalism,** at its simplest, is an economic system based on private ownership and the accumulation of resources. Capitalism, at the beginning of colonialism, was accomplished through the actions of monarchical governments and private individuals. As it grew, corporations emerged.

Capitalism came from a shift from the economic organization called **feudalism.** Under feudalism, people labored on behalf of a landowner, often a noble or royal person. This person owned the land and allowed people to settle on it in exchange for their work on the land. This economic structure was dominant before the Industrial Revolution but began to decline with the emergence of global networks of trade. People could leave feudal townships and sell wares that they made or traded for in cities. This led to the idea of capitalism as a system of private ownership, where individuals owned the means of production and amassed profits from the sale of their goods.

Increasing profit under capitalism thus is premised on the issue of labor, as one can accumulate greater profits by making goods at a lower cost. In modern capitalism, labor is paid a wage and this is calculated as one of the costs of production. At the beginning of capitalism, free labor was often plentiful, particularly for those in power. Spain and Portugal, through the expansion of the Ottoman Empire, regularly enslaved those they conquered. England enslaved Irish people at the end of feudalism, and during colonialism, it established penal colonies where people convicted of crimes were forced to labor for the profit of the Crown. "Undesirables" including political dissidents, people convicted of being poor, and state charges were regularly enslaved by European nations well into the 1800s. And as dictated by the papal bull above, before the emergence of the Atlantic slave trade and the logic of race, the most significant dividing line between people enslaved and not enslaved was religion.

Free and cheap labor was central to the development of the global capitalist economy, and early capitalists sought to create profit by drawing on one of the most prolific sources of raw materials on earth: people. This exploitation of human resources would serve as the foundation of capitalism and grow wealth across states and countries. It would also serve as the basis for the global capitalist economy for centuries to come, and even today, the exploitation of labor is a necessary component of creating profit. Exploiting labor was necessary to the creation of capitalist profit, and two dominant methods of cheap labor were slowly developing: indentured servitude and slavery. This labor structure was also the expression of emerging racial ideas in the United States and served to create and demarcate racial categories in everyday life. The appropriation of land and resources during the colonial period and the knowledge production that served to legitimize and reinforce colonial rule created racial categories that serve as the foundation for social relations to this day.

Labor, Exploitation, and the Creation of Race in the United States

Servitude was common throughout social contexts, and servants were often considered a class unto themselves, like the nobility or merchants. Slavery, as noted earlier, was also common. However, the development of slavery as the foundational mode of labor exploitation in the United States did not happen overnight, but rather through a series of court hearings, new laws, and the actions of individual colonies. As box 2.1 shows, slavery continues to shape the global economy today. The transformation of the United States from a mercantilist capitalist economy to one based on slavery happened over the course of the seventeenth and eighteenth centuries, with Virginia providing perhaps the best example of how it occurred.

BOX 2.1   Capitalism, Slavery and the Global Economy Today

Slavery has not ended. As we detail in later chapters, slavery continues to be allowed today in the United States for one class of person: people in prison. Globally, it also continues to be practiced on a regular basis as campaigns against human trafficking and seemingly countless exposés have demonstrated.

Consider the global farm production of shrimp, which is influenced by slavery today. A recent United Nations labor report finds that even with new government legislation, trafficking and forced labor aboard Thai shrimp boats continues. Workers are locked up and forced to work on ships, often ones that are fishing illegally. One worker reported being chained by his neck when he tried to escape. Workers also experience debt bondage, working to pay off a continually growing debt at an exorbitant interest rate. Twenty-hour days are normal, as is killing workers when they fail to comply.

Thailand's seafood export industry is over $6.5 billion dollars. And its largest consumer? The United States market.

Slavery still exists today and government agencies not only know about it but have been working to stop it to little avail for years. Why do you think it continues? What do you think it would take to stop it?

Source: Policy Analysis and Research Branch, United Nations Office on Drugs and Crime, *Global Report on Trafficking in Persons*, February 2009, www.unodc.org/documents/Global_Report_on_TIP.pdf.

Virginia and the Creation of a Slavery Economy

In the early years of the Virginia colony, Africans and poor whites often labored together in the fields. Whites were from the working class of England and Ireland, and were conscripted into indentured servitude at the time. **Indentured servitude** is a contractual term of service in which someone agrees to work for another for a period of time in exchange for food, clothing, and shelter. The cost of a trip to the colonies was also often included in the term of service. Indentured servitude was a common way to attract workers to the colonies, and the Virginia Company used it prolifically to settle the Virginia colony.

The historical record is unclear as to exactly when Africans arrived in Virginia and were enslaved. In the early 1620s, a Dutch ship arrived on the shores of Virginia, with cargo stolen from a Spanish ship: twenty human beings from Africa. The ship captain exchanged his stolen cargo for food and set sail. It is unclear what status these people were initially given, but in 1623 and 1624, they were listed as servants.

By the mid-1600s, slavery emerged as a legal category in Virginia. The first mention of slavery in the historical records of the colony was in 1640. Three servants—two white and one black—ran away from their indentured servitude contracts on a farm. When they were captured, the court sentenced the two white men to an additional four years of service, but the black man, named John Punch, was ordered to "serve his said master or his assigns for the time of his natural life here or elsewhere." Though the sentences were based on the difference in skin color, Punch's slavery was not just a product of his skin color but of his "criminal" status.

Courts in Virginia upheld the idea that Africans were not necessarily slaves, and there were no laws distinctly made for black people at the time. For instance, in 1641, the courts granted an African man the right to raise his child as a Christian, even though the mother was enslaved. The court even released Africans from servitude when their contracts were illegally extended. And many of those listed as "slaves" could become free by converting to Christianity.

Laws about slavery also shifted over the 1600s. The first mention of the exceptional status of black people was in 1639 when Virginia excluded "negroes" from being provided with "arms and ammunitions" (Guild 1936). In Maryland in 1664, the law mandated that any free woman who married a slave would become a slave as well, as would their children, thus creating slavery as a condition that could be transferred from one generation to the next (Bennett 1970). In 1667, Virginia passed a law noting that baptism did not free a person from bondage and that "masters freed from this doubt may more carefully propagate Christianity by permitting slaves to be admitted to that sacrament" (Guild 1936). And in 1682, Virginia enacted the first law in the United States creating a racial distinction between servants and slaves:

> Act I. It is enacted that all servants . . . [who] shall be imported into this country either by sea or by land, whether Negroes, Moors [Muslim North Africans], mulattoes or Indians who and whose parentage and native countries are not Christian at the time of their first purchase by some Christian . . . and all Indians, which shall be sold by our neighboring Indians, or any other trafficing with us for slaves, are hereby adjudged, deemed and taken to be slaves to all intents and purposes any law, usage, or custom to the contrary notwithstanding.

This law served as the basis for the transformation of the Virginia economy from a system of indentured servitude to one based on race and forced labor.

Virginia's need for labor increased because of its burgeoning tobacco economy. Initially, the supply of labor for the colonies came from England, but in the 1650s the Great Plague decimated England's population and the supply of labor dried up. The price of tobacco had also dropped, leaving Virginia with both a reduced labor supply and less profit from its primary product. Enslavement proved the solution to the colony's labor shortage, and different skin colors provided a built-in surveillance mechanism for local plantation owners. In 1623, there were only twenty-three black people in Virginia, but by 1700, as the economy turned to enslavement as its primary source of labor, over a thousand Africans were brought to the colony each year.

An early declaration from the Virginia General Assembly in 1705 illustrates the religious basis of involuntary servitude and also provides the first legal document consigning people to perpetual servitude based on the color of their skin. The Assembly declared:

> All servants imported and brought into the Country . . . who were not Christians in their native Country . . . shall be accounted and be slaves. All Negro, mulatto and Indian slaves within this dominion . . . shall be held to be real estate. If any slave resists his master . . . correcting such slave, and shall happen to be killed in such correction . . . the master shall be free of all punishment . . . as if such accident never happened.

Reminiscent of the papal bull declaring non-Christians and pagans the property of the Portuguese Crown, the Virginia act emphasizes the religious distinction of enslaved person but also proscribes a blanket enslavement of all nonwhites, not just non-Christians, in the territory. The 1705 declaration also introduced the slave codes, and the legal category of slave as "real estate" was soon entrenched throughout Virginia law and society.

Virginia's Slave Code

Slave codes were separate legal codes for enslaved people that generally, as demonstrated above, considered both white and black people in their application (Johnson 1997). As the declaration above demonstrates, Virginia so thoroughly defined the enslaved person as property that even if that person were "killed in . . . correction," the owner would be "free of all punishment . . . as if such accident never happened." This legal construction is the ultimate act of defining enslaved people as less than human—they could even be killed with impunity. Enslaved people were consigned to a category that was little more than the plants, animals, or other beings of the natural world that were regularly killed without any forethought.

The Virginia code served as a model for the other colonies in North America, and it imposed harsh, brutal punishments on enslaved people. Punishments included whipping, placement in the stocks, and bodily mutilation, such as having ears or hands cut off, branding, and maiming. It also created a status of permanent imprisonment and developed one of the first techniques of state surveillance by requiring enslaved people to possess written permission when they were away from their plantations. Prior to the 1705 code, enslaved people could bring disputes with owners to the courts and could even be set free based on the court case, but the Virginia code removed this legal status. The Virginia slave code thus provided the legal architecture for the development of a state system based on racial difference. It also provided for the very first explicitly apartheid racial state in North America, where the color of one's skin dictated whether one was placed in the category of human. If placed outside that category, one did not deserve legal status as human and thus could be used and disposed of with little consequence. It was this latter condition that cemented race in the history of the United States.

CREATING THE U.S. IDENTITY: WHITENESS, SLAVERY, AND COLONIAL CONQUEST

Ideas of white superiority not only established slavery but also justified colonial conquest across the United States and the world. Throughout the nineteenth century, the United States rapidly grew from its original thirteen colonies to its current mainland territory. This colonial conquest was enabled by the industrial accumulation of wealth off the backs of enslaved people and the ideas of white superiority popular at the time.

Through both the legal institution of slavery and colonial expansion, white identity is defined through ideas of land, morality, and progress. Slavery, westward expansion, and the U.S. occupation of the Philippines at the turn of the twentieth century were all critical to building the identity of the United States as a white racial state. These examples highlight how processes of colonization and racialization were constituted simultaneously.

Slavery and the Creation of a White Racial State

At their declaration of independence in 1776, all thirteen colonies permitted slavery, though a fierce debate emerged and at least one draft of the Declaration included a passage attacking slavery. Despite this debate, enslaved labor was critical to the Southern and the entire U.S. economy.

Enslaved people were numerous throughout the United States (Dodson 2002). Almost 18 percent of residents in the United States counted by the 1790 census were enslaved. In South Carolina, 43 percent of the population was enslaved, while in Maryland it was 32 percent, and 26 percent in North Carolina. Virginia had a slave population over 300,000, almost 40 percent of its population in 1790. Between 1492 and 1776, 6.5 million people crossed the Atlantic, but only 1 million of these were Europeans. Five and a half million were Africans brought to the United States as part of the vast Atlantic slave trade (figure 2.2 shows the numbers arriving between 1620 and 1866).

The annexation of Florida by the United States reveals just how important enslaved labor was to the economy. In 1825, the United States acquired Florida, a Spanish colony that had long been a point of conflict between the United States, Spain, and Britain. The U.S. interest in Florida was not just the land but the many Africans who had escaped enslavement on American plantations and taken refuge in the Everglades with the Seminole indigenous people. The swamps and dense forests of the Everglades made invasion difficult for U.S. military forces, so people who ran away from slavery could not be easily recov-

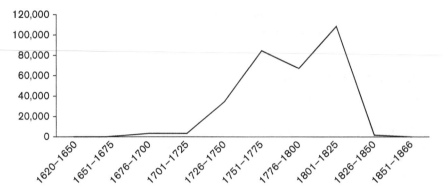

Figure 2.2 Enslaved people arriving in the North American colonies and the United States, 1620–1866. Source: Estimates Database, *Voyages: The Trans-Atlantic Slave Trade Database* (Atlanta, GA: Emory University), www.slavevoyages.org/assessment/estimates.

ered. This posed a serious problem for the U.S. plantation economy. Efforts to acquire Florida were thus also efforts to protect the institution of slavery in U.S. society.

For the first fifty years of the U.S. state, it seemed that slavery would long be protected by legal structures. The nation passed several laws mandating cooperation in "fugitive slave" cases and upholding the right of the Southern people over the bodies of black residents (see figure 2.3). The massive investment in slavery, however, did not necessarily indicate wholehearted support on the part of the U.S. government. Indeed, in the early 1800s, at the same time the United States was protecting the rights of owners of fugitive slaves, it also prohibited U.S. companies from taking part in the slave trade and banned the importation of people. Slavery had to be protected, though, because the profits produced off the backs of enslaved labor fueled the U.S. and global economies.

Slavery as Industrial Production

Slavery was the first example of industrial production in the United States. Profits from production during slavery accumulated wealth not only for plantation owners but also for Northern and British capitalists (Beckert 2015; Blackburn 1998; Johnson 1997). Producing and exporting cotton was one of the first examples of industrial production organized to serve a global market.

Cotton for textiles first depended on British transporters working with slave traders in Africa to take the human beings they had captured across the Atlantic Ocean to the Americas. Once enslaved people arrived, they were bought and sold in slave markets in the South. They were then enslaved in Southern cotton fields, where they grew and picked cotton that was then sent to Britain

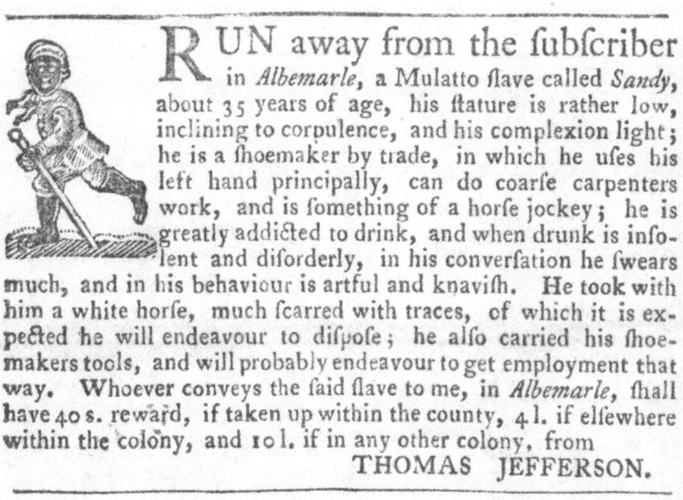

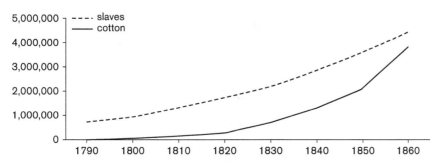

RUN away from the subscriber in *Albemarle*, a Mulatto slave called *Sandy*, about 35 years of age, his stature is rather low, inclining to corpulence, and his complexion light; he is a shoemaker by trade, in which he uses his left hand principally, can do coarse carpenters work, and is something of a horse jockey; he is greatly addicted to drink, and when drunk is insolent and disorderly, in his conversation he swears much, and in his behaviour is artful and knavish. He took with him a white horse, much scarred with traces, of which it is expected he will endeavour to dispose; he also carried his shoemakers tools, and will probably endeavour to get employment that way. Whoever conveys the said slave to me, in *Albemarle*, shall have 40 s. reward, if taken up within the county, 4 l. if elsewhere within the colony, and 10 l. if in any other colony, from

THOMAS JEFFERSON.

Figure 2.3 Runaway slave advertisement placed by Thomas Jefferson in the *Virginia Gazette*, Williamsburg, VA, September 14, 1769. Source: Reproduced by permission of the Virginia Historical Society.

Figure 2.4 Increase of cotton cultivation and number of enslaved people in the United States, 1790–1860. Sources: William H. Philips, "Cotton Gin," EH.net (La Crosse, WI: Economic History Association, February 10, 2004), https://eh.net/encyclopedia/cotton-gin/; Estimates Database, *Voyages: The Trans-Atlantic Slave Trade Database* (Atlanta, Georgia: Emory University), www.slavevoyages.org/assessment/estimates.

to be turned into fabric. This fabric was then often exported back to the United States to be turned into textiles in the industrial centers of the North. Figure 2.4 shows how the growth of the cotton industry in the United States was accompanied by a corresponding increase in enslaved people brought into the country.

Along the way, all sorts of economic benefits accrued to bankers who facilitated transactions, transporters who carried wares across the land and sea, and traders who bought and sold goods—including the enslaved people themselves—

Figure 2.5 "Auction & Negro Sales,"
Whitehall Street, Atlanta, Georgia.
Source: Courtesy of the Library of
Congress, LC-DIG-cwpb-03351.

across the global economic chain (see figure 2.5). Enslaved people were also used
as collateral to secure bank loans, which allowed landowners to acquire even
more land, people, and resources. Although often considered an anachronistic
period in U.S. economic development, slavery in fact provided the blueprint for
the emergence of the factory model of industrial production (Baptist 2016).

Agricultural production in the South of such goods as tobacco and cotton
facilitated the accumulation of wealth nationwide. Cotton was produced through
enslaved labor, while the ports of the Northeast supported a commercial class that
bought that cotton cheaply and sold it to the industrial enterprises in England.
Many others made their living as merchants and tradespeople supporting this
basic economy. Although many states in the North abolished slavery over the first
several decades of the United States, the Northern economy did not directly rely
on enslaved labor and very few enslaved people lived in Northern territories.

Yet, the commercial capitalists of the northeast accumulated great wealth
by selling the South's crops to Europe. They invested that wealth in new

machinery and factories that fueled the industrial revolution. These new industries required wage laborers and resulted in even greater hierarchical differentiation amongst laboring classes. European immigrants filled the role of wage laborers and provided the economic engine of the industrial revolution. They also, as we will discuss in chapter 4, shored up white racial identity as the basis for citizenship. The division of labor was thus entangled with racial hierarchy: broadly speaking, immigrant Europeans served as wage laborers, Africans were enslaved and subject to coerced forms of labor, and indigenous peoples' homelands were appropriated (and the people practically exterminated) to accommodate European settlement.

This industrial production, however, was based on the exploitation of human labor through enslavement. Without enslavement, the United States, Britain, and other countries would not have accumulated the amount of wealth that financed industrial development in the coming decades (Baptist 2016). Slavery was upheld by two different emerging social institutions: white racial violence and knowledge production about race.

Slavery, Productivity, and Violence

Massive productivity gains ensued during slavery, just as they did during industrialization in the late 1800s. This stemmed not from the birth of steam engine nor the development of the factory assembly line but from a different type of technological innovation: how best to violently force the body to work. Gains in cotton production occurred throughout the 1800s due to the extreme violence used against enslaved workers. Edward Baptist (2016) recounts the story of South Carolina cotton plantation that used the "pushing system." This system, which Baptist calls the "whipping-machine" system, was a method of labor control that sought to increase the number of acres cultivated by each person. The pushing system sought to increase the productivity of enslaved workers by increasing their quotas each day. Those who failed to meet their quota were violently whipped, often "as many lashes as there were pounds short," and people who failed multiple days in a row were subjected to all sorts of torture including waterboarding, sexual humiliation, and bodily mutilation (Baptist 2016: 132).

Like industrial production today, slavery was highly organized, and the pushing system was often meticulously recorded in records kept by plantation owners (Baptist 2016). The keeping of records of quotas and whippings was a common practice and reveals how the violence of slavery was embedded within bureaucratic and administrative practices. Violence was routine, and it was through this routinization that racial violence embedded itself within colonial structures. The whipping post was also often kept next to the bushel-weighing station, revealing just how important white racial violence was to creating the U.S. economy. As a result of the pushing system, the Southern cotton harvest grew from 1.4 million pounds per year in 1800 to 2 billion pounds per year in 1860.

Controlling enslaved people was a common topic among traders, plantation owners, and others in the 1800s, and labor management texts and advice proliferated (Roediger and Esch 2012). These texts reveal how white racial violence was seen as key to maintaining labor control. Violence was justified and rationalized through the bureaucratic language of labor control and appeals to the burgeoning attention to individual maladies. Management texts advised "'preventively . . . whipping the devil' out of potential *drapetomaniacs*, and avoiding any possibility of 'negro liberty' to ward of *dysaesthesia*" (Roediger and Esch 2012, 59). Industrial production was not just the production of cotton but also the production of knowledge about race and nonwhite people that justified their perpetual enslavement.

Slavery and Knowledge Production

The trade in humans was highly organized, cross-continental, involved a broad range of occupations (merchants, sailors, buyers, owners, entrepreneurs, etc.), and relied on modern technologies such as the steamboat, railroad, printing press, and telegraph. Marketing and advertising were necessary to slavery, with traders emphasizing body parts and inspection and advertising particular "types" of people. One such type, the "fancy girl," was meant to serve as the "white man's sexual playground" (Baptist 2016), revealing the extent to which slavery, ideas of race, and economic production depend on an intersection of hierarchies like gender and sexuality. Marketing was so important to the trade in enslaved people that those being sold even sought to use this to their benefit, faking injuries when trying to avoid sale or actively trying to convince buyers of the worth of spouses or children (Berry 2004).

The institution of slavery produced all sorts of knowledge that outlasted it and served as the foundation for ideas of racial difference, even today. Plantation owners regularly argued that the very attributes of slavery were found in the biology of the African person: for example, "Africans literally possessed an inherited racial 'instinct,' housed in the feet and knees, to genuflect before whites" (Roediger and Esch 2012, 59). Plantation owners at the time believed that without proper management, this instinct gave way to disease. Slavery, thus, was rationalized as a benevolent act, a system of patriarchal care and tutelage by whites.

Southern writers routinely portrayed slavery as positive, and in doing so, created a benevolent justification for white racial power. For instance, James Henry Hammond, a Southern legislator, argued that one had to have an enslaved class "or you would not have that other class which leads progress, civilization and refinement" (Hammond 1858). He further noted that enslaved people were "well compensated" and "hired for life" compared to their white Northern counterparts, who suffered from starvation, poverty, and unemployment. George Fitzhugh, another Southern legislator, argued that the black person was a "grown up child and must be governed as a child" (Fitzhugh 1850, 91).

Yet, this benevolence did not extend to providing the training that was increasingly seen as necessary for "rational" individuals, such as reading and writing. Slave codes across the South prohibited teaching enslaved people to read or write, a prohibition that is unique to U.S. slavery (Rodriguez 2007, 616–17). Advocates of prohibiting education of enslaved people generally argued that it prevented rebellion and thus it served a critical tool for labor management. Violations could be punished with fines. Uprisings among enslaved people often led to crackdowns on educated free and enslaved people. For instance, the Nat Turner revolt in Virginia in 1831 inspired several states to change their laws to discourage literacy of enslaved people. Mississippi passed a law that required all free black people to leave the territory; Delaware passed a law that prevented meetings of black people at night; and North Carolina strictly prohibited the education of black children.

This vision of white benevolence and African pathology secured a critical aspect of white identity as a rational, reasonable steward of resources and land. In the case of slavery, whites demonstrated this in the case of the management of enslaved people and lauded themselves for the careful control of violence that would "preserve the slaves' 'instinctive and most mysterious love for their masters'" (Roediger and Esch 2012, 60).

Slavery and the white identity it projected might be considered a thing of the past, but these ideas and structures continue to shape us today. A 2016 study found that "whites who currently live in Southern counties that had high shares of slaves in 1860 are more likely to identify as Republican, oppose affirmative action, and express racial resentment and colder feelings towards blacks" (Acharya, Blackwell, and Sen 2016, 622). This suggests that the construction of white identity that was dependent on knowledge produced during the era of slavery still continues to shape the political climate surrounding race today. These same ideas of white identity and the necessary subservience of enslaved people also animated the approach to Native Americans, particularly as the country expanded westward.

Manifest Destiny and Westward Expansion

Westward expansion in the United States was driven by manifest destiny (see figure 2.6). **Manifest destiny** was a concept coined by a newspaper editor in the 1800s to describe the spirit of United States colonization across what is now known as the western United States. This spirit is based on three tenets: white U.S. citizens were especially virtuous; the lands of the "west" were wild and untamed and needed domestication; and it was the destiny of white U.S. citizens to accomplish this domestication. This idea fueled government policies that provided land and titles for whites who would settle lands unclaimed by the United States or other settlers. It also fueled policies of Native American genocide, a practice that had long accompanied U.S. colonial settlement.

Figure 2.6 Manifest destiny illustrated by John Gast's *American Progress,* 1872.
Source: Courtesy of the Library of Congress, LC-DIG-ppmsca-09855.

Native Americans, Colonial Settlement, and Genocide

The occupation of indigenous territories in the United States is of particular importance for understanding the relationship between racialization and colonial conquest. Manifest destiny was the driving ideological force that would lead to the confiscation of Native American homelands in the nineteenth century. This belief not only justified the appropriation of Indian lands, but it also helped to establish whiteness as the ideal expression of humanity. These ideals are captured in Theodore Roosevelt's proclamation that "the most vicious cowboy has more moral principle than the average Indian" (Mieder 1997, 147).

Indigenous peoples were first enslaved by early colonialists and endured a similar status to black people in the United States. The general dispersion of indigenous people and genocide, however, soon meant that there were few indigenous people to supply an industrial slave trade. Despite indigenous people's exclusion from the slave trade, they still were critical to the U.S. economy. However, it was not their labor that enticed U.S. settlers, but their land (see figure 2.7).

Thomas Jefferson began the process of forced removal of all indigenous peoples from the eastern United States. Jefferson's views on indigenous peoples were complicated. He considered indigenous peoples to be "in body and mind

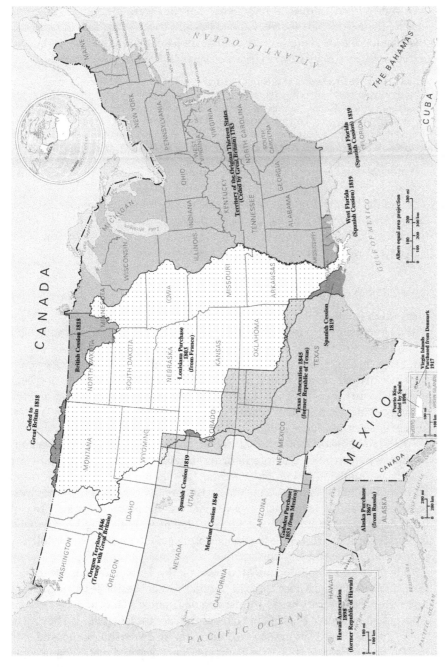

Figure 2.7 Map of the historical territorial expansion of the United States of America. Source: *National Atlas of the United States*, ca. 2005, U.S. Department of the Interior and U.S. Geological Survey, *http://nationalatlas.gov/small_scale/printable/territorialacquisition.html.*

equal to the white man" but still believed that they needed tutelage in agriculture and "refined" modes of living and that they were ultimately "savages." Despite these ideas, Jefferson developed the first strategy for "Indian removal," an explicit policy of the U.S. state to relocate people from the eastern United States to "reservations" west of the Mississippi. In 1803 Jefferson wrote:

> As to their fear, we presume that our strength and their weakness is now so visible that they must see we have only to shut our hand to crush them, and that all our liberalities to them proceed from motives of pure humanity only. Should any tribe be foolhardy enough to take up the hatchet at any time, the seizing the whole country of that tribe, and driving them across the Mississippi, as the only condition of peace, would be an example to others, and a furtherance of our final consolidation. (2000, 22)

Jefferson thus seemingly would permit indigenous peoples to assimilate into U.S. society, but he insisted that this benevolence would end if any were to "take up the hatchet." In that case, the entirety of their land would be seized, and they would be driven past the Mississippi and imprisoned within reservation lands. Jefferson's plan was ultimately enacted by Andrew Jackson when Congress passed the Indian Removal Act in 1830.

Indian Removals and Wealth Accumulation

The **Indian Removal Act** was a piece of legislation that allowed the president of the United States to remove indigenous peoples from the South to federal territory west of the Mississippi (see figure 2.8). Though indigenous people came together to resist this piece of legislation, it ultimately passed. As a consequence of this act, over 75,000 people were resettled and at least 16,000 people died due to the conditions of forced removal. This forced relocation, and the accompanying genocide that occurred during it, is referred to as the **Trail of Tears** (Wallace and Foner 1993).

The Trail of Tears was a series of violent, forced relocations that indigenous peoples were forced to undergo in order to satisfy white settlers' desire for wealth accumulation and profit. Searching for ever more lands to grow cotton prompted white settlers to routinely trespass onto indigenous lands. Once trespassed, white settlers used their own violence and the power of the state to violently expel people from the areas newly settled by whites. Indigenous peoples in North Carolina, Florida, Alabama, Georgia, and Tennessee were violently expelled from these areas in this manner.

One of the most well-documented cases on the Trail of Tears is the case of the Cherokee Nation, whose lands in Georgia became desirable when gold was discovered. Prospectors began trespassing on Cherokee land, and the Georgia government pressured the United States to transfer the Cherokee land claim to itself. The Cherokee Nation sued Georgia to retain ownership of the land, and in *Worcester v. Georgia* (1832), the Supreme Court declared that Georgia could

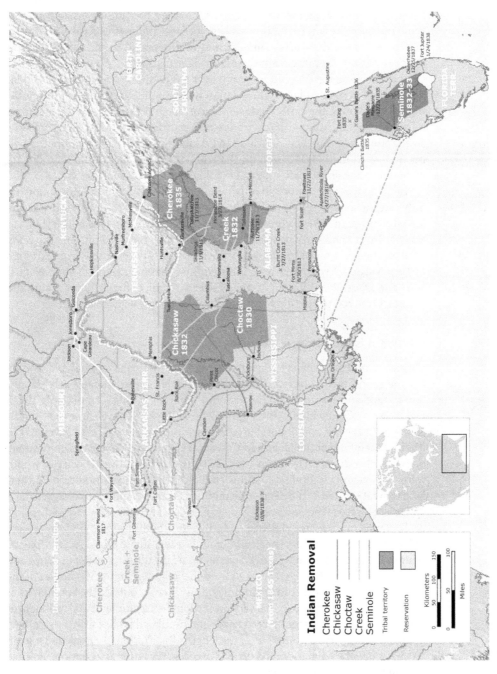

Figure 2.8 Map of removal of native peoples from their land. Source: Nikater, submitted to the public domain. Background map courtesy of Demis, www.demis.nl, and Wilcomb E. Washburn, *Handbook of North American Indians*, vol. 4: *History of Indian-White Relations* (Washington, DC: Smithsonian Institution Press, 1988).

not impose its law on Cherokee land. Yet Georgia persisted, and eventually President Andrew Jackson forced the Cherokee to sign an order for their removal from the land. The removal took place under President Van Buren, with over 7,000 militia, army soldiers, and volunteers taking up arms and forcing over 20,000 Cherokee from their lands (Coates 2014).

The Cherokee were forced to march over 1,000 miles to what today is Oklahoma. They were forced to begin the march in winter, often with just the clothing they had on at the time. Disease, starvation, and exposure to the elements killed thousands. Many Cherokee were also murdered by locals along the way. By the time the group was relocated in Oklahoma, some 8,000—more than 40 percent—had died (4,000 died on the trail, while another 4,000 died during internment and shortly after arrival in Oklahoma) (Gregg 2013).

The Cherokee were not the only people that faced forced removal nor the only ones who suffered mass death. The Potawatomi Trail of Death was the forced removal in 1838 of almost a thousand people from what is now Indiana to Kansas. More than forty people died along the way, mostly children. The Long Walk of the Navajo was the forced deportation of Navajo people from Arizona to New Mexico. Over fifty-three different marches occurred between August 1864 and December 1866, a journey of over 300 miles through mountains and deserts. Over 200 people died and almost 9,000 people were resettled.

Westward Expansion and Genocide

This system of governance considered Native Americans expendable. Events like the Sand Creek Massacre, in which over 150 Native Americans were slaughtered, stand as a testament to the violence inherent in this system (Hoig 1961). Led by Army Colonel John Chivington, who declared, "I have come to kill Indians" and "it is right and honorable to use any means under God's heaven to kill [them]," members of the Colorado Calvary besieged the village of Sandy Creek on November 29, 1864 (Wilson 1998, 273). The victims, the majority of whom were women and children, were murdered after they refused to surrender their land to white settlers. The dead were maimed, scalped, and mutilated; genitalia and fetuses were taken and publicly displayed as war trophies by the soldiers.

This type of excessive violence on indigenous bodies served both to project indigenous peoples as less than human and to legitimate white racial violence against them. The display of body parts signifies the ultimate act of violence and conquest—the widely shared cross-cultural belief in respecting the bodies of the dead is suspended in order to communicate just how far outside the boundaries of humanity the mutilated are. This very projection then legitimates and rationalizes white racial violence, as the severed heads and mutilated bodies serve as signifiers not of the depravity of whites but of the lengths that "rational" people must go in order to tame the wildness of indigenous peoples. With this assumption, violence and land grabbing from indigenous peoples occurred across the United States.

Forced removal was part of westward expansion, a systematic process of colonial violence and conquest organized and authorized at the highest levels of the U.S. government. Lands in the South, Northeast, and the Northwest Territory (roughly the modern states of Ohio, Michigan, Indiana, Illinois, and Wisconsin) were seized from indigenous nations through removal campaigns. Forced violence accompanied legal authorization, and upon removal of indigenous communities, lands were granted to whites by according them "title" to the land. In future court cases, holding "title" documents were necessary to establish legal claim. Thus, the ownership of whites over the land was accomplished through both sovereign force and administrative procedure (Garrison 2002).

As indigenous populations were pushed westward, U.S. expansion followed. In 1889, the Oklahoma Land Rush pushed indigenous populations again from the land, this time from places where they had been resettled (Lynn-Sherow 2004). The land rush was the first of its kind into what were called the "unassigned lands," though these were in the midst of several indigenous settlements. As many as forty different indigenous groups lived in the area. The lands included reservation land, land that indigenous people of the area occupied, and lands that were forcibly taken from indigenous people by the United States during the Civil War. The land rush allowed settlers to claim plots of up to sixteen acres as long as they lived on the land and "improved" it. As many as 50,000 white settlers participated in the land grab, which decimated indigenous people's holdings. Cattle, farm tools, and even wood were also stolen from indigenous people in the land grab, and they were forced again from the areas where settlers laid claim.

The U.S. Congress authorized these acts through series of legal ordinances granting the rights to these lands to whites. Political authorities such as Secretary of State Henry Clay argued that indigenous people "were not an improvable breed and their disappearance from the human family will be no great loss to the world" (Garrison 2002, 25). Congress gave land in the Northwest Territory to whites for the purpose of "civilizing the Indians and promoting Christianity." The hierarchies of race denied indigenous peoples the racial positionality of whites as people who were destined to cultivate and "improve" the land.

It was the myth of indigenous savagery that provided the rationale for the appropriation of their lands and the systematic violence used in the process. Forced removal and usurpation of land and resources, then, depended upon knowledge production about indigenous people that separated them from the class of humanity, just as slavery had done with black Americans. Ideas about white superiority and indigenous inferiority not only justified the execution of these claims, but they became the basis for the system of political rule itself. Laws mandating removal of people from their lands, according property to white titleholders, and encouraging the removal of indigenous children from their homes were all demonstrations of how ideas about savagery were contained within the law. Put very simply, the law of the United States presupposed indigenous savagery, a theme that applied not just to nonwhites in the contiguous United States, but also abroad.

Colonial Conquest in the Philippines

The close of the nineteenth century brought a rapid expansion of U.S. territorial possessions. As the nation pushed west and incorporated California in the mid-1800s, it set its colonial sight on places beyond what is now the contiguous United States. This resulted in the projection of racial narratives onto populations outside the United States' immediate borders and demonstrated just how important ideas of manifest destiny and benevolent enslavement were to notions of white identity.

By 1902, U.S. territories included Cuba, Puerto Rico, Philippines, Samoa, Guam, Hawaii, and Panama. These acquisitions represent an expansion of earlier arguments that it was the moral duty of Americans to bring civilization to "savage" people on the North American continent. Popular rhetoric of the day painted America as the savior of civilization and American imperialism was considered an act of benevolence.

"The White Man's Burden"

Rudyard Kipling, an English poet, first coined the term **white man's burden** in 1899 to argue for the U.S. colonization of the Philippine islands. His poem begins:

> Take up the White Man's burden—
> Send forth the best ye breed—
> Go send your sons to exile
> To serve your captives' need

Immediately, the poem was taken to encourage U.S. **imperialism,** or a policy of expanding U.S. power through military force, as a benevolent civilizing project. The expansion of the United States was seen explicitly as bringing civilization, progress, and "rationality" to untamed places. Yet Kipling implored that this was a burdensome task because it required "patience" to deal with the "blame of those ye better" and "the hate of those ye guard" (see figures 2.9 and 2.10).

This narrative underscored the tenets of white identity first developed through justifications for slavery and westward expansion, but this time it meant colonizing the Philippines. Precipitating the colonial invasion of the Philippines was a three-month war with Spain. Anti-Spanish propaganda spread by newspaper magnates Joseph Pulitzer and William Randolph Hearst (see also chapter 6) called for war against Spain in support of Cuban independence. Attacks on Spanish ships by Cuban, Philippine, and U.S. forces quickly led to Spain's surrender. But the United States and Spain quickly outmaneu-

Figure 2.9 White man's burden cartoon. Source: "The White Man's Burden (Apologies to Rudyard Kipling)," *Judge*, April 1, 1899.

Figure 2.10 Advertisement for Pears' Soap from the 1890s, instructing whites to promote cleanliness among other races. Source: Courtesy of the Library of Congress, LC-USZ62–86352.

vered Cuba and the Philippines, and Puerto Rico, Guam, and the Philippine islands were ceded to the United States by Spain. In exchange, the United States paid $20 million (approximately $575 million today).

After the Spanish-American War ended, President McKinley issued the "benevolent assimilation" policy. This policy proclaimed that "the mission of the United States is one of benevolent assimilation substituting the mild sway of justice and right for arbitrary rule" (McKinley 1898). President of the Philippines Emilio Auguinaldo subsequently issued a proclamation declaring, "My government cannot remain indifferent in view of such a violent and aggressive seizure of a portion of its territory by a nation which arrogated to itself the title of champion of oppressed nations" (McDougall 2016, 126). The three-year Philippine-American War subsequently commenced.

Once the United States acquired the land, arguments soon surfaced that suggested the United States should take up the white man's burden and extend its "civilizing" impulses across the Philippine islands.

In his 1900 plea to Congress in support of the U.S. occupation of the Philippines, Indiana Senator Albert J. Beveridge admonished:

> [God] has made us the master organizers of the world to establish system where chaos reigns. He has given us the spirit of progress to overwhelm the forces of reaction throughout the earth. He has made us adept in government that we may administer government among savage and senile peoples. Were it not for such a force as this the world would relapse into barbarism and night. . . . He has marked the American people as His chosen nation to finally lead in the regeneration of the world. This is the divine mission of America, and it holds for us all the profit, all the glory, all the happiness possible to man. We are trustees of the world's progress, guardians of its righteous peace. (Beveridge 1987, 23)

Beveridge's plea illustrates some of the foundational aspects of white identity. Whites, according to Beveridge, are the "master organizers of the world," an appeal to ideas of rationality, classification, and ordering that were coming to dominate Western Europe and the United States (see further chapters 3 and 4). He also calls upon the "spirit of progress" to "overwhelm the forces of reaction throughout the earth," invoking the idea of the natural world and the need for humans to overcome it. God even provided white people with special skills in government such that they could "administer government among savage and senile peoples." His conclusion demonstrates a very simple expression of benevolent racial superiority, assigning white people to be the "trustees of the world's progress" and "guardians of its righteous peace."

Civilizing the "Savage"

Constructions of white identity as a benevolent imperialism bringing light, improvement, and progress to the United States and the world were comple-

Figure 2.11 School begins. Uncle Sam teaches newly acquired U.S. territories, including the Philippines, Hawaii, Puerto Rico, and Cuba. Source: Courtesy of the Library of Congress, LC-DIG-ppmsca-28668.

mented by racial ideas of Filipinos (see figure 2.11). In support of the occupation of the Philippines, President William McKinley argued that Filipinos "are unfit for self-government—and they would soon have anarchy and misrule. . . . There [is] nothing left for us to do but to take them all, and to educate the Filipinos, and uplift and civilize and Christianize them, and by God's grace do the very best we could by them" (McKinley 1987, 22–23). Racial stereotypes of Filipino inferiority were central to such arguments, which cast U.S. intervention as a moral crusade. In popular culture, Filipinos were often portrayed as black, associating them with racist stereotypes historically reserved for African Americans.

Although the United States' true motives in intervening in nations like the Philippines were to protect American business and military interests, they were rationalized through a racial logic. Moreover, these racial narratives justified a policy of violence used to subdue Filipino resistance. During the Philippine-American War, which lasted from 1899 to 1902, approximately 126,000 American soldiers occupied the Philippines. More than 200,000 Filipinos died as a result of the war over that same three-year period.

The premise of the war, however, was justified and rationalized by all U.S. presidents and their representatives as tutelage. The United States argued that it was "preparing" the Philippines for independence and passed all sorts of legislation from the early 1900s to the early 1940s providing mechanisms for Filipino rule, including elections. This tutelage, however, demonstrates the foundational racial ideology at the heart of U.S. imperialism. Conceived as a benevolent master, the United States set itself up as the arbiter of righteousness, progress, and civilization. In 1945, the United States finally allowed the Philippines its independence.

COLONIAL LEGACIES TODAY

Colonial legacies had a lasting imprint. The wealth accumulated from colonialism facilitated the Industrial Revolution, globalization in the 1970s, and even the technological revolution today. The profits generated by enslaved people resulted in white wealth accumulation, whereas the forced removal of indigenous populations resulted in white land accumulation. As we shall see in chapter 5, landholding today is an important source of white wealth. And the rationalizations of white benevolence allowed the United States to extend its dominance far beyond its shores.

Colonialism and Dehumanization

Historically, colonial dehumanization saw indigenous people as objects to be appropriated. The expropriation of land was justified through the imposition of European legal systems, which cast the colonized as nonhuman. Land was stolen and laws were passed that gave the United States and whites rights to the territories that they seized. Those that had their land stolen were relegated to wage labor or enslavement. At its heart, the colonial process in the United States was inherently violent, depending on the use of violent and brutal methods to secure domination and control. But these systems were also based within legal systems, administrative policies, and the mundane practices of governing everyday life.

This system of exploitation is inherently violent and the structure of colonialist rule, according to Frantz Fanon (1963, 1967), a psychiatrist, philosopher, and revolutionary born in the French colony of Martinique in the early 1920s. For Fanon, European colonialism established a social hierarchy in which the superiority of the colonizer and the inferiority of the colonized are dependent on one another for their expression (Fanon 1963). The white man only knew his "burden" and benevolent rationality through the construction of racial others as inferior, lazy, and savage. In this formulation, the humanity of the colonizer depends upon the inhumanity of the colonial subject. In Fanon's analysis, this relationship is part of the internal logic of colonialism and forms the basis for colonial exploitation. In other words, the process of dehumanization is a fundamental aspect of colonialism.

The racial line serves as the marker that distinguishes the humanity of the European colonial forces from the nonhumanity of indigenous peoples. Under colonialism, if you are white, you are human and your legal rights are recognized. If you are colonized, you are nonhuman and you have no rights. Fanon (1967) refers to these subjectivities as the **zones of being and nonbeing.** In the zone of nonbeing, violence and appropriation are constants. Consider the case of slavery we discussed above. Although violence was not necessarily practiced at all times, on all days against all those enslaved, it was constantly present, possible, and likely if one challenged the social structure. This is quite similar to the criminal justice system. It depends on violence for its work—it can arrest, jail, and remove somebody entirely from society. It can even take someone's life. It isn't necessarily doing this all the time and to everyone, but violence is perpetually able to be called upon.

Fanon (1963) notes that colonial rule "works" because of a perpetual state of violence. As we mentioned earlier, violence as a tool of coercion is a necessary component of colonial rule. Increasing production in the cotton fields or killing revolutionary Filipinos were both necessary to assert U.S. occupation and rule over territory. The violence is justified by relegating colonial subjects to what Fanon calls the zone of nonbeing, where their humanity is denied. This permits the grotesque, brutal, and violent treatment of everyone from enslaved Africans to Filipinos to indigenous peoples. To Fanon and us, this is the origin of the concept of race as a system organizing people in a hierarchy from human to nonhuman, or to use the words of the time, from *civilized* to *savage*.

For Fanon (1967) then, the zones of being and nonbeing are central to the establishment and management of what we call race. As was argued in the Valladolid debate, a person is superior or inferior based on these zones. Superior is human, while inferior is subhuman or nonhuman and relegated to nonbeing and perpetual violence. This structure guides methods of political rule and institutionalizes a racial logic through colonial structures of power. This structure of superiority/inferiority that differentiates humanity from nonhumanity is an essential element of colonialism and the power of coloniality.

Colonialism and Coloniality

To provide a deeper analysis of race and its ties to colonialism, we draw upon the concept of coloniality introduced in chapter 1. Coloniality differs from colonialism in that *colonialism* is the domination and appropriation of a group of people by another and the establishment of colonial administrations. *Coloniality* is the global structure of power that emerged during European and U.S. colonial expansion. This structure of power underwrote enslavement of black Americans, genocide of indigenous people, and invasion of Pacific territories. These structures of power continued even as the formal domination and appropriation of other groups abated. In other words, the end of colonialism does not necessarily mean the end of coloniality.

Coloniality thus allows us to examine the ways that the racial meanings born out of colonialism survive the demise of colonial administrations. Structures of power that were put forward in the 450 years of European colonial expansion are still with us today. We still live under a capitalist economic system; our systems of rule are based on the same political divisions, particularly within Europe; and we still live in a system where the labor of the vast majority of people contributes to and supports wealth accumulation of primarily white industrialists.

This accumulation of wealth, however, was not aided by racial thinking but was in fact the *product* of racial thinking. Whites accumulated wealth because they believed they were more entitled, more deserving, and ultimately, more destined to rule. Whites exploited nonwhites, invaded other countries, and violently extracted wealth and resources because of these beliefs.

Racism today follows the structure of inferiority/superiority and of being and nonbeing that emerged in the colonial period. Through the development of mass incarceration, we see how the zones of being and nonbeing, the human and nonhuman, and between white and black people are remade through the idea of criminals and law-abiding citizens. Criminals are the nonbeings who threaten the civilization of whites, and whites are the benevolent, law-abiding citizens who, once again, face bearing the "white man's burden."

Coloniality is a theoretical tool that will help us rethink marginality in the criminal justice system. Coloniality provides a framework for understanding the link between colonialism, race, and the reproduction of social inequality today in three important ways:

1. Coloniality identifies the creation of race as a tool of domination. By doing so, coloniality provides a specific historical context for the development of racial meaning.
2. Coloniality lets us analyze the resiliency of the racial structure in the absence of formal racial exclusions. Coloniality refers to the structures of power that emanated from colonialism but survived the end of formal colonial rule.
3. Coloniality understands race as a structure with a logic that changes over time and place. Today, we do not use the same language as the colonial era, but many of the outcomes are the same. Coloniality as an analytical framework accounts for these continuities.

Throughout this book, we will examine the ways the power of coloniality continues to circulate, shape, and make the spaces that we inhabit today. Along the way, we examine how and why the racial logics introduced during colonialism continued to shape and inform the U.S. state. In so doing, we argue that the systems of the criminal justice system are today the contemporary manifestations of colonial practice, administration, and racial hierarchies. This is the power of coloniality.

CONCLUSION

Colonial processes initiated a vast conceptualization of society premised on the idea that some people were not quite people and thus could be violently exploited and appropriated. During colonialism, Europeans held the view that they were naturally superior to their subjects. The logic of coloniality became normalized as racial difference and served as a justification for colonial violence.

Coloniality is the foundational logic of race and served to justify and rationalize slavery, genocide, and imperialism. As we show in subsequent chapters, one of the keys to the success of coloniality is its self-reinforcing nature. It is premised on the idea that the agent of conquest is the arbiter of right and good—or "history is written by the victors." In subsequent chapters, we show how the "victors" define the power of the state, the "problems" of cities, and the practices of the criminal justice system in ways that embed racial dominance.

REFERENCES

Acharya, Avidit, Matthew Blackwell, and Maya Sen. 2016. "The Political Legacy of American Slavery." *Journal of Politics* 78, no. 3: 621–41.

Baptist, Edward E. 2016. *The Half Has Never Been Told: Slavery and the Making of American Capitalism.* New York: Basic Books.

Beckert, Sven. 2015. *Empire of Cotton: A Global History.* New York: Vintage.

Bennett, Lerone. 1970. *Before the Mayflower: A History of the Negro in America, 1619–1964.* Harmondsworth, UK: Penguin Books.

Berry, Daina Ramey. 2004. "'We'm Fus' Rate Bargain': Value, Labor, and Price in a Georgia Slave Community." In *The Chattel Principle: Internal Slave Trades in the Americas,* edited by Walter Johnson, 55–71. New Haven, CT: Yale University Press.

Beveridge, Alfred J. 1987. "Our Philippine Policy: Address to Congress, January 9, 1900." In *The Philippines Reader: A History of Colonialism, Neocolonialism, Dictatorship, and Resistance,* edited by Daniel B. Schirmer, and Stephen Rosskamm Shalom, eds. Cambridge, MA: South End Press.

Blackburn, Robin. 1998. *The Making of New World Slavery: From the Baroque to the Modern, 1492–1800.* New York: Verso.

Coates, Julia. 2014. *Trail of Tears.* Santa Barbara, CA: Greenwood.

Dodson, Howard, ed. 2002. *Jubilee: The Emergence of African-American Culture.* Washington, DC: National Geographic Society,

Dussel, Enrique. 1995. *The Invention of the Americas: Eclipse of "the Other" and the Myth of Modernity.* New York: Continuum.

Escobar, E. J. 1999. *Race, Police, and the Making of a Political Identity.* Berkeley: University of California Press.

Fanon, Frantz. 1963. *Wretched of the Earth.* New York: Grove Press.

———. 1967. *Black Skin, White Masks.* New York: Grove Press.

Fitzhugh, George. 1850. *The Universal Law of Slavery.* In *The Black American: A Documentary History,* edited by Leslie H. Fishel and Benjamin Quarles, 91–93. Chicago, IL: Scott, Foresman.

Fox, Cybelle, and Thomas A. Guglielmo. 2012. "Defining America's Racial Boundaries: Blacks, Mexicans, and European Immigrants, 1890–1945." *American Journal of Sociology* 118, no. 2 (September), 327–79.

Garrison, Tim Alan. 2002. *The Legal Ideology of Removal: The Southern Judiciary and the Sovereignty of Native American Nations.* Athens, GA: University of Georgia Press.

Gordon, Lewis R. 2005. "Through the Zone of Nonbeing: A Reading of *Black Skin, White Masks* in Celebration of Fanon's Eightieth Birthday." *C. L. R. James Journal* 11, no. 1 (Summer): 1–43.

———. 2007. "Through the Hellish Zone of Nonbeing: Thinking through Fanon, Disaster, and the Damned of the Earth." *Human Architecture: A Journal of the Sociology of Self-Knowledge* 5, no. 3 (Summer): 5–12.

Gregg, Kelly. 2013. "The Long Trail of Tears." *Geography in the News*. https://blog.nationalgeographic.org/2013/08/25/geography-in-the-news-the-long-trail-of-tears/.

Grosfoguel, Ramón. 2000. "Developmentalism, Modernity, and Dependency Theory in Latin America." *Nepantla: Views from the South* 1, no. 2: 347–74.

———. 2003. *Colonial Subjects: Puerto Ricans in a Global Perspective*. Berkeley: University of California Press.

———. 2007. "The Epistemic Decolonial Turn." *Cultural Studies* 21, no. 2: 211–23.

Guild, June Purcell. 1936. *Black Laws of Virginia: A Summary of the Legislative Acts of Virginia Concerning Negroes from Earliest Times to the Present*. New York: Negro Universities Press.

Hammond, James Henry. 1858. "The 'Mudsill' Theory." Speech to the U.S. Senate, March 4. www.pbs.org/wgbh/aia/part4/4h3439t.html

Hoig, Stan. 1961. *The Sand Creek Massacre*. Norman, OK: University of Oklahoma Press.

Jefferson, Thomas. 2000. "President Jefferson to William Henry Harrison: February 27, 1803," doc. 19. In *Documents of United States Indian Policy*, edited by Francis Paul Prucha, 22–23. Lincoln: University of Nebraska Press, 22.

Johnson, Walter. 1997. "Inconsistency, Contradiction, and Complete Confusion: The Everyday Life of the Law of Slavery." *Law and Social Inquiry* 22, no. 2: 405–33.

Kipling, Rudyard. 1899. "The White Man's Burden." In *Modern History Sourcebook*. New York: Fordham University. https://sourcebooks.fordham.edu/halsall/mod/kipling.asp

Lynn-Sherow, Bonnie. 2004. *Red Earth: Race and Agriculture in Oklahoma Territory*. Lawrence: University Press of Kansas.

Maldonado-Torres, Nelson. 2007. "On the Coloniality of Being." *Cultural Studies* 21, no. 2: 240–70.

McDougall, Walter. 2016. *Tragedy of U.S. Foreign Policy: How America's Civil Religion Betrayed the National Interest*. New Haven, CT: Yale University Press.

McKinley, William. 1898. "McKinley's Benevolent Assimilation Proclamation," December 21, 1898. www.msc.edu.ph/centennial/benevolent.html.

McKinley, William. 1987. "Remarks to Methodist Delegation, January 22, 1903." In *The Philippines Reader: A History of Colonialism, Neocolonialism, Dictatorship, and Resistance*, edited by Daniel B. Schirmer and Stephen Rosskamm Shalom. Cambridge, MA: South End Press.

Mieder, Wolfgang. 1997. *The Politics Of Proverbs: From Traditional Wisdom to Proverbial Stereotypes*. Madison: University of Wisconsin Press.

Mignolo, Walter D. 2002. "The Geopolitics of Knowledge and the Colonial Difference." *South Atlantic Quarterly* 101, no. 1 (Winter).

Mirandé, Alfredo. 1994. *Gringo Justice*. Notre Dame, IN: University of Notre Dame Press.

Mitchell, Timothy. 2002. *Rule of Experts: Egypt, Techno-politics, Modernity*. Berkeley: University of California Press.

Moore, Joan W., and Robert Garcia. 1978. *Homeboys: Gangs, Drugs, and Prison in the Barrios of Los Angeles*. Philadelphia: Temple University Press.

Muñiz, Ana. 2015. *Police, Power, and the Production of Racial Boundaries*. New Brunswick, NJ: Rutgers University Press.

Platt, Anthony M. 1977. *The Child Savers: The Invention of Delinquency*. 2nd ed. Chicago: University of Chicago Press.

Quijano, Aníbal. 2000. "Coloniality of Power, Eurocentrism and Latin America" *Nepantla: Views from the South* 1, no. 3: 533–80.

Quijano, Aníbal, and Immanuel Wallerstein. 1992. "Americanity as a Concept, or the Americas in the Modern World-System." *International Social Science Journal* 134 (November): 549–57.

Roberts, Dorothy. 2012. *Fatal Invention: How Science, Politics, and Big Business Re-create Race in the Twenty-First Century*. New York: New Press.

Rodriguez, Junius P., ed. 2007. *Encyclopedia of Slave Resistance and Rebellion*. Westport, CT: Greenwood.

Roediger, David R., and Elizabeth D. Esch. 2012. *The Production of Difference: Race and the Management of Labor in U.S. History*. New York: Oxford University Press.

Stoler, Ann Laura. 2002. *Carnal Knowledge and Imperial Power: Race and the Intimate in Colonial Rule*. Berkeley: University of California Press.

Wallace, Anthony, and Eric Foner. 1993. *The Long, Bitter Trail: Andrew Jackson and the Indians*. New York: Hill and Wang.

Wallerstein, Immanuel. 1979. *The Capitalist World-Economy*. Cambridge, UK: Cambridge University Press.

———. 2001. *Unthinking the Social Sciences: the Limits of Nineteenth-Century Paradigms*. Philadelphia: Temple University Press.

Wilson, James. 1998. *The Earth Shall Weep: A History of Native America*. New York: Grove Press.

The History of Racial Science: Social Science and the Birth of Criminology

LEARNING OUTCOMES

▶ Outline the scholarly development of the concept of race.

▶ Illustrate how intellectual thinking about race reflected a white, male, propertied perspective.

▶ Explain how intellectual thinking about race shaped the idea of racial superiority and threat.

▶ Summarize how the field of criminology emerged directly from the field of racial science.

▶ Show how theories of racial degeneracy, born criminality, and eugenics contributed to transformations in ideas about race and crime.

KEY TERMS

▶ Enlightenment
▶ social science
▶ scientific method
▶ ideology of objectivity
▶ sociology
▶ positivism
▶ scientific racism
▶ taxonomy
▶ anthropometry
▶ racial naturalism
▶ polygenism
▶ racial historicism
▶ monogenism
▶ phrenology
▶ theory of degeneration
▶ deviance
▶ atavistic criminal
▶ eugenics

Today, most would consider racist the idea that a biological "race" determines criminal activity. The few who still espouse this idea are generally members of fringe entities like neo-Nazis and other white power groups, whose visibility is increasing under the presidency of Donald J. Trump. Although these ideas are no longer mainstream, especially in scholarly communities, academic disciplines—such as criminology—that emerged when these ideas were first espoused live on. This chapter introduces readers to the history of scholarship on race and crime and its influence on the development of the discipline of criminology and the study of social issues.

The ideas covered in this chapter stem predominantly from just one group—white, property-owning, university-educated men. As such, they largely reflect the worldview of this group. Yet these ideas were not restricted to white men and came to influence how many people think about race and crime today. These ideas became the "objective," "rational," and even "right" way to think. While many of the historical iterations of these ideas are today considered outdated and the product of a racist era, they continue to exert considerable influence over beliefs about race, crime, and their connection.

Consider the notion, which emerged directly from racial science, that whites are more rational and less disposed to crime than other people. Today, while few would say such a thing in public, this idea continues to shape how we live and govern our lives. Criminal court statistics show that whites are more likely to receive reduced sentences, have their charges dismissed, and be viewed by probation officers as followers rather than leaders of criminal acts (see chapters 7–9). Everyday citizens express this belief by reporting to researchers that they find neighborhoods of color to be spaces of higher crime, regardless of actual crime rates (Quillian and Pager 2001; Krysan and Bader 2007). Whites are more often acquitted in stand-your-ground cases; their fear is often seen as reasonable and their killing of another as justified (Roman 2013). This connection is reinforced by whites' lack of desire to reside in neighborhoods of color and employers' preference for hiring whites with criminal records over black people without (Pager 2008).

The idea that whites are more rational and less likely to commit crime is directly supported by the field of criminology. Studies of "race and crime" almost invariably focus on the behavior of nonwhites and rarely on others (Harcourt 2008). Indeed, only a few scholarly works examine the criminality of white communities (e.g., Hagan and Foster 2004; Mohamed and Fritsvold 2010). Most studies of "whites and crime" examine not white criminal behavior, but white perceptions of crime and criminality. Crime by whites is often encapsulated as white collar crime, thus foregrounding the connection between whites, wealth, and work. These ideas, however, are not new and date to the birth of criminology during the time of racial science. In this chapter, we trace how the emergence of racial science shaped the birth of criminology and how we respond to and think about crime today.

THE ENLIGHTENMENT AND THE BIRTH OF SOCIAL SCIENCE

Social science, as we practice it today, began in a period in the late seventeenth and eighteenth centuries known as the **Enlightenment,** the era that gave birth to the ideas of rationality, progress, and reason and saw political revolutions against monarchies and religious authority. **Social science** is the use and application of the techniques, rationalities, and ideologies of natural science first developed during the Enlightenment to the study of the social world. The United States' own revolution in the late eighteenth century and its adoption of a liberal democratic form of governance is a product of this period. Liberal, democratic governments were premised on the idea of self-rule, which assumed that citizens were rational, reasonable, and did not need intervention from the state in their daily affairs.

The intellectual revolution of the Enlightenment was not limited to the political and philosophical spheres. It also spawned similar ideas in the study of the natural world, and intellectuals at the time argued that man could use his innate ability to reason to understand the natural world. The scholarly revolution during the Enlightenment was carried throughout western Europe and the emerging United States because of the invention of the printing press in 1440, which allowed scientific discoveries to be widely disseminated.

The Scientific Revolution

From the mid-1500s through the 1600s, a period now known as the scientific revolution, European scientists including Sir Isaac Newton, René Descartes, and Francis Bacon contributed to an explosion of knowledge of mathematics, biology (especially anatomy), and the physical and natural sciences. Their work was premised upon what came to be known as the **scientific method,** a process that produces knowledge about the world through systematic observation and experimentation. Premised on an **ideology of objectivity** that assumes investigations can be carried out without subjective influences or bias, the scientific method was considered the expression of the innate reason and rationality of humans applied to the natural world.

Fueled by the idea that scholars could assess the world independent of the constraints of religiosity, Enlightenment philosophers produced a range of plays, novels, pamphlets, and other literary material arguing that "the application of reason to the affairs of men would encourage a general advance of civilization" (Hamilton 1992, 29). Enlightenment philosophers turned their attention to the social world, or the study of man as a social entity that came to be known as **sociology.** While significant advances in the study of the social world had been occurring in Islamic societies since at least the early 900s, European societies did not undertake the study of sociology until the 1800s.

Auguste Comte is often regarded as the founder of sociology. Comte (1893) argued that knowledge passed through three stages. First was the theological stage, which he considered "fictitious" knowledge. Second was the metaphysical stage (also known as the abstract or philosophical stage), where knowledge about the social world results from practicing reason and rationality, but not from systematic observation or experimentation. The third stage produced knowledge that Comte considered scientific—what he termed "positive" knowledge, which studies the laws of the universe.

While Comte's stages never really caught on, the notion that society could be understood—and even more importantly, governed—through the collection of knowledge about the world did. **Positivism,** or the idea that all rational assertions must be able to be scientifically verified, came to dominate scholarly investigations into the social world. History, for example, one of the oldest disciplines, predating the Enlightenment and the scientific revolution, embraced positivism, and scholars began to insist on the use of primary documents—as opposed to recollections by third parties—as evidence for historical claims (Nora 1989).

Social Science and the Evolutionary Ladder

Colonial conquest brought with it new opportunities for scholars to observe variations within human societies. Charles Darwin's theory of evolution stemmed from his experience observing a landscape utterly unlike the one in which he had been born. Other scholars used encounters with different cultures to question why particular social customs developed in some societies but not others. These encounters were often used to collect stories and examples to help them understand their own social world.

These investigations into the social world, however, assumed that European customs and traditions were far superior to other ways of being. European ideas were seen as having progressed beyond those of other cultures. White men considered themselves enlightened and civilized compared to other social groups. This qualified them for self-rule.

By contrast, European societies saw others as unprepared to take on the tasks that reason, rationality, and political society demanded. Instead, non-Europeans were seen as backward, savage, and irrational. Scholarship began from this premise and sought to find out why other civilizations were not as advanced as the Europeans. This initiated social science as a quest for uncovering why some peoples' predilections and behaviors prevented them from achieving European progress. This further paved the way for constructing race as an evolutionary ladder.

The idea of an evolutionary ladder did not begin with the theory of evolution developed by Charles Darwin but was in fact an idea postulated by Greek philosophers such as Plato and Aristotle to explain the relation of humans to God. Called the "great chain of being," this idea postulated that an almighty and perfect God was at the top of a hierarchical structure of life. Rocks and minerals sat at the bottom of the chain, with organisms above them representing increasing degrees of perfection. Each step up the ladder gained positive attributes, such as motion, appetite, and consciousness. Subdivisions exist, but the basic chain places God at the top, followed by angels, humans, plants, and finally minerals. Though this earliest classification of the natural world did not introduce the idea of race, racial scientists of the Enlightenment drew upon this idea in their work. Races were positioned on an evolutionary ladder, with whites at the top and nonwhites representing various primordial stages believed to be predecessors of "civilized" and "rational" development.

Thomas Jefferson, Race, and Justifications for Slavery

The evolutionary ladder was reflected in the political and material reality of how people of different "races" were treated in political society. Specifically, the United States allowed for the institution of slavery based on skin color, a reflection of political and social belief in the evolutionary ladder of early racial scientists. Yet, the United States was also premised on ideas of equality between "men." Given the ideology of science and objectivity at the time, Enlightenment scholars in the United States sought to reconcile their claims of equality with the reality of slavery. Scientific racism proved critical to this endeavor.

Thomas Jefferson, noted Enlightenment philosopher and U.S. president, demonstrates how Enlightenment scholars attempted to reconcile the idea that "all men are created equal" with the enslavement of men. Jefferson was a noted slaveowner and accumulated significant wealth on the backs of hundreds of enslaved people. But he was also one of the architects of the Declaration of Independence and a fervent proponent of "equality." Jefferson even argued against slavery, while also justifying it by appeal to the scientific method. Jefferson's behavior was not anomalous for the time and instead represents how the ideologies of benevolent governance, the Enlightenment, and capitalism worked together to justify white "freedom" and wealth accumulation and nonwhite enslavement.

In his book *Notes on the State of Virginia* (1787), Jefferson argued *against* slavery, hoping for the "wisdom" to find a way to end the institution, even though he was a slaveholder and what we would today define as a rapist. Jefferson's plantation relied on the labor of enslaved people, including children, and it is well documented that he oversaw severe beatings and violent punishments. He also raped Sally Hemings when she was fourteen and continued for decades. Rape may seem strong language, especially as Jefferson is often represented as someone who "loved" Hemings, but today, we would call someone who raped and impregnated a teenager a "pedophile." Indeed, we reserve even more severe judgment for those who prey upon people in their care—teachers seducing students, for instance. Jefferson's actions are exactly those, taking sexual liberties with someone who was by definition unable to consent because she was *owned* by her rapist. These actions, however, were justified by Jefferson through the language of race.

Jefferson's hypocrisy reflects a common sentiment at the time: that Europeans were distinctly *different* from others, possessing unique and varied traits that science could organize and catalogue. In the chapter titled "Laws," he enumerated the "physical distinctions proving a difference of race" that go beyond color and hair:

> They [black people] have less hair on the face and body. They secrete less by the kidneys, and more by the glands of the skin, which gives them a very strong and disagreeable odour. This greater degree of transpiration renders them more tolerant of heat, and less so of cold, than the whites. Perhaps too a difference of structure in the pulmonary apparatus, which a late ingenious experimentalist has discovered to be the principal regulator of animal heat, may have disabled them from extricating, in the act of inspiration, so much of that fluid from the outer air, or obliged them in expiration, to part with more of it. They seem to require less sleep. A black, after hard labour through the day, will be induced by the slightest amusements to sit up till midnight, or later, though knowing he must be out with the first dawn of the morning. They are at least as brave, and more adventuresome. But this may perhaps proceed from a want of forethought, which prevents their seeing a danger till it be present. When present, they do not go through it with more coolness or steadiness than the whites. . . . Comparing them by their faculties of memory, reason, and imagination, it appears to me, that in memory they are equal to the whites; in reason much inferior, as I think one could scarcely be found capable of tracing and comprehending the investigations of Euclid; and that in imagination they are dull, tasteless, and anomalous. (Jefferson [1787] 1997, 98)

Jefferson's cataloguing of racial differences shows how Enlightenment philosophers used the scientific method of observation. Observations of the "capacities" of peoples were used categorize some as rational men capable of self-rule and others as irrational and thus incapable of self-rule, justifying their subjugation through slavery. Many "enlightened" philosophers thus saw slavery as a moral imperative. Only through enslavement could the irrational and savage be cared for and educated. Jefferson's writings demonstrate how race extended beyond physical attributes and into the realm of reason, imagination, and memory.

Jefferson reconciled the hypocrisy of calling for the natural rights of man while enslaving nonwhite men with an appeal to the scientific basis of race in "Laws":

> The opinion, that they are inferior in the faculties of reason and imagination, must he hazarded with great diffidence. To justify a general conclusion, requires many observations, even where the subject may be submitted to the anatomical knife, to optical glasses, to analysis by fire, or by solvents. . . . To our reproach it must be said, that though for a century and a half we have had under our eyes the races of black and of red men, they have never yet been viewed by us as subjects of natural history. I advance it therefore as a suspicion only, that the blacks, whether originally a distinct race, or made distinct by time and circumstances, are inferior to the whites in the endorsements both of body and mind. It is not against experience to suppose, that different species of the same genus, or varieties of the same species, may

possess different qualifications. Will not a lover of natural history then, one who views the gradations in all the races of animals with the eye of philosophy, excuse an effort to keep those in the department of man as distinct as nature has formed them? (Jefferson [1787] 1997, 102)

Jefferson is initially cautious in his assertions of racial difference, arguing that they should be "hazarded with great diffidence," meaning he lacked scientific confidence in his claims. But should whites "subject" "black" and "red" men to study as one would the natural world, Jefferson was confident that these different gradations and "qualifications" of men would be borne out through science.

Jefferson calls for the creation of what would come to be known as scientific racism. **Scientific racism** is the period of scholarly inquiry in which race was believed to have a biological origin and the scientific method was used to classify people into distinct races. Jefferson's conclusion and scientific racism more generally demonstrate how scientific investigation often began with the assumption that distinctions existed among races. With this assumption, the purpose of scientific investigation was to uncover exactly how and why difference exists. Scientific racism, drawing on the techniques of the natural sciences, especially physiology, resulted in the proliferation of scholars measuring, comparing, and analyzing bodily traits between races. These measurements formed the basis for the modern taxonomy of race as we know it today. They also formed the basis for centuries' worth of work aimed at uncovering why "some" were different from "us" and unable to exhibit the "innate" powers of European rationality.

THE BIRTH OF SCIENTIFIC RACISM

As we detail in chapter 1, the concept of race grew out of the practices of colonialism, particularly the colonial encounter. As Enlightenment theorists grappled with the notions of the "natural rights of man" while also subjugating entire peoples, the concept of race slowly emerged as a justification and rationalization for this complicated and contradictory set of claims and practices.

Classification, Taxonomy, and Race

Given that race emerged from the geographical project of colonialism, it is perhaps not surprising that the concept of race also emerged as a geographical and not a biological phenomenon. One of the earliest theorizations of the modern concept of race came from a Swedish physician, botanist, and zoologist known as Carl Linnaeus.

Linnaeus is considered the father of modern **taxonomy,** a hierarchical system of classification where each order is thought to build upon and extend lower orders. One example of taxonomy is the animal kingdom, thought to begin with simple organisms like bacteria and build toward complex life like birds, fish, mammals, and humans. Linnaeus's defining work is a multivolume tome, revised in over a dozen editions during his lifetime, called *Systemae Naturae,* that provides a detailed taxonomy for plants, minerals, and animals and was the starting point for our modern taxonomic system. Terms you may have learned in school for the classification of the animal kingdom, including *species* and *genus,* were part of Linnaeus's system.

Classifying Humans

As part of his project, Linnaeus created the specimen distinction for humans: *Homo sapiens.* Linnaeus's classification placed *Homo sapiens* within the order of primates, resulting in considerable controversy at the time. Today, however, the controversy surrounding Linnaeus concerns his division of *Homo sapiens* into four different "varieties" (see figure 3.1). The four varieties were *Homo americanus, Homo europaeus, Homo asiaticus,* and *Homo afer* or *africanus.* Linnaeus's taxonomy was based on geographical divisions made possible by the colonial encounter, revealing the extent to which race emerges from practices of conquest rather than a preexisting category awaiting "discovery" (Sauer 1993). Though Linnaeus's human varieties corresponded to particular geographical areas, his classifications also contained descriptions of cultural proclivities and behaviors that reveal how the hierarchy of race infused geographical difference.

Homo americanus was described by Linnaeus as having "black, straight, thick" hair and was also labeled "obstinate" and "regulated by customs." *Homo asiaticus* was described as having "hair black, eyes dark," and was distinguished by personality traits such as "haughty," "melancholy," and "covetous." In contrast to *americanus, asiaticus* was "governed by opinions." Linnaeus provided more bodily descriptors for *Homo africanus* than *asiaticus,* including "skin silky" and "nose flat," and assigned personality traits such as "indolent," "negligent," and "governed by caprice." In contrast, *Homo europaeus* was described as "fair, sanguine and brawny" with both "yellow" and "brown" hair that was "flowing." Personality traits were recorded as "gentle, acute, inventive," and the species as a whole was "governed by laws." Varieties are even described by their clothing, with *americanus* painting himself with "fine red lines," *europaeus* "covered with close vestments," *asiaticus* "covered with loose garments," and *africanus* "annoint[ing] himself with grease."

Racial Taxonomies Today

Linnaeus's categorizations are likely familiar to you. Descriptors of Asians as "covetous" are found throughout stereotypical depictions of Asians, such

MAMMALIA.

ORDER I. PRIMATES.

Fore-teeth cutting; upper 4, parallel; teats 2. pectoral.

1. HOMO.

Sapiens. Diurnal; varying by education and situation.

   2. Four-footed, mute, hairy.   *Wild Man.*

   3. Copper-coloured, choleric, erect.   *American.*

      Hair black, straight, thick; *nostrils* wide, *face* harsh; *beard* scanty; *obstinate,* content free. *Paints* himself with fine red lines. *Regulated* by customs.

   4. Fair, sanguine, brawny.   *European.*

      Hair yellow, brown, flowing; *eyes* blue; *gentle,* acute, inventive. *Covered* with close vestments. *Governed* by laws.

   5. Sooty, melancholy, rigid.   *Asiatic.*

      Hair black; *eyes* dark; *severe,* haughty, covetous. *Covered* with loose garments. *Governed* by opinions.

   6. Black, phlegmatic, relaxed.   *African.*

      Hair black, frizzled; *skin* silky; *nose* flat; *lips* tumid; *crafty,* indolent, negligent. *Anoints* himself with grease. *Governed* by caprice.

Monstrosus Varying by climate or art.

   1. Small, active, timid.   *Mountaineer.*
   2. Large, indolent.   *Patagonian.*
   3. Less fertile.   *Hottentot.*
   4. Beardless.   *American.*
   5. Head conic.   *Chinese.*
   6. Head flattened.   *Canadian.*

The anatomical, physiological, natural, moral, civil and social histories of man, are best described by their respective writers.

Vol. I.—C   2. SIMIA.

Figure 3.1 Carl Linnaeus's taxonomy of humans. Source: Carl Linnaeus, 1806, *A General System of Nature*, translated by William Turton, 10th ed., London: Lackington, Allen, 9, https://books.google.com/books?id=I 3QZAAAAYAAJ&source=gbs_ navlinks_s.

as the Fu Manchu character, a brilliant supervillain intent on world domination who coveted the scientific progress of the United States. His fictional exploits were featured in dozens of books, movies, and TV shows in the twentieth century and have even reappeared in advertisements today (Young 2013). Stereotypes of black Americans as lazy permeate U.S. culture and have been used over the centuries to justify slavery, Jim Crow legislation, and welfare reform in the 1990s. *Homo europaeus* exhibited many of the same traits we have come to associate with "civilization" and whiteness: rule of law; European formal attire, predecessor to the modern tuxedo or ball gown; and advanced technology.

The Proliferation of Racial Science

Though Carl Linnaeus might also be considered the father of modern racial taxonomies, his ideas about how to divide people into categories underwent substantial revision over the next century. Johann Friedrich Blumenbach, a German physician, naturalist, and anthropologist, used Linnaeus's work as a starting point to create racial categories still used today.

Geography and Race

The first edition of Blumenbach's graduate thesis in 1775 identified four varieties of humans, very similar to Linnaeus's categories. By 1781, he had created five geographical distinctions: people from Europe (including North India), North Africa, and North America; people from the rest of Asia (that is, east of the Ganges); people from Africa; people from Central and South America; and people from the southern world (e.g., the Philippines). By 1795, however, Blumenbach dropped the geographical distinctions and identified five distinct races, applying labels that are used by some to this day: Caucasians, Mongolians, Ethiopians, Americans, and Malays.

Blumenbach's decision to expand the varieties of humans into five stemmed from his work of measuring human skulls—from noses and face length to the size of bones and other physical characteristics (examples of Blumenbach's skull drawings are shown in figure 3.2). The practice of measuring bodily traits is called **anthropometry**. Blumenbach wrote: "Formerly in the first edition of this work, I divided all mankind into four varieties; but after I had more actively investigated the different nations of Eastern Asia and America, and, so to speak, looked at them more closely, I was compelled to give up that division, and to place in its stead the following five varieties, as more consonant to nature." Figure 3.3 illustrates how racial scientists imagined these different "races." Because race was "observable" to early racial scientists, anthropometrical techniques were the first methods used to try to find evidence for racial differences.

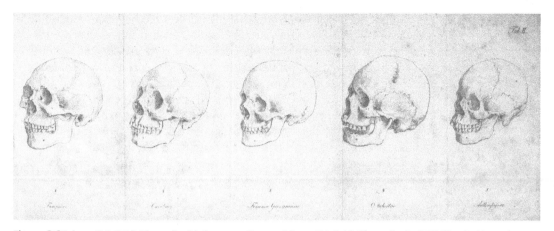

Figure 3.2 Johann Friedrich Blumenbach's five races. Source: Johann Friedrich Blumenbach, 1795, "On the Natural Variety of Mankind," 3rd ed., in *The Anthropological Treatises of Johann Friedrich Blumenbach,* 1865, translated and edited by Thomas Bendyshe, London: Longman, Green, Longman, Roberts, & Green, Plate 4 (foldout), https://archive .org/details/anthropologicalt00blum.

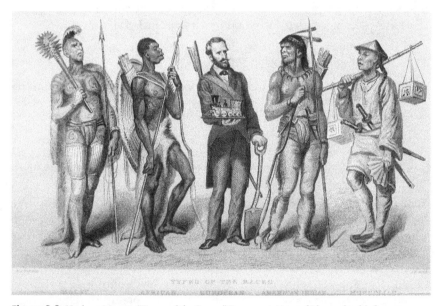

Figure 3.3. Herbert Morris, "Types of the Races." Representatives of Blumenbach's five races. Source: Herbert Morris, 1875, *Present Conflict of Science with the Christian Religion; Or, Modern Scepticism Met on Its Own Ground,* Philadelphia: P. W. Ziegler, 327, https://archive.org/details /presentconflicto00morr.

Blumenbach revolutionized the study of race, and his taxonomy would be the basis of scientific racism until its demise. Prior to Blumenbach, race was conceived as a geographical phenomenon and thus was considered the development of natural processes. In the same way that flowers developed differently depending on light, soil, and temperature conditions, Blumenbach, Linnaeus, and their contemporaries largely viewed differences among people as the result of environmental conditions. For this reason, Blumenbach did not necessarily believe that his five races stemmed from different variants of human, but rather from a single type cultivated in varying environments. This belief, however, did not reflect the entirety of racial scientists, and soon, notions of white racial distinction and superiority were born.

The Birth of White Supremacy

Despite Blumenbach's belief in the common history of humans, his work demonstrates a fundamental transformation from a geographic concept of race to one based upon European superiority. In developing his classification system, Blumenbach used two axes upon which to grade all humans: beauty and moral/intellectual development. Caucasians he placed at the pinnacle of both categories—the most beautiful, moral, and intellectual of all the races:

> I have taken the name of this variety from Mount Caucasus, both because its neighborhood, and especially its southern slope, produces the most beautiful race of men, I mean the Georgian...
>
> I have allotted the first place to the Caucasian because this stock displays the most beautiful race of men which makes me esteem it the primeval one. This diverges in both directions into two, most remote and very different from each other; on the one side, namely, into the Ethiopian, and on the other into the Mongolian. The remaining two occupy the intermediate positions between that primeval one and these two extreme varieties; that is, the American between the Caucasian and Mongolian; the Malay between the same Caucasian and Ethiopian. (Blumenbach 1795)

Though Caucasian is based on a geographical formation of mountains, Blumenbach's reasoning for choosing the name is aesthetic: he believed the people who lived in that area were the most beautiful. This decision marks a shift from a geographical definition of race towards an aesthetic and, importantly, hierarchical concept of race.

Linnaeus and Blumenbach both demonstrate how a purportedly rigorous scientific process can produce results that reflect the predispositions of a culturally specific group—in this case, white, upper-class men. Their taxonomies also provided the scholarly evidence of racial difference that came to dominate social science and the development of modern society. Over the next century, Linnaeus's and Blumenbach's work inspired scientists to measure, exhibit, and connect race to the social world in ways that invigorated the myth of European superiority and confirmed the inferiority of others.

MEASURING RACE

Creating racial taxonomies were important techniques for providing a veneer of scientific objectivity to Europeans' ideas about those they conquered. Scientific racism's theories of race can be divided into two broader ideas: racial naturalism and racial historicism. **Racial naturalism** is the belief that race stems from innate, biological differences and not from social, geographical, or cultural conditions. Proponents of racial naturalism during the era of scientific racism subscribed to the polygeny theory of racial origin. **Polygenism** is the idea that the various races emerged independently, each from its own original type. Figure 3.4 shows one attempt by scholars to articulate this idea in a picture, noting that distinct types of flora and fauna also surrounded the emergence of particular races.

Unlike racial naturalism, which assumes a natural, innate, and preexisting racial difference, **racial historicism** reflects a belief that races developed from unique historical circumstances. The hierarchical ranking of races emerges from different positions within the historical and even evolutionary ladder, rather than innate biological differences. Racial historicism was developed by scientists who subscribed to **monogenism,** or the idea that all races stemmed from a single species. Unlike polygenism, which argues races are distinct species, differences between races in monogenism arise as the result of historical circumstances.

Racial Naturalism

Throughout the 1800s, racial scientists used the growing tools of measurement and classification to justify and demonstrate the biology of racial difference. Measurements of the head, skull, organs, and other body parts provided evidence for racial scientists to assert the truth of racial difference. While polygenist and monogenist theories originated from different ideas of the world, racial scientists were united in the contention that race referred to significant differences between groups. Though most of the measurements and techniques developed by racial scientists are no longer in use, they demonstrate an early and crude attempt to link race with crime and to use science to do so.

Phrenology

One of the most infamous examples of racial science is phrenology. German scientist Franz Joseph Gall is credited with the birth of **phrenology,** a short-lived racial science, popular only from about 1810 to 1840. Phrenology used anthropometric measurements of the human skull to generate insights into a person's character, potential, and moral development. As figure 3.5 shows,

Figure 3.4 Polygenism based on region. Source: "Tableau to Accompany Prof. Agassiz's 'Sketch [of the Natural Provinces of the Animal World and Their Relation to the Different Types of Man],'" in Josiah Clark Nott and George R. Gliddon, 1854, *Types of Mankind; or, Ethnological Researches, Based upon the Ancient Monuments, Paintings, Sculptures, and Crania of Races, and upon Their Natural, Geographical, Philological and Biblical History,* 7th ed., Philadelphia: Lippincott, Grambo, plate following lxxvi, https://quod.lib.umich .edu/m/moa/aja7398.0001.001?view=toc.

phrenology is based on the idea, common to modern neuroscience, that the brain controls particular behaviors, ideas, and emotions, but for phrenologists, this was revealed through the shape of the head. Phrenologists measured the skull's shape and charted its bumps and crevices to reveal an individual's propensities and weaknesses. Gender and race, as figures 3.6 and 3.7 show, were even supposedly reflected in phrenological readings.

Nott & Gliddon's Types of Mankind, 1854.

Phrenology gained wide acceptance during its relatively short life. Monarchs had their children's heads read by popular phrenologists, and even a professional association, the Phrenological Society of Edinburgh, was established. It was one of the first scientific theories to gain mass popularity, spreading throughout the working and middle classes due to the dissemination of phrenology charts (McCandless 1992).

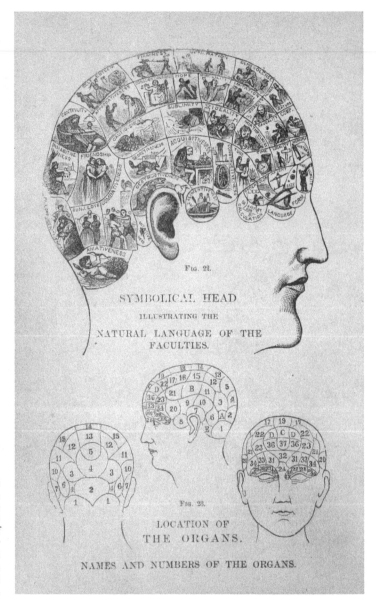

Figure 3.5 Phrenological chart of the faculties. Source: Samuel R. Wells, 1890, "Phrenological chart of the faculties," in *How to Read Character: New Illustrated Hand-Book of Phrenology and Physiognomy for Students and Examiners,* New York: Fowler and Wells, 36, https://books.google.com/books?id=JAJNAQAAM AAJ&source=gbs_navlinks_s.

ful. It is elevating and chastening in its influences, and acts in co-operation with the strictly religious group, to which it is closely allied.

9. The Religious Group has the highest office of all, and tends to elevate man into fellowship with angels, and beget aspirations after holiness and heaven, while making him at the same time meek and humble—even as a little child—

LARGE.   SMALL.

FIG. 20.—EMANUEL KANT.   FIG. 21.—A NEGRO.
REFLECTIVE GROUP.

toward God. When large and active, and holding the leading place which belongs to it, all the other groups are sanctified through its action.

Our illustrations, so far as they go, tell their own story too well to need much comment. We select extreme cases when we can, in order to make the contrast as great as possible, and thus impress the fact illustrated upon the mind. Some of the sub-groups are not susceptible of pictorial illustration.

CLASSIFIED LIST OF ORGANS.

I.—THE PROPENSITIES.

I. THE SOCIAL GROUP.

1. Amativeness.   3. Adhesiveness.
2. Philoprogenitiveness.   4. Inhabitiveness.
         5. Continuity (not grouped).
                    2*

Figure 3.6 "Reflective group" of organs: supposed racial differences based on phrenological head size. Source: Samuel R. Wells, 1890, "Phrenological chart of the faculties," in *How to Read Character: New Illustrated Hand-Book of Phrenology and Physiognomy for Students and Examiners,* New York: Fowler and Wells, 33, https://books.google.com /books?id=JAJNAQAAMAAJ& source=gbs_navlinks_s.

3. The External Senses have for their appropriate work the conveying to the brain of intelligence concerning the world of material things outside of the brain itself, acting, therefore, in direct co-operation with the perceptive faculties.

4. The Perceptive Group, through the senses, brings man into direct communication with the physical universe, gives a correct judgment of the properties of things, and leads to the practical application of the knowledge obtained.

5. The Function of the Reflective Group is to analyze, compare, and classify the facts collected by the perceptives, and to philosophize, contrive, invent, and originate ideas.

LARGE.   NOT LARGE.

FIG. 18.—LOUIS AGASSIZ.   FIG. 19.—MISS CARMICHAEL.
THE PERCEPTIVE GROUP.

6. The Literary Group imparts memory, and the ability to communicate ideas and feelings by means of written or spoken words. (Included among the perceptives in diagram, fig. 15.)

7. The Group of Selfish Sentiments gives regard for character, love of distinction, self-reliance, independence, stability, and perseverance. They have an aspiring and governing tendency.

8. The Semi-Intellectual Group has for its function self-improvement, and the love and production of whatever is beauti-

Figure 3.7 "Perceptive group" of organs: supposed gender differences based on phrenological head size. Source: Samuel R. Wells, 1890, "Phrenological chart of the faculties," in *How to Read Character: New Illustrated Hand-Book of Phrenology and Physiognomy for Students and Examiners,* New York: Fowler and Wells, 32, https://books.google.com/books?id=JAJNAQAAM AAJ&source=gbs_navlinks_s.

Morton's Skulls

One of the most popular figures in skull measurement was a U.S. physician named Samuel Morton, considered the founder of physical anthropology. Morton is also considered by some to be the true founder of scientific racism. He was the first to articulate a theory of race entirely based in a hierarchical ranking of intellectual and moral ability rather than geographic difference (Fredrickson 1987). Morton developed his theory by measuring skulls and showing that white Europeans had larger skulls and thus, he postulated, larger brains.

Morton used skull measurements to create racial classifications that were rooted in biology and the body and not the result of an environmental phenomenon. He reasoned that "the physical characteristics which distinguish the different Races, are independent of external causes" (Morton 1839, 6). Morton's measurements were combined with narratives of colonialist encounters to create a hierarchy that placed whites at the top and black people at the bottom, with other races in between. For example, Morton measured Egyptian skulls and decided that ancient Egyptians were in actuality Caucasian and not African. While Morton's classification was not based in geography, it did replicate the same ideas about race, revealing just how thoroughly the cultural biases of white, male, upper-class Europeans pervaded scientific investigations.

This shift in raciological thinking was an important moment in the development of hierarchical ideas of race. While Morton's theories have been widely disputed, his initiation of the idea that race marked different *biological* capacities remained. Morton's work articulated a theory of race based on innate and immutable bodily characteristics. Under a geographic conception, race is the product of different environmental conditions producing the most adaptable forms, as with plants and species in the natural world. Under a biological conception, race marks not where one is from but rather one's capacity for engagement in the social world. It is this connection between capacity and race through which the ideas of racial scientists were remade in subsequent eras (see the discussion of DNA databases and racial bias in box 3.1), even as they were discredited.

Racial Historicism

Though some racial scientists subscribed to an idea of race rooted in biological difference, a polygenistic theory of racial development, their ideas did not significantly differ from monogenistic racial scientists. Blumenbach was one of the first to articulate a theory of race based in monogeny, arguing that all races stem from the same biological predecessors. Differences arose as a result of what he termed *Bildungstrieb*. He defined this as a force within organisms that acts on them until they reach final form. Bildungstrieb produced negative racial characteristics through the **theory of degeneration,** which posits that

BOX 3.1   DNA Databases and Racial Bias

In 2004, California voters passed Proposition 69, a law that established a statewide DNA database of people who have committed a felony. Failure to provide one's DNA became a crime, punishable by up to one year in county jail. By September 2016, over 2.5 million DNA samples had been collected.

Law enforcement agencies contend that storing DNA information results in less crime and cite the number of "hits" they have gotten for murder, rape, and assault cases that came from people convicted of lesser felonies—such as DUI or felonious theft. Advocates argue that DNA is an invaluable tool in the arsenal against crime and that it helps to reduce the risk of racial disparity based on individual bias.

Opponents argue that the database further targets people of color as criminal. Since people of color are disproportionately represented in arrest statistics, they argue, their DNA will also be disproportionately represented in the DNA database. Because whites are less likely to be arrested for crimes in general and more likely to benefit from prosecutorial and police discretion by, for instance, being charged with a misdemeanor instead of a felony, their DNA is less likely to be in the database. This means the DNA of a white person who rapes or murders is less likely to be included. By contrast, since police concentrate in urban neighborhoods of color, crime in these neighborhoods is subject to greater police intervention, and thus, the DNA of people of color is more likely to end up in a database of samples from convicted felons. One argument for collecting a wide sampling of DNA, and not just that from people who commit infamous crimes like rape and murder, is that DNA from a low-level felony, like theft, can be used to identify those people if they go on to commit more heinous crimes.

Should California continue collecting DNA samples from those convicted of felonies, including juveniles? What dangers might result from operating such a database? Do you think the database is likely to exacerbate or ameliorate practices of racial bias in the criminal justice system? Why or why not?

Source: Joe Khalil, "Officials: California Criminal DNA Database Dwindling Because of Prop 47," Fox 40, Sacramento, updated September 17, 2016, http://fox40.com/2016/09/17/officials-california-criminal-dna-database-dwindling-because-of-prop-47/.

the environment and other external factors can cause the decline of an organism. Regarding variations in human height, Blumenbach wrote:

> We must allow then that there is no entire nation of giants or pigmies. But the racial variety of nature . . . seems to be confined within smaller limits in proportion than those which have everywhere observed it the case of other domestic animals; and this will easily be understood by a consideration of what has been said about the causes of degeneration. That climate has something to do with it, besides many other proofs, is seen from a comparison of the Laplanders with the Hungarians, who are two colonies from one race, but have reached a very different stature under a dif-

ferent climate. Physiology also clearly shows the great influence of diet in augmenting or diminishing the stature. Hence the tall bodies of the nobles of Otaheite is ascribed to the more generous diet in which they indulge. (Blumenbach 1795, 256)

Here, Blumenbach argues that stature (or height) is subject to environmental influences, even within the same racial groupings. For Blumenbach, degeneration could be brought about by climate, diet, or any of a host of other variables (such as sunlight) that influence not only physical attributes but also moral development and custom.

This idea of race as a consequence of environmental influence was taken up repeatedly throughout the nineteenth century and was not necessarily subscribed to only by those who believed in the inferiority of nonwhites. The noted U.S. antiracist Samuel Stanhope Smith invoked this theory when he argued that "the complexion in any climate will be changed towards black, in proportion to the degree of heat, in the atmosphere, and to the quantity of bile in the skin" (1810, 16). Smith worked to defeat slavery and believed in the equality of races, yet his support for the environmental theory of racial difference revealed just how widespread the ideas of racial scientists were.

Degeneration and Racial Historicism

Blumenbach did not develop his theories of degeneration in much detail. It was Bénédict Morel who provided the first elaboration of the idea of degeneration in 1857 in his *Treatise on Degeneration of the Human Species* (Dean 2010). Morel was a psychiatrist who developed the idea of mental degeneration based on his clinical experience working in a psychiatric hospital. In his treatise, Morel proposed that there was an ideal human type and that "degenerations are deviations from the normal human type, which are transmissible by heredity and which deteriorate progressively towards extinction" (Dean 2010, 161). For Morel, degeneration led to elimination of undesirable traits.

Morel introduced the idea that the environment could render changes in the body and in behavior. While some monogenists used the idea of a single origin to explain similarities among people, those committed to establishing a hierarchy of racial differences postulated that Europeans were the ideal type from which all others degenerated. For instance, the blackness of African skin was a "degeneration" from the ideal white type because of exposure to different climates and environmental conditions. These theories demonstrated, to Europeans, why whites were much more advanced than others. Some racial scientists even believed that black people could turn white when thoroughly "enlightened" by European ideals (Dean 2010)! For racial scientists, these changes could also be passed to offspring, resulting in intergenerational transfer of degenerate conditions.

Monogenism might have unseated the idea of race by recognizing the common heritage of all humans. It could have been a uniting force, rather than one that sparked divisions. Instead, monogenism declared race as the by-product of historical circumstances. The consequence of history was the degeneration of some races while others thrived, prospered, and became civilized, all as a consequence of the environment.

Morel's idea of degeneration is quite like racial historicist arguments today. One common contemporary example of racial historicism is the argument that where one lives, the culture one is raised in, and one's environmental influences shape one's capacities. Particular environments support or hinder intellectual and moral development, and these variances are even expressed in the body (in IQ, for instance).

Monogenists who saw race as the result of degeneration retained the essence of racial distinction that also shaped polygenists: that the white race was at the top of a great chain of being or evolutionary ladder and others were deviations and degenerations from this ideal type. The notion of environmental degeneration thus introduced the idea that although race may not be biological, racial differences are nevertheless long lasting, significant, and determinative of behavior. Though Morel did not fully develop the connections between degeneration and race, early criminologists quickly drew on these ideas in trying to explain the development and persistence of crime. Drawing on the concept of degeneration, the field of criminology first emerged as a social science.

THE BIRTH OF CRIMINOLOGY

Charles Darwin's publication of *On the Origin of Species* in 1859 significantly changed the shape of racial science. By postulating a theory of evolution in which natural selection chooses beneficial traits in advancing species development, Darwin's ideas resulted in a proliferation of studies aimed at understanding the impact of degeneration on the human species. Racial taxonomies provided a framework to move from cataloguing plants and animals to cataloguing and classifying "social disorders" such as crime, madness, and other deviances (Nadesan 2010). Medical authorities such as Morel used their clinical experiences to describe, identify, and recommend treatment for such individuals. These taxonomies provide one of the first examples of how delinquents, criminals, and the insane were considered the result of degeneration and environmental imprint.

These techniques, though crude, formed the basis for the modern study of deviance. In sociology, **deviance** is defined as behaviors or actions that violate social norms. Criminology as a scholarly field is concerned with the study of deviances that are defined as crime by a society. Today, taxonomic tools continue to be used to measure, classify, and assess "deviants." Criminology is particularly predisposed to this practice, often working with local agencies to create assessment instruments that group, classify, and recommend sentencing for particular types of cases.

Cases are grouped into typologies of offenders that are well-known throughout U.S. society. The "at-risk youth," the "sex offender," the "recidivist," and the "gang member" are just a few of the types that dominate crime policies today. Policy makers have developed guidelines for sentencing each type, often requiring specific sentences for gang or sex crimes and even lifetime classification into these groupings through registries. Though gradations of deviance are more sophisticated today—often grounded in the current best practices of scientific thought—they owe their origin to the very first taxonomies of deviance in the latter half of the nineteenth century.

Degeneration and the "Criminal"

In the first studies of "degenerates," scholars primarily limited their inquiries to institutionalized populations, especially those considered mad. By the second half of the nineteenth century, the study of degenerates encompassed many segments of society. Alexander Johnson, the head of the National Conference of Charities and Correction described the class of degenerates in the late 1800s:

> The insane, the epileptic, the hysterical, the paralytic, the imbecile and idiotic of various grades, the moral imbecile, the sexual pervert, the kleptomaniac; many, if not most, of the chronic inebriates; many of the prostitutes, tramps, and minor criminals; many habitual paupers, especially the ignorant and irresponsible mothers of illegitimate children, so common in our poorhouses; many of the shiftless poor, ever on the verge of pauperism and often stepping over it; some of the blind, some deaf-mutes, some consumptives. All of these in varying degree, with others not mentioned, are related as being effects of the one cause—which itself is the summing up of many causes—degeneracy. (Johnson 1898, 328–29)

Degeneracy was a category so broad that it encompassed most anyone in society who was considered deviant. Many of these categories were also linked to criminality, a practice that continues even today. For instance, it is today common for politicians, scholars, and other commentators on crime to assert delinquency stems from the problem of single-parent families or families headed by women. Visible poverty is also criminalized today when electorates define the survival behaviors of poor people, such as sleeping outside, as crimes. In the nineteenth century, however, scholarly investigation connecting these conditions to social issues and crime was just beginning.

This model of degeneracy had a second impact on the study of the social world. As Morel conceived it, degeneracy could be acquired through social environment and then passed on biologically through procreation to one's offspring. Even if the children of degenerates were isolated, quarantined, or otherwise segregated from deleterious social influences, they could still develop degeneracy. And exposure to these influences—through the mere presence of degenerates—could harm otherwise "normal" children and adults (as we will see in chapter 4, this belief provided considerable urgency to social reformation programs that warned of the danger to the "normal type" if degeneracy went unchecked).

Morel's notion of degeneracy revolutionized the study of social science and provided one of the first ways for conceiving of the interaction between the social and natural worlds. Unsurprisingly, scholars of the social world—concerned about issues that today we might name as poverty, crime, and racism—drew upon natural concepts to understand how and why the social world included criminality, even in the era of Enlightenment. Two different racial theories of degeneracy and crime dominated in the 1800s and early 1900s: the notion of the "born criminal" developed by Cesare Lombroso and the emerging theory of eugenics.

Cesare Lombroso and the Criminal Man

Cesare Lombroso (1835–1909) was an Italian physician and is considered the founder of criminology. Prior to Lombroso, scholars such as Cesare Beccaria (1738–1794) and John Locke (1632–1704) theorized how crime and criminality should be responded to in an "enlightened" society. Beccaria outlined a comprehensive theory of what today we call deterrence that articulated how punishments should be developed to convince the rational person not to engage in criminality. Locke used the criminal as foil to the rational person and the development of a criminal justice system as evidence of the giving up of the individual right to violence and the ascendance of the social contract. For Beccaria and Locke, crime could be prevented through rational punishments and the realization of the social contract. Despite these philosophies, however, criminality persisted.

Positivist Criminology

In contrast to the ideas developed by Beccaria and Locke, known as the classical school of crime, Lombroso advanced a theory of positivist criminology that examined crime in much the same way disease and other afflictions were studied. Following Morel's concept of degeneracy, Lombroso contended that criminals were born into their roles and inherited their destiny from their forebears. For Lombroso, the ailments of criminality were manifest in the physiological appearance of the body.

Lombroso's most significant work in this field was a tome entitled *L'uomo delinquente,* or *Criminal Man,* which was revised five times between 1876 and 1897, and was based on his study of patients in a psychiatric hospital. Lombroso begins with a review of how he came to his "two fundamental ideas": that the "essential point" of study is "the criminal himself" and not "crime in the abstract" and that the "congenital criminal" is "an anomaly, partly pathological and partly atavistic, a revival of the primitive savage" (Lombroso 2006, 31). His ideas, he wrote, "came to [him] in 1864" when, as an army doctor, he noticed that the "honest soldier" was "distinguished" from the "vicious comrade" by the absence of indecent tattoos.

As a psychiatrist confronted with the inadequacy of "the methods hitherto held in esteem" and the necessity "in studying the insane, to make the patient, not the disease, the object of attention," Lombroso took up practices of measuring the body. Using the esthesiometer and craniometer, he discovered the "atavistic being," or what is now known as the **atavistic criminal.** Atavism in biology is the reappearance of an evolutionary trait that was thought to have disappeared generations earlier, such as a human being born with a tail. An atavistic criminal, according to Lombroso, was one "who reproduces . . . the ferocious instincts of primitive humanity and the inferior animals" (1911, xv).

Race and Atavistic Criminals

In Lombroso's taxonomy, criminals were akin to primitives and savages in the racial order. Characteristics believed to have been left behind as humanity developed could reappear in the atavistic criminal, such as smaller skulls. Criminals were divided into typologies: the arsonist was stereotyped as a homosexual with feminine hairstyle and dress, while rapists and the most violent criminals all had "jug ears, thick hair, thin beards, pronounced sinuses, protruding chins, and broad cheekbones" (Lombroso 2006, 53). Male criminals had abnormally sized heads, often smaller, though female criminals had oversized ones. Lombroso believed that these traits had been characteristic in primitive humans, but that refinement and civilization had bred them out. They remained only as a marker of deviance and degeneration.

Lombroso explicitly connected degeneration supposedly exhibited by criminal types to racial hierarchies and nonwhite people. After a comprehensive accounting of the physiognomies characteristic of criminals, he concludes:

> Those who have read this far should now be persuaded that *criminals resemble savages and the colored races.* These three groups have many characteristics in common, including thinness of body hair, low degrees of strength and below-average weight, small cranial capacities, sloping foreheads, and swollen sinuses. Members of both groups frequently have sutures of the central brow ridge, precocious synostes or disarticulation of the frontal bones, upwardly arching temporal bones, sutural simplicity, thick skulls, overdeveloped jaws and cheekbones, oblique eyes, dark skin, thick and curly hair, and jug ears. Among habitual criminals as among savages, we find less sexual differentiation than between normal men and women. In addition, in both we find insensitivity to pain, lack of moral sense, revulsion for work, absence of remorse, lack of foresight (although this can at times appear to be courage), vanity, superstitiousness, self-importance, and finally, an underdeveloped concept of divinity and morality. These facts clearly prove that the most horrendous and inhuman crimes have a biological, atavistic origin in those animalistic instincts that . . . resurface instantly under given circumstances. (Lombroso 2006, 91, emphasis added)

Lombroso combines several aspects of racial science in this single quote. First, he connects criminality to more "primitive" life forms—"savages and the colored races"—revealing his belief in racial hierarchies. Second, he identifies degeneration within the body—thin body hair, sloping forehead, swollen sinuses.

Lombroso's construction of the criminal borrowed techniques and ideas first developed by racial scientists. He places crime and those who commit it on an evolutionary ladder, just as whites were placed above other races. He invokes bodily attributes and scientific ideology through his measurements that provide evidence of the "difference" of criminals. He further connects this to racial differences, and while criminals are deviant from a normal ideal, they are remarkably similar to those considered racially inferior. Lombroso's treatise provided the definitive investigation into degeneracy and criminality of the time and provided a blueprint for the social reformation policies that would be enacted in the early twentieth century.

Lombroso's work demonstrates that the birth of criminology emerged from the convergence between scientific racism and the theory of degeneration. Importantly, though, as the pictures of Lombroso's "criminal man" attest (see figure 3.8), the study of criminality was not necessarily a study of criminals *from other races*. While not strictly a racial historicist or naturalist, Lombroso's work bridges these two worlds through the figure of the white criminal and the tools of measurement and classification that began with phrenology (see figure 3.9). Criminology developed as the study of how one race—the white race—produced and created more savage, primitive, and uncivilized states of being. By defining criminality as a less advanced and less civilized form of whiteness, Lombroso effectively associated nonwhite people, already seen as less developed, with criminality. This primitive state was considered the starting position of the "colored races," to use Lombroso's terminology. While Lombroso's work is today discredited, it led to ideas of racial degeneracy and crime that remain salient within criminology today.

Frederick Hoffman on Racial Degeneracy and Crime

The first explicit consideration of nonwhites and crime came from a compilation of racial crime statistics produced by Frederick Hoffman in a treatise titled *Race Traits and Tendencies of the American Negro* in 1896. Hoffman's work "was the first book-length study to include a nationwide analysis of black crime statistics" and considerably influenced the study of race and crime in the first half of the twentieth century (Muhammad 2011, 35). Scholars in the United States often faced charges of bias in the study of race and crime. Northern scholars were said to be blinded by sympathy for black people, while Southern ones were still steeped in the social relations of the antebellum South. Hoffman, who was German and thus seen as more objective, was thus embraced and his ideas circulated freely in both the North and the South.

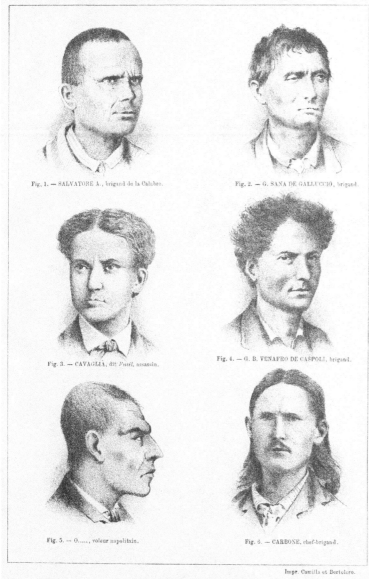

Fig. 1. — SALVATORE A., brigand de la Calabre.

Fig. 2. — G. SANA DE GALLUCCIO, brigand.

Fig. 3. — CAVAGLIA, dit *Pusil,* assassin.

Fig. 4. — G. B. VENAFRO DE CASPOLI, brigand.

Fig. 5. — O....., voleur napolitain.

Fig. 6. — CARBONE, chef-brigand.

TYPES DE CRIMINELS.

Impr. Camilla et Bertolero.

Figure 3.8 Types of criminals, from Lombroso. Source: Cesare Lombroso, 1888, *L'homme criminel: Atlas,* 2nd ed., Turin: Bocca Frères, plate 5. Digital copy courtesy of Royal College of Physicians, Edinburgh.

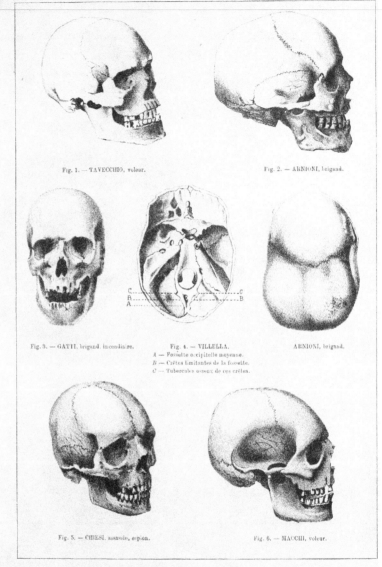

Fig. 1. — TAVECCHIO, voleur.

Fig. 2. — ARNIONI, brigand.

Fig. 3. — GATTI, brigand. incendiaire.

Fig. 4. — VILLELLA.
A — Fossette occipitelle moyenne.
B — Crêtes limitantes de la fossette.
C — Tubercules osseux de ces crêtes.

ARNIONI, brigand.

Fig. 5. — CHIESI, assassin, espion.

Fig. 6. — MACCHI, voleur.

Impr. Camilla et Bertolero.

CRÂNES DE CRIMINELS.

Figure 3.9 Skulls of criminals, from Lombroso. Source: Cesare Lombroso, 1888, *L'homme criminel: Atlas,* 2nd ed., Turin: Bocca Frères, plate 24. Digital copy courtesy of Royal College of Physicians, Edinburgh.

Drawing on the 1890 census, Hoffman sought to identify and understand increasing black mortality rates. Hoffman's study combined a statistical analysis of mortality rates and a consideration of the anthropometric measurements of races. His study, he argued, showed conclusively that the black race was degenerating and undergoing population decline. He linked this decline to the moral "traits and tendencies" of black people, noting that sexual immorality, crime, and racial "impurity" led to economic inefficiency, waste, and decline. He concluded:

> A race may be interesting, gentle and hospitable; but if it is not a useful race in the common acceptation of the term, it is only a question of time when a downward course must take place. All the facts brought together in this work prove that the colored population is gradually parting with the virtues and the moderate degree of economic efficiency developed under the regime of slavery. All the facts prove that a low standard of sexual morality is the main and underlying cause of the law and anti-social condition of the race at the present time. All the facts prove that education, philanthropy and religion have failed to develop a higher appreciation of the stern and uncompromising virtues of the Aryan race. The conclusion is warranted that it is merely a question of time when the actual downward course, that is, a decrease in the population, will take place. In the meantime, however, the presence of the colored population is a serious hindrance to the economic progress of the white race. (Hoffman 1896, 329)

Though Hoffman noted that these tendencies were most pronounced in the Southern cities where African Americans were concentrated, he warned that Northern cities were seeing the development of concentrated urban districts where many African Americans lived. He concluded that the "negro in the North and West therefore presents an even more serious problem than the negro in the South, if mere numbers are disregarded" (Hoffman 1896, 17).

Hoffman demonstrates how the ideas and methods of racial scientists were translated to the study of race and crime. Hoffman used anthropometric measurements, common to methods employed by the field of scientific racism. Hoffman created a hierarchy of races and classified them based on perceived behaviors and traits, much like the taxonomies created by Linnaeus and Blumenbach. And finally, Hoffman explicitly invoked theories of scientific racism, such as degeneration, to conclude that the white population was in danger of corruption and the black population faced imminent extinction. Hoffman's work thus illustrates the very first example of the criminological investigation of race and crime. Unfortunately, rather than demonstrating the absurdity of the work of racial scientists, Hoffman's work, along with Lombroso's, spawned the birth of the field of criminology.

Responses to Hoffman

Hoffman's treatise was the first scholarly work detailing a link between crime and race, and it initiated a national debate about the origins of the supposed race-crime linkage. Khalil Gibran Muhammad writes that the "impact of

Race and Crime Statistics in Canada

In 1992, after concern about how racial crime statistics were being used to claim that nonwhite Canadians committed more crime, the Canadian government banned the collection of racial crime statistics. As a result, no racial statistics have been gathered for twenty-five years.

Today, the very same political group that led the push to ban the compilation of racial statistics is calling for their renewed collection. Given the attention to the #BlackLivesMatter movement in the United States, Canadian media outlets, including the *Toronto Star,* and political agitators have begun calling for the release of racial crime statistics. Yet these statistics do not exist. And trying to determine race through other means—such as news stories about particular incidents—is next to impossible, as media outlets often scrub racial identification. This presents a problem for those concerned about the racial disproportionality of police violence. While many people suspect that black Canadians are overrepresented as victims of police shootings, use of force, and arrest, there exists little data to *prove* it.

Did Canada make the right decision to limit the use of racial crime statistics? Should racial crime statistics be collected? Does our ability to confront crime diminish without the use of racial crime statistics? Does our ability to police the police diminish without racial crime statistics?

Source: Rosie Dimanno, "A Thorny History of Race-Based Statistics," *Toronto Star,* August 17, 2015, www.thestar.com/news/gta/2015/08/17/a-thorny-history-of-race-based-statistics.html.

Hoffman's ideas was detectable immediately following the book's publication" and that the responses "all noted the significance of blacks moving to the urban North, spreading vice, crime, and disease in their wake" (2010, 56). Hoffman's work inspired white researchers to investigate links between biology, race, and crime, with many concluding that Hoffman's findings were indeed correct.

Hoffman's findings were challenged, but for the most part, this challenge was left to black American scholars and reformers like Ida B. Wells-Barnett, W. E. B. Du Bois, and Kelly Miller. Wells-Barnett published pamphlets that chronicled lynchings and lynch law in Southern states, arguing that black Americans were "more sinned against than sinning" and that the "Afro-American is not a bestial race" (Wells-Barnett 1991). Du Bois reviewed Hoffman's book and called it "absurd," while Kelly Miller noted that it was not crime and race, but crime and "condition," like racial discrimination, that resulted in disproportionate rates of black Americans in prisons (Muhammad 2010, 62–63).

Du Bois's *The Philadelphia Negro* (1899) implicitly repudiated Hoffman's findings. This lengthy ethnography of the conditions faced by black people in Philadelphia provides one of the most in-depth considerations of racial reality in a community. Du Bois's work is noted for its significant appraisal of the ways migration, racial discrimination, and "shameful neglect" of black communities contributed to criminality. However, Du Bois's work was hardly consequential in the same ways as Hoffman's: it was not reviewed by the scholarly community, it did not become a bestseller, and it failed to even be recognized as a work of scholarship by his own university until the 1930s, though it today is considered one of the most significant research studies of the period (Muhammad 2010).

Though Hoffman's work is repudiated in most college classrooms today, his work had lasting influence on the field of criminology. It, for the first time, sparked great interest among white scholars in the study of crime (Muhammad 2010). Out of Hoffman's explicitly racialist work came a new generation of scholars seeking to assess, diagnose, and treat what increasingly became seen as "modern urban ailments," like crime. Hoffman's work also amplified the importance of studying crime for whites, who began to see nonwhites in much the same way as Hoffman and as a "serious hindrance to the economic progress of the white race." Degeneration and malady was not confined to nonwhite races but could infect, afflict, and poison the superior positioning of whites. Hoffman's explicitly racial science work thus inspired the entire field of criminology, which would train its lens over the coming century on the poor, nonwhite, and otherwise marginalized populations as it researched crime.

Hoffman's racism did not live on within criminology explicitly, but his conclusions continued to shape the collection of crime statistics, both historically and today (see box 3.2). Within a few decades, Hoffman's explicit racialism and notions of biological degeneracy were replaced by the social-condition and environmental approaches espoused by eugenicists. Though eugenics is normally associated with scientific racism and explicitly racist criminological theories, as we show in the next chapter, eugenic criminology created a perverse and insidious association between social environment and criminality. While eugenic theorists drew upon ideas of biological transmission, this insidious connection created a linkage between urban environments and ideas of degeneracy from which criminology has not yet escaped. Thus, while criminology may not embrace the explicit scientific racism promulgated by Hoffman, as a field, it does have the same effect: to identify nonwhite communities, rather than racialized power structures themselves, as the site and source of what ails modern society. With this in mind, the field of criminology began in the early 1900s to embrace social reformation programs that would do something about the "race problem."

EUGENIC CRIMINOLOGY AND THE DANGER OF DEGENERACY

As we will trace in the next chapter, eugenics had a far-ranging influence on American political life and criminal justice institutions. **Eugenics,** which emerged in the late 1800s, was both a scientific theory and a social program that aimed to improve humanity by breeding out undesirable characteristics. Previous iterations of degeneracy theory relied upon the emerging, crude tenets of evolutionary biology to suggest that deviations from the ideal would eventually result in extinction of that variety of human. Theorists such as Blumenbach thought that degeneration, if taken to the extreme, would result in reduced fertility, until procreation was impossible. Eugenics, however, turned this idea upside down. One of the preeminent eugenicists of the time, Charles Davenport, demonstrated this reasoning when he declared, "The population of the United States will, on account of the great influx of blood from Southeastern Europe, rapidly become darker in pigmentation, smaller in stature, more given to crimes of larceny, kidnapping, assault, murder, rape and sex immorality. And the ration of insanity in the population will rapidly increase" (1911, 219).

Degenerate species would not slowly die out, eugenics proponents argued. Instead, degenerate families were characterized by a higher birth rate and were thus more fertile than the white ideal type. Colonial descriptions of African tribes as overly sexual, with women displaying oversized and prominent genitals are characteristic of this idea. Contact with nonwhites caused alarm among traditional degeneration theorists because of the potential for environmental acquisition of negative traits. Eugenicists contended that degeneracy increased fertility in some instances, which offered a second threat—that of being overtaken by a rapidly increasing population of degenerates. Since eugenicists also believed that negative traits could be acquired, population growth was poised to not only overtake the "normal" population but would more rapidly infect it as well. Eugenics might have gone the way of scientific racism, with little impact on society, but instead of staying within the university, it soon gave way to an entire social program that created institutional structures that are still with us today.

The Birth of Eugenics

Francis Galton, a cousin of Charles Darwin, is credited with coining the term *eugenics* and the scientific theories of heredity and breeding that underpinned eugenic social programs in the 1900s. Galton defined eugenics as

> bearing on what is termed in Greek, *eugenes*, namely, good in stock, hereditarily endowed with noble qualities. This, and the allied words, *eugeneia*, etc., are equally applicable to men, brutes, and plants. We greatly want a brief word to express the science of improving stock, which is by no means confined to questions of judicious mating, but which, especially in the case of man, takes cognisance of all influences that tend in however remote a degree to give to the more suitable races or strains of blood a better chance of prevailing speedily over the less suitable than they otherwise would have had. The word *eugenics* would sufficiently express the idea. (1883, 24–25)

Eugenics was based on the scientific ideas of reproductive biology and the tactics of breeding used in domesticating crops and animals. Eugenic programs would apply these tactics to humans and would work to promote "noble" attributes while breeding out deviance.

Based on his studies, Galton created psychometrics, or the science of measuring mental faculties with tools such as IQ tests. Galton's findings—the psychometric data he collected—supported his conclusion that people with lower scores were more prone to crime and other deviance. Thus, Galton's emphasis on breeding sought to ensure that the mental faculties of "reasonable men" did not degenerate. He advocated policies such as encouraging the most noble to marry young, incentivizing childbirth among the "normal," and establishing criteria to rate family merit.

Galton's theory of eugenics was unique in two respects. First, it contradicted the theory of degeneration: according to Galton, degenerate races would not experience species decline but instead enjoyed extraordinary breeding capacities. Second, it advocated state intervention. As will be discussed further in chapter 4, this was novel. Prior to this moment, the U.S. state was not particularly interventionist, the number of laws was remarkably low, and social supports were practically nonexistent. Galton noted that eugenicists sought "to consider whether it might not be our duty to exert . . . ourselves to further ends of evolution more rapidly and with less distress than if events were left to their own course" (1883, 1). This would soon come to pass, but not until the techniques of scientific racism were again put to use in demonstrating the scientific justification for creating wide-ranging social programs.

Richard Dugdale and the Juke Family

Although Galton did not live to see the full flowering of eugenics, his work inspired a series of studies examining the relationship between heredity and the development of criminality, a practice that continues today in the search for the "criminal" gene (see box 3.3). One of the most influential and widely read eugenic texts in the United States was a study by Richard Dugdale titled *"The Jukes": A Study in Crime, Pauperism, Disease and Heredity* (1877). In 1874, Dugdale was commissioned to visit a series of upstate New York jails and prisons. During these visits, he found six members of the Juke family all imprisoned. Upon further investigation, he found that out of the twenty-nine other male "immediate blood relations" of the Jukes, seventeen had been arrested or convicted of crimes.*

Using interviews and government records, Dugdale created a family tree for the Jukes and found degeneracy spread back to the days of colonization. Further research uncovered 700 relatives, including 18 brothel keepers, 60 thieves, 50–120 prostitutes, 40 women with sexually transmitted diseases (which he

---

* Further investigations found that not all those named Juke in the study were actually related. Regardless, the study reveals the saliency of ideas of degenerate transmission, as bloodlines were less important than the pathogen of close proximity.

BOX 3.3   **"Can Your Genes Make You Kill?"**

The headline in a 2016 issue of *Popular Science* blared "Can Your Genes Make You Kill?" Since the quest to map the human genome began in the early 1990s, questions about the genetic and biological makeup of human traits have resurged. Twenty-five years ago, the National Institutes of Health withdrew funding for a conference on genetics and crime, but today, criminologists are beginning to look at the influence of genetics on criminality, and funding for a new generation of "bio-criminologists" is on the rise. Although "everyone in the field agrees there is no 'crime gene' . . . researchers are looking for . . . inherited traits that are linked to aggression and antisocial behaviors," stated the article.

Criminologists have also returned to the measurement of the head, but they no longer study bumps and crevices on the skull; instead, the brain is studied by neurologists. This research is also finding biological bases to crime—most significantly, in brain scans that reveal that people who have been diagnosed as psychopaths have less developed orbital cortexes than others. One pioneering neuroscientist even discovered that his own brain matched scans of psychopaths, and he found he had killers, including Lizzie Borden, in his family history (Fallon, 2013).

Biological researchers thus are careful to note that genetics does not necessarily presume criminality and that environmental interaction is paramount. For instance, marriage tends to lead to less criminality amongst males, so being married may play a proactive role in limiting the violence of genetically predisposed people. And people with brain scans matching those of psychopaths can become highly respected members of society, like the neuroscientist above.

Given this resurgence in the biological science of crime, should ethicists be worried? Could research like this inspire a new round of scientific racism? Could society ensure that this does not create a new scientific racism, and if so, how?

Sources: James Fallon, *The Psychopath Inside: A Neuroscientist's Personal Journey Into the Dark Side of the Brain* (New York: Current/Penguin); Lois Parshley, "Can Your Genes Make You Kill?," *Popular Science,* April 8, 2016, www.popsci.com/can-your-genes-make-you-kill.

estimated had been spread to 440 others), 30 people prosecuted for having children out of wedlock, 1,200 "bastards," and 2 feeble-minded relatives. In addition, 180 of the Jukes had received a total of 800 hours of poverty relief from poorhouses and other charitable giving. Dugdale estimated that the Jukes had cost the state of New York $1,308,000, the equivalent of over $28 million today.

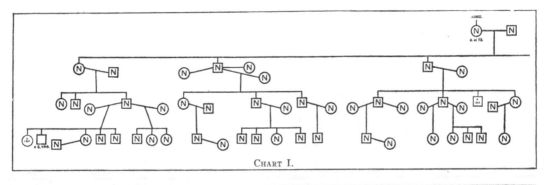

CHART I.

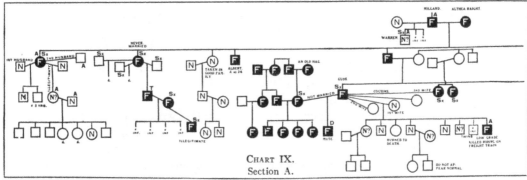

CHART IX.
Section A.

N = Normal.   F = Feeble-minded.   Sx = Sexually immoral.   A = Alcoholic.   I = Insane.   Sy = Syphilitic.   C = Criminalistic.   D = Deaf.
d. inf. = die ! in infancy.   T = Tuberculous.   Hand points to child in Vineland Institution.   For further explanation see pp. 33–35.

Figure 3.10 Family tree of Kallikak Family of New Jersey created by eugenicist Henry Goddard following the methodology developed in Dugdale's *The Jukes*. Source: Henry Herbert Goddard, *The Kallikak Family: A Study in the Heredity of Feeble-Mindedness* (New York: Macmillan, 1913), 45.

Transmitting Degeneracy

Dugdale used a method of scientific investigation based in observation and biological transmission developed by Gregor Mendel. During the period of eugenics, charting the family tree provided evidence for social scientists that degeneracy was transmitted across generations through breeding. Figure 3.10 shows the family tree of another famous family identified by eugenicists, the Kallikaks. Such investigations provided later eugenicists with the necessary tools and scientific legitimacy to fuel the public policy of eugenics until the 1940s. Degeneracy did not stem solely from biology, however, according to Dugdale and eugenicists. The environment played a critical role in transmitting degeneracy.

Through detailed records, Dugdale recounted how the environment that the Jukes grew up resulted in degeneracy throughout the family and non-blood-related kin and neighbors. He proposed that "capacity, physical and mental, is limited and determined mainly by heredity," but "where the conduct depends on the knowledge of moral obligation . . . the environment has more influence than the heredity" (1877, 65). Further, he remarked, "environment tends to produce habits which may become hereditary," and "the logical induction seems to be, that environment is the ultimate controlling factor" (1877, 66). He concluded his tale of the Jukes with these words:

> In the preceding pages I have endeavored to show that the two great factors in a well-balanced life are a healthy body, properly developed, and a sound and broad judgment, resulting in a well-fashioned and powerful will. It now only remains to add that the same methods which will secure the advantages of these for the general community, will also be efficacious when applied to the rectification of unbalanced lives. Indeed, it may be asserted that, inasmuch as the study of the defects of the blind, the deaf mute and the idiotic has resulted in the discovery of some of the most valuable axioms of educational science, so will the steady, careful and masterly training of the criminal add other axioms equally valuable. (1877, 119)

Dugdale's expansive consideration of the Jukes family was one of the most widely read texts of his time and brought the ideas of hereditary, environment, and crime to broader audiences than just the scholarly community. This wide dissemination helped propel eugenics into the political mainstream, and created such a wide base of support that it remained popular in the United States until the 1940s.

Dugdale's text did not just propel eugenics into the mainstream, but it also provided one of the first examples of the argument that the presence of impoverished communities is actually a cost to the state. Calculations such as Dugdale's would continue to be disseminated by eugenicists over the first half of the twentieth century, and some even updated Dugdale's own calculations to argue that the Jukes actually cost the state much more than first estimated (Goddard 1912). These estimates provide some of the very first arguments about the costs—for eugenicists, biological, moral, and monetary costs—if the country failed to fix its "biological problem." However, these arguments did not die away with the decline of eugenics. Assertions of the "cost" of populations is a common tale today—people who are homeless, incarcerated, or poor are frequent targets of these projections. Eugenics arguments thus introduced the idea that those most marginalized and poorest in society also posed the greatest danger and threat to health and prosperity of the nation. In short, eugenics birthed the idea that poor and nonwhite people were ultimately social problems in need of solutions, a belief that continues to this day.

Eugenic philosophy is distinguished by several attributes. First, eugenics builds on the history of scientific racism, which found physical distinctions in the human population to be indicative of differences in moral, intellectual, and creative aptitudes. Second, eugenics is also concerned with the social world and the impact of environment on the creation of degeneracy. Finally, eugenics explicitly connects both the social and the natural world through the concept of racial degeneracy and calls for social programs to quite literally eliminate this threat from society. Chapter 4 details these social programs in depth. Today, eugenic philosophy is dismissed for its role in continuing the antiquated tradition of scientific racism. However, the portions of eugenic philosophy that prophesied national moral, mental, and physical decline because of immigrants and nonwhites and called for intervention to prevent this decline remains.

Social Conditions as the Cause of Racial Degeneration

While today we do not easily talk about biological heritage (or at least when we do, it is often quickly discounted with charges of racial supremacy), we do talk about the role of social conditions in the creation of national issues. This was prevalent during the era when eugenics thrived as well. Franz Boas (1858–1942), who was considered the founder of modern anthropology, was one of the first to articulate a notion of racial degeneration that stemmed not from biological predisposition but from social conditions. Unlike other racial scientists, Boas considered African civilizations to have exceptional achievements—such as controlling fire and creating stone tools—upon which European civilization was based. This, he vehemently argued, demonstrated that black Americans did not have genetic or biological traits preventing them from assuming the rationality of Europeans. Boas argued emphatically against biological racists, including eugenicists, and considered the notion of inherent biological racial traits abhorrent.

Yet Boas concluded that "undesirable traits" existed in the black population and that these *cultural* predispositions had to be eradicated in order for black Americans to assume the mantle of citizenship in parity with white Americans. In a letter arguing to change the racial attitudes of white Americans, Boas illustrated this point:

> All that we can say at the present time is that it seems unfair to judge the Negro by what he has come to be in America, and that the evidence of cultural achievement of the Negro in Africa suggests that his inventiveness, power of political organization, and steadiness of purpose, equal or even excel those of other races of similar stages of culture. Mixture of races in Africa has always been concurrent with the establishment of great and powerful states and the production of strong individualities, who put their stamp upon the culture of large areas and long periods. Those vices and undesirable qualities of the Negro which are generally brought forward do not exist in Africa except where it is ravaged by the slave trade. (1906, 317)

Boas's point is instructive in several respects. First, he is writing *against* racism, but he still constructs black Americans as defined by "vices and undesirable qualities." Second, he articulates these vices as exceptional and brought about by social conditions, such as the slave trade. Finally, he foregrounds the notions of racial historicism by arguing that these conditions stem not from innate capacities—as demonstrated by past accomplishments—but from the particular social conditions—or culture—surrounding black Americans.

Boas's work foregrounded an idea of race based not in racial naturalism but in racial historicism. This shift emphasized the social and cultural conditions that gave way to racial differences. This switch from biology to culture, however, did not undo the notion of African inferiority that existed among scientific racists. Rather, it reframed it as characteristics particular to black Americans but which stemmed not from biology but from social conditions. As we show in the next chapter, this had important consequences for the social reforms initiated in the early twentieth century and that continue to shape society today.

CONCLUSION

Beginning with the age of colonialism, race emerged as an important category for determining which people were classified as "human" and which were considered "nonhuman." With the emergence of the Enlightenment, the tools of the scientific method were used to demonstrate these supposed differences and provide an objective scientific veneer to colonial exploits. From Blumenbach's skulls to Lombroso's criminal types, the field of racial science and criminology worked together to create the idea that the "criminal" was somehow different from the "normal human." Further, the field of criminology provided support for the field of racial science by arguing that criminals were atavistic reminders of primitive races.

What is remarkable about racial science is the way that all sorts of scientific investigations—carried out with rigor and genuine curiosity—were still tainted by the cultural, economic, and political positioning of the scientists. Consider, for instance, how closely Lombroso's conclusions—based supposedly on systematically collected evidence—resemble those of Thomas Jefferson quoted at the beginning of this chapter. Jefferson calls for scientific inquiry into the difference between races by pointing to differences in hair, nose, and skin that supposedly reveal the bodily basis for differences in intellectual and moral capacity. Almost one hundred years later, Lombroso after studying, measuring, and classifying various bodily characteristics came to a similar conclusion: races are distinguished by bodily types. Lombroso did offer something of an advancement over Jefferson's conclusion by connecting racial types to social problems like crime, yet this does not change the fundamental crux of their arguments: that different races have different capacities for reason, rationality, and importantly, self-rule.

The history of racial science is also the history of the birth of criminology and social science. Without racial science and concern about degenerates, it is quite possible that the field of criminology might never have developed. Yet this history also reveals important ways that scientific racism continues to influence conceptions of criminality today. As we see in the next chapter, scientific racism did not continue to be the dominant framework used to explain criminal behavior. However, the idea that crime stems from the cultures of the poor, the working class, and the nonwhite continued to dominate social scientific investigations and state interventions.

Although *degeneracy* lost its biological connotations during the 1900s, it continued to dominate considerations of crime's causes. As we show in the next chapter, even as biology gave way to culture as an explanation for criminality, the idea that whiteness represents the normal human type and all else is a deviation continued and, notably, was broadly disseminated in the new century. While early racial scientists labored in the obscurity of academia, the advent of the Progressive Era in the United States saw the fruits of racial science move into the realm of social policy and come to define the actions and practices of the state.

REFERENCES

Blumenbach, Johann Friedrich. 1795. *De generis humani varietate nativa.* 3rd ed. Göttingen: Vandenhoek. https://archive.org/details/degenerishumaniv00blum.

Boas, Franz. 1906. "Changing the Racial Attitudes of White Americans." Letter to Andrew Carnegie. In *A Franz Boas Reader: The Shaping of American Anthropology, 1883–1911,* edited by George W. Stocking, Jr., 316–18. Chicago: University of Chicago Press.

Comte, Auguste. 1893. *The Positive Philosophy of Auguste Comte.* Translated by Harriet Martineau. London: Kegan Paul, Trench, Trübner & Co. https://archive.org/details/positivephilosop01comtuoft.

Darwin, Charles. 1859. *On the Origin of Species by Means of Natural Selection, or the Preservation of Favoured Races in the Struggle for Life.* London: Murray. https://archive.org/details/B-001-004-417.

Davenport, Charles. 1911. *Heredity in Relation to Eugenics.* New York: Henry Holt. https://archive.org/details/heredityinrelati00dave.

Dean, Mitchell. 2010. *Governmentality: Power and Rule in Modern Society.* Thousand Oaks, CA: Sage.

Du Bois, William Edward Burghardt. 1899. *The Philadelphia Negro: A Social Study.* University of Pennsylvania, Series in Political Economy and Public Law, No. 14. Boston, MA: Ginn & Co.

Dugdale, Richard Louis. 1877. *"The Jukes": A Study in Crime, Pauperism, Disease and Heredity; Also Further Studies of Criminals.* 3rd ed. rev. New York: G. P. Putnam's Sons. https://archive.org/details/jukesastudyincr00dugdgoog.

Fredrickson, George M. 1987. *The Black Image in the White Mind: The Debate on Afro-American Character and Destiny, 1817–1914.* Middletown, CT: Wesleyan University Press.

Galton, Francis. 1883. *Inquiries into the Human Faculty and Its Development.* New York: Macmillan. http://galton.org/books/human-faculty/FirstEdition/humanfacultydeve00galt.pdf.

Goddard, Henry Herbert. 1912. *The Kallikak Family: A Study in the Heredity of Feeble-Mindedness.* New York: Macmillan Company. https://archive.org/details/kallikakfamilyst00godduoft.

Haeckel, Ernst. 1897. *The Evolution of Man: A Popular Exposition of the Principal Points of Human Ontogeny and Phylogeny.* Vol. 1. New York: Appleton. https://books.google.com/books?id=yE7Ub-oHUNgC&pg=PA25#v=onepage&q&f=false.

Hagan, John, and Holly Foster. 2006. "Profiles of Punishment and Privilege: Secret and Disputed Deviance during the Racialized Transition to American Adulthood." *Crime, Law and Social Change* 46, no. 1–2: 65–85.

Hall, Stuart, and Bram Gieben, eds. 1992. *Formations of Modernity.* Cambridge, UK: Polity Press. https://archive.org/details/PHILOSOCIOLOGY.irFormationsOfModernityUnderstandingModernSocietiesAnIntroduction.

Hamilton, Peter. 1992. "The Enlightenment and the Birth of Social Science." In *Formations of Modernity,* edited by Stuart Hall and Bram Gieben, 36–45. Cambridge, UK: Polity Press.

Harcourt, Bernard E. 2008. *Against Prediction: Profiling, Policing, and Punishing in an Actuarial Age.* Chicago: University of Chicago Press.

Hoffman, Frederick L. 1896. *Race Traits and Tendencies of the American Negro.* Publications of the American Economic Association 11, nos. 1–3 (August). New York: Macmillan. https://archive.org/details/racetraitstenden00hoff.

Jefferson, Thomas. (1787) 1997. "The Difference Is Fixed in Nature" (from *Notes on the State of Virginia*). In *Race and the Enlightenment: A Reader,* edited by Emmanuel Chukwudi Eze, 95–103. Malden, MA: Wiley-Blackwell.

Johnson, Alexander. (1898). "Concerning a Form of Degeneracy. I. The Condition and Increase of the Feeble-Minded." *American Journal of Sociology* 4, no. 3, 326–34. www.jstor.org/stable/2761515.

Krysan, Maria, and Michael Bader. 2007. "Perceiving the Metropolis: Seeing the City through a Prism of Race." *Social Forces* 86, no. 2: 699–733.

Linné, Charles. 1806. *A General System of Nature. Vol. 1, Animal Kingdom: Mammalia, Birds, Amphibia, Fishes.* Translated by William Turton. London: Lackington, Allen. https://books.google.com/books?id=I3QZA AAAYAAJ&printsec=frontcover#v=onepage&q&f=false.

Lombroso, Cesare. 1911. *Criminal Man.* Briefly summaried by his daughter Gina Lombroso Ferrero. New York: G. P. Putnam's Sons. https://archive.org/details/criminalmanaccor00lomb.

———. 2006. *Criminal Man.* Translated by Mary Gibson, and Nicole Hahn Rafter. Durham, NC: Duke University Press.

———. 1888. *L'homme criminel: Atlas.* 2nd ed. Turin: Bocca Frères. https://archive.org/details/b21929427.

———. 1896. *L'uomo delinquente in rapporto all'antropologia, alla giurisprudenza ed alle discipline carcerarie. 1896–1897.* Vol. 1. 5th ed. Turin: Fratelli Bocca. https://hdl.handle.net/2027/nyp.33433061814202.

McCandless, Peter. 1992. "Mesmerism and Phrenology in Antebellum Charleston: 'Enough of the Marvellous.'" *Journal of Southern History* 58, no. 2: 199–230. www.jstor.org/stable/2210860.

Morton, Samuel. 1839. *Crania Americana.* Philadelphia: J. Dobson.

Mohamed, A. Rafik, and E. Fritsvold. 2010. *Dorm Room Dealers.* Boulder: Lynne Rienner.

Muhammad, Khalil Gibran. 2011. *The Condemnation of Blackness: Race, Crime, and the Making of Modern Urban America.* New Haven, CT: Harvard University Press.

Nadesan, Majia Holmer. 2010. *Governmentality, Biopower, and Everyday Life.* New York: Routledge.

Nott, Josiah Clark, and George R. Gliddon. 1854. *Types of Mankind, Or Ethnological Researches, Based upon the Ancient Monuments, Paintings, Sculptures, and Crania of Races, and upon Their Natural, Geographical, Philogical, and Biblical History.* London: Trübner. https://books.google.com/books?id=kN03EGxwVLU C&source=gbs_navlinks_s.

Nora, Pierre. 1989. "Between Memory and History: Les lieux de mémoire." *Representations* 26: 7–24.

Pager, Devah. 2008. *Marked: Race, Crime, and Finding Work in an Era of Mass Incarceration.* Chicago: University of Chicago Press.

Quillian, Lincoln, and Devah Pager. 2001. "Black Neighbors, Higher Crime? The Role of Racial Stereotypes in Evaluations of Neighborhood Crime." *American Journal of Sociology* 107, no. 3: 717–67.

Roman, John. 2013. *Race, Justifiable Homicide, and Stand Your Ground Laws: Analysis of FBI Supplementary Homicide Report Data.* Washington, DC: Urban Institute. www.urban.org/sites/default/files /publication/23856/412873-Race-Justifiable-Homicide-and-Stand-Your-Ground-Laws.PDF

Sauer, Norman J. 1993. "Applied Anthropology and the Concept of Race: A Legacy of Linnaeus." *Napa Bulletin* 13, no. 1: 79–84.

Smith, Samuel Stanhope, with White, Charles. 1810. *An Essay on the Causes of the Variety of Complexion and Figure in the Human Species.* 2nd ed. New Brunswick, NJ: Simpson; New York: Williams and Whiting. https://archive.org/details/essayoncausesofv00sm.

Wells, Samuel R. 1874. *How to Read Character: A New Illustrated Hand-Book of Phrenology and Physiognomy, for Students and Examiners.* New York: Samuel R. Wells. https://catalog.hathitrust.org/Record/000473935.

Wells-Barnett, Ida B. 1892. *Southern Horrors: Lynch Law in All Its Phases.* New York: The New York Age Print. www.gutenberg.org/files/14975/14975-h/14975-h.htm.

———. *On Lynchings: Southern Horrors* [1892], *A Red Record* [1895], *Mob Rule in New Orleans* [1900]. 1991. Salem, NH: Ayer.

Young, Ian. 2013. "The Racist Curse of Fu Manchu Back in Spotlight after Chevrolet Ad." *South China Morning Post,* May 3. www.scmp.com/news/world/article/1228548/racist-curse-fu-manchu-back-spotlight-after-chevrolet-ad.

Social Problems and the U.S. Racial State

LEARNING OUTCOMES

▶ Explain why the United States is called a racial state.
▶ Summarize the role of urbanization and industrialization in the emergence of new state institutions and powers and the transformation of racial governance.
▶ List the key political, economic, and geographical conditions that led to the emergence of criminal justice institutions.
▶ Analyze how new state powers institutionalized racial governance and led to the creation of the juvenile court and the uniformed urban police.
▶ Describe the transition from racial domination to racial hegemony in state governance.

KEY TERMS

▶ social problems
▶ racial state
▶ state racism
▶ racial hegemony
▶ whiteness
▶ industrialization
▶ urbanization
▶ tenements
▶ Progressivism
▶ ideology of expertise
▶ race suicide
▶ white slavery
▶ black codes
▶ vice districts

Consider the term *social problem.* What is a social problem? What makes something a problem? Who decides if something in society is a problem? Are all problems social problems or are problems that are specifically *social* unique?

When sociologists talk about **social problems,** they are referring to problems considered so undesirable that they should be corrected, such as poverty and domestic abuse. The processes through which social problems are defined and corrected are large and complicated. These processes represent how governance works in action. Based on the idea that we are a government of the people, the state's primary role is to act in response to citizen agitation. This often revolves around what we call social problems. What constitutes a social problem and what types of state interventions are necessary are set within a larger social, political, economic, and, as we have been arguing, racial context.

In this chapter, we examine how the proliferation of social scientific knowledge, within a context of rapid urbanization and industrialization, set the stage for the emergence of key pillars of the **racial state** today. At the dawn of the United States, the racial state was explicitly made through prohibitions on nonwhite citizenship and the enslavement of black and indigenous peoples. Today, the racial state continues, but it works through policies and programs that often seem far removed from the explicit racism of the slavery-era state.

We trace this transition to the early twentieth century and what is called the Progressive Era (1897–1920), which initiated and accelerated a new conception of state power that called for more active intervention in citizens' lives. Through Progressive Era social reformers, key institutions, including public education and state-funded children's clinics, were born. In the criminal justice system, this period birthed the juvenile court and the uniformed public police that we know today. Through the birth of these institutions, Progressive Era reformers defined state power through a white lens and subsequently targeted state interventions at "social problems," which were defined as nonwhite and poor communities' deviations from a white, middle-class norm. This targeting of nonwhite and poor communities as the site and source of social problems, we argue, is how the racial state continues today. In this chapter, we explore the new forms of the racial state that began in the early twentieth century and set the stage for the emergence of racialized mass incarceration.

SOCIAL PROBLEMS AND THE RACIAL STATE

The United States is often called a **racial state,** meaning that the institutions of government—such as the legal system and state and federal agencies—work to maintain racial hierarchies, homogeneity, and racial power. At its birth, the U.S. state was explicitly defined in the Constitution as exclusively the province of white men, which is the most crude and explicit form of racial statehood. Yet the United States remained a racial state after the end of slavery and even after the civil rights victories of the 1960s. Structural white supremacy continues to reign, despite a more inclusive definition of citizenship, and state policies continue to be implicated. How does this happen?

In part, it happens through the definition of social problems and their state interventions. Take the example of the disproportionate police killings of black men, who are two and half more times likely to be killed in police encounters than whites ("The Counted" 2016). You might argue that these killings are the result of the actions of a few individual racists in police agencies or the tendency of one group to challenge police more often than others. However, this is not borne out by empirical data, which shows that whites are more likely to use force against police officers and that police officers—as well as the general public of all races—are more likely to shoot black men than any other group (Eberhardt et al. 2004; Correll et al. 2006; Hyland, Langton, and Davis 2015). Moreover, data shows that nonwhite police officers also use force against nonwhites more than they do against whites (Hyland, Langton, and Davis 2015). Where does the propensity to use force more against black victims—regardless of circumstances—come from then? It comes from the definition of social problems and how we deploy police.

Take gang membership as an easy example. This is a social problem seen as occurring predominantly within black, Latinx, and Asian communities. It is not seen as a white phenomenon. Thus, we get all sorts of state interventions—gang task force units, laws against gang congregation, and gang intervention programs—targeted exclusively at nonwhite communities.

This targeting has two effects. First, it defines the issue as a problem created by one community and not as the product of the social structural forces that create distinct communities in the first place. Second, it deploys state resources to respond to this "social problem" solely in the community identified as the source of the problem. This has the circular effect of working to further define that very community as the problem. In the case of gang policing, this targeting works to deploy additional police resources over black and Latinx communities, resulting in increased surveillance, arrest, and use of force. Given that gang task force units are often part of the more militarized apparatuses of policing agencies, this also means that black and Latinx communities are more likely to witness and experience police use of force, from tanks rolling down neighborhood streets to militarized raids. The increased surveillance of and arrests in these communities then justifies even further police deployment and often greater criminal justice sanction—and force—in these areas.

Challenging this construction of gangs would force us to reconsider both the racially biased definition and enforcement as well as the broader political forces giving rise to any disproportionate criminalities that do exist. For instance, it would force the state to take account of the racially biased definition of gangs that misses all the ways that crime is repeatedly committed by white groups who are not labeled gangs, or the way that white nationalist organizations are often omitted from popular characterizations of gangs. Further, it would require us to take account of how the lack of employment opportunities and deindustrialization created the underground drug economy as the only choice for employment for some youth. We would have to grapple with the ways in which our popular conceptions of gangs miss how those groups we label as gangs were created in response to white racial violence and how even today, white racial gangs continue to openly congregate, gather, and be protected by police, even when carrying torches and killing counterprotesters, as in Charlottesville, North Carolina, in 2017. By responding to socially constructed social problems such as the issue of youth gangs, the state reinforces, re-creates, and solidifies the boundaries of race.

The practice of defining social problems produces what Michel Foucault called **state racism,** or what we might consider the active production of the logic of the racial state. Foucault defines state racism as the logic that "society must be defended" from a "race that is ceaselessly infiltrating the social body" (Foucault 2003, 61). The state is set up to defend against this "ceaselessly infiltrating" outsider that threatens to undermine national stability. While the outsider is traditionally seen as a foreigner who is physically separate from the nation, the outsider is also those internal foes defined by commonly regarded social problems. Indeed, it is not unusual to hear statements like "if we don't do something about social problem X, the future of society is at stake." Practices of government that seek to counteract this threat are examples of state racism as they seek to eradicate, expel, and eliminate those internal foes, who so often happen to be black and brown people, from the very fabric of society.

Although the racial state shifted away from explicit racial domination (through slavery, Jim Crow, and the like), the practice of state racism continued in the form of **racial hegemony.** Hegemony is the process whereby the cultural worldview of a dominant class is imposed and proliferated as the norm. Often, what we consider "common sense" is the product of hegemonic norms, such as the notion that everyone should drink cow's milk, a mythology promoted after World War II through the confluence of state agencies and the dairy industry. Racial hegemony is the process whereby dominant racial worldviews—such as whiteness in the United States—are reproduced through state and social practices. The eras of racial domination and racial hegemony both sought to purge those "ceaselessly infiltrating" threats, defined as the racial other. In the modern era of social science, however, the tools are not overt domination but rather the securing of racial hegemony through the definition of social problems.

IMMIGRATION AND THE RACIAL STATE

One of the most important ways we see the United States act as a racial state is through the control of immigration, first defined as a social problem in the late

1800s. During the 1800s, the United States experienced several waves of immigration. From about 1800 to 1860, over ten million people arrived in the United States. Most of these immigrants were from Northern and Western Europe. Swedish immigration rose in the 1840s as a result of famine and agricultural decline in Europe. A potato blight brought almost one million German immigrants between 1845 and 1849. Although German and Swedish immigrants were often objects of derision for upper-class white Americans, they were mostly seen as provincial, rather than violent or stupid, and these prejudices did not lead to wide-scale attempts to bar their immigration. By the late 1800s, however, the sources of immigration to the United States changed, as did the country's approach to immigration.

In the late 1800s, immigrants from Europe continued to arrive, but instead of coming from Western and Northern Europe, they came from Southern and Eastern Europe, especially from Italy, Portugal, and Poland. As figure 4.1 shows, immigration from Southern and Eastern Europe increased exponentially after the 1890s, and it came to dominate all immigration by the beginning of the 1900s. Asian immigrants, especially the Chinese, began arriving on the West Coast in the mid-1800s, but between 1885 and the early 1900s, Asian immigration almost completely ceased; then it steadily rose until the 1910s, before tapering off in 1915. These shifts in immigration patterns were not due to events like famines, which had influenced waves of immigrants in the early and mid-1800s, but were a direct result of a new tool of the racial state: immigration restrictions.

Immigration Restrictions

Immigration law is perhaps one of the most brute tactics of the racial state. The very first immigration act in the United States, the Naturalization Act of 1790, limited citizenship to "any Alien being a free white person." Excluded from citizenship, therefore, were American Indians, white indentured servants, enslaved persons, free black people, Asians, and of course all women. For the following century and half, immigration law created whiteness as a coveted prerequisite for citizenship in the United States.

During the nation's first century, immigration laws primarily limited the definition of who could be a U.S. citizen and said little about who was allowed to enter the country. Immigrants, even those who could not be citizens, continued to come to the United States. In the late 1800s, however, the first laws were passed restricting entry, thereby "closing" the border for the first time in U.S. history. Today, the idea of restrictive immigration law is commonplace, but in a country birthed by immigrants, immigration restrictions did not become a reality for almost a hundred years until lawmakers sought to use the tools of the state to shape the racial character of the nation.

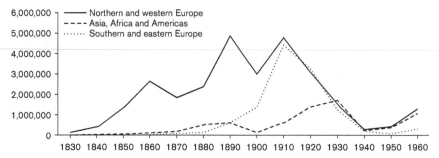

Figure 4.1 Immigration to the United States, 1870–1930, by region of origin. Source: U.S. Department of Homeland Security, *Yearbook of Immigration Statistics, 2013* (Washington, DC: Department of Homeland Security, Office of Immigration Statistics, 2014).

The Page Act and Chinese Exclusion

The Page Act of 1875 was the first racially restrictive immigration law and barred forced laborers, Asian "prostitutes," and all convicts. The Page Act was enacted during a period of anti-Chinese sentiment and a flurry of state-level legislation restricting the activities of Chinese arrivals. Newspapers, politicians, and popular media depicted Chinese men as deceptive and devious and Chinese women as prostitutes who preyed on the virtuous nature of white men. The American Medical Association argued that Chinese immigrants "carried distinct germs to which they were immune, but from which whites would die if exposed" (quoted in Luibhéid 2002, 37). Even as the act focused on immigration controls, it was spurred by concern about the white race and the emerging notions of degeneration and racial infection found in scientific explanations of racial difference.

The Page Act primarily restricted immigration of Asian women, who were seen as threatening white marriage. Men from China, however, continued to emigrate to the United States, until the Chinese Exclusion Act of 1882. The Exclusion Act suspended Chinese immigration for ten years, but was renewed in 1892 and made permanent in 1902. It remained in effect until repealed in 1943. The 1882 act barred "skilled and unskilled laborers and Chinese employed in mining," a category so broad it included almost everyone. Chinese people who were already settled in the United States were excluded from U.S. citizenship, and those who left the United States for any period of time had to be formally certified as a "nonlaborer" to reenter. This effectively cut off Chinese male immigrants from their families and wives in China.

Immigration controls reflected the widespread animosity toward Chinese, who were often used as cheap labor by industrialists. Anti-Chinese sentiment first arose in the mid-1800s in the West; as the California gold rush declined, animosity increased. Chinese people were often driven from their homes in rural California and forced to take up residence in cities. Labor leaders drew upon the constructions of scientific racism and argued that the "devious" and "deceptive" Chinese threatened whites' employment possibilities. When the Chinese were excluded, Japanese immigrants soon replaced Chinese ones, but the National Origins Act, which banned immigration from East Asia entirely, cut off Japanese immigration in 1924.

Immigration and Creating a White National Identity

Immigration law reveals how legal structures worked to solidify a white racial national identity, a reality that continues today (see box 4.1). This identity, however, extended beyond skin color and defined **whiteness** as a particular collection of traits and predilections, just as racial scientists and criminologists did in chapter 3. For instance, the Immigration Act of 1903 barred entry to anarchists, epileptics, and beggars, thus defining whiteness as something shaped by political affiliation, health, and wealth. The Naturalization Act of 1906 made knowledge of English a requirement for citizenship. The 1907 Immigration Act created a new requirement for measuring and tabulating immigrants even before they set foot on American soil: arriving ships now had to produce registries with age, gender, occupation, national origin, and residence for all passengers.

Immigration law continued to be used to control the racial development of the nation into the twentieth century. The Immigration Act of 1917 introduced reading tests for citizenship. In 1921, the Emergency Quota Act limited immigrants arriving from any country in a year to 3 percent of the population of that nationality currently in the United States (based on 1910 Census numbers). In 1924, the Immigration Act reduced that 3 percent to just 2 percent of the population currently in the U.S., again based on 1910 Census numbers. This act extended restrictions to Southern and Eastern Europeans, along with Arabs and Africans and imposed a national-origins quota system and made permanent numerical limits on immigrants. Together, these restrictions effectively stifled immigration, especially from places that did not have strong immigrant communities already present in the United States in 1910.

Defining Whiteness beyond Skin Color

Extensive restrictions on immigration reveal how a white national identity was also defined by particular mental, physical, and economic characteristics. The 1907 act excluded immigration of the following:

> All idiots, imbeciles, feebleminded persons, epileptics, insane persons, and persons who have been insane within five years previous; persons who have had two or more attacks of insanity at any time previously; paupers; persons likely to become a public charge; professional beggars; persons afflicted with tuberculosis or with a loathsome or dangerous contagious disease; persons not comprehended within

BOX 4.1   Urbanization, Immigration and the New Politics of Crime

The 2016 presidential campaign was rife with examples of how concern about immigration and crime often work together to target nonwhite citizens as threats to the nation. Take Donald Trump's infamous characterization of Mexican Americans as "bringing crime," "bringing drugs," and being "rapists." Doubling down, he reiterated his comments and said "tremendous crime is coming across" the border from Mexico into the United States. While Trump's comments certainly caught national attention, they are not the first time accusations like this have been made against immigrants. In 1990, for instance, Congress passed a law to automatically deport any immigrant convicted of a crime. In much the same way that Trump singled out immigrants as a key source of crime, Congress created a dividing line among immigrants, with criminal conviction signaling permanent ineligibility for inclusion in the nation-state. With native-born citizens, however, this standard does not apply.

Despite the rhetoric around immigrants and crime, the evidence paints a vastly different picture. One recent study showed that urban neighborhoods that are recipient of new immigrant residents actually have less crime than neighborhoods of white, native-born citizens (Ewing, Martinez, and Rumbaug 2015). Newcomers to the United States are less likely to commit crime than native-born citizens, and this "holds true especially for the Mexicans, Salvadorans, and Guatemalans who make up the bulk of the undocumented population" (Riley 2015). Studies show further that incarceration rates are lower among the undocumented, with native-born citizens between two and five times more likely to be incarcerated than immigrants.

Though this reality has been demonstrated over the long term and for at least four decades, immigration policy is relentless in deporting permanent residents who have committed even minor crimes. This has resulted in deportations for traffic offenses of people who have lived nearly their entire lives in the United States (Guliani 2014). Gerardo Hernandez-Contreras, who entered the United States when he was fifteen, was pulled over when he was twenty-six for talking on his cell phone while driving; just one day later, he was deported to Mexico. Or Adam Crasper, whose juvenile record forced him to leave his wife and children thirty-seven years after he was brought here by his adoptive parents at the age of two (who later abandoned him and never applied for naturalization).

Some cities, like San Francisco in the 1980s, have responded to this type of enforcement by declaring "sanctuary city" status and instructing all city officials not to cooperate with federal officials regarding immigration enforcement. Sanctuary status means that if someone undocumented is arrested, city officials decline to notify immigration authorities.

Should the federal government continue its practice of deporting any immigrant who is convicted of a crime? Should cities continue to adopt sanctuary policies, or should city authorities be forced to cooperate with federal immigration officials? Should sanctuary cities have their federal funding cut? How does the debate about sanctuary cities and immigration illustrate the contestation over the racial state?

Sources: Walter E. Ewing, Daniel E. Martínez, and Rubén Rumbaut, *The Criminalization of Immigration in the United States,* American Immigration Council Special Report, July 2015, www.americanimmigrationcouncil.org/sites/default/files/research/the_criminalization_of_immigration_in_the_united_states.pdf; Neema Singh Guliani, "How a Father Gets Deported for a Traffic Violation," Speak Freely, ACLU, April 4, 2014, www.aclu.org/blog/how-father-gets-deported-traffic-violation; Michelle Ye Hee Lee, "Donald Trump's False Comments Connecting Mexican Immigrants and Crime," *Washington Post,* July 8, 2015, www.washingtonpost.com/news/fact-checker/wp/2015/07/08/donald-trumps-false-comments-connecting-mexican-immigrants-and-crime/; Jason Riley, "The Mythical Connection between Immigrants and Crime," *Wall Street Journal,* July 14, 2015, www.wsj.com/articles/the-mythical-connection-between-immigrants-and-crime-1436916798.

any of the foregoing excluded classes who are found to be and are certified by the examining surgeon as being mentally or physically defective, such mental or physical defect being of a nature which may affect the ability of such alien to earn a living.

Barring "idiots," "insane persons," and "mentally or physically defective" people conceives of whiteness as embodying a particular rationality and physicality, often defined by Enlightenment principles.

Though property ownership was no longer required for citizenship, the class status of a person was still scrutinized. Outlawing "persons likely to become a public charge" even provided a mechanism for assessing whether the particular economic position of a person was likely to change, guarding against degeneracy *in the future.* Those convicted of "a felony or other crime of misdemeanor involving moral turpitude," polygamists, and revolutionaries were also barred by the 1907 act, meaning particular political and religious ideals were also necessary for claiming whiteness.

Industrialization and Urbanization

Despite immigration restrictions, the economic pull of industrialization resulted in nearly 12 million immigrants arriving between 1870 and 1900 and another almost 19 million arriving between 1900 and 1930. **Industrialization** is the transformation of a society from one based largely on farming to one based on manufacturing. In Europe and the United States, industrialization was the result of the invention of the steam engine and the factory model of production; it began in the late 1700s and accelerated in the late 1800s.

When arriving, over 70 percent of immigrants came through a single entry point: New York City. (Immigrants from Asia primarily entered through San

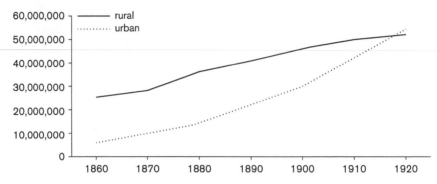

Figure 4.2 U.S. urban to rural shift, 1860–1920. Source: U.S. Census, 1993, Table 4. www
.census.gov/population/censusdata/table-4.pdf.

Francisco.) Immigrants soon found the city hostile to their resettlement, and
many struggled to find housing and work. Cities around the country, however,
sought to lure particular immigrant communities in the hopes of expanding
the laboring population. Eventually, many immigrants found work outside of
New York in the various industries pulling residents to urban centers such as
Detroit, St. Louis, and Chicago.

This resulted in a sevenfold increase in the population of cities over the
course of just one hundred years. This is the process known as **urbanization,**
which happens when primarily rural-based societies transform into ones
where the majority of people live in cities. Urbanization is generally brought
about by economic forces, such as the increased need for labor in the industrial
factory model and the decreased need for agricultural workers. In a period of
just twenty years, from 1890 to 1920, the United States went from being a
majority rural population to a majority urban population (see figure 4.2). New
York City almost doubled in population between 1880 and 1900, and Chicago's
population tripled (see figure 4.3). Economic forces were pulling people to
cities to work in the new industrial manufacturing centers, producing everything from clothes and books to food and housewares.

The consequences of the mass influx of immigrants in the early 1900s were
immediately felt in cities. Incoming immigrants found wholly insufficient
urban systems. As we will see in chapter 5, the most immediate crisis immigrants faced was finding housing. Working-class housing was in short supply,
and new immigrants often squeezed into already overcrowded **tenements.**
Tenement apartment buildings, built to maximize occupancy, were typically
dark and stuffy, with often less than a foot of space separating them. The influx
of immigrants often meant several families lived in a single apartment, sometimes using it in shifts, or taking in boarders to help with rent payments. Tenements were often erected by industrial employers quickly, using substandard

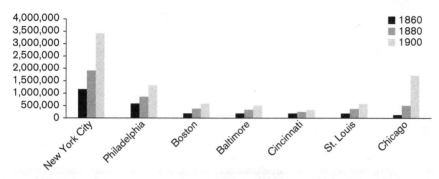

Figure 4.3 Growth of major U.S. cities, 1860–1900. Source: Campbell Gibson, *Population of the 100 Largest Cities and Other Urban Places in the United States: 1790 to 1990,* Population Division Working Paper no. 27 (Washington DC: US Census, 1998), www.census.gov/population /www/documentation/twps0027/twps0027.html.

building materials and with little concern for the health and welfare of residents (Biles 2010).

Additionally, early industrial-era city streets were often heaped with old garbage and the pestilence that came with it (Goubert 1989). Sewage ran down streets and into water sources, making infection and disease a common occurrence among new immigrant populations. Fresh water was in short supply prior to urbanization, and industries dumped pollutants directly into rivers and streams. Despite the crowded, dirty, and disease-ripe conditions, new immigrants had few other places to settle than these areas.

Given the conditions of industrialization and urbanization, plenty of issues emerged to become defined as social problems. These conditions provided an opportunity to redefine the parameters of state power, and remake the racial state through the power of urban interventions. Industrialization and urbanization thus facilitated the emergence of new techniques of state surveillance.

PROGRESSIVISM AND THE NEW POLITICS OF INTERVENTION

Over the first two decades of the twentieth century, as cities grew at extraordinary rates while urban infrastructure stagnated, social reformers known as Progressives invoked these conditions as justification for the state to become more readily involved in shaping and directing society. This ushered in a new era in state power and a new opportunity for the re-creation of the racial state in the post-slavery era.

Much of this power was directed at the issue of the "urban slum" and how to control, thwart, and ultimately govern its development. Like colonial conquest, intervention took a dual approach: the production of knowledge about "urban issues" and a series of projects aimed at "domesticating" the city and remaking its space in the colonial image.

A New Model for State Power

Under the political theory of liberalism, the goal of government is to reduce conflict among people, enforce property rights, and respect the "natural rights of man." This means limited governmental intervention. John Stuart Mill, one of the most famous liberal political philosophers, explained, "The sole end for which mankind are warranted, individually or collectively, in interfering with the liberty of action of any of their number, is self-protection. . . . The only purpose for which power can be rightly exercised over any members of a civilized community, against his will, is to prevent harm to others" (Mill 1869). This principle guided political development for the first hundred years of the United States and meant that state practices were often directed at protecting private property, facilitating trade, and providing national security, practices that meant the brute subjugation of black people, Native Americans, and other nonwhites.

Between 1877 and 1932, however, the U.S. state expanded and transformed its role in U.S. political life (Novak 2012). From 1899 to 1900, 18,243 bills and resolutions were passed by the federal and state governments. Between 1909 and 1914, another 62,000 statutes were passed nationwide and the U.S. Congress passed between 1,700 and 2,000 laws per session. New York and other large states averaged 500 new laws a year during this period (Novak 2012: 33). The immigration laws described above were also products of the expanding role of the U.S. state. Between 1798 and 1870 not a single new piece of immigration law had been passed at the federal level. By contrast, between 1870 and 1924, sixteen new pieces of federal immigration legislation were approved.

The Emergence of Progressivism

This frenzy of legislation signaled a new era in U.S. political life and the use of state power. Prominent intellectuals such as Roscoe Pound, John Dewey, and Jane Addams launched attacks on individualistic conceptions of justice envisioned by John Locke and John Stuart Mill. These late-nineteenth-century intellectuals envisioned a very different role for government power. They saw governmental power as less distant, less reactive, and more interventionist. John Dewey, writing in 1932, described these "new liberals" as foster[ing] the idea that the state has the responsibility for creating institutions under which individuals can effectively realize the potentialities that are theirs. . . . [T]he majority who call themselves liberals . . . are committed to the principle that organized society must use its powers to establish the conditions under which the mass of individuals can possess actual as distinct from merely legal liberty. They define their liberalism in the concrete in terms of a program of measures moving towards this end. They believe that the conception of the state which limits the activities of the latter to keeping order as between individuals and to securing redress for one person when another person infringes the liberty existing law has given him, is in effect simply a justification of the brutalities and inequities of the existing order. (Dewey 2008, 21–22)

The new approach to government Dewey described had been remaking state practice since 1890. This new style was called **Progressivism.**

Progressivism was a theory of government that, at its core, envisioned the state as responsible not just for protecting society by, for instance, providing national security but for making the future of society through active intervention. Progressives sought to use state power to, as Dewey put it, "establish the conditions under which the mass of individuals can possess actual . . . liberty" (2008, 21). This meant not just protecting liberty but actually creating the conditions for the realization of the liberty of the masses, including the poor and, to some extent, the nonwhite. It also meant an opportunity to identify and define social problems, and in so doing, to protect and produce whiteness through state interventions.

Theodore Roosevelt, perhaps the most famous of the Progressives, observed that industrialization and urbanization had brought about changes in society—social problems—to which the state needed to respond:

The tremendous and highly complex industrial development which went on with ever accelerated rapidity during the latter half of the nineteenth century brings us face to face, at the beginning of the twentieth, with very serious social problems. The old laws, and the old customs which had almost the binding force of law, were once quite sufficient to regulate the accumulation and distribution of wealth. Since the industrial changes which have so enormously increased the productive power of mankind, they are no longer sufficient.

Progressives, like Roosevelt, sought to use state power to create programs and state practices that would result in particular desired outcomes, such as the spread of English through education or special institutions for quarantining the "mad." For Progressives, these benevolent intentions were built upon the foundation, as they were for racial scientists, of the particular cultural predilections of their base—white, middle- and upper-class, urban elites. To foster liberty, Progressives advocated education, which often took the form of promoting ideas of whiteness. For instance, important lessons were morality and "industriousness," encouraging people to set aside savings so as not to become a burden to the state. This education, being based in a white, middle-class worldview, ignored the realities of capitalist production that drove wages down, permitted rampant poverty to develop, and concentrated wealth in the hands of whites.

Consequences of Progressivism

This new conception of the state had several consequences for the relationship between the state and citizens. First, it paved the way for a much more interventionist government, where the state played a critical role in ensuring the development of a healthy, educated citizenry. For instance, during the Progressive Era the state actively used public education programs to promote practices like regular physical activity, not keeping animals in houses, and good hygiene. These were early precursors to state campaigns that today encourage citizens to read to their children, eat fruits and vegetables, and save for retirement.

Second, the newly emerging state form also meant that these interventions could be harnessed in ways that prepared people for citizenship—immigrant education classes, for example. Progressive Era reformers sought to actively create citizens in their own ideal, and interventions such as English classes for immigrants, urban parks, and child health centers all aimed to promote a model of citizenship based on white, middle-class idealizations.

Finally, Progressive reformers extended the state into previously uncharted realms: maternal health, child-rearing, urban planning, and public health, to name just a few. This new conception, however, did not change the meaning of citizenship. Instead, these new interventions provided a mechanism for ensuring that even in times of demographic changes—when foreign residents often constituted a majority of urban residents—the white racial state would reign.

Progressive Social Reforms

Perhaps the most famous Progressive work is *The Jungle* by Upton Sinclair. Written after Sinclair spent time working secretly in a meatpacking plant in Chicago, the novel chronicles the life of an immigrant factory worker in the early 1900s. In doing so, Sinclair exposed the brutal conditions of the meatpacking industry, including routine worker injury and deformity, bleaching of spoiled food products for future sale, and crowded, unsafe, and unsanitary living conditions in tenements. Sinclair's work also exposed deep corruption throughout the industrial world and highlighted the brutality of industrial capitalists trying to secure cheaper wages for their factories. The public outcry Sinclair's novel prompted is said to have inspired the establishment of the Food and Drug Administration and the first inspections of meat factories.

Sinclair's work is considered an exemplar of Progressive Era social reform. It combined outcry about the living and working conditions of the poor, while also championing social reforms. In this case, the social reforms were improved working conditions, including increased safety measures, fewer working hours, and more days off. Progressive reforms like these are often associated with creating better working conditions and promoting the betterment of all.

While Progressive regulations did create better working conditions, they also consolidated power in the hands of white industrialists. One of the key tools of Progressive reforms was state regulation. These regulations, however, did not impact all members of an industry equally. For instance, regulations on doctors were aimed at ensuring that medical practitioners had the necessary qualifications. This meant passing state legislation requiring practicing doctors to graduate from accredited medical schools, which sounds perfectly sensible. The problem? Only white medical colleges were accredited, immediately disqualifying African American physicians and colleges (Leonard 2005).

Progressives were also responsible for a slew of other legislation, most importantly several amendments to the U.S. Constitution. Progressives championed amendments introducing a federal income tax, direct election of senators, alcohol prohibition, and women's right to vote. They were instrumental in creating laws against child labor and promoting universal education.

Progressive Era legislation is also credited with creating the mechanisms for the racial state to flourish post-slavery. Progressive reforms were oriented toward making society "better," which often meant whiter and more middle-class, both culturally and demographically. For instance, Progressives supported immigration laws like those discussed above as one way to ensure the nation would have only "fit" citizens. Progressive union reformers advocated exclusionary labor laws, to exclude labor, employment, and citizenship for "parasites," "the unemployable," and "low-wage races" (Leonard 2005).

These types of laws were directly oriented toward ensuring Progressive morality, eradicating degeneracy, and continuing white supremacy. They also institutionalized these ideas through legislative reforms and the creation of new state powers, such as the juvenile court and the uniformed urban police, discussed later in the chapter. First, however, we detail how Progressive reforms re-created the racial state by returning to the topic of eugenics and considering its impact on the Progressive Era.

PROGRESSIVE REFORMS AND THE
METAMORPHOSIS OF THE RACIAL STATE

Progressives believed that the tools of science could be used to solve social problems they identified. This meant that Progressive reformers often relied on the **ideology of expertise,** or the idea that we should defer to people who have expert knowledge or skills. This is not necessarily a bad idea. During the Progressive Era, however, the ideology of expertise meant that governmental interventions were often premised on the insights of scholars, many of whom were racial scientists (discussed in chapter 3).

Progressive appeals for reform often mixed insights from scholarly work with popular appeals to morality and identity. Progressives who espoused eugenic philosophy often decried how the biological lessons of heredity would affect social conditions, particularly as cities continued to swell. Thus, while not all Progressives subscribed to eugenics—like Franz Boas in chapter 3— both Progressives and eugenic-minded social reformers were focused on what they considered the preeminent social problem: urban slums. Under both groups, the racial state flourished through state policies that were targeted at poor, often nonwhite, urban communities.

The Rise of Eugenics

The work of racial scientists in the eighteenth and most of the nineteenth century was limited primarily to scholarly circles and the urban elite. Ideas of racial hierarchy and superiority were commonly held, but the work of racial scientists was not widely known. Eugenics changed that.

As we described in chapter 3, eugenics was the belief that degeneracy is hereditary and that instead of leading to decline of the subgroup, degeneracy could actually infect society and proliferate the unfit through breeding and environmental contamination. Eugenics was fundamentally different than other racial science because it was not only a scholarly theory but a theory of social reform, and it gained considerable traction during the Progressive period.

With the proliferation of textual material and the emergence of mass culture in the late 1800s, eugenic ideas were disseminated to a much broader audience. Eugenics was first proposed in the United Kingdom in the 1890s, and U.S. scholars and social reformers began taking up its cause shortly after. By the 1920s and 1930s, eugenic philosophy was pervasive in U.S. society and considerably shaped how reformers conceived of, thought about, and approached social problems.

State-Sponsored Sterilization

As one proponent, Francis Amasa Walker, put it, eugenics was meant to tackle some of the most pressing social problems, such as poverty:

> We must strain out of the blood of the race more of the taint inherited from a bad and vicious past before we can eliminate poverty, much more pauperism, from our social life. The scientific treatment which is applied to physical diseases must be extended to mental and moral disease, and a wholesome surgery and cautery must be enforced by the whole power of the state for the good of all. (1899, 470)

Walker's logic provides an explicit example of state racism in eugenic discourse, where the elimination of some—that is, the surgical cauterization of a "bad and

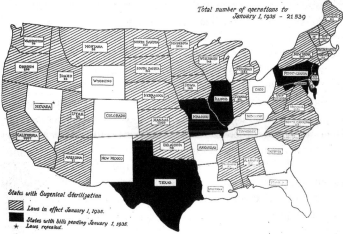

Figure 4.4 Legislative status of eugenical sterilization, by U.S. state, 1935. Source: Harry H. Laughlin Papers, Truman State University.

vicious past"—benefits the health and welfare of others—that is, "for the good of all." It also provides an example of how the social world was seen as in need of the instruments developed in the scientific world—namely, "surgery and cautery."

Eugenic state policy was quite explicitly a logic of state racism. It was the philosophical foundation supporting genocide in Nazi Germany. It informed efforts to sterilize the poor and nonwhite in the United States. And it successfully used the power of the state to make its biological racial vision of society reality.

The practice of eugenic sterilization in the United States was challenged in a lawsuit, *Buck v. Bell* (1927). Justice Oliver Wendell Holmes provided one of the most famous quotes regarding eugenics in his decision for the case: "It is better for all the world, if instead of waiting to execute degenerate offspring for crime, or to let them starve for their imbecility, society can prevent those who are manifestly unfit from continuing their kind. . . . Three generations of imbeciles are enough." Eugenicists were successful in passing compulsory sterilization laws in over thirty states (see figure 4.4). People were often sterilized after contact with state authorities, often when institutionalized for being "insane" or "imbecilic." Sterilization was part of many juvenile court programs of reform (Chávez-García 2012). By the 1960s, over 60,000 people had been sterilized in the U.S. (Reilly 1987).

Racial difference was often the basis for sterilization, and it is likely not surprising to any reader that those deemed threats to society and unable to be saved were most often from disenfranchised, marginalized, impoverished, and nonwhite communities (Ladd-Taylor 1997). One-third of all Puerto Rican women who had children were sterilized by 1965 and a quarter of Native American women between the ages of 15 and 44 were sterilized by the 1970s (Krase 2014). North Carolina sterilized 7,600 individuals between the 1930s and 1970s, predominantly African Americans. Sterilizations continue to be uncovered today. Mexican women undergoing childbirth in Los Angeles in the 1970s were forced to consent to sterilization in order to receive pain medication (Stern 2005). In 2013, evidence emerged that California prisons had sterilized women inmates without proper consent during the 2000s (Roth and Ainsworth 2015).

Other state programs sought to foster eugenic practice throughout society. IQ tests were originally created by a eugenicist, as were some types of genetic screening, birth control, and forced abortion practices (Reilly 1987). Marriage restrictions were a form of eugenics seeking to prevent the downfall of society by outlawing marriage between those who were fit and those unfit. English education and even compulsory education were also advocated by eugenicists as state policies important to ensuring the biological continuation of the most desirable traits in the population.

Displaying Civilizational Progress

Eugenicists conducted extensive education campaigns about the problem of the unfit. These efforts illustrate how eugenicists' opinions of fitness reinforced the social, political, and cultural presuppositions of white identity. Eugenic campaigns communicated what it meant to be white and defined the attributes that demonstrated civilization, refinement, and aptitude (see figure 4.5).

In 1893, the World's Columbian Exposition in Chicago provided an opportunity for everyday people to encounter eugenic ideas. Over 13 million people attended the fair, which attempted "to prove that 'the wonderful progress of the United States, as well as the character of the people' is the result of natural selection" (Blumenthal et al. 2002, 99). As demonstration, the "White City" section of the exposition featured gleaming white modern buildings. The achievements of U.S. culture were, in the eyes of the organizers, reflected in this replication of a utopic city defined by clean streets, endless consumption opportunities, model sanitation facilities, uniformed patrol, an electric railroad, and flawless (and poverty-less) modern landscapes.

Across the street, fairgoers could follow the path of degeneracy away from civilization and quite literally descend into the depths of savagery, according to eugenicists. Organized like the "great chain of being," fair exhibits proceeded through stages of development, with savagery at one end and the civilizational achievements of whites at the other. Villages for each "race" were provided: German and Irish villages were located close to the White City and, as patrons moved farther away, they would head down the supposed evolutionary ladder to Middle Eastern, West Asian, East Asian, African, and finally North American Indian villages.

Figure 4.5 Eugenics social reformers. Source: Wisconsin Historical Society: Classified 6728; Negative no.: W Hi (x3) 14579.

For the 1904 St. Louis World's Fair, organizers brought two thousand people from other places to the event and staged them in "native habitats" and wearing "indigenous" garb that reflected neither what people traditionally nor contemporarily wore. Alongside exhibits of "natives" and their "primitive" ways, the fair exhibited the progress of European nations in art, science, and the humanities and offered lectures on race. At one of the lectures, a prominent scholar argued that though the groups of the world could be classified into "several races," there were only "four culture grades of savagery, barbarism, civilization, and enlightenment" (Rydell 2013, 161). Directly invoking the Age of Enlightenment, the speaker articulated a vision of race that was not necessarily biological but rather culturally based—this time, though, in the context of evolutionary progress.

Ubiquity of Eugenics

Eugenics, while today often considered a fringe and inconsequential moment in U.S. history, was widespread and had lasting consequences for both state and society. By 1928, there were over 376 courses on the subject in American universities and over 20,000 college students received eugenic instruction. It was part of the curriculum in many high schools and in "one survey of 41 textbooks, nearly 90 percent of all high school biology textbooks published between 1914 and 1948 endorsed the movement" (Blumenthal et al. 2002, 182). Courses in other subjects also taught eugenics. Eugenics permeated popular culture. Cartoons, pulp fiction, and social reformers routinely promulgated images of white progress and nonwhite decline and degeneration. Steven Selden describes where students might encounter eugenics messages during one week:

> On a given Saturday evening in the 1920s, . . . school students could go to the movies to see the pro-euthanasia film *The Black Stork*. The following morning, while attending church services, they might listen to a eugenically oriented sermon recommending marriages of "best" with "best." On Monday, the newspaper might warn of a "rising tide of feeblemindedness" and recommend restricting immigration from Eastern and Southern Europe. On Tuesday, the press could report on the attractive winners of "better babies contests." Sitting in class on Wednesday, these same students might open their biology textbooks to a chapter on eugenics. Finally, on Thursday and Friday, while visiting a state fair with their hygiene class, they could participate in a Fitter Families competition. If they were judged as having superior heredity, they might return home bearing a medal with a biblical inscription (Psalms 16.6), "Yea, I have a goodly heritage." (2005, 205)

Eugenics abounded throughout U.S. life. Several eugenic inspired organizations were founded: the Immigration Restriction League was established in 1894, the American Breeder's Association in 1904, the Eugenics Record Office in 1911, and the American Eugenics Society in 1921. Eugenics conferences were held regularly in the United States and internationally. Several nations (including Belgium, Brazil, Canada, Japan, and Sweden) adopted eugenic practices of sterilization. And the rise of Nazi Germany is eugenic philosophy writ large.

Eugenics for the Masses

Popular eugenic events included the "fitter family" and "better baby" contests (see figure 4.6). In these contests, a family or baby was selected from a pool of entrants for their supposed genetic wealth. First held in Kansas City in 1920, the "Fitter Families for Future Firesides" began as a forum to promote breeding and knowledge of eugenics. Participants were subject to a panoply of assessments to demonstrate their fitness, including social and medical history; personality, IQ, and temperament tests; blood and urine samples; and anthropometric measurements, such as height, weight, and bodily "defects." Better baby contests were used as an opportunity to educate mothers on child-rearing and to promote a particular definition of a healthy normal baby (Selden 2005). Like the measurements of scientific racists, eugenicists used better baby and fitter family contests to establish the "normal healthy type" and its deviations.

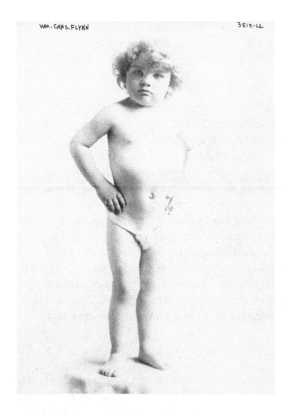

Figure 4.6 William Charles Flynn, a winner of perfect "eugenic baby" contests. Source: Courtesy of the Library of Congress, LC-DIG-ggbain-19313.

Though they typically promoted whiteness, it was not only white social reformers who subscribed to eugenic ideas. Black social reformers also sought to encourage those with the "fittest" traits to marry one another, and the NAACP even held "fit baby" contests. Black intellectuals from W. E. B. Du Bois to Thomas Wyatt Turner and Marcus Garvey promoted theories of black liberation based in eugenic philosophy (Dorr and Logan 2011, 69).

Eugenicists believed that if they did not educate middle-class, nondegenerate people about the hereditary impacts of degeneration, the nation would be committing "race suicide." Coined by Edward Ross in 1901, **race suicide** was a "Progressive Era term for the process by which racially superior stock ('natives') is outbred by a more prolific, but racially inferior stock (immigrants)" (Leonard 2005, 209). Preventing race suicide was the expressed goal of eugenic and Progressive approaches to public policy, and each intervention sought to cultivate those who could become upstanding citizens and separate them from those whose barbarism and savagery threatened cultural demise. Called "the greatest problem of civilization" by Theodore Roosevelt, race suicide revealed anxieties about the status of whiteness in society. In 1910, this anxiety culminated in the passage of the Mann Act, also known as the White Slave-Traffic Act.

The Mann Act

The Mann Act was passed in 1910 after media and political elites bemoaned what they saw as the emergence of **white slavery.** According to the white slavery narrative, women were kidnapped, transported to the cities, and forced into sexual slavery. The Mann Act sought to end this practice by making it a federal felony to transport between states "any woman or girl for the purpose of prostitution or debauchery, or for any other immoral purpose." Though the law theoretically applied to all women, both the name White Slave-Traffic Act and the media hysteria surrounding white slavery demonstrated otherwise. States also adopted what came to be called "white slavery" laws, aimed at stemming the moral furor surrounding urbanization, gender, and race.

The Mann Act came about due to urbanization. The large influx of single young men into the cities gave rise to thriving, often open-air prostitution districts, commonly called "red-light" districts. Population growth often led these districts to push against their boundaries, inciting social reformers to act.

Constructing White Femininity

White women were constructed as inherently virtuous, chaste, and virginal. Consequently, they were also seen as inherently dependent and in need of the protection and guidance of white men. This was the reason for denying women the right to vote, restricting their inheritance rights, and condoning violence and rape in intimate relationships. While not enslaved, women were in many ways the property of men. Urbanization's working opportunities meant that some women could challenge the patriarchal conditions of their lives (Odem 1995).

Concern about "white slavery" resulted from the assumption that detachment from traditional supervisory structures—such as living with their parents until marriage—would result in women's moral downfall (Odem 1995). Dance halls common in Progressive cities were considered major contributors to the ruination of young women, and much of the white slavery literature and propaganda identified spaces of amusement as predatory sites for white slavers. Books and pamphlets were published with titles such as *The Tragedies of the White Slave* (1910) and *From Dance Hall to White Slavery* (1911), and a movie was even made called *Traffic in Souls.* The feared scenario was that young, virtuous white women were being plucked from their homes and forced into prostitution by nefarious traffickers. Traffickers were not readily identified, but as the prosecution of the Mann Act revealed, the feared scenario was predominantly interracial relationships between white women and black men.

Jane Addams, one of the most famous Progressives in Chicago in the early 1900s, described the dangers of the city for young (white) women:

> Perhaps never before have the pleasures of the young and mature become so definitely separated as in the modern city. The public dance halls filled with frivolous and irresponsible young people in a feverish search for pleasure, are but a sorry substitute for the old dances on the village green in which all of the older people of the village participated. Chaperonage was not then a social duty but natural and inevitable, and the whole courtship period was guarded by the conventions and restraint which were taken as a matter of course and had developed through years of publicity and simple propriety.
>
> The only marvel is that the stupid attempt to put the fine old wine of traditional country life into the new bottles of the modern town does not lead to disaster oftener than it does, and that the wine so long remains pure and sparkling. (1909, 5)

Notions of women as "pure and sparkling" underscore the gendered presuppositions of Addams's lament. In the city, women were unsupervised and lacked convention or restraint to guide them. White slavery demonstrated the disaster of this arrangement.

Reformers working to combat white slavery insisted that the freedom women experienced in the city was actually a cover for a more nefarious practice—prostitution (Abrams and Curran 2000). One researcher at the time claimed that young women in the city might not be telling their parents of their plight:

> Another significant fact brought out by the examination of these girls is that practically everyone who admitted having parents living begged that her real name be withheld from the public because of the sorrow and shame it would bring to her parents. . . . In a word, the one concern of nearly all of those examined who have homes in this country was that their parents—and in particular their mothers—might discover, through the prosecution of the "white slavers," that they were leading lives of shame instead of working at the honorable callings which they had left their homes and come to the city to pursue. . . . The mother who has allowed her girl to go to the big city and work should find out what kind of life that girl is living and find out from some other source other than the girl herself . . . You owe it to yourself and to her and it is not disloyalty to go beyond her own words for evidence that the wolves of the city have not dragged her from safe paths. (Bell 1910: 50–51)

Figures 4.7 and 4.8 are illustrations from this report. For proponents of the Mann Act, industrialization and urbanization did not bring greater sexual and economic freedom for young women but rather their enslavement at the hands of sex traffickers. As one might imagine, the idea that white women were being routinely sold into slavery in urban environments generated a considerable amount of concern among the white urban elite.

The Mann Act is still law, and the most recent scholarly recounting of prosecutions under it revealed that as of 1997 there had never been a single prosecution of a white man for the (more common and socially acceptable) sexual

DANGEROUS AMUSEMENTS—THE BRILLIANT ENTRANCE TO
HELL ITSELF
Young girls who have danced at home a little are attracted by the blazing lights,
gaiety and apparent happiness of the "dance halls," which in many instances lead to
their downfall. (See page 112.)

Figure 4.7 Political propaganda, Mann Act, warning against the dangers of urban amusements.
Source: Ernest Albert Bell, *Fighting the Traffic in Young Girls, or The War on the White Slave
Trade* (Chicago: G.S. Ball, 1910), https://archive.org/details/fightingthetraff26081gut.

degradation of a black woman (Mumford 1997). The act has been most often
used to prosecute interracial couples, especially targeting black men romanti-
cally linked to white women (Pliley 2014). This relationship held perhaps the
greatest taboo in U.S. society for it explicitly violated the narrative that an
entire state and country was built upon. The act reveals how moral panics
about women and crime were used to define and demarcate the social and
physical boundaries of race, gender, and sexuality.

The Mann Act provides a glimpse of how racial hegemony works through
gendered narratives about white women's sexuality. Gender norms at the time
of the Mann Act's passage were shifting as a result of the greater freedom that
many women enjoyed as a consequence of urbanization and industrialization.
No longer were working-class women necessarily confined to the home and
farm, and many young women, like young men, migrated to the cities in search
of work. Single women in the city considerably disrupted ideas of virtuous
white womanhood, and the Mann Act worked to reinforce the traditional
model.

"MY GOD! IF ONLY I COULD GET OUT OF HERE"
The midnight shriek of a young girl in the vice district of a large city, heard by two worthy men, started a crusade which resulted in closing up the dens of shame in that city. (See page 450.)

Figure 4.8 Political propaganda, Mann Act. Source: Ernest Albert Bell, *Fighting the Traffic in Young Girls, or The War on the White Slave Trade* (Chicago: G. S. Ball, 1910), https://archive.org/details/fightingthetraff26081gut.

Reasserting White Supremacy

The passage of the Mann Act and the hysteria over white slavery occurred at a time of great change in U.S. society and provided a moment that state power was wielded to reassert white supremacy in the law. Jim Crow laws were proliferating throughout the South and lynchings were a regular occurrence (Wells-Barnett 1969). Antimiscegenation laws were passed throughout the United States. Much of this was premised on the national myth that African American men were hypersexual and inherently desired white women.

The Mann Act resulted from this hysteria. With both women and African Americans migrating to cities in the North, the campaign against white slavery borrowed long-standing narratives used in the South to justify lynching and violent punishment of black men. With ideas that black men were inherently sexually predatory—something supported by the work of racial scientist Frederick

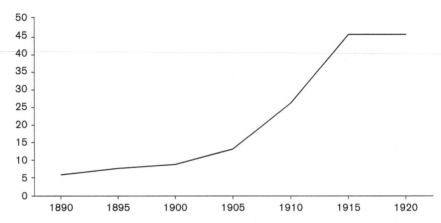

Figure 4.9 Number of states with "white slavery" laws, 1890–1920. Source: Joseph Mayer, The Regulation of Commercialized Vice (New York: Klebold, 1923), 31, https://archive.org/details /regulationofcomm00mayerich.

Hoffman reviewed in chapter 3—Southern society placed strict legal and social restrictions on interactions between them and white women. These boundaries were not as stringent in Northern cities, given the small population of people of color, and the hysteria around the Mann Act worked to fortify those boundaries and the ideology of white supremacy in the North. Exhibitions at the World's Fair and other eugenic educational opportunities provided prolific examples of what "fitness" looked like—white, middle-class, heterosexual, and (for women) sexually chaste—and legislation like the Mann Act aimed to protect and create this normative gender and racialized ideal as a reality throughout society (see figure 4.9).

Cities were not passive in the face of the Mann Act, and many social reformers encouraged the police to actively patrol and surveil women and children in the city. A key tactic in the racial state appeared: what are often today called vice squads but were at the time, in some places, called "purity squads." Purity squads were specialized police divisions responsible for ensuring the moral welfare of women and children. They routinely investigated and patrolled dance halls and saloons and arrested women considered to be in moral peril. In the city of Seattle, the purity squad aimed to clear city spaces of all women and children after sunset by arresting any who were out at night. This short-lived policy soon collided with the reality of women's industrial contribution, as workers whose shifts ended in the middle of the night were routinely arrested (Putman 2008).

The Sexual Infrastructure of Racism

The ease with which this narrative of the virginal white woman and hypersexual black man gained political and popular currency reveals the pervasiveness of what a scholar today calls the "sexual infrastructure of racism" (Meyerowitz 2009, 1280). Racism does not exist separate from other axes of difference, such as class, gender, and sexuality. Concern about white women's virginal and chaste status had long been used to justify enslaving African American men: the narrative was that white women could never be safe if black men were free. It is perhaps the most common racist trope that whites used to justify the lynching of black men. Indeed, during the era of colonialism, "U.S. officials displaced their anxieties about colonialism, immigration, and American masculinity onto dark-skinned foreigners and natives, who were cast as diseased, perverted, and corrupting" by criminalizing interracial relations, including sex and marriage (Meyerowitz 2009, 1279). Prosecutions under the Mann Act suggest that while these anxieties resulted in prosecutions most often against black men, they were widely used to subjugate men of color from many different communities (Mumford 1997).

Ideologies of protecting white womanhood upheld an entire system of intervention that resulted in greater policing of all sorts of people: white women, queer people, and especially, urban nonwhites. Further, this narrative protected the more common sexual degradation routinely occurring at the time: the rape of black women by white men. Though black activists called attention to the hypocrisy of the law, the anti–white slavery movement continued the racist narrative that excluded "black women from the category of the deserving and redeemable" (Mumford 1997, 17–18).

The Lingering Impact of Eugenics

Today, eugenics is seen as an unfortunate period in U.S. history (if it is considered at all), but the racial state practices it created remain (see box 4.2). Better baby contests brought the proliferation of urban child-wellness checkups; concern about the degeneration of society continues to fuel immigration policy; parks as places to ensure the recreation and exercise necessary for a healthy body remain key fixtures in urban communities; and campaigns against white slavery established some of the longest-lasting philanthropic charities with outreach to trafficked women. Though today we see many state programs as benevolent interventions, they also provide a mechanism for the surveillance and control of poor and nonwhite families.

The surveillance and control of poor and nonwhite families continues today through welfare, criminal justice, and even philanthropic practices. "Family caps" that limit how many children a family can have and still receive state welfare aid are one example of how the state continues today to try to prevent breeding of "undesirables." Courts have also ordered those convicted of a crime to undergo sterilization or use long-term birth control. Mothers who have been convicted of child abuse may be ordered to be implanted with Norplant, a contraceptive device that lasts five years, as a term of their probation. Fathers who

BOX 4.2   **Resurgence of Eugenics Today?**

Common in the history of eugenics was the sterilization of "undesirables," often those found within both juvenile and adult institutions. Today, sterilization is considered quite controversial, such as practices discovered in California prisons in the 2000s. However, some courts are today promoting what might be called eugenic strategies and they are not hiding it.

In Tennessee, a judge issued an order providing jail sentence credits for anyone willing to undergo a birth control procedure. Males who got vasectomies and females who had birth control devices implanted that were good for at least four years received thirty days of sentence credit. The judge argued that by providing these credits, he hoped "to encourage [people in jail] to take personal responsibility and give them a chance, when they do get out, not to be burdened with children. This gives them a chance to get on their feet and make something of themselves" (Halloway 2017). He further noted in response to controversy surrounding his plan that "it seemed to me almost a no-brainer. Offer these women a chance to think about what they're doing and try to rehabilitate their life."

Others, like the American Civil Liberties Union, charge that this is hardly a voluntary program, and it coerces those in jail to give up their reproductive rights in order to go free. The Tennessee ACLU wrote that "such a choice violates the fundamental constitutional right to reproductive autonomy and bodily integrity by interfering with the intimate decision of whether and when to have a child, imposing an intrusive medical procedure on individuals who are not in a position to reject it" (2017).

Tennessee has a long history of sterilizing women it considers undesirable and even attempted to enforce a "fetal assault" law in the 1990s and early 2000s. Under this law, women who used drugs while pregnant would be subject to felony prosecution. Because many women consequently avoided prenatal care, which the American Medical Association found more deleterious than drug usage, the state abandoned the law.

Is the Tennessee plan of sterilization and birth control in exchange for sentence reduction a form of modern-day eugenics in your opinion? Given the undeniable racial disparities in prison populations, how is such a law likely to impact racial communities differentially? Is this an example of the racial state in action?

Sources: ACLU Tennessee, "ACLU-TN Statement on White County Inmate Sterilization and Birth Control Program," press release, July 19, 2017, www.aclu-tn.org/aclu-tn-statement-on-white-county-sterilization-program/; Kali Halloway, "Modern-Day Eugenics? Prisoners Sterilized for Shorter Sentences," *Salon,* July 28, 2017, www.salon.com/2017/07/28/modern-day-eugenics-prisoners-sterilized-for-shorter-sentences_partner/.

have been convicted of not paying child support may be ordered by the court, as a condition of probation, to not have additional children (though they are not physically prevented from doing so). Nongovernmental organizations also promote eugenic policies; for example, Project Prevention aims to reduce drug-addicted births by paying women addicted to drugs to use long-term birth control (such as Norplant or Depo-Provera) or undergo sterilization (Paltrow 2003).

Today, though, the continuation of the white racial state framework first envisioned by Progressives and eugenicists happens not through explicit eugenicist policies but from the place where eugenic and progressive ideas converged: the urban origins of degeneration (Currell 2006; Soloway 2014). Both eugenicists and Progressives advocated using state power to ensure the moral development of society by increasing mechanisms of surveillance, especially of the nonwhite and the poor. These efforts led to the formation of urban law enforcement and the juvenile court.

Today many cannot imagine being without urban police or the juvenile court, but it was not until the early 1900s that the responsibilities of these two institutions were assumed fully by the state. Although antecedents of each of these existed, the Progressive Era redefined the power of the state to incorporate the responsibilities of these institutions. These two institutions provide just two examples of how the practices and knowledge of the racial state were institutionalized in the United States, and in particular, the justice system. Given the history of each institution, it is unsurprising that both the juvenile court and urban police are critical agents in the continuing link between race and crime today.

THE BIRTH OF THE JUVENILE COURT

Juvenile courts, though today seen as valued social institutions, are important to the continuity of the racial state. At the time of their founding, they were critical for creating racial divisions amongst the juvenile population. Today, those divisions continue as the entrenched problem called "disproportionate minority contact," an issue which even the federal government recognizes. In many places, black and brown youth, like their adult counterparts in jails and prisons, make up the vast majority of juvenile court wards and residents in juvenile prisons. Furthermore, youth of color are much more likely than white youth to be waived to the adult court, replicating the racial tiers that started in the Progressive Era (Kurlychek and Johnson 2004).

The City and the Child

Progressive Era conceptions of urbanization were a critical influence in the development of the juvenile court (Feld 1999). The first juvenile court opened in Chicago in 1899, and by 1925, every state except two had such courts. Juvenile courts, though, were a distinctly urban movement. By 1925, they were found only in cities, and their jurisdiction rarely extended into rural locations. Progressive founders of juvenile courts viewed urban areas as being filled with a type of infectious virus, able to bring about degeneration and social downfall from mere exposure. Progressives feared that children raised in cities would have their growth stunted and their innocence corrupted through exposure to the activities of adults. Cities also violated the separation of adults and children espoused by Victorian culture.

Progressives viewed childhood as a naturally precocious time, and children were often associated with ideas of nature, primitiveness, and even called "little devils" (Platt 1977). In rural areas, children could express their natural precocity with little consequence. Exploring uncharted areas away from the home exposed children to nature, or at least the idyllic version imagined by Progressives. In the city, though, their natural precocity led children directly into the lair of adult amusements. This vision of rural living and the city meant that many of the first state juvenile institutions—what today we might identify as juvenile prisons but were then called "industrial schools," "training schools," and even "reform schools"—were located outside cities. Despite the rural locale, the residents were urban youth, the group Progressives considered most in danger from the rapid urbanization and industrialization of the early twentieth century.

Separation between Home and Work

Industrialization not only changed the conditions of people's jobs, but it introduced a separation between home and work. In agricultural societies, home and work are often located in the same physical space; industrialization introduced the idea of commuting to work and thus meant that adults were away from the home, often for long periods of the day (as they are today). This meant that children were often left alone and without supervision, especially since industrialization often broke up extended families residing together (Clement 1997). Intergenerational homes became less common as adult children began moving away to find work before they started families, leaving fewer adults to care for and supervise the younger children.

One of the consequences of industrialization, according to Progressives, was the increase in wayward children, especially those in the city without supervision. Children were not only left unsupervised, but worse, according to Progressives, went to work. This concern prompted the formation of the juvenile court and created the figure of the juvenile court judge, a court official with the power to do what was considered to be in the best interests of the child (Platt 1977).

The "Best Interests of the Child"

Progressives believed urban centers corrupted children because of the presence of adult amusements and the lack of parental supervision. Young girls were sexually corrupted through exposure to dance halls, as evidenced by the Mann Act. Young boys found companionship among older, more criminally inclined men and developed into criminals themselves. Without intervention, Progressives argued that society would eventually see the creation of a hardened criminal class, whose youthful exposure would make them far more sophisticated than adults:

> In all cities one condition exists which is comparatively unknown in small communities, namely, numbers of children who, through the death, neglect, poverty, weakness, or criminality of parents or guardians, do not attend school, have practically no home training or control, and through such neglect drift into criminality. There are hundreds of such children in Chicago and elsewhere throughout the State, growing up to constitute an ignorant and criminal class, dangerous to the welfare of the whole country. (Clapp 2010, 39)

Prior to the juvenile court, kids who committed crimes were often released with no intervention at all. When the courts did intervene, it was primarily to house children with adults, to send children to the emerging state homes for children, such as "houses of refuge" or training schools, or to send children to one of the many philanthropic organizations.

White Identity and the Juvenile Court

The jurisdiction of Progressive Era juvenile courts was much broader than it is today. In many places, any child who came to the attention of state authorities—whether dependent, as we consider foster children today, or delinquent—was put before the juvenile court. The juvenile court thus served a dual purpose and was even legally conceived as a distinct type of criminal court: one that could address children who committed crimes, but without the trappings of criminal court procedure, while at the same time providing for children who might be orphaned or abused by their parents. The courts were thus often more like the civil or family welfare legal category than the criminal court.

Through this wide jurisdiction, reveals Anthony Platt, one of the premier historians of the juvenile court and author of the seminal text *The Child-Savers* (1977), the history of the juvenile court was also the history of promoting the white, Protestant ethic of Progressive reformers. Training schools were premised on an industrial model, often mimicking military barracks and enforcing a strict routine to teach discipline and thrift, considered key components of enlightened white identity. Court interventions, such as probation and sentences at an industrial training school, provided an opportunity to intervene in the lives of poor working-class and immigrant families.

Children, especially immigrants and Native Americans, were routinely removed from the home and sent to state institutions or boarding schools for proper "civilizing." Progressives promoted rearing children in two-parent homes and frowned on families with children renting rooms to boarders. Progressive courts often employed "domestic" inspectors to ensure that children were raised in suitable homes, defined by particular standards of cleanliness, a mostly stay-at-home mother (a requirement for state aid in some places), segregated spaces for adults and children, and certain types of structures (i.e., a single-family home with yard instead of an apartment). Welfare benefits, called "mother's pension payments" at the time, were often provided by the juvenile court only on the condition that the family meet the requirements of the court for "upstandingness" (Leff 1973). Progressive reformers also advocated for parental responsibility and compulsory education laws, mandating parents to assume financial responsibility and surveillance of their children (Odem 1995).

These interventions institutionalized surveillance of poor and nonwhite families (Platt 1977). Home visits, denial of mothers' pension payments, and even removal of children from the home were all ways the court responded to failure to conform to imagined white, middle-class norms. Through the court, these ideals were translated into policies that promoted the idea that the middle-class, single-family home with two parents (only one of whom worked) was the most correct way to raise children.

A Two-Tiered System of Justice

From its inception, the juvenile court system institutionalized a two-tiered system of justice (Platt 1969, 1977; Ward 2012). This two-tiered system emerged as a direct consequence of Progressive ideologies about childhood, the family, and the attributes of citizenship. For Progressives, a child who committed crime was not necessarily wayward. Many prominent Progressives even recalled times they themselves had been involved in delinquencies and noted the "significance in the confession of useful men that they spent time being bad boys" (Merrill 1914).

This meant that the court could exercise the power to *not* intervene with children brought before it and instead release the children to the custody of their parents. This continues today. The decision to incarcerate a young person, then, is based not on his or her behavior but the parents' behavior. Homes that the court or the police viewed as morally upright did not have to fear juvenile court intervention. Unsurprisingly, this meant that the court largely allowed the delinquencies and crimes of white middle- and upper-class children to go without censure or punishment (Schlossman 1977).

Some parents, however, were not trusted by the court to deal with their children properly, and thus these children were subject to a different tier of justice

(Brown 2011). At least three broad categories of youth lived in Progressive Era cities: (1) the archetypical Progressive child who could be helped by the more benevolent and social-welfare-oriented mechanisms of the court (such as probationary oversight or charitable intervention); (2) the recidivist, or the older child who could *not* be helped by the softer side of the juvenile court and required institutionalization by the state; and (3) children for whom the juvenile court did not apply: primarily black, Native American, Chinese, and Latinx youth throughout the United States.

The Progressives' Archetypal Child

Youth who needed the court's intervention due to parental neglect (in both delinquency and dependency cases) are perhaps the archetypal children of Progressive America and the juvenile court. These children benefited from the social welfare mechanisms of the court, largely through probationary services or charitable accommodations. These children (invariably white—and not from the more degenerate white classes) were regarded with sympathy; their predicaments and circumstances stirred the generous and philanthropic tendencies of the middle and upper classes.

White youth and their salvation came first, and this group was the primary recipient of judicial benevolence. Interventions were oriented toward educating immigrant white families on how to assume the proper moral and cultural attitudes of middle-class, white families. These interventions, though benevolently premised, still increased the surveillance of poor and immigrant families. These children were also often the younger versions of those who would become the problem children for the juvenile court.

The Progressives' Recidivist Child

The second group, the recidivists, were too advanced in their delinquency—whether they had committed delinquent acts or not—to be housed with more civilized children (often denoted by age but also by class, race, and gender). These youths were often sent away to state training schools and often came from working-class immigrant communities. State training schools, though often premised on the same ideals as the juvenile court, were often called "academies of crime" by Progressive social reformers and were considered a last resort before imprisonment in adult facilities. Yet they served a critical purpose in the juvenile court as the place where "proper training" could occur that would "counteract the impositions of poor family life, a corrupt environment, and poverty, while at the same time toughening and preparing delinquents for the struggle ahead" (Platt 1969, 31).

The Progressives' Unchild

Finally, there existed a group of children for whom the juvenile court did not apply—these were mostly black, Latinx, and Native American children. As Steven Schlossman (1977) notes, it is essential to recall that the juvenile court, even with its antiquated, cruel, and most torturous practices, was primarily considered an institution for the saving of *white* youth only. Indeed, "however unfortunate their [poor white and European immigrant youth] disproportionate encounters with early juvenile institutions proved to be, their access reflected racial privileges in an unyielding white democracy" (Ward 2012, 73).

Children in this category who did make it into juvenile institutions could face sterilization. California juvenile institutions have always housed predominantly Latinx and black youth (especially after WWII). One of the earliest institutions, Whittier State School, was the site of extensive eugenic experimentation and policy in the first half of the twentieth century (Chávez-García 2012). The superintendent from 1912 to 1927, Fred C. Nelles, advocated sending fieldworkers and institution staff to eugenic training and created the reformatory as "a nationally and internationally recognized social laboratory." Fieldworkers for the institution were trained at the Eugenics Record Office and visited their charges' families to determine the hereditary lineage of their delinquency.

Once institutionalized, youth in California and elsewhere deemed potentially unfit endured psychological, intelligence, and physical testing. Young women were also repeatedly queried about their sexual history and subject to pelvic examinations. Through these tests, Whittier staff determined who was fit to return to society and who was so unfit that they required long-term institutionalization and sterilization. Through this process, "Mexicans, Mexican Americans, and African Americans in particular were disproportionately identified as mentally defective and feebleminded youth who needed permanent care and ideally sterilization" (Chávez-García 2012, 13).

Accusations of feeblemindedness, insanity, or incorrigibility were frequent justifications for sterilization, but they hid court officials' real reasons for institutionalization. For instance, one young man who came before the court for truancy and incorrigibility was sentenced to Whittier and determined to be feebleminded because of his ethnic heritage and failure to remember key details of his life. But the interview was conducted in English and the young man spoke only Spanish (Chávez-García 2012, 79). The famous, though unsuccessful, challenge to eugenics in the court case *Buck v. Bell* (1927) involved Carrie Buck, who was facing sterilization for the charge of feeblemindedness. However, Buck was in reality of normal intelligence and had been institutionalized by the court (a disposition sought by her foster parents) for getting pregnant out of wedlock as a result of a rape by her foster brother (Lombardo 2008).

Juvenile court practices during the Progressive Era were key to re-creating the racial state after the downfall of slavery. Court practices worked to sort children based on their deservingness, a category that largely reflected racial boundaries. Further, the ideologies of whiteness animating juvenile court interventions were used to increase surveillance and policing of youth and families of color. Though benevolently premised, the court is an institution critical to remaking the racial state, even today.

The Juvenile Court Today

Today, the juvenile court is little different than the Progressive Era court in terms of its outcomes, even as the state makes efforts to end disproportionate racial outcomes, as discussed in box 4.3 (Feld 1999). Black and Latinx youth continue to be subject to much greater surveillance by the court than their white counterparts (Cochran and Mears 2015). Further, court assessments of the home, family, and social life of delinquents continue to fuel greater interventions into the lives of poor and nonwhite youth (Bridges and Steen 1998). Finally, the various tiers of justice—from diversion out of the system to transfer to adult court—also reflect racial tiers. The most disadvantaged often face the greatest penalties and intervention, while white, middle-class youth frequently have their cases diverted out of the system (Fader, Kurlychek, and Morgan 2014). White youth often enjoy the status of being "secret delinquents": in anonymous surveys they self-report participating in criminal behaviors at similar rates to nonwhite youth, yet they escape notice and surveillance by authorities (Hagan and Foster 2006). Though the intention is not explicitly to create and exacerbate racial divisions, the juvenile court continues to arbitrate the futures of children based on race and contribute to the maintenance of the white racial state.

Incarceration in the juvenile justice system is also not a single event, but rather initiates youth into a cycle of incarceration that considerably affects their future as adults. Far from preventing future criminal legal system involvement, incarceration initiates a cycle of incarceration. White youth who are diverted from the system are likely to escape this cycle. One study found juvenile incarceration resulted in lower high school graduation rates and a higher likelihood of adult incarceration for violent crime (Aizer and Doyle 2015). Juvenile courts, while benevolently intentioned, are thus key mechanisms for the continuation of the racial state. Ideas of delinquency as a social problem that stems primarily from black and brown youths is the contemporary remaking of racial scientists' ideas that nonwhite races are degenerate. Both juvenile incarceration today and eugenics in the early twentieth century resulted in the increased surveillance of poor, nonwhite families. And the approach to delinquency both in the early twentieth century and today results in the continuation of futures predicated on the racial composition of the electorate. This is how the racial state continues, even in the postracial era, in a system

BOX 4.3   Challenging the Racial State in the Juvenile Court?

The fact that juvenile court practices disproportionately affect communities of color is itself considered a social problem. It has garnered countless studies, commentaries, interventions, and since the start of the mass incarceration buildup in the mid-1980s, it has been the subject of federal legislation. Federal authorities mandate that all juvenile court jurisdictions address what is called "disproportionate minority contact/confinement," or DMC for short. As a consequence of receiving federal funding for a juvenile court system, the court system must collect racial statistics, study the issue, and implement reform strategies.

Since the mid-1980s, efforts to counteract racial disproportionality in the juvenile court system have garnered considerable interest. Researchers have found that the disproportionality often results from court personnel assessments that tend to see the exact same crime very differently when committed by a white youth and by a black youth. White youth are often seen as the Progressives' archetypal child—the child whose delinquency results from bad decision-making as the result of peer pressure, bad home life, and/or community influences. Black youth, by contrast, are seen as leaders of criminal activity, actively seeking out crime, and generally remorseless. They are seen as the unchild of the juvenile court, for whom intervention for either them or their families is a waste of court resources. These two poles direct white youth toward diversion and rehabilitative interventions, while subjecting black youth to harsher punishment and transfer to the adult court.

Efforts to remedy this disparity, however, have resulted not in their elimination but rather in the concentration of youth of color in the system. This is due, in part, to the creation of juvenile-risk taxonomies that define the structural conditions of youth of color—more likely to know someone labeled as a gang member, less likely to attend an engaging and quality school, and more likely to be growing up in a high-risk environment—as the attributes of risk (Brown 2007).

Do federal efforts to challenge DMC demonstrate a weakening or challenging of the racial state? How do the unintended consequences of DMC interventions work to re-create the racial state? What would be a state intervention that might challenge the racial state in the juvenile court?

Sources: George S. Bridges and Sara Steen, "Racial Disparities in Official Assessments of Juvenile Offenders: Attributional Stereotypes as Mediating Mechanisms," American Sociological Review 63, no. 4 (August, 1998): 554–70; Elizabeth Brown, "'It's Urban Living, Not Ethnicity Itself': Race, Crime and the Urban Geography of High-Risk Youth," Geography Compass 1, no. 2 (2007): 222–45.

ostensibly dedicated to the "best interests of the children" and to ending "disproportionate minority confinement."

THE BIRTH OF THE UNIFORMED POLICE PATROL

The Progressive Era birthed another institution critical to the racial state today: the uniformed urban police. Policing at the turn of the twentieth century was quite different than it is today. Urban politics was defined by "political machines" (Fogelson 1977). Political machines were often neighborhood or district based and run by a "boss" or a small group of elites. Urban police in places like Boston had been under the control of and funded by these groups since the mid-1800s and often served as enforcers for the particular urban order that neighborhood bosses desired. Police were more akin to organized crime enforcers than the urban police we have today. When police did play an organized, public role, it was primarily to stem riots and other mass uprisings.

During the Progressive Era, this all changed (Kelling and Moore 1989). Instead of police serving at the behest of political bosses, police became a centralized force under the command of the state. Police also began to play a different role in urban society and took on the task of regular patrol and surveillance. The introduction of a centrally controlled, uniformed urban police in the Progressive Era thus extended the racial state through the regular surveillance and patrol of those deemed undesirable by society.

The Antecedents of Patrol

The earliest models that we might associate with today's uniformed urban police departments were slave patrols that operated in Southern states from the colonial period forward. The first slave patrol developed in the colony of Carolina in 1704; patrollers would roam travel routes at night to watch for Native Americans and people escaping from slavery. The stated purpose of today's police is to prevent crime and enforce the law; slave patrols had no such mandate. They enforced a single set of laws: those against runaway slaves. Yet, slave patrol practices provided the basis for the development of urban patrol and surveillance in the early twentieth century.

Between 1689 and 1865, Virginia's only uniformed police force was the slave patrol, which enforced 130 statutes related to slavery and was permanently established in response to an uprising by enslaved people in 1800. In 1837, South Carolina had a slave patrol with over a hundred officers, the largest "police force" at the time, and far larger than any Northern force (Carter 2015). Slave patrols played a critical role in quashing political dissent and protest by attending meetings of enslaved people to prevent any "inappropriate" discussions or plans.

This was not just a southern affair, either; Connecticut, New York, and the U.S. Congress all passed laws to control enslaved people in their territories, and temporary slave patrols arose for this purpose (Browne 2015). Further, nonwhites were the subject of increased surveillance throughout the North through legislative tactics such as "lantern laws" which mandated that black people could move throughout public spaces at night only if they held lanterns to their faces. During this time, Northern police forces generally followed the "night watchman" model from the United Kingdom. This meant that they generally stayed at their posts throughout the city until called upon to act. The function of patrol—moving through an area looking for signs of trouble—did not arise in Northern cities until the mid-1800s.

Modern Police and the Slave Patrollers

Modern police are certainly not the same as slave patrollers. Yet there are similarities between the two institutions in terms of their functions (Reichel 1988). Slave patrollers formalized the idea of regular patrol and surveillance of a geographical area, a practice that is common to modern policing. The term *beat*, which refers to the area that a police officer patrols, originated during the era of slavery and referred to the regular routes covered by officers in the slave patrols.

Slave patrollers carried out many of the same functions as police officers today (Williams 2015). They had the power to arrest anyone they suspected of being a runaway; they could stop people and check documentation to ensure they had permission to be away from their plantation; they searched enslaved people's houses; they inflicted corporal punishment in order to gain compliance; and they suppressed insurrections. While modern police are not slave patrollers, they do carry out the same functions of arrest, surveillance, and patrol, using force, searching private property, and controlling crowds and protests. Patrols were also allowed to enter any plantation they desired to pursue their functions. While modern police often need probable cause, slave patrollers would not have maintained their regional legitimacy if they wantonly abused this power since it challenged the private property of plantation owners. Certainly, modern police also have many differences from the slave patrols of the past, but the slave patrols represented the initial formation of these powers as a function of the state.

Slave patrols were also justified under the logic of deterrence. Their mere presence—plus their infiltration of meetings of enslaved people—was meant to deter any potential disruption to the Southern economy and the industrial machine of slavery. Regular patrol was intended to instill fear and compliance in the enslaved population.

This is hardly different than modern police today. Many people experience fear when they see a police officer in their rearview mirror, and it is not at all uncommon to hear people, most often black or Latinx, talk about fearing for

BOX 4.4   Examples of "Black Codes"

Mississippi Vagrant Act **(1865):** All freedmen, free Negroes, and mulattoes over the age of eighteen years, found with no lawful employment or business, or found unlawfully assembling themselves together, either in the day or night time . . . shall be deemed vagrants, and on conviction thereof shall be fined . . . and imprisoned. In case any freedman, free Negro, or mulatto shall fail for five days after the imposition of any fine . . . to pay the same that it shall be . . . the duty of the sheriff . . . to hire out said freedman, free Negro, or mulatto to any person who will, for the shortest period of service, pay said fine.

Louisiana Farm Labor Act **(1865):** Bad work shall not be allowed. Failing to obey reasonable orders, neglect of duty, and leaving home without permission will be deemed disobedience; impudence, swearing, or indecent language to or in the presence of the employer, his family, or agent, or quarreling and fighting with one another, shall be deemed disobedience. . . . All difficulties arising between the employers and laborers shall be settled by the former.

Florida Act on Public Places **(1866):** If any Negro, mulatto, or other person of color shall intrude himself into any religious or other public assembly of white persons, or into any railroad car or other public vehicle set aside for the exclusive accommodation of white people, he shall be deemed to be guilty of a misdemeanor, and upon conviction shall be sentenced to stand in the pillory for one hour, or be whipped.

Mississippi Apprentice Law **(1865):** It shall be the duty of all . . . civil officers . . . to report to the probate courts . . . all freedmen, free Negroes, and mulattoes under the age of eighteen . . . who are orphans, or whose parent or parents have not the means or who refuse to provide for and support said minors . . . the clerk of said court shall apprentice said minors to some competent and suitable person. . . . the former owner of said minors shall have the preference.

Source: Kathy Sammis, *Focus on U.S. History: The Era of the Civil War and Reconstruction* (Portland, ME: J. Weston Walch, 1997), 84.

Creating the Modern Police: Surveillance in the Progressive Era

Slave patrollers, modern police, and even the juvenile court are all oriented toward a single set of practices: surveillance and control. Surveillance scholars note that the techniques of mass surveillance of communities—such as through periodic patrol—first arose in response to a desire to control nonwhites. John Fiske notes the racial history of surveillance and defines surveillance as an explicit "technology of whiteness" where surveillance works as "a way of imposing norms" that reinforce the dominance of white racial ideas (1998, 69, 81). Simone Browne has extended this to look at the practices of racializing surveillance by uncovering how "enactments of surveillance reify boundaries and borders along racial lines" (2012, 72). Early police were engaged in surveillance exclusively of those with little or no formal political rights: black Americans, Native Americans, and "degenerate" immigrants, and early practices sought to ensure dominance over these groups in perpetuity.

This tradition continued in the Progressive Era, even as reformers sought to end the rampant corruption and brutality in police departments. Indeed, the Progressive dream of the modern police was a system of intricate surveillance operating through cities that would ensure the moral integrity of society for generations to come. A Progressive Era police reformer explained what needed changing: "Under the old system, police officials were appointed through political affiliations and because of this they were frequently unintelligent and untrained, they were distributed through the area to be policed according to a hit-or-miss system and without adequate means of communication; they had little or no record keeping system; their investigation methods were obsolete, and they had no conception of the preventive possibilities of the service" (Vollmer 1933, 161). The vision of Progressive reformers was a modern police force based in the powers of surveillance that Vollmer laments were missing in older systems. Now, police would patrol systematically, could communicate with one another across space, keep records, conduct investigations, and attempt to prevent crime through patrol.

This vision of policing was vastly different from earlier models of urban policing and helped institutionalize a network of surveillance across urban space, especially in places deemed the source of social problems. While hardly sophisticated or all-encompassing, the surveillance strategies of Progressive Era police sought to ensure social stability in the face of urbanization and industrialization. Doing so also meant ensuring the stability of white supremacy, capital accumulation, and the racial state. It is thus hardly surprising that this resulted in both a systematic process of patrolling the leisure lives of the working class and colluding with whites in campaigns of terror against nonwhites.

Policing Leisure

Urban police were often much more integrated into the general practices of urban regulation than they are today. For instance, Progressive police forces often provided trade licenses and made regulations on "immoral" businesses such as dance halls, theaters, movie houses, and billiard halls. As the agency responsible for the moral development of society, the police also used their power to monitor the leisure-time activities of the working class (Williams 2015).

Most Progressive police arrests were oriented not toward felonies but toward misdemeanors. Police routinely patrolled urban centers, and their activities were concentrated in adjacent slums—the places where the poor, the working class, and immigrants resided. Most arrests were for offenses against Progressive morality: drunkenness, vagrancy, loitering, disorderly conduct, and suspicious behavior (Williams 2015). This mirrors what brought most youths before the juvenile court: vagrancy, licentious behavior, sexual delinquency, and incorrigibility (Platt 1977).

In New York, a group of private citizens formed the Committee of Fourteen in 1905 to shape police work in fighting crime and vice near saloons. By investigating, patrolling, and surveilling places where white women could be in the company of nonwhites, the committee drew city attention to places that "emboldened miscegenators, forced white women to descend from the perch of Victorian morality and put them in dangerous proximity with treacherously libidinous black men bent on exploiting them as prostitutes and sex slaves" (Flowe 2014, 66). Liquor licenses were denied or revoked for black-owned saloons that permitted whites and for white-owned saloons that permitted patrons in interracial relationships (Flowe 2014). Newspapers carried tales of the dangers of mixing white and black people, cautioning white racial violence would ensue.

Cleveland's "Golden Rule"

Policies criminalizing the leisure activities of the poor and nonwhite combined with newly empowered police forces led to enormous increases in arrests. In Cleveland in 1906, police made 30,418 arrests, only 938 of which were for felonies. Lacking the resources to cope with this volume, the police introduced the "Golden Rule" in 1907. Rather than arrest drunks or other public order offenders, patrol officers simply walked them home. In the year after the new policy was enacted, they made only 10,095 arrests, slightly more than 1,000 for felonies, suggesting that some 20,000 arrests the year before had been for public-order offenses. Other cities with similar policies saw a 75 percent decrease in the number of arrests.

The Golden Rule policy in Cleveland was enacted by Fred Kohler, a Progressive police chief whom President Theodore Roosevelt called the "best Chief of Police in America." Chief Kohler was an outspoken critic of the rampant powers of arrest used by police in Progressive cities, decrying it as driving "young men and weak men to the haunts and association of habitual and expert criminals, who have taught them the ideals and practices of crime" (Howe 1910, 815). Kohler's policy created the same types of distinctions promoted by the juvenile court: between those who were corrupted by exposure to the criminal justice system and those who were members of the "criminal class." This helped to establish that those who were deemed "desirable" or "savable" should not be policed. Instead, policing surveillance should be reserved for the criminal class, identified by Kohler as the "hoboes" and "vagrants," two categories often used to police immigrants coming to Northern cities (Williams 2015).

Kohler did not permit licentious activity in Cleveland, though. At the same time he enacted the Golden Rule policy, he also increased surveillance of establishments believed to promote "immorality." His tactics included placing police officers at the front doors of saloons and taking the names and addresses of every person entering. He also sent police officers armed with axes to break up gambling and other licentious activity. The criminal class that remained he forcefully expelled from the city. Despite his Golden Rule, Kohler did not end the policing of leisure but rather used the powers of police surveillance to more effectively quash its public expression, particularly when, as in New York, this meant establishments that permitted racial "mixing."

Policing and Defining Whiteness

Policing the leisure activity of undesirables was particularly concentrated in places where race, class, gender, and sexual boundaries were transgressed. Cities throughout the United States sought to use police power not just to crack down on what Progressives considered immoral behavior but to actively promote racial segregation in leisure activities.

Policing played a critical role not just in creating and enforcing racial boundaries in the city but in integrating the more "degenerate" white races into the category of whiteness. Irish and Italian Americans were the dominant ethnic groups in many police forces, and in many Northern cities, they were often contained in cramped quarters in the same neighborhoods as black Americans. Ascendance into the ranks of the police provided one way for Irish and Italian Americans to assimilate into mainstream society, to take on the mantle of whiteness, and even create stark divisions in urban society between themselves and black communities.

Chicago and the Creation of Racial Space

In Chicago, prior to 1914, vice districts were some of the most integrated areas within the city. **Vice districts,** areas where "immoral" amusements predominated, were common in Progressive cities. These amusements were contained in saloons, dance halls, brothels, gambling establishments, and other licentious spaces. Progressive opposition to vice districts gave police the freedom to create racial segregation in Chicago neighborhoods.

Captain Max Nootbaar, of the Chicago Police Department, was tasked with cleaning up vice in the cafes and cabarets of Chicago in 1912. He issued an order prohibiting interracial socializing, dancing, and sex in the Black Belt neighborhoods on Chicago's South Side (the neighborhoods where black Chicagoans predominated). He then instructed his officers in the surveillance of the neighborhood, instituting regular and frequent foot patrols, rampant arrests, and the use of force against violators—common tactics first employed by slave patrollers. Nootbaar's success stemmed from his tapping into several political currents: Progressive definition of nonwhite spaces as the source of societies "problems"; anxiety about white womanhood in urban centers and a need to "protect" it from forces such as "white slavery"; and the definition of nonwhites as inherently licentious, immoral, and degenerate, thus able to lure and entrap white women.

By promoting whiteness as a sacred identity necessitating police protection, Nootbaar effectively transformed himself from a German immigrant into a white American. Rashad Shabazz notes, "Policing helped Nootbaar, a first-generation immigrant from Germany, shore up his own racial identity through reinforcing racist heteronormative masculinity. By placing boundaries around white women's sexuality and using policing as a tool to do so, Nootbaar was able to shed his ethnic identity and enter whiteness" (2015, 15). Nootbaar was one of many officers who used their identity as police to enter the world of whiteness. By providing this opportunity, the police force reinforced the racial state as a place where securing whiteness from the threat of the racial other was foundational. As we will see in more detail in chapter 7, this function of the police did not end with the Progressive Era but continues today. Critical to progressive era policing, however, was not just the function of patrol, but police collusion in white racial violence. While police are not today often regularly involved in *mass* violence against black communities, as Jay Ellis noted above, the campaign of racial violence that police initiated in the Progressive Era continues.

Police Collusion in Racial Violence

The backdrop to the intensive policing of leisure spaces where black and white people came together and the reason so many black business owners willingly complied was police collusion in white racial violence. Policing race in Progressive cities was not limited to the practices of patrol. Instead, police forces were often used to support and bolster attacks by white mobs against nonwhites. Progressive Era cities are riddled with historical examples of how police fostered and supported white mob violence. Police were implicated in white violence directed at black residents in New York; Evansville, Indiana; Springfield, Illinois; St. Louis, Missouri; and Chicago, to name a few. In St. Louis in 1917 for instance, one hundred black residents were killed by a white mob that had the protection and participation of the police.

In Progressive Era New York in 1900, Irish and black Americans were living in the same part of the city due to housing discrimination and the limited stock available to newly arriving immigrants. Both groups were poor, but the majority of the police force was Irish. A young black couple was walking when an Irish police officer accused the woman of being a sex worker. The man objected to this characterization and was subsequently beaten up by the police. Prompted by this single encounter, the police force spent the next few days beating black residents they encountered, injuring hundreds of black Americans and killing several. This violence was not uncommon in New York, as Irish animosity to African Americas was well-documented and even fostered by the elite (Flowe 2014).

In 1921 in Tulsa, Oklahoma, a group of whites attempted to lynch a nineteen-year-old black man. When the lynching failed, white mobs erupted into violence and set fire to the black neighborhood—1,256 homes and over 200 business were torched (Halliburton 1972). In response, the National Guard rounded up black residents and placed them in internment camps. White rioters continued their reign of terror, unimpeded by the police, by dropping kerosene and dynamite on the camps from airplanes, some of which were reportedly owned by the police. Some 300 people are estimated to have been killed in the violence. Nationwide, more than 3,700 people were lynched between 1889 and 1930, and not a single person faced prosecution for any of these crimes (Lieberson and Silverman 1965).

This violence also served the purpose of creating, solidifying, and physically marking the boundary between white and black to include many whites who had previously been excluded from the benefits of whiteness. It also firmly placed the police within the power of the white racial state.

The Riots of Red Summer

Following World War I, the increased competition for jobs, combined with the history of labor tensions between white and black people, led to what is known as the "red summer" of 1919 (McWhirter 2011). The riots began in Charleston, South Carolina, when white U.S. Navy sailors attacked a group of black men. Riots broke out in thirty-eight cities across the nation. In Chicago, police allowed white beachgoers to stone and drown a young man who accidentally drifted into the "white" section of water (Tuttle 1970). This led to more extensive rioting by whites, and in the end, over 1,000 black families had been left homeless, 537 people had been injured, and 23 black people and 15 white people had been killed. In Elaine, Arkansas, a white militia descended on a meeting of black sharecroppers and killed between 100 and 237 black people (Williams 2008). The local government brought charges, but against 79 black people who were all convicted by all-white juries. Twelve were sentenced to death and others received prison terms of up to twenty-one years.

During this wave of violence, nearly all victims and arrestees were black Americans. Police often played a critical role in both condoning and participating in the violence. Police permitted mobs to take control of black prisoners, released white prisoners who had been arrested for violence against black people, and even watched and aided in the violence. Local police in Bisbee, Arizona, even attacked an African American army unit, the Buffalo Soldiers (McWhirter 2011). Police refused to intervene when black people were being randomly beaten and pulled off streetcars in Washington, DC.

Police collusion in white racial violence provides an important demonstration of how Progressive Era reforms are also embedded within the practice and reproduction of the white supremacist racial state. Concerns about morality, debauchery, and crime were often the cover for creating, marking, and reinforcing the line between whites and other races in Progressive cities. While direct police participation in white racial violence might be a thing of the past, the reality is that police continue to focus on the same places and spaces they did during the Progressive Era: neighborhoods of color. And in doing so, the power of the racial state is revealed as the power to define social problems as the province of the marginalized and disenfranchised and deploy the tactics of state violence—in this case, police—in order to surveil, correct, contain, and ultimately eliminate this threat, which so happens also to be people.

CONCLUSION

At its inception, the United States initiated one of the crudest versions of the racial state: an explicit embrace and enfranchisement of whiteness in the form of slavery. Today, crude racial exclusions are considered unconstitutional and are not widely embraced. But the power of white supremacy continues on through the practices of racial hegemony that identify most social problems with poor and communities of color, often in cities. This singular focus unites both the crude racial state and the subtler one that exists today. It also demonstrates the power of the Progressive Era.

Progressive Era legislation represented an expert wielding of legal and state power to redefine the nation through whiteness. Immigration law represented an explicit attempt to define the nation through the mantle of whiteness, a practice that continued at the local level through the surveillance and control of urban spaces. Together, these tactics charted a new direction for state power that was more interventionist, regulatory, and ultimately, controlling of communities of color. This power continues today through the institutionalization of Progressive Era reforms in the juvenile court and the uniformed urban police.

Sydney Harring, a historian of the working class, wrote that the "criminologist's definition of 'public order crimes' come perilously close to the historian's description of 'working-class leisure-time activity'" (1983, 198). Urbanization and industrialization may have created a wage-labor working class, but without the development of Progressives and eugenicists, we may never have developed agencies to reinforce, re-create, and continue the racial state into today. Critical to this creation is the category of whiteness, a system of unearned advantage that results in less police surveillance and greater opportunity for some.

Whiteness as a construct was actively created and promoted by early Progressives. It was the basis for the creation of a Progressive morality and the exemplar of fitness for eugenicists. It defined the state interventions developed during the Progressive Era that are still with us. And it provided the basis for integrating some members of the working class into the racial state, while often violently and forcefully excluding others through the mechanisms of the juvenile court and the uniformed police. This history continues, as we shall see in the next chapter when we turn to the issue of housing and its regulation that stemmed from the industrial city.

REFERENCES

Abrams, Laura S., and Laura Curran. 2000. "Wayward Girls and Virtuous Women: Social Workers and Female Juvenile Delinquency in the Progressive Era." *Affilia* 15, no. 1: 49–64.

ACLU Tennessee. 2017. "ACLU-TN Statement on White County Inmate Sterilization and Birth Control Program." Press release, July 19, 2017. American Civil Liberties Union Tennessee. www.aclu-tn.org /aclu-tn-statement-on-white-county-sterilization-program/.

Addams, Jane. (1909) 1972. *The Spirit of Youth and the City Streets.* Reprint, Urbana and Chicago: University of Illinois Press.

Aizer, Anna, and Joseph J. Doyle Jr. 2015. "Juvenile Incarceration, Human Capital, and Future Crime: Evidence from Randomly Assigned Judges." *The Quarterly Journal of Economics* 130, no. 2: 759–803.

Ashkenas, Jeremy, and Haeyoun Park. 2015. "The Race Gap in America's Police Departments." *New York Times,* April 8, 2015. Retrieved July 17, 2017: https://www.nytimes.com/interactive/2014/09/03/us/the-race-gap-in-americas-police-departments.html.

Bell, Ernest Albert. 1910. *Fighting the Traffic in Young Girls; Or, War on the White Slave Trade, a Complete and Detailed Account of the Shameless Traffic in Young Girls.* Chicago: G. S. Ball. https://archive.org /details/fightingtraffici00bell.

Biles, Roger. 2010. *From Tenements to the Taylor homes: In Search of an Urban Housing Policy in Twentieth-Century America.* University Park, PA: Penn State Press.

Blumenthal, Thomas W., Paul C. Gannon, Scott A. Nathan, and Samuel Plimpton. 2002. *Race and Membership in American History: The Eugenics Movement.* Brookline, MA: Facing History and Ourselves. www .facinghistory.org/sites/default/files/publications/Race_Membership.pdf.

Bridges, George S., and Sara Steen. 1998. "Racial Disparities in Official Assessments of Juvenile Offenders: Attributional Stereotypes as Mediating Mechanisms." *American Sociological Review* 63, no. 4: 554–70.

Brown, Elizabeth. 2011. "The 'Unchildlike Child': Making and Marking the Child/Adult Divide in the Juvenile Court." *Children's Geographies* 9, no. 3–4: 361–77.

Browne, Simone. "Race and Surveillance." 2012. In *Routledge Handbook of Surveillance Studies,* edited by David Lyon, Kirstie Ball, and Kevin D. Haggerty, 72–75. New York: Routledge.

———. 2015. *Dark Matters: On the Surveillance of Blackness.* Durham, NC: Duke University Press.

Carter, Stephen. 2015. "Policing and Oppression Have a Long History." *Bloomberg News,* October 29, 2015. www.bloomberg.com/view/articles/2015–10–29/policing-and-oppression-have-a-long-history.

Chávez-García, Miroslava. 2012. *States of Delinquency: Race and Science in the Making of California's Juvenile Justice System.* American Crossroads 35. Berkeley: University of California Press.

Clapp, Elizabeth Jane. 2010. *Mothers of All Children: Women Reformers and the Rise of Juvenile Courts in Progressive Era America.* University Park: Pennsylvania State University Press.

Clement, Priscilla Ferguson. 1997. *Growing Pains: Children in the Industrial Age, 1850–1890.* Woodbridge, CT: Twayne Publishing.

Cochran, Joshua C., and Daniel P. Mears. 2015. "Race, Ethnic, and Gender Divides in Juvenile Court Sanctioning and Rehabilitative Intervention." *Journal of Research in Crime and Delinquency* 52, no. 2: 181–212.

Correll, J., B. Park, C. M. Judd, B. Wittenbrink, M. S. Sadler, and T. Keesee. 2007. "Across the Thin Blue Line: Police Officers and Racial Bias in the Decision to Shoot." *Journal of Personality and Social Psychology* 92, no. 6: 1006.

"The Counted: People Killed in 2016." 2016. *Guardian*. www.theguardian.com/us-news/ng-interactive/2015 /jun/01/the-counted-police-killings-us-database.

Currell, Susan. 2006. *Popular Eugenics: National Efficiency and American Mass Culture in the 1930s*. Athens: Ohio University Press.

Dewey, John. 2008. *1932: Ethics*. Introduction by Abraham Edel and Elizabeth Flower. Vol. 7 of *The Later Works, 1925–1953*, edited by Jo Ann Boydston. Carbondale: Southern Illinois University Press.

Dorr, Gregory Michael, and Angela Logan. 2011. "Quality, Not Mere Quantity Counts: Black Eugenics and the NAACP Baby Contests." In *A Century of Eugenics in America: From the Indiana Experiment to the Human Genome Era*, edited by Paul A. Lombardo, 68–94. Bloomington: Indiana University Press.

Du Bois, William Edward Burghardt, with Isabel Eaton. 1899. *The Philadelphia Negro: A Social Study*. Political Economy and Public Law 14. Philadelphia: Ginn for University of Pennsylvania.

Eberhardt, J. L., P. A. Goff, V. J. Purdie, and P. G. Davies. 2004. "Seeing Black: Race, Crime, and Visual Processing." *Journal of Personality and Social Psychology* 87, no. 6: 876.

Ewing, Walter E., Daniel E. Martinez, and Ruben Rumbaug. 2015. *The Criminalization of Immigration in the United States*. Special Report, July 2015. Washington, DC: American Immigration Council. www .americanimmigrationcouncil.org/sites/default/files/research/the_criminalization_of_immigration_in_ the_united_states.pdf.

Fader, Jamie J., Megan C. Kurlychek, and Kirstin A. Morgan. 2014. "The color of juvenile justice: Racial disparities in dispositional decisions." *Social Science Research* 44: 126–140.

Feld, Barry C. 1999. *Bad Kids: Race and the Transformation of the Juvenile Court*. New York: Oxford University Press.

Fiske, John. 1998. "Surveilling the City: Whiteness, the Black Man and Democratic Totalitarianism." *Theory, Culture and Society* 15, no. 2: 67–88.

Flowe, Douglas J. 2014. *"Tell the Whole White World": Crime, Violence, and Black Men in Early Migration New York City, 1890–1917*. PhD diss., Department of History, University of Rochester, New York.

Fogelson, Robert M. 1977. *Big-City Police*. Cambridge, MA: Harvard University Press.

Foucault, Michel. 2003. *"Society Must Be Defended."* Edited by Mauro Bertani and Alessandro Fontana. Translated by David Macey. Lectures at the Collège de France, 1975–1976, 3. General editors: François Ewald and Alessandro Fontana. English series editor: Arnold I. Davidson. New York: Picador.

Goubert, Jean-Pierre. 1989. *The Conquest of Water: The Advent of Health in the Industrial Age*. Cambridge, UK: Polity Press.

Guliani, Neema Singh. 2014. "How a Father Gets Deported for a Traffic Violation." Speak Freely, April 14, 2014. ACLU. www.aclu.org/blog/how-father-gets-deported-traffic-violation.

Greenblatt, Alan. 2014. "Rural Areas Lose People But Not Power." *Governing*, April 2014. www.governing.com /topics/politics/gov-rural-areas-lose-people-not-power.html.

Hagan, John, and Holly Foster. 2006. "Profiles of Punishment and Privilege: Secret and Disputed Deviance during the Racialized Transition to American Adulthood." *Crime, Law and Social Change* 46, no. 1: 65–85.

Halliburton, Rudia, Jr. 1972. "The Tulsa Race War of 1921." *Journal of Black Studies* 2, no. 3: 333–58.

Halloway, Kali. 2017. "Modern-Day Eugenics? Prisoners Sterilized for Shorter Sentences." *Salon*, July 28, 2017. www.salon.com/2017/07/28/modern-day-eugenics-prisoners-sterilized-for-shorter-sentences_ partner/.

Harring, Sidney L. 1983. *Policing a Class Society: The Experience of American Cities, 1865–1915*. New Brunswick, NJ: Rutgers University Press.

Howe, Frederic C. 1910. "A Golden Rule Chief of Police." *Everybody's Magazine* 22: 814–23. https://books .google.com/books?id=J2oXAQAAIAAJ&dq=fred%20kohler&pg=PA814#v=onepage&q&f=false.

Hyland, Shelley, Lynn Langton, and Elizabeth Davis. 2015. *Police Use of Nonfatal Force, 2002–11*. Washington, DC: Bureau of Justice Statistics, U.S. Department of Justice. www.bjs.gov/content/pub/pdf/punf0211.pdf.

Kelling, George L., and Mark Harrison Moore. 1989. *The Evolving Strategy of Policing*. Washington, DC: US Department of Justice, Office of Justice Programs, National Institute of Justice, 1989. www.innovations .harvard.edu/sites/default/files/114213.pdf.

Krase, Kathryn. 2014. "History of Forced Sterilization and Current U.S. Abuses." *Our Bodies, Ourselves*. October 1. www.ourbodiesourselves.org/health-info/forced-sterilization/.

Kurlychek, Megan C., and Brian D. Johnson. 2004. "The Juvenile Penalty: A Comparison of Juvenile and Young Adult Sentencing Outcomes in Criminal Court." *Criminology* 42, no. 2: 485–515.

Ladd-Taylor, Molly. 1997. "Saving Babies, and Sterilizing Mothers: Eugenics and Welfare Politics in the Inter-War United States." *Social Politics* 4, no. 1: 137–53.

Lee, Benjamin. 2017. "Insecure's Jay Ellis: Every Time I've Been Pulled Over, I Thought I Was Going to Get Killed." *Guardian*, July 20, 2017. www.theguardian.com/tv-and-radio/2017/jul/20/jay-ellis-insecure-interview-black-male-characters.

Leff, Mark H. 1973. "Consensus for Reform: The Mothers'-Pension Movement in the Progressive Era." *Social Service Review* 47, no. 3: 397–417.

Leonard, Thomas C. 2005. "Retrospectives: Eugenics and Economics in the Progressive Era." *The Journal of Economic Perspectives* 19, no. 4: 207–24.

Lieberson, Stanley, and Arnold R. Silverman. 1965. "The Precipitants and Underlying Conditions of Race Riots." *American Sociological Review* 30, no. 6: 887–98.

Lombardo, Paul A. 2008. *Three Generations, No Imbeciles: Eugenics, the Supreme Court, and Buck v. Bell.* Baltimore, MD: Johns Hopkins University Press.

Luibhéid, Eithne. 2002. *Entry Denied: Controlling Sexuality at the Border.* Minneapolis: University of Minnesota Press.

Mayer, Joseph. 1922. *The Regulation of Commercialized Vice: An Analysis of the Transition from Segregation to Repression in the United States.* New York: Klebold Press. https://archive.org/details/regulationofcomm00mayerich.

McWhirter, Cameron. 2011. *Red Summer: The Summer of 1919 and the Awakening of Black America.* New York: Henry Holt.

Merrill, Lilburn. 1914. "Are Bad Boys Bad?" *Work with Boys: Boys' Clubs of America* 14 (January–December): 249–53.

Meyerowitz, Joanne. 2009. "Transnational Sex and US History." *American Historical Review* 114, no. 5: 1273–86.

Mill, John Stuart. 1869. *On Liberty.* 4th ed. London: Longmans, Roberts, and Green. www.bartleby.com/130/.

Mumford, Kevin J. 1997. *Interzones: Black/White Sex Districts in Chicago and New York in the Early Twentieth Century.* New York: Columbia University Press.

Novak, William. 2012. "Making the Modern American Legislative State." In *Living Legislation: Durability, Change, and the Politics of American Lawmaking,* edited by Jeffery A. Jenkins and Eric M. Patashnik, 20–45. Chicago: University of Chicago Press.

Odem, Mary E. 1995. *Delinquent Daughters: Protecting and Policing Adolescent Female Sexuality in the United States, 1885–1920.* Chapel Hill, NC: University of North Carolina Press.

Paltrow, Lynn. 2003. "Why Caring Communities Must Oppose C.R.A.C.K/Project Prevention." *Journal of Law in Society* 5, no. 11: 11–117.

Platt, Anthony. 1969. "The Rise of the Child-Saving Movement: A Study in Social Policy and Correctional Reform." *The Annals of the American Academy of Political and Social Science* 381, no. 1: 21–38.

———. 1977. *The Child Savers: The Invention of Delinquency.* Chicago: University of Chicago Press.

Pliley, J. R. 2014. *Policing Sexuality: The Mann Act and the Making of the FBI.* Cambridge, MA: Harvard University Press.

Putman, John C. 2008. *Class and Gender Politics in Progressive-Era Seattle.* Reno: University of Nevada Press.

Reichel, Philip L. 1988. "Southern Slave Patrols as a Transitional Police Type." *American Journal of Police* 7, no. 2: 51–77.

Reilly, Philip R. 1987. "Involuntary Sterilization in the United States: A Surgical Solution." *Quarterly Review of Biology* 62, no. 2 (June): 153–70.

Riley, Jason. 2015. "The Mythical Connection between Immigrants and Crime." *Wall Street Journal,* July 14, 2015, www.wsj.com/articles/the-mythical-connection-between-immigrants-and-crime-1436916798.

Roth, Rachel, and Sara L. Ainsworth. 2015. "If They Hand You a Paper, You Sign It: A Call to End the Sterilization of Women in Prison." *Hastings Women's Law Journal* 26 no. 1: 7–49.

Rydell, Robert W. 2013. *All the World's a Fair: Visions of Empire at American International Expositions, 1876–1916.* Chicago: University of Chicago Press.

Schlossman, Steven. 1977. *Love and the American Delinquent.* Chicago: University of Chicago Press.

Selden, S. 2005. "Transforming Better Babies into Fitter Families: Archival Resources and the History of the American Eugenics Movement, 1908–1930." *Proceedings of the American Philosophical Society* 149, no.2 (July 2005): 199–225.

Shabazz, Rashad, 2015. *Spatializing Blackness: Architectures of Confinement and Black Masculinity in Chicago.* Urbana: University of Illinois Press.

Soloway, Richard A. 2014. *Demography and Degeneration: Eugenics and the Declining Birthrate in Twentieth-Century Britain.* Chapel Hill: University of North Carolina Press.

Stern, Alexandra Minna. 2005. "Sterilized in the Name of Public Health: Race, Immigration, and Reproductive Control in Modern California. *American Journal of Public Health* 95 no. 7: 1128–38.

Tuttle, William M. 1970. *Race Riot: Chicago in the Red Summer of 1919.* Vol. 82. Urbana: University of Illinois Press.

Vollmer, August. 1933. "Police Progress in the Past Twenty-Five Years." *American Institute of Criminal Law and Criminology* 24 (May-June): 161–75. https://scholarlycommons.law.northwestern.edu/cgi/viewcontent.cgi?article=2378&context=jclc.

Walker, Francis Amasa. 1899. *Statistics, National Growth, Social Economics.* Vol. 2 of *Discussions in Economics and Statistics.* New York: Henry Holt. https://catalog.hathitrust.org/Record/000204391.

Ward, Geoff K. 2012. *The Black Child-Savers: Racial Democracy and Juvenile Justice.* Chicago: University of Chicago Press.

Wells-Barnett, Ida B. 1969. *On Lynching: Southern Horrors* [1892], *A Red Record* [1895], *Mob Rule in New Orleans* [1900]. New York: Arno Press and the New York Times.

Williams, Kristian. 2015. *Our Enemies in Blue: Police and Power in America.* Oakland, CA and Edinburgh, UK: AK Press.

Williams, Lee E. 2008. *Anatomy of Four Race Riots: Racial Conflict in Knoxville, Elaine (Arkansas), Tulsa, and Chicago, 1919–1921.* Jackson: University Press of Mississippi.

Housing Inequality and the Geography of Residential Racial Segregation

LEARNING OUTCOMES

▶ Summarize the role of law and policy in creating the geographies of racial segregation both historically and today.

▶ Analyze the role of housing in white wealth accumulation.

▶ Describe the transition from legally mandated to private-market-driven racial segregation.

▶ Explain why segregation continues today and how it contributes to the issues of mass incarceration.

KEY TERMS

▶ Jim Crow laws
▶ neighborhood effect
▶ urban planning
▶ zoning
▶ exclusionary zoning
▶ expulsive zoning
▶ blockbusting
▶ restrictive covenants
▶ redlining
▶ white flight
▶ public housing
▶ urban renewal
▶ blight

In 1896, the U.S. Supreme Court decided *Plessy v. Ferguson*, a case challenging enforced racial segregation. Homer Plessy lived in Louisiana, which had passed a law mandating the separation between whites and "coloreds" in railway cars. Louisiana's Separate Car Act was one of a growing number of legal innovations for protecting white supremacy called Jim Crow laws.

Jim Crow laws emerged throughout the southern United States after the Reconstruction era and created a separate legal code specifically targeting nonwhites, especially black people and Native Americans. These laws also spread to the Southwest and the West Coast, where legal codes were used to mandate separation between whites and Mexican Americans and Chinese Americans. These laws prohibited and criminalized a vast range of behaviors, including racial intermarriage, "vagrancy," and "unemployment" (see chapter 4 on black codes). Laws also mandated racial segregation in education and public places such as restrooms, restaurants, and drinking fountains.

Plessy asked the court to consider whether these types of law violated the Equal Protection Clause of the Fourteenth Amendment to the Constitution. The court said no, reasoning that "the assumption that the enforced separation of the two races stamps the colored race with a badge of inferiority" was a "fallacy," and that if this reality emerged, it was not because of the "separate but equal" facilities but "because the colored race chooses to put that construction upon it." The *Plessy* decision codified an emerging approach to the state management of race in the United States—separation, containment, and exclusion—institutionalized through the idea of racial segregation.

Brown v. Board of Education in 1954 began the erosion of *Plessy*'s precedent, and the Civil Rights Act in 1964 formally struck down mandated public racial segregation. Yet the practice of separate but equal did not end in 1964. Instead, as a result of decades and centuries of racial wealth accumulation, racial segregation continues. Indeed, schools today are more segregated than they were at the time of *Brown* (Reardon and Owens 2014; Nowicki 2016). Many factors contribute to this, but one of the most important is the legacy of housing policy and the racial preferences that this continues to engender.

Though seemingly distinct, housing is a significant predictor of one's experience of crime. It shapes who is subject to heightened surveillance and policing, which is then reflected in crime rates justifying even more surveillance and policing. And it determines whether one has to navigate through crime networks and witness the routine application of police use of force. Housing is extremely consequential to the study of race and crime, and in this chapter, we trace how it created the intense racial residential segregation that facilitated the development of mass incarceration and the transformation of the racial state.

WHY IT MATTERS WHERE YOU LIVE

Think back to the neighborhood you grew up in. What was it like?

Neighborhoods construct our experience of the world and communicate to us. Our friends, our schools, and our professional aspirations are shaped by where we grew up. Our neighborhood also shapes our knowledge of the world and the forms we expect families, people, and the built environment to take. Our ideas of what makes "good" and "bad" neighborhoods are connected to our own experiences. The neighborhood where we grow up also, importantly, shapes our experiences themselves.

Neighborhoods and Life Experience

Neighborhoods affect experiences as different as health, employment opportunities, and access to financial services. Where you live determines how long you live, the quality of the air you breathe, your proximity to toxic waste sites, and your exposure to trauma and violence (Brooks and Sethi 1997). Depression, anxiety, and feelings of happiness are all affected by where you live.

Something as simple as air quality can have lasting consequences far beyond the experience of breathing itself. One study found that children living in impoverished New York City neighborhoods were three times as likely to be hospitalized for asthma as wealthy children (NYC Department of Health and Mental Hygiene 2003). In many cities asthma is the leading cause of missed school, emergency room visits, and hospitalization (Corburn. Osleeb, and Porter 2006).

When neighborhood residence makes some more likely to get asthma and other respiratory diseases, it makes those same people less likely to thrive in other ways. School and work days are missed due to illness, resulting in less academic and economic success. People with respiratory illness not only lose money by missing work but have to go to the doctor more often, resulting in yet more missed work time and greater health care costs. Visits to the emergency room are common, taking still more economic, health, and time tolls on afflicted residents. The cost of living in some areas is more than just the cost of housing, something demonstrated by the geographical distribution of crime.

Neighborhoods and Crime

Crime is a geographical phenomenon. People living in a poor neighborhood are more likely to be exposed to crime. This is not because poor people are more likely to commit crime—they most certainly are not. However, they *are* more likely to live in places where crime congregates. Marcus Felson describes the link between poverty and crime as shaped by land use:

> Poor people, having less money for rent and less chance to buy homes move to areas with nonresidential land uses[:] . . . shopping malls, commercial strips, warehouses, loading docks, parking lots and structures, tram yards, truck yards, factories, bars and taverns, medical facilities, and parking structures and lots, as well as wide and busy streets not under private supervision. These places provide more to steal and fewer people at night to watch things, as well as stragglers who are easy to attack (1994, 35)

Felson notes that these types of spaces pull people—most often nonresidents—who are looking for easy places to hide criminal activity or easy targets. These neighborhoods are also often central places for the market in stolen goods and thus further attract people looking to dump, sell, or chop stolen items. This leads to increased police surveillance of these neighborhoods, subjecting residents to greater control by police than their wealthier and whiter counterparts. Moreover, the crime rates we see are often the result of this increased surveillance, rather than different criminal propensities based on race and class, despite perceptions to the contrary.

The concentration of the policing of crime in some neighborhoods exposes children to several deleterious effects. Those who grow up in high-crime neighborhoods experience more negative interactions with police and are more often exposed to incidents of trauma related to crime—having a loved one killed or incarcerated, witnessing violent crime, and even seeing dead bodies at a young age. This often leads to skepticism of police (even though the majority of people in high-crime neighborhoods often support police and desire greater police protection) and criticism of public policies promoting increased incarceration in response to social problems.

By contrast, those who grow up in low-crime neighborhoods, which tend to be whiter, are often the most fearful of crime from "outsiders." It is not even necessarily true that these neighborhoods have less interaction with crime. Rather, crimes in these neighborhoods are often committed in private spaces and they often do not have the open-air markets for drugs and other illegal goods that are common in poorer, less white neighborhoods (Kennedy 2011).

The "Neighborhood Effect"

While the fact of neighborhood differences may be unsurprising, the strength of the **neighborhood effect,** as Robert Sampson (2012) calls it, is remarkable. Sampson, a Harvard sociologist who has long studied juvenile delinquency in Chicago, writes that despite changing policies, economic contexts, and political transformations, neighborhoods have an enduring effect on the lives of people who live in places of high residential mobility, concentrated poverty, and invidious racial discrimination. This effect leads some people and places to be regarded as more criminal by police, the public and policy makers.

This effect was illustrated in an experiment that was conducted by the federal Department of Housing and Urban Development (HUD) to see how neighborhood impacted outcomes for those living in poverty. HUD provided monetary housing assistance to some families in poor neighborhoods but relocated others to middle-class neighborhoods. The result? Increased student achievement, decreased health problems, and greater economic stability for the families who moved (Popkin et al. 2002). The study found that *just changing where a family lives* raises the level of scholastic achievement of children, reduces the likelihood of living in poverty as an adult, and increases the economic wherewithal for families. It also decreased exposure to the deleterious effects of crime management. Other studies have verified these results, demonstrating that where you live not only matters in the present but has enormous consequences for the future.

Perhaps unsurprisingly, race also maps onto neighborhood differences, and what Harvard sociologist William Julius Wilson (2012) called "landscapes of concentrated disadvantage" are present throughout the United States. These landscapes are places where unemployment rates are far higher than in the nation overall, where many men are under some sort of criminal justice supervision, and where women are incarcerated at much higher rates than average. These landscapes contrast with the landscapes of the middle class, where

Table 5.1   Neighborhood racial makeup for the average white, black, Asian, and Hispanic resident in the United States, 2010

	White neighbors (%)	Black neighbors (%)	Asian neighbors (%)	Hispanic* neighbors (%)	Other neighbors (%)
Average white resident	77	7	4	9	3
Average black resident	36	45	2	14	3
Average Asian resident	48	8	20	19	5
Average Hispanic resident	37	10	5	45	3

SOURCE: Frey, 2014, 189.

*The U.S. Census uses the term *Hispanic,* which is historically problematic due to its origination with colonial history and Spanish colonization. In the text, we use *Latinx,* but these terms refer to the same populations.

police find it "pleasant" to patrol and few residents have interacted with the criminal justice system, much less seen the violence of the criminal justice system in action. Our ideas of what make "good" and "bad" neighborhoods are thus situated within very different environmental experiences depending on where we live.

Where one lives is not a random accident or the result of choice or economic capability. Take the fact that poor white families are much more likely to grow up in a middle-class neighborhood surrounded by whites than are middle-class black families, who are much more likely to reside in poor neighborhoods (Massey and Denton 1993; Galster 2017). As table 5.1 shows, the average white resident grows up in a mostly white neighborhood, while the average black and Hispanic residents live in much more integrated neighborhoods. This happens despite preferences among racial groups to live in middle-class, integrated neighborhoods. So why do neighborhoods look the way they do? The answer, and why it matters to the study of race and crime, is the subject to which we now turn.

URBANIZATION, WHITE RACIAL VIOLENCE, AND THE RISE OF SEGREGATION

Many are surprised to learn that residential racial segregation did not emerge until years after slavery ended. Yet almost every major city saw increased racial segregation after the end of slavery, a trend that continued steadily in most major cities until the 1970s and in many Northern metropolitan areas still continues today (see table 5.2). The emergence of racial segregation was not an accident or by-product of industrialization but rather a concerted effort by

Table 5.2   Indices of black-white segregation in Northern cities, 1860–1970

City	1860	1910	1940	1970
Boston	61.3	64.1	86.3	79.9
Chicago	50.0	66.8	95.0	88.8
Cincinnati	47.9	47.3	90.6	83.1
Cleveland	49.0	69.0	92.0	89.0
Indianapolis	57.2	n/a	90.4	88.3
Milwaukee	59.6	66.7	92.9	83.7
New York	40.6	n/a	86.8	73.0
Philadelphia	47.1	46	88.8	83.2
St. Louis	39.1	54.3	92.6	89.3
San Francisco	34.6	n/a	82.9	55.5
Wilmington	26.1	n/a	83.0	n/a
Average	46.6	59.2	89.2	81.4

SOURCE: Massey and Denton, 1993, 21, 47.

NOTE: 100 would indicates complete segregation; 0 would indicate complete integration.

white Americans to separate themselves—racially, culturally, and geographically—from those they considered less than themselves. They did this through two predominant mechanisms: extralegal violence and formal law (which had its own violence as well).

In the late nineteenth century, it was common in the North for whites to provide the primary clientele for free black people; black attorneys, for instance, primarily depended on white clients. Even free black people in the South often subsisted because of the business of white clients. Immigration of Southern black people to Northern cities, however, brought about not only demographic shifts in the composition of cities but shifts in the tactics of racial management in northern areas.

Urbanization also had a second consequence: the tight quarters of the cities brought urban elites and immigrant communities physically closer together. This brought about considerable cultural and economic anxiety among white residents about their place in the social hierarchy and the potential disruption of the system of white supremacy that had marked the first hundred years of the nation. Consequently, race riots were common in Progressive U.S. cities as whites used violence, fear, and intimidation to ensure that nonwhite, especially black, communities—both poor and middle-class—were spatially contained. These events were critical for consolidating the idea of whiteness and for using fear and terror to create the white middle-class city.

Building White Supremacy in Wilmington, North Carolina

In 1898, Wilmington, North Carolina, was a relatively integrated urban community. During the decade before, the black population had expanded, eventually surpassing the white population, and black people frequented the same establishments as whites, managed and owned many thriving businesses, held political office (both appointed and elected), and lived in the same neighborhoods (Collins 2012, 36). White and black people served together in the police forces and the postal service.

Concern about the power of black people in North Carolina, however, led a group of nine white Democrats to meet secretly to "reestablish Anglo-Saxon rule and honest government in North Carolina." They cast black leaders as a "corrupting" influence on U.S. democracy, and black police officers were singled out as practicing unnecessary brutality against whites. White leaders suggested that if reforms were not enacted, violence would be "'rigidly and fearlessly performed' . . . even 'if we have to choke the current of the Cape Fear with carcasses'" (Collins 2012, 37).

Orators drew upon what are now common tropes in white supremacist discourse: the moral supremacy of whites, the threat of black masculinity to white femininity, and, importantly for this chapter, the impact of inaction to these supposed threats on property values. With an upcoming election, Democrats charged that any win by a populist or Republican candidate would surely spell race war, and to rile up anti-black sentiment, they gave out free food and whiskey at their rallies and meetings.

After the election, Democrats called for a meeting of all white men, where they unveiled a "Wilmington Declaration of Independence" that would completely disenfranchise black citizens and banish elected black leaders from the city. The following day Democrat leaders along with upwards of five hundred armed white men set out to expel black leaders from the city. Local militiamen who had been waiting in another part of the city soon joined the mob and a full hunt for any black person in the city ensued.

Overnight, black citizens left the city in droves, and Democrats seized power from the democratically elected mayor, aldermen, and chief of police. White and any remaining black political leaders from the Republican establishment were banished from the city and ordered never to return. By 1900, the black majority that had been established in 1890 was gone, Wilmington became a majority white city, and the proportion of whites would steadily grow. The Wilmington coup and massacre accomplished exactly what the secret nine set out to do: claim urban space as white space.

We might have expected Wilmington to have withstood the racial violence of the Progressive era, given its integrated urban political structures. Instead, it revealed the political power of white supremacy. Though ideas of race as biology were on the decline, the twentieth century saw the redefinition of the "racial problem" as one of property values, morality, and culture, organized around and through where people lived. The Wilmington massacre and mass expulsion shows the colonial power of the ideology of white supremacy to mobilize groups through specific types of knowledge about the "danger" and "threat" some pose, and then make this a geographical reality through the colonization and appropriation of space.

White Racial Violence and Remaking the City

White racial violence was central to remaking cities into the segregated geographies we know today. The violence chronicled in chapter 4 was often directed at neighborhoods, businesses, and homes that encroached on white space. For instance, in the Chicago riot, whites roamed the streets for days, attacking black people at will, but their violence was primarily directed at middle-class black people who lived in white neighborhoods. Chicago's violence quickly became targeted; the home and office of one black real estate agent was bombed seven times in one year. Chicago experienced fifty-eight bombings of black homes and offices between 1917 and 1921, a rate of one every twenty days.

After the torching of black neighborhoods in Tulsa in 1921 (1,256 homes and over 200 businesses destroyed), black citizens were rounded up the by the National Guard and put into internment camps. White rioters continued the reign of terror by dropping kerosene and dynamite on the camps. A white race riot in Longview, Texas, destroyed the black section of town, and in Omaha, Nebraska, more than 10,000 whites attacked black neighborhoods and stores, leading to occupation by federal troops.

Black citizens were not the only people targeted by this violence. Members of almost all nonwhite communities experienced brutal treatment. The genocide of Native Americans at the hands of settler colonialists is just one example of the common use of violence by white society, something we explored in detail in chapter 2. Other examples include the expulsion of Chinese-Americans (see chapter 6) and white riots against Mexican communities in the Southwest and California (see chapters 6 and 7). Unfortunately for the history of the United States, white racial violence against nonwhites is normal, sustained, and, through the modern criminal justice system, ongoing.

Each of these examples shows, however, how the campaign to "purify" the city and rid it of deleterious forces was also a push to remake the city in the image of middle-class, white ideals. Containment, exclusion, and violence all worked to demarcate white spaces and write race into the geography of urban areas. And the result of this violence was exactly that: the containment of black people, whether poor, middle, or upper class, in a small portion of the city, one that had to absorb newcomers as well. While white extralegal violence helped create this reality of racial segregation in Progressive Era United States, it was the force of formal legal mechanisms—themselves backed by the violent force of the law discussed in chapter 4—that carried this reality into the post-WWII era.

FORMALIZING WHITENESS: URBAN PLANNING AND THE EMERGENCE OF RACIAL RESIDENTIAL SEGREGATION

White racial violence accelerated the processes of urban transformation that produced racial segregation. Yet it was the practices of urban planning—a less obvious form of racial violence—in the Progressive Era that provided the foundation for the continuation of residential segregation throughout the twentieth century. As discussed in chapter 4, the industrial city at the turn of the century was ill-equipped to handle the influx of immigrants. Employers rushed to provide housing for them and erected cheap, often substandard, multifamily buildings. These tenements were extremely crowded and had little ventilation, natural light, or protection from noise. They often lacked access to sewer lines, bathrooms, and running water.

Terming these areas "slums," elites considered these communities a virus in the city, threatening to infect the health and longevity of white, middle-class citizens. Political, media, and social elites associated this virus not with the lack of infrastructure but with the moral and racial failings of poor, immigrant, and nonwhite residents.

To remedy the perceived threat of disease and societal degeneration, cities sought to isolate, contain, and quarantine poor residents. Urban governments established city planning departments in this pursuit, informed by newly emerging expertise in universities. Urban planning was heralded by Progressive Era elites, who wanted the city to reflect their sociocultural ideals. Proponents of **urban planning** encouraged cities to develop comprehensive plans to impose order: creating residential, business, and industrial zones; mandating the forms buildings, sidewalks, and the built environment could take; and creating arterial roads and enabling mobility through the city. Key to this process was preventing the development of slum areas and containing and eliminating existing ones.

Baltimore's Residential Segregation Ordinance

The story of residential segregation and urban planning began in Baltimore, which passed the first formal racial segregation ordinance in the country. From there, this legal innovation spread and was a common tactic in the organization of metropolitan areas across the United States. The justification was that racial segregation protected property values, revealing how individual capitalist wealth accumulation trumped the commitment to equal protection under law.

Baltimore represents one of the most important places for understanding the power of white supremacy in the twentieth century to remake urban landscapes. Today, it is often known as the place where rates of incarceration are far higher than other cities—or as the place where police officers took Freddie Gray on a "rough ride," killing him. At the turn of the twentieth century, however, its notorious racial history was just beginning, and its position as one of the most segregated cities was not yet secured. This was all to change in 1911, when Baltimore passed the first residential segregation ordinance in the country (Power 1983).

The path to the 1911 ordinance had begun much earlier, with elite urban reformers' concern about the impact of the development of "slum" areas on public health in the late 1800s. In 1903, the Baltimore Association for the Improvement of the Conditions of the Poor and the Charity Organization Society commissioned an investigation into the city's housing conditions (Kemp 1907). The culminating report used the growing ideologies of social science, public health, and the scientific method to investigate slums. The report concluded by entreating Baltimore to remedy rapidly developing slum conditions through city planning and removal of offending spaces.

The ensuing reforms did create greater public health regulations that arguably were beneficial to residents—such as requiring an individual water supply and toilets in every new apartment. But there was no plan or funding for retrofitting the existing housing stock with these amenities. Some reforms, like regular "sanitary inspections," applied *only* to housing where most black Baltimoreans lived—neighborhoods known as the "alleys"—leading to greater surveillance of the poor and nonwhite. These new requirements effectively rendered the alley apartments and housing of most black Baltimoreans condemnable and led the city to raze the predominantly black neighborhood in the city (Power 1983). Instead of remedying slum conditions, this action squeezed black residents into an even smaller portion of housing stock.

This also occurred at a time when the population of black Baltimore was increasing, resulting in even greater difficulties finding housing. Many were pushed into white neighborhoods in search of shelter. One such neighborhood was called Druid Hill. Figure 5.1's picture of Druid Hill was a piece of political propaganda used by Baltimore elites to demonstrate the threat that black residents seemingly posed to the geography of white supremacy. Druid Hill was where most of the black middle class in Baltimore lived, and it was on the eastern edge of the black neighborhood and butted up against an exclusive white neighborhood. It was also across the street from the "best" white girls public school (Power 1983).

Based on the transformation of Druid Hill, in July of 1910, a meeting was held and a petition circulated demanding that the mayor and city council "take some measures to restrain the colored people from locating in a white community, and proscribe a climate beyond which it shall be unlawful for them to go"

LOOK At These Homes NOW!

An entire block ruined by negro invasion.   Every house marked ''X'' now occupied by negroes.   ACTUAL PHOTOGRAPH OF 4300 WEST BELLE PLACE.

SAVE YOUR HOME! VOTE FOR SEGREGATION!

Figure 5.1 United Welfare Association postcard, 1915, encouraging a vote for mandated racial segregation in Baltimore, Maryland. Source: Courtesy of the Missouri History Museum, St. Louis, Race Relations Collection, 1914–1970, D02323.

(quoted in Power 1983, 299). Eventually, a law was drafted that applied to the entire city and mandated that neither black people nor whites could move to a block where over half the residents were of another race.

The then-mayor explained that "blacks should be quarantined in isolated slums in order to reduce the incidence of civil disturbance, to prevent the spread of communicable disease into nearby White neighborhoods, and to protect property values among the white majority" (quoted in Power 1983, 301). The city attorney further argued that the ordinance was constitutional "because of irrefutable facts, well-known conditions, inherent personal characteristics and ineradicable traits of character perculiar [sic] to the races, close association on a footing of absolute equality is utterly impossible between them, wherever negroes exist in large numbers in a white community, and invariably leads to irritation, friction, disorder and strife" (quoted in Power 1983, 300).

The two arguments proffered by Baltimore political elites were tropes common at the time to justify racial segregation and inequality. First, racial segregation was claimed to be actually *good* for the black community, to prevent both whites killing them and disease. Second, proponents feared declining property values, probably the most common reason whites cite for not wanting to live in integrated neighborhoods today. This paternalistic logic of protection, coupled with the logic of state racism, fueled housing policy for most of the twentieth century.

The Death of Mandated Residential Racial Segregation

Baltimore's residential segregation ordinance was quickly copied around the United States. Though Baltimore was the leader in publicly enforced racial segregation, it was Louisville, Kentucky's ordinance that proved constitutionally fatal to the idea. In 1915, Louisville passed a racial segregation ordinance copied almost verbatim from the first iteration of Baltimore's law. The NAACP immediately took action and challenged the law on both civil and criminal grounds. Municipal policing powers allow cities to draw up ordinances to shape the growth and expression of the city, but *Buchanan v. Warley* (1917) challenged whether these powers could mandate racial segregation (Rice 1968).

The Supreme Court's opinion ignored the history of racial segregation precedents, such as in *Plessy,* and instead interpreted the case as one about the abridgement of property. The court reasoned that police power could be limited when it violated the Fourteenth Amendment's promise of equal protection. However, the court did not interpret this case as a violation of the Fourteenth Amendment because of race, where the *Plessy* or *Berea College* decisions might have applied. In *Plessy,* the Supreme Court ruled that the state could legally segregate. In *Berea,* the Supreme Court ruled that the state could even mandate that integrated universities, such as Berea College, racially segregate. Instead, it argued that "the case presented does not deal with an attempt to prohibit the amalgamation of the races. The right which the ordinance annulled was the civil right of a white man to dispose of his property if he saw fit to do so to a person of color and of a colored person to make such disposition to a white person." By invoking the rights of property, the court argued that the Louisville ordinance went too far and violated the inalienable right to not only own property but also to use, occupy, and dispose of it as one saw fit. Protecting people's ability to profit from property but not protecting people from racial discrimination was ultimately the court's logic in overturning mandated racial segregation.

Zoning for Race

Despite the Supreme Court striking down mandated racial segregation ordinances, city councils continued to use policing powers to create racial segregation. They did this through the power of **zoning,** the process by which cities determine appropriate land uses. Lobbying by neighborhood associations led many city councils to implement zoning restrictions that created racial segregation.

Figure 5.2 "Hell's Half Acre" in Birmingham, Alabama. Famed photographer Lewis Hine described this 1910 photo for the National Child Labor Committee as "a row of disreputable houses at the edge of the mill settlement at Avondale. These houses harbor the scum of the negroes and whites of the vicinity, and are separated from the mill village by a shallow ditch, which gave Gov. Comer, owner of the mills, the excuse that they were not on the mill property when the question of their removal was taken to him a while ago. A prominent social worker told me that not only do the mill people patronize these resorts, but that the broken down mill girls end up in these houses and that there are, on court record, three cases within a year of girls under fourteen years of age ruined in Hell's Half Acre. Told me, that there are innumerable instances showing the bad moral influence of the cotton mill settlement." Source: Courtesy of the Library of Congress, LC-USZ62–84579.

To do so, city councils attacked the types of dwellings accessible to non-whites through the use of exclusionary zoning (Silver 1997). **Exclusionary zoning** is using the local power to regulate building stock and land uses in order to prevent certain types of uses and character. Cities "studied" the conditions of poor communities, found rampant vice, and responded by enacting zoning restrictions on multifamily units and apartment complexes, even outlawing them completely in some areas. Figure 5.2 comes from a report on the conditions of Avondale, a neighborhood in Birmingham, Alabama, described as a place with "three cases within a year of girls under fourteen years of age ruined in Hell's Half Acre." Drawing on narratives of urban and racial decline, cities around the nation limited building heights and corner grocery stores in an effort to thwart the development of low-income neighborhoods and foster neighborhoods of single-family homes (Baar 2007). Cities restricted the number of residents per square feet and even outlined what relationships the residents could have to one another. In San Francisco, for instance, only members of the immediate family one generation out could live together, with exceptions made only for live-in servants (San Francisco Planning Code §102.8). This barred multigenerational households common among the poor and recent immigrants.

Additionally, cities targeted hotels and rooming houses. By zoning neighborhoods as single-family-home residential, cities prohibited these types of businesses from taking root. Exclusionary zoning was accompanied by **expulsive zoning,** which expelled controversial land uses—industrial manufacturing centers, public works projects, and dumps—from "desirable" neighborhoods and located them in "undesirable" neighborhoods (Rabin 1989). This not only exposed the least enfranchised members of society to greater health hazards but also created systematic investment in white neighborhoods. As exclusionary and expulsive zoning accumulated in cities, white neighborhoods were desirable not just because of the systematic investment in them but because of their distance from undesirable land uses. This simultaneously created investment in white neighborhoods and systematic disinvestment in nonwhite ones.

Mandated residential segregation ended, but not residential segregation in general or the city's role in it. By interpreting mandated residential segregation as an issue of property rights, the Supreme Court crafted a rationale that would provide an even more enduring and insidious mechanism of racial segregation than public ordinances. Racial segregation would now be accomplished through the power of private individuals acting in their economic interests. Over the coming decades, the Supreme Court routinely protected these powers, providing a tangible material benefit to whiteness in the form of property and wealth accumulation.

THE POWER OF PRIVATE PROPERTY: RESIDENTIAL SEGREGATION AND PRIVATE INDIVIDUALS

Given the state of segregation today, it should be unsurprising that the end of public residential segregation laws in 1917 did not lead to more racially integrated housing during the twentieth century. Instead, the power of the private market combined with the federal government to create even more wealth accumulation in white communities. By contrast, nonwhite, especially black, communities experienced systematic disinvestment and disenfranchisement, and the power of geography served to stymie gains acquired through the political process.

Real Estate and Lending Practices

Blockbusting emerged at the turn of the twentieth century as a common practice among real estate agents. Blockbusting was a practice that profited off white racial fears and black economic exclusion. Demand for housing was high, while supply was tight. This positioned realtors to make considerable profits. In mixed neighborhoods, agents would go to white houses telling the owners of an impending "black invasion" and offering to buy the home quickly and easily. In this way, realtors were able to obtain homes for much less than their market value.

Once the neighborhood turned over, agents would subdivide the houses into multiple units. The units would be sold to members of the black community, who because of the short supply of available housing and Jim Crow laws criminalizing homelessness were desperate for any shelter. Now, however, the selling price for only a fraction of the home was exorbitant, particularly when compared to the rock-bottom price paid by the realtor (Orser 2015). This is how realtors "busted" the racial heterogeneity of many urban neighborhoods and turned blocks over to one racial group or another.

Though the national realty associations never explicitly endorsed blockbusting practices, in 1922 the National Association of Real Estate Brokers (NAREB) published principles that included the caution that "the purchase of property by certain racial types is very likely to diminish the value of other property", thereby encouraging realtors to guide clients to a particular racialized set of neighborhoods (Power 1983, 318). Until 1950, not engaging in blockbusting-type practices was considered a violation of the NAREB code of ethics, which stated: "The realtor should not be instrumental in introducing into a neighborhood a character of property or occupancy, members of any race or nationality or any individual whose presence will clearly be detrimental to property values in the neighborhood" (Guzman 1956, 14). Realtors' attempts to maintain and establish racial homogeneity in neighborhoods demonstrated how even without mandated residential segregation, racial division still flourished.

Realtors were also aided by private lenders, who often refused loans to black borrowers, thus keeping black families from settling into white neighborhoods through the mortgage process. When loans were offered, they often carried different terms and conditions than loans to similarly situated white debtors. Black loans were often not mortgages at all but "contracts" (Burns 2017). Contract loans were installment loans: A black family would pay a portion of the cost each month, in the same way someone who had a mortgage would. The difference, however, lay in ownership. Black families would not own any portion of the house until the house was entirely paid. Payments did not build housing equity. If the family had to relocate or missed a payment, their investment in the property evaporated.

Racially Restrictive Covenants

Neighborhood associations also acted to ensure that neighborhoods remained racially exclusive. Associations organized and raised funds in order to buy vacant houses or houses owned by black people in white neighborhoods to ensure that whites moved in and prevent racial turnover (Gotham 2000). Neighborhood improvement associations also enacted restrictive covenants to guard against the selling of property to undesirable residents. Racially **restrictive covenants** were defined in 1946 as "agreements entered into by a group of property owners, sub-division developers, or real estate operators in a given neighborhood, binding them not to sell, lease, rent or otherwise convey their property to specified groups because of race, creed or color for a definite period unless all agree to the transaction" (Silva 2009). Covenants barred owners from selling to whomever they chose, based on racial background, and often applied to entire neighborhoods or property developments. *Corrigan v. Buckley* (1926) ruled that since covenants were private contracts—supposedly entered into willingly by property owners—they were constitutional.

Restrictive covenants were widely adopted across the nation. In the city of Seattle, where fewer than half a million people lived in 1950, researchers found over 414 neighborhood-based racially restrictive covenants had been adopted between 1924 and 1948, covering over 90 percent of the city (Silva 2009). Chicago is estimated to have been 80 percent covered by restrictive covenants, and Los Angeles is estimated at 95 percent (Delaney 2010, 151; Avila 2014a). Racially restrictive covenants were widely adopted and used in almost every new development. Even residents of already existing neighborhoods organized covenants.

From Covenants to Redlining

The Supreme Court extended the power of racially restrictive covenants in the first half of the twentieth century by enforcing what is known as the "doctrine of changed conditions" (Delaney 2010). This doctrine allows property owners to sue other owners for recoupment of their losses when the conditions of the neighborhood change. This doctrine is often used, for instance, when the surrounding conditions of the neighborhood have changed such that restrictions on property use are no longer applicable. For instance, this might occur today when a property is contractually residential but the surrounding properties have all transformed into businesses. Until 1948, the Supreme Court contended that the settlement of black persons within a white neighborhood could create such a "changed condition." Indeed, in one famous case, Clara Mays and her family were forcibly expelled from their home when residents decided that the Mayses' arrival changed the racial conditions in the neighborhood. This was in spite of black families living on adjacent blocks.

Racially restrictive covenants were declared unconstitutional in 1948 in the case *Shelley v. Kraemer.* Yet by that point, almost a half century of wealth accumulation by whites, thanks to racially restrictive zoning, had occurred. Further, the practices of the various players in the private property market and the federal government in the post-WWII years ensured that racially restrictive covenants continued to be informally enforced well into the 1960s (Delaney 2010; Massey and Denton 1993; Silva 2009).

MASTER PLANNING WHITENESS: THE FEDERAL GOVERNMENT, HOUSING, AND THE SUBURBS

Prior to the 1930s, the federal government played very little role with respect to the housing finance market. If one wanted to buy a house during this time, often one had to provide a down payment of at least 50 percent, and the repayment period for the loan stretched over just five or ten years (Collins and Margo 2001). Today, it is common for buyers to put down little to nothing to buy a house and repayment terms often stretch over thirty years; some markets even provide fifty-year repayment terms. This considerable shift is due to the role the federal government played in the market during the Depression and the post-WWII era.

The Power (and Price) of Home Ownership

Prior to the 1940s, only about 40 to 50 percent of households owned their homes. At its peak in the early 2000s, that rate was almost 70 percent, and it has not dipped below 60 percent since the 1950s. A more granular look at rates of home ownership, however, reveals the power of race.

According to a 2011 survey, 73 percent of white families own their home, while just 45 percent of black families and 47 percent of Latinx families do (Misra 2015). Homes are an important source of wealth, especially for the middle class. Wealth is different than income; wealth is one's entire net assets. A family's wealth is the total of its assets minus its debts. Houses account for a great majority of wealth as they are an expensive asset. One study notes that "since 1983, for the richest 20 percent of U.S. households, the principal residence as a share of net worth has been around 30 percent. For the next 60 percent—most of us—housing has risen from 62 percent to 67 percent of total wealth" (Greeley 2013). Lower rates of home ownership mean less family wealth.

A report from Brandeis University found that in 2011, the median wealth of a white household was $111,146, while it was just $7,113 for black people, and $8,348 for Latinxs (Sullivan et al. 2015). Given that a majority of white wealth is held in property, the report found that the racial wealth gap would be reduced by over 30 percent if the racial gap in home ownership was eliminated. Even more, it found that if houses invested in by black families appreciated at the same rate as houses invested in by white families, then the wealth gap could decrease as much as 41 percent!

In contrast, eliminating the racial college-attendance-and-graduation gap would shrink the racial wealth gap between black and white households by only 1 percent. Equalizing the impact of a college education on one's future earnings across racial groups would decrease the racial wealth gap by an estimated 10 percent at most. Eliminating racial disparities in income would reduce the racial wealth gap by only 11 percent. While a home may be where the heart is, it also holds, for white families, the key to continuing their economic stability, wealth accumulation, and racial supremacy (Sullivan et al. 2015).

Redlining, Maps and a New Deal for Housing

New Deal reforms in the 1930s and post-WWII federal housing policies were instrumental in the accumulation of wealth in white households through home ownership. Federal policies lowered mortgage rates, required smaller down payments, provided longer terms, and insured private banks against default on home loans. In 1933, Congress created the Home Owners' Loan Corporation (HOLC), which refinanced mortgages to prevent a wave of foreclosures brought on by the Depression. The HOLC bought mortgages from private lenders and refinanced the loans by offering lower rates and longer time frames. Generally, the HOLC provided for fifteen-year loans, whereas commercial banks provided loans of three to six years, and building and loan associations offered only ten-year terms. The federal government also created the Federal Housing Authority (FHA), the Federal Savings and Loan Insurance Corporation, and the United States Housing Authority.

From their creation, these federal agencies played an instrumental role in creating and continuing racially segregated residential communities. In the 1930s, the HOLC produced a series of "residential security maps" for all U.S. cities with more than 40,000 people. These maps color-coded the risk each area of a city presented for private mortgage investment; places that were considered highest risk were colored red, hence the term **redlining** (see figure 5.3). The HOLC defined four grades of city space: green, blue, yellow, and red (Hillier 2003). Only loans offered on properties in green or blue spaces were insured by the federal government, which made them much more attractive for private lenders.

The HOLC defined each color with a range of demographic and built environment characteristics that prioritized racial homogeneity, new construction, and "well-planned" communities. Green areas were "well-planned sections of the city," "homogeneous" and "in demand . . . in 'good times' or 'bad.'" Blue areas were "like a 1935 automobile still good, but not what the people are buying today" (quoted in Goldberg 2009, 72).

Yellow and red areas, however, were places the urban planning experts of the early twentieth century warned against. Yellow areas were "characterized by age, obsolescence, and change of style; expiring restrictions [i.e., racially restrictive covenants] or lack of them; *infiltration of a lower grade population;* . . . as

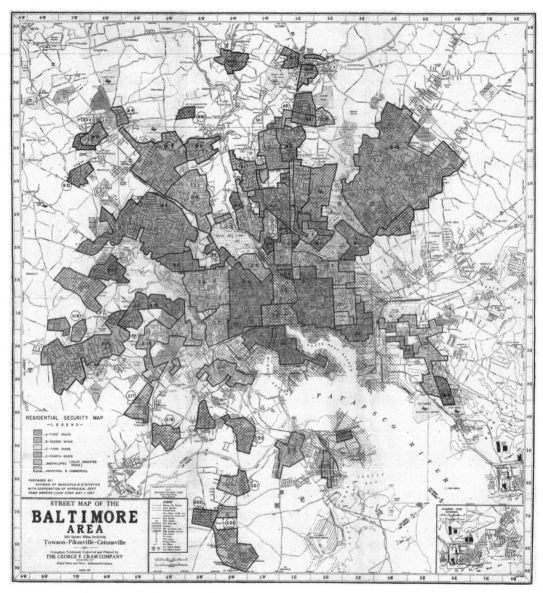

Figure 5.3 Residential security map of Baltimore, Maryland, 1937. Source: HOLC, Division of Research and Statistics, via Johns Hopkins Sheridan Libraries.

Examining Racial Segregation Historically and Today

Ever wonder why your neighborhood looks the way it does? After you've read about the federal policies that created racial segregation in the United States, it should be clear that many of the neighborhoods we grew up in are implicated within this history.

To learn more, visit the Testbed for the Redlining Archives of California's Exclusionary Spaces at http://salt.umd.edu/T-RACES/. Under the Regional Redlining link, check out the before-and-after maps of racial segregation. You can also visit the Demo link to peruse the residential security maps and urban redevelopment ratings for various neighborhoods in California and North Carolina. Choose a neighborhood to explore in greater detail. How is the neighborhood you chose characterized? How are race and class assessed in the neighborhood? Can you see the legacies of these maps within the built environment of the neighborhoods by looking at satellite imagery on Google Maps? Were you surprised by any of the documents related to your chosen neighborhood?

Next, choose a neighborhood that was rated differently than the one you initially chose. How do the residential security maps and urban redevelopment documents compare to the place you initially chose? How were race and class represented in these areas? Can you see this in the built environment or the reputation of the neighborhood? How do you think these two different places impact the futures of residents?

Finally, visit maps at socialexplorer.com and map the racial distribution of your chosen neighborhoods. Has the racial makeup of the neighborhood changed over time? If so, how? If not, what do you think accounts for its stability? Can you see similarities between how these neighborhoods were represented by urban redevelopers and how they are represented in the popular press today? This will require a bit of internet sleuthing at newspaper databases like proquest.com.

Source: R. Marciano, D. Goldberg, and C. Hou, T-RACES: A Testbed for the Redlining Archives of California's Exclusionary Spaces, n.d., accessed December 4, 2017, http://salt.umd.edu /T-RACES.

well as *neighborhoods lacking homogeneity*" (quoted in Goldberg 2009, 72–73, emphasis added). Red areas were the future of yellow areas and "characterized by detrimental influences in a pronounced degree, undesirable population or infiltration of it." Red areas were not just the slum areas but also those areas adjacent to them—which were often the only places outside of the slum where middle-class or more affluent nonwhites could reside. These were the neighborhoods of undesirable populations, who threatened the supremacy of whiteness in the urban landscape. Though these classifications are no longer used, they still shape the composition of neighborhoods (see box 5.1).

The FHA and the Birth of the Suburbs

The Federal Housing Authority (FHA) used these color codes of urban space to guide financing loans, insuring mortgages, and determining interest rates. Importantly, this meant that if the FHA insured a particular mortgage, there was virtually no risk for the bank. The guidelines, in addition to favoring whites, new construction, and planned neighborhoods, also favored single-family homes. Loans to fund renovation were not insured by the FHA, and many found it cheaper to buy new houses than renovate older ones, leading to further deterioration and disinvestment of urban housing stock.

The FHA Underwriting Manual also explicitly recommended "prohibition of the occupancy of properties except by the race for which they are intended" and insisted that houses not be sold to "inharmonious racial and nationality groups" (quoted in Shu 2015). For these reasons, the FHA manual recommended deed restrictions:

> Deed restrictions are apt to prove more effective than a zoning ordinance in providing protection from adverse influences. Where the same deed restrictions apply over a broad area and where these restrictions relate to types of structures, use to which improvements may be put, and racial occupancy, a favorable condition is apt to exist. Where adjacent lots or blocks possess altogether different restrictions, especially for type and use of structure and racial occupancy, the effect of such restrictions is minimized and adequate protection cannot be considered present. (FHA Underwriting Manual, sec. 228, quoted in McGann 2014)

FHA underwriters thus set in place a system of racial segregation, where strict divisions between places were necessary for "adequate protection."

While redlining maps were produced in the 1930s, the 1940s and 1950s saw the creation and expansion of "green areas" through the development of the suburbs. At the end of WWII, there was both pent-up demand for housing and lack of sufficient investment in it to provide for the growing middle class. Returning young servicemen also desired to start families and settle in housing of their own, and the federal government created low-interest loans specifically for veterans, called Veterans Administration loans.

In 1948, Congress passed the Housing Act, which stimulated production of private real estate development. This act guaranteed loans for builders but made no provision for low-income borrowers or housing revitalization. This act, along with the FHA underwriting guidelines, meant that the United States embarked on real estate development on an unprecedented scale, transforming rural and agricultural land into planned residential communities.

Given the FHA underwriting guidelines' preference for new construction and planned communities far from undesirable elements, real estate development concentrated on the outskirts of metropolitan areas, in what are known today as the suburbs. It should be no surprise that suburbs developed into predominantly white neighborhoods, with single-family homes and with planning that emphasized separation between residential and commercial uses, much like the popular representation of suburbs today. Developers even had to commit to excluding black people from these neighborhoods in order to secure federal insurance and financing (Shu 2015). Most of these developments both explicitly and implicitly gave preference to white residents and denied access to brown and black Americans.

Levittown: Planning Whiteness in Suburban New York

One of the most archetypal and famous suburban towns that emerged during this time is Levittown, on Long Island. Little more than potato fields in 1940, by 1951 this site had 17,447 new houses. Levittown's fame started right from the outset of development, and it was frequently featured in housing stories in New York newspapers. Commercials lauded the modern efficiency of Levittown, with each new home boasting a refrigerator, washer, and dryer. The community was marketed as a homogeneous neighborhood, with little individuality from home to home, making life supposedly predictable, stable, and safe (see figure 5.4). Unlike the pestilence brought by living in substandard housing in many urban neighborhoods, suburban living promised the Progressive and eugenic vision of modern society: single-family homes, separation from boarders and tenants, private outdoor space in backyards, and uniform regularity in the homes, the landscapes, and perhaps even more importantly, the people.

Levittown was based on a "master plan that plotted the location of virtually every sapling, screw, and shingle," fulfilling the builder's vision for "the most perfectly planned community in America" (State Museum of Pennsylvania 2003). Instead of the chaos of the city with its "unsightly commercial districts" and haphazard development, Levittown was the culmination of Progressive urban planning.

In Levittown, each social function had a space, separated from the other parts of the community. "Master blocks" clustered residences around community activity centers; churches were along the main parkway; schools were placed inside residential blocks in order to ensure that children did not walk far or cross major streets to attend; and large, separated shopping centers, with ample parking and bucolic landscaping, beckoned drivers. Each house had standardized features, including modern appliances, often expandable attics, and in later models, two-car garages. Landscaping was standardized, and each house received the same number of trees, plants, and shrubs. One commentator at the time remarked, "Your first impression . . . and it stays with you . . . is one of quiet, spacious beauty. The gently curving streets with modern lighting are uncluttered by cars. . . . Everywhere you look, your eyes rest on the loveliness of well-kept lawns, majestic shade trees, fruit trees and flowering shrubs" (State Museum of Pennsylvania 2003).

Figure 5.4 Levittown house. Note the manicured landscaping, single-family homes, and strictly residential zoning. Source: Courtesy of the Library of Congress, LC-G613–72793.

Levittown's vision was set against another vision equally as strong—the vision of the city as a place of degeneration, undesirables, and instability. The *Saturday Evening Post* said of Levittown in 1954 that "everybody lives on the same side of the tracks. They have no slums to fret about, no families of conspicuous wealth to envy, no traditional upper crust to whet and thwart their social aspirations" (State Museum of Pennsylvania 2003). To avoid deterioration, the developer himself inspected homeowners' gardens in the early years and distributed information on how to care for the plants to each new homeowner. The bucolic façade of Levittown, however, was not created by only master planning and landscaping. Ultimately, an important part of Levittown's homogeneity was its racial makeup. This model was so successful that the developer branched out, creating a second Levittown in Pennsylvania as soon as construction in New York was completed.

Every contract for a Levittown house prior to 1948 contained a "whites only" clause, that stated the house "could not 'be used or occupied by any person other than members of the Caucasian race'" (Lambert 1997). When racial covenants were overturned in 1948, Levittown continued informally barring non-whites. Though some protested these racial restrictions, when William and Daisy Myers, a black couple with three small children, attempted to move in to the Levittown community in Pennsylvania in 1957, white mobs again used violence and intimidation to thwart integration. These tactics of racial management ensured that as late as 2000, both Levittown, Pennsylvania, and Levittown, New York, remained over 94 percent white.

Levittown's creation of white suburbia was hardly unique, and nonwhites trying to move into suburbs across the United States had similar difficulty. In

Figure 5.5 Concrete wall in Detroit, Michigan, separating a black neighborhood from a new suburban development for whites, August 1941. Source: Farm Security Administration–Office of War Information Collection, courtesy of the Library of Congress, LC-USF34-063680.

Detroit, black families seeking housing often ended up creating small homes on the outskirts, where the city had yet to extend infrastructure, such as paved roads and water and sewer lines. In 1941, a developer sought to build a suburban development for white families just west of this area. However, the presence of the black neighborhood meant he would be unable to secure FHA funding. The solution? Build a wall. What today is a common trope for the violent exclusion of "undesirables"—a wall—was in suburban Detroit a sign that at least one community (the white one) was certified secure and desirable by the federal government. The developer erected a half mile-long structure that has come to be known as by some as Detroit's Wailing Wall (see figure 5.5). After the wall was built, the FHA agreed to insure the mortgages of white residences in the new housing development (Lee 2016).

White Flight

The movement of whites from the city has come to be known as **white flight** and marks the creation of a new era of metropolitan racial segregation. Nonwhites became concentrated in the city, while whites occupied the surrounding suburbs. Discussions of the "inner city" and its notoriety (see chapter 6) invoke this racial geography. The color-coded mapping system initiated by the HOLC and used by the FHA to determine housing financing created a system of racial valuation that systematically invested in white families and communities, while systematically undervaluing racially mixed and nonwhite neighborhoods. Communities with predominantly nonwhite residents almost never received loans, and suburban communities were prized and valued above those in the central city. The suburbs around St. Louis, for example, received almost five times as many FHA loans and six times as much dollar investment as the city itself, despite St. Louis having a much larger population. Between 1945 and 1959, black families received only 2 percent of FHA loans (Hanchett 2000).

Given the federal government's focus on promoting new construction rather than home repair, housing stock in the city suffered a steep decline. White flight also emptied the city of prosperous residents whose tax dollars and property investments had buoyed urban economies. With white flight, the tax base of most industrial cities declined. Together, white mob violence, the formal and informal policies and practices of real estate, and the logics of capital accumulation led to a new geography of racial segregation: whites in suburban American and nonwhites left behind in disinvested—and soon to be deindustrialized—urban spaces.

Transporting Whiteness: Freeway Construction and the Decline of Black Neighborhoods

Federal authorities further invested in white suburban spaces through freeway construction with passage of the Federal Aid Highway Act of 1956. The act paid for upwards of 90 percent of the cost of freeway construction ("Roads to Somewhere" 2006). New suburban residents needed a way to get to urban centers of employment, and state authorities cut through the heart of poor communities—under the guise of slum clearance—to make this happen (Rothstein 2017). Recognizing that freeway construction would lead to displacement, the Bureau of Public Roads in 1939 declared that "there exists at present around the cores of the cities, particularly of the older ones, a wide border of decadent and dying property which has become, or is in fact becoming, a slum area." Land acquisition in these areas and subsequent slum clearance for highway construction and urban redevelopment would result in "the elimination of unsightly and unsanitary districts where land values are constantly depreciating" (Mohl 2002, 6).

Constructing freeways meant repurposing city space—and across the United States, this offered the opportunity to remake the city, just as nine Democrats did in Wilmington, Delaware at the turn of the twentieth century. Arguments about the threat that dilapidated housing and blighted urban conditions posed to urban development led cities to raze black neighborhoods, supposedly for the betterment of all. In Baltimore, for instance, the city condemned a black neighborhood for freeway development on the basis of its being a slum. The freeway was never built, but the city created a fashionable district for gentrifying whites to occupy (Mohl 2002).

Across the country, low-income housing was destroyed in order to build freeways and never replaced, despite a housing availability crisis. Given the political disenfranchisement of black communities, resistance to these plans was often futile, in contrast to wealthier white communities that succeeded in rerouting federal freeway construction through black neighborhoods and out of theirs (Mohl 2002). In some communities—such as Nashville, Charlotte, Atlanta, and Kansas City—city planners even worked with white supremacist organizations to determine freeway placement (Avila 2014b). Black and brown communities were often divided by a freeway and then subjected to political redistricting that further diluted the residents' political power (Avila 2014a).

Federal investment in housing in the post-WWII era was also an investment in a particular geography of race and a vision of the planned community where homogeneity, uniformity, and white middle-class values reigned. Through investment in housing, the federal government created an important system for the intergenerational transfer of wealth based on race. Indeed, the federal government did not just invest in the postwar generation but in generations to come. Rising equity in white suburban homes, made more valuable by suburbanization, provided the funds for many children of the first suburban residents to attend college. Without the ability to attend primary and secondary schools in federally subsidized areas, these white students would not have had an academic advantage over those who attended schools in disinvested urban centers. Furthermore, without the benefits that come from living within a wealthier and white community—higher-performing schools and higher educational outcomes; access to wealth, better food and housing; and greater eventual earning power—the intergenerational transfer of wealth could not have happened.

At the same time the federal government was investing in suburban communities, it was investing in urban ones—yet the net effects of these investments look very different and contributed not to the upward mobility of citizens but rather to their downward mobility. In contrast to the creation of suburban America, this is the story of what is called urban renewal.

URBAN RENEWAL

Federal support for slum clearance emerged from the uneasy coalition between two opposing groups of housing reformers in the 1930s. On the one hand, there were social workers who worked in tenements and slums who advocated their clearance for the moral and physical health of the poor. They desired poor neighborhoods to be replaced with alternative housing stock. On the other side were urban-planner housing reformers who argued that slum clearance would likely only diminish existing housing and advocated creating housing for the poor on the outskirts of the city. These two camps converged in 1934 by agreeing that "slum clearance was an important goal of their movement but that, as a practical matter, inner-city land cost too much to be the first choice for sites to develop new housing" (Von Hoffman 2000, 302).

By privileging slum clearance, housing reformers made way for a radical reorganization of city space through the creation of public housing. **Public housing** is housing provided by state agencies and is generally provided to low-income residents at little or no cost. By emphasizing the construction of new housing, often away from slum areas, reformers also laid a foundation for segregating the poor in isolated parts of the city, often in cheap, poorly made but new housing. This resulted in the concentration of poverty and the isolation of poor communities. Further, it contributed to an image of these communities as part of an underclass. Public housing developments were defined as places with high rates of dependency, criminal wrongdoing, and other immoral behaviors, a notoriety that continues today. Over the coming decades, the Progressive idea that these issues stemmed from the culture of the poor took root, ignoring the systemic violence that created variegated neighborhoods in the first place (Wilson 2012). Without public housing isolating the poor into what came to be called "vertical ghettos" and slum clearance ensuring that vestiges of a multiracial urban past were scrubbed from the built environment, the emergence of mass incarceration, as we show in the next chapter, might never have come to pass.

Slum Clearance

Slum clearance officially became a federal priority with the passage of Housing Act of 1937, which established a public housing authority. As part of that authority, the law required that "one slum unit be demolished for every public housing unit built" (Von Hoffman 2000: 302). The 1937 act, however, never realized its promise as funding was cut off for public housing from 1938 until 1949. City officials, however, pressed ahead to remove these areas from city space. Although the vehicle of public housing failed to achieve slum clearance, the process surged ahead under the auspices of urban redevelopment.

Urban redevelopment was not just a government program, but was actively promoted and advocated by private developers. The National Association of Real Estate Brokers (NAREB), the professional association of realtors, began advocating in 1941 for cities to acquire slums through eminent-domain processes and then sell them to developers at below-market prices (Von Hoffman 2000, 304). Eminent domain is the power of the federal government to take private property for public use. While the federal government failed to act until the end of the 1940s, during that decade twenty-five states passed urban redevelopment laws aimed at eradicating slums from city centers. Two states subsidized slum clearance projects directly.

Stuyvesant Town

One early redevelopment project was Stuyvesant Town in Manhattan. With support from the New York Urban Redevelopment Act of 1943, the Metropolitan Life Insurance Company (MetLife) carried out a massive redevelopment scheme that demolished eighteen blocks of housing and other buildings.

Twenty thousand residents were displaced during the construction, and when the new 24,000-unit housing complex was opened, the rents were twice what previous residents had paid.

As part of the development deal, MetLife received a twenty-five-year property tax break and when the break ended, the tax rate was based on the "blighted" valuation of the site. The state also guaranteed MetLife a profit of at least 6 percent each year (Von Hoffman 2000, 303–4). Though Stuyvesant Town stemmed from activists' desires to see greater housing for poor and racial minorities, it opened its doors only to white residents. Black former residents were offered housing in a much smaller complex developed by MetLife in Harlem. Courts found that MetLife, as a private developer, was entitled to racially discriminate among its residents. This permitted private development to systematically reorganize the racial landscape of New York City and helped to further establish Harlem as a black neighborhood.

Slum Clearance versus Public Housing

With the passage of the Housing Act of 1949, housing advocates finally achieved legislation that would, as the synopsis of the act put it, "provide Federal aid to assist slum-clearance projects." While the act also aided public housing projects "initiated by local agencies," the public housing provisions merely reauthorized previous legislation that had gone unfunded for years. The crux of the act was the $1 billion in loans allocated to cities to acquire slum land and another $100 million per year for five years for "write-downs" between the cost of the land and the reuse value. As a result, the 1949 act initiated a process of large-scale urban transformation throughout the nation.

In 1954, urban redevelopment was renamed **urban renewal** and the federal government began allowing rehabilitation and conservation of existing structures. It further provided for relocation of displaced residents and citizen participation in renewal planning. While these revisions to the mechanisms of slum clearance offered some protections for residents, they provided mostly for the defense of white neighborhoods against the incursion of redevelopment projects like freeways (Mohl 2002). Neighborhoods of color often faced a far different fate, which is why James Baldwin famously dubbed urban renewal "negro removal."

"Negro Removal" and San Francisco's Fillmore Neighborhood

Cities around the nation have stories of how urban renewal transformed city spaces to the detriment of communities of color and the poor. San Francisco's Fillmore neighborhood provides just one example of these schemes, and demonstrates the limits of citizen participation in the urban renewal planning process. The population of black families in San Francisco's Fillmore neighbor-

Figure 5.6 Advertisements for San Francisco redevelopment, "reclaimed from blight." Source: Mel Scott, 1947, *New City : San Francisco Redeveloped* (San Francisco: City Planning Commission), https://archive.org/details/newcitysanfranci1947scot.

hood grew 1,000 percent between 1940 and 1950, since it was one of the few areas of the city without restrictive covenants. Two-thirds of the area's residents had been white in 1940, but white flight in the 1940s and 1950s led to a steady decline of whites in the neighborhood. This was the very same neighborhood that had housed a large number of Japanese residents, who had been emptied from city space due to forced incarceration—called internment—during World War II.

San Francisco political elites began complaining about blight in the Western Addition, a large neighborhood encompassing the Fillmore, in the late 1940s. **Blight** is a word planners often use to refer to neglected urban areas. According to the city, the Fillmore would be "reclaimed from blight" by a redevelopment plan and "replanned and rebuilt" into "one of San Francisco's most attractive residential areas," presumably populated by white families (Scott 1947; see figure 5.6). Inside the booklet, a white couple dressed in business attire looks over the city with the caption "You get a view of tomorrow from this San Francisco apartment [planned with urban renewal]" (Scott 1947, 1). This racialized vision of urban renewal ignored how the Fillmore was the primary place that newly arriving black residents to the city could find housing and, thus, formed the majority of people who were supposed to be served by the plan's vision.

Over the next two decades, San Francisco turned this vision into reality. In the classification of the city to determine which areas should undergo renewal, San Francisco graded the city on its deviations from an imagined white, middle-class, suburban geography (Opperman 1955). Penalties were assigned for the "absence of setbacks from front and rear lot lines" and "deterioration." Neighborhoods were similarly penalized for having apartments of less than 300 square feet, for "deficiencies in neighborhood facilities," and for high traffic. These descriptions of blight in the city were accompanied by a similar grading of occupants, with "high penalties for overcrowding and monthly rent under $40" and the number of new residents. The city even rated the nonwhite population and assigned penalty points to any neighborhood where the nonwhite population exceeded 2.4 percent, with any neighborhood over 29.6 percent receiving the largest penalty (see figure 5.7). After entire city blocks were razed for the purposes of urban renewal, even many decades later, they were little more than parking lots (see figures 5.8 and 5.9).

By the time housing was completed in 1985, almost two decades later, most residents had moved on and even if they had remained, they likely could not afford the new luxury apartments. By the lowest estimate, at least 10,000 black people had moved out of the area. Though the first phase of the project created 2,009 units of housing, only a third was set aside for low- and moderate-income residents. The director of the resident-founded and housing-act-mandated Western Addition Community Organization concluded: "In the end, urban renewal became what we feared it would: it became black removal" (Stein 1999).

Urban Renewal around the United States

Between 1949 and 1968, the federal government approved 1,946 urban renewal projects in 912 communities. Urban renewal in Kansas City tore down a number of buildings associated with jazz and African Americans in the city. Pittsburgh, Pennsylvania, used urban renewal to tear down a multiracial neighborhood, uprooting and displacing more than 5,000 families. Boston officials cleared forty-eight acres of a poor Italian American community to make way for a private developer to build luxury housing (Von Hoffman 2000). Los Angeles cleared thousands of Mexican American families from the Bunker Hill area, razed the area, and eventually gave the land to the Los Angeles Dodgers for construction of a baseball stadium (Mohl 2002). Urban renewal efforts were bolstered by the Supreme Court, which ruled many times that public entities could use the power of eminent domain for the actions of private developers.

4. <u>Non-white population</u> (no plate)

    <u>Source</u>: 1950 Census of Population

    <u>Scoring</u>: Non-white percentage of total population was scored. Non-white occupancy is high in areas of poor housing. The median for the city is 2.4 per cent and the average is 11.7.

<u>Reading</u>	<u>Penalty points</u>
Non-white, % of total	
0 - 2.4	0
2.5 - 11.6	1
11.7 - 29.6	2
29.7 - 98.7	3

5. <u>New residents</u> (no plate)

    <u>Source</u>: 1950 Census of Population

    <u>Scoring</u>: The per cent of the total of new residents, reported with a 1949 residence in a different county or abroad, was scored. The median for the city is 5.4 per cent. This item identifies areas with newcomers or transients and a high turnover of residential occupancy.

<u>Reading</u>	<u>Penalty points</u>
New residents, % of total	
0 - 5.4	0
5.5 - 7.2	1
7.3 - 44.4	2

20.

Figure 5.7 San Francisco neighborhood ratings example. Source: *Housing and Neighborhood Conditions in San Francisco: A Classification of Areas for Urban Renewal,* 1955 (San Francisco: Department of City Planning), https://archive.org/details/housingneighborh1955sanf.

A 1966 National Commission on Urban Problems survey noted that out of 1,155 urban renewal projects, 67 percent were residential before urban renewal, but only 43 percent were residential after. This net loss in housing was further compounded by the fact that most new residences were too expensive for the residents displaced. The attempt to solve the problem of housing ended up exacerbating these very conditions. By 1967, 400,000 residential units had been demolished nationwide, but only 10,760 of the housing units replacing them were affordable for low-income people (Weiss 1985, 254).

Figure 5.8 Redevelopment plan for the Western Addition, approved redevelopment project area A-1. Source: San Francisco Redevelopment Agency, San Francisco History Center, San Francisco Public Library.

Figure 5.9 Vacant lots between Post and Geary Streets, San Francisco, after redevelopment. Source: Courtesy of Al Canterbury.

Public Housing and the Isolation of the Poor

Though new housing was often a goal of urban reformers, and many sought to change the conditions of slum housing (see figure 5.10), the focus on slum clearance stymied these plans. Instead of providing more and upgraded housing, efforts to reform urban conditions were often coopted by political elites and developers to further goals of slum clearance. Further, the federal regulations on housing meant that when public housing did get built, it exacerbated, rather than relieved, the problem of housing. In 1949, the federal government provided loans and grants to build 810,000 low-rent housing units in six years; it actually took twenty years to develop that many units, while the number of people in need of affordable housing continued to grow.

Public housing intentionally concentrated the poor by restricting public subsidy and providing primarily for large-scale apartment projects. Local authorities were compelled to enforce income limits, and many stable and upwardly mobile tenants were expelled from housing units. These included many families of white servicemen who had returned from the war, settled in public housing units, and were now forced by the mandate restricting public housing to the poor to engage in the practice of white flight. Too prosperous to qualify for public housing but not wealthy enough to pay market rate for homes in city centers, they relocated to the suburbs. This created an immediate economic segregation between public housing residents and others. Mixed-income developments were entirely prevented by federal housing acts promoting the construction of new public housing.

Further, a "neighborhood composition rule" in effect from 1935 until 1949 banned federal housing projects from altering the racial composition of a neighborhood. This meant that public housing had to house the poorest members of the community, in isolation and separated from other economic classes, and had to be entirely racially homogeneous.

Public housing was also not politically popular and thus did not enjoy wide support for its efforts to create the more just vision that some urban reformers desired. Real estate professionals challenged public housing at the local level and lobbied city governments to close local housing authorities, veto housing projects, and reject housing appropriations and bonds (Gotham 2002; Massey and Denton 1993). While they were less successful in the North and East, the lack of public housing in many communities in the South and West is a direct result of this advocacy.

NIMBYism and Chicago's Public Housing

Throughout the post-WWII era, public housing policy continued to exacerbate and accelerate the process of racial segregation. Public housing was subject to not-in-my-backyard (NIMBY) politics, where whites protested the placement

Figure 5.10 CORE (Congress of Racial Equality) pickets in front of 125 North St., New York City(?), protesting slum housing conditions. Source: Courtesy of the Library of Congress, LC-USZ62–115077.

of slum housing in their communities. Wealthier and more influential communities successfully petitioned authorities to locate public housing far from their homes (or backyards), which meant that most of the new units were built in the already poorest and most disenfranchised communities.

Chicago public housing was heralded at the end of the 1940s as the best in the country (Ziemba 1986). At that time, the Chicago Housing Authority (CHA) was relatively independent from local authorities. The federal provision that insisted public housing not change the racial composition of the neighborhood meant that housing for whites was largely confined to white neighborhoods, while housing for black people remained within black neighborhoods. With the authorization of more housing units and the removal of the clause, however, the CHA sought to spread public housing through Chicago's neighborhoods. The city council successfully lobbied the legislature to provide it the authority to approve new sites. Subsequently, the city's white political establishment decided where public housing was located. Not surprisingly, the vast majority of Chicago public housing was subsequently constructed in black neighborhoods.

Robert Taylor Homes

One notorious housing project, the Robert Taylor Homes, illustrates the conditions of public housing in the post-WWII era. Completed in 1962, the project was the largest in the country at the time. Instead of being in a neighborhood

Figure 5.11 The Robert Taylor Homes in Chicago. Source: John White, DOCUMERICA, Environmental Protection Agency, courtesy of National Archives and Records Administration, 556179, https://catalog .archives.gov/id/556179.

center, the project was isolated, bounded by expressways, the Chicago River, industrial zones, and railyards. It was also in an area reserved for public housing projects called the State Street Corridor, which included four other housing projects.

The Robert Taylor Homes was not only part of a large public housing complex but was a massive undertaking in itself. The project had a total of almost 4,500 units. These units were spread across twenty-eight high-rise buildings, each sixteen stories, that stretched for two miles. The idea that public housing constituted "vertical ghettos" is demonstrated poignantly by the Robert Taylor Homes, which spatially isolated poor, predominantly black residents from the rest of the city. This was only possible through the large-scale razing of land, the building of freeways, and the containment and exclusion of some from the metropolitan space of others (see figure 5.11).

Rashad Shabazz's (2015) examination of the Robert Taylor Homes project reveals just how integral the practices of city planning were to creating the racialized landscapes of Chicago and paving the way for mass incarceration. He examines how the project was based on the ideas of the renowned urban planner Le Corbusier and also attempted to use the organization of the complexes to facilitate racial management of the population. The State Street Corridor projects illustrated the segregation of public housing by race and neighborhood: a "consequence of using high-rise housing structures to enable racial segregation is that they made it possible to keep Blacks in certain parts of the city, effectively cutting them off from the resources that would enable social and economic growth" (Shabazz 2015, 63).

Public Housing's Carceral Landscapes

The Robert Taylor Homes acted not just as a site of physical containment, exclusion, and separation of black communities in Chicago but also as a key space in which the security strategies of the mass incarceration era could be developed and practiced (Shabazz 2015; Venkatesh 2009). Onsite police and security guards were a fixture in the projects from the 1970s on but had little impact as crime continued to rise. Surveillance tactics were also implemented and perfected, with "enclosures at the ground floor to force pedestrians to enter and exit through a central location, video surveillance in the lobbies, curfews, more police, lighting systems, controlled visitation, metal detectors, turnstiles in the lobbies and 'perimeter patrols'" (Shabazz 2015, 67). Residents were also issued unique identification cards and were barred from entering the buildings without theirs.

Public housings have also been likened to urban prisons, a comparison strengthened by the motif of the Robert Taylor Homes. Balconies were covered by cages and chain link fencing, and residents were subjected to all sorts of security mechanisms common to criminal justice surveillance: video surveillance, perimeter patrols, stop and frisk techniques, regular apartment sweeps, and constant police surveillance. Residents were also forced to pass through metal detectors, subject to curfews, and required to use special issued identification cards to access buildings. Coupled with the frequent sweeping security tactics that suspended Fourth Amendment protections in public housing (constitutional under *Wyman v. James* [1971]) and the creation of onsite courts, the Robert Taylor Homes was under "a state of siege" (Shabazz 2015, 68). These intrusions in the life of the Taylor Homes residents also failed to deliver benefits, and as Sudhir Venkatesh (2009) has shown, they actually destabilized the relationships among residents that contributed to safety in the building. Further, they undermined the citizen mechanisms of ensuring safety—such as the building-based residents' associations, which were able to negotiate with and moderate local drug networks—as police invaded and occupied the building.

Decline of Public Housing

Chicago was not alone. Most local housing authorities segregated people by race, and projects in St. Louis, San Francisco, New York, and elsewhere were often located on the far outskirts of the cities, often adjacent to industrial areas and far from urban amenities. Projects were often spatially isolated by using urban topography, transportation networks, and industrial centers to contain people away from whiter spaces in the city. With deindustrialization in the 1970s, public housing became the place for housing the chronically underemployed, as blue-collar jobs were lost and few opportunities arose to replace them.

Public housing was short-lived, however, as President Nixon placed a moratorium on federal housing programs in 1973. When he signed the Housing and Community Development Act of 1974, he shifted the federal government's involvement from providing direct housing units to providing housing allowances. Section 8 of the act authorized the government to provide subsidies to families for rent. The act further insisted that every single person on federal aid should be required to pay rent. Poor families were now dependent on the private market to provide their housing. This meant they were subject to greater decentralization over the conditions in which they lived and greater opportunity for "slumlords" to take advantage and profit from their economic deprivation. Today, the federal government retains its commitment to the Section 8 voucher program and has participated mostly in razing public housing, rather than building anew.

Public support for the poor was further eroded by media- and political elite–created scandals surrounding public benefits. One example is the idea of the "welfare queen" that dominated political discourse in the 1980s (Kohler-Hausmann 2007). The scandal centered on Linda Taylor, who was alleged to have two hundred aliases in twelve different states and to have collected over $200,000 in public assistance. This was far from the truth of Taylor's four aliases and $8,000 in benefits. The result of the Taylor scandal? Welfare recipients had to be fingerprinted and often had to pick up their checks at welfare offices that had limited hours and were often in inaccessible places instead of having the checks sent to their home. A fraud hotline was established, and neighbors took to reporting on their neighbors who they suspected of welfare fraud. Despite little proof that fraud was widespread, this scandal helped to further erode support for the poor and transition public benefits from a culture of provision to one of surveillance and security, something we detail in the next chapter.

SEGREGATION AND THE LANDSCAPE OF CRIME

As we said at the outset, in many places the United States is more segregated today than one hundred years ago. Yet this is not the result of any explicit or legal mandate to segregate, as demonstrated by subprime mortgage lending and the 2007 foreclosure crisis (see box 5.2). In fact, because public mandates have now been unconstitutional for a hundred years, the question becomes, why does segregation continue? And what consequences does this have for the geographies of race and crime today?

Several studies note that segregation is critical to the assessment of crime problems in neighborhoods, which further fuels segregation, urban disinvestment, and hyperpolicing in these neighborhoods. One study even found that the assessment of the crime level of one's neighborhood was influenced by how many young black men lived there (Quillian and Pager 2001). Neither the actual crime rate nor the poverty rate was correlated with the assessment—just demographics. Robert Sampson (2012) found the same thing: the idea of a disorderly neighborhood is not influenced by actual crime rates, or what he calls "objectively observed disorder," but by the race of residents.

BOX 5.2   Race, Subprime Mortgage Lending, and the Foreclosure Crisis

The most recent U.S. recession, which began in 2007, was fueled by a larger housing crisis. Key to this crisis were subprime loans. These were loans that had lower lending standards (i.e., reduced income requirements, higher debt-to-loan value ratios, little to no down payment, and "interest only" loans) and were often adjustable rate mortgages. Subprime lending increased from 8 percent of all mortgages in the early 2000s to upwards of 20 percent by 2006. When the recession hit and people began losing their jobs, many could no longer afford the mortgages on their houses. Those with adjustable rate mortgages saw their payments skyrocket, often to unsustainable amounts. Housing values plummeted, in some places as much as 75 percent, and many were "underwater" on their loans, meaning they owed more than the house was worth and were unable to refinance their loans to gain relief from high adjustable rate mortgages. This situation led to the foreclosure crisis, in which at its height, 83,000 homes per month were being foreclosed upon, compared to 21,000 per month prior to the crisis.

This crisis, however, was not race or class neutral; it was felt most acutely by those living in landscapes of concentrated disadvantage. Low-income residents of color were hardest hit by both subprime lending and the foreclosure crisis, and neighborhoods of concentrated disadvantage were often left reeling from the vacancies, foreclosures, and devaluation. Rugh and Massey (2014) note that "ongoing residential segregation and a historical dearth of access to mortgage credit in American urban areas combined to create ideal conditions for predatory lending to poor minority group members in poor minority neighborhoods" (631). As a consequence, "black borrowers who received loans in 2006 were three times more likely to receive a subprime than a prime loan (74% versus 26%) and Hispanics were twice as likely to receive a subprime than a prime loan (63% versus 37%). In contrast, whites were slightly *more likely* to get a prime than a subprime loan from the same lenders (46% versus 54%)" (632).

To see this in real time, review maps of racial and economic segregation at www.umich.edu/~lawrace/seg.htm and socialexplorer.com. Compare these to maps of foreclosures at real estate sites like RealtyTrac and Zillow, and maps of neighborhood valuation historically at T-Races (http://salt.umd.edu/T-RACES /colormap.html. How do the maps of racial segregation compare to maps of foreclosures? How do the contemporary maps compare to the historical valuation of city spaces? How are the geographies of urban disinvestment created by the foreclosure crisis related to the redlining maps created by the Home Owners' Loan Corporation in the 1930s?

Source: Jacob S. Rugh and Douglas S. Massey, "Racial Segregation and the American Foreclosure Crisis," *American Sociological Review* 75, no. 5 (2010): 629–51.

This perception means that white Americans are less likely to invest in neighborhoods of color and more likely to leave when a nonwhite family moves into the neighborhood (Massey and Denton 1993). Whites also see black people as a threat to property values and routinely devalue the cost of housing in neighborhoods when black families are present (Harris 1999; Krysan and Bader 2007). Maria Krysan (2002a) also notes that black and white people disagree on measures of community desirability. When asked to rate various communities, the race of the respondent is the most consistent predictor—not actual racial or social class composition of the residents—of how a particular neighborhood will be rated. In another experiment, Krysan, Farley, and Couper (2008) asked subjects to evaluate neighborhoods. The neighborhood conditions stayed the same; the only thing that changed was the race of the families pictured. The result? Pictures of white families elicited positive assessments of the neighborhood among whites, while black families elicited negative reactions.

Real estate agents still play a critical role in continuing segregation, as do financial institutions. Whites tend to move out of a neighborhood as black people move in, and agents often steer clients to communities dominated by their own race (Massey and Denton 1993; Krysan 2002b). Advertisements are also critical: those for low-income communities often show a diverse clientele, while luxury developments depend on white models (Williams, Qualls, and Grier 1995). Lending practices still favor whites, as black people are less likely to get loans, more likely to get higher interest rates, and are offered longer repayment periods and thus pay more interest over the life of the loan (Howell 2006; Wyly et al. 2006). The foreclosure crisis in 2009 exacerbated these practices, as the majority of those targeted by the subprime lenders were low-income families of color, who were also disproportionately subject to foreclosure (Dymski, Hernandez, and Mohant 2013; Rugh and Massey 2010).

CONCLUSION

Where we grow up is extremely consequential for the lives we lead. It continues to influence life outcomes today, and the racial geographies outlined in this chapter are invoked repeatedly when considering issues of crime and violence. Is this an accident? No, as we detailed in this chapter, this is a direct result of law, public policy, and the private real estate market. Through these forces, racial segregation emerged at a time when formal, legally mandated racial segregation was on the decline. Today, residential racial segregation continues inequalities throughout the nation through schooling, policing, and the combined hypersurveillance and hyperneglect of low-income neighborhoods of colors.

Through the power of housing, white supremacy becomes entrenched through wealth accumulation and wealth maintenance practices of white families. Most white families can sell their houses for more than they paid for them because of the neighborhoods they live in. Subsequently, they seek out white neighborhoods for further investment due to fear of declining property values. This wealth accumulation, though, is responsible for a large part of the racial gap in achievement in the United States. As a consequence of housing wealth, whites are more likely to be able to afford college, invest in their futures, and raise children in healthy environments, leading to generational transfer of the privileges of whiteness and the re-creation of the structuring logic of white supremacy.

Today, the power of the private market is integral to the continuation and intransigence of racial segregation. By itself, racial segregation might not necessarily have resulted in mass incarceration. However, given the history of the pathologizing of urban spaces and community that we detailed in chapter 4, along with the economic and political transformation of white supremacy, racial segregation was critical to advancing the next stage of racial management: police and prisons. We turn in the next chapter to this history.

REFERENCES

Appleton's Annual Cyclopaedia and Register of Important Events of the Year 1898. 1899. Third Series, vol. 3. New York: Appleton. https://hdl.handle.net/2027/mdp.39015053690668.

Avila, Eric. 2014a. *The Folklore of the Freeway: Race and Revolt in the Modernist City.* University of Minnesota Press.

———. 2014b. "Why the Road to Ferguson Was a Freeway." *Time,* December 17, 2014. http://time.com/3636171/road-to-ferguson-freeway/.

Baar, Kenneth. 1992. "The National Movement to Halt the Spread of Multifamily Housing, 1890–1926." *Journal of the American Planning Association* 58, no. 1: 39–48.

Bourgois, Philippe. 2003. *In Search of Respect: Selling Crack in El Barrio.* Structural Analysis in the Social Sciences 10. Cambridge, UK: Cambridge University Press.

Brooks, Nancy, and Rajiv Sethi. 1997. "The Distribution of Pollution: Community Characteristics and Exposure to Air Toxics." *Journal of Environmental Economics and Management* 32, no. 2: 233–50.

Burns, Rebecca. 2017. "The Infamous Practice of Contract Selling Is Back in Chicago." *Chicago Reader,* March 1. www.chicagoreader.com/chicago/contract-selling-redlining-housing-discrimination/Content?oid=25705647.

Collins, Ann V. 2012. *All Hell Broke Loose: American Race Riots from the Progressive Era through World War II.* Santa Barbara, CA: Praeger.

Collins, William J., and Robert A. Margo. 2001. "Race and Home Ownership: A Century-Long View." *Explorations in Economic History* 38, no. 1: 68–92.

Corburn, Jason, Jeffrey Osleeb, and Michael Porter. 2006. "Urban Asthma and the Neighbourhood Environment in New York City." *Health and Place* 12, no. 2 (June): 167–79.

Delaney, David. 2010. *Race, Place, and the Law, 1836–1948.* Austin: University of Texas Press.

Dymski, Gary, Jesus Hernandez, and Lisa Mohanty. 2013. "Race, Gender, Power, and the U.S. Subprime Mortgage and Foreclosure Crisis: A Meso Analysis." *Feminist Economics* 19, no. 3: 124–51.

Felson, Marcus. 1994. *Crime and Everyday Life: Insight and Implications for Society.* Thousand Oaks, CA: Pine Forge Press.

Ford, Richard Thompson. 1994. "The Boundaries of Race: Political Geography in Legal Analysis." *Harvard Law Review* 107, no. 8 (June): 1841–921.

Frey, William H. 2014. *Diversity Explosion: How New Racial Demographics Are Remaking America.* Washington DC: Brookings Institution Press.

Galster, George C. 2017. *The Metropolis in Black and White: Place, Power and Polarization.* New York: Routledge.

Goldberg, David Theo. 2009. *The Threat of Race: Reflections on Racial Neoliberalism.* Malden, MA: Blackwell.

Gotham, Kevin Fox. 2000. "Urban Space, Restrictive Covenants and the Origins of Racial Residential Segregation in a U.S. City, 1900–50." *International Journal of Urban and Regional Research* 24, no. 3: 616–33.

———. 2002. *Race, Real Estate, and Uneven Development: The Kansas City Experience, 1900–2000*. Albany: State University of New York Press.

Greeley, Brendan. 2013. "U.S. Homeowners Are Repeating Their Mistakes." *Bloomberg News* February 14, 2013. www.bloomberg.com/news/articles/2013-02-14/u-dot-s-dot-homeowners-are-repeating-their-mistakes.

Greenberg, Stanley B. 1996. *Middle Class Dreams: The Politics and Power of the New American Majority.* New Haven, CT: Yale University Press.

Guzman, Ralph. 1956. "The Hand of Esau: Words Change, Practices Remain in Racial Covenants." *Frontier* 7 (June): 13.

Hamilton, Joseph Grégoire de Roulhac. 1919. *North Carolina since 1860*. Vol. 3 of *History of North Carolina*. Chicago: Lewis Publishing Company. https://archive.org/details/historyofnorthca03conn_0.

Hanchett, Thomas W. 2000. "The Other 'Subsidized Housing': Federal Aid to Suburbanization 1940s-1960s." In *From Tenements to the Taylor Homes: In Search of an Urban Housing Policy in Twentieth Century America,* edited by John F. Bauman, Roger Biles, and Kristin M. Szylvian, 163–79. University Park: Pennsylvania State University Press.

Harris, David R. 1999. "'Property Values Drop When Blacks Move In, Because . . .': Racial and Socioeconomic Determinants of Neighborhood Desirability." *American Sociological Review* 64, no. 3: 461–79. www.academicroom.com/article/property-values-drop-when-blacks-move-because-racial-and-socioeconomic-determinants-neighborhood-desirability.

Hillier, Amy E. 2003. "Redlining and the Homeowners' Loan Corporation." *Journal of Urban History* 29, no. 4: 394–420.

Howell, Benjamin. 2006. "Exploiting Race and Space: Concentrated Subprime Lending as Housing Discrimination." *California Law Review* 94, no. 1: 101–47.

Katznelson, Ira. 2005. *When Affirmative Action Was White: An Untold History of Racial Inequality in Twentieth-Century America.* New York: Norton.

Kemp, Janet. 1907. *Housing Conditions in Baltimore: Report of a Special Committee of the Association for the Improvement of the Condition of the Poor and the Charity Organization Society.* Baltimore: Federated Charities. https://catalog.hathitrust.org/Record/100895399.

Kennedy, David M. 2011. *Don't Shoot: One Man, a Street Fellowship, and the End of Violence in Inner-City America.* New York: Bloomsbury USA.

Kohler-Hausmann, Julilly. 2007. "'The Crime of Survival': Fraud Prosecutions, Community Surveillance and the Original 'Welfare Queen.'" *Journal of Social History* 41, no. 2: 329–54.

Krysan, Maria. 2002a. "Community Undesirability in Black and White: Examining Racial Residential Preferences through Community Perceptions." *Social Problems* 49, no. 4 (November): 521–43.

———. 2002b. "Whites Who Say They'd Flee: Who Are They, and Why Would They Leave?" *Demography* 39, no. 4 (November): 675–96.

Krysan, Maria, and Michael Bader. 2007. "Perceiving the Metropolis: Seeing the City through a Prism of Race." *Social Forces* 86, no. 2 (December): 699–733.

Krysan, Maria, Reynolds Farley, and Mick P. Couper. 2008. "In the Eye of the Beholder: Racial Beliefs and Residential Segregation." *Du Bois Review: Social Science Research on Race* 5, no. 01 (Spring): 5–26.

Kushner, David. 2009. *Levittown: Two Families, One Tycoon, and the Fight for Civil Rights in America's Legendary Suburb.* New York: Bloomsbury USA.

Lambert, Bruce. 1997. "At 50, Levittown Contends with Its Legacy of Bias." *New York Times,* December 28, 1997. www.nytimes.com/1997/12/28/nyregion/at-50-levittown-contends-with-its-legacy-of-bias.html.

Lee, Ardelia. 2016. "The Detroit Wall: A Tale of How Federal Policy Helped Divide a City." *Daily Detroit,* June 6, 2016. www.dailydetroit.com/2016/06/06/detroit-wall-federal-policy/.

Massey, Douglas S., and Nancy A. Denton. 1993. *American Apartheid: Segregation and the Making of the Underclass.* Cambridge, MA: Harvard University Press.

McCrary, Lacy. 1997. "Trauma of Levittown Integration Remembered." *Baltimore Sun,* August 21, 1997. http://articles.baltimoresun.com/1997-08-21/news/1997233064_1_daisy-myers-levittown-epithets.

McGann, Shaun. 2014. "The Effects of 'Redlining' on the Hartford Metropolitan Region," ConnecticutHistory.org. March 18, 2014. http://connecticuthistory.org/the-effects-of-redlining-on-the-hartford-metropolitan-region/.

Misra, Tanvi. 2015. "Why America's Racial Wealth Gap Is Really a Homeownership Gap." CityLab. March12, 2015. www.citylab.com/housing/2015/03/why-americas-racial-wealth-gap-is-really-a-homeownership-gap/387427.

Mohl, Raymond A. 2002. *The Interstates and the Cities: Highways, Housing and the Freeway Revolt.* Research Report. Washington DC: Poverty and Race Action Council.

Nall, Clayton. 2015. "The Political Consequences of Spatial Policies: How Interstate Highways Facilitated Geographic Polarization." *Journal of Politics* 77, no. 2: 394–406.

New York City Department of Health and Mental Hygiene. 2003. "Asthma Can Be Controlled." *NYC Vital Signs* 2 (April): 1–4. www1.nyc.gov/assets/doh/downloads/pdf/survey/survey-2003asthma.pdf.

Nowicki, Jacqueline. 2016. *Better Use of Information Could Help Agencies Identify Disparities and Address Racial Discrimination.* Washington, DC: Government Accounting Office. https://www.gao.gov /assets/680/676745.pdf.

Olson, Sherry H. 1997. *Baltimore: The Building of an American City.* Rev. ed. Baltimore, MD: Johns Hopkins University Press.

Opperman, Paul. 1955. *Housing and Neighborhood Conditions in San Francisco: A Classification of Areas for Urban Renewal.* San Francisco: Department of City Planning. https://archive.org/details/ housingneighborh1955sanf.

Orser, W. Edward. 2015. *Blockbusting in Baltimore: The Edmondson Village Story.* Lexington: University Press of Kentucky.

Popkin, Susan J., Diane K. Levy, Laura E. Harris, Jennifer Comey, Mary K. Cunningham, and Larry Buron. 2002. *HOPE VI Panel Study: Baseline Report: Final Report.* Washington, DC: Urban Institute. https:// www.urban.org/sites/default/files/publication/60626/410590-HOPE-VI-Panel-Study-Baseline-Report.PDF.

Power, Garrett. 1983. "Apartheid Baltimore Style: The Residential Segregation Ordinances of 1910–1913." *Maryland Law Review* 42, no. 2: 289–328. http://digitalcommons.law.umaryland.edu/mlr/vol42/iss2/4.

Prather, H. Leon, Sr. 1998. "We Have Taken a City: A Centennial Essay." In *Democracy Betrayed: The Wilmington Race Riot of 1898 and Its Legacy,* edited by David S. Cecelski and Timothy B. Tyson, 15–41. Chapel Hill: University of North Carolina Press Books.

Purcell, Mark. 1997. "Ruling Los Angeles: Neighborhood Movements, Urban Regimes, and the Production of Space in Southern California." *Urban Geography* 18, no. 8: 684–704.

Quillian, Lincoln, and Devah Pager. 2001. "Black Neighbors, Higher Crime? The Role of Racial Stereotypes in Evaluations of Neighborhood Crime." *American Journal of Sociology* 107, no. 3: 717–67.

Rabin, Yale. 1989. "Expulsive Zoning: The Inequitable Legacy of Euclid." In *Zoning and the American Dream: Promises Still to Keep,* edited by Charles Haar and Jerold Kayden, 101–21. Chicago: American Planning Association Press.

Reardon, Sean F., and Ann Owens. 2014. "60 Years after Brown: Trends and Consequences of School Segregation." *Annual Review of Sociology* 40: 199–218.

Rice, Roger L. 1968. "Residential Segregation by Law, 1910–1917." *Journal of Southern History* 34, no. 2: 179–99.

"Roads to Somewhere." 2006. *Economist,* June 22, 2006. www.economist.com/node/7087458.

Rothstein, Richard. 2017. *The Color of Law: A Forgotten History of How Our Government Segregated America.* New York, NY: Liveright.

Rugh, Jacob S., and Douglas S. Massey. 2010. "Racial Segregation and the American Foreclosure Crisis." *American Sociological Review* 75, no. 5: 629–51.

Sampson, Robert J. 2012. *Great American City: Chicago and the Enduring Neighborhood Effect.* Chicago: University of Chicago Press.

Scott, Mel. 1947. *New City: San Francisco Redeveloped.* San Francisco: City Planning Commission. https:// archive.org/details/newcitysanfranci1947scot.

Shabazz, Rashad, 2015. *Spatializing Blackness: Architectures of Confinement and Black Masculinity in Chicago.* Urbana: University of Illinois Press.

Shu, Wayne. 2015. "Baltimore's Legacy of Racial Discrimination." *Stanford Review* May 19, 2015. https:// stanfordreview.org/baltimores-legacy-of-racial-discrimination/

Silva, Catherine. 2009. "Racial Restrictive Covenants: Enforcing Neighborhood Segregation in Seattle." Seattle Civil Rights and Labor History Project. http://depts.washington.edu/civilr/covenants_report.htm.

Silver, Christopher. 1997. "The Racial Origins of Zoning in American Cities." In *Urban Planning and the African American Community: In the Shadows,* edited by June Manning Thomas and Marsha Ritzdorf, 23–42. Thousand Oaks, CA: Sage.

State Museum of Pennsylvania. 2003. *Levittown.* http://statemuseumpa.org/levittown/.

Stein, Peter L., producer and writer. 1999. "The Fillmore." Episode in *Neighborhoods: The Hidden Cities of San Francisco.* San Francisco: KQED. http://www.pbs.org/kqed/fillmore/program/index.html.

Sullivan, Laura, Tatjana Meschede, Lars Dietrich, Thomas Shapiro, Amy Traub, Catherine Ruetschlin, and Tamara Draut. 2015. *The Racial Wealth Gap.* Waltham, MA: Institute for Assets and Social Policy, Brandeis University; New York: Demos. http://www.demos.org/sites/default/files/publications /RacialWealthGap_1.pdf.

Venkatesh, Sudhir Alladi. 2009. *American Project: The Rise and Fall of a Modern Ghetto.* Cambridge, MA: Harvard University Press.

Von Hoffman, Alexander. 2000. "A Study in Contradictions: The Origins and Legacy of the Housing Act of 1949." *Housing Policy Debate* 11, no. 2: 299–326.

Weiss, Marc Allan. 1985. *The Origins and Legacy of Urban Renewal.* In *Federal Housing Policy and Programs: Past and Present,* edited by J. Paul Mitchell, 253–76. New Brunswick, NJ: Center for Urban Policy Research, Rutgers University.

Williams, Jerome D., William J. Qualls, and Sonya A. Grier. 1995. "Racially Exclusive Real Estate Advertising: Public Policy Implications for Fair Housing Practices." *Journal of Public Policy and Marketing* 14, no. 2 (Fall): 225–44.

Wilson, William Julius. 2012. *The Truly Disadvantaged: The Inner City, the Underclass, and Public Policy.* Chicago: University of Chicago Press.

Wyly, Elvin K., Mona Atia, Holly Foxcroft, Daniel J. Hamme, and Kelly Phillips-Watts. 2006. "American Home: Predatory Mortgage Capital and Neighbourhood Spaces of Race and Class Exploitation in the United States." *Geografiska Annaler: Series B, Human Geography* 88, no. 1 (March): 105–32.

Ziemba, Stanley. 1986. "How Projects Rose to Failure." *Chicago Tribune,* December 2, 1986. http://articles.chicagotribune.com/1986-12-02/news/8603310330_1_chicago-housing-authority-high-rise-projects-public-housing.

The Problem of Urban America: Race and the Emergence of Mass Incarceration

LEARNING OUTCOMES

▶ Explain how the criminalization of drugs set the stage for the racialization of crime and the emergence of mass incarceration.

▶ Describe the emergence and development of the law and order discourse and its impact on the criminal justice system.

▶ Summarize the role that political elites and repression played in creating mass incarceration.

KEY TERMS

▶ social problems
▶ postwar racial liberalism
▶ War on Poverty
▶ culture of poverty
▶ Southern strategy
▶ law and order discourse
▶ Moynihan Report
▶ COINTELPRO
▶ War on Drugs
▶ Law Enforcement Assistance Administration (LEAA)

Picture an urban place. What are you picturing?

Consider the term *urban*. It's a moniker used to describe all sorts of things. There's urban fashion, urban policy, urban problems, urban myths, and there's even an urban dictionary. What does the word mean though? Why would a dictionary be urban?

This question of what *urban* exactly means is something that urbanists—scholars who study urban life—grapple with regularly. One of the most famous urbanists, Robert Louis Werth, defined urban living as a "way of life" in 1938. What way was this? If it's not referring to some quantitative measure, then what qualitatively was Werth referring to?

If we return to the ideology of Progressives and the post-WWII era, *urban* was predominantly negative. It brings filth and pestilence according to Progressives, and it necessitates slum clearance according to urban redevelopers. It's the site of biological downfall according to eugenicists, and it contributes to social upheaval and violence according to the premise of urban renewal. Through each of these definitions, *urban* reveals its power, its ability to organize complicated ideas into a single five-letter word.

This chapter is about how the invocation of urban social problems in the 1960s mobilized and transformed the U.S. racial state. As shown in the previous chapter, concern about urbanization in the Progressive Era remade cities, state institutions, and even citizens. In this chapter, we examine how in the 1960s some of these same forces proved instrumental in the remaking of the U.S. criminal justice system and the emergence of mass incarceration and the War on Drugs. This remaking, however, is not without precedent, so before we turn to the 1960s, we detail the very first attempts to regulate drugs and the racialization that defined *some* drug usage as a social problem necessitating state intervention.

RACE, DRUGS, AND CRIME: THE EARLY HISTORY

Prohibiting drugs did not begin with the War on Drugs in the 1970s. Instead, drug prohibitions have a long history in U.S. state policy. And this history reveals just how integral racial hysteria has been to drug prohibition.

Defining drugs as a social problem necessitating prohibition happens through a rather common set of steps. Often a social problem is *discovered,* such as when the eugenicists discussed in chapter 3 discovered the supposed problem of biological heritage. The discovery of the social problem gains traction among other groups, politicians, and media elites and the issue is *amplified.* Often, there are archetypal characters—the feeble-minded child, for example, discussed by eugenicists (see chapter 4)—who play the stereotypical role of threatening the very fabric of society. Eventually, there is often a resolution to the problem in the form of state intervention. Special committees may be formed to investigate the issue; politicians may fight over what is the most appropriate solution, sometimes for years and decades; and laws and policies may be passed, overturned, reauthorized, and amended. This is the process of defining **social problems.**

This considerable amount of social activity related to issues that were often not seen as issues in the months, years or decades before is important not just for the changes in how we govern but for the consequences to how we envision ourselves and others. Examining how issues attain status as a "social problem" provides an opportunity to see how disparate ideas are consolidated, broadcast, and politicized. Often, defining a particular issue as a social problem is also a way that powerful entities are able to deflect an issue, such as labor competition in a capitalist market, onto other people and places.

The history of drug prohibition demonstrates how this happens. Drug usage by all racial groups was quite common in the late 1800s and early 1900s. In each case below, we see the elements necessary to define drugs as a problem necessitating state intervention against *some* groups: amplified threat, stylized "folk devils," rampant public reaction, and deployment of extraordinary governmental violence towards just some groups (Cohen 1972). In the three cases below, this was done quite explicitly to oppose upward mobility by Chinese, black, and Mexican people. When explicit racist discourse subsided somewhat in the post-WWII era, however, the emergence of the War on Drugs and mass incarceration drew upon these same rhetorical strategies—without the explicit racism—to define crime and drugs in urban areas as the "most important" social problem facing the United States.

Opium, the Chinese, and Protecting White Womanhood

In the late 1800s, opium dens were commonplace in the urban United States. One English travel writer describing San Francisco's Chinatown community even wrote about the local opium dens not as a deviant undertaking but rather as places to sate one's "curiosity" (Day 1886, 53). The traveler remarked that "although there is supposed to be a law against the sale of opium, it is openly exposed in many of the shops, and smoking dens abound." The traveler further noted that the police paid attention to the opium shops only "when the police are short of funds . . . but as a rule the proprietors are left unmolested." However, in the late 1890s, the situation in San Francisco changed, and by 1920, San Francisco was having public "opium burnings" that attracted crowds of revelers.

Early Anti-Chinese Legislation

Fervent anti-Chinese immigrant sentiments in the United States were all too common in the 1800s. Chinese workers often immigrated to the United States for large projects such as the transcontinental railroad and were often openly vilified by their white working-class counterparts. As anti-Chinese sentiment mounted, state action was sought to deal with this "racial problem" (Craddock 2000; Shah 2001).

State action first began by forbidding Chinese workers through both immigration law and other state tools (Salyer 1995). For instance, in the 1850s, California passed a "foreign miners' tax" to suppress Chinese gold miners; in 1854 the California Supreme Court ruled that Chinese were ineligible to testify in court against whites; and in 1855, a law was passed that specifically forbade Chinese immigration to the state. The U.S. Congress soon took California's lead and passed the Anti-Coolie Act, which banned ships from carrying people from China. This law's title even used an anti-Chinese slur.

Attacks on the Chinese and anti-Chinese worker riots occurred periodically throughout the 1860s and 1870s. Fervent anti-Chinese sentiment was also responsible for the creation of Chinatown, as Chinese residents were excluded from housing throughout the city. As a consequence, Chinese in San Francisco were contained within just a few blocks. Laws were made to specifically target the Chinese without explicitly mentioning them by name, a common practice today as well. For instance, in 1873, the city passed a law taxing laundries. Launderers using horse-drawn vehicles, who were largely white, were taxed $4 per year; those without vehicles, who were predominantly Chinese, were charged $60 per year. This tactic of using the law disparately was also used to criminalize Chinese residents while protecting white opium users during the surge in opium laws in the 1870s.

Criminalizing Opium

In 1875, San Francisco passed the very first anti-drug law, aimed at ending the consumption of opium, a practice commonly associated with the Chinese section of town. The *Sacramento Daily Record* reported: "It was stated the other day, before the San Francisco Board of Supervisors, that as many as eight Chinese opium smoking houses had been fitted up in that city for the use of white men and women, and the announcement has created a good deal of discussion, and elicited from the press recommendations for the suppression of these places" ("The Opium Habit" 1875). Importantly, the law did not outlaw opium use, only opium dens. Ingestion in other settings, which was common in upperclass white society, continued unregulated.

The law continued the common narrative that Chinese immigrants were contributing to the ruin of whites, but this time the narrative was less about labor and more about the downfall of white womanhood. Nayan Shah describes the outcry:

> Moreover, the spectacle of white women in opium dens horrified white male observers. Kane [a San Francisco physician who testified to the California legislature on the dangers of opium] argued that "many females are so much excited sexually by the smoking of opium during the first few weeks [that] . . . many innocent and over-curious girls have thus been seduced." The San Francisco physician Winslow Anderson described the "sickening sight of young white girls from sixteen to twenty years of age lying half-undressed on the floor or couches, smoking with their 'lovers.'" The opium habit resulted in the "downfall of girls and the debasement of married women." Addicted white women often prostituted themselves in exchange of the drug, often seeking Chinse opium den operators as their principal clients. The damage to white women's virtue was irreversible from the perspective of physicians and journalists. The women were dismissed as "disreputable" and "fallen" by their very presence in a semipublic lounge and considered lost to good society. (2001, 94)

Opium as a social problem was supposedly discovered by San Francisco because of the social ruination that resulted from its use. But for San Franciscans, the real issue of opium was not the drug itself but rather the blurring of sex, race, and class lines as whites and Asians, men and women, and the poor and the wealthy converged in opium dens.

A popular photograph demonstrating the issue of opium—that was most likely staged—showed two young white women lying in opium den with a menacing Asian figure watching over them. These racist tropes were repeated again and again in propaganda about the dangers of opium (for an example, see

Figure 6.1 Joseph Jarrow, "The Queen of Chinatown." Note the white women strewn about and the racist caricature of the Chinese business owner. Source: Courtesy of the Library of Congress, LC-USZ62–128694.

figure 6.1). With such images, we can see how the definition of opium as a social problem drew upon the age-old racial discourse of virginal white womanhood and predatory nonwhite men, while invoking the moral and even physical decline of whiteness.

Opium continued to dominate local concerns in San Francisco until its outright prohibition in the early 1900s. A writer in the *San Jose Mercury* described the urgency of prohibition as early as 1881. He wrote:

> This pernicious habit is on the increase, of late, all over this State, especially in the large cities. Many bright young men, including two, at least, graduates of our universities, have died from its effects within the past year. The police records of San

Figure 6.2 Chinatown Squad of the San Francisco Police Department posing with sledgehammers and axes in front of August Pistolesi's grocery store at 752 Washington Street. Source: San Francisco History Center, San Francisco Public Library.

Francisco show the arrest of hundreds of both sexes annually—many of them youth of respectable exterior—in the vilest of Chinese "joints." Opium-smoking, in ninety-nine cases out of a possible hundred, means the mad-house or the morgue, and not far off, either. (quoted in Kane 1881, 77)

Authorities used the anti-opium-dens law to strictly police the lines between the Chinese and whites in San Francisco. The local police department created a special "opium squad," which doubled in size in just a few years (see figure 6.2). Police frequently raided Chinatown establishments under the auspices of rooting out opium dens. Frequent accusations of disease in the area also led to strict quarantines and continued cordoning off of the area from the rest of San Francisco (Craddock 2000).

City hall further commissioned investigation into the Chinese neighborhood and deployed state agents to map the neighborhood (see figure 6.3). This map provided a spatial articulation of the issue of racial degeneration by marking places of "general Chinese occupancy" alongside common issues identified as social problems: prostitution, opium 'resorts', and gambling. Tellingly, the map disaggregated prostitution to provide sites of both Chinese and white prostitution. The map provided the scientific artifact necessary to establish claims of objective and rational state action and is one of the many tools of those working to define particular issues as social problems.

The San Francisco Opium Ordinance represented both the first prohibition against drugs in the nation and the ability of moral panics to consolidate power and remake urban space. Whereas white and Chinese people often interacted before the anti-opium crusades, afterward, the opportunities for interaction were greatly diminished. Now whites in Chinese spaces were considered degenerate and suspicious, and racial restrictions and violence quarantined Chinese in the confines of the newly emerging "Chinatown," a neighborhood that continues to demarcate racialized space in San Francisco today. Further, the labor of Chinese workers was marginalized and devalued, making way for white racial domination of newly emerging industries.

Race and the Criminalization of Cocaine

Cocaine was another widely used drug at the end of the 1890s. Famously, Sigmund Freud, the father of psychology, promoted using the drug and used it himself several times a day. Other famous figures, including Thomas Edison, Robert Louis Stevenson, and Howard Hughes, were all noted cocaine users. As figure 6.4 shows, cocaine was so widespread that it was even widely sold and marketed as a cure-all.

In the early 1900s, tellingly during a period of high unemployment, newspapers began carrying worrisome stories of a new cocaine user who contrasted sharply with previous portrayals (Siegel 1984). Previously, the cocaine user was represented as an upper- or middle-class white person, and the primary problem stemming from drug use was addiction, not violence or crime. By the early 1900s, however, this representation changed. No longer was cocaine a problem of the white upper class, manifested in sickness and a wasting body. Now, cocaine took on extraordinary powers, exemplified by what at the time was called the "negro cocaine fiend."

"Cocaine Fiends"

Reports of the emergence of cocaine fiends first began appearing in the early 1900s (Cohen 2006). In 1911, the *New York Times* published an extensive exposé of the problem, writing:

> It is the unanimous opinion of every state and municipal organization having to do with the enforcement of state and municipal pharmacy laws that the misuse of cocaine is a direct incentive to crime; that it is perhaps of all factors a singular one in augmenting the criminal ranks. The illicit use of the drug is most difficult to cope with, and the habitual use of it temporarily raises the power of the criminal to a point where in resisting arrest, there is no hesitation to murder. (Marshall 1911)

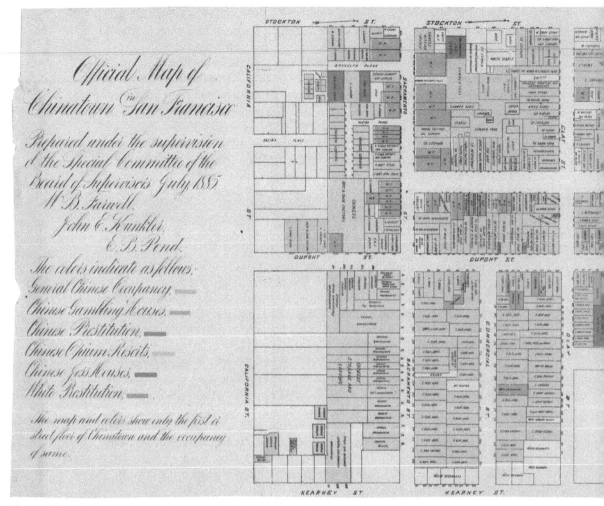

Figure 6.3 Map of San Francisco's Chinatown showing businesses of disrepute—gambling, prostitution, and drugs. Also included are joss houses, which are Chinese temples or shrines. Source: Willard B. Farwell, 1885, *Official Map of Chinatown in San Francisco* (San Francisco: A.L. Bancroft). Image download courtesy of Cartography Association.

This was not the first report of a cocaine fiend, however; as far back as 1901 one scholar noted in the *American Pharmaceutical Journal* that black people were "made wild by cocaine" (quoted in Streatfeild 2003, 140). This view of the power of cocaine was in stark contrast to its representation as a common household and first aid item among whites.

While all statistics from this time reveal that whites were the vast majority of drug users and that black people rarely used cocaine, it was the figure of the black cocaine fiend that prompted its widespread prohibition (Cohen 2006). In

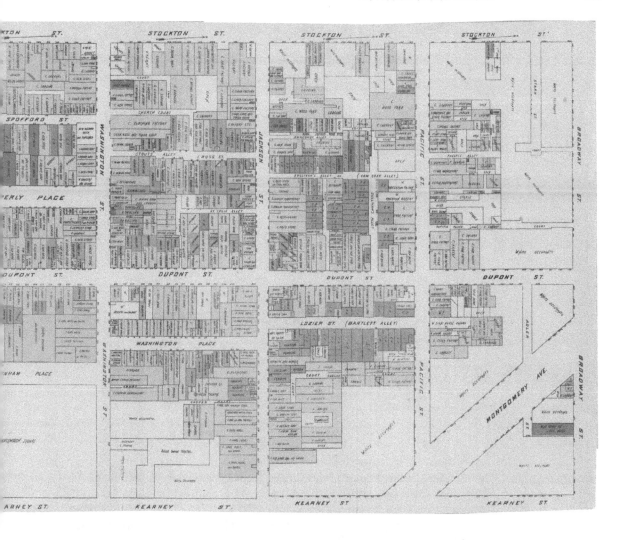

1914, the *New York Times* published an article titled "Negro Cocaine 'Fiends' Are a New Southern Menace" (see figure 6.5):

> The drug produces several other conditions that make the "fiend" a peculiarly dangerous criminal. One of these conditions is a temporary immunity to shock—a resistance to the "knock-down" effects of fatal wounds. Bullets fired into vital parts, that would stop a sane man in his tracks, fail to check the "fiend"—fail to stop his rush or weaken his attack. (Williams 1914)

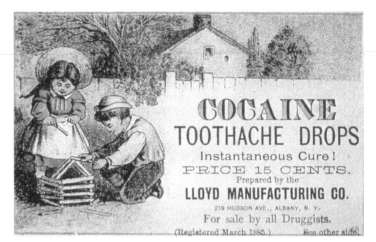

Figure 6.4 Advertisement for cocaine tooth drops, March 1885. Source: Digitized by the National Library of Medicine, Set 72157629315957473, ID 6875689573.

NEGRO COCAINE "FIENDS" ARE A NEW SOUTHERN MENACE

Murder and Insanity Increasing Among Lower Class Blacks Because They Have Taken to "Sniffing" Since Deprived of Whisky by Prohibition.

Figure 6.5 "Negro Cocaine 'Fiends' Are a New Southern Menace," declared a national newspaper headline. Source: Edward Huntington Williams, *New York Times,* February 8, 1914.

The authority of this description was amplified by a large portrait of the white author, identified as a doctor, who carried the social and cultural attributes of whiteness and masculinity through his parted, combed hair, glasses, and trimmed facial hair. Eventually, this tale was carried throughout the nation, and newspapers began reporting on the "horrible crimes" committed in the South by the cocaine fiend. Reports linked cocaine usage to numerous killings, rape, and other crimes. Other reports connected cocaine to the "white slave trade" (see chapter 4) and prostitution.

The mythological cocaine fiends also prompted considerable political activity. Doctors testified at Congressional hearings that "cocaine is the direct incentive to the crime of rape by the Negroes of the South and other sections of the country" (Streatfeild 2003, 145). The idea that cocaine fiends were impervious to bullets led police departments to change their guns from .32 to the more powerful .38 caliber, which was said to be able to stop the superhuman cocaine fiend. Congress eventually passed the Harrison Narcotics Act, one of the first federal legislative attempts to regulate drugs in the United States.

Yet, why did the cocaine fiend gain such prominence in the media and legislative realm and lead police departments to change their guns? Historians find no evidence that black cocaine fiends actually existed, and the cost of cocaine at the time made it prohibitively expensive for the poor (Hart 2014). But there were considerable racial anxieties that the focus on cocaine fiends served to mask. Industrialization spurred black migration to predominantly white Northern communities, and the cocaine fiend narrative masked white anxiety about racial boundaries. The narrative, set amid a context of white racial violence and terror described in chapters 4 and 5, served to justify white racial anxieties and legitimate the use of extraordinary violence to secure white supremacy in the city.

Mexicans and "Reefer Madness"

Cocaine and opium were not the only drugs considered to have extraordinary effects when ingested by nonwhites or to have consumption by nonwhites defined as a social problem. During the 1930s, newspapers and political elites argued that cannabis was particularly dangerous when used by Mexicans. This narrative was pioneered by two very powerful individuals: Henry J. Anslinger, the first head of the Federal Bureau of Narcotics, and William Hearst, a powerful newspaper magnate in California, whose publications reached a peak circulation in the 1930s of over 20 million readers in eighteen cities. Hearst was also an avid racist, well-known for his vitriolic attacks on Mexicans in California (Lusane and Desmond 1991).

Constructing the Racial Threat through Drugs

Newspapers also carried widespread tales of the damage done by Mexicans under the influence of cannabis (see figure 6.6). Hearst newspapers in particular reported sensational stories of cannabis-fueled violence. Stories contended that cannabis was a "short cut to the insane asylum" and that "hashish makes a murder who kills for the love of killing out of the mildest mannered man who ever laughed at the idea that any habit could ever get him." One particularly hyperbolic column reported that marijuana, "the new Mexican drug," was responsible for the fact that "THREE-FOURTHS OF THE CRIMES of violence in this country today are committed by DOPE SLAVES—that is a matter of cold record" (cited in Sanna 2014, 38, emphasis in original).

Anslinger crusaded against cannabis throughout his career and was a key source of misinformation on the drug, even creating federal advertisements warning that it was a "killer drug." In arguing for drug legislation, he contended that "the primary reason to outlaw marijuana is its effect on the degenerate races," noting that it "produces in its users insanity, criminality, and death." His comments explicitly targeted nonwhites, and he even contended that one of the

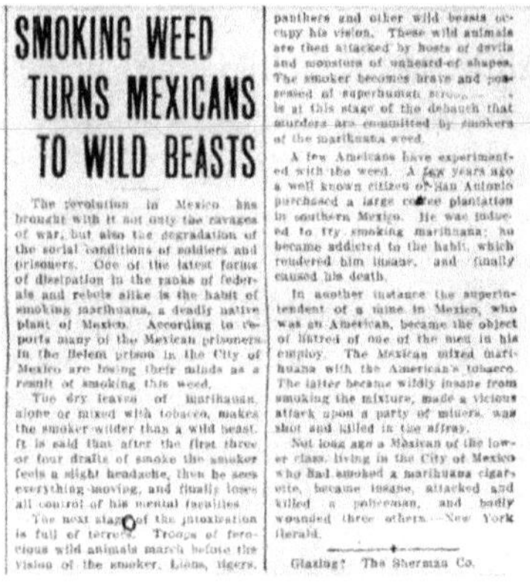

SMOKING WEED TURNS MEXICANS TO WILD BEASTS

The revolution in Mexico has brought with it not only the ravages of war, but also the degradation of the social conditions of soldiers and prisoners. One of the latest forms of dissipation in the ranks of federals and rebels alike is the habit of smoking marihuana, a deadly native plant of Mexico. According to reports many of the Mexican prisoners in the Belem prison in the City of Mexico are losing their minds as a result of smoking this weed.

The dry leaves of marihuana, alone or mixed with tobacco, makes the smoker wilder than a wild beast. It is said that after the first three or four drafts of smoke the smoker feels a slight headache, then he sees everything moving, and finally loses all control of his mental faculities.

The next stage of the intoxication is full of terrors. Troops of ferocious wild animals march before the vision of the smoker. Lions, tigers, panthers and other wild beasts occupy his vision. These wild animals are then attacked by hosts of devils and monsters of unheard-of shapes. The smoker becomes brave and possessed of superhuman stre[illegible] is at this stage of the debauch that murders are committed by smokers of the marihuana weed.

A few Americans have experimented with the weed. A few years ago a well known citizen of San Antonio purchased a large coffee plantation in southern Mexico. He was induced to try smoking marihuana; he became addicted to the habit, which rendered him insane, and finally caused his death.

In another instance the superintendent of a mine in Mexico, who was an American, became the object of hatred of one of the men in his employ. The Mexican mixed marihuana with the American's tobacco. The latter became wildly insane from smoking the mixture, made a vicious attack upon a party of miners, was shot and killed in the affray.

Not long ago a Mexican of the lower class, living in the City of Mexico who had smoked a marihuana cigarette, became insane, attacked and killed a policeman, and badly wounded three others.—New York Herald.

Glazing? The Sherman Co.

Figure 6.6 "Smoking Weed Turns Mexicans into Wild Beasts." Source: *Cheyenne State Leader,* March 29, 1913. Courtesy of Wyoming Newspapers, Wyoming State Library.

primary dangers was that it disrupted white supremacy, telling audiences that "reefer makes darkies think they're as good as white men." He further noted that it "leads to pacifism and communist brainwashing" and that if you "smoke a joint . . . you're likely to kill your brother" because "marijuana is the most violence-causing drug in the history of mankind" (Blecha 2004, 79; Sanna 2014, 39)

Containing the Racial Threat

As a result of Anslinger and Hearst's efforts, cannabis use by Mexicans was defined as a social problem and its consumption was soon criminalized. Anslinger testified about the law to Congress, using as evidence reports of violence and cannabis use profiled in Hearst's newspapers. Though medical authorities opposed the new regulation, upon Anslinger's testimony, Congress acted swiftly and in 1937, the Marijuana Tax Act was passed, effectively banning the use and sale of cannabis in the United States.

Like opium and cocaine, the moral panic about cannabis served to scapegoat Mexican immigrants for broader social, political, and economic changes. At the time of the hysteria around cannabis in the 1930s, the United States was in the throes of the Great Depression and had experienced large-scale migration, especially from Mexico, during the preceding decade. As the labor supply and unemployment increased in tandem, anti-Mexican hostilities in the Southwest also increased.

The criminalization of cannabis was a remarkable feat, accomplished only through racial hysteria, because hemp was widely used and produced throughout the United States. Indeed, the only way the law was able to pass was by using *marijuana* in its name, because marijuana was associated with Mexicans, rather than *hemp* or *cannabis,* which were used by whites (Coughlin-

Bogue 2016). Hearst opposed hemp, a viable alternative to paper, because it threatened his business empire. Further, DuPont Chemical Company sought to criminalize cannabis in order to thwart the competition hemp presented to its new patented product, nylon. In banning the use and sale of marijuana, the act effectively ended the widespread hemp industry in the United States and remade its economic landscape—at least with regard to cannabis—by appealing to racial hysteria.

Drugs and Racial Hysteria

Urbanization, industrialization, and immigration all brought demographic, political, and economic challenges to white supremacy. Social concern about cocaine, opium, and marijuana masked white racial anxieties about these changes and channeled this anxiety into racial hysteria about drugs. In each of the cases above, criminalizing drugs serve to invigorate, stimulate, and re-create the boundaries of white supremacy.

These boundaries were both physical and legal. Legal tactics were used to criminalize nonwhites under the guise of drug enforcement and mythologies of violence. White anxieties about competition from Chinese in the West, Mexicans in the South, and black people in the North were sublimated through gendered and sexualized discourses of depraved nonwhites preying on virtuous white women. These moral panics addressed demographics shifts and competition for housing and space by, under the guise of cleaning up the city, expelling "deviants." And the hysteria about crime and violence invoked the society-must-be-defended logic discussed in chapter 4, which urgently authorized the state's use of violence and force—in place of the due process and measured contemplation used often with whites—to respond to transgressors with new police forces, weapons, and laws.

Criminalizing drug use brought narratives about drugs that are still integral to defining social problems today, as we will see in greater detail below. These narratives, however, existed side by side with narratives of whites and drugs, which considered most drug usage normal and in extreme cases, a representation of sickness necessitating treatment. Instead of images evoking threats of violence or criminal actions, whites were represented as wasting away, languid, and pale, hardly a criminal threat.

Each of these cases provided an opportunity to produce knowledge about race and the exceptional character of particular groups. Though explicit racial exceptionality faded, the idea of racial exceptionality in drug use did not. Instead, the discourse of racial exceptionality transformed into a discourse of *urban* exceptionality. Only now, *urban* did not represent encounter and contact between groups as it had in the Progressive Era, but the racial geographies created by suburbanization and urban disinvestment chronicled in chapter 5.

THE WAR ON POVERTY AND THE CRIMINALIZATION OF RACE

During the post-WWII era, the U.S. state embarked on an ambitious agenda to solve the social problems defined by the Progressive Era. As discussed in chapter 5, this agenda resulted in massive federal investment in suburbanization and urban revitalization. These efforts were predicated on solving social problems such as poverty, housing, and slum development. But as we saw in chapter 5, the political will to solve dilapidated housing oscillated, and when it did appear, it primarily saw the issue as one stemming from inadequate planning and race and class heterogeneity. Thus, although often benevolently intentioned, even such endeavors as slum clearance helped contribute to the eventual remaking of the criminal justice system under mass incarceration.

This becomes clear with an examination of how federal efforts sought to address urban problems in the 1950s and 1960s. Poverty was interpreted in this period as a social issue that could be solved through governmental intervention, such as Democratic President Lyndon Johnson's War on Poverty. By the end of the 1960s, however, cities were in crisis, racial uprisings plagued the United States, and poverty had been reinterpreted. While the War on Poverty often seems far removed ideologically from the wars on crime and drugs, these bellicose endeavors are united in their geographical imagination of the social problems confronting the United States.

The War on Poverty and the Issue of Crime

Common accounts paint a historical picture of mass incarceration as an aberration in the U.S. political scene. It is often seen as vastly different from the War on Poverty promoted by President Johnson that preceded it. Yet the War on Poverty was instrumental in shaping an understanding of U.S. life that led not to the racialization of crime but to the criminalization of race.

Mass incarceration is often regarded as a particular instance in which crime is interpreted as needing ever increasing punishment. Often, this orientation is seen as antithetical to the more rehabilitative-oriented understandings of punishment that preceded it. Yet, this was not the only understanding of punishment. The call for increased punishment, common in the era of mass incarceration, began immediately after World War II as a way to stem *white* racial violence and respond systematically to centuries of racial oppression.

Postwar Racial Liberalism

Examining the racial management strategies of the post-WWII era forces us to examine "how political actors come to obscure racial power through vocabularies of bland administrative reform and soft racial paternalism" (Murakawa 2014, 12). **Postwar racial liberalism,** in contrast to postwar conservative ideology, viewed race as the product of personal and psychological battles, not as a "systemic problem rooted in specific social practices and pervading relations of political economy and culture" (Von Eschen 1997, 157). While the focus on biological origins of racial differences subsided, a new, equally virulent conceptualization of race arose: race as the product of cultural—even racist culture—differences.

Two examples illustrate this point. First, the call for increased imprisonment first stemmed from *liberals* and not conservatives. President Truman, when addressing the issue of race domestically in 1947, called out white racial violence, arguing that "too many of our people still live under the harrowing fear of violence or death at the hands of a mob or of brutal treatment by police officers. Many fear entanglement with the law because of the knowledge that the justice rendered in some courts is not equal for all persons" (quoted in Murakawa 2014, 1). Truman's words reflected a hopeful vision of race relations in the United States and were considerably different from the earlier words of racial scientists, Progressive reformers, and eugenicists. Yet, his words also prefaced an approach to white racial violence that viewed racism as the province of fringe, aberrant, and even criminal members of society. They did not reflect the broader structures of white supremacy that shaped U.S. society. Postwar racial liberalism contended that criminalizing fringe racists would eradicate the problem of racism.

Second, the problems of racism were seen as distinctly contained within white attitudes and black pathology. Whites who held racist views were seen as the predominant problem of racism, and thousands of groups and initiatives formed to educates whites about racial prejudice. By contrast, the problem of racism for black communities was not structural white supremacy but rather the physical and psychological impacts of racism. *Brown v. Board of Education* (1954), for instance, ended segregation not because of the structural ways it protected white advantage but rather because of the psychological impact it (supposedly) had on black children. This "soft racial paternalism" meant that most of the governmental interventions in racial segregation were limited to interventions within the lives of nonwhite communities, not within the social structural conditions that advantage some while disadvantaging others.

Pathologizing Race in the United States

Liberal constructions of race positioned nonwhite, especially black, communities as pathological aberrations that happened as a consequence of racial discrimination. The personifications of the consequences of racial discrimination were remarkably consistent with those of conservatives: the black criminal, the impoverished black child, and the black slum community. Crime, for instance, arose as a consequence of racism and racial deprivation, but it still arose, according to postwar racial liberals, from black communities. Indeed, "liberals relied on a political strategy of compelling reform by making black people seem damaged and potentially violent" (Murakawa 2014, 13). The causes of these particular constructions might be different, but it was black communities and black people themselves that were in need of intervention, transformation, and revitalization. It was not white communities or the state that needed to change.

The **War on Poverty** illustrates the problem of postwar racial liberalism precisely. It was a wide-ranging governmental approach started under President Johnson in 1964. Major parts of the plan included the preschool Head Start program; a federal food stamp program; Medicare and Medicaid; federal funding for primary and secondary education; and job training programs. It also provided funding for retooling the police (a subject we cover below) and for addressing crime and delinquency in urban areas.

Approaches to crime and delinquency during the War on Poverty are often seen as attacking the "root causes" of crime. These approaches built on President Kennedy's efforts against delinquency and crime and turned into a full-scale federal approach to end poverty, crime, and violence.

Yet, what Kennedy, Johnson, and, as we'll come to see, both Democratic and Republican politicians after them had in common was a pathological construction of racial difference. Instead of seeing race as biological, racial difference was seen as the product of growing up in different realities, or cultures, much like the view of proponents of racial historicism in the early twentieth century. Consequently, Kennedy, Johnson, and the War on Poverty programs sought to provide counseling, job training, and remedial education to affected communities. These programs were often seen as part of broader urban redevelopment schemes, such as the 1968 Model Cities programs that sought to entirely remake "blighted" communities.

To qualify for these grants and, even further, to justify their authorization, liberals and urban reformers alike painted a picture of urban areas as rife with crime, violence, and deviant and pathological personalities—what is often called the **culture of poverty.** Communities of color were described as sites breeding pestilence and depravity, reminiscent of eugenic and Progressive constructions of the city, resulting in pathological cultural conditions. Solutions to these conditions included a range of antipoverty programs, such as preschool and free school lunches, but they also included more police surveillance, criminal justice programs specifically targeting these neighborhoods, and increased use of military tactics in urban communities. Together, the political solutions to the problem presented by postwar racial liberals set the stage for the redefinition of the criminal justice system.

Postwar Racial Conservatism

While Kennedy and Johnson fought a war on poverty, the post-WWII era also saw the emergence of a new type of racial conservatism not based in biological understandings of race. The issue of crime was largely absent from national political rhetoric until the 1960s (Beckett 1999, 30). By contrast, the issue of race dominated political rhetoric due to active organizing against white supremacy by nonwhite groups, which came to be known as the civil rights movement.

One of the commonly used tactics of the civil rights movement was civil disobedience to unjust laws. Activists sat at lunch counters reserved for whites, rode interstate buses in mixed-race groups to protest segregation in the South, and used sit-ins to protest racial discrimination in education, employment, and private facilities. These tactics alienated many Democrats, and most white Southerners were conservative Democrats in those days. Support for the War on Poverty and what came to be known as Johnson's Great Society programs further alienated these voters, who saw them as disrupting the white racial power structure. Southern political officials quickly called for a "crackdown on the 'hoodlums,' 'agitators,' 'street mobs,' and 'lawbreakers' who challenged segregation and black disenfranchisement" (Beckett 1999, 30).

The Republicans' "Southern Strategy"

As Democrats throughout the United States moved toward supporting civil rights (albeit reluctantly, in many cases), white voters in the South became dissatisfied with the party and even sought to create their own political party. To win over white voters in the South, Barry Goldwater, the 1964 Republican presidential nominee, ran on what has come to be known as the Southern strategy. The **Southern strategy** was a discourse of crime that would become known as the law and order discourse; it redefined crime as the province of pathological people, rather than social conditions, and called for a strong, punitive response from the state. While Goldwater did not win the presidency, the speech in which he first articulated the Southern strategy would serve as a model for both parties for the next forty years of crime discourse. The appeal of the Southern strategy lay in its geographical imagination of crime and violence that defined crime as a social problem particularly within cities, and not elsewhere. This would not only racialize ideas of crime and orient the tactics of state violence toward nonwhite urban communities but also work to define political protesters as criminals.

Goldwater's articulation of the Southern strategy began with a broad assessment of the problems that faced the United States. This assessment did not differ structurally from the apocalyptic rhetoric of the War on Poverty. In his speech accepting the Republican nomination for president, he began with an appeal to freedom:

> Now, my fellow Americans, the tide has been running against freedom. Our people have followed false prophets. We must, and we shall, return to proven ways—not because they are old, but because they are true. We must, and we shall, set the tide

running again in the cause of freedom. And this party, with its every action, every word, every breath, and every heartbeat, has but a single resolve, and that is freedom—freedom made orderly for this nation by our constitutional government; freedom under a government limited by laws of nature and of nature's God; freedom—balanced so that liberty lacking order will not become the slavery of the prison cell; balanced so that liberty lacking order will not become the license of the mob and of the jungle. (1964)

There are several things to note about Goldwater's characterization. While seemingly about "freedom," Goldwater referenced the civil rights movement by calling out "false prophets" that are seeking to transform society. This is further reinforced by insisting on the necessity of returning "to proven ways," the ways that presumably existed before the rise of those false prophets and the "tide . . . running against freedom." And finally, Goldwater invoked the classic racial imagery of the "jungle." Like his predecessors in the colonial era, Goldwater saw the actions of black and brown citizens as threatening civilization and the "proven ways" of freedom, liberty, and nature. The solution for Goldwater? More order.

The Racial Imagination of "Law and Order"

Goldwater's speech continued to highlight the issues of crime, disorder, and social change, as he sought to emphasize the need for greater "respect for law." He identified this need as especially acute "in our great cities":

> Tonight there is violence in our streets, corruption in our highest offices, aimlessness among our youth, anxiety among our elders and there is a virtual despair among the many who look beyond material success for the inner meaning of their lives. . . . The growing menace in our country tonight, to personal safety, to life, to limb and property, in homes, in churches, on the playgrounds, and places of business, particularly in our great cities, is the mounting concern, or should be, of every thoughtful citizen in the United States. (1964)

Goldwater's characterization of cities as the particular source of the "growing menace" in our midst provided him an opportunity to articulate the issue of crime and order as an issue of black and brown communities without explicitly invoking these groups. Instead, the geography of metropolitan segregation, financed by the federal government, served as the backdrop for his remarks, and the frequent news reports on "urban crises" provided confirmation of his ideas.

Further, Goldwater noted the connection between street violence, corruption, and the aimlessness of urban youth and those, presumably like his opponent Lyndon B. Johnson, who supported Americans who sought "redress . . . through lawlessness, violence, and hurt of his fellow man or damage to his property" (quoted in Beckett 1999, 31). Goldwater further called out government programs for the poor as exacerbating issues of crime and violence in the country, remarking:

If it is entirely proper for the government to take away from some to give to others, then won't some be led to believe that they can rightfully take from anyone who has more than they? No wonder law and order has broken down, mob violence has engulfed great American cities, and our wives feel unsafe in the streets. (1964)

Goldwater's speech demonstrates the colonialist logic of racial difference. He invokes poverty and welfare—or the government's taking "away from some to give to others"—and creates a causal link between them and the issue of crime. He then invokes the racial geographies of great cities "engulfed" in "mob violence." This is not the result of racism, the lack of civil rights, or poverty, in Goldwater's view, but because "law and order has broken down." And perhaps the worst? "Our wives feel unsafe in the streets." Goldwater's invocation of the classic imagery of white womanhood reveals just how important the definition of crime as a social problem is to the consolidation of white supremacy and coloniality in the contemporary moment.

This rhetorical strategy positioned the role of government in a very particular way. Goldwater continued:

Security from domestic violence, no less than from foreign aggression, is the most elementary and fundamental purpose of any government, and a government that cannot fulfill that purpose is one that cannot long command the loyalty of its citizens. History shows us—demonstrates that nothing—nothing prepares the way for tyranny more than the failure of public officials to keep the streets from bullies and marauders. (1964)

Goldwater's speech is the first articulation of what has come to be known as the **law and order discourse.**

This law and order discourse dominated political constructions of crime for the next fifty years, facilitated mass incarceration, and is still, as evidenced by the 2016 presidential election, an important rhetorical tool. As Goldwater demonstrated, it is defined by several components. First is a longing for a return to traditional values, where the words *traditional* and *return* refer to systems of white supremacy and male patriarchy. Often, the phrase "breakdown in the family" is used, which refers both to the women's rights movement and the "depravity" of the single-parent family. Second, he denigrates social programs, blaming them for increasing disorder, which is most often found in "the streets" or the "jungle." These programs are too "permissive" and encourage crime and violence by failing to punish "dangerous" individuals and rewarding those who do not work for a living. Finally, the appropriate response is an increase in order, represented by appeals to increased "security" and legal violence promulgated by the police and the criminal justice system. Goldwater's law and order discourse, then, is one of the first articulations of crime and drugs as a social problem using the postracial language that would become common in the post–civil rights era.

A New Racial Language

Goldwater's speech was one of the first articulations of a new lexicon of racial language, where instead of speaking explicitly about the problems of race, the problems of *urban* crime, violence, and disorder take precedence. While race was always coded geographically, the invocation of this geography in the Goldwater speech reveals how well it works to shift the focus from urban slums being a consequence of racial oppression to urban disorder being the consequence of slum inhabitants—the nonwhite racial threat lurking in the subtext of Goldwater's speech.

Goldwater's invocation of the civil rights movement provided an opportunity to bring white Southern voters critical of racial justice into the Republican party, a ploy that largely worked and that continues to be replicated today. Further, however, Goldwater provided a model of how to talk about race without using the explicit associations pioneered by racial scientists. Goldwater's speech also served as a model for the law and order discourse that Richard Nixon would use to win the presidency in 1968 and helped fuel a substantial reorganization of federal and state criminal justice systems under Reagan, Bush, and Clinton.

Importantly, though, Goldwater's speech also did not stray from the liberal characterization of urban areas. Years of rhetoric about solving the problems of our "great cities" had squarely positioned the issues of crime and violence within urban areas. These areas, as we know from chapter 5, were not racially heterogeneous places; instead, stark racial geographies had emerged throughout U.S. metropolitan regions. This rhetoric provided continuity across the political spectrum, such that no political party or initiative was focused on solving the problems of the racial social order but rather focused on defining social problems as the result of just one part of this racial social order: the spaces inhabited by nonwhites, especially black communities.

Social Science and the Criminalization of Race

As in the Progressive Era and the time of scientific racism, ideologies of objectivity and expertise soon provided evidence for the claims of both postwar conservatives and liberals. The focus on poverty, racial strife, and urban social problems in academia provided fuel for the conceptualizations of urban nonwhite communities as pathological, aberrant, and ultimately criminal.

The "discovery" of poverty in the 1960s by political elites was aided by the publication and widespread dissemination of the ideas in the infamous **Moynihan Report.** It was produced in 1965 by Assistant Secretary of Labor Daniel Patrick Moynihan for the Department of Labor. Titled *The Negro Family: The Case for National Action,* the report examined the "widening" gap between black people and whites in the United States. He attributed this gap to the "tangle of pathology" found in black communities, which began with a supposedly matriarchal structure:

> A community that allows large numbers of young men to grow up in broken families, dominated by women, never acquiring any stable relationships to male authority, never acquiring any set of rational expectations about the future—that community asks for and gets chaos. Crime, violence, unrest, disorder are not only to be expected, but they are very near to inevitable. And they are richly deserved. (Moynihan 1965, 44).

Moynihan attributed the logic that a community is *deserving* of crime, violence, unrest, and disorder to the pathology supposedly inherent in the black family.

Though liberals used the Moynihan Report as part of the architecture of the War on Poverty, it was also embraced by conservatives as evidence of the pathology of black America. It further revealed the place where liberals and conservatives converged: on the racial imaginary of U.S. society. While Moynihan's report may not be a common text for study of white nationalism, it nevertheless helped to consolidate a vision of white racial identity as law-abiding, traditional, patriarchal, and orderly, and black identity as pathological, deviant, and depraved, not least because of its supposedly matriarchal structure. While Moynihan did not invoke biological racism or eugenics, his conclusions and those of postwar racial liberals and conservatives largely echoed scholars from earlier periods: the problem of race lies not in the construction of a racial society but within the personalities and "cultures" of those most marginalized.

LAW AND ORDER TAKES HOLD

Scholars often trace the legal changes that precipitated mass incarceration to the Omnibus Crime Control and Safe Streets Act signed by President Johnson in 1968. Prior to this bill, *federal* crime policy was largely nonexistent. Agents of the Federal Bureau of Investigation primarily investigated white-collar crimes and were viewed with considerable suspicion by local law enforcement and large portions of U.S. society (Beckett and Sasson 2004).

With the 1968 act, however, the role of the federal government relative to local law enforcement changed, and federal enforcement shifted dramatically. As a consequence of this shift, urban police became more uniform, more militarized, and importantly, more prolific. With this widening web of surveillance, the remaking of the criminal justice system as a primary tool for racial governance was not far behind.

The passage of the Omnibus Act was only four years after the passage of the Civil Rights Act in 1964. Though only four years had passed, 1968 was a dramatically different social context. Resistance against the Vietnam War was gaining momentum, the civil rights movement was transforming to address systematic economic injustice, and radical politics were on the rise. With the election of President Nixon in 1968, the nation again turned to the issue of drugs and found panic about drugs to be an important tool in the new era of racial governance.

Political Repression and the New Urban Order

On August 6, 1965, President Lyndon Johnson signed the Voting Rights Act. Designed to protect the voting rights of African Americans, the bill was seen as a major victory for the civil rights movement and its method of nonviolent civil disobedience. The promise of achieving racial progress through nonviolent means was short-lived, however. Only five days after the Voting Rights Act was signed, the Watts neighborhood in Los Angeles went up in flames as thousands of residents took to the streets to protest police brutality. Watts soon became a symbol for urban unrest, and municipal governments throughout the United States worried that their city would be next.

Watts and the Making of a Black Neighborhood

Watts is a neighborhood of a little over two square miles located in southeastern Los Angeles, California. Watts was originally its own city but was incorporated by the city of Los Angeles in 1926. It was one of the few areas not covered by the racially restrictive covenants that formally governed 95 percent of the city until 1948, which were then informally enforced well into the 1970s (Avila 2014).

As a consequence, many African Americans settled in Watts during the second phase of the Great Migration. This second phase occurred during WWII when many Southern black people relocated to serve wartime industries in the North and West. Los Angeles during the war, and after, was a center of shipping and aircraft industries, and millions of people immigrated to the city between 1940 and 1950. During this ten-year period, the African American population nearly tripled. Between 1940 and 1965, the number of black residents in the city increased from 63,000 to about 350,000, a rise in the proportion from 4 percent to 14 percent (Simpson 2012).

As these new residents arrived, they were met with housing and labor restrictions, forcing many of them into established black communities such as Watts. Overcrowding in black communities led many to search for housing in areas previously reserved for whites in the hopes of escaping geographic, economic, and social isolation. However, blockbusting and racial discrimination prevented black people from joining whites in fleeing the city and experiencing the promise of suburban living.

To ease overcrowding, the state stepped in and built public housing to shelter many of the new arrivals. In 1944, a new public housing complex opened in Watts, and between 1940 and 1950, the black population of Watts grew from just under 9,000 residents to over 92,000. This meant that over 42 percent of the total black population of Los Angeles resided in Watts. This made Los Angeles the third most segregated American city in the 1960s, a notoriety derived from measuring the extent to which white and black people live in the same places (Von Hoffman 2004).

White Violence and the Making of Watts

As their numbers grew, African American residents were increasingly met with hostility and violence from white residents nearby. Crosses were burned, houses were bombed and shot at, and white gangs routinely accosted black people who traveled through white neighborhoods.

The Spook Hunters, for example, was a gang of white teenagers that became notorious for violently enforcing racial segregation (Alonso 2004). The Spook Hunters policed the borders of the black areas of Los Angeles and enforced racial boundaries by violently attacking any black youth who dared to cross the racial line. To protect themselves, black youths in Los Angeles formed social clubs. Groups like the Haciendas, the Slausons, and the Gladiators were organized to resist the violence of the Spook Hunters.

By the 1960s, Watts was also marked by the systemic violence of unemployment and housing discrimination. Middle-class black people were often unable to move from the area due to housing discrimination, while at the same time the high rate of unemployment in the neighborhood led to deteriorating conditions for all residents. By 1965, the poverty rate was 30.9 percent in Watts, and the unemployment rate for black males was 10.9 percent (Cohen 1967). "Slum clearance" resulted in razing a portion of the neighborhood for freeway construction, which also cut Watts off from its southern neighbors.

Police violence was commonplace in Watts and other neighborhoods of color in Los Angeles, and it "strictly limited the mobility of black residents." In patrolling the city, police officers routinely

> prohibited blacks from traveling north of Beverly Boulevard and west of La Brea Boulevard, in the affluent part of town. If officers found a black man near the Hollywood station, they interrogated him, checked for outstanding warrants or tried to match him with a crime report. Sometimes they would take him to a call box at Outpost Canyon and Mulholland Drive, a good distance northwest of the central city, where most blacks lived, and far from public transportation. If they could not find the means to arrest the man, they told him to walk back. (Kramer 2007, 250)

Housing available to black residents was segregated and very scarce, and the Los Angeles Police Department (LAPD) ensured that even without laws enforcing segregation, black residents were considerably restricted in their mobility.

Watts Explodes

Decades of mistreatment and excessive violence by the LAPD against black and Latinx communities finally boiled over in 1965 in what is known popularly as the "Watts rebellion," but the riots were not the first protests of conditions by people of color in Los Angeles. In the previous two years, over 250 demonstrations against racial injustice had taken place in the city. Over a thousand people had come out for a protest against the LAPD in 1961 when an officer killed a young man, and black leaders in Los Angeles regularly called for the resignation of the LAPD's chief. In 1963, the NAACP issued a twelve-page memo to the police commission protesting LAPD's treatment of black and Latinx people, naming several officers who routinely engaged in misconduct. This attempt to redefine the social problem of urban poverty as one of police violence, however, failed to gain traction, and Watts soon erupted into a full-scale rebellion.

On August 11, 1965, police pulled over a young black man on suspicion of drunk driving, and a fight broke out between police and the motorist. News of the event spread throughout the neighborhood, which was already concerned about the excessive rates of police brutality in the community. Anger and unrest soon erupted into a full-scale rebellion that lasted for five days and caused over $40 million in property damage (see figure 6.7).

Immediately, the rebellion was cast in the language and practice of war. The chief of the LAPD, William Parker, referred to the rebellion as an "insurgency" and compared Watts residents to the Viet Cong. He further suggested a "paramilitary" response would be necessary to return peace to Los Angeles and referred to residents using animal imagery common to racist characterizations and the law and order discourse.

Watts soon took on the character of an occupied country (see figure 6.8). With the deployment of the National Guard, the number of officers in the neighborhood reached over two thousand. The police response was also extremely aggressive. Thirty-one of the thirty-four people killed during the rebellion were killed by police. A policy of mass arrests and a curfew were instituted in the neighborhood, and nearly four thousand people were arrested (Kramer 2007).

Research directly following the Watts rebellion reveal the extent of aggressive policing in the neighborhood. In one survey by UCLA researchers in the late 1960s, residents reported frequently witnessing police in the neighborhood beating up suspects in custody, "rousting and frisking," using insulting language and unnecessary force in arrests, and showing a general lack of respect (Hahn and Feagin 1970). Further, residents reported that they were unable to access the protective services of the LAPD and that crimes they reported frequently were never investigated. They were, as the today's lexicon puts it, both overpoliced and underpoliced, something common to the professional era of

Figure 6.7 Aerial view of two buildings on fire on Avalon Blvd. between 107th and 108th Streets during Watts Riots, 1965. Source: *Los Angeles Times* Photographic Archive, UCLA Library. Copyright Regents of the University of California, UCLA Library.

policing that continues to shape the culture of policing today (Epp, Maynard-Moody, and Haider-Markel 2014).

The Rise and Suppression of Radical Politics

For many black youths, Watts signaled the formal death of nonviolence as a legitimate political strategy, and some youth who organized against the Spook Hunters formed new radical organizations. For instance, the head of the Slausons, Bunchy Carter, became one of the leaders of the Los Angeles Black Panthers (Umoja 1999).

While the civil rights movement had long focused on inequalities and formal segregation in the South, black youth in the major urban centers of the North and West, such as Los Angeles, were experiencing their own forms of invidious racial discrimination. Los Angeles, for instance, did not have formal Jim Crow laws, so the tactics of civil disobedience were not entirely applicable. Further, many Northern youth were disaffected with the strategies of the civil rights movement, which they saw as overly conciliatory. These new radical

Figure 6.8 Armed police officers guard street in Watts. Source: *Los Angeles Times* Photographic Archive, UCLA Library. Copyright Regents of the University of California, UCLA Library.

politics led to a more explicit approach to confronting racial inequality, found within the more militant and direct-service-oriented platforms of groups like the Black Panther Party (Umoja 1999).

Formed in Oakland, California, in October 1966 by Huey Newton and Bobby Seale, the Black Panther Party was one organization that appealed to black youth in Los Angeles. For Carter and those who followed his trajectory, the state was responsible for their suffering and thus not an entity that could be called upon to end it. Only radical political action would result in transformation and an end of suffering. The Panthers enjoyed rapid success in Los Angeles and quickly drew the attention of the federal government.

As organizations like the Black Panther Party grew in popularity and stature, local and federal law enforcement began employing strategies to dismantle the revolutionary threat. The Black Panther Party would soon find itself defined by law enforcement as one of the most pressing social problems that necessitated violent intervention. Led by J. Edgar Hoover, the FBI designed a strategy of systematic violence to dismantle the Black Panther Party and its influence in Los Angeles. In Hoover's mind, the Black Panther Party had become the "greatest threat to the internal security of the United States" (Grady-Willis 1998). He aimed to counter that threat through his Counter Intelligence Program (**COINTELPRO**), a series of covert operations leveled at U.S. citizens who had been deemed subversive by the FBI. COINTELPRO's tactics against the Panthers included the use of undercover informants, torture, and assassinations. Though considered an overextension of state power today, COINTELPRO represented a successful attempt by the federal government to define black communities as a social problem necessitating ever more state surveillance.

In a 1967 letter issued to FBI headquarters, Hoover described COINTEL-PRO as an "endeavor to expose, disrupt, misdirect, discredit, or otherwise neutralize the activities of black nationalist hate-type organizations and groupings, their leadership, spokesmen, membership, and supporters, and their propensity for violence and civil disorder" (quoted in Van Deburg 1997, 134). In Los Angeles, the FBI and the LAPD worked together to discredit and suppress members of the party. Attacks on the Southern California chapter of the Black Panther Party included the August 1968 killing of three Panthers by the Los Angeles Police Department, the arrests of forty-two Panthers in May 1969, the September 8, 1969, police raid on the Breakfast for Children Program in Watts, and the October 10, 1969, killing of a Panther by the LAPD. The FBI further undermined revolutionary political activity by instigating violence between members of various revolutionary organizations. In Los Angeles, this tactic would end with the murder of Panthers Bunchy Carter and John Huggins on the campus of UCLA on January 17, 1969. In Chicago, police raided a home and intentionally murdered Fred Hampton, the chair of the Illinois chapter of the Black Panther Party.

Surveillance and the Transformation of Policing

The decimation of radical political organizations accompanied the expansion of the surveillance state, which soon aimed paramilitary methods of policing at the day-to-day life of black communities. Like the extension of surveillance in the slavery and Progressive eras, the transformation of modern policing served to create further surveillance, which Simone Browne, a black feminist scholar, calls a "fact of blackness" that works to "reify boundaries along racial lines . . . and where the outcome of this is often discriminatory and violent treatment" (2015, 16).

Although FBI surveillance began with political organizations, it soon extended itself over the urban community. Domestic educators, uniformed urban police, and the juvenile court were some of the institutionalized mechanisms of surveillance historically. Repression of political dissent in the 1960s and 1970s extended this surveillance over the urban community—particularly communities of color—through the War on Drugs.

Drugs and the Remaking of U.S. Criminal Justice

Events around the nation in cities like Watts provided fodder for national political elites to continue the law and order discourse. Although Goldwater failed to win the presidency, concern with law and order endured, and crime remained a central issue for political elites well into the 1970s. Despite defeating Goldwater, President Johnson declared a "war on crime" and helped transform criminal justice in the United States by moving the enforcement and regulation of drugs from the Treasury Department and Food and Drug Administration to a newly created Bureau of Narcotics and Dangerous Drugs within the Justice Department. This was an important moment in the policing of drugs, as it transitioned drugs from a public welfare issue to one of crime, justice, and public suppression. Johnson also signed into law the Omnibus Crime Control and Safe Streets Act of 1968, which President Nixon would use to continue the reorientation of the nation's criminal justice apparatus.

Nixon's Law and Order Campaign

Following Goldwater, Nixon ran on an explicit law and order agenda that directly connected the issues of civil rights protesters, specifically civil disobedience, to crime. In 1966, he argued that "the deterioration of respect for the rule of law can be traced directly to the spread of the corrosive doctrine that every citizen possesses an inherent right to decide for himself which laws to obey and when to disobey them" (quoted in Beckett and Sasson 2004, 48). This directly invoked events occurring around the nation in neighborhoods like Watts, where residents were rising up against decades of mistreatment at the hands of the police. Nixon further argued, like Goldwater, that welfare programs were of little help in the fight against crime: "I say that doubling the conviction rate in this country would do more to cure crime in America than quadrupling the funds for [Democratic candidate Hubert] Humphrey's war on poverty" (quoted in Parenti 2000, 8). Invoking urban protesters and declaring the need for a strong, forceful, and violent response demonstrated just how race had become criminalized.

Nixon's campaign reportedly viewed two groups as enemies of the state: antiwar protesters and black people (LoBianco 2016). Nixon's racial views were documented in a diary kept by one of his aides, H. R. Haldeman. In his diary, Haldeman wrote that Nixon "emphasized that you have to face the fact that the whole problem is really the blacks. The key is to devise a system that recognizes this while not appearing to. Pointed out that there has never in history been an adequate black nation, and they are the only race of which this is true" (Associated Press 1994). Nixon's explicit racism gave way to a political strategy where instead of openly decrying the degeneration of nonwhites, he instead appealed to a particular racialized geography shaping the nation.

Nixon's clear-eyed view of this strategy is further evidenced by a letter he wrote to one of his mentors right before he won the 1968 election: "I have found great audience response to this [law-and-order] theme in all parts of the country, including areas like New Hampshire where there is virtually no race problem and relatively little crime" (quoted in Parenti 2000, 7). In an inadvertent recording of a candid statement to his staff made after reviewing a campaign advertisement about law and order in schools in 1968, he said, "It's all about law-and-order and the damn Negro-Puerto Rican groups out there" (Murakawa 2014, 8).

Nixon's War on Drugs

Nixon, however, faced a dilemma upon assuming office. While he campaigned on a war on crime, the office of the president has almost no role in the day-to-day governance of crime. This is a responsibility usually carried out by local authorities. This twist—especially for a federalist politician who supported smaller federal government—meant that Nixon faced an unusual predicament when he assumed office. To address it, he "devised a system" that recognized the real problems "while not appearing to": the criminalization of drugs (Associated Press 1994; see also Baum 1996).

Just six months after he assumed office, Nixon addressed Congress and set the stage for the emergence of the **War on Drugs,** arguing:

> Within the last decade, the abuse of drugs has grown from essentially a local police problem into a serious national threat to the personal health and safety of millions of Americans. . . . A national awareness of the gravity of the situation is needed: a new urgency and concerted national policy are needed at the federal level to begin to cope with this growing menace to the general welfare of the United States. (quoted in Parenti 2000, 9)

This "growing menace," while unsupported by the evidence, would form the basis for a vast reorientation of the federal approach to law enforcement and the creation of a unified system of surveillance throughout the nation. Going far beyond the policing of drugs, these changes targeted a vast network of political activists.

Creating an Occupying Force

The Omnibus Control Act in 1968 was riddled with references to the need for increased riot control and law enforcement, a direct response to political unrest created by the civil rights movement. When Nixon assumed office in 1969, an emphasis on riot control and increasing urban police would provide the foundation for the remaking of urban law enforcement and the criminal justice system.

One of the most important provisions of the Act was the establishment of the **Law Enforcement Assistance Administration (LEAA).** The LEAA was a federal agency tasked with providing monetary, educational, and technological assistance to local law enforcement agencies. Its importance grew considerably when Congress quadrupled its funding from $59.4 million in 1968 to $268 million just two years later. Through the LEAA, the federal government was not only able to shape the direction of local policing but to harness the power of local police to connect and extend networks of surveillance across the nation (Blauner 1969).

LEAA and Police Militarization

Through the LEAA, local police underwent a process of "modernization," which was also militarization. Notably, an early precedent of the LEAA in 1965 was sponsored by a Democratic senator who noted that it would address racial justice by not only modernizing police through education and adherence to uniform procedures and policies but also teaching "slum children [to] have respect for the law" (quoted in Murakawa 2014, 80). Prior to the LEAA, very few police agencies had officer training programs. In 1965, for instance, only four states in the entire nation required any police training, and more than twenty states did not even have educational or literacy standards for officers (Parenti 2000, 15). At the time, the majority of Detroit's officers came from the bottom 25 percent of their high school classes (Parenti 2000).

With funding from the LEAA, states and localities around the nation created training standards, criminal codes, and police academies (Beckett 1999). The FBI also worked with local police to create criminal history databases that could be monitored and compiled by the FBI. One reason that the FBI rates of crime show increases in the 1970s and 1980s is that this modernization project led to rising rates of crime *being reported* to the FBI by previously off-the-grid agencies. These modernization tactics were critical to addressing claims of racial injustice in policing, since the often particularistic and haphazard enforcement of laws at the local level was carried out against primarily communities of color. Modernization thus provided a moment for imbuing policing with a scientific ideology of objectivity and rationality; through the LEAA, the United States attempted to create a nationwide network of modern police.

These modern police, however, were trained not just in the supposedly objective enforcement of the law but also in military tactics. The LEAA provided local agencies with paramilitary tools, such as high-tech dispatch, radios, and mobile command and control centers. With funding from the National Highway Safety Act of 1966 and the LEAA, local agencies were supplied with police helicopters at a 75-percent discount. Further, the LEAA promoted the formation of "special weapons and tactics units" (which usually operated out of the mobile command units also provided by the LEAA) by providing training and funding through the FBI. These changes brought together a "patchwork, disparate, and sometimes overlapping police agencies . . . into a single, coherent, smooth-running informational and surveillance network" (Parenti 2000, 19). Further, these innovations have continued: a program authorized in 1997 provides police agencies with military-grade weapons such as armored vehicles, tanks, grenade launchers, and aircraft. This is why places such as Davis, California—a small college town—have tanks.

SWAT and the Militarization of Police

One of the most widespread new programs was for Special Weapons and Tactics, or SWAT, teams. SWAT was born out of the era of political repression and first created by LAPD Chief of Police Daryl Gates. SWAT is a paramilitary unit equipped with submachine guns, sniper rifles, and armored vehicles that descends upon a community and takes control in much the same way an occupying force would do in a foreign context—often going door to door raiding and searching homes, rounding up groups of residents, and providing overt displays of force, something reinforced even in the "riot gear" uniform of the officer.

SWAT was created to deal with the perceived threat posed by radical organizations like the Black Panther Party. After his involvement in suppressing the 1965 Watts uprising, Gates became convinced that the LAPD needed to develop a unit that could deal with urban armed insurrections. Inspired by the counterinsurgency campaigns of the U.S. military in Vietnam, Gates envisioned SWAT as an occupying army. To establish the LAPD SWAT team, officers began training with U.S. Marines and members of the Army's Delta Force.

SWAT's inauguration was the December 8, 1969, raid on the Black Panther office in Los Angeles, a raid that was eerily similar to the one carried out in Chicago that had killed Black Panther Fred Hampton just a few days earlier (Umoja 1999). At 5:30 in the morning, SWAT team members burst through the doors of the office and began shooting—no warrant was provided. Armed with automatic rifles, helicopters, tear gas, and dynamite, four hundred police officers surrounded the Panthers' office and a shoot-out ensued. After the Panthers shot back and refused to surrender, Gates was granted permission by the Pentagon to bomb the office with a grenade launcher borrowed from the United States Marines. Only the Panthers' decision to surrender before the grenade launcher was used saved them from obliteration.

SWAT raids on Black Panther organizations, as well as others challenging racial oppression, such as Native Americans, reveal how modernization efforts resulted in a more organized, better equipped, and more technologically sophisticated police force (Churchill and Vander Wall 2002). But these modernization efforts were nevertheless deployed to more efficiently and effectively police urban communities. While commonplace for the period, these efforts also reveal how the highest levels of the U.S. government conspired to bomb U.S. citizens in an effort to repress political dissonance. Even further, these

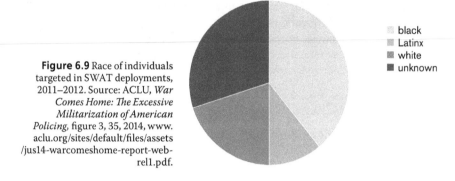

Figure 6.9 Race of individuals targeted in SWAT deployments, 2011–2012. Source: ACLU, *War Comes Home: The Excessive Militarization of American Policing,* figure 3, 35, 2014, www. aclu.org/sites/default/files/assets /jus14-warcomeshome-report-web-rel1.pdf.

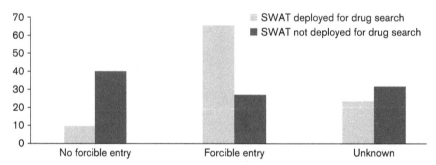

Figure 6.10 Disparities in use of force when SWAT is deployed and not deployed for drug searches, 2011–2012. Source: ACLU, *War Comes Home: The Excessive Militarization of American Policing,* figure 7, 38, 2014, www.aclu.org/sites/default/files/assets/jus14-warcomeshome-report-web-rel1.pdf.

actions—along with the destruction of housing and neighborhood ties to make way for a freeway—are considered the origins of the formation of gangs in Los Angeles (Shelden, Tracy, and Brown 2012).

For the first time, a local police force had created a military unit to be employed solely against U.S. citizens. Although SWAT was originally envisioned as a mechanism to crush the threat of revolution, it has become integrated into everyday policing. SWAT soon became a key tactic in the War on Drugs, and communities were routinely subjected to full-scale military occupation by local police (see figures 6.9 and 6.10). What started as an attempt to professionalize police soon became a full-scale domestic military operation, disproportionately jailing and occupying nonwhite communities.

Today, every major city in the United States has a SWAT team and some estimate that SWAT is deployed as many as 80,000 times per year. Local SWAT teams' weapons are supplied directly by the U.S. Department of Defense and have cost $4.3 billion since the 1990s (Sanburn 2014). While police may not openly engage in the routine killing of political dissidents as they did in Los Angeles, Chicago, and elsewhere in the late 1960s and 1970s, SWAT remains. And it, along with the broader militarization of the police, was instrumental in the reconfiguration of racial repression through the criminal justice system.

Empowering Local Law Enforcement

The targeting of political activists was openly espoused at the highest levels of government. Nixon, as we have seen, openly hated political activists. An article in the *FBI Bulletin* warned, "New tactics and techniques have been developed in the United States by a small number of criminals who style themselves urban guerrillas" (quoted in Parenti 2000, 17). This is how political activists and nonwhite communities became equated with criminals in the national discourse. Likewise, FBI director J. Edgar Hoover wrote, "Never before in the history of American law enforcement has our profession faced such inflamed bitterness and hostility and such purposive intentions to wreak havoc against the police officers through injury, maiming, and outright murder. . . . Ideological and revolutionary violence in the nation is on the increase" (quoted in Parenti 2000, 17). These ideas served, in the context of the racial geographies of metropolitan areas, to target the ideologies and practices of the military toward governing communities of color. It did this through the emerging War on Drugs.

One of Nixon's top advisors reported that the War on Drugs was explicitly created to target "blacks and hippies" (Baum 2016). To do so, Nixon pushed through legislation that increased funding for drug interdiction and policing. With the passage of the Comprehensive Drug Abuse Prevention and Control Act of 1970, an additional $220 million was provided to local law enforcement to fight drugs. That same year, Congress allocated $3.55 billion to the LEAA for the next three years, or over $1 billion per year, and almost four times the budget of the LEAA in 1970 (which had already been quadrupled since 1968). Until the end of the 1970s, the LEAA routinely had an annual budget of over $1 billion. Together, the LEAA and federal emphasis on drugs worked to encourage local police to make drugs a priority and to use military instruments to do so.

Law enforcement was also aided by the federal assault on due-process protections for those accused of crimes. Nixon appointed three Supreme Court justices in his first term, and they helped to roll back constitutional restrictions on confessions, wiretaps, and other law enforcement surveillance. Further, the government targeted organized crime through the Organized Crime Control Act of 1970, which created what are known as Racketeer Influenced and Corrupt Organizations (RICO) charges. RICO charges allowed the government to target organizations, such as the Mafia or a gang, and hold their members accountable for crimes even if they had nothing to do with the criminal act itself. While RICO was ostensibly created to address organized crime groups like the Mafia, it was soon deployed against urban communities through the War on Drugs.

In the era of the drug war, RICO allowed even the lowest-level street pusher to be charged with the crimes of the cartel leader. Consequently, someone with a very small role in a drug transaction could receive a life sentence, even several of them (Blakey and Roddy 1995). RICO created secret "special grand juries" that could interrogate anyone, including defense attorneys, and could jail any "uncooperative" witness for up to eighteen months (Parenti 2000). RICO also allowed for asset seizure from organizations, lengthened possible sentences, and loosened rules on the use of illegally obtained evidence by prosecutors.

THE CONTINUING WAR ON CRIME AND THE RISE OF MASS INCARCERATION

After Nixon's brief foray into the war on crime, few national politicians took up the issue in the 1970s. Nixon's involvement in the Watergate cover-up undercut his anticrime message. The decision by his successor, Gerald Ford, to pardon him made crime a touchy issue for the new administration. However, under the leadership of Presidents Ronald Reagan and George W. Bush, the war on crime finally ascended as a social problem that could substantially transform law enforcement and prison systems into the systems of racialized mass incarceration we know today.

Reagan and the New Federal Role in Law Enforcement

Reagan reinvigorated the issue of crime in the 1980s, and he began his first term by emphasizing that "the war on crime will only be won when . . . certain truths take hold again . . . truths like: right and wrong matters; individuals are responsible for their actions; retribution should be swift and sure for those who prey on the innocent" (Beckett 1999, 47). Reagan also believed that crime was an individual choice and unrelated to social conditions, arguing: "Choosing a career in crime is not the result of poverty or of an unhappy childhood or of a misunderstood adolescence; it is the result of a conscious, willful choice made by some who consider themselves above the law, who seek to exploit the hard work and, sometimes, the very lives of their fellow citizens" (Beckett 1999, 47).

Like Goldwater and Nixon before him, Reagan drew on the now-classic tenets of the law and order discourse by invoking a return to traditional authority, people who commit crime as predators, and the need for increased violence and punishment: when "certain truths take hold again"; "swift and sure" retribution; and notions of innocence "preyed" upon by threatening outsiders who "choose" crime. This logic resulted in a theory of crime that delegitimized rehabilitation, emphasized punishment, and sought longer and more severe prison sentences for those convicted.

Reagan, like Nixon, faced the federalist dilemma of how to address crime with the tools of the federal government. One of the first things he did upon assuming office was task his attorney general with considering ways the federal government could combat violent crime (Beckett 1999, 47). The attorney general's solution was to shift the FBI's focus away from white collar crime and toward street crime. In October 1981, the Justice Department cut by half those assigned to white collar and corporate crime. Further, Reagan authorized the FBI to play a role in drug interdiction efforts, alongside local law enforcement and the Drug Enforcement Agency (DEA; created in the 1970s).

During a time of cuts to federal agencies, only law enforcement agencies saw their budgets increase. Under Reagan, the FBI antidrug funding increased from $8 million to $95 million, and the DEA's budget increased from $215 million to $312 million between 1980 and 1984. And in 1982, Reagan officially declared his "war on drugs," calling drugs "an especially vicious virus of crime" (Reagan 1982). He outlined a "bold and confident plan" that would "beef up" the number of prosecutors and law enforcement and utilize overseas military strategies to attack drugs in the United States. In Congress, legislators sought to have military planes shoot down suspected drug traffickers. In all, nine departments and thirty-three federal agencies were assigned to fight drugs (Beckett 1999).

The War on Crack

The story of the war on crack cocaine, one of the most racialized and virulent examples of political agitation during the war on drugs, often begins with the tragedy of Len Bias's death in 1986. Bias was the number-one pick in the NBA draft and was thought to be a potential all-time great, but before he played a single professional basketball game, he died from a drug overdose. Members of Congress reported when they returned from their session break that Bias's death was all their constituents were talking about (Baum 1996). Though Bias died of a cocaine overdose, rumor spread that he died from taking crack cocaine, a drug that was rapidly gaining public attention.

Working quickly, Congress soon passed the Anti-Drug Abuse Act of 1988, one of the most controversial drugs laws that remains in force (though in a slightly softened form) today. The hallmark of the act was the creation of mandatory minimums for drug crimes, where a particular sentence is required if one is convicted of a given crime. Possession of five grams of crack meant a five-year mandatory minimum prison term. By contrast, one would need to possess 500 grams of cocaine, the more expensive drug from which crack is made, to receive a similar sentence (Beckett and Sasson 2004). Recent court cases have led to a lessening of this mandatory minimum, but not before many were sentenced under this draconian law.

The consequences of this law were devastating. Though whites were 78 percent of crack users and sellers, over 94 percent of convictions were of black Americans (Beckett and Sasson 2004). Crack devastated the black community—but not for the pharmacological reasons generally cited. Instead, the policing and the suspicion of crack led to news stories that continued the reframing of crime as an issue of nonwhite Americans and very few others (Barlow 1995).

Publicizing Drugs

Sensational media stories began to focus on drugs, particularly crack cocaine, identifying it as the drug of choice of the inner city. Between 1984 and 1987 alone, over a thousand articles appeared in major newspapers on the topic of crack cocaine. News organizations ran special coverage of the crack crisis and pseudo-documentaries about life on crack such as *48 Hours on Crack Street* (which launched the weekly program *48 Hours*) were produced. Television news outlets increased coverage of drugs from 73 stories in the latter half of 1985 to 283 in the same period of 1986 (Beckett 1999, 56).

Media coverage reinforced the law and order vision of crime as something committed primarily by nonwhites in cities. News stories that involved crime and violence were almost twice as likely to feature African American suspects (Entman 1994). Further, "studies of local and national news have found that African Americans arrested for violent crimes were more likely to be depicted in the physical custody of police (e.g., spread-eagled against the side of a police cruiser) and to be dressed sloppily" (Beckett and Sasson 2004, 76). The most unusual cases—such as a white woman victimized by a black man—are the ones most represented in the media. One study in Los Angeles found that 37 percent of the suspects portrayed on the news were black, despite the fact that they made up only 21 percent of arrests (Ghandnoosh 2014, 118). Further, the association between blackness and crime, especially violence, in the news media found that when research participants were asked to recall news stories about crime, they often recalled seeing a mug shot of a black or Latinx person even if they had not been shown a mug shot (Beckett and Sasson 2004).

"The Most Serious Problem"

Alongside media elites, political elites continued to argue that drugs were the number-one issue facing the United States. Just after assuming office, President George H. W. Bush addressed the nation about drugs, illustrating just how important he found the issue:

This is the first time since taking the oath of office that I felt an issue was so important, so threatening, that it warranted talking directly with you, the American people. All of us agree that the gravest domestic threat facing our nation today is drugs. Drugs have strained our faith in our system of justice. Our courts, our prisons, our legal system are stretched to the breaking point. The social costs of drugs are mounting. In short, drugs are sapping our strength as a nation. Turn on the evening news or pick up the morning paper and you'll see what some Americans know just by stepping out their front door: Our most serious problem today is cocaine, and in particular, crack. (Bush 1989)

This identification of drugs as "the most serious problem" justified extraordinary criminal justice powers, and the claim that "all of us agree" placed the onus of responsibility on the entire nation.

Bush went on to dangle a baggie of white rocks on television, purportedly crack cocaine itself:

This is crack cocaine seized a few days ago by Drug Enforcement agents in a park just across the street from the White House. It could easily have been heroin or PCP. It's as innocent-looking as candy, but it's turning our cities into battle zones, and it's murdering our children. Let there be no mistake: This stuff is poison. Some used to call drugs harmless recreation; they're not. Drugs are a real and terribly dangerous threat to our neighborhoods, our friends, and our families. (Bush 1989)

While he failed to note that it took DEA agents several days to secure the drugs for the sole purpose of making this claim on TV, this moment served as evidence for many people that crack itself was the greatest threat to the United States (Baum 1996).

Bush's use of his first televised address to highlight the issue of drugs demonstrates just how important politicians are to the framing of social problems. As Katherine Beckett, a sociologist of mass incarceration, demonstrates, after a political address about drugs—including Bush's first—public concern about drugs as a social problem increased considerably. In fact, most of the time, polls found unemployment and the economy to be far greater issues facing the United States than drugs or crime (Beckett 1999). But, as Beckett deftly illustrates, when political elites defined drugs as a social problem, suddenly so did the public.

Defining Crack as a Social Problem: Two Narratives

Elevating the issue of crack cocaine in the national discourse and defining crack as a social problem proceeded through two predominant narratives that are recast today in the definition of meth as a social problem (see box 6.1). First, there was the idea that crack makes people violent—just like the "cocaine fiends" and "reefer madmen" of the 1910s and 1930s. Little evidence supports this idea; instead, the vast majority of violence related to drugs happens because of participation in the drug market. Indeed, homicide rates are primarily a product of prohibition, as they shift with changes in the drug market and

BOX 6.1   Defining Drugs as a Social Problem Today

Moral panics about whites and crime are commonly cited to counter the idea that drugs and crime are racialized. A recent example is the discourse around methamphetamine (meth) usage. The figure of meth is a white, often rural user, unlike the stereotypical user of crack, opium, cocaine, and marijuana historically. Does meth undermine the idea that drug prohibition is one of the dominant ways that racialization works today?

Travis Linnemann and Tyler Wall (2013) say no. They review the popular campaign Faces of Meth. You've probably seen examples in the media, on Facebook, or elsewhere online. These are before-and-after pictures, often mug shots, that show first a face largely devoid of physical deformities—what some might call healthy—and contrast that with the face of the same person after using meth. The "after" photo is an exercise in projecting the grotesque, showing physical maladies that we often associate with disease and dirt and that elicit disgust and unease within us: missing teeth, visible malnutrition, stringy and greasy hair, and faces riddled with sores. These images are supposed to induce within us the feeling of "who would do that?"

Linnemann and Wall identify this as a type of racialization, with whiteness at the core of this identity. In particular, they recognize this as a construction of "white trash" that "polices moral boundaries and fabricates social order through the specter of a 'white trash' Other who threatens the supposed purity of hegemonic whiteness and white social position" (2013, 4). Victorian ideologies of purity and cleanliness are positioned alongside the threatening other—the dirty, diseased "face of meth"—providing an aesthetic representation of the boundaries of whiteness. White trash, like the black cocaine fiend and the Chinese opium denizen—are threats that lurk in our midst and must be rooted out for hegemonic whiteness to continue unabated. Meth provides the "stigmata" identified by Lombroso as the biological sign of degeneracy, and whiteness is imagined through this as an unblemished and pure representation.

View *Frontline's* episode on meth, "The Meth Epidemic," at www.pbs.org/wgbh/pages/frontline/meth/. How does this documentary contribute to what Linneman and Wall identify as the racialized politics of meth? How does it reflect the discourses of law and order used to criminalize black and brown communities? Reflecting on the social construction of white identity, are there other types of moral panics that work in the same way that campaigns against meth do?

Sources: Carl Byker, "The Meth Epidemic," *Frontline,* WGBH Educational Foundation and Oregon Public Broadcasting, 2006 and 2011, www.pbs.org/wgbh/pages/frontline/meth/; Travis Linnemann and Tyler Wall, "'This Is Your Face on Meth': The Punitive Spectacle of 'White Trash' in the Rural War on Drugs," *Theoretical Criminology* 17, no. 3 (2013): 315–34.

Figure 6.11 LAPD battering ram after being used on a suspected crack house. Source: Photographer, Jack Gaunt. Copyright 1986. *Los Angeles Times.* Used with permission.

not with changes in the types of drugs available (Beckett 1999; Werb et al. 2011). However, this narrative still had considerable impact, and as figures 6.9 and 6.10 showed, the war on drugs defined communities of color as needing extraordinary militaristic police intervention. This even resulted in special militarized policing tools, such as the LAPD's "battering ram," routinely rolled out in South Central LA to raid "crack houses" (see figure 6.11).

The second narrative that generated concern about crack cocaine was "crack babies." Newspapers around the nation carried alarming stories about the rise of such babies, with *Rolling Stone* writing that these babies are "like no others, brain damaged in ways yet unknown, oblivious to any affection" (Hopkins 1990). The *Washington Post* editorialized that "the inner-city crack epidemic is now giving birth to the newest horror: a bio-underclass, a generation of physically damaged cocaine babies whose biological inferiority is stamped at birth" (Krauthammer 1989). Ross Perot, a third-party presidential candidate (who won 18.9 percent of the popular vote), invoked the crack baby crisis as a reason why he could not support easing prohibitions on drugs, declaring in the first 1992 presidential debate, "Anytime you think you want to legalize drugs, go to a neonatal unit, if you can get in. They're between 100 and 200 percent capacity up and down the East Coast. And the reason is crack babies being born. The baby's in the hospital 42 days, the typical cost to you and me is $125,000. Again and again and again the mother disappears in three days and the child becomes a ward of the state because he's permanently and genetically damaged. Just look at those little children and if anybody can even think about legalizing drugs, they've lost me" ("Transcript" 1992). The so-called epidemic sparked many of the same fears that the eugenicists had claimed stemmed from racial degeneracy: charity hospitals overwhelmed by patients, harm to the genetic makeup of the United States, and a large cost to the state. In response, organizations offered crack users money to get sterilized, providing both a cash incentive and paying for the procedure.

The problem with the crack-baby narrative, however, was that it was found to be overblown by the American Medical Association (AMA) (Lyons and Rittner 1998; Frank et al. 2001). Scientific claims for "crack babies" were based on a study of just twenty-eight women who used crack while pregnant. These women did experience a rise in infant mortality, but so did the rest of the United States in the 1980s. In 1981, cuts to Medicaid and other public assistance led by Reagan left 1 million people without coverage. The authors concluded that increases in infant mortality had more to do with cuts in health care under Reagan than drugs, and drug addiction was not as dangerous as other factors affecting pregnant women.

Further, a review of the literature found that heavy drinking while pregnant was far worse for babies than drug use and that the real culprit in infant mortality was giving birth without insurance coverage (Frank et al. 2001). The authors concluded it was actually safer to be a drug-using mother who sees a doctor than a non-drug-using mother who never visits the doctor. Yet, the ability of women to see the doctor was significantly corroded through the rollback of social supports, accomplished through the invocation of discourses like the "crack baby." Perot's claim, as well as other sensationalized reports of crack babies, thus did not come from medical evidence but from political and media elites, just as tales of racial degeneration had during the era of eugenics.

The narratives of crack violence and crack babies had considerable consequences. The first was used to push the idea that punishment for drug crimes should be much longer and much more severe. This led to a vast rise in the imprisonment of people for drug crimes in the 1980s. The second resulted in a view of mothers of color—since the popular conception, though not reality, was that crack users were people of color—as morally deficient and in need of sterilization and repression. Perhaps unsurprisingly, imprisonment and sterilization were the same remedies that eugenicists proposed early in the century.

Mass Incarceration and the Transformation of the U.S. Criminal Justice System

While drugs fell off Bush's radar as the Gulf War got underway, under Bill Clinton, mass incarceration received the greatest push, due largely to the criminalization of drugs. By the end of the 1990s, the United States was incarcerating close to 2 million people, accounting for over 25 percent of the world's prisoners, far more any other nation (see figure 6.12). In the federal system, new drug crimes fueled imprisonment growth, with over half the prisoners

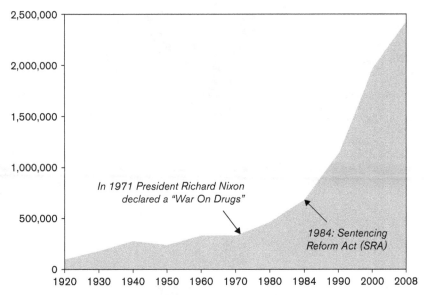

Figure 6.12 U.S. incarceration, 1920–2008. Source: The November Coalition, 2017, https://commons.wikimedia.org/wiki/File:US_incarceration_timeline.gif.

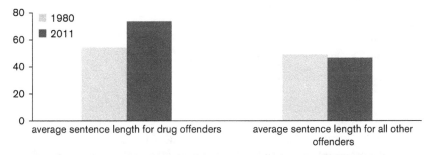

Figure 6.13 Average sentence length for federal drug and other crimes, 1980 and 2011. Source: Data courtesy of the Administrative Office of the U.S. Courts, Judicial Business of the U.S. Courts Series, Table D-5, 1980–2014; and Pew Charitable Trust, www.pewtrusts.org/en/research-and-analysis/issue-briefs/2015/08/federal-drug-sentencing-laws-bring-high-cost-low-return.

incarcerated for drug crimes (Carson 2015). The average sentence for drug crimes had risen over 36 percent since 1980, and almost all people convicted of federal drug crimes went to prison rather than on probation (see figures 6.13, 6.14, and 6.15). As a consequence of the war on drugs, the number of people in jail for drug crimes has increased by almost 1,100 percent in state prisons,

1980

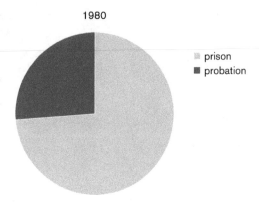

Figure 6.14 Sentences of prison or probation for federal drug crimes, 1980. Source: Data courtesy of the Administrative Office of the U.S. Courts, Judicial Business of the U.S. Courts Series, Table D-5, 1980–2014; and Pew Charitable Trust, www.pewtrusts.org/en/research-and-analysis/issue-briefs/2015/08/federal-drug-sentencing-laws-bring-high-cost-low-return.

2014

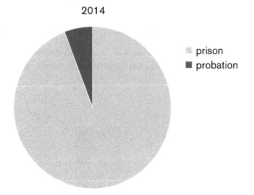

Figure 6.15 Sentences of prison or probation for federal drug crimes, 2014. Source: Data courtesy of the Administrative Office of the U.S. Courts, Judicial Business of the U.S. Courts Series, Table D-5, 1980–2014; and Pew Charitable Trust, www.pewtrusts.org/en/research-and-analysis/issue-briefs/2015/08/federal-drug-sentencing-laws-bring-high-cost-low-return.

almost 2,000 percent in federal prisons, and almost 1,000 percent in jails since 1980 (see figure 6.16). Today, police make a drug arrest every twenty seconds.

Drug policies were premised on deterrence and retributive punishment first outlined as a goal of the state in the Southern strategy. The result was a considerable increase in the use of state violence to address drug usage, premised on a discourse of state racism as discussed in chapter 4. Common tactics through which this occurred included mandatory minimums, determinate sentencing, and habitual-offender statutes like three-strikes laws (discussed in greater detail in chapter 9). As a result, people began serving much longer prison terms, often for lower-level crimes. Between 1985 and 1991, Congress enacted twenty new mandatory-minimum laws. By 1993, twenty-three states and the federal government had enacted increased penalties for subsequent offenses.

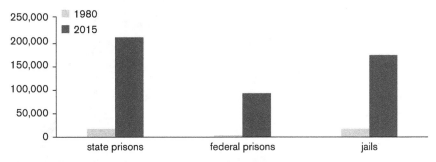

Figure 6.16 Prisoners in state and federal prisons and local jails for drug crimes, 1980 and 2015. Source: The Sentencing Project, 2017.

Every jurisdiction in the 1990s made it easier for states to try youths as adults. The death penalty resurged, with Texas's rapid rate of execution the exemplar. Parole was abolished entirely in the federal system.

Federal grants encouraged prison construction, which resulted in super-maximum-security prisons throughout the United States, despite little need for super-maximum-security beds (Beckett and Sasson 2004). States were required to adopt "truth in sentencing" provisions, which guaranteed inmates would serve 85 percent of their sentences before release, in order to be eligible for federal support to build new prisons. Life in prison was adopted as a mandatory minimum for all sorts of crimes, especially drugs. Retribution also resurged as a goal of punishment, with the creation of a prison encampment in Arizona where people are forced to serve out their sentences in tents and men wear pink underwear as a condition of punishment. The gendered and racialized dimensions of this type of punishment are clear.

The war on drugs created a range of grants and incentives (such as more military equipment, computers, and funding) to encourage local police departments to focus on drug crimes. Departments were permitted to keep any proceeds from the seizure of drug assets, which supplemented police budgets and helped fund the ongoing militarization of law enforcement. Further, the war on drugs worked to redefine funding priorities, and state expenditures on corrections grew almost 900 percent during this time (see figure 6.17).

CONCLUSION

Defining drugs as a social problem is not new, but the most recent war on drugs initiated unprecedented changes in the criminal justice system in the United States and elevated the criminal justice system as the newest state institution

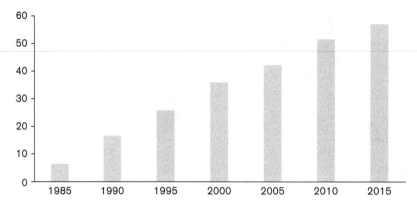

Figure 6.17 U.S. states' expenditures on corrections, 1985–2015, $ in millions. Source: National Association of State Budget Officers, *State Expenditure Report* series (1985–2015), www.nasbo.org/reports-data/state-expenditure-report/state-expenditure-archives.

organizing and managing racial difference today. As the history of drug prohibition shows, defining social problems provides an opportunity to frame issues in ways that engender very specific outcomes. In the history of racialized drug scares, these moments have served to reorient legal apparatuses, funnel anxieties about economic and demographic transformation into justifying increased surveillance, and define social problems as the province of nonwhite communities. In so doing, the criminalization of drugs also provided an opportunity to consolidate white identity and continue the practices of white supremacy, an intention articulated explicitly by Richard Nixon in his quest for the presidency and suppression of civil rights claims.

While the racialized drug panics of the 1880s through the 1950s had major impacts in their times, they also laid the framework for a much more significant use of these ideas through the law and order discourse that emerged in the 1960s. Even further, this framework provided the tools necessary to reframe challenges to the supremacy of whiteness in the United States as acts of crime, rather than political protest. Those who sought economic and racial justice—from the Black Panthers to other organizations not chronicled here—were met with stiff political repression, surveillance, and criminalization of their communities. What started as an attempt to win electoral votes and mount political repression against the civil rights movement transitioned into the latest tactic of racial management and governance: mass incarceration. Drugs and crime provided a way to make the racialized arguments of coloniality without explicit references to racial identities. That this could happen in the post–civil rights era reveals the power of racialization over the nation-state, the identity of the United States, and criminal justice system institutions, to which we now turn.

REFERENCES

Alonso, Alejandro A. 2004. "Racialized Identities and the Formation of Black Gangs in Los Angeles." *Urban Geography* 25, no. 7: 658–74.

Associated Press. 1994. "Haldeman Diary Shows Nixon Was Wary of Blacks and Jews." *New York Times,* May 18, 1994. www.nytimes.com/1994/05/18/us/haldeman-diary-shows-nixon-was-wary-of-blacks-and-jews.html.

Avila, Eric. 2014. *The Folklore of the Freeway: Race and Revolt in the Modernist City.* Minneapolis: University of Minnesota Press,

Barlow, Melissa Hickman. 1998. "Race and the Problem of Crime in *Time* and *Newsweek* Cover Stories, 1946 to 1995." *Social Justice* 25, no. 2 (Summer): 149–83.

Baum, Dan. 1996. *Smoke and Mirrors: The War on Drugs and the Politics of Failure.* Boston: Little, Brown.

———. 2016. "Legalize It All: How to Win the War on Drugs." *Harper's Magazine,* April. https://harpers.org/archive/2016/04/legalize-it-all/.

Beckett, Katherine. 1999. *Making Crime Pay: Law and Order in Contemporary American Politics.* New York: Oxford University Press.

Beckett, Katherine, and Theodore Sasson. 2004. *The Politics of Injustice: Crime and Punishment in America.* Thousand Oaks, CA: Sage.

Blakey, G. Robert, and Kevin P. Roddy. 1995. "Reflections on *Reves v. Ernst & (and) Young:* Its Meaning and Impact on Substantive, Accessory, Aiding, Abetting and Conspiracy Liability under RICO." *American Criminal Law Review* 33: 1345.

Blauner, Robert. 1969. "Internal Colonialism and Ghetto Revolt." *Social Problems* 16, no. 4 (Spring): 393–408. http://socrates.berkeley.edu/~tochtli/blackstudies129/Blauner.pdf.

Blecha, Peter. 2004. *Taboo Tunes: A History of Banned Bands and Censored Songs.* San Francisco: Backbeat Books.

Browne, Simone. 2015. *Dark Matters: On the Surveillance of Blackness.* Durham, NC: Duke University Press.

Bush, George H. W. 1989. "Address to the Nation on the National Drug Control Strategy." The American Presidency Project. September 5, 1989. www.presidency.ucsb.edu/ws/?pid=17472.

Carson, E. Ann. 2015. "Prisoners in 2014." *Bulletin* (September). Bureau of Justice Statistics, U.S. Department of Justice. NCJ 248955. www.bjs.gov/content/pub/pdf/p14.pdf.

Churchill, Ward, and Jim Vander Wall. 2002. *Agents of Repression: The FBI's Secret Wars against the Black Panther Party and the American Indian Movement.* Boston: South End Press.

Coughlin-Bogue, Tobias. 2016. "The Word 'Marijuana' versus the Word 'Cannabis.'" *The Stranger,* April 13, 2016. www.thestranger.com/news/2016/04/13/23948555/the-word-marijuana-versus-the-word-cannabis.

Cohen, Michael M. 2006. "Jim Crow's Drug War: Race, Coca Cola, and the Southern Origins of Drug Prohibition." *Southern Cultures* 12, no. 3: 55–79.

Cohen, Nathan E. 1967. "The Los Angeles Riot Study." *Social Work* 12, no. 4: 14–21.

Cohen, Stanley. 1972. *Folk Devils and Moral Panics: The Creation of the Mods and Rockers.* London: MacGibbon and Kee.

Craddock, Susan. 2000. *City of Plagues: Disease, Poverty, and Deviance in San Francisco.* Minneapolis: University of Minnesota Press,

Day. 1886. "Chinatown." *The Cornhill Magazine* 7, no. 37: 50–60. https://archive.org/details/newcornhill07londuoft.

Entman, Robert M. 1994. "Representation and Reality in the Portrayal of Blacks on Network Television News." *Journalism and Mass Communication Quarterly* 71, no. 3: 509–20.

Epp, Charles R., Steven Maynard-Moody, and Donald P. Haider-Markel. 2014. *Pulled Over: How Police Stops Define Race and Citizenship.* Chicago: University of Chicago Press.

Espiritu, Yen Le. 2004. "Ideological Racism and Cultural Resistance: Constructing Our Own Images." In *Race, Class, and Gender: An Anthology,* edited by Margaret L. Andersen and Patricia Hill Collins, 175–184. Belmont, CA: Wadsworth.

Frank, Deborah A., Marilyn Augustyn, Wanda Grant Knight, Tripler Pell, and Barry Zuckerman. 2001. "Growth, Development, and Behavior in Early Childhood following Prenatal Cocaine Exposure: A Systematic Review." *Journal of American Medical Association* 285, no. 12: 1613–25.

Ghandnoosh, Nazgol. 2014. *Race and Punishment: Racial Perceptions of Crime and Support for Punitive Policies.* Washington DC: Sentencing Project.

Goldwater, Barry. 1998. "Goldwater's 1964 Acceptance Speech." *Washington Post,* May. www.washingtonpost.com/wp-srv/politics/daily/may98/goldwaterspeech.htm.

Grady-Willis, Winston. 1998. "The Black Panther Party: State Repression and Political Prisoners." In *The Black Panther Party Reconsidered,* edited by Charles E. Jones, 363–90. (Baltimore: Black Classic Press).

Hahn, Harlan, and Joe R. Feagin. 1970. "Riot-Precipitating Police Practices: Attitudes in Urban Ghettos." *Phylon (1960–)* 31, no. 2: 183–93.

Hart, Carl. 2014. "How the Myth of the 'Negro Cocaine Fiend' Helped Shape American Drug Policy." *Nation,* February 17, 2014. www.thenation.com/article/how-myth-negro-cocaine-fiend-helped-shape-american-drug-policy/.

Hopkins, Ellen. 1990. "Childhood's End: What Life Is Like for Crack Babies." *Rolling Stone*, October 18, 1990. www.rollingstone.com/culture/features/childhoods-end-19901018.

Kane, Harry Hubbell. 1881. *Opium-Smoking in America and China*. New York: G. P. Putnam's Sons. https://catalog.hathitrust.org/Record/001581484.

Kramer, Alisa Sarah. 2007. "William H. Parker and the Thin Blue Line: Politics, Public Relations and Policing in Postwar Los Angeles." PhD diss., American University.

Krauthammer, Charles. 1989. "Children of Cocaine." *Washington Post*, July 30, 1989. Reprinted in *Congressional Record* 135, no. 106 (August 1, 1989). http://digitalcollections.library.cmu.edu/awweb/awarchive?type=file&item=410809.

LoBianco, Tom. 2016. "Report: Aide says Nixon's War on Drugs Targeted Blacks, Hippies." CNN, March 24, 2016. www.cnn.com/2016/03/23/politics/john-ehrlichman-richard-nixon-drug-war-blacks-hippie/.

Lusane, Clarence, and Dennis Desmond. 1991. *Pipe Dream Blues: Racism and the War on Drugs*. Boston: South End Press.

Lyons, Peter, and Barbara Rittner. 1998. "The Construction of the Crack Babies Phenomenon as a Social Problem." *American Journal of Orthopsychiatry* 68, no. 2: 313.

Marshall, Edward. 1911. "Uncle Sam is the Worst Drug Fiend in the World." *New York Times*, March 12, 1911: 48.

Moynihan, Daniel P. 1965. *The Negro Family: The Case for National Action*. Office of Policy Planning and Research, United States Department of Labor, March 1965. https://web.stanford.edu/~mrosenfe/Moynihan%27s%20The%20Negro%20Family.pdf.

Murakawa, Naomi. 2014. *The First Civil Right: How Liberals Built Prison America*. New York: Oxford University Press.

"The Opium Habit." 1875. *Sacramento Daily Record*, November 20, 1875: 4. https://cdnc.ucr.edu/cgi-bin/cdnc?a=d&d=SDU18751120.2.30.

Parenti, Christian. 2000. *Lockdown America: Police and Prisons in the Age of Crisis*. London: Verso.

Reagan, Ronald. 1982. "Radio Address to the Nation on Federal Drug Policy." American Presidency Project. October 2, 1982. www.presidency.ucsb.edu/ws/?pid=43085.

Reinarman, Craig. 1994. "The Social Construction of Drug Scares." In *Constructions of Deviance: Social Power, Context, and Interaction*, edited by Patricia A. Adler and Peter Adler, 92–105. Belmont, CA: Wadsworth.

Salyer, Lucy E. 1995. *Laws Harsh as Tigers: Chinese Immigrants and the Shaping of Modern Immigration Law*. Chapel Hill: University of North Carolina Press.

Sanburn, Josh. 2014. "This Is Why Your Local Police Department Might Have a Tank." *Time*, June 24, 2014. http://time.com/2907307/aclu-swat-local-police/.

Sanna, E. J. 2014. *Marijuana: Mind-Altering Weed*. Illicit and Misused Drugs series. Broomall, PA: Mason Crest /Simon and Schuster.

Shah, Nayan. 2001. *Contagious Divides: Epidemics and Race in San Francisco's Chinatown*. American Crossroads 7. Berkeley: University of California Press.

Shelden, Randall, Sharon Tracy, and William Brown. 2012. *Youth Gangs in American Society*. 4th ed. Belmont, CA: Cengage Learning.

Siegel, Ronald K. 1984. "Cocaine and the privileged class: a review of historical and contemporary images." *Advances in alcohol & substance abuse* 4, no. 2: 37–49.

Simpson, Kelly. 2012. "The Great Migration: Creating a New Black Identity in Los Angeles." KCET: History and Society. ww.kcet.org/history-society/the-great-migration-creating-a-new-black-identity-in-los-angeles.

Streatfeild, Dominic. 2003. *Cocaine: An Unauthorized Biography*. New York: Picador.

"Transcript of First TV Debate Among Bush, Clinton and Perot." 1992. *New York Times*, October 12, A14. www.nytimes.com/1992/10/12/us/the-1992-campaign-transcript-of-first-tv-debate-among-bush-clinton-and-perot.html.

Umoja, Akinyele Omowale. 1999. "Repression Breeds Resistance: The Black Liberation Army and the Radical Legacy of the Black Panther Party." *New Political Science* 21, no. 2: 131–55.

Van Deburg, William L., ed. 1997. *Modern Black Nationalism: From Marcus Garvey to Louis Farrakhan*. New York: NYU Press.

Von Eschen, Penny M. 1997. *Race against Empire: Black Americans and Anticolonialism, 1937–1957*. Ithaca, NY: Cornell University Press.

Von Hoffman, Alexander. 2004. *House by House, Block by Block: The Rebirth of America's Urban Neighborhoods*. New York: Oxford University Press.

Werb, Dan, Greg Rowell, Gordon Guyatt, Thomas Kerr, Julio Montaner, and Evan Wood. 2011. "Effect of Drug Law Enforcement on Drug Market Violence: A Systematic Review." *International Journal of Drug Policy* 22, no. 2: 87–94.

Williams, Edward Huntington. 1914. "Negro Cocaine 'Fiends' Are a New Southern Menace." *New York Times*, February 8, 1914: 12. www.druglibrary.org/schaffer/history/negro_cocaine_fiends.htm.

Policing the City

LEARNING OUTCOMES

▶ Examine the evidence for race-based policing, and explain why the specific practice of the investigatory stop contributes to the continuation of coloniality through policing practice.

▶ Illustrate how race-based policing practices are justified in constitutional cases.

▶ List the major components of the professional era of policing, and identify how this reform movement created the mechanisms for institutionalized racism in police today.

▶ Describe the impact of the policing transition from the professional era to the order maintenance era on policing urban communities.

▶ Summarize how the culture of policing today shapes the hyperpolicing of communities of color.

KEY TERMS

▶ drug courier profile
▶ investigatory stop
▶ stop and frisk
▶ pretextual stop
▶ territoriality
▶ professional era
▶ ideology of bureaucracy
▶ militarization
▶ Zoot Suit Riots
▶ culture of policing
▶ broken windows policing
▶ order-maintenance policing
▶ disorder
▶ zero tolerance

In recent years, one of the most visible manifestations of coloniality is the relationship between the uniformed police and communities of color. The twinned practices of coloniality, knowledge production and territorial occupation, are present throughout police practices—from arrest, the creation of police reports, and the generation of crime statistics to patrolling surveillance, and interrogation. In each of these practices, criminals, crime, and bad neighborhoods are often cast as the site and source of what ails U.S. democracy. These villains are seen as an outside presence perpetually seeking to undermine the prosperity and safety of our towns, cities, and the nation. Police, by contrast, are cast as the moral protector, if not authority, of the nation. This stark vision of society is consequential not just for the victims of police violence but for the individuals who become police officers as well.

This chapter tells the story of how the colonial imperative that founded the police, as we detailed in chapter 4, led to the structure, organization, and controversies in policing that we know today. As arbiters of social order, police officers are often tasked with responding to situations informed by forces much larger than the individuals involved. (Bourgois 2003; Padilla 1992; Sánchez-Jankowski 2008; Venkatesh 2008). Police are placed on the front lines of social problems such as poverty and the structural effects of invidious racial discrimination and provided primarily the tools of force and violence—batons, tasers, guns, and arrest, among others—to effect change. Given this context, is it any surprise that race and policing is one of the most controversial topics today?

Recent high-profile deaths of people of color at the hands of police are just one form that the controversy over race and crime has taken. Though no complete, official count of police killings exists, *The Guardian*, a British newspaper, began compiling reports of police killings ("The Counted" 2016) after a young man named Michael Brown was killed in Ferguson, Missouri. Brown was walking home and, after an encounter with a police officer in which he was alleged to have reached into the officer's car, Brown was shot. In 2016, *The Guardian* identified 1,092 people who were killed by police in the United States. These figures reveal that black people are 2.5 times more likely to be killed by police, while Native Americans face death more than ten times as often (see figure 7.1).

Police are the most visible representatives of the state's use of violence, and data on police killings illustrate how that power is disproportionately applied to black and brown people. But police killings reveal only one part of the equation and are one of the most extreme examples. The nature of the police relationship with communities of color means that race-based policing seeps into the everyday life of both police and communities of color. The phrases "driving/walking/etc. while black or brown" and "racial profiling" hint at the impact of the relationship, and figure 7.2 shows that black men are by far the most likely group to be injured during encounters with police. But even these terms and this data do not adequately convey the depths to which nonwhites are

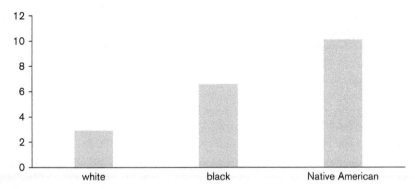

Figure 7.1 People killed by police by race, number per million, 2016. Source: The Counted Project, *Guardian,* www.theguardian.com/us-news/ng-interactive/2015/jun/01/the-counted-police-killings-us-database.

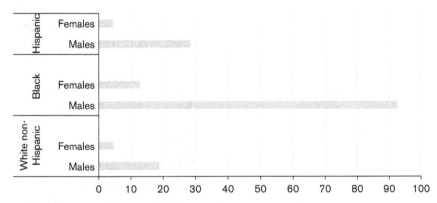

Figure 7.2 People injured due to law enforcement intervention, by race and gender, per 100,000, 2000–2015. Source: Centers for Disease Control, WISQARS, Nonfatal Injury Report, www.cdc.gov/injury/wisqars/nonfatal.html.

subject to both disproportionate surveillance and violence at the hands of the state, reproducing one of the most oppressive experiences of colonialism. This is why Ruth Wilson Gilmore (2007) calls mass incarceration one of the most profound institutions for subjecting black bodies to "premature death."

RACE-BASED POLICING: THE EVIDENCE

While the relationship between police and communities of color has been heavily scrutinized in the media, police departments still remain relatively understudied on this issue. One explanation is the simple mechanics of these types of studies—they need a data set that includes race as a variable. However, most police departments do not collect racial data on all stops, and many agencies are quite resistant (for a number of both practical and protective reasons) to allowing researchers to study them.

But experimental studies suggest that race indeed affects policing. Studies of split-second decisions to shoot possible assailants reveal that both regular citizens and police are much more likely to use lethal force against those they perceive as black than those they perceive as white (Eberhardt et al. 2004; Correll, Urland, and Ito 2006). In studies of race, people are much more likely to perceive objects in the hands of black people as guns and react accordingly, while they take much longer to react to the presence of an actual gun in a white subject's hand (Correll, Urland, and Ito 2006). Police officers and citizens are also more likely to shoot people if primed with a subliminal racist image—such as a gorilla (Goff et al. 2008).

One problem with studies of the practice of race-based policing is that the agencies most likely to be studied are the ones least likely to be involved in the day-to-day practices of patrol, arrest, and incarceration. State highway patrols are well studied, for instance, but those agencies do not typically confront the variegated racial geographies we detailed in chapter 5. Urban police units, in contrast, are understudied, and they are often resistant to releasing data and information about everyday police activities. Because of this difference, highway patrol studies offered some of the first evidence of the extent of racial profiling in the practice of patrol.

Highway Patrols and Drug Courier Profiles

Some of the most extensive studies of racial profiling are of state patrol. For instance, Maryland, California, and New Jersey state patrols have all had to admit in court that they used a **drug courier profile** based on race to identify likely suspects (Gross and Barnes 2002). In these cases, officers were actively using race as a determination of who to stop on the interstate for suspected drug trafficking. In Maryland, black people constituted 17 percent of those driving, but were 72 percent of those stopped and searched (Lange, Johnson, and Voas 2005). In California, the ACLU brought a class-action lawsuit against the California Highway Patrol (CHP) that alleged racial profiling practices. The ACLU demonstrated clear racial disparities in enforcement, to which the CHP responded that these motorists were pulled over as a result of individual officers' "suspicion" or "hunches." As a result of the ruling in *Rodriguez v. CHP* (2003), the CHP was forced to articulate a reason for all drug stops and demonstrate legally justifiable "probable cause or reasonable suspicion."

In 1998, after three officers in New Jersey shot three unarmed men of color at a traffic stop, officials were forced to admit that they used race as a basis for stops. Training documents described "Colombian men, Hispanic men, Hispanic men and black men together, and Hispanic men and women posing as couple" as some of the "common" drug courier types. Officials argued that their efforts merely reflected the greater involvement of these groups in drugs. Yet state troopers of color testified that they were trained to actively racially profile. This resulted in two precincts where over 80 percent of those stopped and searched were black, even though black people represented only 30 percent of motorists (Kocieniewski and Hanley 2000; Lange, Johnson, and Voas 2005).

Urban Police and the Investigatory Stop

Urban police are much less studied, but they play a more prolific role in the process of racial profiling. Urban police, like the highway patrol, are adept at what is called the **investigatory stop,** or stopping citizens in order to investigate crimes. This type of stop ranges from what is called **stop and frisk,** or stopping and patting down pedestrians, to pulling drivers over to investigate drug crimes. In New York City, one study found that black people are more than twice as likely as whites to be stopped for suspicion of possessing a weapon, a charge that allows police officers to do a pat-down search of those they stop (which can lead to other charges as well) (Fagan and Davies 2000). This disparity in who is stopped happens despite possession rates being equal across racial groupings. A quarter of Los Angeles Police Department officers report that racial bias plays a role in policing, and countless other "whistleblowers" have alleged the same in California, Georgia, and Florida, as well as other states (Harris 2003).

In Seattle, a study of the city police found that 57 percent of drug arrests and 79 percent of buy-bust arrests were of black people, even though they made up just 8 percent of the population. Researchers' analysis of the arrests found that the disproportionate focus on crack cocaine over other drugs, the priority on policing outdoor drug areas, and the concentration of police in racially hetero-geneous neighborhoods led to a disproportionate focus on policing drug crimes of black residents (Beckett, Nyrop, and Pfingst 2006). In this sample, race shaped not only how police responded to drug crime in terms of their choices of places to patrol and target. It also shaped how police *conceptualized* drug crimes: black dealers in heterogeneous neighborhoods were singled out as the most threatening and criminogenic of all drug dealers, according to who police decided to target and arrest. These results have far-ranging impact, not just for those who are stopped and searched but for their communities, the larger townships, the police departments, and even the legitimacy of policing and democracy itself.

When disaggregated, data about police behavior suggests an interesting paradox. On the one hand, there is some evidence that there are not racial dis-proportionalities in actual traffic stops and that these are primarily based on driver behavior. This suggests that when the intent of policing is to enforce traffic violations, law enforcement officers are looking not at race but at how someone is driving. Race becomes a factor, however, when the intent shifts to a desire to investigate. Police use traffic stops as the basis for investigatory stops, and the data suggests that when police make a traffic stop, if the person stopped is black or brown, the stop is much more likely to lead to an investigation. Thus, the investigatory stop is the latest surveillance tactic that society aims at black and brown communities.

Whren v. United States (1996) and the Pretextual Stop

Urban residents and police alike know that not all traffic stops are simply that. Often, these stops are to investigate other activities, most often drugs or weapons. Investigatory stops are also known as **pretextual stops,** since they often use traffic violations as a pretext for investigating further crimes. This allows police to bypass the need for reasonable suspicion or probable cause before stopping someone, because the traffic violation is the primary rationale.

This practice was scrutinized in *Whren v. United States* (1996). The case considered the arrest and conviction of Whren for cocaine possession by plainclothes officers in an unmarked car who pulled Whren over for failing to signal when turning. The defense asked whether this conduct was reasonable, particularly given that the police department also had a general order that read, "Members who are not in uniform or are in unmarked vehicles may take enforcement action only in the case of a violation that is so grave as to pose an immediate threat to the safety of others." If this was the case, why was Whren stopped?

Whren was stopped because police use traffic stops as a pretext for enforcing other crimes. According to police, they observed Whren leave a known drug house, followed him until he made a traffic error, and pulled him over. Police did not have probable cause or reasonable suspicion to investigate Whren for a drug crime, but by using the traffic code, they were able to stop and investigate him for exactly that. Pretextual stops are often based on traffic violations but can also include stop and frisks, where officers very broadly interpret their power to pat down someone they suspect of possessing a weapon. Whren was pulled over for violating traffic laws but was ultimately convicted of a drug crime for which police had been conducting surveillance. Upon appeal, the Supreme Court ruled that the stop was constitutional and that police—even plainclothes officers in unmarked cars instructed not to by the department—could use traffic stops as a justification to investigate drug crimes.

While this may seem like smart police work to some, the problem is that, as in the study in Seattle discussed above, people whom police see as threatening is racialized, and thus who they stop in order to investigate also results in race-based policing. *Whren* gives police nearly unbridled power because they now have the power to stop anyone at any time (Moran 2002). Indeed, the police rule of thumb is that average driver cannot go three blocks without violating some sort of traffic regulation (Harris 2003). Yet that power is not likely to be used against all of us equally, and as both distant and recent history have shown, it is used to police black and brown communities more often than not.

Even without *Whren*, there would still be ample opportunity for race-based policing. Neither reasonable suspicion nor probable cause are robust protections against police power, because unverifiable contexts are often considered sufficient for establishing these legal constructions. In *Ornelas v. United States* (1996), the Supreme Court even referred to the imprecision of this legal fiction:

> Articulating precisely what "reasonable suspicion" and "probable cause" mean is not possible. They are commonsense, nontechnical conceptions that deal with the factual and practical considerations of everyday life on which reasonable and prudent men, not legal technicians act. As such, the standards are not really, or even usefully, reduced to a neat set of legal rules. . . . They are instead fluid concepts that take their substantive content from the particular contexts in which the standards are being assessed. (*Ornelas v. United States*, 1996, 517 U.S. at 695–96 [and other citations omitted])

On this basis, the drug courier profile checklist in table 7.1 is sufficient to establish reasonable suspicion to stop someone and investigate further. Yet who has not met at least one of these criteria at some point in the airport? Even the sight or smell of illegal drugs has been found to constitute both reasonable suspicion and probable cause. Furthermore, the location of the incident combined with perceived evasion constitutes probable cause (Harris 2003). So if you are someplace that an officer defines as suspicious and turn and walk away at the wrong time, it is probable cause for the officer to stop and search you. Given the geographies of racial segregation discussed in chapter 5, this amounts to de facto sanctioning of different standards of policing by race and class, and a status of perpetual suspicion of those who are not white.

Consequences of the Investigatory Stop

The investigatory stop is thus an important continuation of coloniality into modern life. In previous eras, the mechanisms of surveillance meant that non-whites were often stopped and forced to produce documents or identification. Slave patrollers, for instance, could require any black person to produce evidence of freedom or permission to be away from the supervision of whites. Lantern laws in New York City required that after dark, nonwhites carry a lantern illuminating their face, thus providing perpetual surveillance of black and brown bodies by white bodies (Browne 2015). Today, Arizona is infamous for passing a law that requires anyone suspected of not being a citizen to produce citizenship papers, a reality that is unlikely to affect anyone outside of the Latinx community.

Table 7.1   Racially "neutral" drug courier profile used at airports

Checklist items	Checklist items (cont.)
Arrived late at night	Carried a small bag
Arrived early in the morning	Carried a medium-sized bag
Arrived in afternoon	Carried two bulky garment bags
One of the first to deplane	Carried two heavy suitcases
One of the last to deplane	Carried four pieces of luggage
Deplaned in the middle	Disassociated self from luggage
Purchased ticket at airport	Traveled alone
Made reservation on short notice	Traveled with a companion
Bought coach ticket	Acted too nervous
Used round-trip ticket	Acted too calm
Paid for ticket with cash	Made eye contact with officer
Paid for ticket with small-denomination currency	Avoided making eye contact with officer
Paid for ticket with large-denomination currency	Wore expensive clothing and gold jewelry
Made local telephone call after deplaning	Dressed causally
Made long distance telephone call after deplaning	Went to restroom after deplaning
Pretended to make telephone call	Walked quickly through airport
Traveled from New York to Los Angeles	Walked slowly through airport
Traveled to Houston	Walked aimlessly through airport
Carried no luggage	Left airport by taxi
Carried brand-new luggage	Left airport by limousine
	Left airport by private car

SOURCE: David Cole, 1999, *No Equal Justice: Race and Class in the American Criminal Justice System* (New York: New Press), 49.

Each of these practices has increased the surveillance and cast a perpetual suspicion onto nonwhite communities. The investigatory stop reflects a considerable incursion into a citizen's life, and the fact that this negative experience is disproportionately felt by nonwhites is significant by itself. But it also contributes to significant racial differences in attitudes about police conduct. With whites largely stopped for legitimate reasons but black drivers often stopped for pretextual reasons, this considerably shapes one's experience of policing. Technically, people have the right to say no to consent searches, but the history of race and policing in the United States means those who are subject to it often do not feel they can say no and exit their encounter with the state. Coercion, then, leads many to say yes (Harris 2003). And given the history of police violence, this fear is often justified.

INVESTIGATORY STOP RECEIPT | Event
CHICAGO POLICE DEPARTMENT | No.

You were the subject of an Investigatory Stop by the Chicago Police Department.

Officer _____

(Print) Name   Star No.

Officer _____

(Print) Name   Star No.

Reason(s) for the Stop (Check all that apply).

☐ ACTIONS INDICATIVE OF ENGAGING IN DRUG TRANSACTION

☐ FITS DESCRIPTION FROM FLASH MESSAGE

☐ FITS DESCRIPTION OF AN OFFENDER AS DESCRIBED BY VICTIM OR WITNESS

☐ ACTIONS INDICATIVE OF "CASING" VICTIM OR LOCATION

☐ PROXIMITY TO THE REPORTED CRIME LOCATION

☐ GANG/NARCOTIC RELATED ENFORCEMENT

☐ OTHER (Specify) _____

CPD-11.912 (Rev. 6/16)

Figure 7.3 Investigatory Stop Receipt from Chicago Police Department. Source: Chicago Police Department.

Investigatory stops also subject black and brown communities to disproportionate exposure to police violence. Investigatory stops are so widespread that in response to a complaint by the ACLU, the Chicago Police Department created an investigatory stop receipt (see figure 7.3). Stops often mean use of force, such as searching, frisking, and handcuffing, even without a crime having been committed. Countless stories abound of people being frisked, searched, handcuffed, and forced to sit on the side of the road while police "investigate," only to be released with no charges. This type of experience, according to police researcher Charles Epp and his colleagues (2014), defines black and brown people, regardless of criminal history, as greater threats and thus as people from whom the rest of society must be protected—and, as has been evidenced by recent events, as people who can be killed, often with impunity, for the safety of the United States.

Legal challenges to the investigatory stop have largely fallen short. In *Schneckloth v. Bustamante* (1973), the Supreme Court affirmed that police could legally exploit ignorance of the law in order gain consent for "legitimate need for such searches." David Harris (1997), legal expert on consent searches and racial profiling, reminds us that whether we *feel* we can say no to a police officer without incurring further state violence is largely dependent on our race and class status. One statistical review of court cases found that "voluntariness is a legal fiction that facilitates balancing the needs of law enforcement against the rights of citizens" (Sutherland 2006, 2194). One might also question whether someone who is handcuffed and speaking from the back of a police car does so voluntarily (Chotvacs 2001). And more recently, in *Utah v. Strieff* (2016), the Supreme Court ruled that even if a motorist is illegally stopped by the police, a legal search can still ensue. The ruling in *Strieff* established that police no longer need probable cause to stop someone if a crime is found. In effect, police can illegally stop you, search your car, and if they find evidence, the *Strieff* ruling renders the initial stop legal. And since these types of tactics are much more commonly applied to black and brown individuals, it makes it even less likely that they feel free to deny police officers' investigatory attempts.

Institutionalizing Race-Based Policing

Investigatory stops are consequential for understanding the extent to which police surveillance is disproportionately targeted at black and brown communities, just as it was during slavery and the Progressive Era. This persistence may seem surprising because of the widespread attention to how race inflects policing. This attention, however, has led not to the erosion of race-based policing but rather to its institutionalization. Race-based policing today is hidden behind policies and procedures that make it more likely that police will target communities and individuals of color. Many departments in fact train "their officers to be unfailingly respectful when stopping people," yet the practices of disproportionate policing and greater incursions and use of force in black and brown communities continue (Epp, Maynard-Moody, and Haider-Markel 2014, 5).

The problem is the use of the investigatory stop itself, a "deliberate creation of police leaders, led by police professional associations, policing researchers, and police chiefs" (Epp Maynard-Moody, and Haider-Markel 2014, 7). The reason? To continue policing the "bad guys," even as the courts seek to protect people from the over-incursion of municipal law enforcement. The investigatory stop today is entrenched and institutionalized in police departments and taught as part of the curriculum on investigation in police academies. The investigatory stop and its use against black and brown communities is also the institutionalization of racialized ideas of threat that lead people to more readily and willingly shoot nonwhites. And given that investigatory stops are used to generate police statistics, it is also a tool whereby racialized policing is translated into a rational and scientifically objective practice.

Not only does the investigatory stop create greater incursions into some people's lives, but it also is an ongoing assault on the dignity and privacy of individuals. Even further, it also allows an entire segment of society to move through life—even while committing crimes—relatively free from surveillance (Harcourt 2008; Hagan and Foster 2006). While horrendous acts of police violence show that this extraordinary surveillance can result in death, as it did for Michael Brown in 2014, it can also reveal the extraordinary cost that communities of color must bear, which extend far beyond highly publicized incidents of violence. Indeed, the investigation into Michael Brown's death revealed a community in Ferguson under siege from the state itself.

The Experience of Racialized Policing: Ferguson, MO

The case of Ferguson, Missouri, where Michael Brown was killed, illustrates the widespread effect of racialized policing. A recent Department of Justice (DOJ) investigation into the Ferguson Police Department reveals impacts not just on individuals, who in this case were mostly black, but also on the city itself (2015).

Ferguson is a suburb struggling under white flight, which led to economic weakening and a precipitous decline in city revenue. The DOJ found that city revenue generation was a primary motivator of police activity, and the investigatory stop was used predominantly against black residents by the Ferguson Police Department (see figure 7.4). Indeed, the police department disciplined officers who failed to issue an average of twenty-eight tickets per month. Officers competed to see who could give the most tickets, and one winner was able to write fourteen tickets in a single encounter. In 2012, the city collected $2 million as a result of police tickets, and the city manager even sent a thank-you note to the chief. Tickets accounted for 23 percent of the total city revenue, and fines were routinely raised to generate even greater funding. With this structure, the entire city benefited from racial profiling, even as those profiled suffered devastating consequences.

In Ferguson, between 2012 and 2014, black people were 67 percent of the population, but subject to 85 percent of all traffic stops, 90 percent of citations, and 93 percent of arrests (DOJ 2015). As figure 7.5 shows, Ferguson was predominantly black but had an almost all-white police department. One case discussed by the DOJ involved a man who was sitting in his car after playing basketball. Officers blocked him in so he could not leave, accused him of pedophilia without any cause, and ordered him out of the car for a pat-down. When they asked to search the car, he objected. In response, he was arrested at gunpoint, charged with eight violations, including a false declaration for saying his name was "Mike" instead of "Michael" and giving an address different than on his driver's license (even though it was a legitimate address). He was also given a ticket for not wearing a seatbelt, despite the fact that he was sitting in a parked car.

Ferguson's system created more and more revenue for the city. A woman who parked her car illegally in 2007 ended up paying $1,000 and spent six days

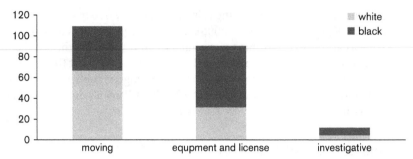

Figure 7.4 Reasons for stops by police in Ferguson, Missouri, by race, %, 2013. Source: Office of the Missouri Attorney General (2014), Racial Profiling Data, 2013, Ferguson Police Department, quoted in Sentencing Project, *Black Lives Matter: Eliminating Racial Inequity in the Criminal Justice System,* 2015, www.sentencingproject.org/publications /black-lives-matter-eliminating-racial-inequity-in-the-criminal-justice-system/. NOTE: Exceeds 100 percent because some stops were for more than one reason.

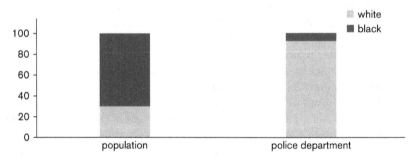

Figure 7.5 Ferguson's population by race compared to police department by race, %. Source: Jeremy Ashkenas and Haeyoun Park, "The Race Gap in America's Police Departments," *New York Times,* April 8, 2015, www.nytimes.com/interactive/2014/09/03 /us/the-race-gap-in-americas-police-departments.html.

in jail for a failure to appear. A single missed, partial, or late payment could mean jail time. Arrest warrants were used as threats for payments, and jail time was not recorded by the court. Dogs were routinely used by the Ferguson police; in every dog-bite incident the DOJ examined in its investigation, the victim was black. Officers ordered a dog to attack an unarmed 14-year-old and then struck him while he was lying on the ground. The DOJ found a pattern of police officers shouting racial epithets as they passed residents. Further, all charges filed of resisting arrest were for black people, and on fourteen occasions, the only charge was for resisting arrest, an oddity given that one must be charged with a crime in order to resist arrest.

The DOJ report did not reveal anything new to those who live this on a daily basis, but it did document quite explicitly how race-based policing was critical to creating the color line in Ferguson. Yet this happened not through the overt or explicit actions of city administrators but rather through the institutionalization of race-based policing. The report also revealed the true costs of profiling, including the fines and time in jail that provide revenue to cities and jobs for city workers.

The Costs of Profiling

In addition to potential emotional costs of being stopped or harassed by the police, racial profiling has real economic costs. The most glaring example is the cost of punishment: incarceration equals lost wages in the communities most impacted. If you are pulled over, you will likely lose at least a half-hour of your time. The police can also detain you while they bring a drug dog to the scene if you refused to consent to a search. If a dog "alerts" the officer, a search can ensue (Harris 2003). Even if nothing is found, that stop can take several hours. If you are cited or arrested, the costs begin mounting even if you are never convicted. Costs include lost employment (as many cannot take time off without losing their jobs), lost wages from missing work, lost free time, reputation damage, fines and court costs—and that is even if you aren't convicted (Harris 2003). While marijuana for most people is hardly criminalized, for black and brown youth it is one of the primary crimes that begins their path through the juvenile justice system and into the cycle of incarceration (Kutateladze and Andiloro 2014).

Beyond economics, there is also the ever-present racial tax that is paid through violence perpetrated against black bodies (Geller and Fagan 2010). Police are more likely to use or threaten to use force against black people than any other group (Smith et al. 2009). One study of stop-and-frisk encounters revealed that black people were more likely to be pushed into a wall or onto the ground, handcuffed when not arrested, have a weapon drawn on them, and be pepper sprayed or hit with a baton (Fryer 2016). Another study found that over the first six months of 2010, a black person died at the hands of police every thirty-six hours (Eisen and Akuno 2012). Over half did not have a weapon on them, and in the other half, canes and BB guns were considered deadly weapons. The vast majority of those killed were young: over 70 percent of those shot in that period were under the age of 30. While most police encounters—over 97 percent—do not include the use of force, those that do involve force most often involve men of color.

Some readers might wonder whether this results from whites complying more readily with police than black people. Yet whites actually pose the greater threat to police safety. They are the group most likely to violently resist arrest (but not most likely to be arrested for it), most likely to evade police, and even

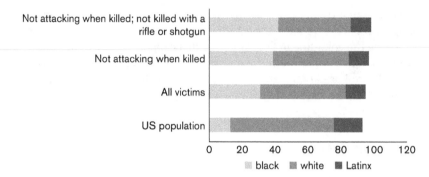

Figure 7.6 People killed by police during arrest, by context and race, 2010–2012, %. Source: FBI, 2012 Supplementary Homicide Report, quoted in Dara Lind, "The FBI Is Trying to Get Better Data on Police Killings," *Vox*, updated April 10, 2015, www.vox .com/2014/8/21/6051043/how-many-people-killed-police-statistics-homicide-official-black.

the most likely to use force against police officers (see figure 7.6; Gabrielson, Sagara, and Jones 2014). Even though whites are objectively the greatest threat to police safety, they are much less likely than African Americans, Native Americans, and Latinxs to be killed in a police encounter (Smith et al. 2009; "The Counted" 2016).

One of the most surprising costs of race-based policing, however, is for policing itself: the loss of police legitimacy. Today, the perception of police legitimacy largely breaks down along racial lines. According to aggregated Gallup polls between 2014 and 2016, only 29 percent of black people "have a great deal or quite a lot of confidence in police" compared to 58 percent of whites. Almost half of black people felt racial minorities are treated unfairly by police, whereas 75 percent of whites thought racial minorities are treated fairly (Newport 2016).

To explain how race-based policing such as that in Ferguson came to be institutionalized throughout society, we turn in the next section to an exploration of the single most significant reform in modern policing: the professional era. This reform movement sought to elevate the status of policing in society while also responding to the widespread belief and reality that police power was often arbitrary and capricious.

POLICE PROFESSIONALISM AND ENFORCING THE COLOR LINE

As we discussed in chapter 4, police developed in order to maintain social order, a practice fraught with the class, gender, and racial politics of industrialization and urbanization. They did this through what we can refer to as practices of territoriality. **Territoriality** refers to the social, cultural, economic, political, and other processes by which space is claimed by one particular group or entity and that claim is communicated to both insiders and outsiders (see further Delaney 2008). For instance, the state communicates its claim on the physical space of the nation in many ways. Border crossings are one of the most obvious: people have to be admitted into a territory by agents of the state. Language is another way territory is claimed, as are subdivisions such as state, cities, and counties. In this sense, space becomes territory through a process of social construction, definition, and often contestation. That process gets written onto the environment.

This happens in cities in part through the actions of the police. Police seek to advance their territorial claim on spaces. When police respond to a call for service, for instance, they respond with the expectation that their authority will dominate the situation, and if this is not the case, additional officers are called in until their authority is fully dominant. Take for instance any escalation of armed conflict—a robbery, a hostage situation, or a riot—that results in calls for backup, whether from more officers, specialized divisions of the police, or other policing agencies (National Guard, FBI, etc.). Police are territorial agents, given the task of making, marking, and claiming space. Policing in this sense is critical to securing the state, because "the process of internal pacification depends on the capacity of the police to mark and enact meaningful boundaries, to restrict people's capacity to act by regulating their movements in space" (Herbert 1997, 13).

By marking and enacting boundaries, police are critical to defining space, and as we saw above, today that often means communicating to some that they are deserving of increased violence, surveillance, and suspicion. This happens today not because of overt mob violence enabled and fostered by the police, as we saw in chapter 4, but rather because of efforts to reform the police since the Progressive Era.

The Professional Era

Efforts to reform the police began in the Progressive Era with a vision of police modeled on the military. Uniform practices and military hierarchy informed some of the first attempts to unseat the widespread corruption and brutality that plagued early forms of the police. With the growth of professional organizations such as the American Medical Association and the American Bar Association, an ideology of professionalism slowly emerged. Expertise is at the core of a professional identity, and reformers sought to establish police as experts on crime through such tactics as specialization and objective distancing. In doing so, they also created a distinctly different type of police force than had previously existed.

The **professional era** of policing lasted from the 1930s to the 1980s, and was primarily an insider-led movement. Police professionals such as J. Edgar

Figure 7.7 LAPD Gangster Squad, ca. 1948, epitomized specialization in the professional era. Source: Silentjacob98, Wikimedia.

Hoover of the FBI and William Parker, a chief of the Los Angeles Police Department (LAPD), dominated the direction of these reform movements. The LAPD in the post-WWII era was seen as the exemplar of the professional model (see figure 7.7). Notably, however, this era of LAPD policing is also associated with some of the most egregious examples of race-based policing.

In the professional era, police agencies sought to establish territorial dominance through new technologies, such as the automobile. Cars were seen as an important tool in the professionalization of policing for two reasons. First, they provided a way for police to deploy across large distances in ways they could not do on foot. Second, cars seemingly allowed police to respond more quickly to crimes. And finally, by removing officers from neighborhood beats, cars provided police with a veneer of objectivity and a sense of being removed from the society they supervised. Police, in this context, were simply professionals doing a job and responding to situations.

This veneer of objectivity was further enabled by other technological innovations such as radios, centralized dispatch, and helicopters. Each of these positioned police as outside crime and its conditions. Under the professional model, police are merely arriving at a scene, responding to a call, or deployed in response to a centralized unit's command. This understanding of policing created a distinctly different image of policing—as one that is professional, expert, and simultaneously objective, rational, and divorced from social mores. This view of police as detached and unbiased experts on crime was also influenced by the **ideology of bureaucracy,** where the chain of command—sergeants, lieutenants, and chiefs—suggested vigilant oversight and management.

Militarization

The **militarization** of the police, which began in the Progressive Era as reformers sought to create more-uniform public agencies, continued during the professional era. It was during this time that Special Weapons and Tactics (SWAT), a military strategy, seeped into urban policing, as we detailed in chapter 6. This borrowing of military strategies was advocated by the top reformers, such as Parker and Hoover, and was meant to bolster the idea that urban police were just as expert as the military in responding to threats.

Frequent invocations of police fighting "wars" on crime reinforced this professional identity, and reformers during the professional era encouraged embedding the tactics of guerrilla warfare and occupation into the everyday tactics of the police. Police training emphasized "thinking like soldiers" and adhering to a strict hierarchical structure, as in the military. Today, antiguerrilla tactics and SWAT teams, as discussed in chapter 6, are commonly used for drug crimes, and the vast majority (79 percent) of SWAT raids are to issue search warrants, not for the commonly imagined scenario where people are under siege or held hostage (ACLU 2014). SWAT raids steadily grew from their beginning in the late 1960s to 3,800 a year in 1980, and then to 45,000 a year by the early 2000s (Kraska 2007). The ideology of professionalism gave these practices a veneer of objectivity, rationality, and *necessity* such that today they are often seen as integral to police work.

The vision of police as expert crime fighters was also reinforced by other aspects of the reform movement. Police reformers emphasized the law enforcement aspect of police functions, suggesting that when police made an arrest, it was based on the enforcement of the law and the bureaucratic rules and regulations guiding their actions. When police did not make an arrest, the ideology contended that the decision was based on the tactical expert knowledge of the police that is not contained in law. Police, in this view, *know* more about crime than can be contained within the law or by lay persons. Police expertise was also confirmed through a reorganization of police functions in which police came to specialize in much the same way doctors and lawyers do; vice, gang, trafficking, juvenile, and drug units are just some examples.

Police as Producers of Crime Knowledge

Professional police expertise was also bolstered by the tactics of knowledge production that were advanced during this era. The professional era saw the emergence of elaborate systems of record keeping through the routine creation of police reports, police statistics, and local databases on crime suspects; the national gathering of police data; and the release of these statistics to the public (Kelling and Moore 1989). During this time, police often released annual reports with little to no narrative, providing only the quantitative measures of those arrested and for what various crimes. This served to further emphasize the ideology of science and objectivity within policing.

Some jurisdictions even aimed to disconnect the police entirely from their social and cultural positions by making it illegal for police to live in the areas they patrolled (Escobar 1999). The idea was that police should be isolated from political influences, building the identity of a patrol officer as an impersonal, objective, bureaucrat, reflecting the ideology of bureaucracy common in policing (Kelling and Moore 1989). Officers also began to be evaluated based on criteria like arrest rates, felony stops, and other measures of police activity. Other scientific technologies of knowledge production served to further this identity, such as crime labs, fingerprinting, and ballistics (Escobar 1999).

Police as Bureaucrats

Together, these policing reforms created an agency identity as one of organizational efficiency, fairness, and neutrality. But they also created a self-reinforcing pattern of arrests, crime, and police activity that continue to shape policing today. Crime knowledge produced by the police, for instance, is not really necessarily about crime per se. Instead, crime knowledge produced by the police is actually a measure of police activity. Producing statistics that say that more crime is connected to some areas and some races can also mean that police look at those areas and people more. This is borne out by some measures of crime such as the National Crime Victimization Survey, which has, since the early 1970s, shown three times more crime than is reflected in the Uniform Crime Report released by the FBI (Beckett and Sasson 2007). This creates a circular logic where locating police in communities of color and then using measures of police activity to describe conditions of crime in these neighborhoods justifies deploying more police to these neighborhoods (Shabazz 2015).

Creating the Color Line in Los Angeles

Bureaucratization and professionalism, then, did not substantially unmake the role of police with respect to the racial geographies of the Progressive Era. The development of the police officer's professional identity as someone distant and removed, focusing only on the facts did not improve the treatment of communities of color. Instead, police continued to play a critical role, even under the professional ideology, in making, marking, and claiming space for white supremacy.

Professionalism and Distance

Police professionalism was predisposed to alienate communities by the very tactics it embraced. Emphasis on the automobile removed police from the day-to-day life of a neighborhood. Preventing rather than reacting to crime meant aggressively targeting it, as we saw in chapter 4, often to the detriment of those who were supposedly being protected. Citizens were considered amateurs on the issues of crime, and thus, police engaged them primarily as the "eyes and ears" of police and not as equal partners in creating safe neighborhoods (Escobar 1999).

These changes created a distinctly proactive organization, seeking to target "enemies" in order to protect the moral vision of society from which policing stemmed. Writing about the Los Angeles Police Department (LAPD), Edward Escobar notes that police professionalism meant

> aggressively confronting the "criminal elements" in society and through a show of force that convinced potential criminals that violation of the law brought swift and severe punishment . . . created an "us against them" mentality within the law-enforcement community. . . . Every time police gave out traffic citations or made arrests for violation of the sumptuary laws, they not only angered an otherwise law-abiding citizen, they provided further evidence for themselves that the population at large disregarded the law. (1999, 173–74)

With the professional era's reliance on crime knowledge, this created a self-reinforcing pattern. Police saw themselves as the moral defense against dirty, diseased, and blighted communities threatening democracy, the nation, and civilization itself. Communities of color were cast as spaces of moral decay, and increased surveillance by the police in these places instead of others generated crime statistics that were geographically disproportionate. These statistics then justified deploying ever more police in these neighborhoods (along with a whole host of other state surveillance programs), and the cycle began—and begins—anew. The professional era then did not undermine or radically transform ideologies of race present in the Progressive Era, but rather built them into the very structure of policing, a strategy seen in the territorial actions of the police.

One of the most common ways the LAPD sought to exert territorial dominance through the professional identity ethos was through the frequent use of dragnets. A dragnet today often means any systematic police investigation, but during the professional era of policing it meant cordoning off an area and systematically investigating all occupants. In Los Angeles, this type of police tactic was frequently used in both Latinx and black communities, with civilians subject to frequent stops and searches by police (Escobar 1999). While today the Fourth Amendment provides a modicum of protection against unreasonable search and seizure and rampant police harassment, it did not apply to local police until *Mapp v. Ohio* (1961). Frequent dragnets in communities of color thus meant an organized system of surveillance, harassment, and violence carried out by the police.

The Zoot Suit Riots

These tactics are demonstrated in the way police responded to what have been called the **Zoot Suit Riots** during WWII. During the 1930s, Mexican immigration to California increased, and discrimination against Mexican Americans dominated newspaper and political discourse. As we detailed in chapter 6, Henry Anslinger, the head of the Bureau of Narcotics, and William Hearst, one of the richest men in California and the owner of its major newspapers, made a concerted effort to stir up fear and hatred of Mexicans. These efforts often invoked statistics about crime and criminality within the Mexican community, and police often targeted Mexican American youth for increased policing. During the war, Los Angeles newspapers and politicians frequently made accusations that a crime wave by Mexicans was overtaking the city (Escobar 1999). While this was factually inaccurate, these claims fueled a perception that police should aggressively patrol and monitor the Latinx community.

During this time, Mexican American neighborhoods were subject to aggressive policing tactics by the LAPD (Escobar 1999). Reports show a marked increase in complaints about police brutality, with beatings and displays of force frequent in encounters between police and Latinxs. Further, the common use of field interrogations, where police stopped and searched residents often for very little reason, led to increasing tensions between Mexican Americans and the police. In the late 1930s and early 1940s, community leaders exposed the LAPD's practice of arresting Mexican American women and demanding sexual favors and conducting street stops that included pat-downs. Frequent use of arrest meant that Latinxs were often held for seventy-two hours by police for no reason, and officers' frequent use of force led to a marked rise in complaints throughout the 1940s. During the war, Latinxs' foremost political issue was police brutality.

Against this backdrop was also a serious housing shortage. During WWII, the federal government invested heavily in the defense industry in Los Angeles. This further increased migration to the city, but little to no housing was created for newcomers. Any available housing was in white neighborhoods, leading to intense overcrowding in nonwhite portions of the city and concerted efforts by whites to maintain the racial homogeneity of their neighborhoods. Restrictive covenants covered over 95 percent of Los Angeles in the early 1940s (Bernstein 2011, 108). This segregation made it much easier for the LAPD to target communities of color and extend the rapidly developing techniques of professional surveillance. Police use of force often had the effect of removing Latinxs and black people from white spaces and ensuring that Latinx and black youths did not breach the color line between urban neighborhoods and rapidly emerging suburban Los Angeles.

During the war, conflict between police and the Latinx community emerged around zoot suiters. These were second-generation Mexican youths in Los Angeles whose baggy zoot suits were often ridiculed in the white press and denigrated by police who equated the style with crime. Some zoot suiters were also explicitly antiestablishment and adopted the style as a political expression against the racism and discrimination Latinxs experienced. The political

Figure 7.8 Zoot suiters lined up outside Los Angeles jail en route to court after feud with sailors, June 9, 1943. Source: Courtesy of the Library of Congress, LC-USZ62-113319.

component of the zoot suit phenomenon in particular caused concern for police. Despite crime rates likely decreasing during the wartime era, police arrests of Mexican Americans increased, and zoot suit–wearing youth were frequent targets (Escobar 1999, ch. 9).

Police and zoot suiters engaged in several altercations, before one night when tensions between white and Latinx youth escalated into several days of rioting. The riots began when over two hundred white sailors marched into East Los Angeles and began beating up zoot suit–wearing youths, stripping them of their clothes, and burning the suits. The LAPD did nothing to intervene and over the next few days, the riots escalated as civilians joined white sailors in assaulting zoot suiters. Filipino American, African American, and Mexican American youths, all of whom wore zoot suits, were pulled off city buses and beaten mercilessly.

The LAPD accompanied the rioters perpetrating this racial violence and had orders not to arrest any of the rioters. The press described the attacks as having a "cleansing effect" on the city, once again invoking the language of slum clearance characteristic of urban planners in the Progressive Era (McWilliams 2001). At the end of the violence, police had arrested five hundred Latinxs (see figure 7.8), and over 150 people, mostly Latinxs, had been injured.

White racial violence against zoot suiters might be seen simply as a continuation of the decades of white racial violence that marked the Progressive Era. While it certainly was a continuation of that violence, it also was an important moment in the transformation of racial management tactics in policing. Instead of indiscriminately shooting, chasing, and making door-to-door searches, as law enforcement had done and had assisted civilians in doing during the Progressive Era, the LAPD showed all the elements of territorial dominance. The officers descended on the neighborhood of East Los Angeles in automobiles, with instruments of force ready if needed. They engaged in mass arrests instead of mass killing, and they followed orders to dragnet the neighborhood to prevent escape and claim territorial dominance. And finally, they followed a bureaucratic chain of command and obeyed other orders, such as not to arrest white sailors but instead to concentrate on arresting zoot suiters. This was the beginning of the professional-era police, and with the expanding tactics of militarization, the occupation of some communities intensified. With their new professional identity, police achieved a role that had historically eluded them: as members of the moral authority of society, rather than threats to it as they had been during the rampant and widespread corruption and brutality of the Progressive Era.

Police Autonomy in Los Angeles

During the 1950s and 1960s, the LAPD continued to develop as the national model for the professionalized police force. Under the direction of William Parker, the longest-serving chief in Los Angeles, the department accelerated its move toward the professionalized model. Parker emphasized a police force divorced from the political system and advocated administrative reforms in the management and oversight of policing. Parker also encouraged a paramilitary system of policing, where professional crime-fighting police swooped into defend communities against criminals.

Parker's reforms also emphasized the crime-fighting orientation of patrol and investigation by abandoning police investment in social programs, such as work with juveniles. This resulted in police work being much more narrowly defined than it had been in the Progressive Era. As part of an effort to eliminate the corruption and graft that had plagued law enforcement when it was closely tied to political machines, Parker also ensured that the LAPD had autonomy over disciplinary proceedings. Thus, as complaints against the police from black and Latinx residents piled up in the 1950s and 1960s, it was the agency itself that was tasked with responding. The professional orientation established the police as separate from society and with little civilian oversight of the day-to-day operations of the police.

When communities protested against police mistreatment, Parker routinely (and successfully, given his public relations prowess) warned of the fall of democracy in the face of supposedly rapidly escalating crime. He also denied that incidents of police brutality occurred in the department, despite highly publicized events like the "Bloody Christmas" of 1951 (Escobar 2003), where around fifty police officers severely beat seven Latinx youths who were being held for underage drinking. Investigations into the incident were stymied by Parker. Internal affairs investigated the abuse, but found no evidence to support the claim that officers had acted inappropriately (Kramer 2007). Rather than ending Parker's career, Bloody Christmas raised Parker's status and furthered the spread of Parker's vision of a distinctly professional type of policing throughout the nation.

Efforts to resist Parker's control of the LAPD and his officers' handling of black and Latinx communities led Parker to oppose public oversight of his agency even further. When the only African American on the police commission asked Parker about the clearly disproportionate arrests of black men for gambling (in 1958, over 5,200 African Americans were arrested for gambling compared to 482 whites), Parker refused to release statistics about arrests or allow the police commission to interview his officers (Hahn and Feagin 1970).

Parker continued through the 1950s and 1960s to deny allegations of police misconduct against black and Latinx communities, even as his officers engaged in flagrant policing of color lines in Los Angeles. In May 1964, the Congress of Racial Equality (CORE) demanded Parker's resignation, only to be met with charges that it was "playing Russian roulette with the peace and security of the community" (Kramer 2007, 254). In response, the chief was commended by the city council, the Los Angeles County Grand Jury, the Veterans of Foreign Wars, and the Police Commission, who noted that he protected Los Angeles against "'organized vice, hoodlumism and anarchy'" (Kramer 2007, 255). This bolstered the LAPD's role as enforcer of white racial geography, something that continues to shape policing in Los Angeles today.

The quest by Parker and other professional-era reformers for police autonomy had far-reaching effects that are still felt. Most cities have no formal mechanism for direct citizen review of the police, and citizen commissions are most often solely advisory. The only direct role of citizens is appointment of the police chief through the political process. Police handle investigations into their own misconduct, and only rarely is this misconduct investigated by a third party, a party that is still a police agency. Unsurprisingly, one study found that in 2002, only 8 percent of complaints about the police were sustained; 34 percent were not sustained, 25 percent were unfounded, and 23 percent resulted in officers' exoneration (see figure 7.9) (Hickman 2006). The final 10 percent of complaints were dealt with by other mechanisms, including being withdrawn.

A more recent study of complaints against the police found that in eight cities, only 11 percent of complaints were sustained, but this varied considerably from a low of 2 percent in one city to a high of 29 percent in another (Terrill and Ingram 2016). When focusing on just use of force, the study further found that just 2 percent of all complaints were sustained, with a high of just 5 percent and a low of 0 percent. Further, the study of eight cities found that when

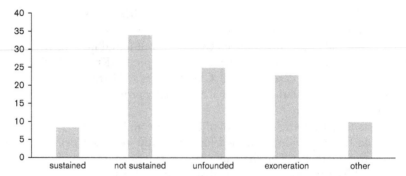

Figure 7.9 Results of complaints against police in large municipal departments, %, 2002. Source: Matthew Hickman, June 2006, *Citizen Complaints about Police Use of Force*, Bureau of Justice Statistics, Department of Justice, https://www.bjs.gov/content /pub/pdf/ccpuf.pdf.

rates of sustained complaints were disaggregated by race, black people were 43 percent less likely to have their complaints sustained. These numbers are hardly surprising given the wide latitude police have been given to do their work since the professional era began. Indeed, places where citizens have more responsibility for investigating complaints had a much higher rate of sustainment than cities where the police took the entire lead on the investigation (Terrill and Ingram 2016; see further box 7.1).

Police professionalism, while not the dominant mode of organizing police today, nevertheless had lasting effects on police organization. Ideologies of bureaucracy and scientific objectivity continue to pervade policing. Police continue to play a critical role in policing the color line of major cities. And police are largely immune to outsider-led change, as the ideology of expertise has resulted in an organizational structure that detaches police from the oversight mechanisms of democratic control. Professionalism has thus institutionalized a vision of society where police play the role of everyday enforcers of the moral order, protecting society from the ceaselessly infiltrating threat of those deemed "criminal," a task that is not largely different than the one envisioned for police by eugenicists and Progressive Era politicians.

BEYOND THE PROFESSIONAL ERA: THE CULTURE OF POLICING TODAY

The professional era of policing reform began to die away in the 1980s in large part as a consequence of the strain between police and communities. As the promised benefits of the professional ideology failed to materialize, it became increasingly clear that without the cooperation of the community, law enforce-

BOX 7.1   Governing the Police

Attempts to control police actions are often stymied by police officers themselves through the power of police unions and institutional legacies. While citizen police commissions are now common throughout the United States, these commissions often operate with little to no power over the actions of the police. For instance, some commissions cannot even investigate police complaints or have zero authority to discipline police officers. Commissions are often only advisory to police leadership, and in many places, commissions are even populated by people selected by police leadership themselves.

Arguments for retaining police authority over complaints stem from the concern about the politicization of police commissions. Many argue that police officers would be unfairly disciplined and instead subject to the whims of popular opinion about policing. Arguments against retaining police authority claim that internal affairs divisions of law enforcement are too close to the issue to fairly adjudicate. Here, scholars argue that police internal investigators are often friends with those they investigate, and they often came up in the same academy class or served together in the agency. Scholars are also concerned that internal investigators are embroiled in the code of silence found within the "thin blue line."

Who do you think should police the police? Should citizens' groups be provided control over police disciplinary proceedings, or should only police chiefs be able to dole out police discipline?

Source: Priyanka Boghani, "Is Citizen Oversight the Answer to Distrust of Police?" Frontline, July 13, 2016, www.pbs.org/wgbh/frontline/article/is-civilian-oversight-the-answer-to-distrust-of-police/.

ment could never achieve its vision of itself as an efficient crime fighting organization. Despite the diminishing of the professional ideology within police reform circles, the tenets of the professional era continue to dominate the organization and culture of policing today. The **culture of policing** refers to how the organizational structure—as well as the behaviors, attitudes, and cultural mores—of policing influences the everyday actions of law enforcement officers and the community. While cultural influences on the police shift, the broader culture of policing is reflected in how police respond to the variegated geographies they confront on a daily basis.

Police Worldviews

Steve Herbert, an ethnographer of the LAPD, provides a complex explanation of how the supposedly race-neutral tactics of policing result in racially disparate policing tactics through the culture of policing. After spending considerable time embedded with the LAPD, Herbert (1997) revealed how geography influences the actions of police and how their behavior changes according to the geographical location they inhabit. For instance, whether a space is private or public, a distinction enshrined in law, will shape how police approach it—for example, by asking permission to enter (as in a private space) or by entering freely (as in public). But space also gets interpreted by police as different places with varying levels of threat, safety, and possibility. Racialized policing and the larger implications for the continuation of coloniality emerge from this translation of perceptions of geographical space into policing practice. The backdrop is a cultural conception of police work that is largely derived from the professional era: a stark moral understanding that police are the authoritative representation of all that is good and right in the world, while the "criminals" they police represent the sources of bad and evil.

Safety and Adventure

Herbert details how a desire for both safety and adventure in police work leads to very different behaviors depending on whether the officer is in a neighborhood defined as propolice or antipolice. Officers, for instance, adopt more "safety" measures when they are in a place they define as antipolice: rolling down the window, taking a gun from its holster, and frequent use of *Terry* stops. Consider the following description of a common use of safety tactics by two officers in a traffic stop:

> As she walks towards the suspect's car, the sergeant pulls his flashlight into one hand and shines it into the car. His other hand rests on his gun. The officer writes down the identification number and returns to the patrol car. When she emerges a second time, the sergeant suggests to her that, in the future, she should require all the passengers to get out of the car. There are he says, three "gangster-looking" guys in the back seat, any of whom might be willing to surprise her. (Herbert 1997, 105)

These tactics might seem mundane or inconsequential, but they result in subjecting residents to more aggressive policing tactics, a key complaint of black and brown communities. Consider the above scenario—if someone is "gangster looking," then he will be viewed with greater suspicion and subject to greater police coercion. Asking someone to step outside the vehicle for a pat-down during a routine traffic stop happens more often in "antipolice" communities. Police justify it as a safety procedure, but as the case of stop and frisk in New York demonstrated, such measures can also be applied broadly to subject entire communities of color to increased surveillance, suspicion, and exclusion from the political community.

While seeking to maximize safety, the more interesting parts of police work often stem from more adventurous encounters. Officers pursuing more adventurous shifts often elect to patrol places perceived as dangerous. Two selections from Herbert's ethnography (1997) reveal what this type of policing looks like on a daily basis:

The senior lead officer is checking on a few "problem locations" in her area on a relatively peaceful weekday morning. She is interested in monitoring an apartment building where she is attempting to wipe out gang graffiti, and also an alley way where stolen cars are being deposited. En route, however, she hears an undercover detective's radio report of gunplay at a gang member's funeral in the southern end of the division. The senior lead decided to respond, even though she is not officially compelled to respond to radio calls. Nor is the incident occurring in her area. (82)

Another patrol officer is assigned to police one beat, but spends most of his spare time in another. More specifically, he heavily monitors one particular rental house, out of which he believes many drug sales are occurring. He watches the house, speaks frequently to its residents, and to its owner. He also speaks to those non-residents who stop by to visit. (113)

These officers sought these locations as spaces where danger lurked and where they could best enact the vision of the gunfighter officer swooping in to save society from the evil lurking in the shadows. Adventure-seeking behaviors—like excessively patrolling black and brown neighborhoods, stopping youth in groups, and using displays of force to generate submission—create a vision of urban spaces as something necessitating violent containment and constant surveillance. This presents a quite troubling picture of the policing of urban space, where police go searching for adventure in the same place where they are likely to use aggressive policing tactics to ensure their safety.

In areas that are propolice, police are much less likely to take safety measures and much more likely to approach residents calmly and pleasantly. Herbert (1997) offers this example:

It is a quiet weekday afternoon, with few calls broadcast on the radio. The sergeant is patrolling exclusively in the Hancock Park area, a quiet, wealthy residential neighborhood that is the source of very few calls even on a busy day. This is my first time with this sergeant. Previous ride-alongs with other sergeants involved many trips to the Smiley and Hauser area. When I asked why he, too, did not head to Smiley and Hauser, the officer merely gestured toward the residents he was passing. Why not, he asked, patrol where it is pleasant? (112)

Patrolling where it is "pleasant" is quite a different experience than patrolling in the places one officer defined as "dirty, filthy, dirty," invoking Progressive Era discourse about the immorality and filth of nonwhite neighborhoods. Instead of frequent displays of force, approaching residents with suspicion and seeking out adventure and adrenaline-producing experiences, patrolling in Hancock Park leads to smiles, pleasantry, and little suspicion of neighborhood residents.

Morality and Getting the "Bad Guys"

Adventure and safety are coupled with the normative order of morality, where police work is shrouded in an understanding of antipolice areas as dirty and needing cleansing. Police work is constructed as virtuous, and arrest, jail, and use of force are seen as moral goods. Here is another example from Herbert (1997):

> A senior lead on patrol points out a hamburger stand that is of interest to him because young men he considers gang members loiter there and because the owner is reputedly involved in dealing drugs. The officer suspects that drugs are distributed at the stand by the owner to the gang member customers. The place, he says, is "dirty, filthy dirty." (147)

This sharp distinction between good and evil, coupled especially with the normative orders of safety, morality, and enacting territorial competence, reveal a world of policing remarkably similar to the one Parker constructed in the 1950s. Police are an expert crime-fighting organization, able to decide when, where, and how to best deploy force, supposedly outside the subjective associations that shape the general public. Resistance to this narrative is met with a stark morality where police are necessarily always working on the side of good.

When problematic events happen, like the Rodney King beating by the LAPD in 1991, this stark morality prevents us from attending to the complexity of the situation (Herbert 1996). The only options available to us are that the individual police officers are corrupt or that the use of force is justified. Yet this belief largely reflects a racialized world view where antipolice neighborhoods are populated by dangerous threatening gang members, and propolice white communities are pleasant, safe, and reflective of the good and moral community. Attempts to understand how the culture of policing works to embed suspicion of black and brown communities into everyday police work are undermined by the presumption that police work should not be scrutinized, lest it undermine the confidence of police.

Factors that are external to the police—the characteristics of neighborhoods, white flight, and urban disinvestment—and those that are internal to the police—the culture of policing—shape how police view neighborhoods and communities and why police behave differently in different places. Neighborhoods that are viewed as antipolice, which often attract aggressive policing by those oriented toward adventure and other extra measures of security that are easily interpreted by community members as aggressive policing.

The culture of policing itself results in the "hyperpolicing" of urban neighborhoods, places where we often see police congregate and where a disproportionate number of police incidents occur. Two professors at Minnesota State have found that a higher incidence of African American residents in a neighborhood correlates with a higher incidence of police misconduct cases in that neighborhood (Lopez and Thomas 2004). This stems not from overt racial animus (which does exist but is not the defining reason for continued racialized policing), but rather from the way police approach space, their cultural and moral positionality, and the continuous definition and redefinition of especially black, indigenous, Asian, and Latinx communities as criminal. As police have moved from the professional era to the era of order-maintenance policing, we will see how the vestiges of the Progressive Era combine with the professional era to infuse a robust machine in the policing of race and crime.

POLICING DISORDER, GENTRIFICATION, AND THE NEW URBAN POLICE

In contrast to the insider-led professional-era reform movement, the "due process" revolution in U.S. courts in the 1950s, 1960s, and 1970s sought to reform the police and tried to put limits on their power. *Mapp v. Ohio* (1961) extended Fourth Amendment protections to the actions of the local police. *Miranda v. Arizona* (1966) provided procedural protections for suspects and sought to decrease the use of physical force to induce confessions. *Mallory v. United State* (1957) ruled that police could not detain suspects longer than forty-eight hours in order to extract a confession, and *Fahy v. Connecticut* (1963) ruled that evidence obtained illegally could not be used in court. Despite these procedural protections, however, urban police became more, not less involved in creating the experience of racial inequality in the United States. To understand why, this section traces how race-based policing grew from the combination of the changing sociopolitical context of urban America, including the growth of private policing (see box 7.2), and the latest reform movement in policing: order-maintenance policing.

Cities, Suburbanization, and Deindustrialization

Suburbanization, white flight, and urban renewal created a distinctly new urban landscape in the 1980s. Modern cities, unlike their industrial predecessors, were entering the period known as "deindustrialization." Rather than centers of economic livelihood and prosperity, cities in the 1980s had become sites of public disinvestment, declining tax bases, and unemployment. Industry no longer sought out urban areas to settle, and between the 1970s and the great recession in 2011, suburbs outpaced cities in job growth. During this time, union jobs declined and industrial manufacturing moved away from traditional centers of production. This created a "spatial mismatch" between employment and unemployment: those experiencing underemployment were in different places than employment opportunities. Given the patterns of federal highway transportation investment, the resistance to public transportation in suburban communities (for fear that poor people would move in), and the disinvestment in urban public transportation overall, there were few economic opportunities for those physically cut off from employment.

Police, by contrast, were entering one of the most significant reform movements in their history—the move toward order-maintenance policing—as a

BOX 7.2   Private Policing

While urban police agencies are central to the issue of mass incarceration, today the vast majority of growth in policing is within the private policing sector. Nationwide, there are three private security officers for every one police officer. Private policing is also bolstered by the networks of surveillance that are more prolific in the private sector, such as gated communities, private security, and personal alarms.

Ethnographies of private policing reveal that private officers are not immune from the practices of racial profiling. For instance, Kevin Walby (2005) conducted an ethnography of video surveillance operators in a private space and found that they relied on racist stereotypes in order to narrow down the list of who to target.

Private policing also blurs the lines between public and private powers, because many police officers moonlight as private security agents. As private security, these officers are not bound by the restrictions on public police. However, as off-duty police officers, they still retain the powers of public police: to arrest and carry a concealed weapon.

In Washington, DC, there is even a category of police officers called "special officers." They are private citizens commissioned to act like a police officer with full arrest powers, and they can be authorized to carry a weapon. Although their authority is restricted to the private places they operate within—such as apartment buildings, colleges, and hospitals—they are allowed to use force. Thus, the special officers have greater power than private security agents who cannot arrest, carry weapons (unless authorized), or use force except in self-defense.

Should the powers of public policing be permitted to be used by private police officers? Should private security officers be restricted from using force, or should they have the same powers as the special officers in Washington, DC? Should the vast industry of private policing be regulated, and if so, how?

Source: Kevin Walby, "How Closed-Circuit Television Surveillance Organizes the Social: An Institutional Ethnography," *Canadian Journal of Sociology* 30, no. 2 (2005): 189–214; Law Enforcement Officers Security Unions–DC, n.d., "Frequent *[sic]* Asked Questions about Washington D.C. Special Police Officers & Training," www.leosudc.org/faq-about-washington-dc-special-police.

result of growing dissatisfaction with urban police agencies. Urban police departments, which had modeled themselves on the military and worked to create a professional ethos, had positioned themselves as crime experts, swooping in to save society from itself. This had alienated many communities, especially those of color, because the use of targeted dragnet-type tactics frequently were aimed exclusively at the poor and nonwhite. A series of key Supreme Court cases challenged the carte blanche often given to urban police and extended essential protections to suspects and the accused.

Two trends in police work illustrate how race-based policing extends beyond the individual decision-making of the police officer to the entire system, culture, and training of police. First was the emergence of "broken windows" policing in the 1980s. Second was the continued militarization of the police, combined with an emphasis on drugs and gangs. These trends were significant not just because they refer to new policing emphases and practices but because they also occurred during an explosion in the number of police in the urban United States.

Between 1987 and 2003, the number of full-time employees in local police departments grew almost 35 percent (Reaves 2015). Further, the growth of police departments also led to considerable growth in police spending—between 2003 and 2013 public-safety spending in cities in California increased 43 percent (Sforza 2014). Cities such as Dallas and Phoenix spend over sixty percent of their municipal budgets on policing and emergency services (Rajwani 2016). And to fund this? Cities increasingly rely on the same tactic used in Ferguson: the policing of disorder.

Broken Windows and Policing Disorder

One of the most significant movements in modern policing is what is known as **broken windows policing.** The term comes from a short article published by sociologists James Q. Wilson and George Kelling in 1982 in *Atlantic Monthly* titled "Broken Windows Policing." From this, an entirely new framework for policing emerged. However, **order-maintenance policing** wasn't exactly new; it was a new way of framing policing practices that had begun with the very first police force. This new framework focused police not on infamous crimes—murder, organized crime, or violence—but rather on **"disorder"** and tasked them with maintaining aesthetic order in the city.

Wilson and Kelling (1982) begin the story of broken windows policing by recounting policing history. In particular, they tell how urban areas confronted crime and the role police and neighborhood residents played in that process:

> The process we call urban decay has occurred for centuries in every city. But what is happening today is different in at least two important respects. First, in the period before, say, World War II, city dwellers—because of money costs, transportation difficulties, familial and church connections—could rarely move away from neighborhood problems. When movement did occur, it tended to be along public-transit routes. Now mobility has become exceptionally easy for all but the poorest or those who are blocked by racial prejudice. Earlier crime waves had a kind of built-in self-correcting mechanism: the determination of a neighborhood or community to reassert control over its turf. Areas in Chicago, New York, and Boston would experience crime and gang wars, and then normalcy would return as the families for whom no alternative residences were possible reclaimed their authority over the streets.
>
> Second, the police in this earlier period assisted in that reassertion of authority by acting on behalf of the community, sometimes violently. Young toughs were

roughed up, people were arrested "on suspicion" or for vagrancy, and prostitutes and petty thieves were routed. "Rights" were something enjoyed by decent folk—and perhaps also by the serious professional criminal, who avoided violence and could afford a lawyer. (36)

Wilson and Kelling construct a very particular history of the city, reminiscent of the construction of the professional era of policing. Cities are places people flee, but those who stayed were able to assert control over the forces of crime and gangs. The role for police in this scenario was simply "acting on behalf of the community, sometimes violently." Here, cities are under threat of "decay" from crime, but with the help of police, they keep it at bay.

In the modern era, Wilson and Kelling contend, decent people who might helped tamp down a crime wave have simply moved away to escape the violence, and police are handicapped in doing more than watching decay take root. Wilson and Kelling's construction of urban America was not entirely off. Those who could leave, due to racial advantage, did so as part of white flight and suburbanization; those who were left behind often remained due to economic disadvantage or racial discrimination. Wilson and Kelling note that the techniques required for police to create the order sought by neighborhood residents "would not withstand a legal challenge." In short, police used to be able to "kick ass" and restore order to the community (Wilson and Kelling 1982, 34), but they are now hamstrung by legal challenges.

Wilson and Kelling's theory grew from, and was named after, a study done by Philip Zimbardo, in which researchers abandoned cars in various neighborhoods. The car abandoned in the poor neighborhood was quickly dismantled for parts. When the car abandoned in the wealthy neighborhood failed to attract the neighborhood's attention, Zimbardo and his associates broke a window. Soon, that car also was dismantled. This was the spark for Wilson and Kelling's theory: if broken windows or, by extension, signs of disorder are left untended, then crime will inevitably enter a neighborhood.

To remedy this, Wilson and Kelling argue for a return to police foot-patrols, but not because they were better at decreasing crime than officers in patrol cars. Rather, Wilson and Kelling contend that most people fear violent crime, but there is another important source of fear: "the fear of being bothered by disorderly people. Not violent people, nor, necessarily, criminals, but disreputable or obstreperous or unpredictable people: panhandlers, drunks, addicts, rowdy teenagers, prostitutes, loiterers, the mentally disturbed" (Wilson and Kelling 1982, 29). Broken windows and the field of order-maintenance policing then is not about crime, but about disorder—and not about things, but about people. Ridding the city of disorderly people—a goal reminiscent of eugenicists and Progressives—became the stated aim of policing.

Wilson and Kelling's article influenced the development of a whole generation of policing techniques that broadly fall under the rubric of order maintenance or quality-of-life policing. These range from relatively sporadic and situational programs such as graffiti paint-outs to wholesale reorientations of police departments. But the common characteristic is that instead of focusing on felony crimes—murder, rape, assault—police are redirected to focus on low-level and minor crimes, some of which are not crimes at all but infractions such as violations of the traffic code. Wilson and Kelling never intended many of the effects that came from the ideas of broken windows policing and have even explicitly condemned some of the more famous iterations of it, but it took over police agencies nevertheless.

In each iteration, order-maintenance policing has the same goal that prompted expansion of the first public policing agencies during the Progressive Era: maintaining urban order. Yet when it comes to defining order and disorder, we find that these terms, while often legally neutral, are in fact steeped in middle-class white patriarchal visions of society.

Disorder and Its Meanings

Though Wilson and Kelling have argued that zero tolerance is not an appropriate broken windows approach, one of the most famous examples of an attempt to apply it was the zero tolerance policy of the New York City Police Department (NYPD) (Greene 1999). **Zero tolerance** is an iteration of policing that emphasizes swift punishment and repression in response to a first encounter. Under the NYPD policy, officers were instructed to aggressively, with a "kick ass" mentality, police lower-level offenses in order to remove "disreputable" people from urban space. To this end, police focused on people perceived to bring fear and avoidance in the white middle class: youth of color, who were targeted through anti-truancy roundups; the homeless; squeegee men; people drinking or urinating in public; low-level drug dealers; and those visiting sex markets. New York also conducted background checks on all those arrested in the hope that more severe crimes would be revealed.

Other iterations of broken window policing focus on similar types of disorder. In Portland, Oregon, police banned women suspected of prostitution from particular neighborhoods, and their mere presence in a neighborhood was grounds for arrest and prosecution (Sanchez 2001). Men soliciting sex in these neighborhoods faced no similar prohibition or control. In Chicago, middle-class residents concerned about a public housing complex lobbied police to focus on the disorderly behaviors of its residents, which included such thing as barbequing in the park, working on cars outside, and loitering (Pattillo 2008). Only three items on the entire list generated by residents' complaints in the study dealt with behavior identified in criminal law: drug sales, violence, and gangs (and only tangentially). Public housing is often cited as a form of disorder, even when there are no tangible problematic behaviors (Pattillo 2008; Griffiths and Tita 2009). In Chicago, neighbors lobbied the public housing authority to require credit checks and drug tests, home visits, housekeeping requirements, and ten years without a felony conviction for all residents (Pattillo 2008).

Criminalizing Disorder

Reformers were not the only drivers of the law enforcement focus on disorder. Cities around the country passed laws *instructing* police to focus on these types of issues. Residents passed laws criminalizing two of the most commonly cited signs of disorder: visible signs of homelessness and young people gathering in public. Yet cities could not criminalize these behaviors outright; *Papachristou v. City of Jacksonville* (1972) outlawed direct prohibition on "vagrants" in response to similar ordinances common during Jim Crow. *Papachristou* defined a distinction in the law between "status" and "conduct" and struck down a statute that criminalized status. Consequently, a rash of city ordinances emerged that focused on practice rather than status.

One of the most popular legal innovations was the criminalization of homelessness through the prohibition of sitting or lying on the sidewalk (Mitchell 1997). This type of law targets those without a place to live and makes perpetual motion or private space a prerequisite for avoiding police surveillance. Cities such as Seattle, New York, and Los Angeles have sought to expel "disorderly" people surviving in public by regularly stopping, moving, and arresting those without private space (Sparks 2010). In one study of Los Angeles, a woman had been stopped by police over a hundred times, arrested over sixty times, and spent over a year of her life in jail on one-week stays for the crime of sitting on the sidewalk (Stuart 2016). (The author of the study was himself stopped fourteen times in one year by the police.) In some cities, including Seattle, violators are banished from particular areas of the city, which limits their access to services, social networks, and safety (Beckett and Herbert 2009). The combination of increased suspicion and surveillance with disproportionate rates of being unhoused and the criminalization of homelessness is yet another way that cities seek to re-create geographies of white supremacy (Stuart 2011).

Homeless people are not the only ones subject to criminalization. Gangs are another target of urban policy, and one that more explicitly targets race in the city. Chicago pioneered the "gang loitering ordinance" which (after several constitutional challenges) allows police to designate areas of the city as "gang areas," where hanging out with more than two people can constitute "gang loitering" (Roberts 1999). As we will discuss in chapter 8, cities are even turning to civil courts to criminalize gangs in the absence of criminal behaviors. *Gang* is often a code word for *race*, and indeed, even gang experts note that "there is no widely or universally accepted definition of a 'gang' among law enforcement agencies" (National Gang Center n.d.). The gang designation is also based solely on police officers' perceptions. The National Gang Youth Sur-

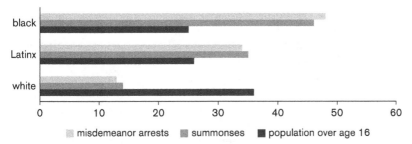

Figure 7.10 New York City population, summonses, and misdemeanor arrests by race, %, 2001–2013. Source: Data retrieved from P. Chauhan, A. G. Fera, M. B. Welsh, E. Balazon, and E. Misshula, *Trends in Misdemeanor Arrests in New York* (New York, NY: John Jay College of Criminal Justice, 2014), 25–27; Sarah Ryley, Laura Bult, and Dareh Gregorian, "Daily News Analysis Finds Racial Disparities in Summonses for Minor Violations in 'Broken Windows' Policing," *New York Daily News,* August 4, 2014, www.nydailynews .com/new-york/summons-broken-windows-racial-disparity-garner-article-1.1890567.

vey periodically surveys *law enforcement* to find out the racial composition of gangs, and unsurprisingly, given the popular culture construction of the term, upwards of 80 percent of gang youths are identified as black or Latinx.

Disorder, for the most part, is not really about actual broken windows but is instead about disorderly *people.* And studies suggest that the *people* who cause the most discomfort are young men of color, something demonstrated by the fact that order-maintenance policing often increases the policing of communities of color for very low-level crime (see figure 7.10). This is demonstrated by an extensive study by Harvard sociologist Robert Sampson. Writing in 2012, he describes how what he calls "objectively observed disorder" is different from "perceived disorder." His study suggests that while objectively observed disorder exists throughout society, it is perceived as disorder only in a nonwhite environment. In other racial contexts, it goes simply unnoticed by residents.

Expelling people from the city, containing those who remain, and subjecting them to increased surveillance are long-standing practices, as we have shown throughout this book, which continue through the language of safety, crime, and disorder today. The gendered, racial, class, and heteronormative dimensions of the colonial narratives of race are today remade through the policing of disorder, as we show next in the case of Antioch, California, during the housing crisis.

Enacting the Color Line in Antioch, California

Antioch, California, was hard hit by the housing crisis in 2008. As a city on the far outskirts of the San Francisco Bay Area, there was rapid development of new housing stock in the years before the crash. When the crisis hit, rental homes sat vacant. Landlords began renting these properties to Section 8 residents, an affordable housing voucher program described in chapter 5. The number of households in Antioch using Section 8 vouchers doubled in just a few years, and while only 4 percent of households in Antioch were black, they made up 56 percent of Section 8 recipients.

These residents were part of a demographic shift in Antioch. In the 2000 census, 65 percent of Antioch residents identified themselves as white. By 2010, however, the white population had dropped to 49 percent of city residents. Meanwhile, those ten years had seen the black population grow by 100 percent, and the Latinx population by 62 percent.

In response to these changes, residents and politicians invoked familiar themes of urban decline and moral bankruptcy (Ocen 2012). Newspaper articles, city council meetings, and even one city report described the newcomers as "criminal," "lazy," and "scary," arguing that failure to act meant the city was doomed to be "just like" Oakland and Richmond, two nearby cities with large African American populations (prior to gentrification). Citizens formed an organization named United Citizens for Better Neighborhoods with a goal of reducing the number of Section 8 residents. The city council formed a specialized police unit called the Community Action Team (CAT) designed to accomplish this same goal.

The CAT solicited complaints about Section 8 residents by placing hang tags on doors asking for neighbors to call the police on quality-of-life issues. Upon receiving complaints, the CAT targeted Section 8 recipients for surveillance and punishment, seeking noncriminal information that could lead to termination of a tenant's housing. If this information included the fact that the resident was a welfare recipient, the CAT could then search the home without consent or a warrant, since searches of welfare recipients are considered "administrative" and thus outside Fourth Amendment protections (*Wyman v. James* [1970], *Sanchez v. County of San Diego* [2006]). The CAT also parked squad cars on blocks where voucher holders lived and sent any evidence it collected to the county housing authority.

Citizens also privately monitored the conduct of black households suspected of using Section 8 and posted signs on their doors saying, "No more Section 8. Save Antioch NOW. We THE RESIDENTS are watching YOU." The citizen group also compiled complaints and submitted them to the CAT, such as the presence of barking dogs, kids playing basketball in the street, and loud music.

The CAT also used calls to the police by Section 8 residents as a reason to investigate these households. One Section 8 recipient called police for help in a domestic violence situation. When police arrived, they did not investigate the domestic violence but instead focused on the complainant's Section 8 status. Another resident reported a break-in, but instead of investigating, the police searched her home. Some reportedly stopped calling police in order to avoid harassment. The CAT also sent threatening letters to landlords suggesting they could be prosecuted if anything amiss occurred on their properties and warned them against renting to African Americans. As a result, at least one landlord forced a woman to leave her home. African Americans were two-thirds of those investigated by CAT officers (Ocen 2012).

This increased surveillance of Section 8 residents is reminiscent of lantern laws requiring black people to light their face at night in New York, community groups that formed in response to black residents in Baltimore and Levittown, and the outright prohibition of black residents through racially restrictive covenants. But the events in Antioch did not occur during slavery or the Progressive Era, or even in the last vestiges of Jim Crow. They occurred in the recent past, less than a decade ago, and provide an example of how order-maintenance policing strategies recreate the racial exclusions common to earlier historical periods. Order maintenance, like events chronicled in earlier chapters, is how coloniality continues today through the institution of policing and how whiteness conquers space. Tellingly, white Section 8 residents were not targeted in Antioch, revealing how the perception of what constitutes disorder depends largely not on class, but on racial composition, something emphasized in chapter 5's discussion of the neighborhood effect (Sampson 2012). Given the racialized construction of disorder, it's hardly surprising that order-maintenance policing has led to the continued surveillance of and violence against black and brown communities (Roberts 1999).

The Experience of Order Maintenance

Implicit stereotypes associating nonwhites with violence and criminality are at the heart of contemporary order-maintenance policing strategies. Under the guise of protection, the police, the public, and city legislatures seek to continue banishing black bodies from public space, and if they remain, subject them to increased surveillance, suspicion, and, importantly, violence.

Studies of broken windows are mixed with regards to their impact on crime, but there are two definitive results of police agencies embracing order-maintenance policing: fear of crime among whites decreased (even when actual crime rates did not) and rates of violence against black residents increased (Harcourt 2009). In every precinct except one, the NYPD's "zero-tolerance policing" increased rates and complaints of police brutality. Filing of civil rights claims against the police increased by 75 percent in four years during the zero-tolerance period (Greene 1999). Citizen complaints to the review board increased 60 percent between 1992 and 1996, and these complaints showed a marked increase during the first year of the program.

Infamous and extremely brutal cases such as Amadou Diallo, who was shot and killed by police, or Abner Louima, who was beaten by police and sodomized with a broom handle, underscore the consequences of broken windows policing.

BOX 7.3   The "Criminology of Place"

A recent publication drew attention to a new field in criminology called the "criminology of place." This entails a different approach to policing, which legal scholar Joseph Margulies refers to as the paradox that "the key to community well-being and public safety is to use police less, not more." This approach is largely part of what is called "crime prevention through environmental design," which instead of arresting and punishing criminals, aims to change the micro-places—not neighborhoods—where crime congregates.

As an example, Margulies tells the story of a corner store in Cincinnati where drugs and guns were often sold. Police caught the sellers on tape and even had an informant who could testify against the dealers. But, instead of arresting the dealers and prosecuting a case that was pretty much a slam dunk, the police took another tack by encouraging change in the market itself. How and why did this happen?

In part, it happened because crime prevention through environmental design emphasizes changing the environment, not people. According to the theory, a different environment can push out crime altogether, without a police response. In Cincinnati, the owners of the market were encouraged by police to replace the employees. The owners chose to staff the store themselves, which increased the number of "place managers." Place managers are people who actively care for a particular place and take steps to protect it. The owners did this by clearly sign-posting that the store no longer sold illegal goods.

Other places have used similar strategies. A gas station in Florida that was fre-quently robbed in the middle of the night when it had few customers increased the number of eyes and ears by offering free coffee to taxi drivers. Increasing lighting and replacing graffiti with murals by local artists helped one neighbor-hood in San Francisco banish drug users and others. These tactics tend to address social problems in urban space very differently than those premised on broken windows theory or order-maintenance policing.

What is the conception of place, people, and crime in the criminology of place? How does the criminology of place challenge the tenets of broken win-dows theory? In your opinion, does the criminology of place have the potential to challenge the coloniality of modern life with respect to policing?

Source: Joseph Margulies, "Changing Places," *Verdict*, Justia, March 6, 2017, https://verdict.justia.com/2017/03/06/changing-places.

Yet these cases are just the extremes of a more robust and everyday practice of aggressive enforcement. This enforcement results in such practices as stop and frisk, where *Terry* stops are widely used (in violation of their constitutional application) to increase the surveillance of nonwhite communities (Fagan and Davies 2000). It also leads police to focus on very minor crimes. And as Eric Garner unfortunately found out in New York, interactions with police for minor crimes, like selling loose cigarettes, can be deadly. Order-maintenance policing, then, is in actuality a type of policing that systematically subjects the poor and communities of color to increased surveillance, intrusion, policing, and violence (Roberts 1999). An alternative approach is discussed in box 7.3.

Even further, the focus on the poor and communities of color is built into the very logic of order-maintenance policing. The logic goes that in order to build the robust cities of tomorrow, citizens must not live in fear as they go about their daily activities, a logic reinforced by the dependence of urban economies on tourism. Anything that induces fear must be removed from the urban environment. One might say that signs of disorder spell fear for all people and thus are irreducible to class or race dimensions. And yet disorder is neither objectively perceived nor immune from the racial and class hierarchies that dominate U.S. society. Instead, order is directly a part of these hierarchies, and the notion of disorder is not only a window into how fear of the other shapes public policy but also how that fear is raced and classed.

When Wilson and Kelling lamented the inability of police officers to "kick ass," they were mourning for a time when the subjugation of some for the health and safety of others was legally sanctioned. During slavery, for example, the violent oppression and killing of some was justified for the economic health and livelihood of others. What order-maintenance policing does, both in logic and application, is re-create this logic by positing that the fear that some feel when faced with the visible manifestations of city life—such as poverty, teens hanging out on the street, and racial segregation—should be met with aggressive suppression unbridled by constitutional regulation. People perceived as disorderly are cast as undesirables incapable of membership in political society and expendable to the continuation of that society. That the people who are expendable continue to be black, brown, and poor demonstrates not only the deeply racialized and classed basis of order-maintenance policing but also that it is a tool for the continuation of the racialized and classed politics of suppression that have long made the United States exemplary.

CONCLUSION

Policing today is integral to the maintenance and continuation of the racial state, even though the recognition of this is increasing. Through a veneer of objectivity, procedure, and bureaucratic formality honed in the professional era, the investigatory stop, broken windows approaches, and the culture of policing continue the logics and practices of coloniality into the current era.

Much of this might be expected. Tell a group of people that they are moral crusaders against disorder and vice. Give them the power of force, coercion, and violence. Then direct them to target the disorder aggressively. Deploy them primarily to communities that are segregated by race and class. Fuel them with popular images of race and crime that reinforce white imaginings of black pathology. It would be naïve to expect anything other than what is happening in policing today. In a recent dissent to a case rolling back protections from police, Supreme Court Justice Sonia Sotomayor wrote, "This case tells everyone, white and black, guilty and innocent, that an officer can verify your legal status at any time. It says that your body is subject to invasion while courts excuse the violation of your rights. It implies that you are not a citizen of a democracy but the subject of a carceral state, just waiting to be cataloged" (*Utah v. Strieff* 2016). But the carceral state and cataloguing practices of surveillance would not apply to everyone, she continued, writing, "It is no secret that people of color are disproportionate victims of this type of [police] scrutiny." Investigatory stops, order-maintenance policing, and the criminalization of disorder all provide ample evidence of why police are considered an occupying army by some communities. They also demonstrate how the issues of policing extend far beyond individual police themselves and implicate the very society and structure that authorizes, deploys, and trains police.

REFERENCES

American Civil Liberties Union (ACLU). *War Comes Home: The Excessive Militarization of American Policing.* New York. https://www.aclu.org/sites/default/files/field_document/jus14-warcomeshome-text-rel1.pdf

Beckett, Katherine, and Steve Herbert. 2009. *Banished: The New Social Control in Urban America.* New York: Oxford University Press.

Beckett, Katherine, Kris Nyrop, and Lori Pfingst. 2006. "Race, Drugs, and Policing: Understanding Disparities in Drug Delivery Arrests." *Criminology* 44, no. 1: 105–37.

Bernstein, Shana. 2011. *Bridges of Reform: Interracial Civil Rights Activism in Twentieth-Century Los Angeles.* New York: Oxford University Press.

Browne, Simone. 2015. *Dark Matters: On the Surveillance of Blackness.* Durham, NC: Duke University Press.

Bourgois, Philippe. 2003. *In Search of Respect: Selling Crack in El Barrio.* Structural Analysis in the Social Sciences 10. Cambridge, UK: Cambridge University Press,

Chotvacs, Charles W. 2002. "The Fourth Amendment Warrant Requirement: Constitutional Protection of Legal Fiction: Noted Exceptions Recognized by the Tenth Circuit." *Denver University Law Review* 79: 331–52.

Correll, Joshua, Geoffrey R. Urland, and Tiffany A. Ito. 2006. "Event-Related Potentials and the Decision to Shoot: The Role of Threat Perception and Cognitive Control." *Journal of Experimental Social Psychology* 42, no. 1: 120–28.

"The Counted: People Killed by Police in the U.S." (interactive database). 2016. *Guardian.* Accessed April 17, 2017. www.theguardian.com/us-news/ng-interactive/2015/jun/01/the-counted-police-killings-us-database.

Cummings, Scott L., ed. 2011. *The Paradox of Professionalism: Lawyers and the Possibility of Justice.* New York: Cambridge University Press.

Delaney, David. 2008. *Territory: a short introduction.* Malden, MA: Blackwell Publishing.

Department of Justice (DOJ). 2015. *Investigation of the Ferguson Police Department.* March 4, 2015. Washington, DC: Department of Justice. https://www.justice.gov/sites/default/files/opa/press-releases/attachments/2015/03/04/ferguson_police_department_report.pdf

Eberhardt, Jennifer L., Phillip Atiba Goff, Valerie J. Purdie, and Paul G. Davies. 2004. "Seeing Black: Race, Crime, and Visual Processing." *Journal of Personality and Social Psychology* 87, no. 6: 876–93. http://fairandimpartialpolicing.com/docs/pob5.pdf.

Eisen, Arlene, and Kali Akuno. 2012. *Report on the Extrajudicial Killings of 120 Black People.* Oakland, CA: Malcolm X Grassroots Movement, Accessed April 17, 2017. https://mxgm.org/wp-content/uploads/2012/07/07_24_Report_all_rev_protected.pdf.

Elinson, Zusha, and Dan Frosch. 2015. "Cost of Police-Misconduct Cases Soars in Big US Cities." *Wall Street Journal*, July 15, 2015. www.wsj.com/articles/cost-of-police-misconduct-cases-soars-in-big-u-s-cities-1437013834.

Epp, Charles R., Steven Maynard-Moody, and Donald P. Haider-Markel. 2014. *Pulled Over: How Police Stops Define Race and Citizenship.* Chicago: University of Chicago Press.

Escobar, Edward J. 1999. *Race, Police, and the Making of a Political Identity: Mexican Americans and the Los Angeles Police Department, 1900–1945.* Latinos in American Society and Culture 7. Berkeley: University of California Press.

———. 2003. "Bloody Christmas and the Irony of Police Professionalism: The Los Angeles Police Department, Mexican Americans, and Police Reform in the 1950s." *Pacific Historical Review* 72, no. 2: 171–99.

Fagan, Jeffrey, and Garth Davies. 2000. "Street Stops and Broken Windows: Terry, Race, and Disorder in New York City." *Fordham Urban Law Journal* 28: 457–504.

Foucault, Michel. 2003. *"Society Must Be Defended."* Edited by Mauro Bertani and Alessandro Fontana. Translated by David Macey. Lectures at the Collège de France, 1975–1976 3. General editors: François Ewald and Alessandro Fontana. English series editor: Arnold I. Davidson. New York: Picador.

Fryer, Roland G., Jr. 2016. *An Empirical Analysis of Racial Differences in Police Use of Force.* NBER Working Paper No. 22399. Issued in July 2016. Cambridge, MA: National Bureau of Economic Research. www.nber.org/papers/w22399

Futterman, Craig B., H. Melissa Mather, and Melanie Miles. 2007. "The Use of Statistical Evidence to Address Police Supervisory and Disciplinary Practices: The Chicago Police Department's Broken System." *DePaul Journal for Social Justice* 1: 251.

Gabrielson, Ryan, Eric Sagara, and Ryann Grochowski Jones. 2014. "Deadly Force, in Black and White." *ProPublica*, October 14, 2014. www.propublica.org/article/deadly-force-in-black-and-white.

Geller, Amanda, and Jeffrey Fagan. 2010. "Pot as Pretext: Marijuana, Race, and the New Disorder in New York City Street Policing." *Journal of Empirical Legal Studies* 7, no. 4: 591–633.

Gilmore, Ruth Wilson. 2007. *Golden Gulag: Prisons, Surplus, Crisis, and Opposition in Globalizing California.* Berkeley: University of California Press.

Goff, Phillip Atiba, Jennifer L. Eberhardt, Melissa J. Williams, and Matthew Christian Jackson. 2008. "Not Yet Human: Implicit Knowledge, Historical Dehumanization, and Contemporary Consequences." *Journal of Personality and Social Psychology* 94, no. 2: 292.

Greene, Judith A. 1999. "Zero Tolerance: A Case Study of Police Policies and Practices in New York City." *Crime and Delinquency* 45, no. 2: 171–87.

Griffiths, Elizabeth, and George Tita. 2009. "Homicide in and around Public Housing: Is Public Housing a Hotbed, a Magnet, or a Generator of Violence for the Surrounding Community?" *Social Problems* 56, no. 3: 474–93.

Gross, Samuel R., and Katherine Y. Barnes. 2002. "Road Work: Racial Profiling and Drug Interdiction on the Highway." *Michigan Law Review* 101, no. 3: 651–754.

Hagan, John, and Holly Foster. 2006. "Profiles of Punishment and Privilege: Secret and Disputed Deviance during the Racialized Transition to American Adulthood." *Crime, Law and Social Change* 46, no. 1: 65–85.

Hahn, Harlan, and Joe R. Feagin. 1970. "Riot-Precipitating Police Practices: Attitudes in Urban Ghettos." *Phylon* 31, no. 2 (Second Quarter): 183–93. http://www.jstor.org/stable/273723.

Harcourt, Bernard E. 2008. *Against Prediction: Profiling, Policing, and Punishing in an Actuarial Age.* Chicago: University of Chicago Press.

———. 2009. *Illusion of Order: The False Promise of Broken Windows Policing.* Cambridge, MA: Harvard University Press.

Harris, David A. 1997. "'Driving While Black' and All Other Traffic Offenses: The Supreme Court and Pretextual Traffic Stops." *Journal of Criminal Law and Criminology* 87, no. 2: 544–82.

———. 1999. "The Stories, the Statistics, and the Law: Why Driving While Black Matters." *Minnesota Law Review* 84: 265.

———. 2003. *Profiles in Injustice: Why Racial Profiling Cannot Work.* New York: New Press.

Herbert, Steve. 1996. "Morality in Law Enforcement: Chasing" Bad Guys" with the Los Angeles Police Department." *Law and Society Review* 30, no. 4: 799–818.

———. 1997. *Policing Space: Territoriality and the Los Angeles Police Department.* Minneapolis: University of Minnesota Press.

Hickman, Matthew. 2006. *Citizen Complaints about Police Use of Force.* Washington DC: Bureau of Justice Statistics, U.S. Department of Justice. June 2006. www.bjs.gov/content/pub/pdf/ccpuf.pdf.

Kelling, George L., and Mark Harrison Moore. 1989. *The Evolving Strategy of Policing.* Perspectives on Policing 4. November 1988. Washington, DC: National Institute of Justice, Office of Justice Programs, U.S. Department of Justice. https://catalog.hathitrust.org/Record/011328412.

Kocieniewski, David, and Robert Hanley. 2000. "An Inside Story of Racial Bias and Denial; New Jersey Files Reveal Drama behind Profiling." *New York Times,* December 3, 2000. www.nytimes.com/2000/12/03 /nyregion/inside-story-racial-bias-denial-new-jersey-files-reveal-drama-behind-profiling.html.

Kramer, Alisa Sarah. 2007. "William H. Parker and the Thin Blue Line: Politics, Public Relations and Policing in Postwar Los Angeles." PhD diss., American University.

Kraska, Peter B. 2007. "Militarization and Policing—Its Relevance to 21st Century Police." *Policing* 1, no. 4: 501–13.

Kraska, Peter B., and Victor E. Kappeler. 1997. "Militarizing American Police: The Rise and Normalization of Paramilitary Units." *Social Problems* 44, no. 1: 1–18.

Krysan, Maria. 2002. "Community Undesirability in Black and White: Examining Racial Residential Preferences through Community Perceptions." *Social Problems* 49, no. 4: 521–43.

Kutateladze, Besiki Luka, and Nancy Andiloro. 2014. *Prosecution and Racial Justice in New York County.* Report submitted to National Institute of Justice, January 31, 2014. New York: Vera Institute of Justice. www .ncjrs.gov/pdffiles1/nij/grants/247227.pdf.

Lange, James E., Mark B. Johnson, and Robert B. Voas. 2005. "Testing the Racial Profiling Hypothesis for Seemingly Disparate Traffic Stops on the New Jersey Turnpike." *Justice Quarterly* 22, no. 2: 193–223.

Leo, Richard A. 1996. "Miranda's Revenge: Police Interrogation as a Confidence Game." *Law and Society Review* 30: 259–88. https://ssrn.com/abstract=1134050.

Lopez, Jose Javier, and Pedro M. Thomas. 2004. "The Geography of Law Enforcement Malpractice: National Patterns of Official Misconduct in the United States, 1989–1999." *Journal of American Studies* 38, no. 3: 371–90.

MacDonald, John, Robert J. Stokes, Greg Ridgeway, and K. Jack Riley. 2007. "Race, Neighbourhood Context and Perceptions of Injustice by the Police in Cincinnati." *Urban Studies* 44, no. 13: 2567–85.

McWilliams, Carey. 2001. *Fool's Paradise: A Carey McWilliams Reader.* Edited by Dean Stewart and Jeannine Gendar. Berkeley, CA: Heyday Books.

Mitchell, Don. 1997. "The Annihilation of Space by Law: The Roots and Implications of Anti-Homeless Laws in the United States." *Antipode* 29, no. 3: 303–35.

Moran, David A. 2002. "The New Fourth Amendment Vehicle Doctrine: Stop and Search Any Car at Any Time." *Villanova Law Review* 47: 815.

National Gang Center. n.d. *National Youth Gang Survey Analysis.* Accessed September 28, 2017. www .nationalgangcenter.gov/Survey-Analysis.

NBC News. 2004. *Dateline.* "A Pattern of Suspicion." Broadcast April 9, 2004. https://vimeo.com/31737378.

Newport, Frank. 2016. "Public Opinion Context: Americans, Race and Police." Gallup blog. July 8, 2016. www .gallup.com/opinion/polling-matters/193586/public-opinion-context-americans-race-police.aspx.

Ocen, Priscilla A. 2012. "The New Racially Restrictive Covenant: Race, Welfare and the Policing of Black Women in Subsidized Housing." *UCLA Law Review* 59: 1540.

Padilla, Felix M. 1992. *The Gang as an American Enterprise.* New Brunswick, NJ: Rutgers University Press.

Pager, Devah. 2008. *Marked: Race, Crime, and Finding Work in an Era of Mass Incarceration.* Chicago: University of Chicago Press.

Parenti, Christian. 2000. *Lockdown America: Police and Prisons in the Age of Crisis.* London: Verso,

Pattillo, Mary. 2008. *Black on the Block: The Politics of Race and Class in the City.* Chicago: University of Chicago Press.

Quillian, Lincoln, and Devah Pager. 2001. "Black Neighbors, Higher Crime? The Role of Racial Stereotypes in Evaluations of Neighborhood Crime." *American Journal of Sociology* 107, no. 3: 717–67.

Rajwani, Naheed. 2016. "Dallas Officials Wonder If We Spend Too Much on Public Safety, but How Do We Fare against Other U.S. Cities?" *Dallas Morning News,* September 20, 2016. www.dallasnews.com/news /dallas-police/2016/09/20/dallas-officials-wonder-spend-much-public-safety-fare-us-cities.

Reaves, Brian. 2015. *Local Police Departments, 2013: Personnel, Policies and Practices.* BJS Bulletin, May 2015. Washington DC: Bureau of Justice Statistics, U.S. Department of Justice. www.bjs.gov/content/pub /pdf/lpd13ppp.pdf.

Roberts, Dorothy E. 1999. "Foreword: Race, Vagueness, and the Social Meaning of Order-Maintenance Policing." *Journal of Criminal Law and Criminology (1973-)* 89, no. 3: 775–836.

Sampson, Robert J. 2012. *Great American City: Chicago and the Enduring Neighborhood Effect.* Chicago: University of Chicago Press.

Sanchez, Lisa E. 2001. "Enclosure Acts and Exclusionary Practices." In *Between Law and Culture: Relocating Legal Studies,* edited by David Theo Goldberg, Michael Musheno, and Lisa C. Bowers, 122–40. Minneapolis: University of Minnesota Press.

Sánchez-Jankowski, Martín. 2008. *Cracks in the Pavement: Social Change and Resilience in Poor Neighborhoods.* Berkeley: University of California Press.

Sforza, Teri. 2014. "Public Safety Devours City Budgets." *Orange County Register,* September 14, 2014. www .ocregister.com/2014/09/14/public-safety-devours-city-budgets/.

Shabazz, Rashad. 2015. *Spatializing Blackness: Architectures of Confinement and Black Masculinity in Chicago.* Urbana: University of Illinois Press.

Simpson, Kelly. 2012. "The Great Migration: Creating a New Black Identity in Los Angeles." History and Society. February 14, 2012. KCET. www.kcet.org/history-society/the-great-migration-creating-a-new-black-identity-in-los-angeles.

Sparks, Tony. 2010. "Broke Not Broken: Rights, Privacy, and Homelessness in Seattle." *Urban Geography* 31, no. 6: 842–62.

Stuart, Forrest. 2011. "Race, Space, and the Regulation of Surplus Labor: Policing African Americans in Los Angeles's Skid Row." *Souls* 13, no. 2: 197–212.

———. 2016. *Down, Out, and Under Arrest: Policing and Everyday Life in Skid Row.* Chicago: University of Chicago Press.

Sutherland, Brian A. 2006. "Whether Consent to Search Was Given Voluntarily: A Statistical Analysis of Factors That Predict the Suppression Rulings of the Federal District Courts." *NYU Law Review* 81: 2192.

Smith, Michael R., Robert J. Kaminski, Geoffrey Alpert, Lorie Fridell, John MacDonald, and Bruce Kubu. 2009. *Multi-Method Evaluation of Police Use of Force Outcomes: Final Report to the National Institute of Justice.* Washington DC: National Institute of Justice.

Stamper, Norm. 2006. *Breaking Rank: A Top Cop's Exposé of the Dark Side of American Policing.* New York: Nation Books.

Terrill, William, and Jason R. Ingram. 2016. "Citizen Complaints against the Police: An Eight-City Examination." *Police Quarterly* 19, no. 2: 150–79.

Venkatesh, Sudhir Alladi. 2008. *Gang Leader for a Day: A Rogue Sociologist Takes to the Streets.* New York: Penguin.

Wilson, James Q., and George L. Kelling. 1982. "The Police and Neighborhood Safety: Broken Windows." *Atlantic Monthly* 127, no. 2 (March). www.theatlantic.com/magazine/archive/1982/03/broken-windows/304465/.

The Colonial Order of the Court

LEARNING OUTCOMES

► Describe the role that courts played in advancing colonial conquest and illustrate how that continues through court practices today.

► Explain how courtrooms are organized in ways that reinforce social, economic, political, and racial inequalities.

► Analyze how racial inequality in court practice is systematically embedded in plea bargaining and court players.

► Summarize how key court players are shaped by racial prejudice in ways that continue colonial and slavery era practices, such as the all-white jury.

► Analyze the role that courts play in the creation of urban racial and class geographies.

KEY TERMS

► fiction of objectivity
► courtroom working group
► pretrial detention
► plea bargain
► prosecutorial upcharging
► trial penalty
► peremptory challenge
► *Batson* challenge
► stand-your-ground laws
► spatial governmentality
► gang injunction

C ourts are often viewed differently than police agencies, but as we show in this chapter, they are critical institutions organizing and producing race and coloniality in society today. Courts are purveyors of crime knowledge and enact colonial conquest by controlling the physical, financial, and social mobility of those who pass through their doors. While often seen as static institutions, courts are in fact the arbiters of the geographical boundaries of the law—boundaries that affect people, places, and movement.

Courts, however, one might argue, are places where we can challenge the biased practices of state authority and have been critical for achieving gains in racial justice. This is most certainly the case. But as scholars studying colonialism show, while courts provide a mechanism for resisting state power, they also reproduce, bolster, and extend the power of the conqueror.

On closer inspection, this should be unsurprising. European identity is premised in part on the "rule of law," and establishing courts was one way to advance European identity and rule over others. Having courts meant Europeans were "advanced," "civilized," and lacked "caprice" (Anghie 1999). Take, for instance, the Linnaean racial descriptions in chapter 3: "homo Americanus" is "regulated by customs"; "homo Asiaticus" is "governed by opinion"; "homo Africanus" is "governed by caprice"; and "homo Europeanus" is "governed by laws." Courts thus play an important role in advancing white identity as an invisible organizing power animating the social world.

Courts continue the colonial endeavor through the production of knowledge about crime and through the territorial imprint of court practices. Courtrooms, for instance, are organized in ways that re-create the very social, political, economic, and racial inequalities that many legal cases seek to remedy. Court practices also imprint themselves on surrounding communities through the concept of jurisdiction, where orders can have far-ranging impacts on how places look and how people move through space. Nowhere is this clearer than in the many court orders compelling people, places, and things to relocate, clear out entirely, or exist in public only under very specific conditions. Courts, though seemingly static buildings only concerned with interpreting the law, are in fact critical sites for consolidating colonial geographies and the territorial control of people, places, and resources (Villanueva 2013).

COLONIAL CONQUEST AND THE RULE OF LAW

The statement that courts are an agent of colonial enterprise might seem hyperbolic at first. But courts themselves have long recognized their role in colonial conquest. In 1823, the Supreme Court heard the case *Johnson v. M'Intosh*. The plaintiff, Johnson, claimed that he had bought a parcel of land from the Piankeshaw people. M'Intosh claimed he bought the same parcel of land from the United States government and thus held title. The court unanimously ruled for M'Intosh. Chief Justice Marshall's written decision exposes how integral colonial practices were to the construction, legitimacy, and power of law: "We will not enter into the controversy, whether agriculturalists, merchants, and manufacturers, have a right, on abstract principles, to expel hunters from the territory they possess, or to contract their limits. Conquest gives a title which the Courts of the conqueror cannot deny, whatever the private and speculative opinions of individuals may be." As a legal precedent for property law, *Johnson* revealed that the Supreme Court itself was an institution important for the consolidation and codification of colonial conquest.

Producing Colonial Knowledge in the Court

The law of the conqueror was not based solely on conquest but also the production of knowledge about the conquered, particularly indigenous peoples. Members of the Supreme Court did consider that there could be competing sovereign claims in which they would arbitrate. The court opined that "conquest is acquired and maintained by force" but that "humanity . . . has established . . . that the conquered shall not be wantonly oppressed." It reasoned that the conquered are "more usually . . . incorporated with the victorious nation, and become subjects or citizens of the government" and that "when the conquest is complete . . . the conquered inhabitants can be blended with the conquerors or safely governed as a distinct people." However, the opinion justified state racism by providing reasoning for why this was not possible in the case of indigenous peoples:

> But the tribes of Indians inhabiting this country were fierce savages, whose occupation was war, and whose subsistence was drawn chiefly from the forest. To leave them in possession of their country, was to leave the country a wilderness; to govern them as a distinct people, was impossible, because they were as brave and as high spirited as they were fierce, and were ready to repel by arms every attempt on their independence.

It was the particular construction of Native Americans as a warmongering race that prevented their inclusion within the "universal" rule of law that conquered Europeans would presumably enjoy. Indigenous peoples, by this particularly pejorative construction, could not rightly hold title to land because they had not yet achieved the "reasonable" or "rational" disposition supposedly innate to whites, illustrated by their refusal to accept the law of the conqueror. To the court, prohibiting purchases from indigenous peoples demonstrated the "soundest principles of wisdom and national policy." Yet M'Intosh's title to the land was the triumph of conquest, not the removed, dispassionate, and neutral positionality often accorded to the rule of law or courts.

"The English Mode of Warfare"

Land claims, however, are only the most visible manifestation of the colonial territoriality of courts. Court practices are also critical to conquest as a "tool for pacifying and governing . . . colonized peoples" (Stamp 1991, 810). This point has not been lost on indigenous peoples. For example, Tswana-speaking people in South Africa referred in the nineteenth century to courts as "the English mode of warfare" (Mackenzie 1887, 77–78). John Comaroff named this phenomenon "lawfare," or the "effort to conquer and control indigenous peoples by the coercive use of legal means" (2001, 306).

Courts served this purpose in the United States not just through upholding the land claims of colonizers but through the overt criminalization of indigenous peoples, practices, and beliefs. Customs such as traditional dancing, drumming, speaking indigenous languages, and having long hair were all criminalized in various places in the United States (Ross 1998). Indigenous peoples were included in Jim Crow laws and often specifically prohibited from purchasing and possessing alcohol (Mawani 2010). Indigenous peoples faced genocidal brutality at the hands of colonizers, ranging from wholesale massacres to sustained campaigns of terror, and disproportionately faced execution by the state (Banner 2009). The "law" of the conqueror was anything but objective or dispassionate but instead, through each of these types of laws, was concerned with enforcing white identity—measured in language, dancing, hair style, and ability to imbibe—as the normative prerequisite for citizenship.

As Comaroff further notes, this role for courts reveals how "almost everywhere, cultures of legality were *constitutive* of colonialism", meaning law was necessary to enact and continue the mechanisms of conquest (2001, 309). Colonies were mapped "by an appeal to a specifically legal sensibility . . . transforming the landscapes of others . . . into territory and real estate." Legal documents—such as titles and contracts—were used to establish the idea of "rights" over land and territory and to usurp material resources and carry that claim into the present day. European legal rule is considered in the courts, as Marshall's reasoning suggests, as the only right way to govern—as "progress" over other forms of rule. Even further, by placing themselves outside the violent powers of conquest, courts claim to be the institutions of "reason" and "rationality" characteristic of liberal, democratic society.

Courts and the Universal Conception of the Human

Indeed, conceptualizations of humanity are often intertwined with legal reasoning. We are offended when human rights are under attack, but this reveals how our conception of humanity is inseparable from the Western legal construction of "rights." Rights are said to be "universal" as in the United Nations Universal Declaration of Human Rights and Declaration of the Rights of the

Child. Yet, rights themselves are historically and geographically situated ideas and reveal the inseparability of Western legal concepts from white, middle-class, heteronormative identity.

The continuity of this identity shapes the court through the its structure and practice. *Looking White People in the Eye* (1998), Sherene Razack's consideration of the courtroom as a place for the creation of racial and gender identity, illustrates this continuity. She begins her account of what this means by quoting Franz Fanon:

> And then the occasion arose I had to meet the white man's eyes. An unfamiliar weight burdened me. A real world challenged me. In the white world the man of color encounters difficulties in the development of his bodily schema. Consciousness of the body is solely a negating activity. It is a third-person consciousness. The body is surrounded by an atmosphere of certain uncertainty. . . . And I was battered down by tom-toms, cannibalism, intellectual deficiency, fetishism, racial defects. . . . I took myself far off from my own presence. . . . What else could it be for me but an amputation, an excision, a hemorrhage that spattered my whole body with Black blood. (Fanon 1952, 112)

When gazed at by a white man, Fanon is aware that he is perceived not as himself but as a third person, one defined by "tom-toms, cannibalism, intellectual deficiency, fetishism, racial defects." Razack begins with Fanon in order to draw attention to how practices that are often taken as simply "respectful" or "proper" are in fact laden with historical raced, classed, gendered, and sexualized relations between colonizer and colonized.

Let's take Razack's claim seriously. What does it mean to look someone in the eye? This is often associated with truthfulness, while looking away or down is considered evasive. This association has no inherent connection, yet it is commonly used to determine who among us is trustworthy. It also misunderstands what looking someone in the eye meant historically. For black men, looking white people, especially women, in the eye could result in violence and death. In cultures where people have been taught to be deferential, looking someone in the eye can also signal defiance or aggression.

"Looking white people in the eye" then is shorthand for how the colonial encounter is reproduced through even the most minute interaction in the court: the look that passes, or doesn't, between the accused and the judge, between the attorney and the jury, between the jury and the accused. This results in what Razack calls the **fiction of objectivity** associated with court processes. She writes that this fiction "obscures that key players in the legal system have tended to share a conceptual scheme," and "they are not seen to possess the norms and values that derive directly from their social location" (1998, 38). Legal practices are steeped in subjective considerations, yet we see these practices as arbiters of truth and not as reproductive of the colonial order.

Marshall's opinion in *M'Intosh* reveals how the fiction of objectivity shaped property law and instead revealed the normative logics of the colonial order. According to Marshall, indigenous peoples were unassimilable and thus could be denied property, land, and even existence. As the opinion noted, colonizers provided "ample compensation . . . by bestowing on them civilization and Christianity." This "branding . . . announces that Indigenous people are subhuman, the kind of human one can only deal with through force" (Razack 2015, 6). The court organizes this knowledge through its everyday practice, paying less attention to the nonwhite victims, casting the racialized criminal "other" as someone knowable, pathological, and inherently deviant, and re-creating the language, structure, and everyday practice of the court as an opportunity for the performance of the colonial order (Lazarus-Black 2007).

The Colonial Order of the Court

Today, the colonial order of the court is institutionally manifest through the organization of what is known as the **courtroom working group**: the norms and values that unite, rather than divide, the court players—especially the judge, prosecutor, and defense attorney—despite their apparently adversarial positions. Although the members may be viewed as ideologically opposed to one another (with the judge positioned as neutral arbitrator), these figures are instead remarkably homogeneous. All usually have advanced degrees. All usually come from the same social class. All usually depend on each other in order to get their day-to-day work done, an everyday reality that exists long after any one case is heard. And all, usually, are white (see figures 8.1 and 8.2).

Walk into any courtroom today and its colonial legacies are immediately apparent. In today's court, "conquerors"—the attorneys and judge—are predominantly white, usually dressed in conservative suits, and arguing on behalf of the "colonized," whose voices are silenced by the requirements of legal language and process. The colonized are often dressed differently, representing their status in different race and class hierarchies, and in the extreme, they are fully othered from court norms by appearing in court in uniforms reserved for prison and jail inmates.

Everyday practices of the criminal court further legitimize this colonial order by pathologizing defendants as people who can be understood through the production of legal knowledge. Defendants become "murderers," "gang members," or "drug addicts," and the histories and contexts of their lives beyond these particular labels are largely excluded from court practices (sentencing hearings in capital trials being a notable exception). Knowledge that contradicts or complicates the legal knowledge is often cast out of the court, and crime becomes the result not of larger social conditions but of the individual pathologies of the angry, the alcoholic, and the criminal. This knowledge that claims to look people in the eye and "know" their truth is the practice of

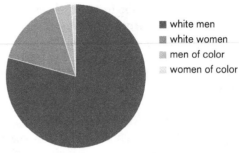

Figure 8.1 Percent of prosecutors by race and gender, United States, 2006. Source: Mark Motivans, *Federal Justice Statistics 2006* (Washington, DC: Bureau of Justice Statistics, 2009), www.bjs.gov/content/pub/html /fjsst/2006/fjs06st.pdf.

Figure 8.2 Percent of judges by race, California, 2016. Source: Judicial Council of California, "Race of Judges in California, 2016," December 31, 2016.

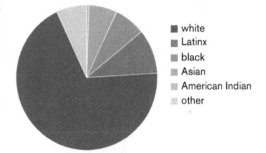

power. With the casting of judgment, the "truth" of the colonial order is remade, re-created, and transformed through the workings of the court and the players of the courtroom working group.

DEPENDING ON INEQUALITY: COURTS, DUE PROCESS, AND THE PERSISTENCE OF RACIAL OUTCOMES

Today, colonial practices continue through the exploitation of inequality. David Cole, a leading legal scholar, argues that the criminal justice system "affirmatively depends on the exploitation of inequality" (1999, 5). While perhaps a radical proposition at first read, Cole's thesis is, on further examination, a well-known reality throughout the United States. In *Schneckloth v. Bustamante* (1973), the Supreme Court stopped short of requiring police officers to notify drivers that they have the right to refuse search requests. The reasoning of the court? Although the state has a "legitimate need for such searches and the equally important requirement of assuring the absence of coercion," requiring warnings is "thoroughly impractical" and would "create serious doubt whether consent searches could continue to be conducted." This reasoning codifies police officers' dependence on the exploitation of ignorance in order to catch crime, thus building into the law not hard and discrete legal boundaries but the opportunity for the rights of some to be upheld and the rights of others to be trampled because of their own ignorance.

Courts most certainly exploit inequality in order to operate. Yet this is not because—as Cole's thesis seems to imply—the mechanisms of the court are dependent on inequality. Rather, the court structure itself is premised on inequality. As we show below, the deference given to prosecutors in the peremptory challenge, the necessity of depending on a lawyer in order to be heard in the court, and the role of the jury as able to judge without partiality are all premised on a single colonial logic. And that is the logic of the "courts of the conqueror." These players are provided a moral authority over the process *because* of the logic of colonialism: that they can arbitrate who should be recognized as "human" and who not. The court is not outside the colonial order, but rather is a part of it. How courts adjudicate criminal cases provides just one example of the role the judicial system plays in legitimating, justifying, and rationalizing the colonial order of power.

Race and Court Processes

Like urban police agencies, courts are historically understudied institutions in U.S. society. Studies of race, class, and gender in the courts are especially scarce and methodologically difficult to conduct. Those that do exist, however, point to what one can observe just by walking into any urban courtroom: defendants are primarily drawn from the same raced and classed geographies in the United States discussed in chapter 5 and are 70 percent nonwhite (see figure 8.3).

Studies of criminal court processes find significant biases built into every stage of the criminal court system. One study found sentences for black defendants are 10 percent longer than those of comparable whites for the exact same crimes (Rehavi and Starr 2014). White juries convict black defendants almost 16 percent more often than white defendants (Anwar, Bayer, and Hjalmarsson 2012). Black men are more likely to face incarceration when convicted in the criminal court, and overall they are incarcerated at six and a half times the rate of whites, resulting in comparatively longer times of incarceration (see figure 8.4; Sabol, West, and Cooper 2009).

Black defendants are up to 18 percent more likely to be sentenced to prison than whites, and when they are sentenced to prison, the average sentence difference between whites and blacks is about ten months (Abrams, Bertrand, and Mullainathan 2012). Even the neighborhood one comes from affects one's likelihood of incarceration, with black defendants from higher-status neighborhoods facing a greater likelihood of incarceration than defendants overall

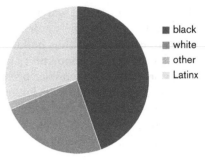

Figure 8.3 Court defendants charged with felonies by race, 2009. Source: Brian Reaves, *Felony Defendants in Large Urban Counties, 2009—Statistical Tables,* U.S. Department of Justice, Office of Justice Programs, Bureau of Justice Statistics, December 2013, www.bjs.gov /content/pub/pdf/fdluc09.pdf.

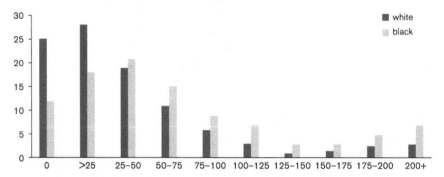

Figure 8.4 Length of prison sentences for black and white prisoners, in months. Source: M. Marit Rehavi and Sonja B. Starr, "Racial Disparity in Federal Criminal Sentences," *Journal of Political Economy* 122, no. 6 (2014): 1329.

(Williams and Rosenfeld 2016). Further, if one fits the stereotypical vision of the drug trafficker—black, male, used a weapon, and convicted of crack cocaine—the prison sentence is typically much longer than for one who does not embody this stereotype (Spohn and Sample 2013).

Studies of the juvenile court reveal that racial disparities increase at every stage in the court process, from the determination of pretrial detention and the charges brought to the charges convicted and the sentences assessed (Cole 1999; Sampson and Lauritson 1997). In the criminal court, the processes of bail, pretrial detention, sentence, and jury trials all are riddled with race and class disparities (Mustard 2001; Schlesinger 2005; Steffensmeier, Ulmer, and Kramer 1998; Gau 2016). This is not something that is unknown to court actors, and the impact of social class on juvenile court procedures is also well documented (Shelden 2012; Shelden and Horvath 1987).

Race and the Criminal Court Value of Whiteness

Studies of criminal defense attorneys are particularly instructive about how race, class, and gender influence the court process. As a court case progresses, both the defense attorney and prosecutor begin engaging in the negotiation process, and the first part of this process is to assess the "value" of a case. This means negotiation over the facts of the case (e.g., whether something was malicious or accidental) as well as over the expected outcome. In assessing this value, lawyers routinely use race and class in their negotiations and know that when the defendant is white, it is likely to influence the negotiation. Consider the following interview with a public defender:

> Kathy: I go in [to the judge's chambers] and say [to the prosecutor] "What's the offer on this case, Rick?" He tells me, and I usually respond "Geez Rick! You can give me something better than that!" And give the D.A. information about the client, information about the case—mitigating factors in essence.
> Interviewer: For example?
> The client has no record. The client is young. Actually, to be quite truthful, the client's white.
> Interviewer: Actually?!
> I do indeed. If I've got a young blonde kid out there, you think I'm not gonna tell the D.A. that I've got a young blonde kid out there. You better believe I do!
> Interviewer: Wow!
> I tell the D.A., "This kid's really middle-class." (Emmelman 2003, 103)

Similarly, a San Jose public defender revealed to the *Mercury News* in the early 1990s that utilizing race was a commonly accepted practice in the court process (Schmitt 1991). He explained: "If a white person can put together a halfway plausible excuse, people will bend over backward to accommodate that person. It's a feeling, 'You've got a nice person screwing up,' as opposed to the feeling that 'this minority person is on track and eventually they're going to end up in state prison.' It's an unfortunate racial stereotype that pervades the system. It's an unconscious thing."

Unconscious or not, this "feeling" or negotiating strategy has grave consequences for how people are punished. A review of studies of racial disparities in the courtroom revealed just how important race, gender, and class are to who gets into the system, finding that those punished most harshly are young black and brown men (Sun and Wu 2006). One study even found that "if probation eligible blacks had been treated like their white counterparts, more than 8,000 fewer black defendants would have received prison in that two-year period, resulting in a five percent decline in the percentage of blacks sentenced to jail as a percentage of the entire sentenced population" (Weich and Angulo 2000, 4). Given the inequalities in policing and patrol that introduce considerable racial disparities in terms of defendants and their charges in the first place, the continued compounding of inequality in the court reveals just how integral court processes are to the reproduction of race and class in U.S. society today.

This bias is built into the very structure of the criminal court. Court processes are well-established to disadvantage defendants in ways much like indigenous peoples were disadvantaged in the *M'Intosh* case. Bail decisions, the plea-bargaining system, the application of defense and prosecutorial discretion, and the selection of juries all provide a moment for remaking the colonial structure within the everyday practices of the court.

ADJUDICATING COLONIAL PRACTICE: JAIL, BAIL, AND THE PLEA BARGAIN

Colonial court practices presumed that colonizers were rational and the colonized were pathological—and adjudicated accordingly. Today, that structural relationship continues to shape the criminal court, where the vast majority of defendants are presumed to be guilty and processed through a system that some have likened to a conveyor belt (Packer 1964). The bureaucratic organization of the court process is particularly well-suited for providing a veneer of organizational credibility to proceedings, while executing a structural system that disproportionately incarcerates, constrains, and classifies as criminal the poor and nonwhite. Three structures work in tandem to do this: the jail, bail, and the plea bargain.

At each stage in the system, racial disadvantages manifest, and together these create a "cumulative disadvantage" that makes it 26 percent more likely that a black or Latinx will go to prison than a white person (Sutton 2013). Beginning with the decision to detain someone prior to trial, these cumulative disadvantages mean that a poor, black defendant is more likely to have bail set and at a higher amount, a disparity that is exacerbated by the fact that black people are more likely to have a public defender, whose cases are also set at higher bails (Wooldredge et al. 2015). Further, this cumulative disadvantage continues across the criminal court system: a person who faces incarceration is also subsequently more likely to face future arrest, conviction, and incarceration. Greater policing of black and brown neighborhoods thus initiates an entire process of concentrating poor nonwhites in the criminal court system.

A recent investigation into plea bargaining in Manhattan by the Vera Institute of Justice found a surprising fact: black people and Latinx were the most likely defendants to have their cases dismissed (Kutateladze and Andiloro 2014). Out of context, this fact could be taken to mean that the criminal court is more lenient with black and Latinx defendants, but the study suggests otherwise: in Manhattan, despite being less than 40 percent of the population, black people and Latinxs are 80 percent of the criminal court defendants.

Frequent dismissal did not mean that black people and Latinxs had sentences on par with whites, however, or were convicted less often. Rather as we discuss further below, these showed considerable racial disproportionalities. What the frequent dismissal finding showed was not leniency, but the overpolicing of black and Latinx groups that results in a greater likelihood of winding up in the criminal court in the first place, often charged with a crime for which there is little evidence (and for which a white person likely would not have faced prosecution). Race biases, then, are not just built into the courtroom but shape the structural conditions of court work. Once in the court, however, these biases worsen, beginning with an arrest and the decision whether to detain someone pretrial in jail.

Jail and "Managing the Underclass"

One now classic study of the jail in 1985 by John Irwin, a renowned criminologist and ex-prisoner, famously argued that jails were designed to manage society's "rabble," those Irwin defined as the "underclass": people incarcerated for relatively low-level offenses whose real crimes are being "detached" and "disreputable." According to Irwin, jail is actually a key means of producing the "rabble class," whose frequent incarcerations only serve to entrench them further into this social setting.

Studies of overpolicing show that courts compound these disproportionalities; black people are more likely than whites to be detained prior to trial, denied bail, and convicted and sentenced to jail (Alexander 2012). Take the example of marijuana arrests (Golub, Johnson, and Dunlap 2007). For white defendants, a marijuana conviction is little to fear in many places, because they are the least likely to be arrested, the most likely to have their case diverted, and the least likely to get prison or jail time if convicted. Since 2000, smoking marijuana in public in New York has been the most common misdemeanor arrest. But these arrests are not racially neutral. They are almost entirely confined to black and Latinx defendants. Policing marijuana crimes then provides a mechanism for the frequent arrest, jailing, and ushering of black and brown people into the criminal court process.

Bail and Pretrial Detention

Many defendants are released from jail to await trial on their own recognizance (OR). This means they are released without bail and without providing any monetary bond. Over 52 percent of white defendants get an OR release, compared to just 37 percent of black defendants. By contrast, whites are only 41 percent likely to be jailed prior to trial, compared to 59 percent of black people (see figure 8.5; Kutateladze and Andiloro 2014). The decision to deny someone bail is highly consequential to the outcome of the case. Denial of bail

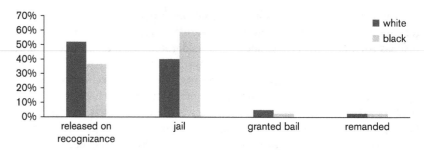

Figure 8.5 Detention status after arraignment for felony convictions, New York County. Source: Besiki Luka Kutateladze and Nancy Andiloro, *Prosecution and Racial Justice in New York County* (New York: Vera Institute of Justice, 2014), www.ncjrs.gov/pdffiles1/nij /grants/247227.pdf.

means the defendant is held in **pretrial detention** pending trial. Pretrial detention is supposedly reserved for defendants who pose a greater threat of absconding, but in reality bail decisions are racially biased. One study found that black people are almost 12 percent more likely than whites to have monetary bail conditions assigned to them, and their bail amounts are on average over $14,000 higher (Arnold, Dobbie, and Yang 2017).

In considering bail, judges weigh whether a defendant is at high risk of fleeing or committing additional crimes before the trial is complete (Arnold, Dobbie, and Yang 2017; Demuth 2003). Black defendants are consistently assigned monetary bail more often and at higher amounts than whites with similar risk factors (Sacks, Sainato, and Ackerman 2015; Arnold, Dobbie, and Yang 2017). This discrepancy exists despite the finding that whites are 18 percent more likely to be rearrested prior to sentencing than similarly situated black defendants (Arnold, Dobbie, and Yang 2017). Another study further found that this stems from racial bias in the assessment of risk, with both black and white judges likely to see black defendants as riskier than whites and detain accordingly (McIntyre and Baradaran 2013). Like racial scientists, Progressives, and eugenicists, judges today see blackness as a sign of risk, danger, and aggression.

Bail may seem like an insignificant part of the criminal court process, but it is very consequential to the outcome of a case. Studies show that black people and Latinxs are more likely to have monetary bail set and set at higher amounts, but that these same groups are least able to economically bear this burden (see figure 8.6; Sacks, Sainato, and Ackerman 2015). The result? Black people and Latinxs are more likely to languish in jail prior to trial, and as we show below, this provides a strong incentive to plead guilty in order to be released. It also, however, has a considerable impact on the eventual disposition of the case.

Detaining a defendant pretrial results in greater punishment, regardless of the facts of the case, than a defendant not detained. Multiple studies have found that pretrial detention increases the likelihood of conviction and length

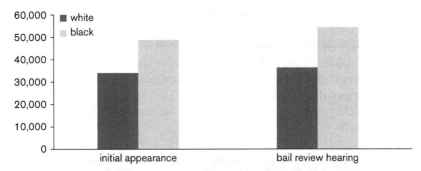

Figure 8.6 Mean bail amount by race, in dollars, 2011–2015. Source: Maryland Office of the Public Defender, *The High Cost of Bail: How Maryland's Reliance on Money Bail Jails the Poor and Costs the Community Millions,* November 2016, 12, www.opd.state.md.us /Portals/0/Downloads/High%20Cost%20of%20Bail.pdf.

of sentence (Oleson et al. 2016; Sacks, Sainato, and Ackerman 2015; Wooldredge 2015). One study found that pretrial detention increased the sentence length by more than a year for black defendants (LaFrentz and Spohn 2006). Thus, denying or setting bail higher for black defendants than white ones does not just influence that one decision, but has cumulative impacts over the entirety of the case.

Issues of bail are further complicated by the plea-bargaining system, where release may eventually mean "copping a plea." One study of the bail system in California found that over half a million people between 2011 and 2015 were incarcerated or paid bail and were never convicted of a crime. Most of them had their cases dismissed or their cases were never filed by the prosecutor office, meaning they spent their time and money on a criminal case that they never should have faced (Human Rights Watch 2017). The cost to the state for incarcerating people who were never charged, had their charges dropped, or had cases dismissed was over $37.5 million for two years.

Plea Bargaining in the Shadow of the Law

The idea of an adversarial court system is far from the truth. Instead of two opposing sides vigorously fighting under the formal guidance of legal precedent and the watchful eye of the judge, the courtroom is often likened to an assembly line of justice. Any examination of the workload of the court would conclude that there is no other way to organize the system. In a single month, the largest seventy-five counties in the United States heard over 56,000 cases (Reaves 2013). If each of these cases went to trial, the court system would undoubtedly come to a grinding halt. Thus, the system depends on *not* enacting due process in order for it to run; as Cole notes, it depends on inequality in order to function. Instead, over 96 percent of cases go through the plea-bargaining process.

Unlike the formal court process, in which due process rights are guaranteed and can be challenged by appeal, the **plea bargain**—the vast majority of court work—happens in the shadow of due process and outside the formal oversight of court procedures. Informal relations dominate the plea-bargaining process. Plea bargains often represent not an adversarial matchup between two attorneys but a negotiation between two colleagues with different goals and assumptions. Given the informality of this system, what may be called "unconscious" bias can dominate.

Even further, this reality is reinforced by the very nature of policing, which brings a far different social class—often young, black or brown, and poor—into a very formal world where the decision-makers are mostly white people who have pursued advanced degrees and been socialized by law school. For these reasons, legal scholars conclude that "blacks, Hispanics, males, older defendants, noncitizens, and high school dropouts receive fewer and smaller substantial-assistance discounts than whites, females, the young, citizens, and high school graduates" (Bibas 2004, 2475).

Given that plea bargaining occurs in the shadow of the law, few comprehensive studies have documented how race affects the process. The Vera Institute of Justice provides one such study of the Manhattan district attorney (Kutateladze and Andiloro 2014). While this study confirmed that attorneys bargain and negotiate over the facts of the case regardless of the demographic outcome, it also revealed that race continues to be a significant independent variable in these negotiations. The study found that when the facts of the case were the same, black people were 19 percent more likely than whites to receive an offer that includes jail time, thus institutionally affirming the social myth that black people are "more dangerous" and thus deserving of greater confinement (see figure 8.7). The normative presupposition of colonial-era courts that white identity was necessary to be given legal protection is thus remade through practices that treat white defendants more leniently and with greater deference than similarly situated nonwhite defendants.

"The Process Is the Punishment"

Race, gender, and class disparities are not the only way that plea bargaining affects groups disproportionately, though. Rather, the plea-bargaining process is often seen as punishment in and of itself. For that reason, many people are induced to plead guilty regardless of actual guilt. Two legal scholars note that "innocent defendants plead guilty quite frequently. It is one of the many dark secrets of the criminal justice system" (Blume and Helm 2014, 161). For many, the choice between a plea deal and persisting to trial is hardly a choice, particularly for those facing pretrial detention. This choice is institutionalized in what is known in forty-seven states as the "Alford plea," where a defendant accepts the terms of a plea deal while also invoking innocence (Blume and Helm 2004).

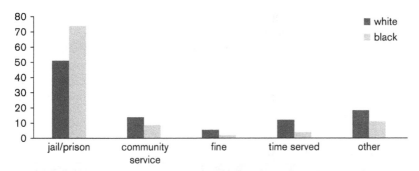

Figure 8.7 Plea offer types for felonies, by race, New York County. Source: Besiki Luka Kutateladze and Nancy Andiloro, *Prosecution and Racial Justice in New York County* (New York: Vera Institute of Justice, 2014), www.ncjrs.gov/pdffiles1/nij/grants/247227.pdf.

Malcolm Feeley, a contemporary legal scholar, noted almost forty years ago that often the criminal court experience does not result in formal punishment sanctions, but regardless of outcome, "the process is the punishment." He elaborates:

> Many defendants are faced with an immediate concern for returning to work or their children, and these concerns often take precedence over the desire to avoid the *remote* consequences that a (or another) conviction might bring. This *relative* lack of concern about conviction is reinforced by the type of employment opportunities available to lower-class defendants. If an employee is reliable, it may make little difference whether or not he pleads guilty to a minor charge emerging from a "Saturday night escapade." Indeed, an employer is not likely to find out about the incident unless his employee has to arrange to miss work in order to appear in court.... When this occurs, the process itself becomes the punishment. (1979, 201)

The costs of the court process include costs to employment and family, as well as the cost of court itself. Without employer-paid vacation or sick time, defendants often miss out on pay altogether and can even lose their employment due to missing too much time. Attending court hearings also requires those with families to find childcare. Defendants may have to pay court costs regardless of conviction. Those with less money are also less likely to receive bail, and if they do receive it, they are less likely to have funds for it (Schlesinger 2005). Those who cannot afford bail must place their lives on hold until their case is resolved, accruing further costs and providing incentive to plead guilty in order to get the case over with. A study in California found that of people incarcerated pretrial, between 77 and 91 percent (depending on the county) pled guilty and were released before the first trial date (Human Rights Watch 2017).

Plea bargaining is the most common practice in the criminal court and is one that provides the most salient example of how court practices provide merely a veneer of justice, impartiality, and truth. For many, getting caught up in the court is exactly that—a dispassionate process that takes hold of their lives and from which it is impossible to escape. For nonwhites in the United States, the court cycle begins with overpolicing and is compounded by the denial of or excessively high bail, and then in order to extricate oneself in some way, one must engage in a plea-bargaining system that sees the defendant as less than human and the case as just one of the many. Consider the two cases we discuss next.

A Tale of Two Cases: Erma Faye Stewart and Regina Kelly

Two defendants from the same case chronicled in the PBS documentary *The Plea* illustrate how court processes criminalize the poor and nonwhite. Erma Faye Stewart and Regina Kelly lived in the same housing complex in Hearne, Texas. In 2000, in a drug sweep based on the word of a confidential informant, both women, along with twenty-five others, were arrested. They were charged with being part of a drug distribution ring. All but one was black and all claimed innocence.

Besides the word of the confidential informant, no evidence was found. There were no drugs, no other witnesses, and twenty-seven people claiming innocence. As the case pushed further into the system, the confidential informant was ultimately deemed unreliable. All the remaining pending cases were dismissed. Be sure you read that correctly. All the *remaining* cases were dismissed. By this point, those defendants with the least resources had already taken plea deals in order to be released. Those convictions stood.

Erma Faye Stewart was one of those defendants. Although Stewart pleaded with her court-appointed attorney to investigate, he had little time for her (even failing to recall she was a client). He urged her to plead guilty and get out of jail. Stewart spent two weeks in jail, trying to fight the charges. On the outside, her two children were bounced from house to house and facing care in the state system. Stewart, concerned about her children and needing to be out in order to care for them, took the plea and was released in an hour. She was sentenced to 10 years' probation and an $1,800 fine.

Regina Kelly, by contrast, waited in jail for several weeks until her parents were able to get her bond reduced to $10,000. Once they posted it, she was released to await trial. Regina never faced trial. No defendant did, because quickly after the first trial began, all the cases were dismissed. Seven defendants in total took a plea bargain, while those who could not post bond waited *five months* in jail for their trials. Those who pled guilty, though, had to continue to serve their sentences.

Stewart, who pled guilty to go home to her children, was destitute three years later. And because she pled guilty to a drug offense, she was no longer eligible for food stamps or federal education grants. She was evicted from public housing for being unable to pay rent and was homeless. The court costs continued to mount, because she faced increased fines for late payments and in addition to her initial fine, she also has to pay probation fees. Without health care, most of her wages from her minimum-wage, part-time job went to pay for her son's asthma medicine, which was also in danger because the court insisted that she remit a portion of her paycheck to the court. In the end her children were placed in foster care, the very outcome Stewart had tried to avoid by taking a plea deal.

These consequences are not unique; Stewart had gotten caught in the structural ways that plea bargaining, jail, and bail disadvantage criminal defendants. Alexes Harris and her colleagues detail how monetary sanctions common to criminal court processes actually create a cycle of "ongoing criminal justice involvement" (Harris, Evans, and Beckett 2010). Defendants like Stewart are induced to plead guilty, and both those who face jail and those who are released are required to pay fines and penalties. These are often high relative to expected earnings and defendants become trapped in a cycle of debt, familial economic insecurity, and arrest due to failure to pay. Indeed, we may have a right to an attorney, but that attorney, even a public defender, can cost us, even if we are found not guilty (Sunne 2014).

Bureaucratic processes, such as the decision to jail, deny bail, or plea bargain, construct the colonial order of the court. It is a systematic process, and one is ushered into it through what actions get defined as laws, how variegated racial geographies get policed, and then how people are placed on a conveyor belt of "justice" that consistently assesses nonwhite defendants as riskier, more dangerous, and deserving of greater punishment—a judgment that also befell the colonized in countless colonial contexts. Black, Latinx, and indigenous defendants face greater punishment, harsher sentences, and suffer more severe economic impacts of incarceration. A system seemingly designed without "caprice," "custom," or "opinion," according to the Linnaean taxonomy of race, is instead found to hide the capricious custom of whiteness within the everyday practices of the court. The bureaucratic indifference provides a veneer of objectivity and rationality to a process that is both marked by a colonial logic, and as we show in the next section, a colonial cast of characters.

EMBODYING THE COLONIAL ORDER: PUBLIC DEFENDERS AND PROSECUTORS

The colonial order of the court is further organized through the structural positioning of two of the court's key players: public defenders and prosecutors. Both are instrumental to the adversarial conception of the court, and the idea that court processes vigorously seek the truth. The reality is far from this conception and both players are caught within political economic structures that contribute to the racial subjugation of nonwhites.

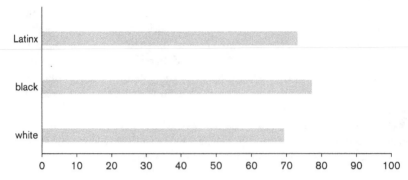

Figure 8.8 Use of public defense by incarcerated people, by race and ethnicity, %. Source: Caroline Wolf Harlow, *Defense Counsel in Criminal Cases* (Washington DC: Bureau of Justice Statistics, 2000).

Public Defense: Institutionalizing Inequity

Public defense is intended as a remedy to the inequality that comes from a lay person, especially a poor one, competing in the adversarial system. Even though not providing counsel is unconstitutional, as found in *Gideon v. Wainwright* (1963), and counsel has to be effective, as found in *Strickland v. Washington* (1984), the reality of public defense is that it can often do little more than process people through the system. Often, the result is prison, where the vast majority of prisoners of any race used a public defender for their case (Owens et al. 2014). But given the lack of wealth of black and brown communities, as detailed in chapters 1, 5, and 6, it is unsurprising that prisoners of color make up the majority of both those who use public defense and those who are imprisoned (see figure 8.8).

The Reality of "Effective Counsel"

Today, the promise of legal reform codified in *Gideon* and *Strickland* is structurally constrained by public defense funding that results in extremely high caseloads. In Florida, for instance, the average caseload per public defender is about 500 felonies and 2,225 misdemeanors; by contrast, the average caseload for prosecutors in large counties is just under 100 cases (Van Brunt 2015; Perry and Banks 2011).

The Department of Justice estimates that over 73 percent of public defense offices are above the recommended maximum limit of 150 felonies or 400 misdemeanors per year (Farole and Langton 2010). In Washington State, public defenders spend an average of less than an hour on each case and have had caseloads of over 1,000 cases per year (Van Brunt 2015). Fourteen out of twenty-three states in a recent survey conducted by the federal Bureau of Justice had no caseload limits for attorneys (Farole and Langton 2010). Due to caseloads, public defenders in Missouri, Kentucky, Louisiana, and Pennsylvania have all, at times, refused to take on new clients (Sunne 2014).

Besides overworking attorneys, large caseloads have another effect. Attorneys must decide where to concentrate their energy, and given the large number of cases, many attorneys are unable to invest much time or energy in determining which clients deserve a more vigorous defense. Thus, many make these decisions in way that reflect implicit bias toward whites, perhaps for the same reasons as the attorneys cited at the beginning of this chapter (Richardson and Goff 2012; Rapping 2013).

Further, few appeals on the basis of ineffective counsel are upheld. Cases where counsel has been ruled effective are jaw-dropping. One attorney was so drunk at trial that he was arrested for driving to court intoxicated. The court's response to the defendant's claim of ineffective counsel? Being drunk can be a trial strategy (Cole 1999). Attorneys who have slept through cases have been considered effective. Using heroin and cocaine during a trial is considered an effective defense strategy, as is the attorney admitting at trial that he or she is not prepared on the law or facts and even simply failing to show up for trial.

Why are these examples considered effective counsel? The Supreme Court has determined that in order for counsel to be ineffective the appeal must show both "deficient performance and prejudice" (Cole 1999, 78). In judging deficient performance, the Supreme Court emphasized deference to court authorities, arguing that reviewing courts "must indulge a strong presumption that counsel's conduct falls within a wide range of reasonable assistance" and should be "highly deferential" (*Strickland v. Washington* [1984]). This deference immediately presumes the moral authority of the court and its actors, while regarding those outside this authority—the defendant arguing for effective counsel—as a pest to the decorum of the court.

Funding Public Defense

Public defense budgets are also precarious. The source of funding varies by state, with some states funding the entire cost, and others splitting the expense with counties. Pennsylvania places the entire burden of the cost on counties, leading to large geographical disparities (Owens et al. 2014). In some counties the use of a forensic expert or a court psychologist would exceed the entire budget for public defense (Feinberg 2011). Most states provide no public defense during the appeal process.

In many places, public defense offices are also resourced technologically with hand-me-downs from the prosecutor's office, and in some states, only prosecutors are eligible for student loan forgiveness (Van Brunt 2015). Some public defense attorneys get paid as little as $2 an hour, when time and compensation are factored in. Many public defenders get a flat fee for every case they take, resulting in a disincentive to put any time into cases.

Public defense is also not free to defendants. Many states require an application fee, which can be as high as $212 (Strong 2016). Some states also require clients to pay back the costs for public defense, and in two states—New Hampshire and New Jersey—clients are compelled to pay even if they have no ability. Louisiana, among other states, actually bases the public defense budget on the ability to recoup these costs.

Lack of funding means few or no support staff, and in several states, including Hawaii, Montana, and New Hampshire, not a single social worker, paralegal, or law clerk is employed for public defense. While prosecutors can rely on police as investigators, several states have only a handful of investigators for public defense. In Wayne County, Michigan, public defenders are given $150 to hire an investigator and just $250 for an expert to meet with their client, assess that client, and testify on their behalf (Whitehurst 2004; see also Casper 1971).

In states without robust public defense systems, clients are often at the mercy of private counsel with little experience in criminal law. Tales abound of tax or real estate attorneys appointed as public defense in death penalty cases or attorneys with little experience in trial law appointed to oversee jury trials. Maine, New Hampshire, and West Virginia do not even have state-run public defender agencies and instead rely on contract counsel, nonprofit public defense corporations, or appointed counsel from the local bar (Strong 2016). The American Bar Association has even coined the phrase "meet 'em and plead 'em" to refer to lawyers so overworked and overloaded they are unable to do much more than meet their clients and enter plea deals *at the same time* (Whitehurst 2004).

Under these conditions, the colonial legacies of criminal courts are unsurprising. Colonial courts silenced colonized subjects through their explicit exclusion from court judgment processes or because those processes were conducted in languages different from the indigenous population. Today, this reality continues. The defendant's voice is often relegated to a court official. Any attempt to elevate one's voice in the courtroom is obscured through the formalities of the court. Without knowledge of the legal language, procedures, and practices of the courtroom, self-represented defendants fare far worse than others. Defendants cannot even implore their public defender to advocate on their behalf, because they may not meet before their trial date. The reality of defense is little more than meet, greet, and plead.

This results in a court system where the colonial imperative of shielding the state from contestation is contained within the court. Courts act to territorially appropriate the lives and resources of black and brown communities through the system of payments, restrictions, and fines levied through plea bargaining and public defense. Resource extraction from the colonized continues apace in the criminal court.

Prosecuting Race: Charging and Trying Cases in the Criminal Court

Prosecutors face a vastly different funding reality than public defenders. In the United States, prosecutors' offices are funded at twice the rate of public defender offices. Prosecutorial budgets further do not need to cover investigators, forensic lab expenses, and other court support personnel since these are provided by police agencies and the court. The U.S. Congress supports the retraining of prosecutors annually but provides no similar training or funding for public defenders. While the median salary for public defenders ranges from $42,000 to $45,000, the median salary for prosecutors is $62,000 (NALP 2010).

Prosecutorial Discretion

The court structure also gives prosecutors a more advantageous position, especially with regard to plea bargaining. Prosecutors have considerable discretion in terms of how they approach a case and can engage in what is known as **prosecutorial upcharging.** Here, a single incident might generate a range of charges and often multiple counts. For instance, a single fight might lead to charges of simple assault, assault with a deadly weapon, aggravated assault, attempted murder, disorderly conduct, and breaching the peace, to name a few. If it's a fight between more than two people, multiple counts of each charge might apply.

Prosecutorial upcharging privileges the prosecutor during the plea-bargaining process because it provides an incentive for defendants to take a lesser charge in a plea deal rather than face a trial on a whole litany of very serious charges. Charges that have mandatory minimum sentences attached or that count as "strikes" are particularly damaging to a defendant and thus of high value for prosecutors in the plea-bargaining process. One study found that much of the sentencing disparity in criminal court processes can be traced to the initial decision by the prosecutor about what to charge. The decision about what to charge results in black arrestees with similar cases to whites facing a mandatory minimum sentence almost two times as often (Rehavi and Starr 2014). Even further, when whites are convicted of mandatory minimums, they are "relieved of application," or waived from receiving the mandatory sentence at greater rates than black defendants (see figure 8.9). Given the racialized construction of punitiveness that prompted the passage of mandatory minimums discussed in chapter 6, it appears that these type of sentences are doing exactly what they were designed to do.

Prosecutors can also enact a **trial penalty** by pursuing the entire range of charges should defendants fail to accept a plea deal, thus subjecting the defendant to a potentially greater sentence. One study found that defendants who went to trial were 8.4 times more likely to face sentencing enhancements than

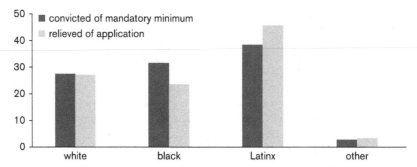

Figure 8.9 Race and mandatory minimums in the federal system, 2016. Source: U.S. Sentencing Commission, *An Overview of Mandatory Minimum Penalties in the Federal Criminal Justice System*, 2017, 37, https://go.usa.gov/xNthU.

those who accepted a plea deal. Sentencing enhancements are laws that require additional time be added to a sentence upon conviction. Enhancements are provided for crimes that involve gangs, guns, or carjacking, among others, and are sought at the discretion of the prosecution (Human Rights Watch 2013). Prosecutors can also interpret the facts of case in ways that advantage white defendants—for instance, interpreting attempted murder as merely assault with a dangerous weapon—and disadvantage black and brown defendants—such as vigorously prosecuting self-defense claims (Davis 1998). For example, a prosecutor might choose to drop a gun charge against a defendant because he is a "rural guy who grew up on a farm," while pursuing charges against a "gun-toting drug dealer" from the city even though these descriptions are inherently racialized, revealing how racial bias impacts prosecutorial discretion (Lu 2007). This is further demonstrated in the comparison between the cases of Renisha McBride and George Zimmerman discussed below. Although penalizing defendants for invoking their right to due process might seem unconstitutional, the Supreme Court ruled in *Bordenkircher v. Hayes* (1982) that using enhancements to punish those who take their cases to trial was constitutional and merely "give and take" in the plea bargaining negotiation (Blume and Helm 2014).

Prosecuting Federal Drug Crimes

The results of this are particularly perverse in the case of federal drug crimes, an issue that has so disproportionately impacted black and brown communities that some groups consider it a human rights violation (Human Rights Watch 2013). With a slew of federal mandatory minimum laws in their arsenal, prosecutors can induce defendants to plead guilty to lesser charges. Consequently, prosecutorial upcharging results in a conviction rate over 93 percent

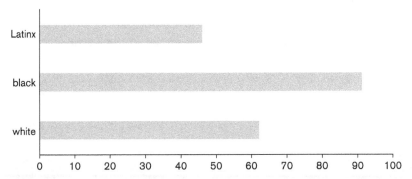

Figure 8.10 Average length of prison sentence, in months, for federal offenders, by race and ethnicity, 2007. Source: U.S. Sentencing Commission, 2007, quoted in Mark Hugo Lopez and Michael T. Light, *A Rising Share: Hispanics and Federal Crime.* (Washington, DC: Pew Research Center, 2009), http://assets.pewresearch.org/wp-content/uploads /sites/7/reports/104.pdf.

for federal drug offenses and vast racial differences in federal sentences (see figure 8.10; Motivans 2009).

Increased sentences for drug crimes mean that defendants often rationally choose a plea deal rather than facing several life sentences for drug crimes (Human Rights Watch 2013). On average, a plea deal for federal drug defendants results in a sentence of 5 years, 4 months. By contrast, a conviction at trial on a federal drug charge results in a sentence, on average, of over 16 years, or three times longer than under a plea deal. Further, there is immense pressure on defendants to provide "substantial assistance" to prosecutors as part of a plea deal, often resulting in people at the lowest ranks of the drug distribution hierarchy receiving the longest sentences (Human Rights Watch 2013).

Take the case of Clarence Aaron (Bikel 1999). Aaron was on a college football scholarship in a neighboring state and introduced some of his cousins from home to his college friends. The cousins and his friends went on to engage in a drug deal, in which Aaron was not involved. Facing many life sentences, Aaron's cousin and college friends all provided "substantial assistance" as part of a plea arrangement and provided prosecutors with names of others involved in drug trafficking. Under this pressure, Aaron's cousin named him as the source of their relationship. Aaron was charged with conspiracy to distribute drugs and faced three mandatory life sentences.

Aaron was not actually involved in the drug trade and thus had no substantial assistance to offer prosecutors. Prosecutors cited his unwillingness to cooperate as justification for charging him with three counts of conspiracy and offered no plea deal. They took the case to trial, where no drugs were ever introduced into evidence. The only evidence against Aaron was his cousin's testimony that Aaron had made the initial introduction.

BOX 8.1   **Jury Nullification and Racial Remedies for the Drug War**

Many framers of the Constitution saw the jury as an opportunity for jurors to not only determine guilt or innocence in terms of what the law said but also to comment on the law itself. In other words, they could ignore the law through what is referred to as jury nullification. Indeed, juries had exercised this right before the Revolution.

John Peter Zenger was a newspaper editor who was prosecuted in 1734 for publishing a newspaper that the colonial authorities claimed was seditious—that is, it incited disrespect for government. His lawyer explicitly told the jury that part of its function was to send messages to the government. He also argued that a vigorous press was needed to thwart overaggressive governments and that the jurors thus needed to acquit Zenger. Zenger was acquitted.

It was also common after the Revolution for juries to be explicitly instructed that they could nullify the law. This was used to thwart fugitive slave cases in the North and Prohibition; it was used in the South in the 1950s and 1960s by all-white juries who refused to convict white supremacists. But the popularity of nullification has waned, and today, even though juries are allowed to use it, they are often instructed only to apply the law to the facts of the case. In only two states, Indiana and Arizona, are they told that they can comment on the law, not just apply the facts of the case to the law. But even if jurors do not know it, juries retain the power to nullify the law. In other words, they can make decisions based not just on how laws apply to the facts of a given case but also in terms of the law itself. This played a role in the trials of former Washington DC mayor Marion Barry for drug use, Oliver North in the Iran Contra affair, and Bernhard Goetz for his subway assault detailed in this chapter.

A prominent legal scholar, Paul Butler, has argued that the black community is predominantly hurt by drug laws and that black jurors should use nullification in prosecutions of nonviolent crimes like drug possession. He writes that "for pragmatic and political reasons, the black community is better off when some nonviolent lawbreakers remain in the community rather than go to prisons. . . . Considering the costs of law enforcement to the black community and the failure of white lawmakers to devise significant nonincarcerative responses to black antisocial conduct, it is the moral responsibility of black jurors to emancipate some guilty black outlaws" (Butler 1995, 678).

Should jury nullification be used in the case of drugs or nonviolent crimes? Why or why not?

Sources: Chris Donovan, "A Case for Jury Nullification," Marquette University Law School Faculty Blog, October 13, 2009, https://law.marquette.edu/facultyblog/2009/10/13/a-case-for-jury-nullification/; Paul Butler, "Racially Based Jury Nullification: Black Power in the Criminal Justice System." *Yale Law Journal* 105, no. 3 (1995): 677–725.

Aaron's case demonstrates the impact of prosecutorial discretion. In a bid to get Aaron to provide names of drug dealers, prosecutors charged him with the maximum possible sentence. When he failed to provide names, prosecutors took the case to trial, where Aaron paid the trial penalty and ended up in prison on three life sentences. Aaron, a college student on scholarship and promising football player, suddenly faced a very different future, one that only changed when a presidential order commuted his sentence over a decade later. Countless others like Aaron continue to languish in prison, a reality that motivates some criminal justice reformers to argue for nullification of drug laws (see box 8.1).

Prosecutors, Sentencing, and Race

Given the racial realities of drug arrests, it is unsurprising that the result of prosecutions like Aaron's are increased punishment and time for black and brown defendants. The black population is just 13 percent of the U.S. population but over 28 percent of those serving life sentences, 56 percent of those serving life without parole (LWOP), and 56 percent of those who received LWOP sentences as juveniles (ACLU 2014). In the federal system, over 71 percent of people serving LWOP are black. Perhaps even more disturbing, over 3,200 people are currently serving LWOP for nonviolent offenses, including petty theft, and almost 70 percent of these prisoners are black; add Latinx prisoners, and over 90 percent of those serving LWOP for nonviolent offenses are people of color (ACLU 2013). The odds of being arraigned, prosecuted, and sentenced are significantly higher for black people and Latinxs than whites, yet the court system is considered the guard against capricious and arbitrary treatment.

As Angela J. Davis, a former prosecutor and legal scholar notes, even when supposedly objective legal considerations are taken into account by prosecutors, racial consequences still apply. This stems from both the context of racialized policing and the nearly all-white composition of prosecutors and judges discussed previously. For instance, a commonly cited reason to charge someone over another is arrest and conviction history. Yet, Davis notes:

> The fact that a white defendant has no criminal arrest or conviction record may not be a reflection of a lack of criminality on his part. If he lives in a neighborhood or attends a school that resolves certain criminal offenses (drug use, assault, etc.) without police intervention, he may be a recidivist without a record. Likewise, a black defendant who lives in a designated "high crime" area may have been detained and arrested on numerous occasions with or without probable cause. Thus, the existence or nonexistence of an arrest or conviction record may or may not reflect relative criminality in black and white defendants. (1998, 37)

Further, victims who can agitate the prosecutor's office the most are likely to have their cases pursued more vigorously, with higher charges and longer potential sentences. Other victims—whose cases can be dismissed or not pursued with little public notice—are left without the protection of the court; it is often black and brown victims of crime whose cases receive the least amount of prosecution and sentenced time (Davis 2007).

LEGITIMATING THE COLONIAL ORDER: JURIES

Once a case reaches the trial stage (only 4 percent of all criminal cases), the jury provides another component in the colonial order of the court. Juries were used in the colonial era to justify and impose white rule. Charges against enslaved and indigenous peoples were often processed through court procedures, but they could not sit on juries or wield court power.

Today, the Sixth Amendment guarantees an "impartial jury," which is interpreted by the Supreme Court to mean a "fair cross section of the community." Yet the selection process continues to result in juries that are very different in racial and socioeconomic status than defendants. Impartiality, as defined by the Supreme Court, means protecting the rights of the defense and prosecution to excuse individuals from the jury for almost any reason. The result? All or mostly white juries continue to dominate the courtroom. While this is not for explicitly legal reasons, the result of jury selection is the re-creation of colonial and slavery-era jurisprudence.

Producing the De Facto White Jury

Juries provide a historical demonstration of how white supremacy was established through the everyday practices of the court. Prior to 1860, black people were entirely prevented from serving on juries, and after Reconstruction, Southern states passed a series of laws mandating only whites could serve on juries. In the late 1800s, the California state legislature passed a law barring Chinese Americans from serving on any juries in the prosecution of whites—though whites could serve on trials of nonwhites. In the Southwestern United States, it was common to forbid Mexican Americans from serving on juries, including those which involved Mexican American defendants.

Explicit, or de jure, exclusion of nonwhites from jury pools was first struck down by the Supreme Court in 1880 in *Strauther v. West Virginia.* But states adapted to this ruling and soon adopted other provisions preventing nonwhites from serving, including tying jury service to voter rolls, which kept out black voters in areas with poll taxes and literacy tests; others gave discretion to jury officials to decide who should be in the pool. Today, 30 percent of all black men are excluded from juries due to federal and state laws that prohibit jury service by those with felony convictions *for the rest of their lives* (Wheelock 2011). Racial composition of juries is further complicated by the economic hardship that jury service presents; black, Latinx, and Asian people are especially likely to be dismissed for this reason (Gau 2016). Despite legal gains, juries continue to be all or

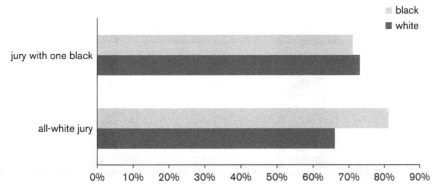

Figure 8.11 Rates of conviction by race of defendant with all-white jury versus jury with one black juror. Source: Shamena Anwar, Patrick Bayer, and Randi Hjalmarsson, "The Impact of Jury Race in Criminal Trials," *Quarterly Journal of Economics* 127, no. 2 (May 1, 2012): 1017–55, https://doi.org/10.1093/qje/qjs014.

mostly white, with the vast majority mostly white, 13 percent all white, and only 14 percent with whites as the minority racial group (see figure 8.11).

Swain v. Alabama (1965) was one of the first cases to address the constitutionality of the de facto composition of the all-white jury. In this case, Swain was convicted in Alabama and sentenced to death. His case was appealed to the Supreme Court on the basis that there were no black jurors, or as decision put it, no black person "within the memory of persons now living has ever served on any petit jury in any civil or criminal case tried in Talladega County, Alabama."

Upon review of the case, the Supreme Court found constitutional Alabama's method of jury selection, which resulted in an all-white jury. Even though 25 percent of the jury-eligible men (only men were allowed to serve on juries at the time) in the county were black, of the one hundred people called for jury selection, only eight were black. Upon prosecutorial dismissal, all eight were struck from participation. The court reasoned: "The overall percentage disparity has been small and reflects no studied attempt to include or exclude a specified number of blacks. Undoubtedly the selection of prospective jurors was somewhat haphazard, and little effort was made to ensure that all groups in the community were fully represented. But an imperfect system is not equivalent to purposeful discrimination based on race." Here, we see one of the first iterations of court racial discrimination jurisprudence that prioritizes remedying *purposeful* discrimination over discrimination built into the very structure of court processes. *Swain* provided constitutional legitimacy to practices that were occurring throughout the United States: the informal striking of black, Chinese, Mexican, and other nonwhite jurors even as the law forbade their explicit exclusion.

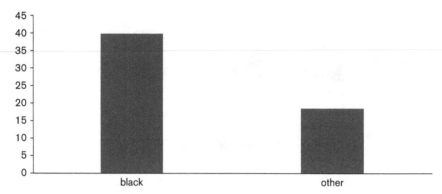

Figure 8.12 Percent of jurors struck from jury pools by race. Source: Barbara O'Brien and Catherine M. Grosso, "Report on Jury Selection Study," Michigan State University College of Law, 2011, https://digitalcommons.law.msu.edu/cgi/viewcontent.cgi?referer=&httpsredir=1&article=1330&context=facpubs.

Voir Dire and the Peremptory Challenge

Two legal processes of jury selection—called the "voir dire" phase of a trial—provide the mechanisms, both historically and today, for prosecutors to create all-white juries (Cole 1999). The first is the **peremptory challenge,** which can be used by either the defense or the prosecution. The peremptory challenge allows the attorney to excuse a potential jury member for any reason. Both prosecution and defense are given a set number of challenges and use these challenges to craft a jury pool they believe will be amenable to their argument. In *Swain*, the prosecutor used peremptory challenges to exclude all black people from serving on Swain's jury, a common practice that has led to calls to abolish the peremptory challenge (see box 8.2).

The second mechanism is striking for cause, which is a more common form of challenge. This challenge is based on a potential juror's answers to questions posed by the prosecution or defense about the juror's potential biases. For instance, the prosecutor might question whether a potential juror has been the victim of police discrimination, which might lead to dismissal from the jury. This is considered striking for cause. The peremptory challenge is the more common type of challenge used to create all-white jury panels (see figure 8.12).

In 1985, the Supreme Court finally ruled against the practice of creating all-white juries through the peremptory challenge in *Batson v. Kentucky*. Batson was a black man convicted by an all-white jury who appealed his conviction on the basis of the Fourteenth Amendment's equal protection clause, which states that a state cannot "deny to any person within its jurisdiction the equal protection of the laws." *Batson* overturned *Swain* when the court ruled that defendants did not have to show that there was discrimination across all cases in the county and instead lowered the standard to showing that the "prosecutor has

BOX 8.2   Abolish the Peremptory Challenge?

As Jacinta Gau (2016) found, the process for selecting racially representative juries is hampered by the efforts of both defense lawyers and prosecutors who are racially selective in their use of peremptory challenges and for-cause dismissals. Some legal scholars argue that abolishing the peremptory challenges would result in greater diversity on jury panels. One scholar notes, "Legal scholars, by and large, revile peremptory challenges. Allowing parties to unilaterally strike prospective jurors without explanation has been attacked as undemocratic, as prone to manipulation, as a potential First Amendment violation, and—most often of all—as racist" (Revesz 2015, 2535). With peremptory challenges, all-white juries continue to operate, and many nonwhite defendants face a jury with very different life experiences than their owns.

In contrast to legal scholars, criminal litigators—both defense attorneys and prosecutors—vociferously argue for retaining such challenges. Litigators argue that it provides an opportunity to secure a fairer jury and allows both sides to eliminate bias in the jury selection pool. Defense attorneys often argue that eliminating peremptory challenges would unfairly disadvantage their clients, especially because conservatives and whites are overrepresented in jury pools, while non-whites are overrepresented as defendants. Prosecutors argue that it allows them to remove bias and jurors who will practice nullification regardless of the facts of the case.

To address the issues of peremptory challenge, two different solutions have been proffered by legal scholars: abolishing peremptory challenges entirely or forcing both sides to agree on a challenge of a juror. Abolishing peremptory challenges entirely would result in only for-cause challenges and jurors being released for reasons such as economic hardship, personal experience with similar cases, or other clear reasons for bias in the jury pool. Caren Myers Morrison (2014) writes that another alternative—forcing both sides to consent to a challenge—would provide the best solution. Both sides would have the opportunity to limit bias, while also providing for the legitimacy of verdicts and enhanced community participation.

Given these two suggestions, what do you think should be done about peremptory challenges? Should they be abolished, reformed so both sides have to consent, or retained in their current configuration?

Sources: Jacinta M. Gau, "A Jury of Whose Peers? The Impact of Selection Procedures on Racial Composition and the Prevalence of Majority-White Juries," *Journal of Crime and Justice* 39, no. 1 (2016): 75–87; Joshua Revesz, "Ideological Imbalance and the Peremptory Challenge," *Yale Law Journal* 125 (2015): 2535; Caren Myers Morrison, "Negotiating Peremptory Challenges," *Journal of Criminal Law and Criminology* 104 (2014): 1.

exercised peremptory challenges to remove from the venire [jury pool] members of the defendant's race." The court shifted the burden to the state to provide an explanation for challenges of jurors of a particular race, creating what is known as the *Batson* challenge.

The *Batson* Challenge and Race

A **Batson challenge** contests the validity of a peremptory dismissal of a jury member based on the belief that the real reason a juror has been struck is because of race or gender. While the decision may seem a victory for equal protection under the law, the reality of the *Batson* challenge has been far different. First, *Batson* cases have been used most often to challenge the denial of a *white* person from the jury pool (Mililli 1996). Second, the justification for a peremptory challenge is wide enough that even the most obtuse of prosecutors are able to find a race-neutral reason for removing someone from a jury.

In *Hernandez v. New York* (1991), the Supreme Court further found that striking jurors because they can speak a particular language (in this case, Spanish) did not constitute racial discrimination. In *Purkett v. Elem* (1995), a prosecutor cited a juror's long hair, moustache, and beard in response to a *Batson* challenge. The court ruled that the challenge required only that the explanation be race neutral, not that it be plausible. One legal scholar concluded, "If prosecutors exist who . . . cannot create a 'racially neutral' reason for discriminating on the basis of race, bar exams are too easy" (Alexander 2012, 122).

Other Supreme Court cases provide troubling precedents to the challenge of all-white juries. In *Georgia v. McCollum* (1992), the court ruled that *Batson* challenges applied to the defense as well. This meant it could be used against black defendants striking white jurors in order to obtain a racially representative jury (Johnson 2014).

Finally, in *Miller-El v. Drekte* (2005), the Supreme Court found in favor of the defense and struck down a conviction on the basis of a *Batson* challenge. Miller-El was convicted and sentenced to death, but the prosecution had successfully challenged ten out of eleven black people in the jury pool. The defense charged that the real basis for the exclusion of these ten jurors was race. In this case, the court permitted evidence of discrimination provided by statistical analysis, demonstration of race-based questioning by the prosecution, and past discrimination by the prosecutor's office. This successful case provided a check on the power of prosecutorial discretion in jury selection.

In *Snyder v. Louisiana* (2008), the court extended this ruling. In *Snyder,* even though 20 percent of the community was black, only nine of eighty-five members of the jury pool were. Four black jurors were dismissed for cause, and the prosecution used peremptory strikes to dismiss the remaining five, resulting in an all-white jury. Prosecutors had cited reasons such as lack of support for the death penalty for their strikes. The defense argued that whites had expressed lack of support in similar language but were not struck. The Supreme Court overturned Snyder's conviction by finding that peremptory challenges were unconstitutional if black jurors were stuck for reasons that whites were not.

Yet in *Jackson v. Felkner* (2011), the court again reinforced the all-white jury by ruling that race-specific experiences—such as the hyperpolicing of black and brown communities detailed in chapter 7—could be used as the basis for a peremptory challenge. In *Jackson,* the court reversed a ruling by the Ninth Circuit that overturned a conviction on the basis that black jurors had been struck due to answering that they had been the recipients of undue attention from law enforcement authorities. Given that this is a common experience among black people, the defense argued this amounted to discrimination based on race. The Supreme Court disagreed and the conviction was affirmed.

Though the Supreme Court has made some strides toward protecting due process, it has routinely adopted the perspective of whiteness when making its ruling. In the *Jackson* case, this perspective considers the experience of racial discrimination at the hands of police by a juror to be aberrational and grounds for dismissal, even though this is a common experience. The result suggests that it is the experience of *whites* that defines the set of "reasonable" experiences that make one eligible for jury selection. One's experience of the common racialized practices of state repression are grounds for yet further exclusion from the political community.

Jurors, Racial Bias, and the Ruse of Impartiality

Though the vast majority of cases never make it to jury trial, once there, the demographic composition of the jury is related to the outcome of the case. Numerous studies have shown that juror demographics are important for ensuring fair trials, because increasing the representation of nonwhite racial groups, particularly those that reflect the defendant, leads to less racial bias in verdicts (Gau 2016). One study even found that having just one black juryperson *eliminated racial gaps in conviction rates entirely* (Anwar, Bayer, and Hjalmarsson 2012). Experiments with juror composition show that race, gender, age, and other sociodemographic variables are important in shaping the verdict. Predeliberation preferences of jurors are also the most likely predictor of eventual verdict, suggesting the ominous conclusion that deliberating over actual evidence is secondary to demographics (Bell and Lynch 2015).

Demographic and personality traits are highly predictive of jurors' eventual verdicts. Experimental studies find that those who are more authoritarian are more likely to convict (Narby, Cutler and Moran 1993). This is complicated by studies of punitive attitudes that show that whites exposed to media and political reports on crime—such as the crack scare in chapter 6—are more likely to espouse punitive and prejudiced attitudes. This set of attitudes also makes them more likely to support guilty verdicts for black people than whites given the same set of facts (Kleider, Knuycky and Cavrak 2012). Supporters of the death penalty—who are also more likely to be white—are also more likely to convict and make premature judgments of guilt (Bowers, Sandys, and Steiner 1997).

One experimental study of jurors also found reason for us to be troubled by how demographics shapes our ideas of who commits crime and who is deserving of punishment. In the experiment, researchers examined how people responded to two different scenarios: a white woman who killed her abusive white husband while he was asleep and a white commuter who killed a black teen who asked him for money on his way home. Findings of guilt were lower for the white commuter than the wife (33 percent versus 47 percent), and whites and political conservatives were significantly more likely to acquit the white commuter (Kahan and Braman 2008).

Juries and Stand-Your-Ground Laws

To those who work in the world of legal defense, these findings are likely unsurprising. The historical practice of killing nonwhites with impunity continues today under the protection of what have come to be called **stand-your-ground laws.** As part of the "castle doctrine" that permits protection of private property, stand-your-ground laws allow someone to use lethal force rather than retreat from danger. These types of laws are instrumental in protecting white racial violence today.

Take the cases of Trayvon Martin and Marissa Alexander. Martin was a black teenager walking home from a convenience store when he was stalked, approached, and ultimately killed by George Zimmerman. Zimmerman initially escaped arrest, but due to public outcry, he was prosecuted for Martin's murder. At trial, he invoked Florida's stand-your-ground law, arguing that though he stalked Martin (multiple times), was not on his private property, and attacked a legal resident of the area, he should be acquitted because Martin fought back against his assailant. The jury agreed, and Zimmerman was set free.

Marissa Alexander also lived in Florida, but she was not found to have stood her ground, perhaps because she was black and in a domestic violence situation. By most accounts, including the one given by her "victim," Alexander was chased throughout the house by her husband. Alexander fired a warning shot into the wall. No one was hurt, no one died. But she was charged, prosecuted, and ultimately received the mandatory minimum twenty years in prison for aggravated assault with a deadly weapon. After she was released due to a trial error, the prosecutor sought to retry her on the same counts, but instead sought sixty years instead of twenty.

By contrast, the same prosecutor failed to obtain a conviction in the case of Michael Dunn, who shot and killed a teenager, Jordan Davis, for playing music too loudly at a convenience store. The difference? Dunn was white, and jurors were convinced that he was so afraid he "reasonably" had to kill Davis (but not his friends who were also at the scene). White racial violence is protected through the reasonable racist legal defense, which results in juries routinely acquitting whites while convicting black people. In cases where a homicide results from a single victim and single shooter, strangers to each other and using a firearm, white-on-black violence is found justified 45 percent of the time, but black-on-white violence only 11 percent of the time (with black-on-black the least justified at just under 10 percent) (Roman 2013).

Renisha McBride suffered a similar fate to Trayvon Martin. McBride was also a teenager, nineteen years old, and black. She was driving late at night and got into a car accident. She approached a home for help, knocked on the door, and was subsequently killed by Theodore Wafer. Wafer discharged his weapon from behind a closed, locked screen door at close range, shooting her in the face. The difference between Wafer and Zimmerman? Michigan has no stand-your-ground law, and Wafer was ultimately convicted and sentenced to seventeen to thirty-two years in prison.

Laws like stand your ground both increase and protect white racial violence. Indeed, jurors and judges are six times more likely to judge a homicide justifiable if a black male is the victim and a white male is the perpetrator. By contrast, they are *ten* times more likely to convict if it's a black perpetrator and a white victim (Roman 2013). One study found that "controlling for population, the number of homicides of Black people that were deemed justifiable in Stand Your Ground states more than doubled between 2005 and 2011—rising from 0.5 to 1.2 per 100,000 people—while it remained unchanged in the rest of the country" (Bell and Lynch 2015, 432). Rates of homicide also increased by 8 percent in states with stand-your-ground laws (Cheng and Hoekstra 2013). Taken cumulatively? Stand your ground increases white racial violence and protects whites from prosecution by the state, a practice reminiscent of colonial era Jim Crow, lynching, and other injustices.

Juries and the "Reasonable Racism" Defense

Stand-your-ground laws are just the latest iteration in the protection of white racial violence by juries. Bernhard Goetz, called the "subway vigilante," shot four unarmed black teens on a subway train in New York in 1984. Goetz alleged that they approached him and asked for money, at which point he shot them multiple times. His defense? "Reasonable racism" (see chapter 1) and protection from the supposedly rampant crime committed by black youths on the subway (Carter 1987). Goetz, like Zimmerman thirty years after him, was acquitted.

Vincent Chin's murder is another example. Chin was stalked, severely beaten, and killed in 1982 in a hate crime by autoworkers that was witnessed by two off-duty police officers. Yet Chin's assailants served no jail time, were given a plea deal that consisted of $3,000 fine, and were cleared by a jury of federal civil rights charges. According to the judge, the sentence was justified because of the ideology of whiteness: "these weren't the kind of men you send to jail," he said (Zia 2000). The consequence of this "glaring double standard" was not just underprotection from the law for the Chinese community. This lack of protection also results in "open incitement to violence," the same result that came from failing to prosecute white violence in previous eras (Walsh 2004).

Unfortunately, over 60 percent of juries are still majority-white or all-white, and the protection of white racial violence has continued unabated (Gau 2016). While we no longer associate courts with the era of colonization, the logic of conquest still pervades the court. Moreover, courts are also important in producing racial geographies outside the courtroom through the power of the court order.

COURT GEOGRAPHIES: CREATING THE COLONIAL ORDER

Court processes, such as plea bargaining and jury trials, are just one kind of court power. Court powers extend beyond the walls of the courtroom and are instrumental in enacting, marking, and making geographies. Courts legitimate some geographical visions of urban life while criminalizing others. The courts have the power to both make and remake urban space.

Courts shape space in several ways. The most explicit is the court order. Through the court order, the court defines not only where people can be but how they can move through their surrounding community. This tactic is reminiscent of colonial era laws that enforced curfews on nonwhites or required their exclusion from "white" spaces. Today, however, the courts remake urban space by attempting to contain the power of the gang. And given the tactics of racialization used in gang policing, it is unsurprising that though groups of people of all races commit crime and violence at the same rates, often only black and brown communities carry the legal stigmata of the gang.

Criminalizing Everyday Life and Racial Governance

In the 1970s, the Supreme Court ruled in *Papachristou v. the City of Jacksonville* (1972) that cities could not criminalize "status" and struck down a statute criminalizing vagrancy because it was considered too vague. Based on the ordinance, vagrant defendants were charged with anything from theft to loitering to vagabondage. The court ruled that this permitted "arbitrary and discriminatory enforcement" and "makes criminal activities which, by modern standards, are normally innocent." Walking at night, wandering, or otherwise being without an obvious purpose could be a crime according to the Jacksonville statute. The court ruled that statutes such as these provide police too much "unfettered discretion" and create a situation in which "even-handed administration of the law is not possible."

As we detailed in chapter 7, police responded to this new legal restriction by shifting to policing low-level crimes and jailing "disorderly" people. Courts have enabled this power and even used court orders to extend the power of the police over the everyday life of some communities. Tactics that explicitly manipulate the spatial order of a community or region and attempt to manage the flow of people are known as **spatial governmentality.** This type of management is used to determine who should be in a particular space or region and is a common tool used today to mount colonial geographies without the explicit barring of unwanted persons. Court orders provide the ability to criminalize everyday life for those deemed gang members.

Through a court order, judges can order someone to do a whole range of things—from attending anger management or counseling to obeying curfews and attending school—that normally would be regarded as state overreach. Violation of a court order results in the same penalties as committing a crime: fines and incarceration. Court orders are thus able to criminalize people in ways that would not be permitted by legislative statute. This phenomenon, in which a person is convicted of a crime for a behavior that would not be considered a crime except for the court order, is known as "backdoor criminalization." Even further, court orders codify the divide between insider and outsider independent of any criminal behavior, thus providing even greater efficiency to the colonial project.

Gang Injunctions

Court orders have been remarkably useful to urban police, whose powers of "unfettered discretion" were limited by *Papachristou*. As discussed in chapter 7, tactics of order maintenance often target gangs as signs of disorder. Yet in many places, gang membership becomes illegal only when accompanied by a crime. For instance, in California, as in many places, committing a crime in the context of a gang can result in a sentencing enhancement, but the mere fact of gang membership is not enough to put someone in prison. Without the ability to convict people for crimes, urban police turned to the civil court and sought what came to be known as "gang injunctions."

A **gang injunction** is a court order similar to a restraining order in cases of domestic violence. It simply mandates that certain conditions be met by the person or people named in the order. The very first gang injunctions were sought in Los Angeles in the late 1980s and targeted anyone named by police as a member of the gangs identified in the order. Today, they are used in many cities. Gang injunctions are filed in civil court by the city attorney, not the district attorney, and are sought based on the testimony of police officers. Because they are filed in civil court, those named in the gang injunction are not eligible for public counsel, and the burden of evidence is considerably lower.

Gang injunctions are sought for a specific geographical area, such as a neighborhood or a few city blocks. An injunction effectively bans a person from a particular space under certain conditions. Common stipulations make it a crime to be with others in a group, to associate with others subject to the injunction, and to be in the injunction area at specific times. Conditions can include a curfew from 10 p.m. to 5 a.m. or even exclusion from a particular space entirely. They can also include stipulations such as not to loiter in public or not to carry "criminal" tools. Injunctions, like those sought in Los Angeles, Oakland, and San Francisco, are typically sought in low-income communities of color. Consider Los Angeles. More than thirty gang injunctions, out of just forty-five, are in South Central LA, home to neighborhoods such as Watts and the geographic concentrations of black and Latinx communities in the city.

Because stipulations are limitless, gang injunctions actually work to criminalize everyday life and, often, prosocial behaviors (Caldwell 2009). One couple was walking down the street and saw a friend who they stopped and talked with: this violated being in a group of three. Another two people were arrested because they showed up at the same job fair. One person lost a job because he could not carpool with a friend who was also on the injunction. Injunctions effectively prevent going to neighborhood recreation centers and public gatherings. In Oakland, two people were arrested for being at a neighborhood fair at the same time.

Territorializing Whiteness

Gang injunctions are key tactics in the territorialization of whiteness in urban space today (Muniz 2014). One study of gang injunctions found little evidence that they did anything about crime other than reducing the public fear of crime (Maxson, Hennigan, and Sloane 2005). The authors noted, "Little evidence was found that . . . translated into larger improvements in neighborhood quality, such as neighborhood social cohesion, informal social control, collective efficacy, and police/community relations" (2005, 520). Though this study of gang injunctions did not racially disaggregate fear of crime, fear is racialized, and as we showed in chapters 5–7, nonwhite youth are often assumed to be the source of crime. The gang label is often a code word for youths of color. Policing these youths leads to a reduction in white racial fear, shown in other contexts, if not actual crime, which then leads police to laud these tactics a success, and institute even more injunctions throughout the urban environment (Caldwell 2009).

Gang injunctions are informed by the colonial tactics that intricately controlled the movement and settlement of the colonized in order to guarantee the free movement, control, and appropriation of space of conquerors, as we saw in *M'Intosh* above. This continues today through gang injunctions, which at their inception were "meticulously designed to control the movement of black youth by criminalizing activities and behavior that is unremarkable and legal in other jurisdictions," just as police agencies such as the LAPD (discussed in chapters 6 and 7) have done in the past (Muniz 2015, 35). Though injunctions appear race neutral, they have been almost exclusively sought for black and Latinx youth and provide a primary tool for police to stop, question, and even threaten this group. Injunctions further expel and exclude black and brown youth from urban space in much the same way as colonial and Progressive Era tactics. Legal scholar Gary Stewart (1998) describes these legal tactics as the "legacy of postbellum vagrancy ordinances" found throughout the "black codes" (discussed in chapter 4) and broken windows policing (discussed in chapter 7). Gang injunctions are an expression of the state racism discussed in chapter 4, where the elimination, exclusion, containment, and displacement of some benefits the health and wealth of others. It is the same colonial logic that determined that Native Americans cannot possess title to the land because of their "heathen" ways. And it is part of the practice of coloniality in the United States today, sanctioned and ordered by the very courts that are supposed to be protecting equal rights for all.

CONCLUSION

Courts, though seen as static institutions, are key agents of the territorial practices and knowledge production that attends to colonial conquest. Courts started as the "courts of the conqueror," where the racial knowledge used to deny humanity to the conquered was codified as the foundation of legal authority. As the criminal justice system developed, this foundation served to protect the supremacy of whites, especially with regard to the criminal court process.

While today, attempts to explicitly racialize court practices are forbidden, racialization continues through the structure and activities of the court. The court structure silences defendants and upholds the routinized and procedural aspects of the law, while ignoring the structural conditions under which the law operates. Courts thereby exploit inequality, reserving the protections of due process for the conquerors—or in today's language, those who can afford legal representation, who can withstand a court trial, and whose outsider status is not visible in a courtroom.

Courts extend these colonial practices into urban society through practices of knowledge production that uphold some urban spaces as more criminal than others. Through a similar function of holding people as more criminal than others, in the absence of any criminal activity, courts extend colonial practices over both the bodies of defendants and urban space. Courts participate in the remaking of urban space through the management of the residents' movement through these spaces, marking some people as criminal simply by their presence in a social space. Through these practices, the court provides legal codification to the geographies of race and class that mark urban society and uses its powers to remake and produce these geographies into the future.

REFERENCES

Abrams, David S., Marianne Bertrand, and Sendhil Mullainathan. 2012. "Do Judges Vary in Their Treatment of Race?." *Journal of Legal Studies* 41, no. 2: 347–83.

Alexander, Michelle. 2012. *The New Jim Crow: Mass Incarceration in the Age of Colorblindness.* New York: New Press.

American Civil Liberties Union (ACLU). 2013. *A Living Death: Life without Parole for Non-violent Offenses.* November 2013. New York: ACLU Foundation. www.aclu.org/files/assets/111813-lwop-complete-report.pdf.

———. 2014. *Racial Disparities in Sentencing.* Submitted to the Inter-American Commission on Human Rights, October 27, 2014. www.aclu.org/sites/default/files/assets/141027_iachr_racial_disparities_aclu_submission_0.pdf.

Anghie, Antony. 1999. "Finding the Peripheries: Sovereignty and Colonialism in Nineteenth-Century International Law." *Harvard International Law Journal* 40: 1.

Anwar, Shamena, Patrick Bayer, and Randi Hjalmarsson. 2012. "The Impact of Jury Race in Criminal Trials." *Quarterly Journal of Economics* 127, no. 2: 1017–55.

Arnold, David, Will Dobbie, and Crystal S. Yang. 2017. *Racial Bias in Bail Decisions.* NBER Working Paper no. 23421. Cambridge, MA: National Bureau of Economic Research.

Banner, Stuart. 2009. *The Death Penalty: An American History.* Cambridge, MA: Harvard University Press.

Beckett, Katherine, and Steve Herbert. 2010. "Penal Boundaries: Banishment and the Expansion of Punishment." *Law and Social Inquiry* 35, no. 1: 1–38.

Bell, Jeannine, and Mona Lynch. 2015. "Cross-Sectional Challenges: Gender, Race, and Six-Person Juries." *Seton Hall Law Review* 46: 419.

Bibas, Stephanos. 2004. "Plea Bargaining Outside the Shadow of Trial." *Harvard Law Review:* 2463–2547.

Bikel, Ofra, writer, prod., dir. 1999. "Snitch." *Frontline.* Air date: January 12, 1999. PBS. www.pbs.org/wgbh/pages/frontline/shows/snitch/.

Blume, John H., and Rebecca K. Helm. 2014. "The Unexonerated: Factually Innocent Defendants Who Plead Guilty." *Cornell Law Review* 100: 157.

Bowers, William J., Marla Sandys, and Benjamin D. Steiner. 1997. "Foreclosed Impartiality in Capital Sentencing: Jurors' Predispositions, Guilt-Trial Experience, and Premature Decision Making." *Cornell Law Review* 83, no. 6 (September): 1476. www.lawschool.cornell.edu/research/cornell-law-review/upload/Bowers.pdf.

Butler, Paul. 1995. "Racially Based Jury Nullification: Black Power in the Criminal Justice System." *Yale Law Journal* 105, no. 3: 677–725.

Caldwell, B. 2009. "Criminalizing day-to-day life: A socio-legal critique of gang injunctions." *American Journal of Criminal Law* 37, no. 3: 241–90.

Carter, Stephen L. 1987. "When Victims Happen to Be Black." *Yale Law Journal* 97: 420.

Casper, J. D. 1971. "Did You Have a Lawyer When You Went to Court? No. I Had a Public Defender." *Yale Review of Law and Social Action* 1 (Spring): 4–9.

Cheng, Cheng, and Mark Hoekstra. 2013. "Does Strengthening Self-Defense Law Deter Crime or Escalate Violence? Evidence from Expansions to Castle Doctrine." *Journal of Human Resources* 48, no. 3: 821–54.

Cole, David. 1999. *No Equal Justice: Race and Class in the American Criminal Justice System.* New York: New Press.

Comaroff, John L. 2001. "Colonialism, Culture, and the Law: A Foreword." *Law and Social Inquiry* 26, no. 2: 305–14.

Davis, Angela J. 1998. "Prosecution and Race: The Power and Privilege of Discretion." *Fordham Law Review* 67, no. 1: 13–67.

———. 2007. *Arbitrary Justice: The Power of the American Prosecutor.* New York: Oxford University Press.

Demuth, Stephen. 2003. "Racial and Ethnic Differences in Pretrial Release Decisions and Outcomes: A Comparison of Hispanic, Black, and White Felony Arrestees." *Criminology* 41, no. 3: 873–908.

Emmelman, Debra. 2003. *Justice for the Poor: A Study of Criminal Defense Work.* Burlington, VT: Ashgate.

Farole, Donald J., and Lynn Langton. 2010. *County-Based and Local Public Defender Offices, 2007.* Special Report, September 2010. Washington, DC: Bureau of Justice Statistics, Department of Justice. www.bjs.gov/content/pub/pdf/clpdo07.pdf.

Fanon, Frantz. (1952) 1967. *Black Skin, White Masks.* Reprint, New York: Grove.

Feeley, Malcolm M. 1979. *The Process Is the Punishment: Handling Cases in a Lower Criminal Court.* New York: Russell Sage Foundation.

Feinberg, Lawrence. 2011. *A Constitutional Default: Services to Indigent Criminal Defendants in Pennsylvania.* Report of the Task Force and Advisory Committee on Services to Indigent Criminal Defendants, December 2011. Harrisburg: Joint State Government Commission. www.nlada.net/sites/default/files /pa_indigentdefensetaskforce_report_12062011.pdf.

Gau, Jacinta M. 2016. "A Jury of Whose Peers? The Impact of Selection Procedures on Racial Composition and the Prevalence of Majority-White Juries." *Journal of Crime and Justice* 39, no. 1: 75–87.

Golub, Andrew, Bruce D. Johnson, and Eloise Dunlap. 2007. "The Race/Ethnicity Disparity in Misdemeanor Marijuana Arrests in New York City." *Criminology and Public Policy* 6, no. 1: 131–64.

Gupta, Arpit, Douglas Swanson, and Ethan Frenchman. 2016. *The High Cost of Bail: How Maryland's Reliance on Money Bail Jails the Poor and Cost the Community Millions.* Maryland Office of the Public Defender. November 2016. www.opd.state.md.us/Portals/0/Downloads/High%20Cost%20of%20Bail.pdf.

Harlow, Caroline Wolf. 2000. *Defense Counsel in Criminal Cases.* Washington DC: Bureau of Justice Statistics, Department of Justice.

Harris, Alexes, Heather Evans, and Katherine Beckett. 2010. "Drawing Blood from Stones: Legal Debt and Social Inequality in the Contemporary United States." *American Journal of Sociology* 115, no. 6: 1753–99.

Harris, David A. 1994. "Factors for Reasonable Suspicion: When Black and Poor Means Stopped and Frisked." *Indiana Law Journal* 69, no. 3 (Summer): 659–88. www.repository.law.indiana.edu/ilj/vol69/iss3/1.

Human Rights Watch. 2013. *An Offer You Can't Refuse: How U.S. Federal Prosecutors Force Drug Defendants to Plead Guilty.* December 5, 2013. https://www.hrw.org/report/2013/12/05/offer-you-cant-refuse/how-us-federal-prosecutors-force-drug-defendants-plead.

———. 2017. *"Not in It for Justice": How California's Pretrial Detention and Bail System Unfairly Punishes Poor People.* April 2017. https://www.hrw.org/report/2017/04/11/not-it-justice/how-californias-pretrial-detention-and-bail-system-unfairly.

Irwin, John. 1985. *The Jail.* Berkeley: University of California Press.

Johnson, Sheri Lynn. 2014. "*Batson* from the Very Bottom of the Well: Critical Race Theory and the Supreme Court's Peremptory Challenge Jurisprudence." *Ohio State Journal of Criminal Law* 12, no. 1 (Fall): 71–90. https://kb.osu.edu/dspace/bitstream/handle/1811/73473/OSJCL_V12N1_071.pdf.

Kahan, Dan M., and Donald Braman. 2008. "The Self-Defensive Cognition of Self-Defense." *American Criminal Law Review* 45: 1.

Lu, Lynn D. 2007. "Prosecutorial Discretion and Racial Disparities in Federal Sentencing: Some Views of Former U.S. Attorneys." *Federal Sentencing Reporter* 19, no. 3: 192–201.

Kleider, Heather M., Leslie R. Knuycky, and Sarah E. Cavrak. 2012. "Deciding the Fate of Others: The Cognitive Underpinnings of Racially Biased Juror Decision Making." *Journal of General Psychology* 139, no. 3: 175–93.

Narby, Douglas J., Brian L. Cutler, and Gary Moran. 1993. "A Meta-analysis of the Association between Authoritarianism and Jurors' Perceptions of Defendant Culpability." *Journal of Applied Psychology* 70, no. 1: 34–42.

Kutateladze, Besiki Luka, and Nancy Andiloro. 2014. *Prosecution and Racial Justice in New York County.* Report submitted to National Institute of Justice, January 31, 2014. New York: Vera Institute of Justice. www .ncjrs.gov/pdffiles1/nij/grants/247227.pdf.

LaFrentz, Chandra D., and Cassia Spohn. 2006. "Who Is Punished More Harshly in Federal Court? The Interaction of Race/Ethnicity, Gender, Age, and Employment Status in the Sentencing of Drug Offenders." *Justice Research and Policy* 8, no. 2: 25–56.

Lazarus-Black, Mindie. 2007. *Everyday Harm: Domestic Violence, Court Rites, and Cultures of Reconciliation.* Urbana: University of Illinois Press.

Locke, Phil. 2015. "Prosecutors, Charge Stacking and Plea Deals." *Wrongful Convictions Blog.* Posted June 12, 2015. https://wrongfulconvictionsblog.org/2015/06/12/prosecutors-charge-stacking-and-plea-deals/.

Lu, Lynn D. 2007. "Prosecutorial Discretion and Racial Disparities in Federal Sentencing: Some Views of Former US Attorneys." *Federal Sentencing Review* 19, no. 3: 192.

Mackenzie, John. 1887. *Austral Africa; Losing It or Ruling It: Being Incidents and Experiences in Bechuanaland, Cape Colony, and England.* Vol. 1. London: Sampson, Low, Marston, Searle, and Rivington. https://hdl .handle.net/2027/uc1.$b58307.

Mawani, Renisa. 2010. "'Half-Breeds,' Racial Opacity, and Geographies of Crime: Law's Search for the 'Original' Indian." *Cultural Geographies* 17, no. 4: 487–506.

Maxson, Cheryl L., Karen M. Hennigan, and David C. Sloane. 2005. "'It's Getting Crazy Out There': Can A Civil Gang Injunction Change A Community?" *Criminology and Public Policy* 4, no. 3: 577–605.

Maxwell, James D. 2013. "And Stay Out: A Look at Judicial Banishment in Mississippi." *Supra* 82: 1.

McIntyre, Frank, and Shima Baradaran. 2013. "Race, Prediction, and Pretrial Detention." *Journal of Empirical Legal Studies* 10, no. 4: 741–70.

Miller, James A. 2009. *Remembering Scottsboro: the Legacy of an Infamous Trial.* Princeton, NJ: Princeton University Press.

Mililli, Kenneth J. 1996. "*Batson* in Practice: What We Have Learned About *Batson* and Peremptory Challenges." *Notre Dame Law Review* 71: 447.

Morrison, Caren Myers. 2014. "Negotiating Peremptory Challenges." *Journal of Criminal Law and Criminology* 104: 1.

Motivans, Mark. 2009. *Federal Justice Statistics 2006*. Washington DC: Bureau of Justice Statistics. www.bjs .gov/content/pub/html/fjsst/2006/fjs06st.pdf.

Muniz, Ana. 2014. "Maintaining Racial Boundaries: Criminalization, Neighborhood Context, and the Origins of Gang Injunctions." *Social Problems* 61, no. 2: 216–36.

——. 2015. *Police, Power, and the Production of Racial Boundaries*. New Brunswick, NJ: Rutgers University Press.

Mustard, David B. 2001. "Racial, Ethnic, and Gender Disparities in Sentencing: Evidence from the U.S. Federal Courts." *Journal of Law and Economics* 44, no. 1: 285–314.

National Association of Law Placement (NALP). 2010. "New Findings on Salaries for Public Interest Attorneys." *NALP Bulletin*, September 2010. www.nalp.org/sept2010pubintsal

Oleson, J. C., Christopher T. Lowenkamp, Timothy P. Cadigan, Marie Van Nostrand, and John Wooldredge. 2016. "The Effect of Pretrial Detention on Sentencing in Two Federal Districts." *Justice Quarterly* 33, no. 6: 1103–22.

Owens, Stephen D., Elizabeth Accetta, Jennifer J. Charles, and Samantha E. Shoemaker. 2014. *Indigent Defense Services in the United States, FY 2008–2012*. Technical Report. Washington DC: Bureau of Justice Statistics, Department of Justice. www.bjs.gov/content/pub/pdf/idsus0812.pdf.

Packer, Herbert L. 1964. "Two Models of the Criminal Process." *University of Pennsylvania Law Review* 113, no. 1: 1–68.

Perry, Steven, and Duren Banks. 2011. *Prosecutors in State Courts, 2007—Statistical Tables*. 2007 National Census of State Court Prosecutors, December 2011. Washington DC: US Department of Justice, Bureau of Justice Statistics. www.bjs.gov/content/pub/pdf/psc07st.pdf.

Rapping, Jonathan A. 2013. "Implicitly Unjust: How Defenders Can Affect Systemic Racist Assumptions." *NYU Journal of Legislation and Public Policy* 16: 999.

Raymond, Margaret. 1999. "Down on the Corner, Out in the Street: Considering the Character of the Neighborhood in Evaluating Reasonable Suspicion." *Ohio State Law Journal* 60: 99.

Razack, Sherene. 1998. *Looking White People in The Eye: Gender, Race, and Culture in Courtrooms and Classrooms*. Toronto: University of Toronto Press.

——. 2015. *Dying from Improvement: Inquests and Inquiries into Indigenous Deaths in Custody*. Toronto: University of Toronto Press.

Reaves, Brian. 2013. *Felony Defendants in Large Urban Counties, 2009*. Washington, DC: Bureau of Justice Statistics, Department of Justice.

Rehavi, M. Marit, and Sonja B. Starr. 2014. "Racial Disparity in Federal Criminal Sentences." *Journal of Political Economy* 122, no. 6: 1320–54.

Revesz, Joshua. 2015. "Ideological Imbalance and the Peremptory Challenge." *Yale Law Journal* 125: 2535.

Richardson, L. Song, and Phillip Atiba Goff. 2012. "Implicit Racial Bias in Public Defender Triage." *Yale Law Journal* 122: 2626.

Roberts, Dorothy E. 1999. "Foreword: Race, Vagueness, and the Social Meaning of Order-Maintenance Policing." *Journal of Criminal Law and Criminology* 89, no. 3: 775–836.

Roman, John. 2013. *Race, Justifiable Homicide, and Stand Your Ground Laws: Analysis of FBI Supplementary Homicide Report Data*. Washington DC: The Urban Institute.

Ross, Luana. 1998. *Inventing the Savage: The Social Construction of Native American Criminality*. Austin: University of Texas Press.

Sabol, William J., Heather C. West, and Matthew Cooper. 2009. "Prisoners in 2008." *Bureau of Justice Statistics Bulletin* 228417: 1–45.

Sacks, Meghan, Vincenzo A. Sainato, and Alissa R. Ackerman. 2015. "Sentenced to Pretrial Detention: A Study of Bail Decisions and Outcomes." *American Journal of Criminal Justice* 40, no. 3: 661–81.

Sanchez, Lisa E. 2001. "Enclosure Acts and Exclusionary Practices." In *Between Law and Culture: Relocating Legal Studies*, edited by David Theo Goldberg, Michael C. Musheno, and Lisa C. Bower, 122–140. Minneapolis: University of Minnesota Press.

Schlesinger, Traci. 2005. "Racial and Ethnic Disparity in Pretrial Criminal Processing." *Justice Quarterly* 22, no. 2: 170–92.

Schmitt, Christopher. 1991. "Plea Bargaining Favors Whites, as Blacks, Hispanics Pay Price." *San Jose Mercury News*, December 8, 1991: 1A.

Shelden, Randall G. 2012. *Delinquency and Juvenile Justice in American Society*. 2nd ed. Long Grove, IL: Waveland Press.

Shelden, Randall G., and John A. Horvath. 1987. "Intake Processing in a Juvenile Court: A Comparison of Legal and Nonlegal Variables." *Juvenile and Family Court Journal* 38, no. 3: 13–19.

Smith, Robert J., and Justin D. Levinson. 2011. "The Impact of Implicit Racial Bias on the Exercise of Prosecutorial Discretion." *Seattle University Law Review* 35: 795.

Sunne, Samantha. 2014. "Why Our Right to a Public Defender May Come with a Fee." *Special Series: Guilty and Charged.* May 29, 2014. National Public Radio. www.npr.org/2014/05/29/316735545/why-your-right-to-a-public-defender-may-come-with-a-fee.

Spohn, Cassia, and Lisa L. Sample. 2013. "The Dangerous Drug Offender in Federal Court: Intersections of Race, Ethnicity, and Culpability." *Crime and Delinquency* 59, no. 1: 3–31.

Stamp, Patricia. 1991. "Burying Otieno: The Politics of Gender and Ethnicity in Kenya." *Signs: Journal of Women in Culture and Society* 16, no. 4: 808–45.

Stewart, Gary. 1998. "Black Codes and Broken Windows: The Legacy of Racial Hegemony in Anti-Gang Civil Injunctions." *Yale Law Journal* 107, no. 7: 2249–79.

Sutton, John R. 2013. "Structural Bias in the Sentencing of Felony Defendants." *Social Science Research* 42, no. 5: 1207–21.

Steffensmeier, Darrell, Jeffery Ulmer, and John Kramer. 1998, "The Interaction of Race, Gender, and Age in Criminal Sentencing: The Punishment Cost of Being Young, Black, and Male." *Criminology* 36, no. 4: 763–98.

Strong, Suzanne. 2016. *State-Administered Indigent Defense Systems, 2013.* Washington DC: Bureau of Justice Statistics, Department of Justice. www.bjs.gov/content/pub/pdf/saids13.pdf.

Sun, Ivan Y., and Yuning Wu. 2006. "Citizens' Perceptions of the Courts: The Impact of Race, Gender, and Recent Experience." *Journal of Criminal Justice* 34, no. 5: 457–67.

Van Brunt, Alexa. 2015. "Poor People Rely on Public Defenders Who Are Too Overworked to Defend Them." *Guardian,* June 17 2015. www.theguardian.com/commentisfree/2015/jun/17/poor-rely-public-defenders-too-overworked.

Villanueva, Joaquin. 2013. "The Territorialization of the 'Republican Law': Judicial Presence in Seine-Saint-Denis, France." PhD diss., Syracuse University.

Walsh, Anthony. 2004. *Race and Crime: A Biosocial Analysis.* Hauppauge, NY: Nova Science Publishers.

Weich, Ronald and Carols Angulo. 2000. *Justice on Trial: Racial Disparities in the American Criminal Justice System.* Washington, DC: Leadership Conference on Civil Rights.

Wheelock, Darren. 2011. "A Jury of One's 'Peers': The Racial Impact of Felon Jury Exclusion in Georgia." *Justice System Journal* 32, no. 3: 335–59.

Whitehurst, Bill. 2004. *Gideon's Broken Promise: America's Continuing Quest for Equal Justice.* Chicago: American Bar Association. www.americanbar.org/content/dam/aba/administrative/legal_aid_indigent_defendants/ls_sclaid_def_bp_right_to_counsel_in_criminal_proceedings.authcheckdam.pdf/

Williams, Joshua H., and Richard Rosenfeld. 2016. "The Impact of Neighborhood Status on Imprisonment for Firearm Offenses." *Journal of Contemporary Criminal Justice* 32, no. 4: 383–400.

Wooldredge, John, James Frank, Natalie Goulette, and Lawrence Travis. 2015. "Is the Impact of Cumulative Disadvantage on Sentencing Greater for Black Defendants?" *Criminology and Public Policy* 14, no. 2: 187–223.

Zia, Helen. 2000. *Asian American Dreams.* New York: Farrar, Straus & Giroux.

Imprisoning Race: From Slavery to the Prison

LEARNING OUTCOMES

▶ Explain how the prison is an institution of coloniality.

▶ Summarize why and how people argue that the prison replicates systems of racialized capitalist expropriation, such as slavery.

▶ Survey the history of prison, why it developed, and how it contributed to a social construction of whiteness.

▶ Describe how and why the prison transformed into the racial management institution it is today.

▶ Compare philosophies of punishment and the new penology with racial dehumanization logics.

▶ Give examples of the impact of imprisonment on individuals after they've served their time.

KEY TERMS

▶ dehumanization
▶ life course
▶ prison industrial complex
▶ private prisons
▶ deterrence
▶ convict leasing
▶ chain gang
▶ rehabilitation
▶ trusty system
▶ indeterminate sentencing
▶ punitive
▶ warehousing
▶ incapacitation
▶ determinate sentences
▶ new penology
▶ civil death
▶ felon disenfranchisement

Prisons lurk in the mind of many as places of violence, victimization, and inhumanity. Prisons are the "other" of civilization, housing those too "savage" to continue in society. Inhabitants are sequestered, unable to participate in the pursuit of happiness or experience liberty or freedom, considered essential attributes of our society, and what we define as civilization. Imprisonment strips people of their social standing, their geographical location, and their bodily autonomy. Prisons are, in effect, systems of **dehumanization,** working to exclude their inhabitants from the category of human.

Prisons are also today one of the most important institutions organizing the racial experience. For this reason, racialized mass incarceration has been likened to a "new Jim Crow" or "neoslavery." These comparisons have merit. This chapter explores why the prison is considered the modern successor to slavery and other institutions of racial management, before embarking on a historicized understanding of how prisons came to play such an integral role today in the remaking of race and racialized experience. This experience, we argue, is produced through the multiple dehumanizing effects of the prison, from actual incarceration to the lasting stigma of a felony conviction to the collateral consequences on affected communities, families, and loved ones.

PRISONS, SLAVERY, RACE, AND THE ECONOMY

Given the considerable racial disparities in imprisonment, prisons have been called the latest in a long line of "peculiar institutions" that organize racial subjugation—including slavery, Jim Crow, and public housing (Davis 1998a; Wacquant 2000). While seemingly a hyperbolic claim, the reality is that prisons are structurally consonant with slavery. Prisons are demographically similar to slavery, both in terms of those imprisoned and those in power, and are a vast economic enterprise, with the prison workforce contributing 6 percent of the GDP of the U.S. (White 2015). Together, these form the structural context of imprisonment such that it fulfills a social and economic function similar to slavery's: wealth accumulation and racial subjugation.

Mass Incarceration as a "Peculiar Institution"

Between 1970 and 2005, there was a 700 percent increase in the population of prisons in the United States (see figure 9.1). During this same time, there was only a 44 percent increase in population overall. Today, the United States is home to just 5 percent of the world's population, but it incarcerates 25 percent of the world's prisoners. We are the world leader in incarceration, with over 670 people incarcerated per 100,000, surpassing even countries such as China and Russia, which come in at 118th and 439th, respectively. Over one in one hundred U.S. citizens are in jail or prison, and just over 2.3 million people are behind bars. Many of these statistics have been cited or alluded to in previous chapters, but given the immensity of mass incarceration, they bear repeating. This monumental growth happened in just a couple of decades, and its most defining characteristic is the racially disproportionate outcome.

As noted in earlier chapters, imprisonment is heavily gendered and racialized (see figure 9.2). Over 60 percent of those imprisoned are black or brown, revealing just how important the prison and criminal legal system is to racial-governance strategies in the United States. Today, 1 in 36 Latinos and 1 in 15 black men are currently incarcerated, while only 1 in every 106 white men faces the same fate. Once on the inside, black prisoners are also subject to greater administrative punishment, such as solitary confinement (Olson 2016).

In 2011, almost 7 million people in the United States were under some sort of criminal justice supervision (see figure 9.3). Nationwide, the rate of supervision for black men is one in three, and in some cities, such as Baltimore and Washington, DC, the number is one in two (Mauer 2011). The rate for whites, by contrast, is just one in twenty-three.

Women, though a much smaller proportion of the prison population overall, are nevertheless its fastest growing constituency, increasing over 800 percent since 1980. The jail population alone increased over 1,400 percent since 1970 (Swavola, Riley, and Subramanian 2016). Black and Latina women are the majority of female prisoners, and almost two-thirds of women imprisoned are nonwhite. One in every 18 black women will go to prison in her lifetime, as will 1 in 45 Latinas, but only 1 in 111 white women. The large majority of women, 82 percent, are imprisoned for nonviolent offenses, including drugs, property, and public order offenses.

Imprisonment is so widespread in some communities that it is considered a part of the life course for poor, black males (Pettit and Western 2004). **Life course** is a sociological term that "views the passage to adulthood as a sequence of well-ordered stages that affect life trajectories long after the early transitions are completed" (Pettit and Western 2004, 154). For young black men without an education, incarceration is now one of these life stages, much like transitioning from school to work then to marriage and parenthood is for other demographic groups. Indeed, 60 percent of young black men without a high school education had gone to prison by 1999. This rate of incarceration has far-ranging effects not just on those incarcerated but on the families, children, and entire neighborhoods that must adjust to the normality of having a loved one incarcerated. Not only are young black men at a much greater risk of incarceration than their white counterparts, but also death (figures 9.4 and 9.5; Pettit and Western 2004). State policies organize this premature death through the practices described in preceding chapters.

Michelle Alexander (2012) has named this imprisonment reality the "new Jim Crow" because it reveals the institutional impact of prisons on social inequality. Black men are not only more likely to be in prison but are more likely to

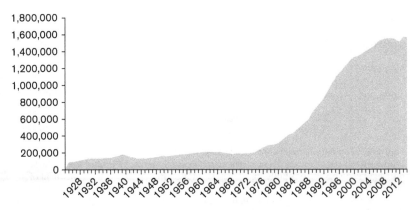

Figure 9.1 Number of people incarcerated in U.S. state and federal prisons (excluding jails), 1926–2014. Sources: E. Ann Carson and Daniela Golinelli, *Prisoners in 2012: Trends in Admissions and Releases, 1991–2012*, Bureau of Justice Statistics Bulletin (Washington, DC: U.S. Department of Justice, December 2013 [revised September 2014]), www.bjs.gov /content/pub/pdf/p12tar9112.pdf; Danielle Kaeble, Lauren Glaze, Anastasios Tsoutis, and Todd Minton, *Correction Populations in the United States, 2014*, Bureau of Justice Statistics Bulletin (Washington, DC: U.S. Department of Justice, December 2015 [revised January 2016]), www.bjs.gov/content/pub/pdf/cpus14.pdf; Margaret Warner Cahalan and Lee Anne Parsons, *Historical Corrections Statistics in the United States, 1850–1984*, NCJ-102529 (Washington, DC: U.S. Department of Justice, Bureau of Justice Statistics, December 1986), www.bjs.gov/content/pub/pdf/hcsus5084.pdf.

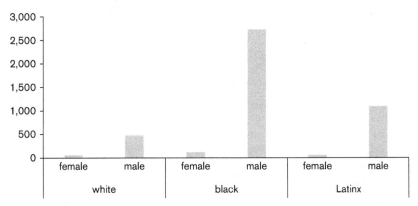

Figure 9.2 Imprisonment rates by gender, race, and ethnicity, per 100,000, 2014. Source: E. Ann Carson, *Prisoners in 2014*, Bureau of Justice Statistics Bulletin, NCJ 248955 (Washington, DC: U.S. Department of Justice, September 2015), www.bjs.gov/content/pub /pdf/p14.pdf.

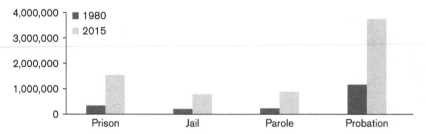

Figure 9.3 Population under control of U.S. corrections system, 1980 and 2015. Sources: Danielle Kaeble and Lauren Glaze, *Correctional Populations in the United States, 2015*, Bureau of Justice Statistics Bulletin, NCJ 250374 (Washington, DC: U.S. Department of Justice, December 2016); *Key Facts at a Glance: Corrections* (Washington, DC: Bureau of Justice Statistics, n.d.), accessed August 26, 2017, www.bjs.gov/glance_redirect .cfm#corrections.

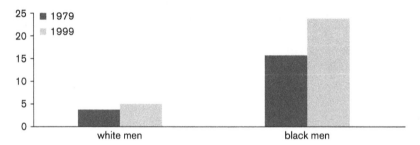

Figure 9.4 Cumulative risk of death or imprisonment by age 30–34 for black and white men, 1979 and 1999. Source: Becky Pettit, and Bruce Western, "Mass Imprisonment and the Life Course: Race and Class Inequality in US Incarceration," *American Sociological Review* 69, no. 2 (2004): 162, table 4.

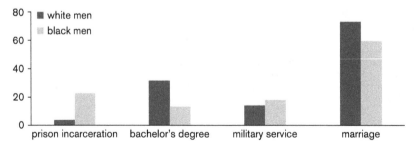

Figure 9.5 Percent of black and white men experiencing major life events. Source: Becky Pettit, and Bruce Western, "Mass Imprisonment and the Life Course: Race and Class Inequality in US Incarceration," *American Sociological Review* 69, no. 2 (2004): 151–69.

die. Slavery, Jim Crow, and residential racial segregation were all mechanisms through which the state created racial inequality, racially subjugated black communities, and subjected them to violence and increased death. These "peculiar institutions" had the ability to effect destructive outcomes on an ongoing and generational basis. Today, imprisonment systematically results in these very same outcomes.

Slavery, the Prison, and Industrial Production

Like slavery, prison organizes a vast amount of wealth accumulation, mainly for whites, due to racial stratification in the prison workforce and corporate ownership. Slavery provided a model of industrial production, as we discussed in chapter 2, and the prison today is no different. It is a sizable industry that plays an integral role in the U.S. economy. State prisons spend $30 billion dollars annually on imprisonment, with federal prisons adding another $5 billion (Myser 2007). Add in the cost of jails, parole, and probation, and the state expends over $80 billion on incarceration. The vast economy that has emerged around imprisonment is called the **prison industrial complex,** a term that encompasses not just the business of imprisonment but also the vast number of private companies supplying goods and services to prisons. Profit is generated not just through the building of prisons but also through both prison labor for multinational corporations and the contracting of services to prisoners on the inside.

The Private Prison

Private prisons are often the most visible way that profit motive is embedded within imprisonment. Private prisons today are corporations that build and operate secure facilities. Corporations enter into contract with the state to house those convicted of crimes. Private imprisonment is not new, and many of the first prisons, such as San Quentin in California, were originally private. Early private prisons were opportunities to "lease" people convicted of crimes from the state, a practice discussed below that was responsible for the reconstitution of slavery in the postslavery era. Michael Hallet observes that one of "the most striking things about the reemergence of for-profit imprisonment in the United States . . . is not simply that it has reappeared, but that it should once again involve the disproportionate captivity of black men" (2006, 4). Hallet calls attention to how both for-profit imprisonment in the late 1800s and early 1900s and private prisons today accumulate wealth from racialized incarceration; whereas historically this meant enslavement, today the mere act of warehousing people can accumulate profit.

Private prisons are a $5 billion industry, and they contain only 8 percent of the entire prison population (White 2015). Companies have an incentive to keep prison admissions high, even in the face of declining crime rates. The 2010 report to the Securities and Exchange Commission by the Corrections Corporation of America states this fact explicitly: "The demand for our facilities and services could be adversely affected by . . . leniency in conviction or parole standards and sentencing practices" (Cohen 2015). Since 1990, the number of people held in private prisons has increased 1,600 percent, and today, private prisons incarcerate around 6 percent of the state prison population and 15 percent of the federal. Profit from private prisons was almost $700 million in 2014, revealing the vast wealth accumulation produced by imprisoning just over 128,000 people (White 2015).

Public and private prisons also have substantially different standards of care. There are fewer programs and opportunities for education in private facilities. Private facilities have higher inmate-to-guard ratios, and guards are better trained and paid in public facilities. Private facilities often have substandard facilities and food. And people imprisoned in public facilities are better able to keep in contact with their families (Dyer 2000). Private prisons are also not bound by the outcomes of lawsuits against the states for better living conditions in prison.

The substandard conditions of private imprisonment, including the profit incentive, are disproportionately borne by black prisoners (Hallett 2006). In order to keep costs down, private prisons will not accept any inmate with significant health issues. This means that older prisoners, who are more likely white given the history of incarceration discussed below, are often excluded from private prisons. By contrast, younger men of color are disproportionately transferred to private prisons. This provides just one more way the disproportionate incarceration of black and Latino men helps fuel profits in the twenty-first century.

Profiting Off Punishment

Prisons, both public and private, offer other opportunities for profit. As a massive system housing over 2.3 million people, there is considerable need for goods and services—food, clothes, laundry, furniture, security instruments, construction, transportation, commissary items, and so on. Each of these items represents an opportunity for a private corporation to profit.

Take phone calls, for example ("Intrastate Collect Prison Phone Rates" 2016). Prisons, both public and private, contract with telephone companies to provide pay phones. These contracts do two things: they set the price of phone calls (since most calls are collect) and provide commission kickbacks to the prison. Contracts are often awarded to the company with the highest kickback, not the lowest cost of phone service. This means that the cost of calls in various prisons is often much more than it would be on the outside. The cost of a fifteen-minute call ranges from just nineteen cents in Nebraska, which does not accept kickbacks, to $5.70 in Kentucky. Phone commissions paid to prison authorities topped $128.3 million in 2012.

Trade shows reveal the vast market in private goods for prisons (Dyer 2000). Companies market all sorts of goods, from new security technologies to cheaper, easier-to-prepare, and less perishable food products. Gas masks, riot gear, and new restraints are often displayed at these shows along with new types of dinnerware, toilets, and bulletproof glass. Private industries also provide health care, pharmaceuticals, and commissary services. At trade shows, enthusiastic vendors hawk their wares with little regard for the human suffering on the other side. One documentary even caught a vendor boasting that her barbed wire caused an inmate an injury that required over 600 stitches to repair (Segal 2015).

Forced Labor in the Prison Today

Prison labor is the practice that most closely resembles slavery, as private corporations profit off the labor of prison inmates. Though the labor is not always "forced" in the sense that prison employment is often considered a privilege and something that inmates spend many years waiting for, the chance to labor for considerably reduced wages hardly represents freedom of employment. By using inmates to perform essential tasks in the prison, such as laundry, labor costs are a fraction of what free labor would be paid, both in terms of hourly rates and the lack of employment taxes, benefits, and other costs. Prison labor is also very advantageous to corporations. State prison systems even boast about the benefits of using their labor: "No strikes. No union organizing. No health benefits, unemployment insurance, or workers' compensation to pay. No language barriers, as in foreign countries" (Davis 1998b: 12).

Numerous corporations make use of prison labor, including Starbucks, Eddie Bauer, Kmart, Dell, Gap, McDonald's, Target, American Airlines, Nike, Microsoft, Bed, Bath and Beyond, Honda, and the Hard Rock Café (see further Shelden and Vasiliev 2018, ch. 7). Since 1993, AT&T has paid prisoners less that $2 per day to staff their call centers (*Workers World* 1993). "American farm raised" tilapia found at Whole Foods is raised by prisoners who earn as little as 74 cents a day, as are the goats for Whole Foods branded goat cheese (Curry 2015). McDonald's uniforms are sewn by prisoners and Walmart purchases produce from prison farms. The list goes on.

The problem with mixing prisons and labor reveals another similarity with slavery. Before the Civil War, the law worked to protect the use of white racial violence for black economic subjugation. Similarly, the prison system works today to protect corporate wealth accumulation. Victoria's Secret is one corporation that depends on prison employees to make its products. Two "employees" of Victoria's Secret revealed to the media that they had been hired, along with their prison peers, to replace "Made in Honduras" tags with "Made in the USA" (Winter 2008). The consequence of this exposure? Both inmates were transferred to solitary confinement.

Further, as we noted in chapter 6, prisoners are the only group that can continue to be subjected to slavery under the Thirteenth Amendment. Many might be surprised by the claim that slavery continues today. Slavery not only continues but is legally and constitutionally sanctioned. When the Thirteenth Amendment was passed, it outlawed slavery except for one class: those convicted of crimes. The text of the amendment reads: "Neither slavery nor involuntary servitude, *except as a punishment for crime* whereof the party shall have been duly convicted, shall exist within the United States, or any place subject to their jurisdiction" (emphasis added). Through this provision, as we show below, the South was able to reconstitute slavery during Reconstruction, and today, prisoners are considered to have no employment protections and to be constitutionally enslaved, which the recent case *McGarry v. Pallito* (2012) confirmed.

Angela Davis remarks that "the practice of disappearing vast numbers of people from poor, immigrant, and racially marginalized communities has literally become big business" (1998b, 13). The racialized assumptions of criminality that emerged in the post-WWII era (described in chapter 6) combined with hyperpolicing of racially segregated urban communities (described in chapters 5 and 7), alongside the disproportionate use of incarceration for black and brown defendants (described in chapter 8), move people into the prison complex who serve as the raw materials for corporate wealth accumulation. Davis sums it up: "Colored bodies constitute the main human raw material in this vast experiment to disappear the major social problems of our time" (1998b, 13). And like slavery, the vast majority of profits from the prison industrial complex are also not distributed in a racially equitable manner, but are instead concentrated in the hands of the majority white owners.

Slavery and the Racial Geographies of Prison

Prisons share another similarity with slavery. They provide an economic boost to white communities through employment and rural economic development. This creates a particular optic that looks remarkably like the labor structure on slavery-era plantations: whites, with legal authorization to use violent force, guarding and controlling disenfranchised blacks (an optic that influences the very issue of race and wrongful convictions, as discussed in box 9.1).

While the majority of those imprisoned are people of color, the prison workforce is 70 percent white (see figure 9.6). Prisons don't just imprison; they are also one of the few places where someone with only a high school diploma can get a job that has health benefits, pays a living wage, and, in some places, provides for retirement. These workers are often white workers or descendants of white workers whose economic trajectories were disrupted by globalization, deindustrialization, and the decline of rural economies (Hallinan 2001). During slavery, lower-status whites were often the direct supervisors, guards, and

BOX 9.1   Race and Wrongful Convictions

Some of the most influential evidence for juries is eyewitness testimony. Yet this is one of the most unreliable types of evidence, often due to the problem of cross-racial identification. This misidentification has contributed to the surge in wrongful convictions in black communities: African Americans make up over 47 percent of those who have been exonerated due to wrongful convictions (Gross, Possley, and Stephens 2017).

Take the case of William Jackson, who spent five years imprisoned on a rape charge before he was released (Rizer 2003). Two white women swore under oath that he had raped them. Despite several alibis, an all-white jury convicted him on the strength of eyewitness testimony. Almost 75 percent of all wrongful convictions overturned by DNA evidence are due to incorrect eyewitness accounts, a relevant issue when considering the research on cross-racial identification.

Cross-racial identification is problematic because of the difficulty that members of one race have in recognizing people of other races. This is a well-established issue in the psychological literature, but juries are not told about the weaknesses of cross-racial eyewitness testimony, and defense attorneys are barred from entering studies about them as evidence. Given that juries are overwhelmingly white, black and Latinx defendants suffer disproportionately from wrongful convictions, especially when the identifier is white (Rizer 2003).

Should defense attorneys be permitted to introduce evidence of the problem with cross-racial identification? Should juror instructions include guidance about the problems with eyewitness testimony?

Sources: Samuel Gross, Maurice Possley, and Klara Stephens, *Race and Wrongful Convictions in the United States* (Irvine, CA: National Registry of Exonerations, Newkirk Center for Science and Society, 2017), www.law.umich.edu/special/exoneration/Documents/Race_and_Wrongful_Convictions.pdf; Arthur L. Rizer III, "The Race Effect on Wrongful Convictions," *William Mitchell Law Review* 29, no. 3, art. 5 (2003), http://open.mitchellhamline.edu/wmlr/vol29/iss3/5.

enforcers on plantations and were even the majority of those who served in slave patrols (see chapter 7). Prison replicates this racial structure.

Urban and Rural Geographies in Prison

Prison is marked by processes occurring in two different geographic spaces. On one hand, imprisonment is spatially concentrated and enabled by the geographies of racial segregation discussed in chapter 5. The places that faced urban disinvestment, renewal, and ultimately a decrease in affordable housing and social service supports are the very same neighborhoods where a high percentage

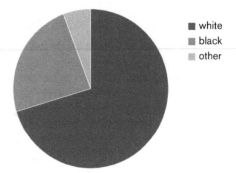

Figure 9.6 Race of correctional officers, jailers, and bailiffs. Source: DataUSA: Bailiffs, Correctional Officers, and Jailers, Dataset: ACS PUMS 1 year estimate, U.S. Census Bureau, accessed October 31, 2017, https://datausa.io/profile/soc/333010/.

of residents are or have been incarcerated. Consider that in 2009 just 19 percent of New York City neighborhoods were responsible for over 50 percent of the prison admissions from the city (Justicemapping.org 2018). And in Chicago, one neighborhood—West Garfield—had a forty times higher rate of admission than the highest ranked white neighborhood (Sampson 2012, 113).

Other places reveal similar disparities: 25 percent of people on probation or parole in Wichita, Kansas, live in just 8 percent of the neighborhoods; three zip codes in Philadelphia cost the state $40 million *each;* and in Austin, Texas, just two of its fifty-three zip codes account for 18 percent of people imprisoned (Justicemapping.org 2018; NAACP 2011; Eames, Terranova, and Kirk 2014). Researchers have identified what are called "million dollar blocks," or single blocks where the state spends over $1 million dollars to incarcerate people. This concentration of state resources in tiny geographical areas, in the very same places that have disproportionately felt the effects of state disinvestment, is all oriented toward incarcerating people.

Imprisonment has a geography, and this geography results from the deployment of state force through housing policy, the war on drugs, and law enforcement in just a few neighborhoods, as discussed in chapters 5, 6, and 7. Prisoners are often from urban areas because of both urban economies and policing. Yet, as a consequence of mass incarceration, where they serve their time is often far from places of home.

Imprisonment, then, is implicated in another geography: rural communities. Consider the geography of California state prisons. The majority of California prisons are found in the eastern, less populated side of the state, many of which have been built since the incarceration boom. Prison towns reflect the racial geography of California, and many of them are, or recently were, majority white and predominantly politically conservative. By contrast, most prison admissions are from metropolitan areas: the Los Angeles region, the San Francisco Bay Area, and Sacramento. California is not alone in this divergent distribution; the same trend has been observed in Michigan and Texas (Shelden 2001). Prison towns reveal a spatial separation between those imprisoned and their loved ones.

The convergence of these two geographies in the space of the prison results in a confrontation between cultural constructions, political affiliations, and demographics that does not normally happen (Halfacree 1993). Compare the stereotypes urban dwellers often have of rural living—backward, inbred, uneducated rednecks—with rural dwellers' stereotypes of cities—dirty, crowded, and crime-ridden. The prison brings together not just blacks and whites but urban dwellers and rural residents. This mix is further complicated by racialized constructions of each of these geographical imaginations. Prisons, then, are microcosms of colonial power relations, with the white rural working class called upon to guard and corral those excluded from urban living.

Prison guards are politically powerful, supporting candidates who advocate increasing punishment and working against those who advocate prison reform (Page 2011). And white prison guards are more punitive in their attitudes than guards of color (Jackson and Ammen 1996). This reality has resulted in a considerable amount of documented racial violence in prisons. In at least six states, guards have been disciplined for appearing in mock Klan attire (Southern Poverty Law Center 2000). Guards have been accused of race-based violence in ten states.

Lawsuits have been filed in thirteen states by black guards alleging racial harassment and violence from white colleagues. For instance, the NAACP filed a lawsuit on behalf of a hundred black employees against Florida prisons for condoning racist violence in the system—such as white officers wearing Klan paraphernalia and other racist symbols, carrying nooses on key chains, and retaliating against employees who challenged these practices. And there are likely an uncounted number of settlements that are sealed by court order in addition to the large number of civil cases filed. This is not to suggest that prison guards are necessarily more prone to racial violence than anyone else. Rather, the prison environment is structured by a history of racial violence that is structurally remade in the prison setting.

The "Prison Fix"

Prisons today are often seen by rural communities as sources of economic development. Prison siting used to be difficult due to NIMBY (not in my backyard) politics. Today, we have YIMBY, or yes in my backyard, with communities lobbying and cajoling legislatures to place prisons in their towns (Bonds 2013). As a result, some of the most depressed economies in the nation have all had significant prison building, creating a situation where the community not only profits from but needs the prison for its economic survival (Gilmore 2007). From a macroeconomic perspective, the prison represents how the survival of some means the subjugation of others.

Rural towns also benefit from prison siting in others ways. Prisoners are counted by the federal government where they reside: in prisons (Lotke and Wagner 2003). The number of prison residents swells the population of the rural community, bringing additional federal payments for schools, hospitals, public housing, social services, and food stamps. Urban communities, by contrast, suffer population losses, and funds are shifted from urban to rural communities. Population is also used to determine how many seats each state has in the U.S. House of Representatives. In Massachusetts, five districts meet the minimum population for a representative only because prisoners are counted (Lavarreda, Wagner, and Heyer 2009). Imprisonment then works to systematically bolster the political power of rural white communities and undermine that of urban nonwhite ones.

From a bird's-eye view then, the prison looks a lot like slavery. They both have been the primary mechanism of racial subjugation in the United States They both have had vast industrial impacts on the U.S. economy and the accumulation of wealth in the hands of a few, mostly white capitalists and communities. Prison is also organizationally synchronous with slavery, because it uses a similar racial power structure in the organization of the subjugated, the watchers, and enforcers—and even the accumulators.

Prisons, however, did not always play this role. At their inception, prisons were considered an enlightened method of punishment, suitable primarily for whites. When the strategies of racial management were accomplished by other state institutions, the prison was actually viewed as a *privilege* reserved for whites. It took considerable twists and turns in the racialized construction of punishment before prisons emerged as the contemporary corollary to slavery.

THE HISTORY OF RACE AND PUNISHMENT

Oftentimes, people are shocked to learn that prisons have not always housed society's most dispossessed—including racial minorities. In the 1700s and 1800s, prisons in many places were not racially integrated, much like the rest of society. Instead, prisons, especially ones oriented toward reform, were reserved for white men. Though brutal and inhumane by today's standards, the institutions that advocated reformation through hard labor, biblical reflection, or enforced silence were all considered the privilege of those that could be reformed. Women and minorities served their time on plantations, in congregate systems, and other warehousing institutions.

Reformation, Whiteness, and the Birth of the Penitentiary

Prior to the eighteenth century, prisons were not seen as places of punishment, even for the purposes of reformation, and were instead often merely holding cells. Minor offenses were generally punished with a fine, while more severe offenses like theft might be punished with public shaming or mutilation. In the most severe cases, death would be imposed. Public punishments were particularly important because they shamed the offender in ways that reinforced compliance and obedience throughout the general population. With the advent of urbanization, shaming lost its power.

As shaming lost its social significance, corporal punishments increased. England in particular began using death as the primary form of punishment. Its legal code came to be known as the bloody code since so many crimes were punished with death. Instead of social stability, however, the bloody code led to social upheaval.

Quakers advocated for the development of prisons as a humane alternative to the rampant use of capital punishment. Enlightenment philosophers questioned whether punishing relatively minor crimes with death might induce a thief or other petty criminal to wantonly take life since the punishment for both crimes was the same. Eventually, the prison emerged as an "enlightened" form of punishment that could preserve the liberty and rationality of the (white) people imprisoned.

The "Enlightened" Prison

The birth of the "enlightened" prison was premised on the philosophy of punishment called deterrence. **Deterrence** is a philosophy that presumes that people commit crime when they are not prevented from doing so by fear of sanctions. Punishment, according to early Enlightenment philosophers such as Cesare Beccaria and Jeremy Bentham, should induce restraint in people committing crime. Social reformers, such as the Quakers, took this idea of the social utility of imprisonment one step further and contended that the experience of imprisonment itself should engender personal reformation (Wines and Lane 1910).

Enlightened prisons developed on what would be called the Pennsylvania and Auburn models of imprisonment. The Pennsylvania model housed everyone in solitary confinement, presuming that this would encourage penitence, reflection, and eventually reformation. The Auburn model, by contrast, forced people in prison to work all day together in silence and then spend the night in solitary confinement. Through work and reflection, prisoners would reform. Critical to these conceptualizations of punishment, however, were that prisoners were first and foremost "rational," which is why most early prisons admitted only white men.

Whiteness and Rationality

The Enlightenment conceptualization of rationality meant that the very first prisons oriented toward reformation were reserved not for just anyone who committed crime. A government report in 1822 in Virginia explained who was and was not eligible for prison: "Although the free white persons usually confined to the penitentiary are for the most part from the lowest parts of society, yet the free negroes and mulattoes are a grade or so below them, and should not be associated with them" (*Journal of the House of Delegates of Virginia* 1822, 18).

Prison officials believed that blacks' presence in the penitentiary seemed to "destroy whatever reformatory effect the institution might exert on either race . . . for it destroyed white men's feelings of pride while dangerously inflating that of the blacks" (Ayers 1984: 62). When erecting a juvenile training school, a governor of Mississippi explained that "it would be degrading to the white children to associate with beings given up to public scorn" (Holloran 1989, 141). This justification of racial segregation in prisons was based wholly on the racist idea that some people—whites, men, property owners and their sons—were inherently rational, while others lacked reformatory capacity.

Most reform-oriented prisons housed white men. Immigrants were sometimes included, but women, blacks, and Native Americans were routinely excluded. Women lived in attics segregated from men, often languishing with little to do. When they were offered "reformatory" options, it was primarily training in domesticity (Rafter 1990). Blacks and Native Americans were segregated from whites, and like women, they were primarily kept in confinement with little concern for their reformation since they were presumed unable to reform. For them, punishment worked with other mechanisms of exploitation and oppression to achieve its ends. Silence and reflection, though brutal and violent in their own right, gave way to violent punishment of the body, which Enlightenment philosophers argued bred resentment and incivility, but only in "rational individuals."

Under the classical theory of deterrence, punishment served the purpose of preserving liberty. In this formulation, the person who commits crime is also someone who can be *prevented* from committing crime, just through the threat of punishment. This idea of punishment may seem inconsequential or even commonplace today. But it also demonstrates the racialized worldview of this idea. Those who had liberty were white, male, and property owning. Usurping the property of others or violent confrontation would not be "rational" in this context. With this formulation, the prison was conceived through a white, upper-class, male worldview—and punishment in the enlightened prison was limited to that group as well.

Permanent Imprisonment and the Reformation of Native Americans

Native Americans, by contrast, were subject to a strategy of permanent imprisonment. The creation of federal reservation lands was the result of a multipronged strategy of state violence. First, through campaigns of terror discussed in previous chapters, the state decimated the population of Native Americans. Then, the state encouraged and condoned the killing of native peoples by citizens in a campaign of "civilization" and "manifest destiny." Finally, the state rounded up native peoples and forced them to reside in federal reservations.

Reservations were not land that Native Americans had used prior to the arrival of whites. Instead, these were tracts of land that were often desolate and unusable for white purposes (at the time). Communities of people were banded together, often with little regard for the social relations that existed prior to genocide and internment, and moved to these areas, which were often hundreds of miles from their homes. Reservations were much like prisons today—people from many different walks of life were brought together into a confined area from which they could not leave and were permanently under the tutelage of an unfamiliar power. Native peoples were forced to remain within the area of confinement, and the borders of reservation land were often violently policed. Those leaving without a "pass" could be subject to death (Hoxie 1979).

This perpetual incarceration complemented a series of "civilizational" programs, including the routine practice in the late nineteenth and early twentieth centuries of removing children from reservation lands in order to raise them in "boarding schools." One of the most famous of these schools was the Carlisle Indian Industrial School in Pennsylvania, which used the assimilation model of schooling (Cooper 1999). Native American children were ripped from their families and subjected to a childhood of education in European American cultural traditions.

At Carlisle, children were forbidden to speak their languages, practice their cultural traditions, or even retain their native names. They were punished—often violently—for violating these rules. Day-to-day life in these institutions was premised not on reformation and restoring the "rationality" of wayward individuals, but on the complete annihilation of native customs (Cooper 1999).

Convict Leasing: Slavery by Another Name

The punishment of black Americans, by contrast, was premised on their role as forced laborers. While some Northern blacks spent their time warehoused in prisons, most black incarceration prior to the Second World War happened in the South. During slavery, plantation owners were given impunity to deal with "crimes" among the black population as they saw fit. When free blacks were punished, it was with very different sentences and punishments than those of whites and presaged the form of punishment that dominated the South post-slavery: convict leasing (Mancini 1996).

Punishment and the Rebirth of Slavery

For fifty years after the Civil War, there were no real prisons in Southern states (Adamson 1983). Some prisons did exist but these were reserved for just a small portion of convicted people and were so rarely used that they were almost

Figure 9.7. Chain gang of convicted persons engaged in road work, Pitt County, North Carolina, autumn 1910. The inmates were quartered in the wagons shown in the picture. Wagons were equipped with bunks and moved from place to place as labor was utilized. Seated in the foreground is J. Z. McLawhon, county superintendent of chain gangs. The dogs are bloodhounds used for running down any attempted escapes. Source: Courtesy of the Library of Congress, LC-USF344-007541-ZB.

entirely superfluous to the state's punishment activities. Prior to the Civil War, convicted free blacks were sentenced to forced labor, a practice that became known as **convict leasing.** After the Civil War, convict leasing was the primary form of punishment used in the South and was critical to reconstituting slavery-era race relations well into the twentieth century.

Convict leasing was a form of punishment where those convicted of crimes were forced to labor for private owners. "Contractors" would pay a fee to the state for the labor of the prisoners. The state would earn both revenue from the lease and save money by not housing and feeding its prisoners. The lengthy sentences given for petty crimes under "black codes" (discussed in chapter 4) meant that those liberated from the plantation were often quickly re-enslaved through the system of convict leasing.

Figure 9.7 shows the conditions under which nonwhite prisoners labored. Leased labor was critical to the Southern economy. Without this labor, plantations, coal mines, and other Southern industries would have collapsed, as would Northern industries that relied on Southern coal and other goods (Lichtenstein 1996). Rates of arrest even increased when more labor was needed, revealing how integral the practice was to the economic self-sufficiency of the South (Mancini 1996).

The Case of Green Cottenham

The story of Green Cottenham reveals the horrors of convict leasing. Cottenham was arrested in Alabama in 1908 and charged with vagrancy. *Vagrancy,* at the time, was a legal term that meant "having no fixed purpose." In 1907, Alabama outlawed vagrancy, which criminalized not being able to show that one was employed. The vagrancy code placed the burden of proof on defendants to show that they were not "guilty of wandering or strolling about in idleness, being able to work, etc." Historical records reveal that this charge was "reserved almost exclusively for black men" (Blackmon 2009, 1).

Cottenham spent three days in jail before he was sentenced to thirty days of hard labor. But prisoners were also commonly charged fees, and since Cottenham was unable to pay these fees, he was sentenced to an additional year of hard labor. Cottenham was sold to a subsidiary of the northern-owned U.S. Steel Corporation, the Tennessee Coal, Iron and Railroad Company. The company, in turn, paid $12 per month to the county.

Cottenham spent his sentence in mines in Tennessee, in what Douglas Blackmon describes as a "shaft in a vast subterranean labyrinth":

> There, he was chained inside a long wooden barrack at night and required to spend nearly every waking hour digging and loading coal. His required daily "task" was to remove eight tons of coal from the mine. Cottenham was subject to the whip for failure to dig the requisite amount, at risk of physical torture for disobedience, and vulnerable to the sexual predations of other miners—many of whom already had passed years or decades in their own chthonian confinement. The lightless catacombs of black rock, packed with hundreds of desperate men slick with sweat and coated in pulverized coal, must have exceeded any vision of hell a boy born in the countryside of Alabama—even a child of slaves—could have ever imagined. (Blackmon 2009, 2)

The conditions of Cottenham's imprisonment reveal the vast gulf between Enlightenment ideas of the prison and the everyday reality of punishment for nonwhites. For Cottenham, there was little distinction between slavery and convict leasing: he was forced to labor by the state under violence and the threat of death. He was subject to inhumane conditions that Enlightenment philosophers would have argued bred incivility and resentment in whites. And he was eventually given over to death.

Disease ran rampant throughout Cottenham's mine, and in the first four weeks of his incarceration, six people died from pneumonia or tuberculosis. By the end of his yearlong sentence, sixty had succumbed to disease or accident. Those who died were buried in mass graves surrounding the mine, a fate to which Cottenham ultimately succumbed. His body, entombed in a mass grave, today represents how people's bodies were exploited, appropriated, and ultimately used and disposed of. Colonial extraction common to slavery continued apace through convict leasing.

Conditions and Demise of Convict Leasing

Convict leasing conditions were often worse than slavery. Conditions were often brutal, with people chained inside railway cars or other open-air cages at night and then forced to work from sunup to sundown, or even later, until they were caged again. Unlike enslaved people, there was little incentive to keep leased convicts alive, and mortality rates were extraordinarily high. For instance, nine times more black prisoners in Mississippi died as a consequence of convict leasing than in northern prisons (Oshinsky 1997).

Through black-code laws that made it a crime for blacks to be in public spaces, white Southerners criminalized the ability of blacks to survive and thus ensured the continuation of white supremacy after slavery (Blackmon 2009). Further, the label of "criminal" provided a modicum of moral authority to white Southerners who argued that the enslavement of black Americans was due to their predilection for crime, and not because of southern ideas of white superiority. These practices continued the colonial logics of slavery, as the "civilized" sought to tame and restrain the "savage" through brutal subjugation and violence.

Convict leasing was critical to reshaping southern incarceration after the Civil War. In Tennessee prior to the Civil War, whites were the majority of prisoners (Shelden and Vasiliev [2018]). After the Civil War, the number of black prisoners steadily increased and that of whites decreased, until blacks were the majority of those imprisoned. This fundamentally shifted the nature of incarceration in the United States and served, long before the era of mass incarceration, to racialize prison populations (Shelden 2001). Convict leasing further presaged the resurgence of private profit and imprisonment, especially in the form of the private prison, which is considerably more dominant in the U.S. South.

By the late 1920s, convict leasing was banned in almost all states because of widespread public criticism of the practice. This criticism started when a plantation owner summarily executed his employees in order to avoid investigation by the FBI. Although the FBI was not actually investigating him, he killed eleven laborers in a single week in a move that shocked even the white community. During his murder trial, reports of convict leasing emerged and scandalized the nation. Widespread outrage led southern states to repeal convict-leasing laws over the next decade, and an Alabama governor even won election partly on the promise to end convict leasing (Mancini 1996). Yet, the use of slavery as a punishment did not go away. Instead, states replaced the private contractor with the state itself, and the chain gang was born.

Forced Labor, Punishment, and the Birth of the Chain Gang

Depictions of **chain gangs** are prolific in U.S. culture. Often, the scene is a group of men working a field in black and white striped jumpsuits, chained at

Figure 9.8 Juvenile chain gang, 1903. Source: Courtesy of the Library of Congress, LC-D428-850 [P&P].

the ankle, with men on horses overseeing. Chain gangs like the one in figure 9.8 were used prolifically throughout the South, both before and after the banning of convict leasing. Chain gangs were responsible for creating much of southern infrastructure, such as public roadways and ditches, and like convict leasing, were integral to the southern economy and accumulation of wealth.

The chain gang changed the owner of enslaved people from the private contractor to the state, but it did little to undo forced labor of African Americans. Progressive proponents of the chain gang saw it "as an example of penal humanitarianism, state-sponsored economic modernization and efficiency and racial moderation," and northerners praised southerners for its invention (Lichtenstein 1993, 86). Progressives considered chain gangs an efficient use of state resources and an opportunity to instill the habits of disciplined work. Yet, they were in reality the re-creation of slavery because almost 90 percent of the prison population in the South was black (Lichtenstein 2001).

The conditions of chain gangs mimicked slavery and convict leasing and were incredibly brutal, with rampant corporal punishment enforcing compliance. Imprisoned people were held in railway cars or trucks at night (as figure 9.7 above depicts) and transported from worksite to worksite. While some toiled at the prison itself, they often did so under harsh conditions with little protection from the sun, lack of water and food, and chains that often weighed over twenty pounds. The chains themselves were a type of punishment, and ulcers and infections on the ankles from the heavy shackles were common (Blackmon 2009).

Chain gangs were used primarily in the South, and they were phased out entirely by 1955. Though chain gangs were abandoned in the 1950s, they resurged in the 1990s, revealing the striking similarities between the tactics of punishment in the past and those under mass incarceration. Alabama was the first state to revive the chain gang in 1995, and others followed suit. Although this was a short-lived experiment, one state, Arizona, continues to use the chain gang. People imprisoned in the Maricopa County Jail can today volunteer to be on a chain gang in exchange for high school credits or to avoid lockdowns for rule violations.

Permanent imprisonment and slavery created through reservations, convict leasing, and the chain gang reveal how the methods of enlightened punishment theorized by the classical school of criminology did not extend to nonwhites. Instead, black and brown communities continued to face the violence and subjugation accorded to the dehumanized and colonized. As formal structures of racial subjugation fell away, however, prisons soon housed people of many races. Nevertheless, even in the era of rehabilitation, the prison continued to perpetuate a stark color line, and practices of racial dehumanization continued.

REHABILITATION, THE "CORRECTIONAL INSTITUTION," AND THE COLOR LINE

Prisons did not become the primary means of confinement in both the North and the South until after WWII, when rehabilitation surged as the dominant punishment ideology. **Rehabilitation** is premised on the idea that someone who commits crime is damaged in some way and can be repaired, reformed, or rehabilitated. Advocates of this idea, which first arose in the Progressive Era, envisioned the prison as a "correctional institution" guided by social service professionals, such as social workers, counselors, and psychiatrists. The idea of prison guards was even transformed and they became known as "correctional officers."

Though the rehabilitative ideology dominated corrections in the post-WWII era, it did not necessarily result in more humane conditions, especially for communities of color. Some states never embraced the rehabilitative ideal—including many in the South—and brutal, violent punishments were commonplace in many prisons. Further, a strict racial hierarchy emerged in prisons, retaining the practices of white supremacy through the institutional benefits of rehabilitation: greater freedoms and early release.

Rehabilitation and the Trusty System

While rehabilitation was the governing ethos of prisons after WWII, this ideology was often missing from the actual day-to-day life of prisoners. For most of the rehabilitation era, prisoners remained segregated in prisons throughout the United States, as they can even be found today. Until the late 1960s, federal and southern prisons were entirely segregated (Adamson 1983).

In prisons that did house both black and white inmates, a system of forced labor endured through what is known as the "trusty" system. The **trusty system** was a method of controlling inmates using the inmates themselves. Through this system, staff designated particular individuals—always white—to control and discipline others. Trusties were permitted to use physical violence and any other method they deemed necessary.

The most famous example of the trusty system was in Mississippi State Penitentiary at Parchman, the only prison in the state. At Parchman, inmates' participation in the trusty system was compulsory, because the state mandated that the prison not only had to pay for itself through the labor of inmates but also had to make a profit that would go back into the state budget (Oshinsky 1997). In 1911, the *New York Times* praised the system, writing that "Mississippi trains negro criminals to be such good farmers that they quickly secure places" of outside employment upon release. Invoking the ethos of rehabilitation, the article further praised Mississippi for demonstrating that through forced labor "a criminal population may be taken in hand, improved mentally and morally, built up physically, taught habits of regularity and industry, and . . . at the end of their terms . . . be eagerly sought by the planters of the state as laborers" (*New York Times* 1911).

The article noted that the trusty system allowed Mississippi to move beyond the "grave scandals" of convict leasing. Calling convict-leasing "infinitely worse than the slavery the war abrogated," it argued that slavery provided an economic incentive to care for enslaved people. Convict leasing provided no such incentive because the cost of the prisoner was the same to the company regardless of whether the leased individual lived or died. There were no repercussions for killing someone leased and companies could easily get new laborers from the court.

The article concluded, "Thus, it seems, Mississippi has solved the problem," through the use of the prison and the creation of the trusty system. The farm generated enough money to run the prison, pay for the court costs of prisoners, and put money back into the state treasury. This profit, however, was created through a system of white supremacy that largely mimicked slavery and colonial relations elsewhere. Almost all of the guarding and disciplining of the prison was done by white prisoners, who numbered fewer than 200 in Parchman, compared to over 1,800 black residents (*New York Times* 1911). Many trusties were supplied with a gun and rode horses, disciplining and beating black laborers in the field. At the end of each day, trusties would whip any laborer who failed to meet his quota. Trusties performed almost all of the work of running the prison, including dispensing medication and medical care, recommending further punishment in solitary units, and undertaking almost all administrative tasks. Whether a black prisoner was to be released was also in the hands of the trusty.

The End of Trusties

While Parchman prison is the most famous example of the trusty system, it was used in many states, including Arkansas, Alabama, New York, Texas, and Louisiana, until the 1970s. Arkansas's trusty system resulted in a national scandal when it was uncovered that endemic sexual assaults, electric torture, floggings, extortion, open sales of alcohol and drugs, and other crimes were being perpetrated by the "guards" of the prison: the armed trusty prisoners (Murton and Hyams 1969). This scandal even inspired the movie *Brubaker*, with Robert Redford.

In 1974, the decision in *Gates v. Collier* finally ended the trusty system. A group of Parchman residents had brought a class-action lawsuit against the state claiming that whites were the only employees at the prison; the majority of those who were armed were prisoners, not civilians; and very few civilians carried guns, making them dependent on the trusties. Charging that the trusty system deprived them of their constitutional rights, the lawsuit sought to end both the system of trusties and the racial segregation of prisoners.

As a result of *Gates*, rampant abuse in the trusty system was documented for the first time. Reports included physical violence, loan-sharking, and extortion. Black prisoners were routinely abused, physically assaulted, and tortured by trusties. Punishments were arbitrary and capricious. The Supreme Court found that trusties were "corrupt, venal, incompetent, and dangerous" and concluded that "the trusty system, which allows inmates to exercise unchecked authority over other inmates, is patently impermissible" (*Gates v. Collier* 1974). As a consequence of the *Gates* decision, the trusty system was replaced with civilian guards, and the final era of convict leasing ended. But this did not end wealth accumulation from punishment, as we saw earlier, and efforts to profit from the labor of prisoners continues today.

Beyond the Trusty System: Rehabilitation and Prison Conditions

Northern prisons embraced rehabilitation more readily than southern ones, and many did not depend on the trusty system explicitly. However, they still organized internal relations in ways that resembled the trusty system, with whites enjoying privileges and benefits denied to nonwhites, such as early release.

One of the tactics of rehabilitation was indeterminate sentencing. **Indeterminate sentencing** is an open-ended sentence, such as a sentence of "from one day to life" or for a range of one to ten years. This shifts discretion from the judge to the warden and the parole board, who determine whether someone is "rehabilitated" and can be released. Early release for "good behavior" was common during the rehabilitative era and had a long history, beginning in the penal

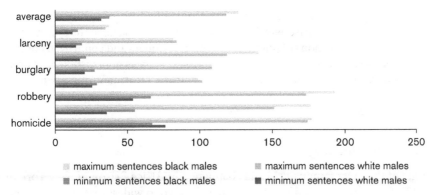

Figure 9.9 Indeterminate sentencing in months by race and charge, 1931. Source: Frederick J. Gaudet, George S. Harris, and Charles W. St. John, "Individual Differences in the Sentencing Tendencies of Judges," *Journal of Criminal Law and Criminology* 23, no. 5 (1933).

colonies of Australia in the 1800s (Shelden and Vasiliev 2018). Perhaps unsurprisingly, this discretion resulted in significant disparities in sentencing and a pattern of imprisonment that saw whites quickly "rehabilitated" while others languished behind bars year after year.

Indeterminate sentencing was long known to be racially discriminatory, even before its rampant use in the post-WWII era (see figure 9.9; Gaudet, Harris, and St. John 1933). In 1935, a researcher revealed that especially with indeterminate sentencing, black men received much longer sentences than either native-born or foreign-born whites for most categories and that "equality before the law is a social fiction" (Sellin 1935). About thirty years later, a 1962 study showed that state and federal sentences were affected by gender, with women receiving more lenient sentences for most crimes; class, with less-well-off people receiving harsher sentences; and race, with blacks receiving prison sentences much more often and longer than whites (Nagel 1969).

This widespread affirmation of the racial disparities shaping indeterminate sentencing, however, did not detail the effects on day-to-day life in prisons. Prisons during this period—even newly built correctional facilities—were brutal places. Black, Native American, and Latinx prisoners, in particular, suffered inhumane conditions because they were often segregated from white prisoners in substandard areas of the prison. Prisons were overcrowded, so nonwhites were often housed in spaces not meant for living, such as converted warehouses, barns, and other utility spaces. They were often denied food and access to clean water and were afforded little protection from high temperatures in the summer or freezing temperatures in the winter.

Prisons in the North mimicked the racial power structure of the trusty system in the South. Prisoners, particularly nonwhites, were frequently subject to violence, including frequent use of force, and some were killed by guards.

Violence against black prisoners at the hands of white prisoners was rarely punished, and white prisoners, like their trusty counterparts in the South, were often placed in positions of power above black prisoners and could even control their release dates in some cases. Medical treatment was nonexistent, and prisoners were subject to near starvation. The brutal treatment of nonwhites in U.S. prisons came to a head in the late 1960s and early 1970s as prisons around the nation were wracked by uprisings.

The Attica Uprising

One of the most famous uprisings happened in Attica Prison in New York in 1971. People imprisoned in Attica were subjected to widespread mistreatment (Wicker 1994; Thompson 2016). Conditions in Attica revealed a similar racial hierarchy to that in Parchman, though in Attica the white guards were civilians rather than prisoners. In a system that was over 60 percent black and Puerto Rican, all of the almost four hundred correctional officers were white (Thompson 2016). Officers were often openly racist and dubbed their batons "n*****r sticks." Prisoners lived in inhumane conditions: they were fed only once per day, they were forced to brave harsh winters without heat, and the guards were brutal. Further, any politicized prisoner often faced violent retaliation from prison guards. People who brought up issues of inhumane conditions or were radicalized often received the most intense punishments and were routinely denied parole.

Documents unsealed in 2015 reveal even more brutality (Thompson 2016). Prisoners were beaten as they lay on stretchers, suffered extensive injuries from grotesque sexual assaults, and were routinely burned with cigarettes. Medical indifference resulted in the deaths of prisoners and was so bad that one group of prison employees even considered taking private action against medical personnel employed by the prison. Violent, invasive strip searches led one prison guard to remark that he would have committed suicide if he had had to undergo it. "It wasn't that conditions in the Depression-era prison were, by prison standards, uniquely horrible," said one writer. "It was that they were *systematically* horrible; procedures designed to instill a minimal humanity had been allowed to degrade in ways that made every day a trial" (Gopnik 2016). Attica, like other prisons, was an institution oriented toward the systematic dehumanization of those imprisoned, just as convict leasing, slavery, and the trusty system accomplished.

In response to these conditions, mostly nonwhite prisoners organized the Attica Liberation Faction and prepared a manifesto calling for twenty-eight reforms, centered on improving the working and living conditions of those on the inside. Despite the humanitarian impulses of these demands, prisons officials responded by subjecting anyone found in possession of the manifesto to sixty days in solitary confinement. Life in Attica continued as before. Two months later, prisoners took a group of guards hostage. For four days, prison officials negotiated with prisoners. On the fourth day, prison officials dropped gas into the prisons, and guards stormed the prison, indiscriminately beating and killing prisoners. Even though the media reported that hostages had their throats slit by prisoners, no medical evidence was found and the testimony of guards contradicted those claims. In fact, one of the surviving guards testified that he would not have survived without the protection of prisoners, including when the guards led their assault on the prison.

Once that violence subsided, the ordinary organized violence and dehumanization of the prison resumed. Black and Puerto Rican prisoners were made to strip naked and crawl through mud under the oversight of white guards. Some were forced to run between guards who violently attacked them with batons as they ran. Beatings were commonplace after the riots. Ultimately, the violence of the uprising was quelled just as colonial uprisings had been—with the massive use of state violence, supported not just by New York State but by the FBI and President Nixon himself.

This *systematic* dehumanization is the hallmark of colonial administration degradation. Violence is normal and routine. Prisons during the rehabilitative era continued the brutal tactics of subjugation and expropriation of people's bodies that had long marked race relations in the United States. This subjugation, though, was not the primary mechanism of racial management. With the decline of rehabilitation, mass incarceration ascended, and it entrenched and expanded the systematic dehumanization of nonwhite prisoners.

MASS INCARCERATION AND THE TRANSFORMATION OF WHY WE PUNISH

The emergence of the prison as the primary institution for the systematic dehumanization of nonwhites in the United States also transformed the purpose of the prison. Under the Auburn, Pennsylvania, and rehabilitation prison models, prison was meant to transform white prisoners. As prison populations swelled in the 1980s and 1990s, the purpose of punishment was also transformed. And the racial constructions of criminality helped propel these ideas forward.

Racist Attitudes and Support for Punishment

Nowhere is the connection between racial attitudes and support for mass incarceration clearer than in studies of punitive attitudes about crime. The term **punitive** refers to the desire to increase the severity of prison sentences, including the death penalty and the idea that imprisonment is for punishment, not for enlightenment, reformation, or other seemingly benevolent intentions.

Surveys of white Americans show that those that hold racist beliefs—even if those beliefs are unconscious and unknown to the respondent—are more likely to support tough, punitive crime policies such as the death penalty (Green, Staerkle, and Sears 2006; Barkan and Cohn 1994). Respondents who believe racial differences stem from internal deficiencies in nonwhites, a logic reminiscent of scientific racists in the 1800s, are more likely to support harsh policies. Those who deny institutional discrimination are also more likely to oppose structural remedies to issues of poverty and racism. Whites who hold racial stereotypes are also more likely to support tough, punitive juvenile justice policies and favor transferring kids to the adult court (Pickett and Chiricos 2012).

When the term *inner-city* is used with a word like *crime* or *violence,* researchers find that racial attitudes also emerge (Hurwitz and Peffley 2005). When white respondents were asked whether they support money for prisons or antipoverty programs, researchers found that just adding the label *inner-city* to descriptions of crime made whites support prisons over antipoverty programs. Without that addition, whites' racial attitudes did not emerge, thus demonstrating the salience of racial code words in political discourse. It also demonstrates the importance of understanding how the geographies of race in metropolitan areas, as discussed in chapter 5, inform ideas about crime, morality, and deservingness.

Scholars have shown that those who hold politically conservative views, are Southern, and have higher-than-average rates of news-media consumption and those who are more concerned than average about crime typically support punitive policies and increasing sentences. Yet when crimes are "racially typified," or associated with racial code words, support for punitive policies expands across the board among whites (Chiricos, Welch, and Gertz 2004; Unnever and Cullen 2010). Support for punitive policies across the racial spectrum is also based on different experiences; whites who hold more racist ideologies and blacks who fear crime are both more supportive of punitive policies (Cohn, Barkan, and Halteman 1991; Welch and Payne 2010).

Without the common association between race and crime in the political lexicon (detailed in earlier chapters), political support for prison expansion and mass incarceration might not have happened. Support for the punitive policies characteristic of mass incarceration reveals not just a desire for increased punishment but also a transformation in why we punish. When the figure of the prison resident was a wayward white, the purpose of prison was salvation and reformation. As the political imagination of crime transformed and as crime became synonymous with "young black man" (Barlow 1998), the demographics of the prison population transformed and so did the purpose of prison.

Theorizing Mass Incarceration: Philosophies of Punishment

Four trends in practices of punishment reveal how systematic dehumanization is justified and rationalized through the social construction of criminality today. As a consequence of the turn to mass incarceration, systems around the nation ended nominally rehabilitative policies and turned to a new era in the practices of imprisonment: what is often called the warehousing era. **Warehousing** refers to the way that people in prison are often merely housed, with little purpose to their incarceration, and often in ways that are hardly different from the warehousing of consumer goods. These practices are supported by the convergence of incapacitation, deterrence, retribution, and managerial institutional philosophies that imagine the criminal much as we imagined the nonwhite racial other of the past—as inherently savage, predatory, and ultimately nonhuman.

Incapacitation, Deterrence, and Retribution

Incapacitation is the ultimate dehumanizing tactic of punishment, because it considers that people who commit crime need to be completely removed from society. Life sentences without parole, the death penalty, and civil confinement (incarceration *after* serving a criminal sentence) are all examples of incapacitation policies. Institutionally, this is best demonstrated in the surge of supermax prisons, in which people are kept in solitary confinement except for one hour a day. Prior to 1984, there was only one prison that qualified as supermax in the United States. By 1999, there were at least fifty-seven supermax facilities throughout the United States.

The era of mass incarceration saw incapacitation policies surge, something we discuss in chapter 10 in the case of the death penalty. The federal system abolished parole, defining a life sentence as someone's entire life (as opposed to twenty or twenty-five years, as it often was when someone was sentenced to life with the possibility of parole), and imposing life as the mandatory sentence for forty-five crimes, many related to drugs. The result? Over 40 percent of those incarcerated for life without parole in the federal system are there for drug crimes, and over 75 percent of those serving life sentences in the federal system are not white (see figure 9.10; Schmitt and Konfrst 2015).

Classical Enlightenment theories of deterrence were also reinvigorated by mass incarceration. Deterrence today is defined not as a rational penal system, as it was in the past, but rather through "swift and sure" punishment accomplished through determinate sentences. In contrast to indeterminate sentences, **determinate sentences** prescribe a fixed amount of time. Determinate sentences are represented by the slogan "you do the crime, you do the time." Typical deterrent policies include habitual offender statutes (like three-strikes laws), mandatory minimums (which prescribe mandatory sentences for convictions of particular crimes), and determinate sentencing guidelines (where offenses are assigned mandated sentencing ranges).

Mass incarceration is also marked by retributive justice, which subjects incarcerated people to public scorn and shame. The most famous example of

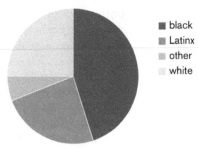

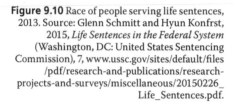

Figure 9.10 Race of people serving life sentences, 2013. Source: Glenn Schmitt and Hyun Konfrst, 2015, *Life Sentences in the Federal System* (Washington, DC: United States Sentencing Commission), 7, www.ussc.gov/sites/default/files /pdf/research-and-publications/research-projects-and-surveys/miscellaneous/20150226_ Life_Sentences.pdf.

retributive justice took place in Maricopa County, Arizona, where until 2016 now-former Sheriff Joe Arpaio forced incarcerated men to wear pink underwear and sleep outside in tents. The entire jail was a tent encampment, where even the most basic requirements of shelter—such as plumbing (prisoners used port-a-potties)—were denied (Jerreat 2014). The return of chain gangs briefly in the 1990s throughout the South and the replacement of meals with "foodstuff," such as manufactured loaves containing the daily minimum requirement of vitamins, minerals, and calories (Hallinan 2001), also reveal the retributive nature of punishment in the era of mass incarceration.

None of these trends were necessarily racialized because on their face, they could apply to anyone subject to imprisonment. Yet, the predominance of nonwhites in prison populations combined with the racialized construction of criminality emerging in political and media constructions since the 1960s suggest otherwise. It's telling that the shift toward policies and practices that look a lot like warehousing happened at the same time that the nation was redefining criminality and the racial composition of U.S. prisons.

The New Penology

As incapacitation, deterrence, and retributive policies reigned, a new theory of punishment was also emerging in prison systems, dominated by a managerial ethos. This was called the **new penology** (Feeley and Simon 1992). In the new-penology era, punishment is not about the individual convicted of crime but about maintaining control and eliminating risk. The primary role of punishment is "herding a specific population that cannot be disaggregated and transformed but only maintained—a kind of waste management" (1992, 470). The goal is to secure and neutralize threats, not to transform behavior. More simply, the aim is "cost-efficient warehousing" (Kempf-Leonard and Peterson 2000, 66). The new penology continues systematic dehumanization by failing to even consider those managed as human, and instead considers them as merely objects to be controlled.

Instead of retributive judgements or clinical diagnoses, new penology punishments emphasize the probability of particular strategies and risk assessments to guide institutional decisions. Corollaries of the science of risk management are insurance and actuarial practices. Efficient control of the system is the goal. Instead of targeting individuals or creating equity or proportionality amongst offenders (i.e., deterrence), the new penology targets offenders as aggregate or population groups: sex offenders, habitual criminals, drug dealers, and so on.

Under the new penology, the task is managerial, not transformative. It replaces a moral or clinical understanding of the person who commits crime with an actuarial understanding of probabilities and statistical distributions applied to populations. For example, California prisons today are differentiated largely by the level of security they maintain, and thus, who is housed in each facility is determined primarily by their "risk" status. Twenty years ago, in contrast, they were differentiated by specialized functions: California Rehabilitation Center, for drug users; California Medical Facility at Vacaville, for the mentally ill; Deuel Vocational Institute, for young adults. Today, these prisons have the same names, but they do not provide these specialized functions and instead are defined primarily by whether they are "minimum," "medium," or "maximum" security. A prisoner's risk level is often defined by the particular population grouping that he or she falls into, such as gang membership, type of crime, or length of stay in the system. In practice, however, these distinctions are often guided more by the availability of institutional beds than other factors.

The new penology also introduces new techniques of punishment, such as electronic monitoring instead of probationary or parole oversight. Probation and parole are now largely concerned with managing whether a client meets certain conditions, not with individual aspects that contribute to their well-being (Simon 1998). Risk management is also found in the emergence of sentencing grids and guidelines based on population risks, not on the individual. Greater use of drug testing than treatment emphasizes surveillance and control, rather than reformation and rehabilitation. Treatment, for instance, is often measured by attendance at a requisite number of meetings rather than by actual cessation of problem behavior. Prison guards are not "correctional officers," tasked with correcting behavior and part of rehabilitation; they now simply maintain control. The new penology systematically organizes dehumanization, seeing prisoners as little more than waste to be managed.

Together, the emergence of these philosophies of punishment reveal the deep entrenchment of colonial narratives in the modern prison system. Instead of the reformative attempts to include an incarcerated person within the political body, as problematic as that aim is, these seek to mark prisoners as different, as threats, as savage. Prisoners are solely objects to be managed, incapacitated, or warehoused. Crime is a "choice" committed by evil villains. They are violent savages, unconvinced by harsh deterrent punishments or retributive shame. They are the nonhumans of classical colonial discourse.

The deep racialization of this view of criminality and its dehumanizing consequences is demonstrated both by the punitive attitudes of whites discussed above and the racialized population of prison. It is further demonstrated through the management of race in prison today.

Managing Race in Prison

Prisons today are often characterized as "hotbeds of racial tension." TV shows about prisons like *Lockdown America* promote this image by focusing on notorious prison gangs that are often organized along racial lines. Images abound of heavily tattooed, sunglass-wearing inmates striking threatening poses. This vision is often called the "commonsense" image—or what we might call the hegemonic image, as discussed in chapters 2 and 4—of prison and its residents. As noted in previous chapters, what is often considered common sense is the reflection of the raced, classed, gendered, and sexual views of the dominant class. This commonsense vision does not just stay in the imagination, though; it shapes prison policies that have far-reaching impacts on the reproduction of racial lines both within and outside prison walls.

Ongoing Racial Segregation in Prisons

One of the most salient example of racial management strategies in prisons is the assigning of cellmates. The most important characteristic in many prisons is the race of the prisoner. Prisons were legally segregated until 1968 when the Supreme Court in *Lee v. Washington* struck down mandatory racial segregation in cellblocks. Despite this and other affirming rulings, many prisons continued to segregate on the basis of race as a form of managing gangs in prisons.

Formal policies of racial segregation are still enforced in prisons. Only recently has California begun to ease its formal policies of racial segregation, which forced someone who is a particular race (and in the case of Latinx prisoners, from particular geographical areas) to be housed with others of the same race. Some states even have yards separated by race. Race is determined by prison administrators, not by the individuals, and researchers have found that this segregation strengthens prison gangs based on race, rather than undermining their control (Goodman 2008; Skarbek 2014).

Even when racial segregation is not formal, prisons continue to be highly racially segregated, a division that is often supported, enforced, and practiced by prison administrators (Hallinan 2001; Skarbek 2014). Oftentimes, prison facilities such as weightlifting or television rooms and even particular outside seating areas are racially segregated. One racial group might dominate these places at a particular time, or if there are multiple areas, they are often informally assigned to a different racial group.

Arguments of prison administrators for racial segregation reveal how commonsense racism pervades accounts of prison life (Robertson 2005). Under *Johnson v. California* in 2005, federal authorities ordered California to integrate its cells. In this case, California argued that its use of racial segregation was constitutional in accordance with *Turner v. Safley* (1987), which allows prison guards to limit the constitutional rights of prisoners if it is "related to legitimate security interests." In defending the practice, the Ninth Circuit decision declared: "Given the admittedly high racial tensions and violence already existing within the CDC [California Department of Corrections], there is *clearly a commonsense connection* between the use of race as the predominant factor in assigning cellmates for 60 days until it is clear how the inmate will adjust to his new environment and reducing racial violence and maintaining a safer environment" (emphasis added).

Though the Supreme Court overturned the Ninth Circuit's decision, the commonsense representation of prisoners reinforces "a historic and widely shared stereotype: the black male as 'fearsome, threatening, unemployed, irresponsible, potentially dangerous and generally socially pathological'" (Robertson 2005, 821–22). No evidence was provided for California's claim that racial violence would result from integration. In fact, the experience of Oklahoma and Texas, which have integrated their prisons, suggests that violence actually *decreases* as a result of integration (Trulson and Marquart 2010). The Supreme Court used this evidence to rule against California, but this did little to quell the commonsense racialization of prisons in the law. Indeed, despite the Supreme Court's ruling, California prisons continued to be segregated as recently as 2016 (Raphael 2016).

Prison Violence and Gangs

According to this commonsense reasoning, prisoners are inherently violent, and racial segregation helps to control prison violence (Robertson 2005). Yet, this reflects a misunderstanding of the role of institutional structures in prison violence. First, some contend that prison gangs actually developed as the internal, private response to the state organization of systematic violence through the trusty system. While the trusties are not considered a "racial gang" by contemporary gang literature, these groups nevertheless were defined by race and organized violence and control, the same charge levied at prison gangs.

In California prisons, Robert Morrill, a former fifty-year career correctional officer wrote that the Mexican Mafia, "like all Security Threat Groups which formed afterward, initially started out as a self-protecting group. They wanted to survive in the prison environment and protect their private property from being taken" (quoted in Skarbek 2014, 52). Today, empirical studies of prison gangs and violence show that "gang members" and unaffiliated prisoners have the same likelihood of engaging in violence. Further, the length of gang membership is negatively correlated with violence, meaning the longer one is in a gang, the less likely one is to be involved in violent incidents (Gaes et al. 2002). Yet, this racialized image of people imprisoned as inherently violent is the one that underwrites the commonsense vision of prison conditions and the surge in punitive policies promoting incapacitation, retribution, and warehousing.

Further, there are many reports of prisons actually *fostering* prison violence and gangs. Until 1996, Corcoran, California, prison guards routinely pitted differing gang members against one another in gladiator-style fights. While this may seem an extreme example, it stemmed from racial governance rationalizations. A prisoner was paired with a member of a rival gang under an official policy of "integration." Implementation of the policy at Corcoran meant staging brawls between the pairs on what came to be called "gladiator days." Guards bet with each other, delayed fights to allow for the greatest attendance of other guards and secretaries, stuffed guards into control towers to watch the fight, and watched armed with gas guns and rifles, ready to shoot if anything went amiss. As one person involved in eleven such fights noted, "I was made aware by officers that there was money riding on me to win. . . . I was even thanked by officers for making them a bit richer" (Cornwell 1996). Fights served both to fulfill institutional integration demands and to provide evidence to be relayed back to prison administrators of why the policy of integration did not work.

Racial governance policies and practices reveal how the commonsense logics of race pervade our ideas about crime, violence, and prison. These contribute to prison environments that undermine and degrade the humanity of the inhabitants and re-create the conditions of coloniality through imprisonment. This experience, however, is not confined to imprisonment and affects people long after they leave the prisons walls.

DEHUMANIZATION BEYOND IMPRISONMENT

Imprisonment marks people, and practices of dehumanization extend beyond the prison walls. Those convicted of crimes are reminded of this each time they attempt to reintegrate back into "civilization." They are systematically denied their humanity when applying for jobs and attempting to vote, practices that affect a much larger number of people than just those incarcerated.

Imprisonment as "Civil Death"

Imprisonment today imparts the status of civil death. The idea of **civil death** comes from medieval Europe, where one who committed a crime was stripped of citizenship and the rights and protections that went along with it. Those who experienced civil death could be killed with impunity. Enslaved black people and Native Americans, among others, were essentially civically dead; they were often killed with impunity, defined as three-fifths of a human being, unable to vote or participate in civic life, and seen merely as property to be exploited.

Today, civil death continues through punishments that continue long after one has left the prison. For instance, a felony conviction in some states is grounds for "at-fault" divorce. Contractual rights can be terminated, as can the right to hold public office. Felons are often restricted from firearm ownership, thus permanently denied Second Amendment rights. Felons can be denied educational loans, public housing, and federal assistance. Noncitizens can be deported.

Imprisoned people can even lose their parental rights and access to their children simply because they are locked up. In California, if no one steps in to care for a child after eighteen months, the child is officially removed from the parent's custody and put up for adoption. In some states, felony conviction can be used in child custody hearings as a basis for denying custody rights (Travis 2005). As a result, a disproportionate number of black and Latina women have had their parental rights terminated, a precedent first established in the mass removal of Native American children from their families (Roberts 2012).

Modern civil death happens through two key mechanisms: the denial of employment to prisoners and the denial of their civic rights of representation. Through these two means, imprisonment accords a nonhuman status on prisoners, a status they can carry throughout their entire lives. Dehumanization thus is not limited to the space of the prison but affects even people who have officially served their time.

Work and Felony Convictions

Employment difficulties following conviction reveal deep racialized conceptions of criminality and the connection between racial dehumanization and imprisonment. Often, we think of the challenge former inmates face in finding a job as due solely to their criminal record. Indeed, by some estimates only one in nineteen people who have been to prison will find stable, full-time employment (Mauer 2006). Other estimates suggest that over 75 percent will not even be able to secure transitional employment. Yet, Devah Pager (2008) found that while the mark of a criminal record certainly reduces opportunities for employment, race is even more consequential.

Pager's study consisted of fabricating résumés and using them to apply for jobs in the greater Chicago area, sometimes delivered in person by college students playing the part. Pager varied the race of applicant and the criminal history revealed on the résumé. The results were striking. As figure 9.11 shows, Pager found that whites with a criminal record were more likely to get called back to an interview than blacks without one.

Even without a criminal record, black applicants faced more discrimination than the white "criminals," revealing how important race is to understanding

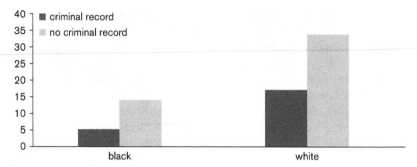

Figure 9.11 Percent of applicants called back, by race and criminal record. Source: Devah Pager, 2008, *Marked: Race, Crime, and Finding Work in an Era of Mass Incarceration* (Chicago: University of Chicago Press), 91.

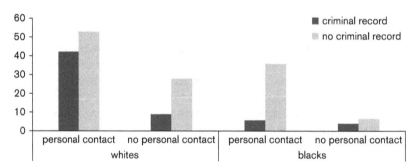

Figure 9.12 Percent of applicants called back, contact versus no contact. Source: Devah Pager, 2008, *Marked: Race, Crime, and Finding Work in an Era of Mass Incarceration* (Chicago: University of Chicago Press), 104–5.

the experience and life course impacts of incarceration. Suburban employers and restaurant owners were particularly reluctant to hire black applicants, and black people with a criminal record were almost entirely excluded from employment in suburban areas—especially consequential given the discussion of spatial mismatch in chapter 7 and how suburban areas outpaced cities in job growth from the 1970s until 2011. Personal contact—that is, an in-person application rather than one submitted online or by mail—mitigated some of the effect of a criminal record for whites, but it had no such effect for blacks, who were less likely to be called back than even whites with a criminal record and no personal contact (see figure 9.12). The clear message? Incarceration hurts employment, but race hurts more.

As with earlier eras of racial management, the reduced employability of ex-prisoners of color is yet one more way that the capitalist system benefits from the exploitation of nonwhites. Ex-prisoners form a disposable labor force, but they also provide downward pressure on wages by creating a class of workers with permanently precarious employment. In the current "flexible economy," where technology facilitates hiring people at low wages to do the work that used to be done by the dwindling middle and professional class, the dual strike against ex-prisoners of color results in a permanent unemployable economic class, a considerable mark of the nonhuman in a capitalist democracy like the United States.

Felon Disenfranchisement

A felony conviction can also lead to permanent civil death, as it does in the case of felon disenfranchisement. **Felon disenfranchisement** is the denial of political rights, including voting, to those convicted of felonies (Manza and Uggen 2008; see further box 9.2). Those who experience it are subject to the rules, regulations, and taxes of citizenship but do not receive the right of participation. Felon disenfranchisement has a long history, but in the United States it was first used vigorously toward the end of the nineteenth century, particularly in Southern states (Behrens, Uggen, and Manza 2003).

During Reconstruction, Southern states' "race-neutral" voting bans for convicts included laws only enforced against blacks. For example, South Carolina disenfranchised those convicted of thievery, adultery, arson, wife beating, house breaking, and attempted rape—crimes only blacks were charged with—but not murder and fighting. Alabama disenfranchised those who committed crimes of "moral turpitude." Felon disenfranchisement laws have also increased in direct response to advances in racial justice (Behrens, Uggen, and Manza 2003).

Today, over 6.1 million citizens are disenfranchised due to criminal convictions. Of these, 3.9 million are out on probation, parole, or otherwise released from the system but still do not have the ability to vote. Felon disenfranchisement considerably decreases the political power of nonwhite communities. Currently, 13 percent of all black males have lost the right to vote due to felony convictions, despite the fact that 74 percent of those disenfranchised are currently working, paying taxes, and sending kids to school (Manza and Uggen 2008). In two states, one in three black men are disenfranchised, and in eight states, it is one in four. If current trends continue, 40 percent of black men will be disenfranchised in states that permit disenfranchisement. This is over five times the rate of disenfranchisement of non–African Americans. And the number of people disenfranchised has increased considerably as a consequence of mass incarceration, starting in the 1990s (see figure 9.13). Thus, any gains in voting power gained by nonwhite communities as a consequence of the Voting Rights Act have been undone by incarceration (Uggen, Shannon, and Manza 2012).

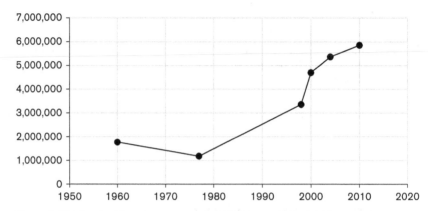

Figure 9.13 Felon disenfranchisement, 1960–2010. Source: Christopher Uggen, Sharon Shannon and Jeff Manza, *State-Level Estimates of Felon Disenfranchisement in the United States, 2010* (Washington, DC: Sentencing Project, 2012), 9, figure 5, https://felonvoting. procon.org/sourcefiles/2010_State_Level_Estimates_of_Felon_Disenfranchisement.pdf.

Felon disenfranchisement varies by state, and some states, like Virginia and Kentucky, bar felons from voting for life. States that do allow felons to regain the right to vote tend to make it difficult to do so. In eight states, a pardon or governor's order is required, and the federal government requires those convicted of federal offenses who are denied the right to vote by state law to obtain a presidential pardon. In two states, the parole or pardons board must act to restore one's rights. Local election officials are also often misinformed about the right to vote among felons, with many insisting upon documents that are not legally required to vote and often do not even exist (ACLU 2006). In effect, once barred from voting, one is not likely ever to restore one's rights.

Felon disenfranchisement also systematically works to decrease the political power of entire communities. One researcher found that neighborhoods with increased rates of incarceration also have lower rates of voter registration among all members of the community, not just those who have been incarcerated (Miles 2004). Researchers also note that this has changed the results of elections, including at least seven U.S. Senate races since 1970 (Manza and Uggen 2008). In each of these cases, had people who served time and were no longer under criminal justice supervision been allowed to vote, the election would have gone the other way. If we included disenfranchised felons on probation and parole, this number would increase considerably.

The 2000 presidential election, in which George W. Bush ultimately defeated Al Gore, hinged on just 537 votes in Florida. If felons who were no longer under supervision had been allowed to vote in Florida, it is estimated that Gore would have beaten Bush by over 30,000 votes (Uggen and Manza 2008). Even further, that election was affected by the stereotypes about race and crime, because

BOX 9.2   Felon Disenfranchisement and the Right to Vote

Arguments against enfranchising those convicted of felonies are often premised on the idea that they will use their voting rights for criminal purposes, such as voting against important crime-control measures. But this actually contradicts the reality of political opinions among those who are or have been incarcerated, which often support harsher penalties for criminal behavior (Manza and Uggen 2008).

Further, many people convicted of felonies say that civic reintegration is key to their rehabilitation and note that losing the right to vote makes them feel as if they are in exile and have no voice in the political process. Preliminary studies of felon disenfranchisement also suggest that those who have voting rights restored upon release are less likely to engage in crime than those who don't (Hamilton-Smith and Vogel 2012).

Today, only two states—Maine and Vermont—allow people currently incarcerated to vote. Why do you think the denial of the right to vote is so widespread? Should people in prison be given the right to vote?

Sources: G. P. Hamilton-Smith and M. Vogel, 2012, "The Violence of Voicelessness: The Impact of Felony Disenfranchisement on Recidivism," *Berkeley La Raza Law Journal* 22: 407; J. Manza and C. Uggen, *Locked Out: Felon Disenfranchisement and American Democracy* (New York: Oxford University Press, 2008).

many African Americans were incorrectly included on lists of those who lost the right to vote even though they had not been convicted of felonies. These were people who had never even been in the criminal justice system! If just their votes had been allowed to be cast, Gore likely would have won.

This disenfranchisement also happened only in African American communities. Manza and Uggen (2008) note that the percentage of black people in a county was the most important predictor of ballot rejection rate. The more African Americans in a county, the more ballots were rejected. Latinxs offer an important insight into this process. If this phenomenon were a consequence of lack of education or poverty, we might expect other similarly positioned groups to experience the same rate of ballot rejection. Yet, ballot rejection rates were actually lower in heavily Latinx counties than in non-Latinx counties. This shows how ideas about race and crime combine to limit the political participation not only of felons but of the black community all together.

CONCLUSION

Prison, while seen as a punishment for a particular crime, is today much more than that. Contemporary punishments are emblematic of the way that we continue to focus on the body as a locus of punishment, especially for communities of color, and serve as a critical source of profit for the prison-industrial complex. Punishment continues to be harsh, violent, and brutal, even as it is philosophically considered to be fulfilling other roles.

Prison also continues to be a key site for the production of knowledge about race. This knowledge is revealed within punitive attitudes, popular conceptions of prisons, imprisonment philosophies, and even prison administration. This knowledge is premised on the colonial logic of race that some people are too dangerous and uncivilized—or, to use historical words, bestial and savage—to exist, even after release, as full equals within society. This knowledge, however, is not about whether someone is actually a criminal or a felon, as we see in the case of employment, but rather about how being black, Latinx, or Native American becomes shorthand for this dehumanizing logic. Through racialized mass incarceration, the prison becomes the place organizing and producing the margins of the colonial state.

This reality—like slavery and other colonial management strategies—continues the tradition of appropriating the lives, resources, and bodies of communities of color. Prisons secure profits and economic viability for many in the United States. Without the prison-industrial complex, the nation would face a severe economic crisis in many communities and corporations. While labor may not always be forced in prisons, slavery remains a common punishment throughout the nation. When Michelle Alexander (2012) calls mass incarceration "the new Jim Crow" or political commentators call the prison "neo-slavery," this is not hyperbolic rhetoric but a description of the structural context of race, crime, and imprisonment in the United States today. In the next chapter, we consider more closely how the nonwhite racialized body is appropriated by the ultimate power of the state: to put someone to death.

REFERENCES

ACLU (American Civil Liberties Union). 2006. *Out of Step with the World: An Analysis of Felony Disenfranchisement in the U.S. and Other Democracies*. www.aclu.org/images/asset_upload_file825_25663.pdf.

Adamson, Christopher R. 1983. "Punishment after Slavery: Southern State Penal Systems, 1865–1890." *Social Problems* 30, no. 5: 555–69.

Alexander, Michelle. 2012. *The New Jim Crow: Mass Incarceration in the Age of Colorblindness*. New York: New Press.

Ayers, Edward L. 1984. *Vengeance and Justice: Crime and Punishment in the 19th Century American South*. New York: Oxford University Press.

Barkan, Steven E., and Steven F. Cohn. 1994. "Racial Prejudice and Support for the Death Penalty by Whites." *Journal of Research in Crime and Delinquency* 31, no. 2: 202–9.

Barlow, Melissa Hickman. 1998. "Race and the Problem of Crime in *Time* and *Newsweek* Cover Stories, 1946 to 1995." *Social Justice* 25, no. 2 (Summer): 149–83.

Beccaria, Cesare. (1764) 2008. *On Crimes and Punishments and Other Writings*. Edited by Aaron Thomas. Reprint, Toronto: University of Toronto Press.

Beckett, Katherine. 1999. *Making Crime Pay: Law and Order in Contemporary American Politics*. New York: Oxford University Press.

Behrens, Angela, Christopher Uggen, and Jeff Manza. 2003. "Ballot Manipulation and the 'Menace of Negro Domination': Racial Threat and Felon Disenfranchisement in the United States, 1850–2002." *American Journal of Sociology* 109, no. 3: 559–605.

Blackmon, Douglas A. 2009. *Slavery by Another Name: The Re-enslavement of Black Americans from the Civil War to World War II.* New York: Anchor.

Bonds, Anne. 2013. "Economic Development, Racialization, and Privilege: 'Yes in My Backyard,' Prison Politics, and the Reinvention of Madras, Oregon." *Annals of the Association of American Geographers* 103, no. 6: 1389–1405.

Chiricos, Ted, Kelly Welch, and Marc Gertz. 2004. "Racial Typification of Crime and Support for Punitive Measures." *Criminology* 42, no. 2: 358–90.

Clear, Todd R. 1996. "Backfire: When Incarceration Increases Crime." *Journal of the Oklahoma Criminal Justice Research Consortium* 3, 7–8.

Cohen, Michael. 2015. "How For-Profit Prisons Have Become the Biggest Lobby No One Is Talking About." *Washington Post,* April 28, 2015. www.washingtonpost.com/posteverything/wp/2015/04/28/how-for-profit-prisons-have-become-the-biggest-lobby-no-one-is-talking-about/?utm_term=.5497feb8c00f.

Cohn, Steven F., Steven E. Barkan, and William A. Halteman. 1991. "Punitive Attitudes toward Criminals: Racial Consensus or Racial Conflict?" *Social Problems* 38, no. 2: 287–96.

Cooper, Michael, L. 1999. *Indian School: Teaching the White Man's Way.* Wilmington, MA: Clarion Books, Houghton Mifflin.

Cornwell, Tim. 1996. "Staged Fights, Betting Guards, Gunfire and Death for the Gladiators." *The Independent,* Los Angeles. www.independent.co.uk/news/world/staged-fights-betting-guards-gunfire-and-death-for-the-gladiators-1310849.html.

Curry, Colleen. 2015. "Whole Foods, Expensive Cheese, and the Dilemma of Cheap Prison Labor." *Vice News,* July 21, 2015. https://news.vice.com/article/whole-foods-expensive-cheese-and-the-dilemma-of-cheap-prison-labor.

Davis, Angela Y. 1998a. "From the Prison of Slavery to the Slavery of Prison: Frederick Douglass and the Convict Lease System." In *The Angela Y. Davis Reader,* 74–95. Cambridge, MA: Blackwell.

———. 1998b. "Masked Racism: Reflections on the Prison Industrial Complex." *Color Lines 1,* no. 2: 11–13.

Dimitri, Carolyn, Anne B. Effland, and Neilson C. Conklin. 2005. *The 20th Century Transformation of U.S. Agriculture and Farm Policy.* Vol. 3. Washington, DC: US Department of Agriculture, Economic Research Service.

Dyer, Joel. 2000. *Perpetual Prisoner Machine: How America Profits from Crime.* New York: Basic Books

Eames, Sandra, Victoria Terranova, and David Kirk. 2014. *Austin/Travis County Reentry Report Card.* Austin /Travis County Reentry Roundtable. www.reentryroundtable.net/wp-content/uploads/2014/08 /ATCRRT-report-card-revised-Sept14-Final.pdf.

Feeley, Malcolm M., and Jonathan Simon. 1992. "The New Penology: Notes on the Emerging Strategy of Corrections and Its Implications." *Criminology 30,* no. 4: 449–74.

Gaudet, Frederick J., George S. Harris, and Charles W. St. John. 1933. "Individual Differences in the Sentencing Tendencies of Judges." *Journal of Criminal Law and Criminology (1931–1951)* 23, no. 5: 811–18.

Gaes, Gerald G., Susan Wallace, Evan Gilman, Jody Klein-Saffran, and Sharon Suppa. 2002. "The Influence of Prison Gang Affiliation on Violence and Other Prison Misconduct." *Prison Journal* 82, no. 3: 359–85.

Gilmore, Ruth Wilson 2002. "Fatal Couplings of Power and Difference: Notes on Racism and Geography." *Professional Geographer* 54, no. 1: 15–24.

———. 2007. *Golden Gulag: Prisons, Surplus, Crisis, and Opposition In Globalizing California.* Berkeley: University of California Press.

Glasmeier, Amy K., and Tracey Farrigan. 2007. "The Economic Impacts of the Prison Development Boom on Persistently Poor Rural Places." *International Regional Science Review* 30, no. 3: 274–99.

Goldberg, David T. 2002. *The Racial State.* Malden, MA: Blackwell.

Goodman, Philip. 2008. "'It's Just Black, White, or Hispanic': An Observational Study of Racializing Moves in California's Segregated Prison Reception Centers." *Law and Society Review* 42, no. 4: 735–70.

Gopnik, Adam. 2016. "Learning from the Slaughter in Attica." *New Yorker,* August 29, 2016. www.newyorker .com/magazine/2016/08/29/learning-from-the-slaughter-in-attica.

Green, Edward. 1964. "Inter-and Intra-Racial Crime Relative to Sentencing." *Journal of Criminal Law, Criminology, and Police Science* 55, no. 3: 348–58.

Green, Eva G., Christian Staerkle, and David O. Sears. 2006. "Symbolic Racism and Whites' Attitudes towards Punitive and Preventive Crime Policies." *Law and Human Behavior* 30, no. 4: 435–54.

Gross, Samuel, Maurice Possley, and Klara Stephens. 2017. *Race and Wrongful Convictions in the United States.* Irvine, CA: National Registry of Exonerations, Newkirk Center for Science and Society. www.law .umich.edu/special/exoneration/documents/race_and_wrongful_convictions.pdf.

Halfacree, K. H. 1993. "Locality and Social Representation: Space, Discourse and Alternative Definitions of the Rural." *Journal of Rural Studies* 9, no. 1: 23–37.

Hallett, Michael A. 2006. *Private Prisons in America: A Critical Race Perspective.* Urbana: University of Illinois Press.

Hallinan, Joseph T. 2001. *Going Up the River: Travels in a Prison Nation.* New York: Random House.

Hamilton-Smith, Guy P., and Vogel, Matt. 2012. "The Violence of Voicelessness: The Impact of Felony Disenfranchisement on Recidivism." *Berkeley La Raza Law Journal* 22: 407.

Holloran, Peter C. 1989. *Boston's Wayward Children: Social Services for Homeless Children, 1830–1930.* Madison, NJ: Fairleigh Dickinson University Press.

Hoxie, Frederick E. 1979. "From Prison to Homeland: The Cheyenne River Indian Reservation before WWI." *South Dakota History* 10: 1–24.

Huling, Tracy. 2002. "Building a Prison Economy in Rural America." In *Invisible Punishment: The Collateral Consequences of Mass Imprisonment,* edited by Marc Mauer and Meda Chesney-Lind, 197–213. New York: New Press.

Hurwitz, Jon, and Mark Peffley. 2005. "Playing the Race Card in the Post–Willie Horton Era: The Impact of Racialized Code Words on Support for Punitive Crime Policy." *Public Opinion Quarterly* 69, no. 1: 99–112.

Jackson, Jerome E., and Sue Ammen. 1996. "Race and Correctional Officers' Punitive Attitudes toward Treatment Programs for Inmates." *Journal of Criminal Justice* 24, no. 2: 153–66.

James, Joy. 1996. *Resisting State Violence: Radicalism, Gender, and Race in U.S. Culture.* Minneapolis: University of Minnesota Press.

Jerreat, Jessica. 2014. "'It Looks Like 21st Century Slavery': Photographer's Images of Arizona's Chain Gangs Evoke a Dark Period in the Country's History." *Daily Mail,* January 29, 2014. www.dailymail.co.uk/news/article-2547778/images-arizona-chain-gang-evoke-dark-history-slavery.html#ixzz4qzxaz6vn.

Journal of the House of Delegates of the Commonwealth of Virginia. 1822. Richmond, VA: Thomas Ritchie, Printer for the Commonwealth. https://catalog.hathitrust.org/Record/100743895.

Justicemapping.org. 2018. Projects: New York City and Wichita, Kansas. www.justicemapping.org/technical-assistance-gallery.

Kempf-Leonard, Kimberly, and Elicka S. L. Peterson. 2000. "Expanding Realms of the New Penology: The Advent of Actuarial Justice for Juveniles." *Punishment and Society* 2, no. 1: 66–97.

Lavarreda, Elena, Peter Wagner, and Rose Heyer. 2009. *Importing Constituents: Prisoners and Political Clout in Massachusetts.* Prison Gerrymandering Project. October 6, 2009. Easthampton, MA: Prison Policy Initiative. www.prisonersofthecensus.org/ma/report.html.

Lawson, Vicky, Lucy Jarosz, and Anne Bonds. 2010. "Articulations of Place, Poverty, and Race: Dumping Grounds and Unseen Grounds in the Rural American Northwest." *Annals of the Association of American Geographers* 100, no. 3: 655–77.

Lichtenstein, Alex. 1993. "Good Roads and Chain Gangs in the Progressive South: 'The Negro Convict Is a Slave.'" *Journal of Southern History* 59, no. 1: 85–110.

———. 1996. *Twice the Work of Free Labor: The Political Economy of Convict Labor in the New South.* London: Verso.

———. 2001. "The Private and the Public in Penal History: A Commentary on Zimring and Tonry." *Punishment and Society* 3, no. 1: 189–96.

Lotke, Eric, and Peter Wagner. 2003. "Prisoners of the Census: Electoral and Financial Consequences of Counting Prisoners Where They Go, Not Where They Come From." *Pace Law Review* 24: 587.

Mancini, Matthew J. 1996. *One Dies, Get Another: Convict Leasing in the American South, 1866–1928.* Columbia: University of South Carolina Press.

Manza, Jeff, and Christopher Uggen. 2008. *Locked Out: Felon Disenfranchisement and American Democracy.* New York: Oxford University Press.

Mauer, Marc. 2006. *Race to incarcerate.* New York: The New Press.

———. 2011. "Addressing Racial Disparities in Incarceration." *Prison Journal* 91, no. 3 (Suppl.): 87S–101S.

Miles, Thomas J. 2004. "Felon Disenfranchisement and Voter Turnout." *Journal of Legal Studies* 33, no. 1: 85–129.

Murton, Tom, and Joe Hyams. 1969. *Accomplices to the Crime: The Arkansas Prison Scandal.* New York: Grove Press.

Myser, Michael. 2007. "The Hard Sell: The Nation's 2 Million Inmates and Their Keepers Are the Ultimate Captive Market: A $37 Billion Economy Bulging with Business Opportunity." *CNN Money Business 2.0 Magazine,* March 15, 2007. http://money.cnn.com/magazines/business2/business2_archive/2006/12/01/8394995/index.htm.

Nagel, Stuart S. 1969. *The Legal Process from a Behavioral Perspective.* Homewood, IL: Dorsey Press.

National Association for the Advancement of Colored People (NAACP). 2011. *Misplaced Priorities: Over Incarcerate, Under Educate.* https://naacp.3cdn.net/01d6f368edbe135234_bq0m68x5h.pdf.

New York Times. 1911. "Convicts Who Are in Demand after Serving Terms: Mississippi Trains Negro Criminals to Be Such Good Farmers That They Quickly Secure Places—Penitentiary Farm Pays and Makes Money." June 4, 1911. www.nytimes.com/1911/06/04/archives/article-14-no-title.html.

Olson, Jeremiah C. 2016. "Race and Punishment in American Prisons." *Journal of Public Administration Research and Theory* 26, no. 4: 758–68.

Oshinsky, David M. 1997. *"Worse Than Slavery": Parchman Farm and the Ordeal of Jim Crow Justice.* New York: Simon & Schuster.

Swavola, Elizabeth, Kristine Riley, and Ram Subramanian. 2016. *Overlooked: Women and Jails in an Era of Reform.* New York: Vera Institute of Justice. www.vera.org/publications/overlooked-women-and-jails-report.

Page, Joshua. 2011. *The Toughest Beat: Politics, Punishment, and the Prison Officers Union in California.* New York: Oxford University Press.

Pager, Devah. 2008. *Marked: Race, Crime, and Finding Work in an Era of Mass Incarceration.* Chicago: University of Chicago Press.

Papachristos, Andrew V., Tracey L. Meares, and Jeffrey Fagan. 2007. "Attention Felons: Evaluating Project Safe Neighborhoods in Chicago." *Journal of Empirical Legal Studies* 4, no. 2: 223–72.

Pettit, Becky, and Bruce Western. 2004. "Mass Imprisonment and the Life Course: Race and Class Inequality in US Incarceration." *American Sociological Review* 69, no. 2: 151–69.

Pickett, Justin T., and Ted Chiricos. 2012. "Controlling Other People's Children: Racialized Views of Delinquency and Whites' Punitive Attitudes toward Juvenile Offenders." *Criminology* 50, no. 3: 673–710.

"Intrastate Collect Prison Phone Rates." Prison Phone Justice, Human Rights Defense Center. Accessed June 16, 2017. www.prisonphonejustice.org/.

Rafter, Nicole H. 1990. *Partial Justice: Women, Prisons, and Social Control.* Piscataway, NJ: Transaction Publishers.

Raphael, T. J. 2016. "California Prisons Struggle to Adapt to Desegregation." *The Takeaway.* April 27, 2016. PRI. www.pri.org/stories/california-prisons-struggle-adapt-desegregation.

Roberts, Dorothy E. 2004. The Social and Moral Cost of Mass Incarceration in African American Communities. *Stanford Law Review* 56, no. 5, 1271–1305.

———. 2012. "Prison, Foster Care, and the Systemic Punishment of Black Mothers." *UCLA Law Review* 59: 1474–1500. www.uclalawreview.org/pdf/59-6-2.pdf.

Robertson, James E. 2005. "Foreword: Separate But Equal in Prison: Johnson v. California and Common Sense Racism." *Journal of Criminal Law and Criminology* 96: 795.

Rizer, Arthur L., III. 2003. "The Race Effect on Wrongful Convictions." *William Mitchell Law Review* 29, no. 3, art. 5. http://open.mitchellhamline.edu/wmlr/vol29/iss3/5.

Sampson, Robert J. 2012. *Great American City: Chicago and the Enduring Neighborhood Effect.* Chicago: University of Chicago Press.

Schmitt, Glenn, and Hyun Konfrst. 2015. *Life Sentences in the Federal System.* Washington, DC: United States Sentencing Commission. www.ussc.gov/sites/default/files/pdf/research-and-publications/research-projects-and-surveys/miscellaneous/20150226_Life_Sentences.pdf.

Segal, David. 2015. "Prison Vendors See Continued Signs of a Captive Market." *New York Times,* August 29, 2015. www.nytimes.com/2015/08/30/business/prison-vendors-see-continued-signs-of-a-captive-market.html.

Sellin, Thorsten. 1935. "Race Prejudice in the Administration of Justice." *American Journal of Sociology* 41, no. 2: 212–17.

Shelden, Randall G. 2010. *Our Punitive Society.* Long Grove, IL: Waveland Press.

Shelden, Randall G., and Pavel Vasiliev. 2018. *Controlling the Dangerous Classes.* 3rd ed. Long Grove, IL: Waveland Press.

Simon, Jonathan. 1998. "Managing the Monstrous: Sex Offenders and the New Penology." *Psychology, Public Policy, and Law* 4, no. 1–2: 452.

Skarbek, David. 2014. *The Social Order of the Underworld: How Prison Gangs Govern the American Penal System.* New York: Oxford University Press.

Southern Poverty Law Center. 2000. "Allegations of Racist Guards Are Plaguing the Corrections Industry." *Intelligence Report,* December 2000. www.splcenter.org/fighting-hate/intelligence-report/2000/allegations-racist-guards-are-plaguing-corrections-industry.

Thompson, Heather A. 2016. *Blood in the Water: The Attica Prison Uprising of 1971 and Its Legacy.* New York: Pantheon.

Travis, Jeremy. 2005. *But They All Come Back: Facing the Challenges of Prisoner Reentry.* Washington, DC: Urban Institute.

Trulson, Chad R., and James W. Marquart. 2010. *First Available Cell: Desegregation of the Texas Prison System.* Austin: University of Texas Press.

Uggen, Christopher, Sarah Shannon, and Jeff Manza. 2012. *State-Level Estimates of Felon Disenfranchisement in the United States, 2010.* Washington DC: Sentencing Project. 2012. https://felonvoting.procon.org/sourcefiles/2010_state_level_estimates_of_felon_disenfranchisement.pdf.

Unnever, James D., and Francis T. Cullen. 2010. "The Social Sources of Americans' Punitiveness: A Test of Three Competing Models." *Criminology* 48, no. 1: 99–129.

Wacquant, Loic. 2000. "The New 'Peculiar Institution': On the Prison as Surrogate Ghetto." *Theoretical Criminology* 4, no. 3: 377–89.

———. 2001. "Deadly Symbiosis: When Ghetto and Prison Meet and Mesh." *Punishment and Society* 3, no. 1: 95–133.

Welch, Kelly, and Allison Ann Payne. 2010. "Racial Threat and Punitive School Discipline." *Social Problems* 57, no. 1: 25–48.

White, Martha. 2015. "Locked-In Profits: The U.S. Prison Industry, by the Numbers." *NBC News.* November 2, 2015. www.nbcnews.com/business/business-news/locked-profits-u-s-prison-industry-numbers-n455976.

Winter, Caroline. 2008. "What Do Prisoners Make for Victoria's Secret?" *Mother Jones*, July/August 2008. www.motherjones.com/politics/2008/07/what-do-prisoners-make-victorias-secret/.

Wicker, Tom. 1994. *A Time to Die: The Attica Prison Revolt*. Lincoln: University of Nebraska Press.

Wines, Frederick H., and Winthrop D. Lane. 1910. *Punishment and Reformation; A Study of the Penitentiary System*. Rev. ed. New York: Thomas Y. Crowell. https://catalog.hathitrust.org/Record/001135391.

Workers World. 1993. "AT&T Exploits Prison Labor." *Prison Legal News*, uploaded April 15, 1993, 8. www.prisonlegalnews.org/news/1993/apr/15/att-exploits-prison-labor/.

"Race to Execution": Lynching, Mass Incarceration, and the Resurgence of the Death Penalty

LEARNING OUTCOMES

▶ Explain the racialized application of the death penalty.

▶ Summarize how the death penalty continues the practices of racial oppression associated with lynching and colonial era slavery relations.

▶ Illustrate how racial disparities are produced through geography and race.

▶ Describe the roles that key court actors play in facilitating racial disproportionalities in the use of the death penalty.

KEY TERMS

▶ aggravating factors
▶ mitigating factors
▶ lynching
▶ death-qualified jury
▶ wrongful convictions
▶ Fourteenth Amendment
▶ *McCleskey v. Kemp*
▶ Baldus study

The United States is alone among industrialized nations in continuing to use the death penalty, and it does so in a racially capricious manner. This latter fact—that has been true since the inception of the United States—is confirmed by over 90 percent of research on the death penalty. The death penalty is also the most brute example of why, today, the criminal legal system is integral to the perpetuation of coloniality in the United States.

Death is the ultimate dehumanization. It literally extinguishes someone's very humanness. Dehumanization is supposed to be used sparingly by a democratic state, as the result of a series of disinterested administrative and bureaucratic procedures. It is to be used only in the last resort and with great regard for its awesome violence.

Yet, the history of the death penalty reveals something very different and suggests that its application is not objective, considered, or disinterested. Instead, it has been a tactic critical to racial governance, something recognized in the post-WWII era as the death penalty moved toward a considered reduction in usage. With the advent of mass incarceration, however, the use of the death penalty resurged, as did its racially capricious application. This chapter considers death's role in racial governance both historically and today.

THE RESURGENCE OF THE DEATH PENALTY

Today, there are over three thousand people on death row, and as figure 10.1 demonstrates, the number of people sentenced to death has risen alongside the imprisonment boom in the United States. Since the reinstitution of the death penalty in 1976, there have been 1,460 executions (see figure 10.2). With the advent of mass incarceration, the use of the death penalty embarked on a steady upward climb, only slowed by the difficulties states faced in securing execution drugs in the early 2000s. The death penalty is not a historical relic, but a tool and technique of modern governance.

One of the most significant hallmarks of mass incarceration is in fact the resurgence of the death penalty. Not only have we become more punitive, but at the height of the imprisonment boom, we also became more and more willing to sentence people to death. Indeed, facing the charge that Democrats were not tough on crime (a charge that doomed the previous candidate), Bill Clinton left the campaign trail in 1992 to go back to Arkansas, where he was governor, to oversee (and widely publicize) the execution of a man with an IQ less than 70 (Beckett and Sasson 2003). Today, executing someone with an IQ that low is unconstitutional, yet its widespread, racially capricious application is constitutionally allowed to continue.

Electorates also continue to be committed to the death penalty, and the most recent Gallup poll showed over 60 percent in favor. California, considered by some to be a liberal bastion that routinely votes heavily Democratic in presidential elections, had two death penalty laws on the ballot in 2016. One would have banned the death penalty. The other limited appeals, eased procedural protections, and sought to speed up the process. It was the second that won, revealing the electorate's deep commitment to death.

This commitment to the death sentence, however, is not racially neutral. Like incarceration, the majority of people put to death by the government in the seventeenth and early eighteenth century were white. During this time, whites were the majority of the population, and extrajudicial killings of non-whites made the legal machinery of death unnecessary. Once slavery ended, however, death ascended as a critical tool in racial governance until the 1930s, when it began to decline. The decline continued throughout the rehabilitative era of the post-WWII period, and was declared unconstitutional by the Supreme Court in the early 1970s. The court reversed itself in 1976, however, and the use of the death penalty followed a steep upward curve similar to imprisonment rates.

Today, the racial composition of those living on death row is 42 percent black, 42 percent white, and 13 percent Latinx, despite black people making up only 13 percent of the general population (see figure 10.3). Of those executed since 1976, almost 45 percent are nonwhite (see figure 10.4). Racial disparity deepens when considering which victim-offender combinations lead to the

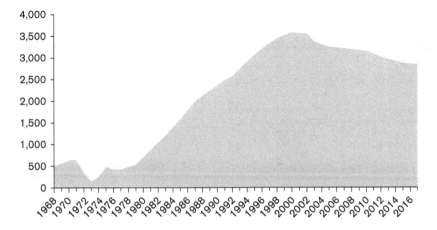

Figure 10.1 Number of people sentenced to death in the United States, 1968–2016. Source: Data from Tracy Snell, *Capital Punishment, 2013—Statistical Tables*, Bureau of Justice Statistics, U.S. Department of Justice, December 2014, www.bjs.gov/content/pub/pdf /cp13st.pdf; NAACP, *Death Row U.S.A.*, Quarterly Report by Criminal Justice Project of NAACP Legal Defense Fund, Spring 2017, www.naacpldf.org/files/about-us /DRUSASpring2017.pdf.

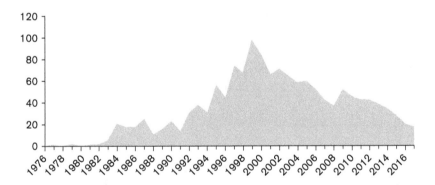

Figure 10.2 Number of executions in the United States since 1976. Source: *Executions in the United States*, Death Penalty Information Center, https://deathpenaltyinfo.org /executions-united-states.

death penalty. Over 76 percent of cases that result in the death penalty are homicides against white victims (see figure 10.5). And as we discuss further below, the most likely cases to lead to the death penalty are ones where the defendant is black and the victim is white (see figure 10.6). This happens despite black-on-white homicide being the *least likely* homicide pairing and African Americans making up 50 percent of all homicide victims.

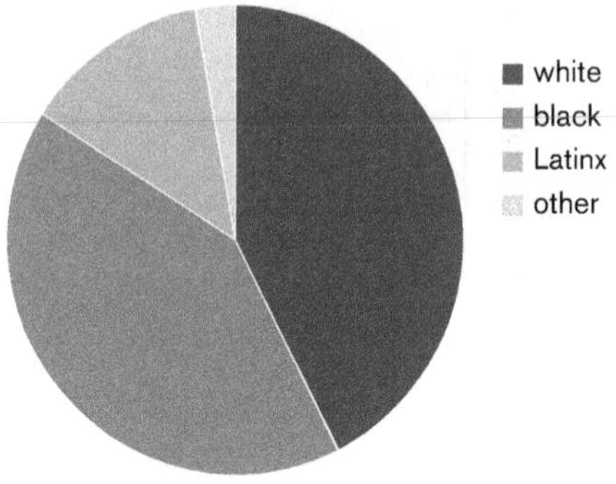

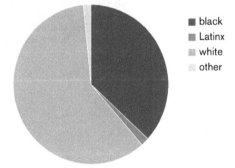

Figure 10.3 Race of death row population in the United States, 2017. Source: NAACP, *Death Row U.S.A.*, Quarterly Report by Criminal Justice Project of NAACP Legal Defense Fund, Spring 2017, www.naacpldf .org/files/about-us/DRUSASpring2017.pdf.

- white
- black
- Latinx
- other

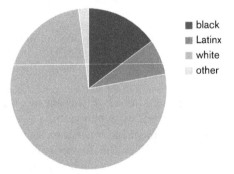

Figure 10.4 Race of people executed in the United States since 1976. Source: NAACP, *Death Row U.S.A.*, Quarterly Report by Criminal Justice Project of NAACP Legal Defense Fund, Spring 2017, www.naacpldf .org/files/about-us/DRUSASpring2017.pdf.

- black
- Latinx
- white
- other

Figure 10.5 Race of victims of those executed since 1976. Source: *National Statistics on the Death Penalty and Race*, Death Penalty Information Center, https:// deathpenaltyinfo.org/race-death-row- inmates-executed-1976.

- black
- Latinx
- white
- other

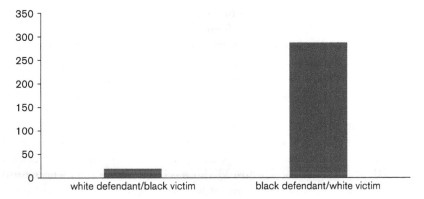

Figure 10.6 Executions for interracial murders since 1976. Source: *National Statistics on the Death Penalty and Race,* Death Penalty Information Center, https://deathpenaltyinfo .org/race-death-row-inmates-executed-1976.

While overall the usage of the death penalty has declined over time in the United States, the proportion of black people executed has increased. In the eighteenth century, the ratio of executions of black people to whites was 6:1, but by 1945, the ratio was 10:1 (Allen and Clubb 2009). This suggests that even though the use of the death penalty has declined overall, our vision of who deserves death remains heavily racialized. This vision is demonstrated by the evidence of racial disproportionality in the administration of death.

Racial Bias in Death Penalty Administration

There is ample evidence of racial disproportionality in application of the death penalty, which has even led several states to declare a moratorium. In Illinois, a Republican governor even cited racial disproportionality as his reason for declaring a moratorium.

In 1990, the U.S. Justice Department reviewed death penalty cases at the federal level and found numerous racial and geographical disparities, a situation that continued ten years later (GAO 1990; Sorensen, Wallace, and Pilgrim 2001). They found that defendants in 80 percent of federal death penalty cases were racial minorities. Over 50 percent of these were black. The U.S. General Accounting Office further found a pattern of evidence indicating racial disparities in the charging, sentencing, and imposition of the death penalty in almost every state.

One metareview of the literature found that in over 96 percent of the studies of the death penalty, some element of racial bias had been revealed (Dieter 1998; Lee, Paternoster, and Rowan 2016). A review of death penalty cases in

Connecticut found racial disproportionalities similar to those in the federal system (Donohue 2014). The study found that the risk of the death penalty did not increase with the type of crime. Instead, the author reported, "cases prosecutors charge as capital are virtually indistinguishable in these measures from cases where prosecutors choose not to bring capital charges" (Donohue 2014, 639). Instead of reserving the death penalty only for the "worst of the worst," studies show that in actuality it is most often administered to those who are poor and nonwhite.

Racial bias in capital punishment is a widespread problem. In Louisiana, people whose victim was white have a 97 percent higher chance of receiving the death penalty than those whose victim was black (Pierce and Radelet 2010). In California, those who killed whites were three times as likely to be given death as those who killed blacks and four times as likely as those who killed Latinxs (Pierce and Radelet 2005). The same has been found for North Carolina and Delaware—that is, the odds of receiving a death sentence rise significantly if one's victim is white (Unah 2011; Johnson et al. 2011).

The Philadelphia Study

One of the most significant studies of the death penalty undertaken in recent history was one conducted in Philadelphia (Baldus et al. 1997). It found that a black person is 38 percent more likely to get the death penalty than defendants of other races on trial for the same crime. Yet this was not the most surprising result of the study.

In looking at the data overall, the Philadelphia researchers came to a shocking conclusion about race and the effects of aggravating and mitigating factors. When thinking about the death penalty, often one considers the severity of the crime. Here, factors such as how the victim was killed, the type of person killed, and any other crimes committed at the same time might affect the case. Such factors might lead prosecutors, juries, legislatures, and others to view one type of murder as more violent, and thus deserving of more punishment, than another. These elements are known as **aggravating factors.** Aggravating factors are of two types: those that are legislatively prescribed (see box 10.1 for examples from Texas) and those that satisfy more subjective assumptions for a jury, such as "heinousness" or "causing great harm."

Mitigating factors, by contrast, are factors that lessen the severity of a crime. In death penalty cases, these are presented in the sentencing phase by the defense attorney, who often draws upon the personal history of the defendant, highlighting abuse or other trauma. Mitigating factors are often critical in humanizing a defendant and convincing the jury to spare his or her life.

The Philadelphia study and others since have found that aggravating factors act very differently for white and black defendants. Shockingly, the color of someone's skin was found to make a crime more heinous in the eyes of

BOX 10.1   Aggravating Factors in Texas Law

(1) The person murders a peace officer or fireman who is acting in the lawful discharge of an official duty and who the person knows is a peace officer or fireman;

(2) the person intentionally commits the murder in the course of committing or attempting to commit kidnapping, burglary, robbery, aggravated sexual assault, arson, obstruction or retaliation, or terroristic threat under Section 22.07(a)(1), (3), (4), (5), or (6);

(3) the person commits the murder for remuneration or the promise of remuneration or employs another to commit the murder for remuneration or the promise of remuneration;

(4) the person commits the murder while escaping or attempting to escape from a penal institution;

(5) the person, while incarcerated in a penal institution, murders another:

    (a) who is employed in the operation of the penal institution; or

    (b) with the intent to establish, maintain, or participate in a combination or in the profits of a combination;

(6) the person:

    (a) while incarcerated for an offense under this section or Section 19.02, murders another; or

    (b) while serving a sentence of life imprisonment or a term of 99 years for an offense under Section 20.04, 22.021, or 29.03, murders another;

(7) the person murders more than one person:

    (a) during the same criminal transaction; or

    (b) during different criminal transactions but the murders are committed pursuant to the same scheme or course of conduct;

(8) the person murders an individual under 10 years of age; or

(9) the person murders another person in retaliation for or on account of the service or status of the other person as a judge or justice of the supreme court, the court of criminal appeals, a court of appeals, a district court, a criminal dis trict court, a constitutional county court, a statutory county court, a justice court, or a municipal court.

Source: *Texas Penal Code,* 19.03.

the jury than factors such as "murder with multiple stab wounds" or "causing great harm, fear, or pain." Just being black is an aggravating factor in a death penalty case (see figure 10.7). Being black was also found to be more influential than other types of aggravating factors, including heinousness of crime and robbery (Pierce et al. 2014).

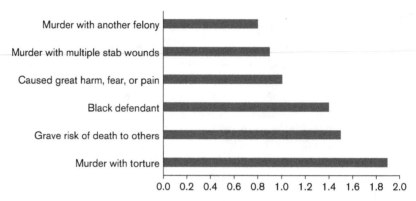

Figure 10.7 Impact of aggravating factors in jury decisions. X-axis numbers represent the relative predictive value of a factor, with 0 indicating no predictive value. Source: Richard C. Dieter, *The Death Penalty in Black and White: Who Lives, Who Dies, Who Decides* (Washington, DC: Death Penalty Information Center, 1998) https://deathpenaltyinfo.org /death-penalty-black-and-white-who-lives-who-dies-who-decides.

Further research into the sentencing stage found that mitigating factors also functioned differently as a result of race. Pennsylvania's death penalty law mandates death in cases where there is no mitigating factor but there is an aggravating one. Mitigating factors are thus necessary to avoid death in capital crimes. Researchers found that the same factor—such as childhood abuse—was seen as a mitigating factor for whites, but not for black people. Mona Lynch and Craig Haney (2011) describe this as the "tendency for White jurors—especially White male jurors—to interpret many common penalty phase facts and circumstances as potentially mitigating for a White defendant but to see those same things as irrelevant or even aggravating for a defendant who is black" (573).

The Philadelphia study also added nuance to our understanding of racial disparities and why racialized assumptions about mitigating and aggravating factors are so important to racial disproportionalities in sentencing. The least severe cases are the least likely to have the death penalty sought, while the most severe cases, the most likely. Little racial disparity exists at these extremes. Racial disparity comes into play in the middle, when the question of the crime is open to more interpretation and contestation. In these cases, race is elevated as a decisive variable, and black people are four times more likely to get the death penalty overall, and up to thirty times more likely if they killed a white person. Thus, the death penalty is given most often to the *least likely* type of crime to occur, while those who experience homicide the most—black victims—are the least likely to have the state seek the highest penalty.

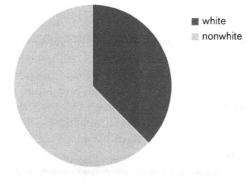

white
nonwhite

Figure 10.8 Percent of white and nonwhite juveniles executed, by race, 18th century. Source: Data from M. Watt Espy and John Ortiz Smykla, *Executions in the United States 1608–2002: The Espy File* (computer file), 4th ICPSR ed. (Ann Arbor, MI: Inter-university Consortium for Political and Social Research, March 2004), https://web.stanford.edu/group/ssds/dewidocs/icpsr8451/cb8451.

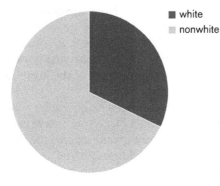

white
nonwhite

Figure 10.9 Percent of white and nonwhite juveniles executed, by race, 19th century. Source: Data from M. Watt Espy and John Ortiz Smykla, *Executions in the United States 1608–2002: The Espy File* (computer file), 4th ICPSR ed. (Ann Arbor, MI: Inter-university Consortium for Political and Social Research, March 2004), https://web.stanford.edu/group/ssds/dewidocs/icpsr8451/cb8451.

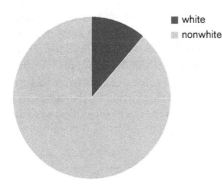

white
nonwhite

Figure 10.10 Percent of white and nonwhite juveniles executed, by race, 20th century. Source: Data from M. Watt Espy and John Ortiz Smykla, *Executions in the United States 1608–2002: The Espy File* (computer file), 4th ICPSR ed. (Ann Arbor, MI: Inter-university Consortium for Political and Social Research, March 2004), https://web.stanford.edu/group/ssds/dewidocs/icpsr8451/cb8451.

Bias in the Juvenile Death Penalty

The racially dehumanizing function of the death penalty is displayed at its most extreme in the execution of juveniles. Between 1642 and 1960, 160 children under the age of eighteen were executed in the United States. Countless other executions of those over the age of eighteen were for crimes committed before they were legally an adult. Victor Streib estimates that since 1642, the United States has executed at least 366 people who committed crimes while under eighteen (2005). Since the 1960s, 23 people have been executed for crimes committed while under eighteen.

Of the 183 juveniles executed, only 45 were white (Linde 2011). Almost 70 percent (125) of the juveniles executed were black. As figures 10.8, 10.9, and 10.10 show, the concentration of nonwhite juveniles executed increased between the seventeenth and twentieth centuries. In the twentieth century, at the same time that states were investing in juvenile courts and other juvenile institutions, the death penalty became reserved for the crimes of nonwhite youths. This reflects the larger societal process by which nonwhite youths were often excluded from the benevolently intentioned practices of the juvenile court, discussed in chapter 4.

Like their adult counterparts, nonwhite youth also faced execution for nonlethal crimes. In the twentieth century, twenty-seven black youth were executed for rape and two for attempted rape. One juvenile was executed for robbery and another for attempted murder. No white children suffered a similar fate, despite being convicted of these same crimes. Of the up to ten young women executed, none were white (Linde 2011). And 91 percent of executions of black youth took place in the South (Streib 2005).

As the twentieth century progressed, the United States soon stood alone among its peers as the only industrialized nation to continue using the death penalty against people who committed crimes as juveniles. This led to falling international esteem, and eventually the practice was outlawed 2005 in *Roper v. Simmons* (Linde 2011). Though outlawed today, the United States for centuries regularly sentenced primarily black children to death. This represents the ultimate act of dehumanization, as the child is not even allowed to fully become a citizen before having his or her life extinguished by the state. That this happened primarily to black children reveals the deep integration of racial dehumanization in the practice of the death penalty.

"LEGAL LYNCHING"

The racialized history of the death penalty, and its resurgence as a tool of racial governance under mass incarceration have led many to consider it "legal lynching." Reverend Jesse Jackson even titled his 2001 book on the history of the death penalty *Legal Lynching.* Austin Sarat writes, "Good people versus bad people, virtue juxtaposed with vice—this simple morality tale, a reassuring sentimental narrative fuels the engine of state killing" (2001, 93). This deceptively simple tale, though, is incredibly persuasive. It is also the tale of racism, animating not just the death penalty but also social support for lynchings and white racial violence.

The history of the U.S. death penalty is, at its heart, a tale of race. It's a tale of who belongs, who does not, and whose existence is a threat. It's the tale of "who lives, who dies, and who decides" (Dieter 1998). It's ultimately a tale of belonging and survival, but one where belonging and survival is integral to creating a particular racial identity and the ideology of white supremacy.

Judicial State Killing and Race

Enlightenment philosophers of punishment largely questioned the utility of the death penalty. Cesare Beccaria, whom we first met in chapter 3 and again in chapter 9 as someone who contributed to deterrence philosophy, considered the penalty "ineffectual because of the barbarity of the example it gives to men" (2008, 17). Thomas Jefferson campaigned against the death penalty, as did Thomas Paine and Benjamin Rush, two other noted Enlightenment figures (Banner 2002). This meant that many states have had a long history of death penalty abolition. Michigan repealed the death penalty for murder in 1847, and Rhode Island and Wisconsin did the same in the 1850s. By World War I, thirteen states had eliminated capital punishment through legislative decree (Jackson, Jackson, and Shapiro 2001). Further, when the death penalty was applied in the early United States, pardoning and commuting sentences by governors was common, and close to fifty percent of all executions were halted through this practice (Jackson, Jackson, and Shapiro 2001).

This "restrained application," however, was not the case when considering a more expansive understanding of state killing. State killing through the death penalty was only one mechanism of violence in the early days of our country. States killed in other ways as well. For instance, at least 555 enslaved persons were put to death by the colony (later commonwealth) of Virginia between 1706 and 1784, but these people do not show up in the official death penalty counts. And in New York, a slave uprising was punished by sentencing thirty enslaved people to death, though the death penalty had been abolished for whites except for murder and treason. The racialized history of the death penalty is at its most extreme, however, in the South.

Killing in the South

Populist outcry against the death penalty led by Enlightenment philosophy did little to curtail its use in the South, where over 90 percent of black Americans resided until the early 1900s (Banner 2002). When many northern states began limiting the use of the death penalty for whites in the late 1700s, southern states did so as well, while simultaneously *expanding* the list of offenses for which black people could be put to death, including crimes such as theft. Prior to the Civil War, the South often maintained separate lists of capital offenses on the basis of race (Steiker and Steiker 2015). Enslaved people could also be killed with impunity by their masters since they were seen as property (Banner 2002; Jackson, Jackson, and Shapiro 2001).

Free black people were also subject to this different standard. Sentences were even formally outlined in the law based on the race of the victim. In Virginia, for example, in addition to the four crimes that whites faced death for, free black people were also subject to the death penalty for rape, attempted rape, kidnapping, and aggravated assault if the victim was white. Enslaved people were subject to death for any of sixty-six crimes in Virginia and thirty-eight crimes in Mississippi (Johnson 2009). Free and enslaved black people in Texas also faced death for crimes like robbery and attempted robbery if their victims were white (Banner 2006). And all southern states had codes that differentiated whether a crime was capital if committed by an enslaved person instead of a white one (Johnson 2009). Further, a black man convicted of raping a white woman was subject to death, but the rape of a black woman was often no crime at all.

Executions during the time of slavery were also different depending on race. When the offender was black, particularly torturous methods, such as burning at the stake, inflicted great violence upon the body prior to death. Whites, by contrast, were often hung or, later, shot. This is what Stephen John Hartnett calls "race-encoding categories of punishment: Who is whipped, who is hanged, and who is burned at the stake?" (2012, 20). The particularly torturous executions were meant to send a "race-encoding" message about the value—or lack thereof—of black life. Black life could be extinguished in a violent, gruesome manner that some whites even celebrated. This celebration served as the linchpin of white supremacy and colonial era governance—one could actually revel in the taking of another's life for one's own gain.

Lynching and the Death Penalty

The death penalty for the first hundred and fifty years of the United States, however, was only one type of violence routinely practiced against people of color. In the South, the real engine of racial terror was extrajudicial killing, sanctioned by state officials, in the form of **lynching.** At no point in U.S. history has the extrajudicial killing of whites been a norm. The ability of particular groups of white people to kill nonwhites extrajudicially has at various times not only been directly sanctioned by the government but condoned and participated in by state actors. The rise of lynching meant that states did not have to rely on the death penalty. But as lynching started to be met with social uproar, states sought to use the death penalty explicitly to replace the practice of lynching.

Almost five thousand people were killed by lynch mobs in the United States, almost all of them nonwhite, and three-quarters of them black (Curriden 1995). Lynchings steadily rose in the early 1900s, and public outcry in the North led to the threat that the U.S. Congress would pass a federal antilynching law. Some argue that it was this threat that pushed the South away from the use of lynching and toward the death penalty, securing sentences of death not by the mob but by the all-white jury. Lynching was a common form of white racial terrorism and increased steadily after the end of slavery, with a peak in the late 1800s. Lynching decreased throughout the 1900s, at the same time that the use of the death penalty for the execution of black people increased.

Rape was a common justification for lynchings. Narratives about hypersexual black males preying on virginal white women has fueled generations and centuries of white racist violence. Legal scholars note:

> Historians of lynching in the South find it difficult to overstate the centrality of the fear of black rapists to the practice of lynching: "Black men were lynched for other crimes, but rape was always the key." Even high-level elected officials in the South publicly endorsed lynching as the only "suitable punishment" for black men who raped white women. Lynching was so entrenched a practice that in the most intense period of lynchings in American history, 1889–1893, considerably more people were lynched than executed nationwide—921 to 556, by one count. (Steiker and Steiker 2010, 647)

Rape was the most common narrative justifying white racial violence, and it was based on one of the oldest narratives about racial difference. The use of this justification directly after the Civil War illustrates how racial anxieties were funneled through ideas about crime and violence, even though the dominant mechanism for responding was outside the criminal justice system.

At the end of the Civil War, the abolition of slave codes meant that white Southerners turned to the law as an outlet for their racial vengeance. While lynching emerged as a critical outlet for this vengeance, the social disgust at the practice meant that eventually it was subsumed under the death penalty. Several proponents of the death penalty even argued for the increased use of the sentence with the logic that if the state did not execute people for crimes deemed particularly morally reprehensible—like those supposedly transgressing racial hierarchies—the mob would take violence into their own hand. Lynching was given as evidence for this view.

Lynching as Justification for the Death Penalty

One social reformer, J. E. Cutler, provided an extended accounting of why lynching demonstrated the need for a death penalty. He began by recounting the various humanitarian reasons for abolishing the death penalty, such as it being a "relic of barbarism" and that the "authority of a government . . . [has] no more right to take human life than one man has" (Cutler 1907, 622). This "abstract justice," however, did not account for the "circumstances and conditions that prevail within the territory of its application." He wrote further: "A noteworthy illustration of this fact is to be found in connection with the history of the lynching of negroes in the United States. In the midst of the increased criminality that has been manifested among the negroes since emancipation, the Southern whites have found the law and its administration utterly unsuited to the function of dealing with negro criminals—hence the frequent adoption of summary and extra-legal methods of punishment" (1907, 622). The author's spurious logic about an "increase in criminality" among black people after the Civil War is remarkably reminiscent of the racialized construction of criminality more generally. Here, the author draws upon this as evidence (yet again) of the extraordinary difference between black and white—so different that legal regimes do not apply across racial lines.

The problem with the law, according to Cutler, was that the judicial system was "adapted to a highly civilized and cultured race" and thus unable to deal with the "wanton, bestial, outrageous, brutal and inhuman" crimes of an "a race of inferior civilization" (1907, 623). A legal system built on "rationality" and "liberty" could not be used for those not evolutionarily ready for it. He concluded:

> We are just beginning to realize that if the lynching of negroes is to cease, there must be much less reliance than in the past on abstract principles concerning the rights of man, regardless of his training and his capacity. . . . Under such circumstances, it is not the part of wisdom to abolish capital punishment. The presence of racial contrasts in the population of the United States, particularly that between the negroes and the whites, must not be omitted from consideration in the legal treatment of crime. (1907, 623)

This argument against the abolition of capital punishment re-creates the colonial order of racism. It argues that Enlightenment principles should not be adhered to, particularly not "regardless of his [the person subject to the penalty] training or his capacity." According to Cutler's logic, in light of lynching, it is inappropriate to give up the death penalty, because whites will just use extra-judicial violence to enact vengeance. Cutler ends by suggesting that given the "racial contrasts" between white and black people, presumably an allusion to the talk of racial capacities common at the time, the death penalty continued to have utility. Since it was not useful in the punishment of "rational" whites, this meant that the legal machinery of death was intended for black people only, something demonstrated by the increased concentration of black people receiving death-penalty sentences over time.

Though Cutler's argument may seem ostentatious and extreme, it was remarkably common for the time. This logic even had legislative impact. In Colorado, for instance, the legislature abolished capital punishment in 1898, only to reinstate it three years later. The reason? In 1900, there were three killings by lynch mobs, and the legislature argued that without the death penalty, mobs would just take matters into their own hands. In this case, the death penalty was literally the expression of mob justice (Banner 2006).

Tennessee was often cited by Progressive activists as proof that death penalty abolition could happen in the South, although the state never actually abolished the death penalty (Galliher, Ray, and Cook 1992). Tennessee significantly curtailed the use of the death penalty in 1915, yet did not actually abolish it. It retained it for two crimes: murder by a prisoner already serving a life sentence and rape, a crime for which African Americans were disproportionately prosecuted and sentenced at the time. Moreover, the law explicitly limited the death penalty for rape to black defendants. Tennessee repealed the law four years later, however, using the same reason as Colorado had: a rash of lynchings. While presumably unfit for white defendants, the death penalty's racial history reveals just why it has been kept for so long in the United States.

Eugenics and the Death Penalty

Another argument for the death penalty also revealed its foundational ties to white racial violence: that of eugenics (Steiker and Steiker 2010). Eugenic proponents of the death penalty saw it as a "conscious artificial selection for the elimination of dangerous biologic stocks from the community" (Bye 1919, 97–98). They argued that life imprisonment meant the possibility of convicts going free, a dangerous proposition if the goal was to purify the racial stock. They even argued explicitly that it would solve the "race question." One member of the Michigan State Bar Association, for example, claimed in 1928: "It has been established beyond any doubt that our modern killer is biologically inferior. Authorities agree upon this fact. To illustrate: Memphis, with its illiterate, defective Negro population, has the highest murder rate of any American city. On the other hand, St. Paul and Minneapolis, of almost pure Scandinavian stock, have the lowest" (Dunham 1939, 193).

The power of coloniality is found within arguments for the death penalty based in eugenics and concern about mob justice. Both these arguments position whites as a more rational, reasonable, and thus less death-worthy form of humanity. Other races, by contrast, failed to display these traits and thus would continue to threaten society if not dealt with savagely. Lynch mobs illustrated not the savage and capricious nature of the mob, but the failure of the state. Killing black people did not end with the decline of lynching and extrajudicial murders. Instead this power was subsumed under the death penalty.

The Death Penalty as Legal Lynching

Due process during the first part of the twentieth century looked a lot like formalized racial violence in the law. As chapter 8 showed, the all-white jury was a key Southern institution, one that persists to this day. Another demonstration of "due process" in the South was one man who was hung immediately after a "trial" that lasted less than an hour (Wright 1996). The local paper considered this event deserving of "special congratulation" as "Kentucky was saved the mortification of a lynching" (Wright 1996, 253).

Between the end of the Civil War and the civil rights movement, there were not any dramatic changes in the southern criminal code. This reveals the continuity of the death penalty as a mechanism for racial violence. As lynching subsided, the South turned to the death penalty as the major instrument of state violence, and the number of black people sentenced to death by the state began to increase (see figure 10.11). Stuart Banner notes that the crimes that were capital offenses for black defendants at the end of the Civil War were still capital crimes a century later: "As of 1954 rape was punished with death in eighteen states, sixteen in the south. . . . Robbery was capital in nine. . . . Burglary was still capital in four" (2002, 228–29). This continuation demonstrates how the mob impulse was so easily subsumed under the death penalty. The law allowed for state execution against the very same purported crimes that often prompted lynchings, especially rape. In order to continue the campaign of white racial terror, the courts merely had to suppress the ability of nonwhites to receive a fair trial. The tools were the all-white jury, mandated racial segregation, and the continued dominance of whiteness in the law.

While many might be shocked by a consideration of the death penalty alongside the practice of lynching, legal scholar Charles Ogletree notes that "the racially disproportionate application of the death penalty can be seen as being in historical continuity with the long and sordid history of lynching in this country" (2002, 19). Why does Ogletree consider the death penalty the continuation of the history of lynching in the United States? He identifies several factors that overlap between lynching, or extrajudicial killing, and the death penalty, or state killing.

First, both are expressions of racism and racial discrimination, with the death penalty merely sublimating the racist expression of mob violence to the formal procedures of due process. This is demonstrated most notably by the people who are most likely to be subjected to these practices: 90 percent of those lynched were black and over half of those killed by the state in the United States have been black. Lynching results in the same outcome as the death penalty, just without the legal process.

Second, lynchings often served in part as a recreational event for white mobs, and "in rural areas . . . offered a degree of 'excitement'" (Howard 2005, 139). Media accounts of the death penalty today—including did-they-do-it news documentaries and the lotteries journalists enter in order to be in the audience for an execution—demonstrate that putting people to death continues to be recreation. Public fascination with "notorious criminals" reveals the excitement and joy that many people gather from knowing about the suffering

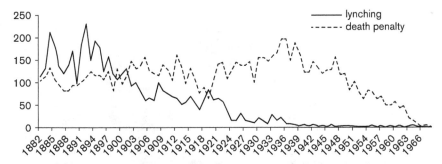

Figure 10.11 Number of lynchings versus death penalty sentences, United States. Source: Data from M. Watt Espy and John Ortiz Smykla, *Executions in the United States 1608–2002: The Espy File* (computer file), 4th ICPSR ed. (Ann Arbor, MI: Inter-university Consortium for Political and Social Research, March 2004), https://web.stanford.edu/group/ssds/dewidocs/icpsr8451/cb8451; Tuskegee Institute, "Lynching, Whites and Negroes, 1882–1968." Tuskegee University Archives, http://archive.tuskegee.edu/archive/handle/123456789/511.

of others. As lynching and the extrajudicial murder of nonwhites declined, the judicial death penalty became "legal lynching."

The death penalty, however, is distinguished from lynching in at least one critical aspect: being embedded within the law. Lynching was supported and condoned by the state, but it was not the formal practice of the state. Though this distinction has little consequence to those killed, it does provide a cover for the use of the death penalty. As one legal scholar puts it, "the contemporary practice of capital punishment contributes to much the same end [as lynching], but without provoking the outrage once incited by its extra-legal counterpart" (Kaufman-Osborn 2006, 23). Thus, while "the death penalty is a direct descendent of lynching and other forms of racial violence and . . . oppression" (Bright 1995, 439), the structural context of the death penalty has proved an important legal cover for the continuation of racial violence in the United States.

Lynching continues through the death penalty not because judges, prosecutors, and other court officials are out to perpetuate white racial violence. Quite the contrary. We would bet that on any measure the vast majority of court officials are well-meaning actors seeking to protect what they believe is right. But even if that is the case, the use of the death penalty continues to result in hugely disparate racial outcomes. This happens not through mass racial violence, as lynching did, but through the structural context of the legal application of the death penalty.

RACE, STATE VIOLENCE, AND THE GEOGRAPHY OF DEATH

In addition to racial capriciousness, the death penalty is geographically capricious. Whether one gets the death penalty is dependent on *where* one is. Just

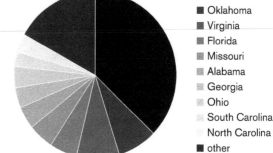

Figure 10.12 Top ten executing states, 1976–2018. Source: *Executions by Region,* Death Penalty Information Center, https://deathpenaltyinfo.org/ number-executions-state-and-region-1976.

- ■ Texas
- ■ Oklahoma
- ■ Virginia
- ■ Florida
- ▓ Missouri
- ▓ Alabama
- ▓ Georgia
- ▒ Ohio
- ▒ South Carolina
- North Carolina
- ■ other

2 percent of counties in the United States account for over 50 percent of the executions (Dieter 2013). In the federal system, almost half of all death penalty cases come from just five of ninety-four jurisdictions. Where you kill can make all the difference. Kill someone in one county and you may eligible for parole in a few decades, whereas if you walk over into another county, you could lose your life.

Of the 1,473 executions carried out since 1972, 83 percent have been carried out by just ten states—just 20 percent of states in the United States. Alabama, Arkansas, Florida, Georgia, Louisiana, Missouri, and South Carolina account for a little under half of the executions, while Texas, Oklahoma, and Virginia account for over half (see figure 10.12).

Perhaps most telling about these states is their geographical proximity to one another and their membership in the cultural region titled the "South." Ogletree observes "that the states of what is often called the "Death Belt"—the southern states that together account for over 90 percent of all executions carried out since 1976—overlap considerably with the southern states that had the highest incidence of extra-legal violence and killings during the Jim Crow era" (2002, 19). However, looking closer at the death penalty also reveals how some seemingly more liberal areas also fuel the racialized engine of death.

Suburban counties, which tend to be whiter, wealthier, and more Republican, are more likely to send people to death row. Take, for example, two counties in the San Francisco Bay Area. San Mateo County, directly south of San Francisco, is much wealthier and more suburban than San Francisco City and County. San Mateo's median household income was just under $100,000 in 2016 and the average household net worth was $1.29 million. By contrast, San Francisco's median household income was just over $70,000. While they may seem like similar wealthy places, they are very different with regard to crime. San Francisco has two times as many murders as San Mateo, yet San Mateo has thirteen people currently serving time on death row and San Francisco has only one (CDCR 2017). There is a similar pattern in Maryland, where suburban Baltimore County produces fifteen times more death sentences than Baltimore City (Paternoster and Brame 2003, 30–31). Yet suburban Baltimore County's average yearly homicides between 2011 and 2015 was 26, while Baltimore City's was 240.

Over half the death row inmates in California come from just three counties—Los Angeles, Riverside, and Orange—at a rate that is twice their proportion of the population (Dieter 2013). In Missouri, St. Louis County pursues the death penalty fourteen times as often as Jackson County, which includes Kansas City (Sloss 2008). In Connecticut, the city of Waterbury sentences people to death at least seven times the rate of other places in the state (Donohue 2014). Further, this discrepancy reflects not a difference in prosecutors seeking the death penalty in Waterbury, but a greater rate of success in securing the death sentence (Beardsley et al. 2015). This success comes in part from the geographical imagination of crime and violence that often results in suburban, whiter, and wealthier counties sentencing people to death more often than people and places that experience homicide and victimization at greater rates.

Producing the "Other" through Geographical Discourse

In Delaware, the Brooks armored car case illustrates how "commonsense racism" fuels the quest for more severe punishments. As discussed in chapter 9, commonsense racism is the assumption that people from the outside—generally nonwhite—are more prone to violence and crime. In 1990, four black men traveled from Philadelphia to Delaware to hold up an armored car and shot the two guards multiple times. They were apprehended and charged with two counts of capital murder, but the jury sentenced them to life without the possibility of parole.

Reaction to the sentences revealed how commonsense racism is expressed through the geographical imagination of crime. Media coverage called the four defendants the Philadelphia Four and "portrayed them as outsiders who *must* receive the death sentence in order to send a message to surrounding states that such conduct will not be tolerated" (Fleury-Steiner, Dunn, and Fleury-Steiner 2009, 11). Newspapers charged that there was a "moral breakdown of community" in the county that failed to sentence the Brooks killers to death. The coverage also portrayed the crime in typical racist logic, with the victims cast as part of "our" community through "detailed backgrounds of the two guards as 'fathers,' 'husbands,' and 'upstanding citizen'" (2009, 11). By contrast, the shooters were cast as marauding outsiders, preying on the moral community with terrorizing crime and violence. No effort was made to humanize them, and instead the enduring trope of "decent" versus "street" with all its racial connotations persisted.

The insistence on the death penalty was underscored by the geographical imagination of the crime, which came up during the ensuing legislative debate about death penalty reform. Local Delaware representative David Merrill declared: "We're talking about a form of organized crime that plots and schemes and comes into this state and commits brutal acts, fully aware of what they're doing. And if one examines the laws in the contiguous states relative to capital punishment or how that is imposed, then the citizens of Delaware are very vulnerable to this sort of activity in the future" (Fleury-Steiner, Dunn, and Fleury-Steiner 2009, 19). This image of the defendants as geographical outsiders facilitates an inherently racialized notion of the crime as perpetuated by the "uncivilized, savage outsiders" who prey on civilized, morally pure communities. Unsurprisingly, this discursive logic was successful in Delaware, which passed death penalty reform without ever considering the consequences of this bill or the consequences of racial bias that might ensue (Fleury-Steiner, Dunn, and Fleury-Steiner 2009, 15). As a result of change in law, four times more people were sentenced to death than before.

Geography structures who receives the death penalty and provides a mechanism for allowing white racial violence to be subsumed in political processes. Suburban counties are often more likely to have white residents who report higher fear of crime, while also being more punitive and supportive of the death penalty. This translates into a judicial system where these counties send more people to death row and perpetuate the narrative that "some places" are more violent, and thus necessitating death, than others. This is the very same narrative that was used against black people by those who argued for the death penalty's use in order to stem the tide (and shame) of lynching. The geographical context of the death penalty is further complemented by the administration of the death penalty, where the racial violence of the past is remade into the seemingly objective and disinterested application of the law.

RACE, KILLING, AND THE ADMINISTRATION OF DEATH

Court practices provide a veneer of impartiality and objectivity to the machinery of death. People are charged, tried, convicted, and sentenced through a series of routine steps, each designed to reveal aspects of the case that could weigh against death. Yet, despite these steps, the outcome of state practices of death continues to be racialized. This happens not usually through the explicit intentions of any court player, but rather through a mechanism by which the status of being nonwhite and poor results in defendants being placed on a conveyor belt of capital justice. And once on the inside, the dehumanization continues.

Public Defense

It is no accident that the vast majority of people on death row were poor prior to arriving there. "People who are well represented at trial," said Justice Ruth

Bader Ginsburg, "do not get the death penalty." The vast majority of people on death row were represented by a public defender, with some estimates suggesting that almost all who face capital trials cannot afford a lawyer (Cole 1999). Further, estimates place the number of people in poverty prior to joining death row at over 99 percent. The problems of public defense detailed in chapter 8 are further compounded during capital trials.

Mounting a Capital Defense

Capital defense budgets are notoriously precarious, because they are often subject to the political whims of legislatures and governors, and criminal defense is not a particularly popular political platform. As such, one of the most significant hurdles public defenders face to providing a strong defense for someone accused of a capital crime is funding for mounting the case. Pennsylvania, which devolves responsibility for the cost of counsel to the counties, provides an exceptional example of the lack of funding for many capital defense trials. In some Pennsylvania counties, the cost of a single consultation with a psychologist or a forensic expert would exhaust the entire budget. Compensation for attorneys is as little as $2 an hour in some counties. Technology, such as office computers, is frequently passed down from the prosecutor's office, and public defenders, unlike prosecutors, are not eligible for student loan forgiveness (Feinberg et al. 2011).

In Alabama, defense attorneys are compensated a maximum of $1,000 for preparing a case. Texas provides court-appointed attorneys with just $5,000 to mount a capital appeal, a figure that often will not cover the cost of even one expert testimony (Cole 1999). The cost of mounting a capital defense can often be in the hundreds of thousands of dollars, or even millions. Capital sentences are often automatically appealed, and appeals can stretch over decades. A state, such as Texas, that provides just $5,000 for appeals, then, provides a considerable structural restraint to mounting a robust capital defense, a burden that disproportionately falls on poor and nonwhite defendants.

Further, several studies suggest that those represented by public defenders often do not get adequate counsel. In Washington, 20 percent of the people who faced execution over the past twenty years were represented by lawyers who had been or were later disbarred, suspended, or arrested, though the state has only a 1 percent disbarment rate (Olsen 2001). Twelve percent of those sentenced to death in Illinois had attorneys who had been or would be disbarred or suspended, and almost 10 percent of death row inmates received new sentencing because of incompetent representation (Armstrong and Mills 1999). One study of 461 cases in Texas found that 25 percent of those on death row were represented by someone who had been disciplined for professional misconduct (Jennings et al. 2000).

The Importance of Experience

Experience with death penalty cases is critical to securing a fair trial, as demonstrated by the case of John Eldon Smith (Bright 2002). Smith was executed in 1983, a death that would have been prevented by a simple change in the random assignment of lawyers. Smith and his codefendant were tried separately and both were convicted. However, both were convicted in a county that barred women from serving on juries. A recent Supreme Court case had overturned this law. Attorneys for Smith's codefendant were aware of this decision and were granted a new trial. The codefendant did not face death in the new trial. Smith, by contrast, did not have the same luck, and his lawyers were unware of the recent decision and failed to challenge the jury composition. The exact same court then upheld his death sentence. Stephen Bright (2002) notes, "Simply switching the lawyers in this case would have resulted in a new trial for Smith—and death for his codefendant" (76).

Nevertheless, death penalty cases are routinely assigned to those with very little experience in criminal trials, much less in capital cases. In Alabama, for instance, many of those on death row are represented by attorneys with less than five years of criminal defense experience, which is the minimum qualification for capital trials recommended by the American Bar Association (Equal Justice Initiative 2017). Tax attorneys, real estate attorneys, and corporate lawyers, as well as new, inexperienced attorneys and those so overloaded with cases that they cannot provide an adequate defense for any case, much less a capital one, have all been assigned to cover death penalty cases (Cole 1999).

Two death penalty reforms show how important inexperience is to a sentence of death. First, in 1987, the U.S. Congress authorized the creation of federally funded death penalty resource centers to provide legal aid and counsel to those facing capital trials. These centers provided lawyers who had the skills and time to "humanize" defendants in the eyes of jurors. As others have shown in death penalty literature more broadly, the ability to provide a human face to the defendant—which public defenders are often unable to do due to high caseloads and lack of resources—is a key factor in avoiding the death penalty (Cole 1999). It's even a necessary component in the Pennsylvania law, which mandates death unless mitigating factors, like those that illustrate the humanity of the defendant, are found. Defendants whose lawyers are able to do the social research to show how a person's life experience contributed to their crime—such as through suffering extreme abuse—are more successful at avoiding death sentences for their clients (Sundby 2002). This, however, takes money, as the second example illustrates.

In Indiana, concern about the quality of representation in capital cases led to fundamental reform of the public defense system (Cole 1999). In every capital case, the state now requires at least two experienced attorneys on the defense team. The lead counsel must have five years of criminal trial experience, and have been lead counsel or co-counsel on at least five completed felony jury trials and one death penalty case. The co-counsel must have three years of trial experience and been lead counsel or co-counsel on three completed felony jury trials. Attorneys are required to undergo twelve hours of capital litigation training every other year and are paid at least $70 per hour. Additionally, capital defenders cannot be assigned any additional cases for one month preceding trial, and there are strict limits on their caseloads overall. The result? Not a single Indiana jury recommended the death penalty for the first three years after implementation. Prosecutors also sought the death penalty 30 percent less often.

The structural context of publicly funded capital defense reveals just how white racial violence is sublimated through the practices of the law. The poor and nonwhite are the most frequent users of public defense, and they are also the most likely to be sentenced to death. Public defense is not funded in ways that allow for the humanity of the defendant to be uncovered and demonstrated at trial, and thus, this group is more often relegated to the role of nonhuman whose life is acceptably extinguished by the state. Wealth accumulation and whiteness, however, work together to define the defendant as human and thus deserving of life, even if imprisoned. The legal cover of public defense suggest that everyone gets a fair trial, but the reality reveals just how racialized a "fair trial" is and how systematically the inexperience of appointed counsel and inadequate funding of public defense work to dehumanize the poor and nonwhite.

Prosecution

The prosecutor is the only figure in the courtroom who can make the decision to seek a death sentence. The prosecutor has also been described as the figure in the U.S. judiciary with "more control over life, liberty, and reputation than any other person in America" (Jackson 1940, 3). Given this broad power, it is not surprising that one of the many sources of racial disparities in the administration of the death penalty stems from the power of the prosecutor.

Consider the cases of Texas, Oklahoma, and Pennsylvania. The first two of these states are well-known for their high rate of execution compared to other states, yet in all three, a simple change of district attorney in three counties led to significant drops in the death penalty (Seiver 2015). In Harris County, Texas (where Houston is located), prosecutors went from seeking the death penalty on average twelve times per year to six times per year to just once per year. Each of these decreases was precipitated by a new district attorney assuming office. In Oklahoma County, the rate went from about 2.5 per year to less than 0.5 per year. In Philadelphia, the rate dropped from 9.5 per year to just 3 death

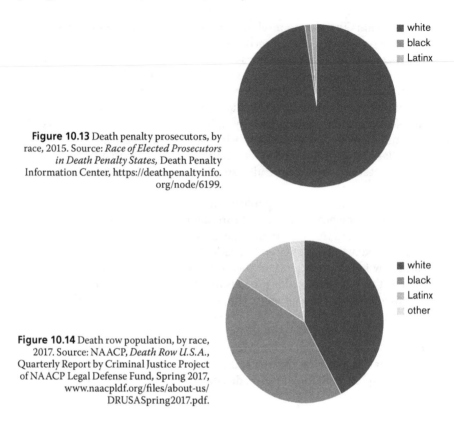

Figure 10.13 Death penalty prosecutors, by race, 2015. Source: *Race of Elected Prosecutors in Death Penalty States,* Death Penalty Information Center, https://deathpenaltyinfo. org/node/6199.

Figure 10.14 Death row population, by race, 2017. Source: NAACP, *Death Row U.S.A.,* Quarterly Report by Criminal Justice Project of NAACP Legal Defense Fund, Spring 2017, www.naacpldf.org/files/about-us/ DRUSASpring2017.pdf.

sentences in five years. These three counties were all once among the 2 percent of counties that were the source of 56 percent of people on death row, but a simple change in prosecutor led to a very different reality of state killing (Dieter 2013).

Seeing Like a (White) Prosecutor

Prosecutorial discretion is also shaped by the racialized structure of prosecution. District attorneys in death penalty counties are over 95 percent white, a stark contrast with the racial makeup of death penalty recipients (see figures 10.13 and 10.14). As noted in chapter 8, this does not significantly differ from prosecutors in general, 95 percent of whom are white (Reflective Democracy Campaign 2015). In thirty-seven of thirty-eight death penalty states (except

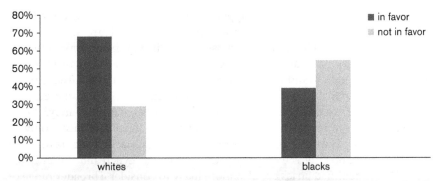

Figure 10.15 Death penalty support, by race, 2015. Source: Data sourced with permission from Gallup Poll, Andrew Dugan, "Solid Majority Continue to Support Death Penalty," Politics, October 15, 2015, http://news.gallup.com/poll/186218/solid-majority-continue-support-death-penalty.aspx.

New Mexico), more than 90 percent of prosecutors were white. And in eighteen states, 100 percent of the death penalty decision-makers were white. In 1997, of the 1,838 identified prosecutors, 1,794 were white (Pokorak 1997, 1817). Two decades later, little has changed, and of the 2,437 identified prosecutors, the concentration of whites in prosecution only shifted 2 percent (Lartey 2015).

Unconscious bias likely pervades death penalty decisions in two ways, as it does other areas of prosecutorial discretion (Pokorak 1997). First, given their white identity, prosecutors are likely to reflect racialized worldviews that see black people as dangerous and violent. Further, prosecutors' decisions to seek capital sentencing more often in cases with a black assailant and white victim are likely the result of identification with the victim and racial fears. Prosecutors can also stoke racial fears through their invocation of particular racialized narratives of crime and violence, something to which "death-qualified" juries are uniquely susceptible.

"Death-Qualified" Juries

As we have seen, juries are shaped by their racial composition. In death penalty cases, the problem of all-white juries is even more acute. In order to sit on a jury for a capital murder case, one must be what is called "death qualified." A **death-qualified jury** is one that is selected from a pool of people who satisfy two conditions: they are not categorically opposed to the death penalty, and they are not in favor of a mandatory death penalty for instances of capital murder. As figure 10.15 shows, the majority of whites support the death penalty and thus are immediately dominant within the pool of death-qualified jurors. Moreover, a majority of black people do not support the death penalty, making them ineligible for service, which structurally leads to a whiter pool of jurors.

Despite decades of Supreme Court cases establishing the unconstitutionality of an intentionally all-white jury, juries still are predominantly white, something with profound consequences in a death penalty trial (see further, box 10.2). When five or more white males sit on a capital trial jury, there is a 70 percent chance of a death penalty outcome (Bowers, Steiner, and Sandys 2001). If there are four or fewer white males, the chance of a death sentence is only 30 percent. In one study, so many white men sentenced black defendants to death that they accounted for the entirety of the race effect (Lynch and Haney 2009, 487). Death-qualified juries are also more likely to consider a broader range of factors aggravating and to dismiss mitigating factors (Butler and Moran 2007). This is further complicated by race, because white jurors also more likely to empathize with white defendants and see themselves in their characteristics, something demonstrated by psychological research on death-qualified juries.

Seeing Like a Juror

Lynch and Haney (2011) illustrate how jurors interpret facts in such a way that they reflect inclusion within the political community for whites but distance, exclusion, and dehumanization for blacks. In the following excerpts, two jurors talk about simulated penalty-phase hearings that were identical except for the race of the defendant.

> I could really identify with the defendant, because that is a story that I hear all too often and have experienced exactly the same thing in my own family that he experienced. I didn't go out and kill anybody and our case may not have been so bad as his family's, but everything that was . . . done in that family by that stepfather was done by my father in my family. So I put myself in that position, if I did snap, like he did. I guess, because I could relate to it so much, I could be more empathic. (Juror 305–5, arguing for a life sentence)

> I don't need to know that this guy was whipped. I feel bad for him. I don't need to know about his three kids. I feel bad for them. I grew up without a dad, so I feel bad for them. All I need to know is that this guy went and came back with his socks [and stuffed them down the victim's throat and killed him]. (Juror 403–4, arguing for a death sentence) (573)

These two excerpts reveal a larger tendency on the part of jurors to use the facts of a case to support leniency and life for whites but severity and death for black defendants. This is further complicated by white jurors' tendency to be more punitive and, as we showed in chapter 8, for juries to continue to be mostly or all white.

This pattern is also illustrated through interviews with jurors who have actually served on capital trials. Ben Fleury-Steiner (2004) details how juror interviews reveal the "insider" and "outsider" narratives so common to racial

BOX 10.2   Juries, Racism, and Overturning Convictions

Though plea bargains are common throughout the rest of the criminal court, almost all capital cases go to jury trial. The reasoning makes sense. Why take a plea if the penalty is not less than death?

This means, however, that juries are more consequential to capital sentences than other verdicts. Yet what goes on in the jury deliberation is secret and is often subject to what is called the "no impeachment" rule that protects deliberations from scrutiny after a verdict is issued. This means that even though there may be allegations of juror misconduct—such as one case where the jury deliberation was described as "one big party"—the actions of juries are not grounds for overturning a conviction. The judicial reasoning is that with twelve jurors, verdicts override the process to arrive at them.

The Supreme Court recently took up the issue of racist jury deliberations in *Pena-Rodriguez v. Colorado* (2017). In this case, two jurors approached defense attorneys and reported that one of the jurors had repeatedly expressed racial bias against the defendant. Here, the Supreme Court ruled that jury deliberations could be unsealed if allegations of racial misconduct were proven and that racism was "especially pernicious in the administration of justice." Critics of the ruling contend that this subjects the jury to unnecessary scrutiny and will likely, as the dissent put it, "erode citizens' willingness to serve on juries."

Do you think this protection by the Supreme Court is a remedy to racial disparities in the death penalty?

Source: Kevin Zhao, "The Choice between Right and Easy: *Pena-Rodriguez v. Colorado* and the Necessity of a Racial Bias Exception to Rule 606 (B)," *Duke Journal of Constitutional Law and Public Policy Sidebar* 12 (2016): 33.

ideas. One interview subject answered the question "During the trial, what were your impressions of the defendant?" this way:

> I saw the defendant as a very typical product of the lower socioeconomic black group who grew up with no values, no ideals, no authority, no morals, no leadership, and this has come down from generation to generation. And that was one of the problems we had, for me, and in the jury. Because some of the jurors were looking at him as your average white kid: he wasn't a white kid. He came from a totally different environment. I'm just saying that he was the one that was the defendant. And I just saw him as a loser from day one, as soon as he was born into that environment, and into that set of people who basically were into drugs, alcohol, illegitimacy, AIDS, the whole nine yards. This kid didn't have a chance. That's how I saw the defendant. And there are ten thousand others like him out there, which is very tragic. (45)

This juror uses distancing language to create a geographical gulf between her and the defendant that served to define the contours of race. He was "totally different," a "loser from day one," "born into that environment." This is contrasted with the implicit image of the white kid from a place of values, ideals, authority, morals, and leaders that "has come down from generation to generation."

As in the study by Lynch and Haney, jurors in Fleury-Steiner's analysis also used their own personal narratives to demonstrate distance from the defendant when they were black, and understanding and empathy when they were white. Further, Jennifer Eberhardt and her colleagues (2006) show that those with "stereotypical" racial characteristics or darker skin are more likely to get the death penalty when the victim is white. This confirms that our ideas of race today are still connected to the biases of early-twentieth-century proponents of the death penalty, who saw it as the only appropriate penalty for groups they considered less rational and, by extension, less human. By contrast, studies of black jurors find that they are able to "keep the sin separate from the sinner" when serving as capital jury members (Garvey 2000, 47).

Wrongful Convictions

The actions of defense attorneys, prosecutors, and juries are not only likely to result in death sentences for more black defendants than white, but they also introduce astonishing racial disparities in **wrongful convictions.** Since 1973, there have been a total of 159 exonerations of people on death row—27 in Florida alone (Death Penalty Information Center n.d.). The nation averaged three exonerations per year between 1973 and 1999; since 2000, that has increased to five per year. Over 70 percent of exonerations are people of color, and black people alone are 63 percent of all exonerations (Grimsley 2012).

Significant disparities are also experienced from one place to another. Take the case of Dallas County in Texas. Between 1995 and 2007, twelve people had their capital convictions overturned because of genetic evidence exonerating them. Barry Scheck of the Innocence Project has noted that nowhere else in the country has had this number of wrongful convictions revealed in such a short time (Scheck 2017). Without the actions of prosecutors in Dallas County, these cases would never have gone to trial for death.

The reasons for racial bias in wrongful convictions are telling. Jurors deliberate for less time in capital cases of nonwhites, suggesting that they are weighing the evidence less carefully and may be motivated by prejudice (Gould 2007). Convictions are often based on eyewitness testimony, and as discussed in box 9.1, cross-racial identifications are often inaccurate (Rutledge 2000). Nearly 75 percent of DNA exonerations are in cases where eyewitnesses misidentified suspects (Grimsley 2012).

Nonwhite defendants are also more likely than white defendants to be convicted on the basis of little solid evidence of guilt (Martin 2001). Police misconduct is also an element in wrongful convictions, and one that affects the cases of black defendants much more often. Indeed, in the vast majority of high-profile cases of rampant and entrenched police misconduct—in places like Los Angeles, Oakland, and Tulia, Texas—almost all of the targeted people were black or brown, revealing how criminal justice inequalities compound in the case of the death penalty (Covey 2012). Further, nonwhites are overrepresented in cases of false confessions, revealing the importance of police tactics and their impact on black and brown communities in securing wrongful convictions (Gould and Leo 2010).

Further, forensic evidence is also unreliable, a factor that affects nonwhite defendants disproportionately due to their greater presence in death penalty trials. Forensic science is second to eyewitness identification in producing the greatest number of false convictions (Innocence Project 2017). Forensic science is often presented as "scientific" but it is often anything but. For instance, the FBI reviewed cases involving microscopic hair analysis prior to 2012. Its findings? Out of 3,000 cases where this type of analysis was used against a defendant at trial, 95 percent were "scientifically invalid" (President's Council of Advisors on Science and Technology 2016, 3). Bite-mark evidence has also been used to convict hundreds of defendants and even led to the execution of at least seven people, but its potential to become a "scientifically valid method" was judged by scientific experts to be "low" (President's Council of Advisors on Science and Technology 2016, 9).

The issue of forensic science is further complicated by prosecutors who encourage forensic experts to testify in ways that mislead about the significance of the analysis, often encouraging their experts to use terms "within a reasonable degree of scientific certainty." Yet this phrase has no meaning, and as the National Academy of Sciences concluded, most forensic sciences "do not meet the fundamental requirements of science" (National Research Council 2009, 43). Despite these findings, forensic science is still used to convict people, a fact that is disproportionately experienced by those who are more likely to have their cases classified as capital, are less likely to be perceived empathetically by jurors, and are most likely to suffer the consequences of faulty testimony: black and brown defendants.

Wrongful convictions do not just demonstrate miscarriages of justice but also confirm the racial narratives told about the world. Eyewitnesses who misidentify defendants, prosecutors out for death, and juries who convict are all likely working hard for justice, yet wrongful convictions ensue anyway and in a clearly racially biased manner. How does this happen? The fictional ideas of black male violence and sexuality, long used to perpetuate white racial violence, still lurk unconsciously in the minds of many. And these ideas are easily confirmed in a court trial. Those who sit in judgment are predominantly from different racial and class backgrounds from those who are judged. They are subjected to narratives and evidence that confirms latent racial ideas. Defendants are subsequently cast as less than human, unable to be redeemed for society, and sentenced to death. And unsurprisingly, wrongful convictions—and executions—of those whom society views as less than human result.

Administrating Death

The obfuscation of racial violence and dehumanization tactics of the death penalty are also accomplished through death administration tactics inspired by the new penology (discussed in chapter 9). Contemporary methods of administration create psychological distance from those incarcerated and in places like Arizona, the death penalty has been likened to "waste disposal" (Lynch 2000).

This invocation of death row residents as "waste" is revealed through practices that reduce any recognition of the humanity of the person being put to death. Practices like a last meal are part of these humanizing impulses. Generally, people being put to death get to eat a meal of their choice with guards and sometimes family and friends. In Arizona, those facing execution do not get to choose a last meal and instead eat the day's standard meal alone in their cell. They also are not allowed to gather in a group, because this can inject emotion into what the state prefers to see as a routine practice (Lynch 2000).

Arizona also changed the time of day of executions (Lynch 2000). Traditionally held at midnight, which signals the gravity and exceptionality of the sentence in the prison, executions are now held in the middle of the afternoon, during normal business hours. The condemned are housed in supermax conditions with no physical contact during visitation and no contact between the condemned and prison staff. Personnel are also changed frequently to avoid any undue closeness that might develop between guards and those condemned. The executed are referred to by number and not name, in perhaps the most telling indication that the prison views them only as waste to be disposed. This transition in Arizona demonstrates the convergence between racial dehumanization and the tactics of criminal justice administration.

Whether death could be administrated in ways that are not racially capricious is an open question, and the history of the death penalty suggests that without the human/nonhuman cleavage initiated by race, we might have found little need for the death penalty in an "enlightened" legal system. Yet, today, we are faced with a legal system that although often racially neutral on its face, is structurally designed to answer the questions of who lives, who dies, and who decides as, respectively, white defendants, black defendants, and white prosecutors and death-qualified juries. This structural and systematic rendering of race in the death penalty is not accomplished just by public defense, elected prosecutors, or death-qualified juries but also extends to the highest court in the nation: the Supreme Court.

ABOLISHING AND REINSTATING THE DEATH PENALTY

The reality that the death penalty is administered in a racially disparate manner has plagued the United States since its founding and has only sped up during the twentieth century. This is curious given the Constitution's **Fourteenth Amendment,** which prevents discrimination on the basis of race. The Fourteenth Amendment was passed shortly after the end of slavery and guarantees citizens that "no State shall . . . deny to any person within its jurisdiction the equal protection of the laws." This is known as the equal protection clause.

Despite this clause, as well as ample criticism of the death penalty's racially capricious application, the law has provided little redress for those seeking to challenge the constitutionality of the death penalty based on racial disparities. Even though the U.S. Supreme Court has used the Fourteenth Amendment to ensure that racism is not formally permitted in other realms, it has stopped short of doing so in the case of capital punishment. In the early twentieth century, it appeared that this might not matter as abolition efforts stepped up and the use of the death penalty declined.

The death penalty began to decline in the 1930s (but the concentration of nonwhites among those executed rose), in large part due to abolitionists' attempts to define the sentence as incompatible with a modern, democratic nation-state. As a result of abolitionists' work, many northern states abolished capital punishment outright. Even president Franklin Roosevelt reported that he would like to see capital punishment abolished throughout the country by the end of the first year of his term (Banner 2002). Reformers routinely challenged the penalty on the basis of the Eighth Amendment prohibition on "cruel and unusual punishment," but these claims were generally rejected by the Supreme Court.

Racial disparities in the administration of the sentence, however, provided another opportunity for Supreme Court review based on the equal protection clause. As the civil rights movement grew in prominence, attention to racial disparities in the imposition of the death penalty did as well. A 1967 presidential commission concluded that the penalty "follow[ed] discriminatory patterns" (President's Commission on Law Enforcement and Administration of Justice 1967, 143). Public sentiment brought death penalties almost to a stop by the mid-1960s, with Michigan, Oregon, Iowa, New York, West Virginia, and Vermont all ending the death penalty by 1965 (Randa 1997). State by state abolition, however, was difficult and death penalty opponents eventually succeeded in getting a case to the Supreme Court in *Furman v. Georgia* in 1972.

Furman v. Georgia

In *Furman v. Georgia* the Supreme Court heard the case of William Henry Furman, who killed someone during a home burglary. The case also consolidated two other cases where men convicted of rape were sentenced to death. The *Furman* case laid out in detail how race affected capital sentencing. Organizations from the NAACP to the Central Conference of American Rabbis filed briefs arguing that the death penalty was administered in a racially biased way.

In a 5–4 decision, the U.S. Supreme Court agreed that the death penalty violated the Eighth and Fourteenth Amendments and found it unconstitutional. In the opinion, there was scant mention of the racial arguments for abolition presented by the defense, but the court still found the sentence to be administered in a biased and capricious manner:

> These death sentences are cruel and unusual in the same way that being struck by lightning is cruel and unusual. For, of all the people convicted of rapes and murders in 1967 and 1968, many just as reprehensible as these, the petitioners are among a capriciously selected random handful upon whom the sentence of death has in fact been imposed. My concurring Brothers have demonstrated that, if any basis can be discerned for the selection of these few to be sentenced to death, it is the constitutionally impermissible basis of race. *But racial discrimination has not been proved, and I put it to one side.* I simply conclude that the Eighth and Fourteenth Amendments cannot tolerate the infliction of a sentence of death under legal systems that permit this unique penalty to be so wantonly and so freakishly imposed. (emphasis added)

Despite evidence that the Georgia death penalty was used almost exclusively for black defendants, the court was not convinced that racial discrimination was the cause. The problem with the death penalty, according to the Supreme Court, was the randomness with which it was imposed. This problem could be remedied with guidelines for what constitutes a death-eligible case (Steiker and Steiker 2015). Until that time, however, the death penalty would be unconstitutional. That time was just four years away.

Gregg v. Georgia

The abolition of the death penalty was not the law of the land for long. Over the next several years, thirty-five states revised their death penalty statutes in response to *Furman.* States mandated separating the guilt and penalty phases, created standards to guide jury discretion, and articulated aggravating factors that made someone eligible for the death penalty. In 1976, the Supreme Court considered these new schemes in *Gregg v. Georgia.*

In this decision, the court again considered whether the process for administrating the death penalty was constitutional and examined newly revised statutes in five states. In particular, the court considered whether these statutes overcame the prohibition on the "wanton" application of the penalty that constituted cruel and unusual punishment in *Furman.*

Two of the states the court examined—North Carolina and Louisiana—mandated death for a range of crimes and were found unconstitutional. The remaining three—Georgia, Florida and Texas—provided guidance for the application of the death penalty and were sustained. These three had one thing in common: they provided guidance in the exercise of discretion but did not remove discretion overall. But the *Gregg* decision failed to consider how this continued to allow for systematic racial discrimination in the application of the death penalty.

McClesky v. Kemp and the Statistics of Death

A decade after the death penalty's reinstatement, legal reformers successfully petitioned the Supreme Court to hear a case contesting the constitutionality of the death penalty on the basis of race. *McCleskey v. Kemp* (1987) was brought by Warren McCleskey, who had been convicted of murder and two counts of armed robbery. His offense was considered an aggravated offense because he killed a police officer, and he was thus eligible for the death penalty in the state of Georgia.

McCleskey's conviction was challenged on the basis that race was a key factor in who is likely to receive the death penalty in Georgia. This argument presented the results of what is known as the Baldus study (Baldus, Pulaski, and Woodworth 1983). The **Baldus study** tested 230 variables in the administration of the death penalty in Georgia, including age, level of education, prior offenses, facts of the case, and importantly, race. This was the first time that such extensive statistical demonstration of racial disparity was presented to the court.

A simple presentation of death penalty statistics shows a distinct disparity: black people made up 12 percent of the population at the time, yet they constituted the majority of people executed in the United States This simple equation, however, is often explained away. Some suggest that black people kill whites with particular vehemence. Or that black communities are more involved in homicide.

Baldus's study was unique in that by testing 230 variables, including elements of the crime, the telling factors that shaped the application of the death penalty would emerge. So criminological variables, such as particularly vicious killings or more black people being charged initially, were tested, as were demographic variables, such as race and gender. If racial bias in the death penalty resulted from disparities in homicide rates between racial groupings or racial differences in how people killed, this study would have found that. But what the Baldus study found was that race—an extralegal, noncriminological measure—was the only variable to have a significant effect on the death penalty. Racial disparity in the application of the death penalty thus did not stem from racial differences in homicide but, rather, from the race of the defendant and victim themselves.

In the study, Baldus found that the race of the defendant made it four times as likely that a black person would receive the death penalty. If the victim was white, a black defendant was eleven times more likely to be sentenced to death. Even though only 9.2 percent of all Georgia homicides involved black defendants and white victims, prosecutors sought the death penalty in 70 percent of those cases. Over 60.7 percent of all Georgia homicides involved black victims, yet prosecutors sought the death penalty in only 34 percent of those cases.

The death penalty was applied to 22 percent of the black defendants convicted of killing white victims versus roughly 12 percent for all the other categories combined (white defendant and white victim, white defendant and black victim, black defendant and black victim). Most notably, a death penalty conviction was given in only 1 percent of the cases involving a black victim and a black defendant. Despite the extensive evidence provided by the Baldus study, the Supreme Court found McCleskey's sentence constitutional.

Disparity versus Discrimination

McClesky thus provides an important lesson for contemporary legal scholars: evidence of systematic racial discrimination is not enough to trigger Fourteenth Amendment protections. In the court's legal reasoning, the Baldus study presented a racial disparity, but not one that rose to the level of racial discrimination. The court reasoned that "at most, the Baldus study indicates a discrepancy to correlate with race, but this discrepancy does not constitute a major systemic defect.... Despite such imperfections, constitutional guarantees are met when the mode for determining guilt or punishment has been surrounded with safeguards to make it as fair as possible." The court concluded that little in McCleskey's case rose to the issue of discrimination as a matter of due process and that without overt animus in his particular trial, he was accorded the due process protections of the law.

Legal scholar David Cole explains the Court's reasoning: "The fact that *other juries* imposed the death penalty more often on blacks who killed whites did not shed light on whether *McCleskey's jury* had been motivated by race" (1999, 135, emphasis in original). Without purposeful intent to discriminate or a particular decision-maker acting with discriminatory purpose that has a demonstrated impact on the case, the Fourteenth Amendment does not apply.

Further, the court created a standard for the finding of racial discrimination that is exceedingly difficult for a defendant to make. Cole explains:

> For one thing, long-standing rules generally bar criminal defendants from obtaining discovery from the prosecution. Thus, unless the prosecutor admits to acting for racially biased reasons, it will be difficult to pin discrimination on the prosecutor. A similar rule bars inquiry into jury deliberations, and generally forbids introduction of evidence about jury deliberations even where a juror has chosen to make it public. So defendants are precluded from discovering evidence of intent from the two actors whose discriminatory intent the *McCleskey* Court required them to establish. (1999, 135)

After setting this impossible standard, the court further disavowed a role for itself in adjudicating cases like these and concluded that these "arguments are best presented to the legislative bodies, not the courts."

Dobbs v. Zant

One case that tried to show racial discrimination in the post-*McCleskey* era reveals the limits of strategies challenging convictions even when there is evidence of overt racist animus. In *Dobbs v. Zant* (1993), the defendant showed that jurors had revealed during pretrial questioning their discomfort with interracial dating and marriage and used the words *colored* and *n****r.* Dobbs further showed that the judge in the case opposed integration and that his own attorney used racial slurs and held negative racial stereotypes. The *McCleskey* standard was still not met. Stephen Bright writes,

> *Dobbs* is only one of many cases that starkly illustrates that racial discrimination not acceptable in any other area of American life today is tolerated in criminal courts. The use of a racial slur may cost a sports announcer his job, but there have been capital cases in which judges, jurors and defense counsel have called an African-American defendant a "nigger" with no repercussions for anyone except the accused. For example, parents of an African-American defendant were referred to as the "nigger mom and dad" by the judge in a Florida case. The judge did not lose his job; the Florida Supreme Court merely suggested that judges should avoid the "appearance" of impropriety in the future. (1995, 447)

Supreme Court jurisprudence has provided little protection from the racial disparity of state violence, and the *Dobbs* case demonstrates just how important the appearance of objectivity is to the working of the law.

Miller-El v. Dretke

The *McCleskey* case provides an important case for understanding the limits of legal protection against racial discrimination. The disparity-versus-discrimination jurisprudence was further reinforced by the *Miller-El v. Dretke* (2005) decision discussed in chapter 8. In this decision, the attorneys for the defense showed a pattern of prosecutors keeping black people off juries.

Evidence presented included prosecutor notes showing the moving of black names in the jury pool to the end of the line. Peremptory challenges also did not apply across all groups, such that some black people were struck for being too old, when whites who were older were retained. A training manual for prosecutors was also uncovered that specifically advised attorneys to remove people of color, arguing that "minorities always empathize with defendant." The court agreed that racial discrimination did influence his case, revealing the extent of overt systematic bias that is necessary for a discrimination claim to proceed in a criminal court case.

BOX 10.3   Racism and the Possibility of the Death Penalty

The evidence makes clear that the death penalty has long been administrated in a racially biased fashion. Few scholarly analyses show anything otherwise. Statistical demonstrations of pervasive racism are deemed unacceptable by the Supreme Court, which has largely left the issue to the states to decide. The result? More geographical complexity in the administration of the death penalty.

Attempts to remedy capital punishment and its racially disparities have led some states, including "red" ones to embrace moratoriums on its administration. Others, though, including more "blue" states, like California, have recently made it easier to put people to death. Few states are significantly committed to the death penalty, but these states are also ones with some of the more entrenched histories of racial violence, punitive tendencies, and white supremacist policies.

Why do you think places like California would align in support of the death penalty with other "red" states in the "death belt"? Why would some Republican administrations, including those in Kansas and Illinois, support death penalty moratoriums and even abolition in some cases? What do you think this says about race and the death penalty in the United States? Do you think it is possible to administer the death penalty without systemic racial bias?

Sources: Frank R. Baumgardner, Emma Johnson, Colin Wilson, and Clarke Whitehead, "These Lives Matter, Those Ones Don't: Comparing Execution Rates by the Race and Gender of the Victim in the US and in the Top Death Penalty States," *Albany Law Review* 79, no. 3 (2016): 797–861; Jacqueline G.C. Lee, Ray Paternoster, and Zachary Rowan, "Death Penalty and Race," in *Wiley Blackwell Encyclopedia of Race, Ethnicity, and Nationalism,* edited by John Stone et al., Wiley Blackwell Encyclopedias in Social Science (Chichester, UK: Wiley Blackwell, 2016).

Despite this finding in *Miller-El,* the court is not always sympathetic to claims that include overt discrimination if it believes that this did not have an impact on the case. In Utah, for instance, William Andrews, an African American man, was executed. A note was found by a juror depicting a stick figure on a gallows with the inscription "hang the n****r." Andrews was tried by an all-white jury. The trial judge never sought to determine who wrote it or how many jurors saw it. The court declined to hear his appeal on this basis.

The jurisprudence of death suggests that the Supreme Court is not a bulwark against unequal protection under the law (see box 10.3). Rather, as the court has shown repeatedly over the past century, evidence of racial discrimination—whether systemic or overt—is of little consequence to equal protection claims. Instead, the court has shown a remarkable willingness to allow the systematic execution of nonwhites in the criminal legal system, revealing perhaps the ultimate example of the perpetuation of coloniality today.

CONCLUSION

Thirty years after *McCleskey* was decided, the death penalty remains with us and continues to be used in a racially discriminatory manner. Today, the evidence of racial discrimination is extensive and undeniable, and the Baldus study is now neither novel nor unique, as it was during the McClesky trial. Further, scholars have moved beyond showing the discriminatory intent and application of the death penalty. Today they show the extensive ways that race shapes the administration of the death penalty, from political arguments for its utilization to the geography of application.

Though there is an extensive body of research on the death penalty showing that those who die are the poor and the nonwhite, not a mythological "worst of the worst," capital punishment continues to play a key role in the criminal legal system today. This role reveals that the death penalty is a primary tool through which to glimpse how the racial state continues. As we saw at the beginning of the chapter, the death penalty demonstrates the limits of the liberal social contract by identifying those for whom the social contract *cannot* apply. This is made real through the administration and application of the death penalty, which puts people to death because of their race, where they are from, and the structural context of court procedures. Whiteness is built into the mechanisms of the law in ways that reinforce commonsense ideas of racism and age-old ideas of race, gender, and sexuality.

For the white "rational insider" imagined by the architects of deterrence, the death penalty reveals the barbarism of the state. As the jurisprudence of death shows, this insider is invariably imagined as white, something recognized by juries, the Supreme Court, and punitive attitudes about the death penalty. For those outside the racial political community, the death penalty is merely the application of sovereign force necessary to sustain, grow, and protect imagined insiders. It is here that the death penalty most completely demonstrates the role that coloniality continues to play in the criminal legal system. It is also with the death penalty that we can continue to see the ways that white supremacy is not only produced but bolstered, condoned, and even hidden through legal procedures and practices. Until we confront the racial menace of white supremacy lurking in the colonial imagination, the death penalty will likely continue to kill some so that others may live.

REFERENCES

Allen, H. W., and J. M. Clubb. 2009. *Race, Class, and the Death Penalty: Capital Punishment in American History.* Albany: State University of New York Press.

Armstrong, Ken and Steve Mills. 1999. "Inept Defenses Cloud Verdict." *Chicago Tribune*, November 15, 1999.

Baldus, D. C., C. Pulaski, and G. Woodworth. 1983. "Comparative Review of Death Sentences: An Empirical Study of the Georgia Experience." *Journal of Criminal Law and Criminology* 74, no. 3: 661–753.

Baldus, D. C., G. Woodworth, D. Zuckerman, and N. A. Weiner. 1997. "Racial Discrimination and the Death Penalty in the Post-Furman Era: An Empirical and Legal Overview with Recent Findings from Philadelphia." *Cornell Law Review* 83: 1638.

Banner, Stuart. 2002. *The Death Penalty: An American History.* Cambridge, MA: Harvard University Press.

———. 2006. *Traces of Slavery.* New York: New York University Press.

Beardsley, M., S. Kamin, J. F. Marceau, and S. Phillips. 2015. "Disquieting Discretion: Race, Geography and the Colorado Death Penalty in the First Decade of the Twenty-First Century." *Denver University Law Review* 92, no. 4.

Beccaria, Cesare. (1764) 2008. *On Crimes and Punishments and Other Writings.* Edited by Aaron Thomas. Reprint, Toronto: University of Toronto Press.

Beckett, Katherine, and Heather Evans. 2016. "Race, Death, and Justice: Capital Sentencing in Washington State, 1981–2014." *Columbia Journal of Race and Law* 6: 77.

Beckett, Katherine, and Theodore Sasson. 2003. *The Politics of Injustice: Crime and Punishment in America.* Thousand Oaks, CA: Sage.

Bowers, W. J., B. D. Steiner, and M. Sandys. 2001. "Death Sentencing in Black and White: An Empirical Analysis of the Role of Jurors' Race and Jury Racial Composition." *University of Pennsylvania Journal of Constitutional Law* 3: 171.

Bright, Stephen B. 1995. "Discrimination, Death and Denial: The Tolerance of Racial Discrimination in Infliction of the Death Penalty." *Santa Clara Law Review* 35, no. 2, https://ssrn.com/abstract=2769644.

———. 2002. "Race, Poverty, the Death Penalty, and the Responsibility of the Legal Profession." *Seattle Journal of Social Justice* 1: 73.

Butler, Brooke, and Gary Moran. 2007. "The Impact of Death Qualification, Belief in a Just World, Legal Authoritarianism, and Locus of Control on Venirepersons' Evaluations of Aggravating and Mitigating Circumstances in Capital Trials." *Behavioral Sciences and the Law* 25, no. 1: 57–68.

Bye, R. T. 1919. *Capital Punishment in the United States.* Philadelphia: Committee on Philanthropic Labor, Philadelphia Yearly Meeting of Friends.

CDCR (California Department of Corrections and Rehabilitation). 2017. "Death Row Tracking System: Condemned Inmate Summary List." Accessed October 3, 2017. www.cdcr.ca.gov/capital_punishment /docs/condemnedinmatesummary.pdf?pdf=condemned-inmates.

Cole, David. 1999. *Unequal Justice.* New York: New Press.

Covey, Russell. 2012. "Police Misconduct as a Cause of Wrongful Convictions." *Washington University Law Review* 90: 1133.

Cutler, J. E. 1907. "Capital Punishment and Lynching." *Annals of the American Academy of Political and Social Science* 29, no. 3: 182–85. https://doi.org/10.1177/000271620702900335.

Curriden, Mark. 1995. "The Legacy of Lynching." *Atlanta Journal-Constitution,* January 15, 1995.

Death Penalty Information Center. n.d. *Innocence and the Death Penalty.* Accessed 16 June 2016. https:// deathpenaltyinfo.org/innocence-and-death-penalty.

Dieter, Richard C. 1998. *The Death Penalty in Black and White: Who Lives, Who Dies, Who Decides.* Washington, DC: Death Penalty Information Center. https://deathpenaltyinfo.org/death-penalty-black-and-white-who-lives-who-dies-who-decides.

———. 2013. *The 2% Death Penalty: How a Minority of Counties Produce Most Death Cases at Enormous Costs to All.* Washington DC: Death Penalty Information Center. https://deathpenaltyinfo.org/documents /twopercentreport.pdf.

Donohue, J. J. 2014. "An Empirical Evaluation of the Connecticut Death Penalty System since 1973: Are There Unlawful Racial, Gender, and Geographic Disparities?" *Journal of Empirical Legal Studies* 11, no. 4: 637–96.

Dunham, J. M. (1929) 1939. "Report of Committee on Capital Punishment, 1928." Michigan State Bar Journal 8: 279. In *Capital Punishment,* edited by Julia E. Johnsen, 192–95. New York: H. W. Wilson.

Eberhardt, J. L., P. G. Davies, V. J. Purdie-Vaughns, and S. L. Johnson. 2006. "Looking Deathworthy: Perceived Stereotypicality of Black Defendants Predicts Capital-Sentencing Outcomes." *Psychological Science* 17, no. 5: 383–86.

Equal Justice Initiative. 2017. *Race and Poverty.* https://eji.org/death-penalty/race-and-poverty.

Feinberg, L. G., K. E. Maynard, G. J. Pasewicz, and D. P. Reese. 2011. *A Constitutional Default: Services to Indigent Criminal Defendants in Pennsylvania.* Task Force and Advisory Committee on Services to Indigent Criminal Defendants, December 2011. Harrisburg: Joint State Government Commission, General Assembly of the Commonwealth of Pennsylvania. http://jsg.legis.state.pa.us/resources /documents/ftp/publications/2011-265-indigent%20defense.pdf.

Fleury-Steiner, Benjamin. 2004. *Jurors' Stories of Death: How America's Death Penalty Invests in Inequality.* Ann Arbor: University of Michigan Press.

Fleury-Steiner, B. D., K. Dunn, and R. Fleury-Steiner. 2009. "Governing through Crime as Commonsense Racism: Race, Space, and Death Penalty Reform in Delaware." *Punishment and Society* 11, no. 1: 5–24.

GAO (General Accounting Office). 1990. *Death Penalty Sentencing: Research Indicates Pattern of Racial Disparities.* Report to the Senate and House Committees on the Judiciary, February 26, 1990. Washington, DC. www.gao.gov/assets/220/212180.pdf.

Galliher, J. F., G. Ray, and B. Cook. 1992. "Abolition and Reinstatement of Capital Punishment during the Progressive Era and Early 20th Century." *Journal of Criminal Law and Criminology* 83, no. 3 (Fall): 538–76.

Garvey, S. P. 2000. "The Emotional Economy of Capital Sentencing." *New York University Law Review* 75: 26.

Gould, Jon B. 2007. *The Innocence Commission: Preventing Wrongful Convictions and Restoring the Criminal Justice System*. New York: New York University Press.

Gould, Jon B., and Richard A. Leo. 2010. "One Hundred Years Later: Wrongful Convictions after a Century of Research." *Journal of Criminal Law and Criminology* 100, no. 3 (Summer): 825–68.

Grimsley, Edwin. 2012. "What Wrongful Convictions Teach Us about Racial Inequality." News. Innocence Project. www.innocenceproject.org/what-wrongful-convictions-teach-us-about-racial-inequality/.

Hartnett, Stephen John. 2012. *Executing Democracy*. Vol. 2, *Capital Punishment and the Making of America, 1835–1843*. East Lansing: Michigan State University Press.

Howard, Walter Thomas. 2005. *Lynchings: Extralegal Violence in Florida during the 1930s*. Lincoln, NE: Iuniverse.

Innocence Project. 2017. "Misapplication of Forensic Science." www.innocenceproject.org/causes /misapplication-forensic-science/

Jackson, Jesse, Jesse Jackson Jr., and Bruce Shapiro. 2001. *Legal Lynching: The Death Penalty and America's Future*. New York: New Press.

Jackson, Robert H. 1940. "The Federal Prosecutor." *Journal of Criminal Law and Criminology* 31, no. 1: 3–6.

Jennings, Diane, Brooks Egerton, Dan Malone, Darlean Spangenberger, Pete Slover, and Howard Swindle. 2000. "Quality of Justice." *Dallas Morning News*, July 16, September 10–11, 2000.

Johnson, S. L. 2009. "Coker v. Georgia: Of Rape, Race, and Burying the Past." In *Death Penalty Stories*, edited by John H. Blume and Jordan M. Steiker, 171–91. New York: Foundations Press.

Johnson, S. L., J. H. Blume, T. Eisenberg, and V. P. Hans. 2011. "The Delaware Death Penalty: An Empirical Study." *Iowa Law Review* 97: 1925.

Kaufman-Osborn, Timothy V. 2006. "Capital Punishment as Legal Lynching?" In *From Lynch Mobs to the Killing State: Race and the Death Penalty in America*, edited by Charles J. Ogletree Jr. and Austin Sarat, 21–54. New York: New York University Press.

Lartey, Jamiles. 2015. "White Men Make Up 79% of Elected Prosecutors in US, Study Says." *Guardian*, July 7, 2015. www.theguardian.com/law/2015/jul/07/us-elected-prosecutors-white-men-criminal-justice-system.

Lee, Jacqueline Ghislaine, Ray Paternoster, and Zachary Rowan. 2016. "Death Penalty and Race." In *Wiley Blackwell Encyclopedia of Race, Ethnicity, and Nationalism*, edited by John Stone et al. Wiley Blackwell Encyclopedias in Social Science. Chichester, UK: Wiley Blackwell.

Linde, R. 2011. "From Rapists to Superpredators: What the Practice of Capital Punishment Says about Race, Rights, and the American Child." *International Journal of Children's Rights* 19, no. 1: 127–50.

Lynch, Mona. 2000. "The Disposal of Inmate #85271: Notes on a Routine Execution." *Studies in Law, Politics, and Society* 20: 3–34.

Lynch, Mona, and Craig Haney. 2009. "Capital Jury Deliberation: Effects on Death Sentencing, Comprehension, and Discrimination." *Law and Human Behavior* 33, no. 6: 481.

———. 2011. "Looking across the Empathic Divide: Racialized Decision Making on the Capital Jury." *Michigan State Law Review* 2011, no. 3 (Fall): 573.

Martin, Dianne L. 2001. "Lessons about Justice from the Laboratory of Wrongful Convictions: Tunnel Vision, the Construction of Guilt and Informer Evidence." *University of Missouri–Kansas City Law Review* 70, no. 4: 847–864.

National Research Council. 2009. *Strengthening Forensic Science in the United States: A Path Forward*. Washington, DC: National Academies Press. www.ncjrs.gov/pdffiles1/nij/grants/228091.pdf.

Ogletree, Charles J. 2002. "Black Man's Burden: Race and the Death Penalty in America." *Oregon Law Review* 81, no. 1: 15–38.

Olsen, Lise. 2001. "Uncertain Justice." 3-part series. *Seattle Post-Intelligencer*, August 5–8, 2001.

Paternoster, Raymond, and Robert Brame. 2003. *An Empirical Analysis of Maryland's Death Sentencing System with Respect to the Influence of Race and Legal Jurisdiction*. Final Report to Maryland Legislature. http:// www.aclu-md.org/uploaded_files/0000/0377/md_death_penalty_race_study.pdf.

Pierce, G. L., and M. L. Radelet. 2005. "The Impact of Legally Inappropriate Factors on Death Sentencing for California Homicides, 1990–1999." *Santa Clara Law Review* 46: 1.

———. 2010. "Death Sentencing in East Baton Rouge Parish, 1990–2008." *Louisiana Law Review* 71: 647.

Pierce, G. L., M. L. Radelet, C. Posick, and T. Lyman. 2014. "Race and the Construction of Evidence in Homicide Cases." *American Journal of Criminal Justice* 39, no. 4: 771–86.

Pokorak, J. J. 1997. "Probing the Capital Prosecutor's Perspective: Race of the Discretionary Actors." *Cornell Law Review* 83: 1811.

President's Commission on Law Enforcement and Administration of Justice. 1967. *The Challenge of Crime in a Free Society*. February 1967. Washington, DC: U.S. Government Printing Office. https://www.ncjrs.gov /pdffiles1/nij/42.pdf.

President's Council of Advisors on Science and Technology. 2016. *Forensic Science in Criminal Courts: Ensuring Scientific Validity of Feature-Comparison Methods*. September 2016. Washington DC: Executive Office

of the President. https://obamawhitehouse.archives.gov/sites/default/files/microsites/ostp/PCAST
/pcast_forensic_science_report_final.pdf.

Randa, L. E., ed.. 1997. *Society's Final Solution: A History and Discussion of the Death Penalty.* Lanham, MD:
University Press of America.

Reflective Democracy Campaign. 2015. "Justice for All?" Women's Donor Network. http://wholeads.us/justice/.

Rutledge, John P. 2000. "They All Look Alike: The Inaccuracy of Cross-Racial Identifications." *American Journal
of Criminal Law* 28: 207.

Sarat, Austin. 2001. *When the State Kills: Capital Punishment and the American Condition.* Princeton, NJ:
Princeton University Press.

Scheck, Barry C. 2016. "Conviction Integrity Units Revisited." *Ohio State Journal of Criminal Law* 14: 705–52.

Seiver, Simone. 2015. "Why Three Counties That Loved the Death Penalty Have Almost Stopped Pursuing
It." News, August 11, 2015. Marshall Project. www.themarshallproject.org/2015/08/11/why-three-
counties-that-loved-the-death-penalty-have-almost-stopped-pursuing-it#.ullaktbvb.

Sloss, D. 2008. "Death Penalty: In Missouri, Where You Live May Matter." *St. Louis Beacon,* May 1, 2008.

Sorensen, J., Wallace, D. H., and Pilgrim, R. L. 2001. "Empirical Studies on Race and Death Penalty Sentencing: A
Decade after the GAO Report." *Criminal Law Bulletin–Boston* 37, no. 4: 395–408.

Steiker, Carol S., and Steiker, Jordan M. 2010. "Capital Punishment: A Century of Discontinuous Debate."
Journal of Criminal Law and Criminology 100: 643.

———. 2015. "The American Death Penalty and the (In)Visibility of Race." *University of Chicago Law Review* 82:
243–94.

Streib, Victor L. 2005. *Death Penalty for Juveniles.* Bloomington: Indiana University Press.

Sundby, S. E. 2002. "The Capital Jury and Empathy: The Problem of Worthy and Unworthy Victims." *Cornell Law
Review* 88: 343.

Unah, Isaac. 2011. "Empirical Analysis of Race and the Process of Capital Punishment in North Carolina."
Michigan State Law Review (2011): 609–58.

Wright, George C. 1996. *Racial Violence in Kentucky, 1865–1940: Lynchings, Mob Rule, and "Legal Lynchings."*
Baton Rouge: Louisiana State University Press.

Conclusion: Futures of Race and Crime?

Throughout this book, we've explored how ideas of race born out of colonialism shape the institutions and practices of the criminal justice system today. Ideas of crime have consolidated structures of racial hierarchy and re-created race as a meaningful category even though legal racial apartheid structures are a thing of the past. This continuous process of racial subordination is the result of the power of coloniality and how logics and practices of humanization/dehumanization work to shape ideas, practices, and institutions. Coloniality as a twinned project of geographical conquest and knowledge production is evident not just in how we organize our society but within the very practices and actions of our institutional structures.

We organize our society such that the places we live and work are marked by considerable racial differentiations. These differences are found not just in exposure to criminal victimization and hypersurveillance but in life expectancies, health outcomes, and wealth accumulation. These divisions are supported and bolstered by ideas that some places are "slums" and that slum conditions arise not from patterns of capital and political investment and disinvestment but from the nature or culture of the inhabitants themselves.

Institutions that are often held dear reflect these ideas through their very conception of the social problems that the United States faces. Juvenile courts and police patrol emerged not from an increase in crime or delinquents but from the practices of racial scientists who defined urban social problems as an issue of racial "degeneration." Unsurprisingly, the first expansive urban criminal justice systems concentrated not on society more broadly but on the perceived pathologies of nonwhites, on groups who just so happened to live in the places defined by urban reformers as slums. While the language around social issues has mutated and transformed over time, this fundamental power dynamic has not changed. People, places, and communities that were seen as pathological, diseased, and "crime-ridden" a century ago are often still seen as the source of what ails society today.

These divisions have become more pronounced over time through federal housing policies seeking to cement the "American dream" for white society while systematically disinvesting from and excluding communities of color. Although these formal racial structures were banished more than fifty years ago, they continue to exert considerable influence on wealth accumulation, college attendance, and life outcomes.

One of the most important life outcomes that these differentiated racial geographies influence is passage through the criminal justice system. Defined by the law and order discourse as "wild" and "jungle-like" spaces, urban communities were soon subject to a militarized police force and a redefinition of poverty as the product of criminals and were besieged by the war on drugs. Social inequalities between racial groups once explained through genetics and natural inferiorities were replaced by a narrative that replaced biology with culture. A "culture of poverty" associated with urban communities served as the independent variable that explained not only inequality but crime itself.

Soon, U.S. prisons filled with people, a vast and unprecedented outcome both historically and internationally. Police fueled the filling of prisons through policing of nonviolent "quality-of-life" crimes, which continued a centuries-long definition of crime and disorder as the consequence of the poor and nonwhite. Stark, sharp dividing lines between "us" and "them" are sustained through practices of knowledge production that equate police activity with objective measures of crime and use the outcomes to further justify concentrating police resources in the very same places that have historically suffered from hyperpolicing. And the widespread application of the term *gang* has only further fueled the engine of racialized policing.

Court practices, idealized as the heart of due process and the place where the search for truth and justice can occur in the criminal justice system, have proven to provide little redress for the vast racial disparities in policing and arrest. Instead, the administrative structure of court processes demonstrates the power of coloniality through a courtroom workgroup that often comes from very different geographies than those who are adjudicated by the court. Courts also do not just respond to these geographies but actively create them through the pathologization of defendants and the control of their mobility.

Racial pathologization and hierarchies are further reinforced in systems of punishment that are structurally reminiscent of chattel slavery. This can be seen both in terms of the profit-making incentives of prisons and the common-sense story of racism that tells us that prisons house the "worst of the worst." And the disproportionate incarceration of black and brown communities just fuels the story that these communities are the site and source of the nation's social ills.

This story that those in prison are the "worst of the worst" fuels not just log-ics of warehousing and "waste" management but a death penalty regime described by many as legal lynching. Considering that extinguishing some-one's life is the ultimate act of state racism, the near centuries-long use of the penalty to disproportionately kill black people—especially children—reveals just how the dehumanizing logics of coloniality continue today.

Coloniality, however, does not stay the same across time or space, and its manifestations today look different than a hundred years ago. But its impacts are nevertheless widespread and, as such, we emphasize coloniality as a logic of human/nonhuman that could look different tomorrow. It could come to be that human/nonhuman is not defined by color. As the criminal justice system shows, color is only a proxy for an entire systematic process of humanization and dehumanization, a process that results in what we identify today as race. Even as the practices of criminal justice shift—as they are certainly doing today—they will likely continue to play a role in mediating this line. The under-lying story to this book is not just about coloniality, race, and crime but also about how the power to define *who* is a criminal (and who is not) is itself often premised on a logic of human/nonhuman. Thus, even though some states have embarked on decarceration, this has not resulted in the abolition of prisons, pathologization, or dehumanization. Instead, it has inscribed them onto the landscape of the community and into the logic of reform.

CRIMINAL JUSTICE, COMMUNITIES, AND "COLLATERAL CONSEQUENCES"

As we have stressed throughout this book, the problem of coloniality and racial dehumanization today is a structural condition that affects people regardless of whether they actually commit crime. Nowhere is this clearer than in the "collateral consequences" of imprisonment. In war, collateral consequences are the unintended destruction of people, property, and places; in the case of crim-inal justice and imprisonment, they are the damage inflicted upon places and people other than the 7 million people under criminal justice supervision.

Mass incarceration not only affects those incarcerated but also the sur-rounding community. While some communities may see positive gains when one or two lawbreakers are removed from the streets, spatially concentrated incarceration has no such positive effects. Instead, the reality is one of diminishing returns, until a tipping point is reached after which incarceration actually fuels crime rates, as it does today (Clear 1996; Liedka, Piehl, and Useem 2006). This subjects communities not only to the destructive influences of imprisonment but to increased victimization and harm.

As noted throughout this book, incarceration isn't just socially concentrated but spatially concentrated as well. Seventy-two percent of all New York State prisoners came from just seven of New York City's fifty-five community board districts (Roberts 2004). Likewise, 53 percent of prisoners released in Illinois return to Chicago, and 34 percent of releases came from just six of Chicago's seventy-seven communities. This clustering of incarceration subjects some communities to increased surveillance even beyond police. Parole and probation officers, for example, frequent areas as a consequence of their supervision caseloads. The reduced Fourth Amendment rights of probationers, parolees, and those in their proximity (such as those riding in a car or living with them) has the effect of placing many communities under perpetual surveillance and suspicion.

Further, police departments also concentrate police resources in neighborhoods known to have a high number of ex-prisoners (Papachristos, Meares, and Fagan 2007). Police justify this as preventing future crime, but it subjects both those who have been in prison and their neighbors to increased surveillance and oversight. Unlike wealthier and whiter communities who can conduct their deviance in private, communities with a high number of people who have been in prison are subject to ongoing intrusions from state actors. This means, for instance, that children experimenting with marijuana are much more likely to escape notice in a white neighborhood than in a black one. And unsurprisingly, demographic groups that face prosecution for crimes like marijuana use are largely not white (Golub, Johnson, and Dunlap 2007; Ramchand, Pacula, and Iguchi 2006)

The effects on young people who grow up in these neighborhoods are far-reaching. These young people have less access to the social networks necessary to secure future educational opportunities and employment. With a significant concentration of the population of potential wage-earners, especially men who earn more than women, taken out of the neighborhood, families of those incarcerated are under tremendous financial strain. Emotional and physical health tolls also ensue, such as from worrying about loved ones' well-being while they are incarcerated.

Black children are nine times more likely than white children to have a parent in prison (Roberts 2004). Children with parents in prison suffer not just from the reduced economic standing of their families but in other ways as well. They are at risk for increased rates of depression, anxiety about their future, and guilt and shame about their family. It is not surprising that this often translates into lower performance at school, when prior to parental incarceration they had excelled. At the macro scale, this produces the very same constructs of coloniality that have been with us since the dawn of the U.S. nation-state, with some cast outside the political community and subject to a society that denies their humanity from birth.

This is clear in the case of immigration law, where questions around race and citizenship can also have dire consequences for communities. In 1996, the Immigration and Nationality Act drastically changed policing of immigration by authorizing local police departments to perform federal immigration enforcement (Chesney-Lind and Mauer 2002). These changes harm communities by saturating areas with high concentrations of immigrants with police.

Local policing of immigration also leads to increased racial profiling, decreases employment opportunities, breaks up families, and creates an environment that ostracizes immigrants. The threat of deportation increases the victimization of not only undocumented immigrants themselves but the community at large. In his study of Latinx perceptions of police in Chicago, Nik Theodore (2013) found that regardless of their citizenship status, many people reported that they would not contact police if they were the victim of a crime. They reported fears that doing so would bring unwanted inquiries about their immigration status or that of people in their community.

The escalation of immigration policing also increases victimization during the process of migration itself. Militarization of the U.S.-Mexico border has caused many immigrants to cross through the most dangerous points in order to avoid detection (NNIRR 2016). In the Donald Trump era, anti-immigration sentiments are likely to further the social isolation and exclusion of many immigrants.

These community effects are shifting, though, and cities are not likely to long be the site and source of massive incarceration or immigration detention. Already this terrain has shifted. Politics have also changed, as have the demographics of metropolitan areas. These shifts, which we describe next, suggest that the mechanisms and practices of coloniality are also shifting, but it does not appear that they are lessening or disengaging from the criminal justice system.

FUTURES OF RACE AND CRIME?

As alluded to in other chapters, racial terrains are shifting, as are forces supporting massive prison expansion. Indeed, the rate of incarceration in the United States has plateaued for at least four years since its peak in 2013, and given the role of state governments in having to pay for incarceration, it might not increase much higher than its current rate. These shifts come from a variety of places and suggest that what we might target in a generation as the most important practices to the continuation of coloniality might be very different than those discussed today.

One of the most important trends currently shifting the terrain of race and crime in the United States is gentrification, or the process of higher-income residents pushing lower-income residents out of neighborhoods. This is going on across metropolitan communities in the United States. What were once urban "slums," "ghettoes," and no-go zones for whites are now bastions of the modern urban entertainment industry. High-end shops, bars, restaurants, and cafes replaced boarded-up storefronts and open-air drug markets in places like New York, Chicago, San Francisco, and Los Angeles. This economic transformation, however, has made major changes in the racial geographies of metropolitan areas.

Consider, for instance, the San Francisco metropolitan area. Gentrification in San Francisco and Oakland has pushed poor and nonwhite people out to the far outer-ring suburbs of Antioch, Pittsburgh, and Brentwood. In San Francisco in 1970, one in seven residents was black, over 14 percent of the population. Today, that number is one in twenty, a drop of more than 9 percentage points! Although blacks are only 5 percent of the city's total population, they make up, for example, 40 percent of the victims of officer-involved shootings (Fuller 2016). Many of these residents are also isolated and confined to public housing and are vastly poorer than whites in the city. Indeed, the median income of black residents in San Francisco is $27,000 compared to $89,000 for whites.

Across the bay in Oakland, the situation is similar. In 1950, Oakland was over 75 percent white. In 1980, Oakland was 47 percent black and, due to white flight, only 38 percent white. By 2010, though, it was only 28 percent black. While the number of whites continued to decline in 1990 and 2000 to a low of 31 percent, by the 2010 census, whites were beginning to return to the city and now make up almost 35 percent of residents, a proportion that is projected to grow.

Many of the people displaced are going to neighborhoods that used to be majority white suburbs, like Antioch, California, detailed in chapter 7. Here, they have been met with white racial violence, just as migrants were in cities one hundred years ago. In these places, like urban areas, the use of criminal justice systems to police the poor continue apace. Black students in Antioch are expelled at greater rates, and as we detailed in chapter 7, police and local residents colluded to subject poor black newcomers to greater surveillance and diminished due process rights. The same conditions that met urban residents prior to gentrification are now those that are used for racial governance strategies in suburbs.

This phenomenon is occurring more broadly. Take for instance the fact that today, the largest contributors to the California prison system are not historically industrial cities but what is known as the Central Valley—cities like Stockton, Modesto, and Fresno. None of these places would have been regarded as the distressed urban areas of the past, but today they are the places that are carrying on the mantle of mass incarceration.

Nowhere is this clearer than in the juvenile justice system. Place like San Francisco have embraced policies of decarceration to keep kids out of juvenile prisons. Yet, the youth population in San Francisco is on the decline, as is the number of people in juvenile hall. This means that as San Francisco's wealth grows and it is able to provide more attention to the economic needs of those incarcerated, those who need it most no longer reside there. Instead, they reside in places like Antioch. These outlying cities, however, are facing many of the structural conditions that large cities faced in the 1970s: declining property taxes, now from the recent housing and foreclosure crisis, lack of industrial base, and the decline of wealth overall.

Further, decarceration is more broadly embraced today than before, so many cities, even those that are not wealthy, are turning toward more community-based strategies. This is even happening in conservative places, where Republicans concerned about fiscal prudence have come out against the expense of funding the criminal justice system at current levels. Recent efforts in New York and California have led to declines in prison admissions overall, but not necessarily in criminal justice supervision.

Residents are released from prison, but are remanded to the community, which seems to be emerging as the new place to serve time (Brown and Smith 2017). Now incarceration is not being in prison but living with the threat of prison if one's urinalysis comes up "dirty," one's ankle monitor is not charged, or one fails to keep a probation or parole appointment. This threat results in a population of people whose mobility is curtailed, and surveillance is enacted not through prison guards or walls but through technological innovations like GPS monitoring and biometric tests. This shift means that we may see the lessening importance of prison as an institutional structure, but not the lessening of logics of coloniality. Instead, coloniality and responsibility for state supervision shift geographies. The walls of the prison are replaced with the prison of the local community.

These trends demonstrate how even when ideas upholding coloniality and racial dehumanization are challenged, the challenge is often still based within racial pathologization. Even without the prison, criminal justice practices continue to racialize and sort human beings into a system of racial classification; now, however, it's the ankle monitor that works alongside race to mark people as outside the political community. This tactic of dehumanization certainly shifts the terrain of coloniality, but not its power.

REFERENCES

Brown, Elizabeth, and Amy Smith. 2017. "Challenging Mass Incarceration in the City of Care: Punishment, Community and Residential Placement." *Theoretical Criminology* 22, no. 1: 4–21. https://doi.org /10.1177/1362480616683794.

Clear, Todd R. 1996. "Backfire: When Incarceration Increases Crime." *Journal of the Oklahoma Criminal Justice Research Consortium* 3: 7–19.

Chesney-Lind, Meda, and Marc Mauer, eds. 2003. *Invisible Punishment: The Collateral Consequences of Mass Imprisonment.* New York: New Press.

Fuller, Thomas. 2016. "The Loneliness of Being Black in San Francisco." *New York Times,* July 20, 2016. www .nytimes.com/2016/07/21/us/black-exodus-from-san-francisco.html.

Golub, Andrew, Bruce D. Johnson, and Eloise Dunlap. 2007. "The Race/Ethnicity Disparity in Misdemeanor Marijuana Arrests in New York City." *Criminology and Public Policy* 6, no. 1: 131–64.

Liedka, Raymond V., Anne Morrison Piehl, and Bert Useem. 2006. "The Crime-Control Effect of Incarceration: Does Scale Matter?" *Criminology and Public Policy* 5, no. 2: 245–76.

NNIRR (National Network for Immigrant and Refugee Rights). 2010. *Injustice for All: The Rise of the U.S. Immigration Policing Regime.* Human Rights Immigrant Community Action Network (HURRICANE). www.racialequitytools.org/resourcefiles/nnir.pdf.

Papachristos, Andrew V., Tracey L. Meares, and Jeffrey Fagan. 2007. "Attention Felons: Evaluating Project Safe Neighborhoods in Chicago." *Journal of Empirical Legal Studies* 4, no. 2: 223–72.

Ramchand, Rajeev, Rosalie Liccardo Pacula, and Martin Y. Iguchi. 2006. "Racial Differences in Marijuana-Users' Risk of Arrest in the United States." *Drug and Alcohol Dependence* 84, no. 3: 264–72.

Roberts, Dorothy E. 2003. "The Social and Moral Cost of Mass Incarceration in African American Communities." *Stanford Law Review* 56: 1271–305.

Theodore, Nik. 2013. *Insecure Communities: Latino Perceptions of Police Involvement in Immigration Enforcement.* Department of Urban Planning and Policy, University of Illinois at Chicago. www .policylink.org/sites/default/files/INSECURE_COMMUNITIES_REPORT_FINAL.PDF.

Index

Printed in the USA
CPSIA information can be obtained
at www.ICGtesting.com
LVHW061442300823
756646LV00013B/1033